RIVER

Buchan Ro...

Blacknook?

DON BRIDGE, one Arch 80 Feet, both sides on a hard rock.

Road to Peterhead High Banks

Inch

Fall

Hill head

Seaton Gate

High Banks

Whitehouse

Seaton Meadows

ABERDEEN

A Bulwark built by the Citizens to divert y Current mor Easterly for better Fish?

Bayliff's Boggs or Marsh

Kings College

Bent Hills

Ditches

Brick holes

Ponies Burn

Brick Kilns

ge Garden

Fenny Ground

Tyle Burn

Spittal Kirk Ruins

Lynks

Corn Fields

or

...s Ditch'd to
... the Marshs

Kings Meadow

...imagin'd that the Don breaking
...rough the Lakes of Cannoswea enter'd
... under y foot of y Broad hill, having
...g but Sands to keep it in its Chanel, it
...nly Changes its Current ..

odey

Gallow Marsh

The Tyde breaking in from Don overflows the Kings Lynks on the Flood & Change.

Lakes of Cannosweat

with

D. FO

By

ABERDEEN
BEFORE 1800

A NEW HISTORY

ABERDEEN

BEFORE 1800
A New History

Edited by
E. PATRICIA DENNISON,
DAVID DITCHBURN
AND MICHAEL LYNCH

Foreword by
Cllr JAMES WYNESS

TUCKWELL PRESS

Published by Tuckwell Press Ltd
The Mill House
Phantassie
East Linton
East Lothian EH40 3DG
Scotland

Copyright © City of Aberdeen Council 2002
First published 2002

ISBN: 1 86232 119 1 *hardback*
ISBN: 1 86232 114 0 *paperback*

British Library Cataloguing-in-Publication data are available

Typeset and originated by Carnegie Publishing Ltd, Lancaster
Printed and bound by Bath Press, Glasgow, Scotland

Contents

List of Figures and Maps

List of Black and White Illustrations

List of Colour Plates

Abbreviations

A. B. Coll.	*Collections for a History of the Shires of Aberdeen and Banff* (Spalding Club, 1843).
A. B. Ill.	*Illustrations of the Topography and Antiquities of the Shires of Aberdeen and Banff* (Spalding Club, 1847-69).
Abdn Chrs	*Aberdeen Charters and Other Writs Illustrating the History of the Royal Burgh of Aberdeen*, ed. P. J. Anderson (Aberdeen, 1890).
Abdn Counc.	*Extracts from the Council Register of the Burgh of Aberdeen*, ed. J. Stuart (Spalding Club & SBRS, 1844-72).
Abdn Ecc. Recs	*Selections from the Records of the Kirk Session, Presbytery and Synod of Aberdeen*, ed. J. Stuart (Spalding Club, 1846).
Abdn Fasti	*Fasti Aberdonenses: Selections from the Records of the University and King's College of Aberdeen, 1494-1854*, ed. C. Innes (Spalding Club, 1854).
Abdn Grads	*Officers and Graduates of University and King's College, Aberdeen MVD-MDCCCLX*, ed. P. J. Anderson (New Spalding Club, 1893).
Abdn Recs	*Early Records of the Burgh of Aberdeen, 1317, 1398-1407*, ed. W. C. Dickinson (SHS, 1957).
Abdn Reg.	*Registrum Episcopatus Aberdonensis*, ed. C. Innes (Spalding and Maitland Clubs, 1845).
Aberdeen Description	James Gordon of Rothiemay, *Abredoniae Utriusque Descriptio 1660*, ed. C. Innes (Spalding Club, 1842).
Aberdeen Friars	*Aberdeen Friars: Red, Black, White, Grey*, ed. P. J. Anderson (Aberdeen, 1909).
ACA	Aberdeen City Archives.
ACL	*Aberdeen Council Letters*, ed. L. B. Taylor (Oxford, 1942-61).
Adv. MS	Advocates' MS (NLS).
AJ	*Aberdeen Journal*.
Ancient Burgh Laws	*Ancient Laws and Customs of the Burghs of Scotland, 1124-1424 and 1424-1707*, ed. C. Innes (SBRS, 1868-1910).

APS	*The Acts of the Parliaments of Scotland*, eds T. Thomson and C. Innes (Edinburgh, 1814-75).
AUL	Aberdeen University Library.
AUR	*Aberdeen University Review.*
Balfour, *Practicks*	Sir James Balfour of Pittendreich, *Practicks*, 2 vols, ed. P. G. B. McNeill (Stair Soc., 1962).
BL	British Library, London.
Boece, *Vitae*	Hector Boece, *Murthlacensium et Aberdonensium Episcoporum Vitae*, ed. J. Moir (New Spalding Club, 1894).
BUK	*Booke of the Universall Kirk: Acts and Proceedings of the General Assemblies of the Kirk of Scotland*, 3 vols, ed. T. Thomson (Bannatyne Club, 1839-45).
Calderwood, *History*	David Calderwood, *History of the Kirk of Scotland*, 8 vols, eds T. Thomson and D. Laing (Wodrow Society, 1842-9).
CDS	*Calendar of Documents Relating to Scotland*, 5 vols, ed. J. Bain *et al.* (Edinburgh, 1881-1986).
Chron. Bower (Watt)	Walter Bower, *Scotichronicon*, ed. D. E. R. Watt (Aberdeen, 1987-98).
Chron. Fordun	Johannis de Fordun, *Chronica Gentis Scotorum*, ed. W. F. Skene (Edinburgh, 1871-2).
Chron. Wyntoun	*The Original Chronicle of Andrew of Wyntoun* (STS, 1903-14).
Cowan & Easson, *Religious Houses*	Cowan, I. B., and Easson, D. E. (eds), *Medieval Religious Houses: Scotland* (2nd edn, London, 1976).
CR	Council Register (ACA).
CSP Scot.	*Calendar of the State Papers Relating to Scotland and Mary, Queen of Scots 1547-1603*, 13 vols, eds J. Bain *et al.* (Edinburgh, 1898-1969).
CSSR	*Calendar of Scottish Supplications to Rome* (SHS, 1934-).
DNB	*Dictionary of National Biography* (1885-).
DOST	*Dictionary of the Older Scottish Tongue, from the Twelfth Century to the end of the Seventeenth Century*, eds W. A. Craigie and A. J. Aitken *et al.* (London, 1937-2002).
Edin. Recs.	*Extracts from the Records of the Burgh of Edinburgh*, 13 vols, eds J. D. Marwick *et al.* (SBRS & Edinburgh, 1869-1967).
ER	*The Exchequer Rolls of Scotland*, 23 vols, eds J. Stuart *et al.* (Edinburgh, 1878-1908).
Halyburton's Ledger	*Ledger of Andrew Halyburton, 1492-1503*, ed. C. Innes (Edinburgh, 1867).

IR	*Innes Review.*
Keith, *Bishops*	Robert Keith, *An Historical Catalogue of the Scottish Bishops, Down to the Year 1688*, ed. M. Russel (Edinburgh, 1824).
Maitland Misc.	*Miscellany of the Maitland Club*, 4 vols (Maitland Club, 1833-47).
Moray Reg.	*Registrum Episcopatus Moraviensis* (Bannatyne Club, 1837).
NAS	National Archives of Scotland, Edinburgh.
New Spalding Misc.	*Miscellany of the New Spalding Club* (New Spalding Club, 1890-1908).
NRA(S)	National Register of Archives (Scotland), Edinburgh.
Old Aberdeen Recs.	*Records of Old Aberdeen*, 2 vols, ed. A. M. Munro (New Spalding Club, 1899-1909).
OSA	*The Statistical Account of Scotland, 1792-99*, ed. Sir John Sinclair (repr. Wakefield, 1982).
P & P	*Past and Present.*
Pitcairn, *Trials*	*Criminal Trials in Scotland, 1488-1624*, 3 vols, ed. R. Pitcairn (Bannatyne and Maitland Clubs, 1833).
PRO	Public Record Office, London.
PSAS	*Proceedings of the Society of Antiquaries of Scotland.*
RCAHMS	Royal Commission on the Ancient and Historical Monuments of Scotland.
RCRB	*Records of the Convention of the Royal Burghs of Scotland*, 7 vols, eds J. D. Marwick and T. Hunter (Edinburgh, 1866-1918).
RGC	Robert Gordon's College.
RMS	*Registrum Magni Sigilii Regum Scotorum*, 11 vols, ed. J. M. Thomson *et al.* (Edinburgh, 1882-).
ROSC	*Review of Scottish Culture.*
Rot. Scot.	*Rotuli Scotiae in Turri Londinensi et in Domo Capitulari Westmonasteriensi Asservati*, ed. D. Macpherson (London, 1814-19).
RPC	*Register of the Privy Council of Scotland*, 38 vols, ed. J. H. Burton *et al.* (Edinburgh, 1877-).
RRS	*Regesta Regum Scottorum*, ed. G. Barrow *et al.* (Edinburgh, 1960-**).**
RSCHS	*Records of the Scottish Church History Society.*
RSS	*Registrum Secreti Sigilli Regum Scotorum*, 8 vols, eds M. Livingstone *et al.* (Edinburgh, 1908-).
SBRS	Scottish Burgh Records Society.

Scot. Stud.	*Scottish Studies.*
Scott, *Fasti*	*Fasti Ecclesiae Scoticanae*, 7 vols, ed. H. Scott (2nd edn, Edinburgh, 1915-61).
SESH	*Scottish Economic and Social History.*
Shore Work Accounts	*Aberdeen Shore Work Accounts, 1596-1670*, ed. L. B. Taylor (Aberdeen, 1972).
SHR	*Scottish Historical Review.*
SHS	Scottish History Society.
SP	*The Scots Peerage*, ed. Sir J. Balfour Paul (Edinburgh, 1906-14).
Spalding Misc.	*Miscellany of the Spalding Club*, 5 vols (Spalding Club, 1841-52).
SRS	Scottish Record Society.
St Nich. Cart.	*Cartularium Ecclesiae Sancti Nicholai Aberdonensis*, 2 vols, ed. J. Cooper (New Spalding Club, 1888-92).
STS	Scottish Text Society.
TA	*Accounts of the Lord High Treasurer of Scotland*, 13 vols, eds T. Dickson *et al.* (Edinburgh, 1877-).
TGSI	*Transactions of the Gaelic Society of Inverness.*
TRHS	*Transactions of the Royal Historical Society.*

Contributors

Ian Blanchard is Professor of Medieval Economic History at the University of Edinburgh.

Stephen Boardman is Lecturer in Scottish History at the University of Edinburgh.

E. Patricia Dennison is Director of the Centre for Scottish Urban History at the University of Edinburgh.

Gordon DesBrisay is Associate Professor of History at the University of Saskatchewan.

H. Lesley Diack is Wellcome Research Fellow at the University of Aberdeen.

Helen M. Dingwall is Senior Lecturer in History at the University of Stirling.

David Ditchburn is Senior Lecturer in History at the University of Aberdeen.

Elizabeth Ewan is Associate Professor of History at the University of Guelph.

David Findlay is Teaching Assistant in Celtic at the University of Aberdeen.

Elizabeth Gemmill is an Associate Lecturer with the Open University and Honorary Research Fellow in the Research Institute of Irish and Scottish Studies, University of Aberdeen.

Marjory Harper is Senior Lecturer in History at the University of Aberdeen.

Gordon Jackson is Honorary Research Fellow in Economic History at the University of Strathclyde.

Michael Lynch is Sir William Fraser Professor of Scottish History and Palaeography at the University of Edinburgh.

James Macaulay was formerly Senior Lecturer at the Mackintosh School of Architecture, University of Glasgow.

Nicholas Mayhew is Reader in Numismatics at the University of Oxford.

Alexander Murdoch is Senior Lecturer in Scottish History at the University of Edinburgh.

Murray G. H. Pittock is Professor of Literature at the University of Strathclyde.

Anne T. Simpson is an independent scholar, based in Aberdeen.

Grant G. Simpson was formerly Reader in History at the University of Aberdeen.

Geoffrey P. Stell is Head of Architecture at the Royal Commission on the Ancient and Historical Monuments of Scotland in Edinburgh.

Robert E. Tyson is Senior Lecturer in Economic History at the University of Aberdeen.

Shona Vance was formerly Postdoctoral Research Fellow at Trinity College, University of Dublin.

Allan White O.P. is Prior Provincial of the English Dominicans and Visiting Lecturer at Blackfriars, Oxford, in Church History and Liturgy.

Ian D. Whyte is Professor of Historical Geography at the University of Lancaster.

Acknowledgements

A work of this size and complexity is not produced without the help of many people. The first debt for the editors to record is that owed to the contributors, who have been prepared to write to a specific brief and, in many cases, also to see their work presented in co-authored chapters. We hope that they will be pleased by the collective results. Most chapters include reference to material held in the City of Aberdeen Archives, the City of Aberdeen Archaeological Unit or in the University of Aberdeen Library. Staff in all three locations - especially Judith Cripps and Iain Gray (of the City Archives), Judith Stones, Alison Cameron, Jan Dunbar and Helen McPherson (of the Archaeology Unit) and Michelle Gait, Caroline Craig and Mike Craig (of the University Library) - have been particularly helpful in the selection and reproduction of illustrations. The staff in the Map Room of the National Library of Scotland have also been characteristically helpful.

Colleagues in Aberdeen University's Department of History - especially Roy Bridges, Grant Simpson and Peter Payne - were very supportive in the early stages of the enterprise, while more recently Andrew Mackillop has been generous in providing both advice and additional data from a variety of unpublished eighteenth-century sources. Alison Sandison, of the Department of Geography, produced several maps with speed and efficiency, despite the tight deadlines we imposed upon her. Judith Stones was particularly generous in her discussions of pre-burghal Aberdeen and this was reinforced by Jan Dunbar's illustrations. In Edinburgh, Mark Mulhern, Martin Rorke and Katie Stevenson, and in Aberdeen Barbara McGillivray and Janet Hendry, undertook various editorial or secretarial tasks, while Eila Williamson (of Glasgow University) and David Worthington (now of University College, Maynooth) made transcriptions of various records for some of the contributors.

In an important sense, however, our greatest debt is that owed to Aberdeen City Council, to the members of the then City of Aberdeen District Council who sat on the Working Party which guided and oversaw the *New History of Aberdeen* project from its inception - Councillors Adam, Adams, Cooney, Farquhar, Massie, Savidge, Third and Urquhart - and to the former Lord Provost, James Wyness, whose idea it first was to commission this book and its companion volume. We are also grateful for all the practical help and support which was given by the late Ann Hughes, then Depute Chief Executive, and Alan Towns, City Solicitor, in making the project a reality.

We hope that the *New History of Aberdeen* will live up to the expectations of those who put their trust in its editors and authors. And, above all, we hope that the book will appeal to Aberdonians throughout the world.

DD
EPD
ML
Dublin, August 2002

Foreword

With the publication of volume 1 of *Aberdeen: A New History* the realisation of the hopes and aspirations of the original Working Party are on the road to fulfilment. It is now up to the City's many historians, amateur and professional, to develop and expand on the themes and topics within the two volumes.

This is the first professionally researched and complete history of the City of Aberdeen. It is, and was always intended to be, as one of our own historians stated 'a quarry into which others will dig and develop more detailed histories'.

It has always been necessary for citizens to keep sight of and nurture a pride in our long history and evolving culture. These volumes will certainly create an awareness on our City that there is a need to understand our roots and, therefore, realise we are, as Aberdonians, unique and remarkable.

Cllr James Wyness,
Town House,
Aberdeen

Preface

Aberdeen has a long and distinctive history. There are many reasons for that. Described in the 1460s as 'beyond the mountains', it was isolated, or at least insulated, from southern Scotland, not so much by the Grampians, as by the barrier of the Mounth, stretching westward from Stonehaven. Aberdeen was recognised in official documents of the fifteenth and sixteenth centuries as the gateway to the 'north pairt' of the kingdom, which lay 'benorth the water of Dee'. And as the political and administrative focus of the Scottish kingdom evolved to the south, geography and geology ensured that the north-east emerged as a distinctive region. Aberdeen – as a market centre, a port, the seat of a sheriffdom and the home of a bishop and a university – became its focal point. Indeed, Aberdeen dominated the largest rural hinterland of any Scottish town for much of the period considered by this volume, its orbit of influence stretching from the Mounth almost as far as Inverness. In this vast expanse, it had few rival towns of any size with which to contend. Inverurie and Kintore, although both enjoyed the status of a royal burgh, were tiny market centres. Elgin had a population considerably less than 1,000, even at the end of the seventeenth century. Inverness, the largest of the other northern burghs, paid, at most, a third of the national taxation paid by Aberdeen. By comparison, Aberdeen's status as one of Scotland's foremost towns was unchallenged throughout the period covered by this volume.

Partly as a result of its location and its regional dominance, Aberdeen witnessed a more complex interaction of town and country than the other major Scottish towns. Local lords and landowners sought preferential access to the town's market, port and professional services. The houses of great nobles and other wealthy landowners jostled for space in the Castlegate, while 'landmen' – ordinary country folk, ranging from farmers to chapmen and peddlars – thronged its large marketplace. For substantial parts of this period, the town was run not by merchants, as in most other burghs of comparable size, but by merchant lairds. Indeed, Aberdeen had fewer large merchants than one might expect for an exporting town but also relatively few craftsmen. Many trades, including textiles and plaiding, were based in the surrounding countryside.

At the same time, however, Aberdeen's horizons stretched beyond its provincial backyard. The twelfth century is the first for which we have anything like adequate documentary records. By then, the town was probably one of a trio of headports, including Perth and Berwick, which acted as a commercial funnel for the main economic regions in Scotland – Moray (which was then far more extensive than now), Scotia and Lothian. By the fourteenth century, Aberdeen's status as one of the 'four great towns of Scotland' was recognised by the authorities of Bruges, the foremost commercial centre in northern Europe. Indeed, Aberdeen was well known to merchants and seamen from Dieppe in north-western France to Stralsund and Danzig (modern-day Gdansk) in the Baltic. The acknowledged word for cod in the streets of seaports in the Low Countries was 'aberdaan'.

Yet, for all its significance – provincially, nationally and internationally – medieval Aberdeen may seem tiny to modern eyes. Growth was not axiomatic. In 1400, Aberdeen's population was probably smaller than that it had been in 1300. The Black Death struck in the mid fourteenth century, leaving Aberdeen with a population of only about 3,000 by 1400. Repeated outbreaks of plague in the following centuries ensured that the population rose to only about 5,500 in the 1570s, and to some 8,300 by the early 1640s, before the last, major outbreak of plague arrived in 1647. The equivalent population figures for Edinburgh at the same dates are about 4,000, 13,500, and 20,000. Demographic uncertainties, however, did not deter physical growth. By 1500, Aberdeen was the home of the largest parish church in Scotland, St Nicholas, which had seen extensive refurbishment and enlargement in the second half of the fifteenth century. By 1600, the royal burgh and the nearby bishop's burgh each had its own university college – a situation which was unique in the British Isles. Between them, Aberdeen's two universities were producing some fifty graduates a year by the 1620s, fully a quarter of the output of all of Scotland's universities.

Such has been the restructuring of landscape over the centuries, present-day Aberdonians must make a concerted effort to imagine the shape of the town as it existed before the fording of the Denburn defile and the building of Union Street – the iconic moment at which this volume ends. What had been main streets and exit points in the period covered by this volume are now back lanes. The original site of the town, probably at the junction of the Denburn and the Putachie Burn, at the foot of St Katherine's Hill, is now obscured by nineteenth- and twentieth-century developments. Many of the eccentricities of the royal burgh's site have been flattened, forded or by-passed over the centuries. The Castlegate has been without a castle since the early fourteenth century. The original line of 'Broad Street', or Broadgate, is where it is at its narrowest. The names of only two of the burgh's four medieval quarters – Green, Futty, Even and Crooked (or Cruikit) – will be familiar to today's Aberdonians. Yet, in the case of Futty, the historic name which dates back to at least the fourteenth century and is based on St Fotin has been superseded in modern times by 'Footdee' - a complete misnomer since, whatever Futty is, it is not, and never has been, at 'the foot of the Dee'.

For the purposes of this volume, what distinguishes Aberdeen's early history above all is the wealth of material to be gleaned from its rich archaeological heritage and its voluminous records. The latter begin at the turn of the fourteenth century, fully a century or more before those of all the other major Scottish towns. This material has been haphazardly used by successive generations of historians, beginning (arguably) with Hector Boece (d. 1536), the first principal of King's College. Boece compiled a biographical compendium of the first bishops of Aberdeen, as well as a more general history of Scotland. His reliability falls well short of the standards expected of modern scholars and he embellished much that was already apocryphal or ill-founded. Amongst these legends is that of 'Bon Accord', claimed to be the secret password used by Aberdonian supporters of Robert I (1306-29) during their assault on the town's English garrison in 1308. On this basis, a special relationship was said to have been established between the royal burgh and the usurper king. In later generations, the special affinity between the now heroic warrior king 'of blessed memory' and the royal burgh was preserved by the motto of 'Bon Accord' and a double tressure on the burgh seal and later coat of arms. In fact, both motto and tressure are not to be found until a century after the events of 1308 - as good an example as any of the collective amnesia which often is historical identity. Yet the double tressure - unique to a burgh in this period - may in fact mark the sacrifice of Aberdonians, not in 1308, but in 1411, at the battle of 'Red Harlaw'. Again, here is an example as good as any of history getting it right, but for the wrong reasons. There *was* a distinctive relationship between the crown and the royal burgh in the late Middle Ages; like other relationships involving king and subjects, it needed mythology to provide it with status.

It was not really until the nineteenth century that a more rigorous, source-based examination began to be undertaken of Aberdeen's records. William Kennedy's two-volume *Annals of Aberdeen from the Reign of King William the Lion to the End of 1818*, published in 1818, began that process. For all his faults as a historian, and he had many, Kennedy trawled the burgh's records for what he regarded as interesting information - and his work remains, to this day, a significant (and surprisingly broad-ranging) point of access to those sources. For most of the nineteenth century, however, historical energies took a different route, focusing above all on the publication of record material. Much of this task, as far as Aberdeen was concerned, was undertaken under the auspices of the Spalding Club and its successors, which published copious extracts from various burgh sources. These collections remain important, and are cited regularly in the pages which follow, although much remained (and remains) hidden in the manuscripts housed in the

City Archive. It has been estimated that there are in the region of a million entries in the unpublished council records of the fifteenth century alone.

It was not until the 1970s and '80s that a cohort of postgraduate students began to investigate the town's records more fully; and it was about the same time that archaeological remains began to be unearthed in substantial amounts. Many of the scholars who used both kinds of evidence had been enthused by the new emphasis on cultural, economic and social history which held sway in contemporary academic circles, but which had not greatly troubled the Spalding Club's editors. The fruits of this new research gradually began to appear in doctoral theses, and then in published format. Hitherto, however, there have been few attempts to produce a holistic account of pre-industrial Aberdeen. Such studies which have been published - such as Fenton Wyness's *City by the Grey North Sea* (Aberdeen, 1966) and Alexander Keith's *A Thousand Years of Aberdeen* (Aberdeen, 1972) - are entertaining, but show little sign of grappling with the voluminous records of the town. Even before their publication, R. Murdoch Lawrence had commented in the *Aberdeen Journal* of 8 August 1953:

> In view of the visit to Aberdeen next year of the British Association, an up-to-date history of the city is essential. It should be the work of several collaborators, each an authority in his [sic] own line of research.

Somewhat belatedly, it is that need which this volume seeks to address - with twenty-four contributors based in two continents, drawn from a range of interests and specialisms, and more than a third of them female. This is not to claim that the following pages constitute the final authority on Aberdeen's early history. Several contributors point to topics upon which much research remains to be done and the rich records preserved in the City Archives have been still only partially exploited. Nevertheless, the detail presented in this volume provides a picture that can be both intimate and revealing. No apology should be necessary for the graphic picture of life and death, health and disease - and particularly venereal disease - which can be gleaned from the uniquely rich records of Aberdeen. Indeed, what else might one expect from a market town, a seaport and a place with not one, but two, sets of university students?

EPD

DD

ML

Introduction:
Aberdeen Before Aberdeen

E. PATRICIA DENNISON

Aberdeen - the solid, confident capital of north-east Scotland, neighbour to a harsh, grey North Sea and the granite lands of Buchan - has a long and hard-working history. It owes its urban origins to two small medieval burghs - Old Aberdeen, set in a crook of the River Don, and New Aberdeen, on the north bank of the River Dee (Fig. 0.1). Before the city existed, these small towns were making their own mark on Scotland and overseas.

But this is not the beginning. Before the burghs were founded, there were small settlements or townships hugging the banks of the Dee and Don, and still earlier, before these small Dark Age settlements established themselves, men were settling, fishing, hunting and clearing fields for agriculture. Before them, yet other peoples were roaming the Aberdeen area in search of food. People have chosen to settle here for thousands of years; and, to this day, evidence of these early Aberdonians stands prominently on the landscape while other traces of their presence is hidden in the ground.

In 1976, an archaeological team working at 45-59 the Green in New Aberdeen unearthed evidence of Mesolithic (literally meaning Middle Stone Age) flint-knapping, the tools that were worked out of nodules picked up on beaches and river beds. This was merely the first of a number of discoveries showing that Aberdeen had been inhabited from at least about 6,000 BC. The site of 67-71 the Green revealed evidence of Mesolithic activity, as did 16–18 Netherkirkgate where several hundred flints were found.[1] Very recently, it was realised that a series of ditches at 12 Martin's Lane, which lay under the earlier Carmelite friary, and still further below the pre-friary layers, also contained flints. Whenever excavations have taken place within the city centre, almost invariably Mesolithic flints have been found in stratified layers below the medieval town. Shell middens in the Nigg Bay area are probably also further evidence that people were in this area up to 8,000 years ago, living off the shellfish they gathered from the shore. All of this is confirmation of communities, possibly in temporary camps, moving around the area that is now the city of Aberdeen, hunting the local animals, gathering from the countryside and fishing for their food.

Beyond the central core of the city, wonderful standing remnants of early man may still be seen. Long Cairn, to the west, overlooking Skene Road, is Neolithic, probably between 6,000 and 4,000 years old. Cairns were built as burial places by Neolithic men, who were gradually becoming more settled and farming the land. There are a number of other, slightly later standing structures, but still of great antiquity, dating from the Later Neolithic to the Bronze Age, that is from roughly the third millennium BC to 600 BC. Recumbent standing stones set in a circle, probably designed as a place of ritual or for lunar observation, occupy a wonderful position, overlooking the twenty-first century airport. The rich prehistory of the

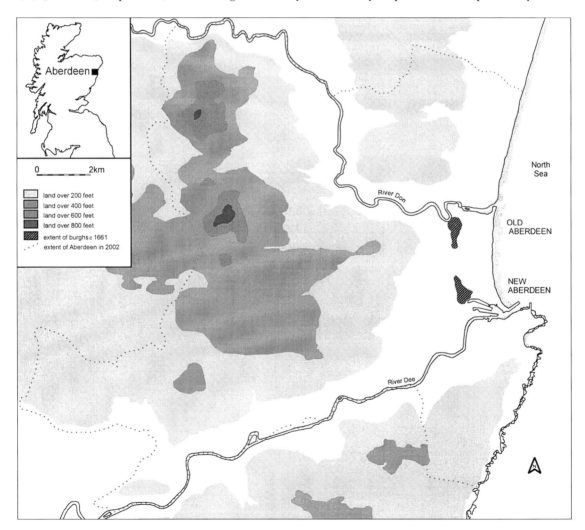

ABERDEEN BEFORE 1800

Aberdeen area is seen in two further stone circles (Fig.0.2). Binghill stone circle, with a nearby cairn, stands in what is now wooded land and Friarsfield circle, although in its present state partially reconstructed, is probably still intact below ground. Individual standing stones of this period may either be remnants of stone circles or way-markers. Dubford Stone (Plate 1), in a fine position with views to the south, may be a survival of a stone circle, whereas Lang Stane at Hilton is thought to be a way-marker for the early people who travelled around the Aberdeen area. It was said that there were once several cup-marked stones, enigmatic prehistoric markings in stone, in the vicinity of Blacktop Stone, but only one is now identifiable.

A number of monuments dating to the Later Neolithic or Bronze Ages still survive. The Aberdeen area is rich with evidence of settlement in this early period. Cults Cairn (Plate 2) is a fine monument. Tullos Cairn dates from the Bronze Age and is one of the four survivors of the best preserved cairnfield in the north-east. The other three, also dating from the Bronze Age, are Crab's Cairn, which was unfortunately damaged during the Second World War and afterwards; Baron's

Figure 0..2
Evidence of
prehistoric people.

Cairn, likewise spoiled by a World War II observation post; and Cat Cairn. In Kirkhill Forest, despite afforestation over many years, there is potentially evidence of considerable activity dating to the Bronze Age and later prehistoric period. Slacks Cairn may still be seen, as well as the remains of hut circles, the bases of huts, and evidence of field clearance, indicating that people were living a settled, permanent existence in the area. Another hut circle can still be identified at Clerkhill Wood; and it is recorded that a further two circles stood nearby. Cists, or stone-lined graves, also date from this period. At the Scotstown Cist (Plate 3), found during house building in 1975, there was a skeleton, a Beaker - a pot with an S-shaped profile and simple rim, usually highly decorated with impressed or incised patterns - two flints and some traces of copper. This has been reconstructed and may be viewed at Provost Skene's House. Six cists were found at Borrowstone. The grave goods here included Beakers, a superb group of barbed and tanged arrowheads and a highly polished greenstone wristguard (Plate 4), all testimony to the skills of workmanship. Marischal Museum contains material from these cists.

Of more recent date, giving clear indication that Aberdeen and its surrounding countryside were consistently favoured settlement sites, is a fragment of a wall, probably part of an enclosure, on the summit of Elrick Hill. Brimmond Hill, likewise, offers clear evidence of prehistoric activity. Field clearance heaps, in the form of up to twenty stony mounds, might imply permanent homes. It was recorded in the 1930s that there were hut circles here, although much of the hillside is now covered with gorse. A single stone, called the Gouk Stone, is of uncertain date but may have been a way-marker. It is also possible that Corby Loch had a crannog dating to this time. Crannogs were fortified homes, set on either a natural or man-made island in a loch, and sometimes set above the water on stilts. Access was by a walkway from the shore or bank. This could be readily defended, or even removed, if attacked.[2]

What was so special about the Aberdeen area that man would choose to settle here over such a huge extent of time? The answer lies in both the geography and the geology of the site. Clearly, the twin estuaries of the Dee and the Don provided not only a route inland but also a source of food, whether gathered from the shores and banks of the rivers or fished for from primitive log boats. To the north of the Don, the coastline takes on the character of dune-fringed beaches, with rocky headlands; south of the Dee, much of the coast is flanked by cliffs. In the north-east, the Dee and Don provided rare embayments, the other examples on the east coast being Montrose and the Ythan. West of the modern city of Aberdeen, between the Dee and the Don valleys, was higher ground, dissected by shallow valleys with small streams. Most of these small streams emptied themselves into the Dee estuary or the lower Dee channel. A series of sand and gravel mounds, formed by meltwater activities during the decline of the last Ice Age, and running in a roughly north-south direction, to some extent impeded these flows of water along what was essentially a slope downwards from west to east. To the east of what would become the city, natural sand dunes, ridges and links, grass-covered, marshy ground, provided further obstacles to the eastwards flow of the waters, so diverting them in a southerly direction, running almost parallel with the sea. As a result there developed small lochs and poorly drained areas. But these small burns and lochans, along with the resultant springs and seepages, were the essential water supply for early man and for the animals that he hunted.[3] Conversely, the gravel mounds might supply dry ground for the building of primitive huts for shelter. The area provided the essentials for living – a food supply, from the rivers and land; a water supply; and some firm ground on which to erect shelters and give protection from marauders, be they human or animal.

Whether settlement was continuous on the Aberdeen site is difficult to prove. Aberdeen's history from the time of the Romans until the eleventh century remains somewhat shrouded. Normandykes Roman camp to the south of New Aberdeen might, speculatively, suggest that there was native settlement nearby which the Roman authorities wished to control. A settlement with the name of *Devana* existed at the time of the Roman occupation of Britain; but whether this can be equated with the site of Aberdeen or, rather, Normandykes itself is unclear.[4]

A possible Iron Age souterrain was discovered in the Netherkirkgate before the building of Marks and Spencer's store in the 1960s. Souterrains were underground chambers, dating to the last centuries BC and early centuries AD. And very recently a cut feature in Shiprow was radiocarbon-dated to the first century AD.[5] Two symbol stones may still be found at the chapel of St Fergus, Dyce.[6] The earlier of these two Pictish stones dates to the seventh century and is a slab incised with a large beast. The second is a ninth-century, finely decorated cross-slab with symbols flanking the knot-filled cross. Smaller grave markers found in the graveyard of the chapel, some of which may date to the seventh century, are further evidence of an early Christian site.

What is very clear from documentary sources is that New Aberdeen was in existence as an important township even before it was given the status of a royal burgh, with specific legal and economic privileges, some time in the reign of David I (1124–53). By then, Aberdeen was of sufficient importance to be visited by the peripatetic king and his court; it is known that David I issued at least one charter from Aberdeen.[7] Although this brought prestige to the settlement, what is important about the royal presence is the inherent implication about the economic status of the settlement on the north bank of the River Dee. The town was clearly capable, by this reign, of housing the king and his household, along with all the magnates and prelates attendant at the royal court. The court had also to be provisioned. This entailed not only basic food supplies, which were largely available from the surrounding countryside, but also luxury items, such as wines, spices and fine cloths. All of these had to be imported. Aberdeen was by this time an established, viable trading post of some standing for it to be able to play host to the royal court.

When, precisely, this trading post was established is difficult to specify. Although evidence of overseas trade before the twelfth century is slight, it is likely that such trade probably never totally died out during the Dark Ages; and there does seem to be some evidence that there was a level of resurgence in the latter half of the eleventh century. According to her contemporary biographer, Queen Margaret, the wife of King Malcolm Canmore (1058-93), encouraged foreign merchants into Scotland; and it is known that Scotland was trading with both Flanders and England in the last decades of the eleventh century.[8] To reinforce this, an assize that has been attributed to David I's reign suggests that as early as the reign of Malcolm Canmore fixed dues had been set on hides for export, implying, at the very least, a steady export trade.[9] There can be no doubt that Aberdeen was one of the participants in this resurgence.

There is, very significantly, specific evidence of the importance of Aberdeen as a trading post before it gained burghal status. As early as the reign of Alexander I (1107-24), it was one of three trading centres cited as being north of the Forth. Because it was considerably further north than the other two - Inverkeithing and Perth - Aberdeen was in the ideal situation to dominate trade in the northern parts of the country.[10] Also, in a grant of c. 1180 by King William the Lion (1165-1214) to his burgesses at Aberdeen, Moray and north of the Mounth, it was quite specifically stated that they should enjoy their 'free hanse', as they had in the time of David I.[11] Here is firm evidence that by the first half of the twelfth century settlements of both foreign and native traders were established in Aberdeen. In 1136, the bishop of Aberdeen received an important concession from the crown: he was granted the tithes, or tenths, of the goods of all ships coming into Aberdeen.[12] Although intended as a mark of favour from the king, this grant confirms that the haven of Aberdeen was well frequented by ships and merchants. Clearly, Aberdeen was already, in the early years of the twelfth century, a thriving port.

But how long had this been the case? It is not likely that Aberdeen suddenly burst upon the mercantile scene in a few years at the beginning of the twelfth century. Given its geographical setting, Aberdeen had offered an excellent site for a trading post for centuries; perhaps back to prehistoric times. It is possible that traders had inhabited Aberdeen from well back into the haar of the Dark Ages. This awaits verification by the archaeologists. But one thing is certain. Aberdeen was an established trading settlement before it was granted burghal status.

What is less clear is whether the parish church of St Nicholas, one of the important landmarks in the twelfth century, was in existence before the township became a burgh. The dedication to this saint, the patron saint of traders and sailors, was certainly favoured on both sides of the North Sea at the end of the eleventh century, as in Berwick, Newcastle, Amsterdam, Kiel and Hamburg. But this does not necessarily indicate that New Aberdeen's church was founded at this time. The first documentary evidence of the church comes as late as 1157, in a papal bull of Adrian IV, when the Bishop of Aberdeen was confirmed in its possession.[13] Such confirmation, however, would argue for an already existing ecclesiastical foundation.

The siting of the church may, on the other hand, offer some clue as to where this small trading settlement clustered. Comment has been made on a number of occasions on the seemingly unusual placement of the church outwith the medieval settlement and the town gates, or ports, to the west of the urban core. A number of explanations have been proffered, but none is entirely convincing.[14] Such a siting outside settlement is not in itself unknown. St Mary's Church, Dundee, for example, when first founded, stood outside and to the west of the town, although as the town expanded westwards the church ultimately stood within the core of medieval settlement.[15] And parish churches were not necessarily urban: rural parishes might in many cases pre-date urban growth, such as St Cuthbert's beside Edinburgh. If the church was an ancient foundation it could originally have been a rural parish church. It does, however, seem very likely, given the proximity of the much larger parish of St Machar's at Old Aberdeen, that the church of St Nicholas was intended to serve the trading settlement at the Dee.

But where, exactly, was this settlement? It might be expected that it would have grown up close to the Dee and the Denburn, the focus of its trading activities, where in early times boats could be pulled up on the shore and, later, primitive harbour works built. A small trading settlement would also want a market and a collection point for all those coming to use that market. The market place would be located in an open area as near as possible to the shore, in order to spare undue portage of the goods to the point of sale. In 1219, there is reference to the 'forum', or market, of Aberdeen and in 1317 the Aberdeen Burgh Court Roll three times refers to a 'tolloneum', the place where tolls or market taxes were collected.[16] There is, as yet, no archaeological or historical evidence that firmly locates this early market and toll collection point. They were not in Castlegate, the later site of the tolbooth and market (see Chapter 1), as the king gave permission for a tolbooth to be built here for the first time only in 1393. Clues to the site of the early tolbooth come as late as the seventeenth century, when Gordon of Rothiemay claimed that the ruins of an old tolbooth were still standing. These he describes as being near the Trinitarian friary site and at the postern gate of the laird of Pitfodels' town house, which opened out on to the shore. Both the friary and the town house stood to the south-west of St Katherine's Hill, at the east end of the Green.

One other small clue which might support this area as the site of the early market and tolbooth, around which the traders would cluster, is partially revealed in cartographic evidence. When open market spaces are eventually abandoned for larger, more commodious sites and they are developed upon or encroached upon with buildings, a process known as 'market repletion' sets in. This can often be detected in later maps in many towns. The same may be true for Aberdeen. Gordon of Rothiemay's mid seventeenth-century map shows a built-up triangular area at the eastern end of the Green (Plate 38). This has all the hallmarks of a classic case of market repletion.[17]

Rothiemay's seventeenth-century map also clearly shows that medieval New Aberdeen was endowed with some major burns or rivulets, including Powcreek Burn to the east, Trinity Burn running along near the shore line, Denburn to the west of the town and the Putachie Burn which ran down the west side of St Katherine's Hill (Fig. 1.1). There may have been springs and seepages, which would have provided adequate water for domestic needs and the Loch to the north-west of the town could also supply water. It has been mooted that the Castlegate area was the original nucleus of the town; but it did not have a ready supply of water. Indeed, it has even been argued that there were no springs at the eastern end of the town.[18] It is, as a result, very unlikely that first settlement was in the Castlegate area. There could readily have been movement to that area once wells were dug; but people did not settle where there was no water. A more suitable site, for first settlement, would have been close to one of the burns. A site beside the Putachie and the Denburn would have provided this absolutely essential basic requirement of early settlers, as long as it was not unduly waterlogged. The prehistoric remains of tools and camps and the subsequent presence of both the Carmelite and the Trinitarian friaries in this area, together with the documentary evidence that throughout the medieval period the majority of those crafts that required water power concentrated to the west side of St Katherine's Hill, all strongly suggest that the east end of the Green was not unduly boggy for the small pre-burghal trading settlement.

There was another essential requirement for early settlement and that was security from potential enemies. Most early settlements concentrated on, or clustered near, a focal point that was psychologically or physically safe, such as an ecclesiastical establishment or a fortified spot. It is known that Aberdeen had a castle by 1264 and that this was probably sited on the later-named Castle Hill, at the eastern end of Castlegate.[19] As late as the mid seventeenth century, however, Rothiemay could write that 'the most considerable part of the city stands on three hills – the Castle Hill, St Katherine's Hill and the Gallowgate Hill'.[20] Any of these three hills could have been readily defensible, although none had the advantage of water. Castle Hill offered no more and no less than the other two. It is hypothetically possible that St Katherine's Hill was at one time topped with a simple wooden fortification, which would have offered a measure of protection to a small settlement at its foot. Interestingly, also, which may be a further hint, the office of constable of the castle was hereditary in the family of Kennedy of Carmuc (Kermuck) until the end of the sixteenth century. There is no apparent connection between the Kennedys and Castle Hill; the Kennedy name, however, is traditionally linked with St Katherine's Hill and here it was that they reputedly founded a chapel in the thirteenth century (see Chapter 1).[21]

Although the western end of the Green at the confluence of the Dee and the Denburn might have been waterlogged - and the nearby lands of the Carmelites sometimes flooded - there was some settlement at the western end of the Green by the end of the twelfth century. It is also possible that the bottom of the steep slope leading down from St Nicholas Church to the Green might have been a bit boggy. But the eastern end of the Green did offer the basic essentials for settlement - a water supply, yet dry ground; ready access to the Dee, the Denburn and the sea; an open market space; and the protection of a church and possibly a primitive fortification. It is very possible, then, that the pre-burghal settlement of traders clustered at the foot of St Katherine's Hill in the streets that became Putachieside, Netherkirkgate and East Green, and perhaps creeping round also into Shore Brae.

But there was one thing this site could not offer - room for expansion. To the west and south was waterlogged land or water, to the east of the Green and Putachieside and south of Netherkirkgate were the steep slopes of St Katherine's Hill. Expansion could be successful only in a north-easterly direction. Archaeological evidence has shown that this was beginning to happen in the mid to late twelfth century in Upperkirkgate. Significantly, sherds of pottery at 30-46 Upperkirkgate, dated to as early as the eleventh century, are firm indication, if not of settlement on this particular site, then at least of nearby settlement at this early period;[22] and by the late twelfth and thirteenth centuries in Broadgate and Gallowgate. A new market centre would be needed as the town flourished. Broadgate and Castlegate, large open sites, could offer what the East Green could not, with its confined situation and winding water courses. There was a shift in focus. The Green ceased to function as the market centre. The medieval nucleus would lie further east, leaving St Nicholas parish church as if outwith the main settlement. This also released land for the foundations in the late thirteenth century of the Carmelite and Trinitarian friaries, both of which favoured sites at the edge of settlement. The possibly original small trading settlement site now appeared as marginal land as the later, more easterly, medieval town plan gradually evolved.[23]

The site of the little settlement to the north, Old Aberdeen, was equally determined by both geography and geology. And, just as with the trading post to the south, there are uncertainties about its history before the twelfth century. There is a well-known legend that its origins lie in the sixth century, when St Machar, a companion of St Columba, left the Christian community at Iona and came to preach and convert in this area. He reputedly built a church on, or very near, where the cathedral now stands, as he was instructed to set his church 'where the river curves in the shape of a bishop's crosier, just before it enters the sea'.[24] That suggests in the loop of the Don where the cathedral of St Machar now stands. Others have argued that Christianity came with the efforts of missionaries led by St Ninian from the south-west of Scotland, but this is now a somewhat discredited view. Only archaeological evidence can establish whether there was an early church founded on the site of the cathedral; but it may be possible that sometime around the end of the sixth century a small fishing community, scattered along the banks of the Don, was converted to Christianity.

What is known is that David I began a programme of reorganisation of the church in his kingdom and specifically laid down diocesan boundaries. It was at this point, in about 1131, that he reputedly transferred the seat of the ancient diocese, centred on Mortlach in Banffshire, to Old Aberdeen and instructed Bishop Nechtan to erect a stone building.[25] Whether this move was to a new building on virgin ground, or to the site of an existing church, has yet to be established.[26]

Undoubtedly, once this new building was underway the size of the little fishing community expanded. A workforce would be needed to help with construction and general services, and food supplies were essential for the religious community. Without archaeological evidence, it must be assumed that the settlement clustered near to the church, as well as to the fortified place now called Tillydrone Motte (Plate 5), just to the west of the cathedral and still readily visible. To the west was the Loch of Old Aberdeen and Kettle Hill, both barriers to settlement. To the south, joined by a tributary flowing out of the loch, running from west to east was the Powis Burn, 'pow' meaning a slow-moving stream, which created marshy areas. This ran just south of where King's College now stands.[27] As with New Aberdeen, first settlement in Old Aberdeen would avoid waterlogged areas.

But geography and geology offered a major advantage. The raised ridge, later called Spitalhill, afforded a firm route to the trading settlement two miles to the south. As the little settlement began to develop, its main street would move southwards from its early ecclesiastical nucleus in a direct line towards the later settlement of New Aberdeen. The skeleton of the City of Aberdeen had been formed.

Part I

LOCATIONS AND LIFESTYLES

1

The Growth of Two Towns

E. PATRICIA DENNISON, ANNE T. SIMPSON
and GRANT G. SIMPSON

The Aberdeen region and its various settlements, 1100–1600

The Introduction has located the probable origins of pre-burghal New Aberdeen and Old Aberdeen within the area between Dee and Don. It is possible to look further into certain details of the landscape, in order to see how some other settlements also emerged (usually at unknown dates) and to suggest why they appeared and were interrelated. The general survey of the topography and geology of the area in the Introduction has emphasised the benefits derived from these in relation to early settlement and development. But it is one of the fascinations of studying the early centuries of Aberdeen's history that there can be balanced against such positive elements a number of negative features which also had an impact. The coastline south of Aberdeen is often inhospitable and composed of rocks, cliffs and creeks. At a period when sea transport was a vital mode of travel, the Dee estuary was a valuable refuge for shipping. But even here problems could hinder, since a sandbar tended to form regularly at the mouth of the Dee. And the inner part of the estuary consisted of low ground called the Inches, which was frequently covered by tidal water (see Chapters 7 and 17).

Inland water and watercourses and their importance for the two settlements have already been mentioned. In addition to the Powcreek, Trinity and Putachie Burns and the lengthy Denburn, a further five (Polmuir Burn, Holburn, Westburn, Spital Burn and Powis Burn) ran through the areas west and north of the built-up core of New Aberdeen (Fig. 1.1). Along with the two lochs, at Old Aberdeen and New Aberdeen, and various boggy areas, these nine streams not only provided water supplies for men and animals, plus industries such as milling and tanning, but also placed hindrances in the landscape. There were geographical minuses as well as pluses.

All this water existed in, or ran through, a terrain which was characterised by numerous awkward hills and mounds. The plan-view of the two towns in 1661, by James Gordon of Rothiemay, identifies about a dozen of them (Plate 38). Intrusive bumps of this sort had an effect on routeways and meant that most of the early street-plan of New Aberdeen was highly irregular in form. The burgh did not possess

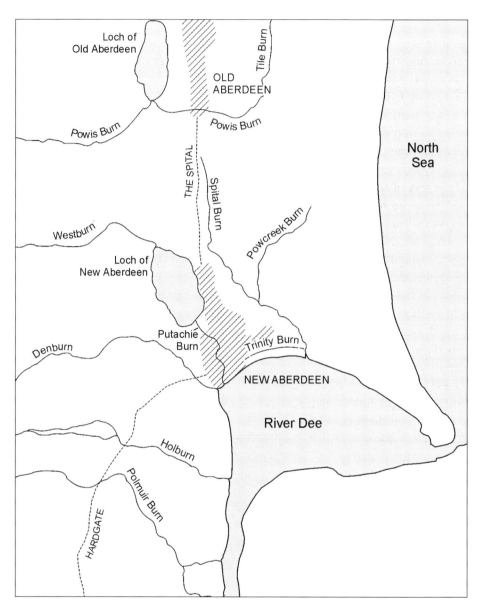

*Figure 1.1
Medieval Aberdeen,
showing
watercourses.
(after J. Smith).*

any open street sufficiently central and prominent to be named the High Street, that is the principal street. This failure to evolve a visible High Street is almost unique among early Scottish towns. In New Aberdeen, there were very few wide, level stretches of ground conducive to extended urban layout and building. Curving streets and steepish slopes were common. The only large, open rectangular area was the Castlegate, which may have been a secondary development (see Introduction).

Given all these topographical troubles, it is in some ways surprising that, from such an early date, human settlement developed in the area as much as it did. The motivations which led the early inhabitants to combat their surroundings must have been powerful, and were certainly varied. Within the landscape there were clusters of activity and a network of routeways to enable people to reach these. Church, harbour, market, defence point, bridge and industrial unit were all vital nodes within the structure. To understand these crux points and the settlements related to them, it may be helpful to follow some of the principal routes of the region. Many medieval travellers along these narrow ways would see New Aberdeen as the goal of their journey. But as this is a history of Aberdeen (Old and New), it will be more revealing to retrace the steps of an early Aberdonian and travel outwards from the centre.

To go south by the coast road, avoiding the difficult passes over the Grampians, a start would be made at the Green.[1] The way went west, by a ford over the Denburn, later replaced by the Bow Brig (Bridge). Immediately came a steep climb up the Windmill Brae on to the Hardgate (meaning a built roadway). This road ran along a ridge - utilised by Union Street many centuries later (see Chapter 18) - then turned south-west down a hill, crossed the Holburn near the Justice Mills, and proceeded south, also crossing the Polmuir Burn. A route involving two steep hills, three mills and three burns was fairly typical of the environs of early Aberdeen. At a point near the western end of the present Fonthill Road, the old road divided, where the right fork passed into the modern Broomhill Road, and continued for many miles as the ancient route along Deeside.[2] At Broomhill Road lies Ruthrieston, the modern form of the name 'Ruadri's toun', meaning settlement of Ruadri, possibly identifiable as the mormaer or earl of Mar in the 1130s.[3] The placename records one of Aberdeen's early peripheral settlements, probably small in extent. The other fork of the road made for the Bridge of Dee, planned in the later fifteenth century, completed in 1527 and still extant. The bridge had seven arches, a port or gateway, much heraldic decoration and a chapel for the use of travellers.[4] Even if the Hardgate route presented problems, the Bridge of Dee made a handsome entry point into the outer lands of the burgh. King James V (1513-42) and his queen, Mary of Guise, passed across it on their progress to the town in 1541.[5]

The medieval Aberdonian who chose to go south by crossing the lower reaches of the River Dee would arrive in the parish of Nigg, in northern Kincardineshire. This parish had some good soils, and its original core was an ancient church centre. This was dedicated to St Fittick, a Celtic missionary, who seems by confusion of names and legends to have had his career erroneously intertwined with that of the French St Fiacre.[6] St Fittick's church of Nigg, with its lands, was granted by King William the Lion (1165-1214) to the abbey of Arbroath. His charter is undated, but must have been issued between 1189 and 1194.[7] Two ferries were available for journeys south. The upper one ran from Ferryhill, also called Clayhills, at an inlet where the Holburn joined the Dee. The available clay here led to the emergence, as early as the fourteenth century, of a settlement of potters: hence the name Potters' Creek.[8] It was customary for some industries, such as this one, to carry out their activities at sites beyond the edge of the built-up urban area.

The lower ferry was much closer to the mouth of the Dee. Its arrival point on the south side of the river in medieval times was the village of Torry, which was the principal settlement within the parish of Nigg. The ferry at Torry, with its profits, was also a possession of the abbots of Arbroath, who may have had a residence there. The village was a flourishing fishing-town and was raised to the status of a burgh of barony in 1495.[9] It functioned as a harbour for larger vessels which could not successfully navigate the awkward channel of the Dee up to the inner harbour at the Quayhead.

Discussion of ferry routes provides a reminder that the River Dee was a principal routeway in the Middle Ages and for long afterwards. Sea transport was essential, not only for journeys to Scandinavia, the Low Countries or further afield but also as the usual mode of travel along the Scottish coast or to England. The original harbour lay at a point near to the marshy confluence of the Denburn with the north-western edge of the Dee estuary. In a geographical sense, that harbour was rather more a Denburn harbour than it was a River Dee harbour. It is striking also that topography has dictated the extent that the innermost point of the greatly developed modern harbour lies very close to the upper point of the old harbour. Stand now at the corner of Trinity Quay and Market Street and you are gazing at the site of at least nine centuries of maritime history.

On the eastern side of the Dee estuary, roughly halfway between the town centre and the river mouth, lay a further outlying settlement. This was Futty, a fishing village which was reached by a roadway from the Castlegate, passing below the Castle Hill. Its modern name, 'Footdee', proclaimed on the destination boards of buses which travel there, is a misnomer. Its earliest form, in the fourteenth century, is 'Fotin' and commemorates St Fotin, to whom a local chapel was dedicated. He and his chapel became forgotten and it was gradually assumed that the name must mean 'Foot of the Dee', which it does not.[10] The town council in 1498 founded a new chapel for the white fishers (fishers of white fish) at Futty, which was dedicated to St Clement. It fell out of use after the Reformation of 1560, but was restored to activity in 1631.[11] The situation was further complicated by the decision of the council in 1808 to move the settlement to a new planned village site actually at the mouth of the Dee.[12]

As the Hardgate was clearly the principal exit out of the town to the south, so the main northern route was the one which aimed for the church of St Machar and, beyond it, a way across the Don. This road once again demonstrates the difficulties of the landscape. From Broad Street (Broadgate), it first avoids the Loch and slopes gently up to the top of Gallowgate Hill, then descends quite steeply down to the marshy area of Mounthooly. Just before that, two ways diverge from it to the west. The first leads to the sparsely settled but significant lands of the Forest of Stocket, granted to the burgh by the crown in 1319 (Ill. 19).[13] The names Foresterhill, Mid Stocket Road and Forest Road, among others, commemorate an area valuable for both timber supply and recreational hunting. The other branch from the Gallowgate begins at Causewayend (that is, the end of the causeway, or built roadway). That led north-west, eventually to Inverurie and the lands of Garioch, formed into a royal dependent lordship in the late twelfth century. Proceeding beyond Mounthooly, the north road climbed again to the top of Spitalhill, then fell sharply down College Bounds, to the boggy stretch where around 1500 Bishop Elphinstone and his cunning masons managed to lay foundations for King's College (see Chapter 15).[14] At the end of the straight and level High Street of Old Aberdeen the road divided. By the left fork it entered through one of the gateways into the Chanonry precinct, surrounding St Machar's Cathedral. To the right it became the modern Don Street, winding and eventually climbing again to the Hillhead of Seaton, overlooking the Don. That river was, in earliest times, crossed by a ford, but a single-arched Gothic bridge was erected nearby about 1300.[15] It still stands, although altered, and is known as the Brig of Balgownie. Beyond it, various roads took the traveller to Buchan and further north.

This northern roadway was one of the most important in the region. Firstly, it had great antiquity. St Machar's church had been visited since the Dark Ages, and even more so after it became a cathedral in about 1131. The harbour of New Aberdeen had traded since before 1100 (see Introduction). The modern no. 20 bus, which today follows the line almost exactly, is successor vehicle to carriages and carts which stretch back in their journeyings to represent over 1,000 years of travel. Secondly, that harbour and the ancient church were two especially vital centres of activity. Old Aberdeen was tiny, but of high status, possessor of both a cathedral and a university. New Aberdeen had the potential to become, as it did, a thriving and expanding community. The hinterland of these two important north-eastern towns may sometimes have been awkward to pass through, but it is perhaps for this very reason that the settlements scattered within it were distinctly varied in size and in origin.

The growing townscape: New Aberdeen, 1100–c. 1560

With the granting of burgh status, probably as early as the reign of David I (1124–53), and the important economic privileges which came with it, New Aberdeen was set to prosper. This increasing wealth was reflected in the townscape. The very first settlement at Aberdeen had probably clustered at the west base of St Katherine's Hill, but this site offered little scope for expansion of the town's market as the burgh grew larger with prosperity (see Introduction). By the fourteenth century the basic street pattern of New Aberdeen had been established; the focal point was the Castlegate, where the market was then held. The market area has remained till today very much as it was in medieval times – a large open space capable of housing a busy, prosperous market. Gordon of Rothiemay in *c.* 1660 described it as 'a rectangular space, of a hundred paces in breadth and 200 in length, nor so far as I know, does Scotland show its equal' (Plate 38).[16]

As already indicated, running north from Castlegate was Broadgate, leading to Gallowgate, and from there northwards to Old Aberdeen. To the west of Broadgate and running parallel with it was Guestrow. It is possible that these two thorough-fares were originally one large open space, which functioned as a market area prior to the move to Castlegate. Westwards from Broadgate and Guestrow ran two streets, Upperkirkgate and Netherkirkgate, giving access to the parish church of St Nicholas. Leading from Upperkirkgate, moving north-westerly out of the town, was Schoolhill.

From the east of Castlegate a road led to the seat of the Justiciar's circuit courts beside Castle Hill and then to Heading Hill. From the south-east corner, at the foot of Castle Hill, ran Futty Wynd, giving access to the separate small fishing settlement of Futty. South from the market area, via Exchequer Row and Shiprow, was the all-important route to the harbourside, Quayhead, and Shore Brae. Skirting the south side of St Katherine's Hill, the road then led westwards to the Green. The Green could also be approached from Netherkirkgate, via Putachieside to the west of St Katherine's Hill.

Many Scottish towns were basically simple single-street settlements throughout the Middle Ages. Such a complex town plan as is found in medieval New Aberdeen is firm indication not only of a clever adaptation of routeways to the contours of the land, but also of the prosperity of the burgh. Lining all these thoroughfares, and running back in a herring-bone pattern, were the burgage plots, or tofts. Tofts were the pieces of land allocated to the burgesses, the privileged members of urban society, on which they might build their homes. These were normally placed at the frontage of the plot and the backlands, at the rear, were used to grow foodstuffs, keep animals and sink wells and midden-pits. In time, as pressure for space in the burgh, especially near the market area, was felt, the backlands began to house the workshops of craftsmen and the homes of poorer people in the town. These backland properties were accessed by small vennels or alleyways. Only the very wealthiest burgesses could afford to retain all their backlands for formal gardens.

This division of the townscape into quite specific burgage plots was not a random process. Tofts were formally laid out by burgh officers called 'liners'. It was their responsibility to measure out the street frontage, prior to land being allocated and, thereafter, to ensure that these delineations were respected by the townspeople and that they did not encroach upon each other's land. The tofts were originally demarcated from each other by either gulleys or simple fences, originally made of wattle; they were later replaced with hedges or small walls of stone.

The built environment of New Aberdeen, 1100–c.1560

Probably the most prominent feature on the townscape was, for a while, the castle, dominating the town from the hill to the east of Castlegate – Castle Hill (Fig. 1.2). When it was built is not clear, but it was certainly in existence by 1264, when the *Exchequer Rolls* detail building works at the castle and its provisioning.[17] The castle did not survive for many decades after this, although it was still standing in 1308, when it was supposedly razed to the ground by the Aberdeen burgesses with their rally-call of 'Bon Accord' (see Chapter 9). On 10 July of that year, Edward II (1307–27) of England instructed that reinforcements be brought from Hartlepool, Newcastle, Berwick-on-Tweed and other strongholds to assist in raising the siege of Aberdeen castle.[18] After this date, however, all documentary references to the castle disappear, so it was possibly destroyed soon after. By whom is equally unclear.

Although the homes of the people were the most personal features on the townscape, as a burgh with trading and marketing privileges, New Aberdeen had three very important urban physical symbols – the market cross, the tolbooth and the tron, or public weighing beam. All stood at the focal point of the burgh, in the market square. According to Gordon, an early tolbooth stood in Shiprow (see Introduction).[19] In the Aberdeen Burgh Court Roll of 1317 this is three times described as 'tolloneum',[20] meaning the place where tolls were collected, rather than 'praetorium', the later Latin word for the vernacular 'tolbooth', so at this stage it may not have functioned as the burgh court assembly rooms, but merely as a toll collection point. But this is not certain. In 1393, Robert III (1390–1406) sanctioned the erection of a tolbooth at the market place on Castlegate, on condition that it did not intrude into the market area itself.[21] It was constructed some time after 1407, when each man of Aberdeen was required to give a day's labour or pay four pence towards its construction.[22] Its design is unknown, other than that it had a steeple, from which the townspeople could keep watch for the safety of their town. It was at the tolbooth that dues to attend the town market were paid, as well as at the town gates. The town weights were housed in the tolbooth and it also functioned as the meeting place for the burgh council and as the town jail. Near to the tolbooth was the market cross. It was here that all market transactions were made, so that all could be seen to be fair and open in the wide public space. Public

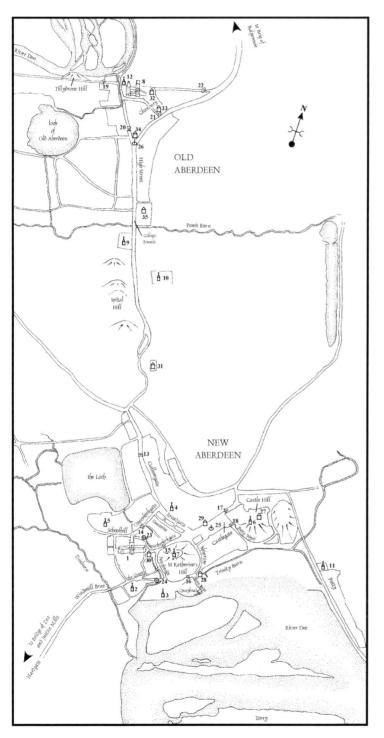

KEY

ECCLESIASTICAL ESTABLISHMENTS

1 St Nicholas Church
2 Carmelite Friary
3 Trinitarian Friary
4 Franciscan Friary
5 Dominican Friary
6 St Ninian's Chapel
7 St Katherine's Chapel
8 St Machar's Cathedral
9 St Maria ad Nives (Snow Kirk)
10 St Peter's Chapel and hospital
11 St Clement's Chapel
12 Hospital in the Chanonry

PORTS

13 Gallowgate Port
14 Upperkirkgate Port
15 Netherkirkgate Port
16 Shiprow Port
17 Justice Port
18 Futty Port
19 Tillydrone Port
20 Cluny's Port
21 Chaplains' Port
22 East Port

MILLS

23 Upper Mill
24 Nether Mill

MARKET CROSSES

25 New Aberdeen
26 Old Aberdeen

OTHER HISTORIC BUILDINGS

27 Castle *(site of)*
28 Early Tolbooth *(poss. site of)*
29 Tolbooth
30 St Thomas the Martyr Hospital
31 Leper Hospital
32 Bishop's Palace
33 Chaplains' Court
34 Town House, Old Aberdeen
35 King's College

Figure 1.2
Conjectural map of
Old and New
Aberdeen, c. 1500.
(After James Gordon
of Rothiemay).

proclamations were also announced from the cross. Close beside the cross and tolbooth was the town weighing machine, the tron.

While these were the most important physical structures in an increasingly economically important burgh, there were other urban features that set New Aberdeen apart from the surrounding countryside. There is no evidence, however, that it was 'walled', in the sense that it was protected by a highly defensible encircling structure. Documentary and archaeological evidence also suggests that the town had no defensive ditching, as some other towns did. The sea to the south, the Loch to the north-west and surrounding marshy areas would have offered some sort of natural defence. There were proposals to ditch the town in 1480, but whether this was achieved is not clear.[23] A licence was granted to the town by James V in 1529, giving it the authority to erect walls of stone and lime and other protective features, such as 'fortalices', ditches and 'munitions', but there is no evidence that this was acted upon.[24] A measure of protection was given to the burgh by contiguous barricading or fencing in wood at the tail-end of the tofts, called the heid-dykes. Archaeological evidence suggests that in the early Middle Ages such fencing was far from substantial,[25] perhaps even being as slight as the palisading at Linlithgow, which used to blow down in high winds. But, importantly, such barricades did serve as psychological barriers to entrance to and exit from the town.[26] Gordon's map of 1661 does suggest the possibility of what might have been a man-made bank along the line of the western ends of Netherkirkgate and Upperkirkgate and the Loch, but no archaeological traces of it have yet been found.[27]

The barricading at the end of the tofts was often punctuated with small 'yetts' or gates, giving access to the town's lands and the countryside. Gordon, in 1661, described the dwellings as having 'their own back gates for particular gardens'.[28] The burgesses were responsible for the security of their tofts' gates, just as strict rules about the shutting of the main town ports, or gates, controlled more public access into and out of the town. In 1435, for example, the town council enacted that 'na man na woman pas out of the portis to b[u]y anything quhil [before] it be brocht on the market'.[29] In this way, all access to the town's markets was controlled, by ensuring full payment for the use of the market either at the ports or in the tolbooth. The ports were also shut at curfew (usually dusk) to provide security in the town and also in times of trouble, be it the arrival of potential enemies or sickness (see Chapter 3).

It is known that by the end of the Middle Ages there were six ports (Fig. 1.2). Whether the area called the Green and the parish church of St Nicholas stood within any ports by this time is uncertain (see Introduction). The entrance to the town from Hardgate and the Green to the south-west was controlled by two ports. One stood on Shiprow. This was sometimes called the Trinity Port because of its proximity to the Trinitarian friary. It monitored entry from the harbour and round the south side of St Katherine's Hill. The other, sited on the Netherkirkgate, controlled the entry from the Green and Putachieside via the north side of St Katherine's Hill. The eastern entrances to the town were channelled through two ports at the east end of Castlegate: Futty Port at the head of Futty Wynd; and the Justice or Thieves Port, so named from its site on the road to the seat of the Justiciar's circuit courts and from the thieves, sentenced to be hanged, who passed through this gate to Heading Hill, one of the places of execution. A port was either being built or was under repair in Castlegate in 1440, when five merks were demanded from everyone entering into the privileges of becoming a burgess or a member of the guild merchant. This funding went 'ad edificationem porte in fine orientali vici castri'.[30] To the north stood the important Gallowgate (or Calsie or Causey) Port, also leading to a place of execution and beyond to Old Aberdeen and the north. The north-west approach was guarded by Upperkirkgate or Schoolhill Port.

The burgh invested heavily in its important buildings – the tolbooth, cross, tron and ports.[31] A further drain on the town's finances was the maintenance of the harbour. The natural sheltered harbour at the mouth of the Denburn, probably used by first settlers in the area (see Introduction), would soon prove to be inadequate for the important trading entrepôt that Aberdeen was in the Middle Ages. Quays were needed for mooring the boats and bulwarks to protect them. It is not known when the first quay was built; it may have been soon after the granting of burghal status. One was constructed sometime before 1399, when the records speak of 'our key of Abirden'.[32] This was probably sited at Shore Brae, beside the Quayhead. A small-scale excavation has already indicated the presence of portions of a late fourteenth-century or early fifteenth-century ashlar-faced harbour wall; and the quay was probably of ash wood.[33] By 1413, the records refer to it as an 'open common space',[34] so stressing its use by all the burgesses.

The documentary evidence makes it very clear that the maintenance of the harbour was an ongoing commitment for the burgh. In 1453, a further £53 was spent on the quay when it was either radically repaired or totally rebuilt, such was its poor state.[35] The guildry accounts for this year detail the purchase of stones and speak of 'makyng the key' and building 'steps' to the quay.[36] It has been suggested that part of the problem was the silting up of the river at the head of the quay.[37] A further opportunity was taken at the same time to improve the harbour facilities, in general, with beacons being erected and a wrecked Spanish ship which obstructed the deeper channel near the south shore being removed (see Chapter 17).[38] Such works continued into the sixteenth century. In 1512, and in 1526, the master of shorework was dispatched to Dundee to purchase 'famous stones' for the harbour works; and in 1549 a stair was built to facilitate loading and unloading from the ships at the quayside (see Chapter 7).[39]

During the Middle Ages, the town was also provided with two mills (Fig. 1.2). The Upper Mill was in existence by the fourteenth century as a meal mill. It was sited in what became called Flourmill Brae, which is now below the St Nicholas Centre. The Nether Mill stood just to the north of the Trinitarian friary and was certainly standing by 1453.[40] These needed maintenance, as did the bridge at the Green and the Bridge of Balgownie, even though it lay well to the north,[41] and, after 1527, the Bridge of Dee.

Another important establishment was the leper house. This was sited to the north of the town on the route to Old Aberdeen, and at a discrete distance from both settlements. It was certainly in existence by 1363[42] and served to keep those suffering from leprosy and other disfiguring skin diseases at a safe remove from the healthy (see Chapter 3).

The principal ecclesiastical building was the parish church of St Nicholas. Its origins may well have been earlier than the granting of burgh status to the settlement at New Aberdeen (see Introduction), although the first documentary evidence comes as late as 1157.[43] Its position west of the urban nucleus, towards or even beyond the edge of settlement, was not unusual; similar examples were at Crail and Dundee. The earliest surviving architectural remains, which date to the late twelfth century, suggest that the church consisted of an aisled nave, with north and south transepts, surmounted by a tower, and with the east end possessing an aisled chancel of three bays and terminating in a semi-circular apse. It is known that the transepts were extended to the south in 1355 and, apparently around the same time, a chapel was added to the east side of the north transept, resulting in the blocking up of a window and the insertion of a door. There is a reference to a chapel in 1445, when it was called the vault of 'Our Lady of Pity'. A new choir was begun to be built around 1477 and in 1495 the town council was loaned money 'to pay Johne Fendour for the making of the ruff and tymmer of the queyr'. By 1508, it was agreed that he would receive a further £200 Scots and a bounty if the work was completed by Michaelmas of that year – a large task as he was to 'big, oupmak, and finally end and complet the xxxiiij stalls in thar queyr, with the spiris and the chanslar dur, and ale uther thingis according tharto'.[44] A further distinguishing feature was the oak steeple over the main body of the church. Being 256 feet (78 metres) long, St Nicholas was not only one of the largest medieval churches in Scotland, but also one of the most prestigious.

Close by the parish church, and with strong links to it, was the song school (see Chapter 14). Its purpose was not merely to give a rudimentary education, but also to provide choristers for the church. The first documentary evidence of it comes in 1483, but it was probably very much older (see Chapter 14).[45] The school was sited at the west wall of the kirk yard, on the east side of what would later be Back Wynd. The town also had at least two chapels. There was a chapel in the castle by

1264, at latest. Some claim that, after the destruction of the castle, it was replaced with a chapel dedicated to St Ninian on Castle Hill. Others, however, argue that it was a new foundation of 1504.[46] Another chapel stood on the top of St Katherine's Hill. It was said to have been built by the constable of Aberdeen in 1242; although this date may have been specified after an over-literal interpretation of a comment of the chaplain of the chapel, Sir John Cuming, in 1542, that it 'was foundit and biggyit iijc yeir syne'.[47] By 1459, the town also had a hospital – dedicated to St Thomas the Martyr.[48] It was founded by John Clat for the care of the poor and infirm and stood to the east of St Nicholas Church and just to the west of the burn flowing from the Upper Mill. A Maison Dieu is referred to in the *St Nicholas Cartulary* in September 1459 and these two may be one and the same.

Prominent in the town were four friaries (Fig. 1.2; Ill. 25). Possibly the first established was the Dominican friary. It was said to have been founded by Alexander II (1214–49) between 1222 and 1249; there is certainly evidence that it existed by 1257. From the fourteenth century, it features regularly in documentary sources. Sited at the edge of settlement, at the later named Schoolhill, the area is now occupied by part of the Robert Gordon University and Aberdeen Art Gallery. As well as their church and the usual residential and domestic buildings, there was also a barn, a kiln, a dovecot, a garden and an orchard.[49]

The house of the Trinitarians stood south-west of St Katherine's Hill. It has been claimed that it was built here as William the Lion in 1211 granted his palace and gardens to this purpose. It is not proven that there was ever a palace in this location. The order, however, was certainly present in New Aberdeen by 1273 and it remained in existence until the Reformation, although by this time the house was in a state of disrepair.[50] Nearby, was the friary complex of the Carmelites. Its northern boundary was the south edge of the Green and it covered from east to west over the twentieth-century Rennie's Wynd, Martin's Lane and Carmelite Street. Presumably, its southern boundary was determined by the confluence of the Dee and the Denburn, as this created flooding, tidal flows and waterlogged conditions that were not suitable for building. In 1273, a grant was made to the Carmelites 'till their buildings should be completed'. Work was certainly under way by the end of the century, although it is possible that their church was not finished until the middle of the following century. The grant of an annual rent in 1355 'for the repair of the fabric of their church' suggests that it was complete by then.[51] The building programme was aided by a number of royal grants.[52] As regular religious orders usually placed their houses on the periphery of towns, the siting of both the Carmelite and the Trinitarian houses to the west and south-west of St Katherine's Hill suggest that, by the time of their establishment, the Green was not the focal point of the main urban settlement. The siting of the Observant Franciscan friary in Broad Street, in the heart of settlement is, therefore, unusual.

Although the Observant Franciscans, or Greyfriars, may have been working in the town by 1461, their house was erected around 1469. This followed the grant of endowments and land from a prominent burgess, Richard Vaus, as well as burgh officials and others; and it may have been that the friary was sited on waste tenements owned by Vaus. Archaeological evidence has shown that from the fourteenth century, and accelerating in the fifteenth, the east side of Broad Street was in decline. In 1518-32, a new church was built for the friars by Bishop Gavin Dunbar.[53] Evidence from a 1584 document indicates that, attached to the church, there was a small 'nether house which [was] entered by the small south gate of the east side of the church, beneath the choir, commonly called the Jowal house, then bounded by four walls'. There was 'also the greater front gate, and also a passage of fifteen feet from the buttresses of the said church, which gave entrance to it by the lesser said entrance'.[54] The site is now occupied by Marischal College.

The growing townscape: Old Aberdeen, 1100–c. 1560

A community in Old Aberdeen grew up beside a church many years before the settlement received burghal status in 1489. Although an older settlement than New Aberdeen, Old Aberdeen remained small; and this was displayed graphically in the townscape (Fig. 1.2). Essentially a single-street town, the footprint of the ancient settlement is still highly visible today. As with New Aberdeen, burgage plots ran back from the street frontage, culminating in the 'heid dykes' with little gates giving access to the fields beyond. Being only a small community, there is no evidence of repletion in the backlands either in the documentary sources or in Rothiemay's map of 1661 (Plate 38). Indeed, a census of inhabitants in 1636 suggests a population figure of no greater than about 830 men, women and children.[55] Even with the further fifty to a hundred personnel at King's College, the total population was probably no greater than 900.[56]

The built environment of Old Aberdeen, 1100–c. 1560

Although the small town was dominated commercially by the entrepôt of New Aberdeen, the burgesses of Old Aberdeen had their own right to hold a weekly market and two annual fairs. The market cross stood in the open area at the head of the High Street, or 'Middle Toun', in front of where the present townhouse is sited. On the Monday market day wooden booths probably lined much of the High Street, there not being a wide open space to function as a market 'square'. Old Aberdeen had, perforce, a linear market place.

At the south end of High Street stood King's College; work on its buildings started in 1500, five years after the college, dedicated to St Mary in the Nativity, was founded by papal bull (see Chapter 15). The nucleus of the college buildings was the quadrangle, bounded to the north by the chapel, to the east by the great hall, to the west by accommodation for the principal, and to the south by chambers for the masters and students. In the north-west corner was the Crown Tower, an open imperial crown, possibly reflecting the Scottish monarchy's imperial pretensions;[57] and in the south-east corner was the Ivy or Round Tower. This was completed in 1525 and it had a wooden spire. Work on clearing the site for the college chapel may have begun in 1498. The ground proved to be so marshy that its foundations had to be laid on rafts of oak. Construction was completed around 1506, with the leading of the roof, undertaken by John Burnel, master plumber to King Henry VII of England (1485-1509). The master mason was either Alexander Gray, who had worked on St Giles Church in Edinburgh, or John Gray, the mason responsible for the nave of St Nicholas Church in New Aberdeen. The interior of the chapel, while displaying Flemish influence, was probably the result of the skills of local master joiners, including John Fendour.[58] Along the south wall of the chapel, within the quadrangle, there were a sacristy, library and jewel house, which were completed some time between 1532 and 1545. The complex was surrounded by a precinct wall, although a few associated buildings stood outside. A manse for the mediciner was sited west of College Bounds and it was originally intended to expand the university complex still further west beyond the Powis Burn.[59]

Prestigious as these academic buildings were, dominating the small town was the cathedral of St Machar with its associated Chanonry (Fig. 1.2). Throughout the Middle Ages the cathedral building was to receive much of the energy and wealth of succeeding bishops, as they extended and beautified it. According to Hector Boece, historian and principal of King's College in the early sixteenth century, the building of the first cathedral was started before the death of King Malcolm IV (1153-65) in 1165. A small Romanesque abacus seems to confirm this. During the episcopate of Henry Cheyne (1282-1328), however, there was some demolition of the early cathedral, in order to replace it with a larger building. A corbel forming part of the inside arch of a large gothic window appears to be the only surviving remnant of Cheyne's work. Bishop Alexander Kininmund (1355-80) began the construction of what was probably intended to be a cruciform church and at the eastern end of the present nave can be seen the fine sandstone western piers of the bell tower constructed at this time. The completion of the nave, in granite, fell to Bishop Henry Lichton (1422-40) and it was at this time that the aisles were covered by a wooden lean-to roof.[60] Bishop Ingram Lindsay (1441-58) was responsible for roofing the nave with slates and paving the floor; and Bishop Thomas Spens (1457-80) completed the glazing of the windows and inserted luxurious features in the interior. The episcopate of William Elphinstone (1483-1514) brought the completion of Lichton's chancel with the addition of a belfry and spire to the central tower, the work of John Fendour. The spire was then covered in lead, and the slate and stone roofs were likewise replaced in lead. Bishop Gavin Dunbar (1518-32) is perhaps best remembered for the addition to the nave of the unique heraldic ceiling, portraying the political situation of Scotland and Christendom about the year 1520. Still extant, it is one of the treasures of St Machar's Church. Further embellishments were subsequently made, such as the replacement of the cap-house roofs on the twin west towers with spires of sandstone, and the south transept was also remodelled. In spite of all these building works, the new choir was incomplete and the ambitious building programme unfinished at the Reformation.

The Chanonry developed around the cathedral. It set itself apart from the small burgh by 'high strong walls and dikes'. Within the walls were the manses and gardens of the canons. The manses were of considerably superior quality to the homes of the townspeople: slated roofs, rather than thatch, and well-dressed sandstone rather than wood.[61] Probably most magnificent was the bishop's palace. This has been described as 'a large court having four towers, one in every corner of the close, and a great hall and chambers'.[62] In the centre of the courtyard was a well and to the south-east a garden. At the southern end of the bishop's garden stood the chaplains' court which held the chambers of twenty or more chaplains. This was constructed about 1519.

Also within the precinct was a small hospital, founded in 1531-2 to care for twelve poor men.[63] It stood at the north end of the Chanonry, with the parson of Tullienessle's manse to the east and that of the rector of Monymusk on the west. The building was one hundred feet long and thirty-two feet wide, with a steeple and a bell and twelve small chambers with chimneys and a kitchen and, at its east end, an oratory. Attached to the cathedral there was also a school to train boys as choristers in music and song. Access to the Chanonry was through any of four ports: Tillydrone Port, so named as it stood near to Tillydrone Motte (Plate 5), Cluny's Port, Chaplains' Port and East Port.

To the south of the town lay two further ecclesiastical buildings and the leper house. St Maria ad Nives, or Snow Kirk, was established in 1498 as part of Bishop William Elphinstone's overall scheme for founding a burgh and a university, and this was to function as a new parish church. A little further south, on the upper slopes of Spitalhill, and to the east of the road called the Spital, was St Peter's Hospital, thus giving the street its name. Founded between 1172 and 1199, it was to sustain 'infirm brethren'. A reference to 'sisters living therein' in 1256 suggests that women were later included. Attached to the hospital were a chapel and a burial ground.[64]

Reformation to Restoration, 1560–1660: decay and growth

Two national events - the Reformation (1560) and the Restoration of the monarchy (1660) - appear to block off neatly a century in which we can observe the two Aberdeens moving into the early modern era. But national occurrences quite often have less sudden effects on particular localities than might be expected. To take a single example: only in 1574, fourteen years after the official date of Reformation, did the authorities at St Nicholas Kirk proceed to the removal of ancient stained glass and the organ and the demolition of parts of the carved choir stalls (see Chapter 10).[65] And, for the historian of Aberdeen, the Restoration is less notable than the creation in 1661 of James Gordon's plan-view of the towns, with an associated description of them. These two documents enable the observer literally to view the towns more precisely than previous documentation permits.

The physical history of the towns during this century has to be presented as a report balanced between some elements of decay and yet also various indications of what must be described as internal growth. The two settlement areas seem to have been very little enlarged, but re-building and change of use does represent positive development at work. Although the events of the Reformation in Aberdeen were not notably violent in respect of either buildings or people, the resulting alterations, based on a new theology, a fluctuating church polity and different forms of worship, had distinct effects, sometimes rather gradually, on the physical kirk (see Chapter 13).

The actual amount of decayed property at this period is difficult to quantify. There are occasional references in legal documentation to 'waste lands', ruined or unused tenements, but how many there were will remain unknown until much more detailed research has been carried out on the semi-official property records, recorded in the burgh's Register of Sasines, which is extant from 1484 (Plate 21). And exactly how 'waste' a ruined property was might be a matter of dispute.[66] The devastation of major structures, such as church buildings, is rather easier to record from contemporary report. The four friaries of New Aberdeen were damaged or despoiled to varying degrees. The Dominican house, lying to the north-west, was described by James Gordon as entirely vanished by 1661, only its ruined precinct wall remaining.[67] He implies that most of the friary's good stonework had been used for housebuilding by townspeople. The town council took a close interest in the fate of the church institutions and possessions. In 1562, it agreed that the chalices and other ornaments of St Nicholas should be sold by public roup and the proceeds were eventually applied to works at the harbour and the Bridge of Don (Ill. 1).[68] In 1561, the council decreed that the place of the Greyfriars should be used for the storage and sale of malt and meal. A crown grant of 1567 conveyed that house to the council for conversion into a hospital; but this never happened.[69] Not

*Illustration 1
Bridge of Don, from
Thomas Pennant,* A
Tour in Scotland
(1774).

surprisingly, there was a good deal of uncertainty about future use of church buildings - the Reformation with its aftermath was totally unprecedented. A degree of pragmatic conservatism is sometimes visible, as in 1574, when the burgesses who were instructed to remove the reredos, or screen, at one of the side altars at St Nicholas protested that it helped to keep the draughts off the congregation during services.[70]

Decay of ecclesiastical buildings would have been even more visible in Old Aberdeen, as a small settlement centred on a cathedral. The Snow Kirk, established as the burgh's parish kirk by Bishop Elphinstone, was annexed to St Machar's in 1583. It presumably ceased to function and is visible as a roofless ruin in Gordon's plan-view of 1661.[71] King's College itself was condemned in a visitation of 1619 for the dilapidation of its buildings.[72] Gordon also reports that most of the canons' manses in the Chanonry lay in ruins by his time.[73] But at least two, facing the cathedral, had been rescued, since George Gordon, marquis of Huntly, acquired them and turned them into his Aberdeen town house, sometime around 1600.[74]

The communal lodging known as Chaplains' Court, formerly a courtyard building, consisted of little more than one wing when it was bought in 1622 by Patrick Forbes of Corse, bishop of Aberdeen (1618–35), who donated it for use by the newly created professor of divinity.[75] Although much altered, it still stands and is the oldest still-inhabited house in Aberdeen. St Machar's Church, still not complete at the east end by 1560, had been at times well maintained since then, but its great central spire was to collapse in 1688, as a result of earlier stone-robbing and inept attempts at repair.[76]

Anyone who visited the two towns, say during the reign of James VI (1567–1625), would certainly find at least in New Aberdeen a bustling and economically thriving urban settlement. But such an outsider could not have failed to observe some elements of physical collapse in both towns. This must be attributed ultimately to the Reformation and all that resulted from it in terms of property use and disuse. Yet there is a distinctly positive counter-balance to these negative aspects. Continuing concerns for civic, educational, religious and charitable activities remain visible, although sometimes now flowing along new channels.

Educational advance occurred in both towns. The most significant development was the establishment in 1593 of Marischal College, based at the house of the Greyfriars in Broad Street (see Chapter 15). Adaptation of the friary buildings and its continuing existence in Broad Street proved to be problematic at times. But, in spite of some duplication of the teaching activities at King's College over the next 267 years, the new university college represented expansion of educational provision within the region.[77] King's itself did recover from its post-Reformation depression and embarked on new building work in the mid seventeenth century. At the north-east corner of the quadrangle a 'skyscraper' tower-house was intelligently planned to provide more accommodation. Erroneously named the 'Cromwell Tower' in later times, it appears in Gordon's plan-view of 1661 as complete to the wall-head at that date, but still lacking its roof.[78]

The post-Reformation kirk had troubles in its early generations in maintaining its buildings and providing a sufficiency of qualified ministers. But at St Nicholas it resorted, as often elsewhere where there was an awkward legacy of large, ancient town churches, to the process of dividing the building. In 1596, a wall was erected to create the East and West churches, each with its own minister. They continued as separate congregations almost to the end of the twentieth century. Two of the town's four administrative quarters were allocated to each church: Green and Crooked to the West Kirk and Even and Futty to the East Kirk (Fig. 1.3).[79] The building alteration was somewhat drastic, but standards of pastoral care in the burgh were presumably raised as a result of the splitting of the parish (see Chapter 13). One further set of former church buildings was turned to charitable use. The Trinitarian friary structures had been acquired by Dr William Guild, later principal

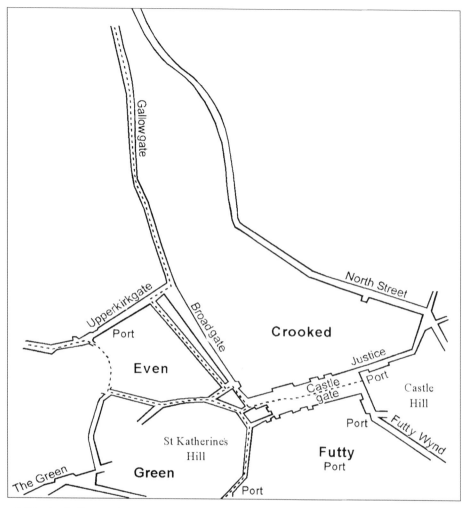

Figure 1.3
The four quarters of
Aberdeen.

of King's College, who about 1632 gifted them to the Seven Incorporated Trades
of New Aberdeen, to serve as a hospital for decayed brethren. He also founded
bursaries at Marischal College for the sons of members. The friary, therefore, became
the headquarters for the Incorporation, which developed into an active and well-
endowed charity, which still exists and flourishes.[80]

Civic concern, and indeed pride, continued to fuel attempts at growth and
improvement. Some were more successful than others. The cramped site of New
Aberdeen militated against physical expansion on any notable scale. Certainly one
street, Back Wynd or Westerkirkgate, laid out in 1594-5, improved access from the
Schoolhill area to the Green.[81] Harbour works to the east of the Quayhead created
by about 1658 a long pier or quay which drained the land to the north of it.
Gordon's plan-view described it as 'drye ground somtyme overflowed by the tyde

before the peer was builded' (Plate 37). In this useful reclaimed area, Virginia Street and other roadways were later laid out.[82]

Other public works, such as water supply and bridge maintenance, were kept in mind, if not greatly advanced. In 1632, the magistrates made a proposal for bringing water to the town by a system of lead pipes, but the project did not materialise.[83] In 1605, Mr Alexander Hay, a clerk of the Court of Session, transferred to the burgh of New Aberdeen funds which were previously annuities of the chaplains of St Machar's. This modest gift of £2 5s 8½d sterling was to be used for upkeep of the ancient Bridge of Balgownie, and became one of the foundations of a fund which enabled a new Bridge of Don to be erected in 1827 and widened in 1958.[84]

For public buildings the council often had beauty, as well as utility, in mind. In 1615 and 1627, a tower with a prison, plus a belfry and spire, was added to the tolbooth: the structure remains visible and elegant.[85] The building has been much altered and added to over the centuries and the complexities of its physical history point both to civic concern for handsome appearance and to the continuing willingness to expend cash on the burgh's headquarters. The longest continuous process of public building work, however, was applied, not surprisingly, to the harbour. From the fifteenth century, taxes to pay for harbour works are repeatedly on record. The difficult mouth of the Dee had been improved and the pier was a notable improvement. The administration of the works can be followed in detail in the extant series of Shore Work Accounts, from 1596 onwards.[86] But the harbour remained an awkward area until modern engineering techniques began to be applied to it in the later eighteenth century.

Towards a modern city, 1660–1800: function follows form

Until *c.* 1750 Aberdeen maintained the basis of its medieval street network. After that, the need for expansion became critical. Aberdeen began to extend beyond the limits of its traditional confines; and new suburbs, mills and early factories developed around the main centre and along roads and the rivers Dee and Don. Aberdeen's development in the period from 1660 to 1800 was not just about 'the most functionally satisfactory arrangement of streets'.[87] Within its physical boundaries, there was at work a complex of political, economic and social impulses which had to embrace forces of change. This period included evidence of both urban growth - an increase in the size of the town - and urbanisation - an increase in the proportion of the population living in the town.[88]

In common with other towns in the British Isles, there was a perception in Aberdeen that urban growth enhanced work opportunities and economic prospects for the bulk of the Aberdeen population. The latter grew steadily, owing to

migration from the countryside, natural increase and overseas immigration, especially from the Low Countries. From approximately 9,000 inhabitants in New
and Old Aberdeen by the early 1690s, the population of New Aberdeen, including
Futty, had climbed to approximately 17,600 by 1801. Suburbs had also probably
increased. The parish of Old Machar grew from a likely 5,000 inhabitants in 1755
to a population of 9,911 by 1801.[89] By contrast, Old Aberdeen was probably no larger
in 1800 than a century previously. In 1790, according to the *Old Statistical Account*,
it had only 1,713 inhabitants.[90] The political functions of the burgh, which was still
working with institutions developed in the later Middle Ages, such as the church
(albeit now 'reformed'), hospitals and grammar school, were based on 'relationships
of proximity'.[91] These facilitated the construction of social networks which helped
bring about the innovative changes in Aberdeen's urban fabric in the last half of
the eighteenth century.

An English commentator, Richard Franck, writing in 1656, stated that Aberdeen
was famed for civility and humanity and suggested that it owed its growth as a
town to that.[92] Gordon of Rothiemay, his contemporary, stressed the importance
of the harbour as well as the Aberdonians' sharp and shrewd intellect.[93] Gordon's
Description of New and Old Aberdeen provides the best authority for the size,
appearance and general layout of the seventeenth-century town. Even so, it must
be viewed with some caution for it was engraved by a Dutchman who had
probably never seen Aberdeen (Plate 38). Gordon presents inconsistently sized
streets, wynds, and rows, with no obvious plan, other than response to geography
and geology. Aberdeen owed its origins to the sea and its prosperity to trade. The
harbour was the key to growth. Geography itself had been Aberdeen's principal
town planner for centuries and also had an impact on burgage plot size. The
infilling of burgage plots with store areas and additional houses was just one way
the morphology of the town could be altered. Although many plots are illustrated
with regimented orchards, which are probably stylised, Gordon's plan-view hints
at occasional infilling known as burgage repletion, which had begun even in the
Middle Ages (see above). That process provides a key to change in approaches to
land use and a signal that a town is undergoing a period of growth.

There is some evidence from Gordon's *Description* that Aberdeen followed
the example of Edinburgh and built upwards, with the result that some mid
seventeenth-century buildings reached three or four storeys.[94] An owner might
have moved into a new house at the rear, drawing an income from the old
high-density housing. Access to burgage plots could be through back lanes or
through houses – although some house owners put in pends or arches in their
properties to allow access from the street.[95] Although G. and W. Paterson's map of
1746 (Ill. 2) shows very stylised burgage plots, the intensity of burgage repletion is
shown in Alexander Milne's 1789 map. In this plan, gardens had almost vanished

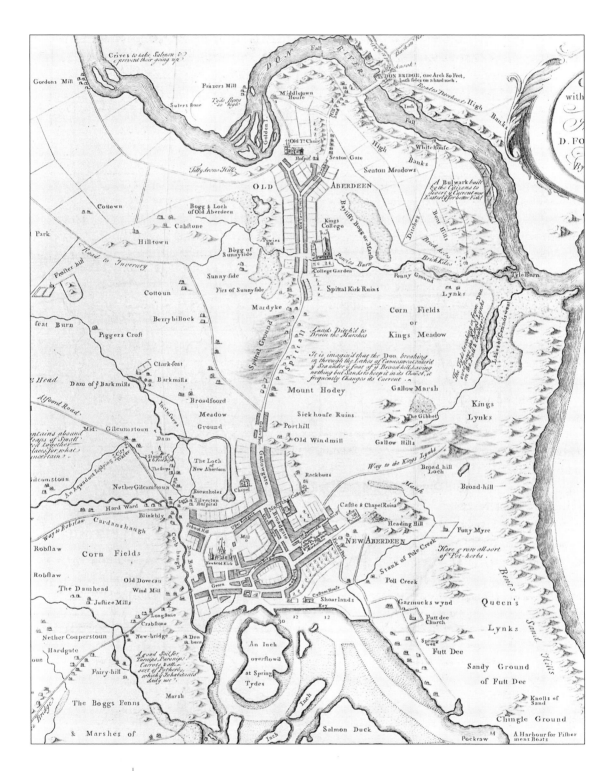

beneath a network of courts, back buildings and purpose-built tenements.[96] It was not only burgage plots which were being developed. Pioneering land reclamation at the shore, already noted, was initially given over to pasture, but by 1715 the Shorelands had become an area of resort and amusement for local townspeople. Over the course of several decades, drainage of the Loch of Aberdeen was undertaken, until by 1838 it had disappeared altogether.

For much of the period from 1660 to 1750, Aberdeen was tightly confined to the streets around the bases of St Katherine's Hill to the west and Castle Hill to the east. To the south, the River Dee formed a natural boundary and to the north and west suburbs were, in Richard Franck's words, 'guarded by hills, as are those levels more easterly saluted by the ocean'.[97] For administrative purposes, the town remained divided into four quarters: the Green, Even, Crooked (or Cruikit), and Futty (Fig. 1.3). There were still the same six ports: Justice, Gallowgate, Futty, Upperkirkgate, Netherkirkgate, Shiprow. It has been suggested that, of all the features of towns inherited from the medieval centuries, the street plan once laid down has proved to be among the most enduring.[98] Certainly, in Gordon's time this was true. On his plan-view there were only about sixteen streets and his description says that all are neatly paved with 'flint or a very hard stone resembling flint'.[99] The principal ones were Castlegate, Shiprow, Netherkirkgate, Upperkirkgate, Broadgate and Gallowgate leading to Old Aberdeen. Small wynds and rows included St Katherine's, Huckster, Correction, Adie's, Futty, the Narrow Wynds, the Exchequer, Ghaist, Ship, and Rotton Rows; leading out of the town were Schoolhill and the Green, from which ran the lane leading to the Bow Bridge and then to Hardgate. It was only in the eighteenth century that all the ports were removed, so as to cope with the increasing amount of wheeled and sedan chair traffic.

Outside the ports, to the east and south of Castle Hill, there were a few houses in the Futty quarter, with its separate church. The Green and outlying Schoolhill were then residential suburbs and Gilcomston a separate hamlet. Because of their secluded position, Futty and Torry kept a separate identity from that of the rest of Aberdeen. Futty, still the abode of fishers and sailors, nestled under the shadow of the great Castle Hill.[100] Torry, once in the hegemony of the abbots of Arbroath but latterly in private ownership, guarded the entrance to the Dee. Thomas Tucker, a Cromwellian official, noted:

> At the end of the foremost neck of the land there is a little village called Footie, and on the other headland another Torye, and both nigh in harbour'mouth, and lyeing very neer unto the place where the ships usually ride ... have given opportunity of much fraude, in landing goods privatly, but prevented of late by appointing the wayters by turnes, to watch those two places narrowly. The trade of this place is ... inwards from Norway, Eastland, Holland and France: and

Illustration 2
G. & W. Paterson, Old and New Aberdeen (1746).

outwards, with the salmon and pladding, commodityes caught and made here-about in a greater plenty then any other place over the nation whatsoever.[101]

According to the map evidence presented by Gordon and the Patersons, both were modest settlements. Torry's strength according to Gordon was the ability of warships and merchantmen to ride at anchor there; small ships called at Futty.[102]

The independence of spirit that Tucker observed in the 1650s appears to have survived later in the same century. In 1675, a restraining order was raised against the inhabitants of Torry for encroaching on Aberdeen's fishings, but eighteen years later the council empowered magistrates to take steps for stopping the white fishers from leaving 'Footy or Torrie' to ply their trade in Newburgh or elsewhere. Clearly, they were damned if they did; and damned if they didn't.

Even though many streets had descriptive names and all were probably filthy, council ordinances in the late seventeenth century were passed against fleshers slaughtering in the streets, the keeping of pigs, and townsfolk tossing out the contents of chamber pots on to the streets. In 1675, the town council appointed 'ane scaffinger' for keeping clean the streets, closes and 'backsyds', or back lanes, on a daily basis (see Chapter 3).[103] Civic responsibility became more pronounced in the period. As the population grew and became more dispersed, the town council gradually took away from individual inhabitants more and more of the burden of keeping the wheels of urban life turning. A fire engine was purchased from London in 1721, an infirmary was opened in 1742 and the town also licensed water carriers. Up until the end of the seventeenth century, Aberdeen's water supply came from the Loch and various wells. The water carriers augmented the supply, which was greatly improved by the enhancement of springs at Carden's Haugh in 1706. Further improvements followed in 1742 and 1766, when water was conveyed from six springs at Fountainhall to the Water House in Broad Street, built in 1769.[104] The shift from individual to corporate responsibility culminated in the Aberdeen Police Act of 1795. One of its elements provided for election of a new ruling authority of thirteen commissioners, who undertook the systematic naming of streets and numbering of houses, supplying the inhabitants with fresh water, street lighting, and the 'removing and preventing [of] all obstructions and annoyances within the city'.[105]

The space within a town may be divided into three kinds: private, institutional and public.[106] Distinctions can be blurred. Private space in Aberdeen largely consisted of houses and gardens. Much business and manufacture prior to 1750 was domestic in operation and so parts of a private house could be open to the public at certain times of the day for the purposes of commerce. Merchants and craftsmen often lived 'above the shop' and were naturally keen, as are modern businesses, to 'catch the passing trade'. Many passageways and courts were shared. Burgage plots were further subdivided and amalgamated.[107]

Institutional space and buildings devoted to trade and commerce took a growing number of forms.[108] Institutional space included those buildings which were the responsibility of administrative and cultural organisations. In Aberdeen, the harbour, bridges, mills, tolbooth and correction house were all maintained from council funds. The new market cross, erected in 1686, was paid for out of the council's wine funds. Castlegate was the commercial centre of the town and was where the principal institutional buildings were concentrated. The tolbooth had new prison cells added in 1718 and was enlarged by William Adam in 1729. Within a few feet of the tolbooth, the New Inn provided accommodation of a different sort - for travellers both obscure and famous, including the two literary giants, Samuel Johnson and James Boswell, and for local personages in masonic meetings. A new record office was opened to replace an earlier one destroyed by fire in 1721.

Opposite the tolbooth, ancient religious met modern secular symbolism in the positioning of the market cross, which had for centuries been the site of 'honest trading', and Plainstanes, the paved area beside the cross. The Plainstanes were laid out in 1752 'as a place of resort of the citizens both for transacting business and for recreation'.[109] The new hexagonal cross, still standing but not in its original position, comprises a series of arches supporting a parapet, decorated with heraldic arms and portrait medallions of the ten Stewart monarchs from James I (1406-37) to James VII (1685-9), punctured by a richly carved column surmounted by a unicorn. It is a credit to Aberdeen that the market cross survived the frenzied period of some forty years between 1760 and 1800, when so many market crosses were destroyed - their main crime being as encumbrances to traffic on the street. After repair in 1821, the market cross was moved to its present position, towards the eastern end of Castlegate.

Aberdeen's public space consisted of the streets, lanes and open spaces, such as the market place and outlying areas such as the Play Green, which some evidence suggests had been used for dramatic performances from the Middle Ages.[110] The public spaces were regulated by the town council. It fought battles against middens, took a stand about the encroachments of forestairs - stairs that intruded on to the thoroughfare, but which gave access to upper storeys of houses. It also regulated stalls in the market place, put out fires and improved the water supply. But public space extended beyond the built environment. In 1693, the council ordered a halt to feeding sheep on the Links, the bent grass hillocks towards the sea, because horses and cattle within the burgh were made 'destitute of grass'. In 1700, the widow Agnes Geddes was continued in her late husband's post as town herd, for keeping the town's cattle on the Links. In 1726, it was ordered that all querns or iron handmills already set up, or to be set up, for grinding malt or any other grain were to be seized and demolished. The town council was certainly not going to encourage private enterprise at the expense of the income it received from local mills.

Was Aberdeen in reality a town, or of the country, or both? In the period under review, the growth of towns and an intensification of what may be called 'the harsh distinction between rural and urban life' have been identified as key issues.[111] Much of Great Britain remained rural in outlook. In 1800, the urban population of the United Kingdom formed only a quarter of its total; by 1851, it made up more than a half. For Aberdeen, it was more than a question of divided landscape. A town ambitious for its future could no longer afford the 'luxury' of swine running amok and untended in its streets.

There were many factors which helped set New Aberdeen in a very urban context. It had a complicated social structure, a dense population, a variety of economic activities and occupations, and a complex political makeup.[112] Old Aberdeen, on the other hand, presents an interesting case study in the question of the divided landscape. Although it passes one hypothetical test for distinguishing town from country - the presence of schools and foreigners (Old Aberdeen had a number of schools and a significant number of Flemish weavers) - its population in 1790 was only 1,713 and economic activity remained modest.[113] Charitable institutions and endowments primarily came from the cathedral and King's College, although there was a masonic lodge and a hospital endowed by the Incorporated Trades of Old Aberdeen. Still, in 1691 Professor Alexander Fraser purchased a narrow strip of boggy land south of the Loch of Old Aberdeen, which had been drained in 1662. His family extended the Powis estate westwards and improved it. Their successors, the Leslies of Powis, underscored the ties of their country estate to the town by building at College Bounds an impressive lodge house and in 1830 a fairy-tale gateway.

Old Aberdeen was a long straggling settlement, its form reflecting natural growth along a well-used route.[114] It may be unofficially divided into four sectors: cathedral, High Street, King's College and Spital. The cathedral and its clergy controlled the urban political system until the late seventeenth century. With the demise of bishops at this period, a political vacuum arose in Old Aberdeen which made - so the official records maintained - for an increase in daily disorders and confusions. There was no longer an official means of electing magistrates. The situation was remedied in 1690 when the magistrates and town council of Old Aberdeen success-fully petitioned to elect their own deacons, hold their own courts and select their own bailies, whose duties included punishing delinquents and 'repressing tumults', as well as monitoring the maintenance of the built fabric of the town.[115]

Prior to the Reformation, the Chanonry was lined with the manses of the canons of the cathedral. The change of religious practice escalated a new approach in the construction of domestic dwellings in the Chanonry. Many of the finest mansions date from the early nineteenth century. The High Street, in contrast, remained largely unchanged, punctuated in a herring-bone fashion with narrow lanes, courts and closes. Few new thoroughfares appeared. However, the built environment had more of a profound influence on the appearance of the burgh. The earliest surviving houses date from the late seventeenth century and many buildings survive from the eighteenth century and have helped to define the picture-postcard tourist magnet we can see today. In the seventeenth century, most houses would have been thatched; only houses in the Chanonry would have been slated. The College did not grow physically in the period between erection of the so-called Cromwell Tower in c. 1660 and New King's in 1913. The Spital had few inhabitants. The ruins of the hospital are visible on Gordon's map of 1661 and a small number of houses lay near them.

Gordon maintained that the buildings of New Aberdeen were of stone and lime with slate roofs, of three or four or even more storeys. He might have been somewhat fanciful in his allegation of the widespread use of stone. It is clear from town records that traditional roofing materials, heather and straw, persisted despite a council ordinance of 1716 prohibiting their use. Timber was a common building material well into the eighteenth century. Slate and locally produced brick (principally from Ferryhill and Seaton) were in more common use in the eighteenth century. Although difficult to work, the use of building granite became more widespread after 1730 as a result of the opening of Loanhead Quarry and the reopening by the town council of Rubislaw Quarry in 1741.[116]

At the Links, which in the seventeenth century were natural duneland, the inhabitants 'strolled every day for the sake of their health', watched horse racing and practised various sports including football, golf and bowls.[117] The Play Green, which is marked on Gordon's map, was a square plot of public space between Gilcomston hamlet and the Loch of New Aberdeen. Below the Play Green, the Denburn passed through an area known as Corby Haugh, meaning crows' meadow, on its way down to the Dee estuary. The area between the Haugh and the main gateway to the burgh at the Green was common pasture land until 1757, when a series of improvements were made, which provided this area with a public bleaching green.[118]

The harbour remained the central character in the drama and the focus of Aberdeen's wealth. In 1686, several improvements had been carried out, including the removal of stones and other debris which had accumulated on the bar of sand and silt. The bar was apparently often dry at low water, and access for large ships was difficult. As part of their civic responsibilities townsfolk were obliged to help in removing obstructions at the harbour mouth, a task which occurred on an annual basis. But in the first half of the eighteenth century little was done to improve either the harbour or the townspeople's growing impatience. Caught by the spirit of the age, and determined to tackle the problem, the town council took action. In 1751, it appointed a harbour overseer; four years later, it approached the great engineer John Smeaton to consider future developments. He proposed the building of a new pier to ward off sand silting into the harbour entrance.[119] Smeaton's pier, shown on a map of 1773 as a 'design', was soon under construction and was finished by the early 1780s. This new pier, the North Pier, was reinforced by Abercrombie's pier built in the last decade of the century. The harbour developments aided shipping and shipbuilding. In 1700, Aberdeen had only two vessels of 60 tons. One hundred years later, the port had at least 150 ships totalling 17,130 tons. Shipbuilding, which began in 1753, quickly became an established part of the local economy (see Chapter 7).[120]

Form follows function

The opening of market opportunities in the surrounding countryside secured Aberdeen's role as a centre for exchange (see Chapter 6). As trade and industry expanded, there was a need for labour and for related road, harbour and, later, canal construction, opening up access to rural communities, inland towns and overseas ports.[121] In 1790, the *Aberdeen Journal* reported that 'the population and extent of this place seems to be going on with increasing speed'.[122] Eighteenth-century Aberdeen was also becoming a safer and more convenient place in which to live. The town was improved by street lighting, an upgraded provision of water, the removal of ports, the laying out of public walks such as at Shorelands, and the creation of whole new streets and widening and straightening of others. All these were underpinned in Aberdeen by an improvement in the commercial wealth of the town.

With wealth came 'a raging thirst for recreation'.[123] In Aberdeen, this translated itself into pleasure areas such as the Shorelands, a theatre (opened by subscription in 1795), a music room and a reading room (the Athenaeum), a golfing society (founded 1780), and dancing masters' studios. While other towns had assembly rooms, Aberdonians used local taverns for dances and other public events (see Chapter 16). In short, Georgian Aberdeen was a home of polite manners, taste and (some) sophistication: 'an arena of human fulfilment'.[124] In Aberdeen, there was also a new urban elite bent on philanthropy, which established charities to fund hospitals and other good works. The Honourable Club was founded in December 1718 to provide 'social intercourse' for members and with the aim of contributing pecuniary assistance to those who were recommended to them.[125] Robert Gordon, merchant of Danzig, in a 1729 deed of mortification, ensured the educational establishment which would bear his name as Gordon's College; and a legacy from Bailie Daniel Cargill at the century's end was used to help fund a lunatic asylum separate from the town council funded infirmary.[126] A number of valuable endowments were allied with St Machar's Cathedral and Marischal and King's Colleges. In addition, Aberdeen possessed a number of charitable friendly societies, including

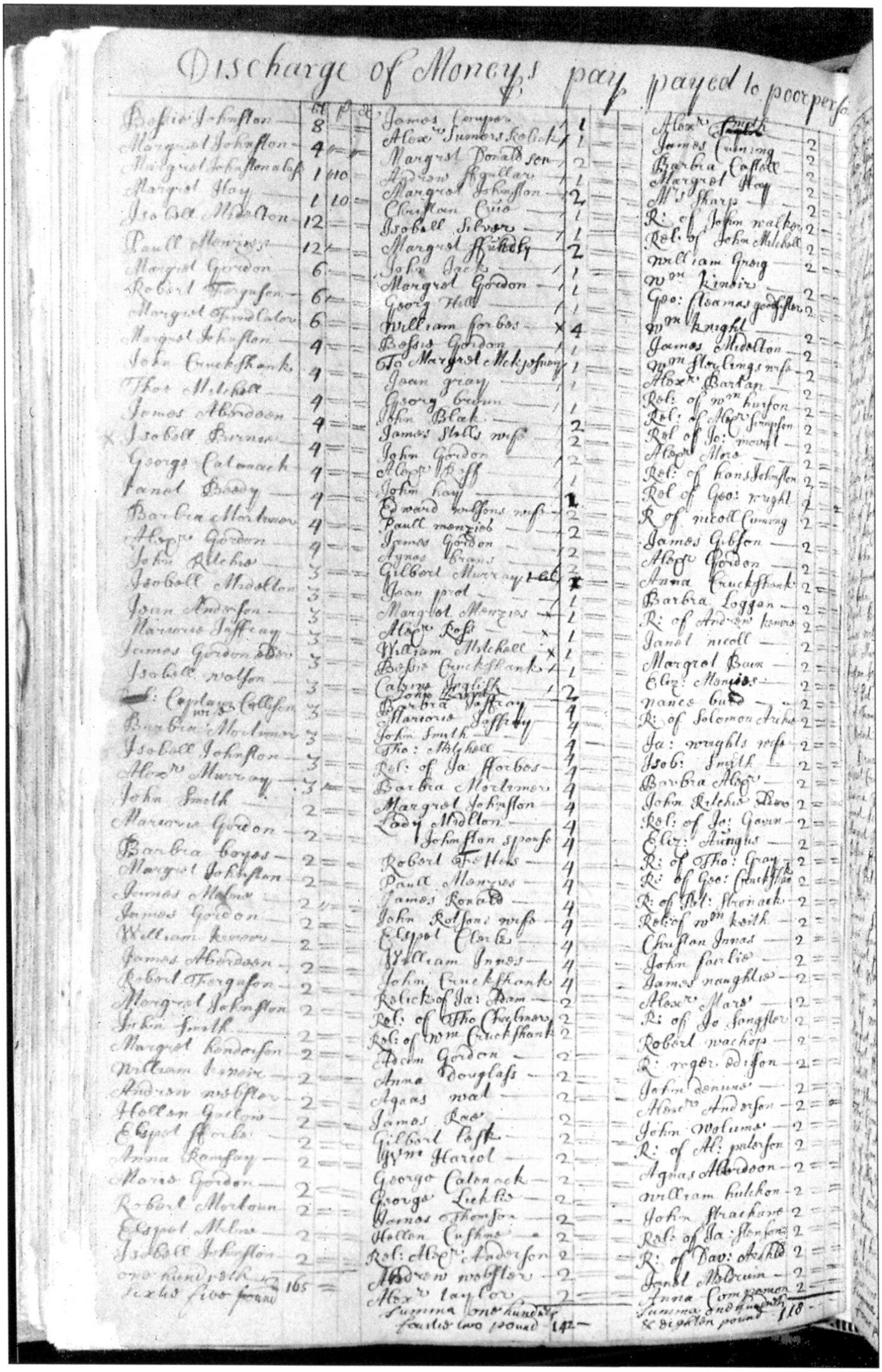

Illustration 3
Robert Johnstoune's
mortifications,
1696-7.

one formed by women for relief of the poor. Aberdeen was becoming a city of widening philanthropic horizons.

Politeness moved to improvement and improvement to Enlightenment thinking. Eighteenth-century equivalents of our modern 'chattering classes' frequented coffee shops, theatres and assembly rooms (even if they were merely taverns) to discuss interrelated ideas of God, reason, nature and man. The questioning of society and of man's role in it was one of the cornerstones of contemporary thought. Ideas of improvement, growing civic pride, the struggle for order, and better town planning all reflected economic progress in general.[127] University dons came out of their ivory towers. It has been suggested that Scottish men of letters consolidated their social position at this time by participating in the informal, voluntary associations of 'polite' urban culture, the clubs and societies which multiplied in Scotland. In Aberdeen's case, the King's College professor Thomas Reid (among others) spearheaded the establishment in 1758 of the Philosophical Society (known by contemporaries as the Wise Club). It met once a fortnight, alternately in tavern rooms in New Aberdeen and Old Aberdeen, and helped in bridging the gap between 'town and gown' as well as spreading new ideas. In the fifteen years of its existence, academics and townsmen debated over 120 subjects. Men of letters were, at last, on equal footing with landed, legal and merchant leaders.[128]

In the second half of the eighteenth century, Aberdeen's town council demonstrated an ability to adapt to change and the town ultimately expanded against heavy geographical odds: hills, marshes and valleys. Aberdeen needed to expand. Form was now going to follow function. And in so doing, Aberdeen would demonstrate vision, assured engineering and confident industrialisation. Marischal Street was one of the first bold leaps, predating Edinburgh's New Town in plan, realisation and impact. Before 1767, there was no easy direct public access from Castlegate to the quay at any point between Futty Wynd on the east and Shore Brae on the west. The growth of trade at the harbour made a new street desirable and, following the purchase and demolition of the Earl Marischal's town house, the new street was laid out in a steep descent to the harbour. The street was an innovative, modern construction, in that it cut through an existing medieval townscape layout; it was an entirely new vision in response to the needs of a central area that contained both market place and harbour. Bannerman's Bridge, which the architect Edward Meldrum described as Scotland's earliest flyover, carried Marischal Street over what became Virginia Street.[129] It was a single arch of some thirty feet, designed by the Marischal Street architect William Law and built by Alexander Bannerman. The bridge was replaced by a concrete structure in 1983, when Virginia Street was widened.

Some eleven new streets (including Marischal Street) were opened or improved in the course of the second half of the eighteenth century. Virginia and James

Streets were opened in the harbour area. Queen Street was constructed in 1775 to provide access from Broadgate to the flesh market, which was situated where the present North Church of St Andrew stands. Carmelite, George, Charlotte, St Andrew, John and Tannery Streets (later incorporated into George Street) formed part of the late eighteenth-century Lochlands development and Littlejohn Street also provided access from Gallowgate and Broadgate to a back lane. Another small lane - Shoe Lane, opposite Queen Street and Lodge Walk - was opened in 1785 as a public street for 'all time coming'.[130] Behind the Town House and the Sheriff Court lies Concert Court, which took its name from weekly concerts held there by the Aberdeen Musical Society for a long period in the eighteenth century. One of Aberdeen's famous old closes, Patagonian Court, leads from Belmont Street, opposite Gaelic Lane, to the Lower Denburn, by a steep flight of steps. It was originally an old lane that led from Back Wynd to the Corby Haugh. Back Wynd (originally Westerkirkgate), which led to the Green, still has many late eighteenth-century buildings.

Another new street, Belmont Street, overlooking the valley of the Denburn, opened a fashionable new suburb. As Aberdeen began expanding westwards in the dying years of the century, some of the more prosperous wished to add physical distance to social distance. But the aim was not to move too far from the city - access to the council chamber and Aberdeen's harbour was vital for merchant princes. One of the wealthiest - Menzies of Pitfodels - moved to Belmont Street in about 1788, surrendering the site of his centuries-old town house to what became the North of Scotland Bank at 5 Castle Street. The westward expansion of the well-to-do was gradual in Aberdeen and the social gulf created in late eighteenth-century Edinburgh and in its New Town development was not replicated.[131]

The difficulties of expanding westwards, and the way in which to achieve this, occupied much attention in the closing years of the century.[132] In 1790, the editor of the *Aberdeen Journal* praised the new Lochlands development, and also clearly understood the bigger picture: 'from the spirit of improvement which so much prevails, there is little doubt but in a few years this will form a populous and elegant addition to Aberdeen. Indeed, it is almost the only quarter where the town can be extended to any great extent.'[133] Expansion was going to be a costly business, for it involved the purchase and demolition of houses, the removal of a hill and the building of a bridge across the Denburn (see Chapter 18). At the same time, consideration was being given to the building of a road to the north that would provide better access than the existing one, which ran from the Gallowgate through Spital to Old Aberdeen.[134] The new street to the west commemorated the Union between Great Britain and Ireland in 1801 and the handsome way to the north, commenced in 1803, gloried in the name of King Street. Aberdeen knew that it was entering the modern era.

2

Life in the Two Towns

GORDON DesBRISAY *and* ELIZABETH EWAN
with H. LESLEY DIACK

By the seventeenth century, visitors to Aberdeen often remarked upon the civility of the townsfolk. Richard Franck, an English gentleman who visited both burghs in 1656, was particularly impressed by a Sunday service in St Nicholas, the parish church of the royal burgh:

> The magistrates sit under the soveraignty of the mace, and every merchant in his peculiar pew; where every society of mechanicks have their particular seats, distinguished by escutcheons, suitable to their profession; so that confusion seldom or rarely happens among them, in quarrelling for places; where strangers are unsuspected for informers and intruders, and the civility of the people such, that no man is left destitute of a seat to sit on, but every one entertained answerable to his quality.[1]

Franck went on to contrast the scene in St Nicholas favourably with that in English churches, 'where a man may stand … till his feet are surbeat, yet nobody proffer him a remove, or a stool to sit on'. He even liked the music, marvelling that the parishioners managed 'to sing a psalm in tune' without, in those Covenanted days, benefit of a choir or choirmaster.[2]

Aberdonians in and out of the pews

Aberdonians would probably have been pleased by Franck's depiction of the various sorts of civic harmony on display that Sunday, but they might also have allowed themselves a wry chuckle. They knew that civility and decorum in church services, as in civic life generally, could not be taken for granted and was not achieved without a good deal of bickering and negotiation. Sunday services brought Aberdonians of all walks of life together under a single roof, and their interactions in church inevitably reflected the divisions and tensions among them.

Seating in the church became a contentious issue in the seventeenth century, much as the order of precedence of the various craft guilds in the Corpus Christi processions had been in the Middle Ages (see Chapter 13).[3] In earlier times, only civic dignitaries and distinguished guests sat in pews, while the rest of the congregation stood, milled about, or sat on portable stools. The reformed kirk's emphasis on preaching, however, required that everyone be able to hear the Word, and that in turn necessitated rearranging the vast interior space of St Nicholas. In 1596, interior walls were erected to divide the church and the congregation in two.[4] The single urban parish of St Nicholas, however, remained intact under multiple ministers and a single kirk session. Once everyone could hear, they were expected to listen attentively to long sermons, something best done while seated.

In the medieval church, wealth and status could be displayed through the foundation and endowment of chantries in St Machar's Cathedral in the old town and in St Nicholas in the new. As well as helping the founder's soul in the afterlife, such benefaction ensured the perpetuation of his or her memory among the living.[5] The altars were swept away with the Reformation, and elaborately carved pews soon became the new spiritual status symbols for the rich.[6] As private pews began to proliferate in the two parts of St Nicholas early in the seventeenth century, the town council acted to maintain order through regulation and enforcement. It licensed approved pews and removed others, collecting 'pew rent', regulating size and style, trying (without much success) to preserve aisles, and insisting that pews be removable to allow for burials under the church floor.[7] In 1663, a 'keeper of pews' was appointed to oversee these matters and, in particular, to ensure that people sat where they belonged.[8] As concerned as the burgh authorities were to preserve the physical integrity of the church, they were even more concerned to maintain the social integrity of the congregation. Where Aberdonians sat and how they behaved in church had everything to do with the relations of rank and hierarchy, wealth and occupation, age and sex that loomed so large in daily life.[9] Apportioning seats involved fixing groups and individuals not only in physical space, but in social space. It was a touchy business: in 1682 the baxters, complaining that the wrights and coopers had elbowed them aside, went to court to reclaim their right to the second place (after the hammermen) in all processions and seating arrangements pertaining to the incorporated trades.[10]

Well-to-do people, naturally, tended to sit towards the front of the church, with most of the central section reserved for burgesses and their wives and older children. Servants, apprentices, the poor and others of the 'meaner sort', along with children under eight, were banished to stand at the sides and rear of the church, while grammar school and Marischal College students sat in lofts overlooking the whole scene. Young children under six were barred altogether because they 'perturbes the Churche'.[11] The one group of humble folk, mostly young people, assured of a seat near the front were penitents, usually fornicators or adulterers making shame-faced appearances before the congregation. (Fornicators and adulterers among the elite tended to be spared this indignity.) As the congregation filed in, penitents stood by the kirk door (barefoot and in sack cloth, if adulterers) before taking their place at the front on a cuckstool, where they sat facing the congregation as the minister railed and prayed at them. Penitents were expected to show suitable, preferably sincere, signs of contrition and remorse. Most played their role properly, put in the requisite number of appearances, and were duly absolved of their sin. A small minority had to be sent back to the kirk session for further admonition and counselling after being caught smirking, flirting, responding to taunts, pulling plaids over their heads, or putting 'sneishen' (snuff) in their eyes to make them shed tears on cue.[12]

The authorities took even seemingly petty breaches of conduct very seriously. They were especially concerned to monitor and control the behaviour of adolescents and young adults, whose spirit, warned Bailie Alexander Skene, 'being naturally in the greatest heat, and consequently fittest for action' would all too easily 'vent it self in Vice' if left unchecked.[13] This threatened civic as well as personal ruin, not just because they were the coming generation, but because God was known to hold communities accountable for misconduct in their midst – especially, perhaps, in His own house. With God looking over their shoulders, the town fathers dealt strictly with the unrepentant penitents, as well as with unruly servants, apprentices, and students who occupied seats above their station or acted in ways that threatened to disrupt the carefully constructed tableaux of order and deference that the community re-enacted for itself each Sunday.

This suspicion of young people was nothing new. From at least 1418, Aberdeen's schools were educating many young men (and some young women) in the finer points of life. By the late sixteenth century, the town authorities were so fearful of disorderly schoolboys that schoolmasters were ordered not to accept a student unless his parents gave a surety for good behaviour.[14] It only got worse as the boys grew up: the rivalry between King's and Marischal College students all too often tipped into violence that threatened innocent bystanders.[15] Servants and apprentices were another potential source of disorder. In 1632, and at regular intervals thereafter the magistrates stormed against 'meane menis sones, prentice boyes and uther persones within this burghe of common sort', who in church 'presumptuouslie takis upon thame to sit in eminent rowmes and honest menis daskis'.[16] In 1661, the complaint was extended to cover 'scollers of the colledge and many of the tradsmen' who had proper seats of their own but still usurped the places of merchants, some of whom were forced to stand during the service.[17] Young men caught trespassing in pews were dragged away ('shamefullie cast furth') and fined.[18] The same applied to female servants, who were especially barred from entering the centre sections of the Old (West) and New (East) Kirks of St Nicholas where many of their mistresses sat. The area was fenced and gated, but servants (who in murky light and the right hand-me-downs could sometimes be mistaken for their mistresses) were known to sneak in 'under pretext of carieing ther mistres books and having libertie from their mistress to sit in their pewes'. This sounds harmless enough. But the town council condemned such 'uncivil and rude cariage' in the strongest language, making the extraordinary claim that tumult in the women's pews could induce premature labour: 'weemen with child are often thereby much wrongit and prejudgit and causit part with their childerin and [are] indangerit of ther owne and childs lyfe'.[19]

The civic officials who assigned seats found it particularly difficult to decide where to put women, who were meant to be segregated on the basis of their sex, but needed to be accommodated according to their rank, and were not always inclined to stay where they were put. In 1640, the magistrates tried to finesse the issue of gender segregation by allowing prominent men to place low benches in front of their pews for their wives.[20] But not every wife was content to sit at her husband's feet and stare into the back of the next pew. In 1660, the council tried to stop wives (aristocrats excepted, of course) from sitting beside their husbands, claiming it was 'only practicable' that men sat in pews, while women sat 'in the body of the churches in litle handsome chairs, or such comodious seats as they find expedient and wes permissable'.[21] But the noise of scraping chairs on the stone floor soon reached intolerable levels, and the next year the council ordered the master of kirk work to build benches so that respectable women could sit in near-male comfort in the centre section of the Old Kirk.[22] Some women still preferred to attend services in the New Kirk; over time their persistence and the pressure of their numbers paid off. In 1677, exasperated magistrates, determined to halt the mushrooming of 'gross and undecent' chairs and stools built 'by weemen at their owne hands', finally agreed to install proper pews for women in the New Kirk as well.[23] These furnishings cost the council money but, because bench seating made more efficient use of space, it freed up several new rows of revenue-generating pews for men.[24]

Aberdonians in trouble

It is just as well that Richard Franck and others provided some rose-tinted accounts of life in Aberdeen, because the town's own public records cast a decidedly less flattering light. This is not so much because Aberdonians were especially turbulent or sinful folk (though the records can certainly give that impression) as because most of the early records were generated by law-enforcement activities of one sort or another. Of the everyday good deeds of neighbours, the sort who shared a kind word or a convivial drink, watched out for one another, and saw each other through hard times, little trace remains in the written records. Imagine trying to reconstruct contemporary Aberdonian life from police blotters or even newspapers: the stories might be accurate in their way, but hardly representative of how most people live – except in the very important sense that they offer exceptions that prove the rule. 'For what is the Origen of a City or Civil Society,' asked Bailie Skene in 1685, 'but an harmonious Concord and Agreement to live together for mutual Aid and Assistance in all common Concernments.'[25] Even without Skene to tell us how things were meant to be, we might still deduce the ideal from the fact that the hard words, sharp blows and low deals that all too often passed between neighbours and even within families were understood to be disrupting that ideal.

From at least the fourteenth century, Aberdeen's elected officials struggled to maintain 'harmonious Concord' by enforcing bye-laws and mediating in disagreements between neighbours.[26] Much of the council's work involved settling property disputes. Most medieval and early modern summers witnessed the 'riding of the merches' or boundaries. On such occasions, the town magistrates and other local worthies inspected the territory over which the town held jurisdiction, including the boundary areas of the 'inner merches' of the burgh proper, and the 'outer merches' of farmland extending westward for about four miles.[27] When matters were unclear, as when the Don changed course in the 1670s, old men with keen memories were called upon to explain where and how things had been.[28] When matters were altogether too clear, legal instruments were invoked on the spot against landlords and tenants found to have planted or grazed or built beyond their bounds, cut more than their share of wood or peat, diverted a stream, ploughed up a road, or meddled with the cruives and nets of the salmon fishing.

Town dwellers were just as likely to encroach upon their neighbours. James Gordon of Rothiemay's 1661 map depicts substantial stone houses with slate roofs, wooden porches and tidy gardens and orchards (Plate 38). But not everyone lived in such surroundings, let alone a magnificent townhouse like that of Provost George Skene (Ill. 7; Plate 29). Neither did everyone maintain their property to a decent standard. Many houses, especially those set back in alleys and wynds off the main streets, were still of the wattle and daub or timber-framed, thatched type that predominated in earlier centuries (see Chapter 4). Such houses drew on the resources of surrounding wood and scrubland and were cheap and easy to build. Floors in these single-storey structures were of sand, clay or gravel, covered with straw, heather or bracken, sometimes sweetened by meadowsweet. Windows were small and covered with wooden shutters. Many seventeenth-century families still lived in a single room, perhaps subdivided by partitions, with most activities focused on a central stone hearth - more likely a chimneyed fireplace by the seventeenth century.[29] In 1642, Margaret Cruden lived in conditions considered shocking even by the standards of the day, as her terrified neighbours discovered when they saw smoke pouring from the cook fire in the unventilated cellar she rented. Fire was a constant threat in pre-modern communities (hence Aberdeen's oft-violated statutes restricting the use of wood and thatch), and Cruden's widowed landlady was found in breach of laws by which 'no fyre should be kepit nor kindled in laich [single-storey] housses within burghs except thair be chimnayis'.[30]

Apart from extreme circumstances like these, the authorities were not much concerned with the interior living conditions of a house, and would intervene only when the exterior fabric posed a threat to others. So, homeowners were required to repair bulging walls before they collapsed, correct gutters or chimneys that poured water or smoke into the house next door, and tear down porches and stairs ('forestairs') that extended so far into the street that a single packhorse or two adults could barely squeeze by.[31] Because people cherished their privacy (even, perhaps especially, in a society of crowded homes and face-to-face contact), they often objected when a new window overlooking their back yard was installed next door without their permission. The council invariably ordered such windows to be walled up. These disputes would not be necessary, argued the widow Janet Anderson after she won her case in 1667, if only 'ilk neighbour should keepe and observe the antient bounds and privileges and not to usurp any new priviliges nor Impose any servitude upon yr neighbors.'[32] If only.

As in any modern town, matters of health and safety were a constant concern. Neighbours called on burgh officials to warn slaters not to leave their ladders out at night, lest they be used by 'theevish persons'. Merchants were reminded not to store gunpowder in booths located on crowded, narrow streets, or anywhere near the tolbooth magazine, and not to sell the stuff at night – least of all by candlelight. Survivors of this last infraction were liable to a punitive £100 fine.[33] Parents lobbied to have abandoned wells covered so as to protect small children, and in 1668 'ane moderate and modest' speed limit was imposed on the town's streets, after a child was injured by a galloping horse that slid on wet cobbles.[34] One irate burgess convinced the council to order Marischal College to move its archery range after he was 'shot in the breaches be ane arrow which did come over the college yard dyk'.[35] Neighbours were pitted against neighbours when the authorities ordered a purge of pigs and dogs. In New Aberdeen, it was said that large mastiffs 'worried and destroyed' sheep grazing in and around the burgh. In Old Aberdeen, meanwhile, it was claimed that dogs in heat ('hot and jollie') attracted so many other dogs that they trampled crops grown in the burgh, destroyed kail yards and pulled thatch off low, sloping roofs.[36] Pigs, too, got into the town's market gardens, menaced small children, soiled streets, rooted around fresh graves, raised an intolerable and 'infectious' smell (disease was thought to be spread by noxious smells), and were an altogether 'unseemelie kynd of beast' to have in the town.[37] No wonder pigs were banished for a fortnight in honour of the Queen Margaret's visit to Aberdeen in 1511 (see Chapter 3).[38]

Most of the mess in Aberdeen was caused by humans. As the two towns prospered in the later Middle Ages, their populations grew; the empty yards and gardens of earlier times were filled with new, often flimsy, housing and workshops. Burgh officials armed with well-intentioned bye-laws, backed by the occasional cautionary fine, did what they could to limit the environmental damage caused by crowding and congestion and the endless detritus of daily life. Household and industrial wastes had to be disposed of. But Aberdonians continued to complain about their less fastidious neighbours who piled middens by their doors, emptied chamber pots in the street, and dumped noxious dye-stuffs and all manner of effluent into a water supply long since deemed 'unsavourie to the taste' and of 'ane greene and uncomelie cullour'. In 1679, the water was so 'putrefied pestit and spoiled' that even cooking or brewing with it was deemed 'Indangaring of yr health and lyves'.[39]

Buying and selling

Buying and selling was the essence of urban life, and in their daily dealings the inhabitants often came into conflict with one another. The economy of medieval and early modern Aberdeen, especially New Aberdeen, was highly regulated. Burgesses of guild and trade jealously guarded their monopolistic and restrictive trade practices, while the town council (burgesses to a man) fixed key wages and prices and dealt with the inevitable contraventions. From an early date, the prices of bread and ale, staples of the urban diet, were set by the council on a regular basis. This was done once a year by the seventeenth century, but as often as every few weeks in earlier times or during later spells of extreme volatility in prices. The fixed prices were meant to balance the interests of producers and consumers, but there were always those who strove to keep a little extra for themselves.[40] Council records abound with complaints about baxters who tried to shave additional profit by baking underweight loaves or by cutting the flour with more filler than usual.[41] Brewers were inclined to sell watery ale, but they had complaints of their own about customers who turned up with oversize 'stoups' or buckets and then objected when the brewer refused to fill them completely.[42] When fishwives or fleshers tried to sell day-old fish or spoiled meat it was confiscated and given to the poor.[43] Cloth buyers complained of weavers who stretched the cloth excessively, or folded it so as to hide imperfections, while weavers complained of buyers' cheating with overlong 'elne wands' or measuring sticks.[44] Merchants exporting salmon worried that the coopers' shoddy workmanship threatened their overseas sales, especially when defective barrels 'spill the pickle and so the salmond are spoillit'.[45] And everyone complained of the wrights, who not only charged 'ane extraordinar rate' for coffins, but refused to keep any on hand, so that when someone died on a

Saturday or Sunday 'and could not be keepit', they charged extra for working (illegally) on the Sabbath.[46]

Much of the buying and selling in Aberdeen was conducted not with cash, but with credit. Medieval and early modern Aberdonians were bound together, and, indeed, to the wider population, through a vast web of credit and debt.[47] Aberdeen's bailie court dealt with hundreds of debt cases a year, many of them involving quite humble people. Most debtors (and some creditors) belonged to the working poor, people who fell beneath the taxable threshold but nevertheless stayed off the poor rolls. They may have been struggling to get by, but they were sufficiently well known and well regarded in the community to be deemed worth lending to. Many of the sums owed were quite small: in 1444, William White took a widow to court for 17d.[48] In 1673, a merchant named William Meldrum took the recently widowed Isobel Massie to court because she owed him 18s for wool, 12s for onions, and £3 1s 4d 'for hir husbands buriall'.[49] In 1687, George Melville, a market gardener, owed £4 to a ship's captain for seeds, and another £4 to a merchant for rent on 150 beds of carrots.[50] Married women routinely lent and borrowed money, sometimes in concert with their husbands, sometimes independently. John Royson and his wife were both summoned to court to answer for a debt of 17s in 1445.[51] In 1673, Bessie Fairlie was married to Robert Nicholson, a mariner who must often have been away. Like many women, Fairlie supplemented the household income by spinning wool and finishing cloth. This was supplied by cloth merchants, in her case a husband and wife team, Walter Shirrone and Margaret Webster, to whom she owed £6 for half a stone of wool and £2 for worsted cloth which she had failed to finish and return.[52] Robert Nicholson's name was recorded because he was legally liable for his wife's debts, but Bessie Fairlie's name came first and the deal was clearly hers; Margaret Webster, co-creditor with her husband, need not have been named at all, unless she had been personally involved.

Violence by hand and tongue

People routinely turned to the magistrates and courts to uphold building codes, enforce safety standards and settle bad debts. But often they took a more direct approach to settling their differences. Violence was a constant factor in urban life, as people with long memories and short fuses, often ignited by drink, lashed out at their neighbours with their tongues, their fists and anything else that came to hand. When the dust settled, it was once again up to the authorities to try to restore peace and harmony. In 1398, the year in which the council records begin, fourteen people were charged with assault in one month alone, and in subsequent centuries dozens of people a year were convicted of assaulting one another.[53]

Sometimes the magistrates mediated a settlement - in 1317 a special court day 'for concord in love' was held – but more often they imposed fines or prison sentences.[54] In such cases they almost always required that the belligerents also made a public apology, both to each other and to the magistrates as representing the community at large. From the late fourteenth to the late sixteenth century, those convicted of 'strublance' (disturbing other town dwellers by word or deed) were sentenced to process through the streets, sometimes barefoot, to High Mass at St Nicholas. There, before the congregation, they were required to make an offering of wax to the altar lights of the church and express their repentance.[55] The post-Reformation church dispensed with the procession and the wax, but kept the public repentance. In the summer of 1684, for example, simmering tensions among three households of weavers boiled over in the Green quarter of New Aberdeen, where most weavers lived (Fig. 1.3). The number involved, eight, was unusually large, but the nature and scale of the violence was all too common. It began, for reasons not disclosed, when one weaver and his servant assaulted two servants of another weaver, igniting 'ane great tumult on the streit'. Another weaver and all the wives soon joined in. Combatants of both sexes pulled hair, tore clothes, dashed heads and called each other horrible names. When constable John Hendrie tried to intervene, the weaver who instigated the whole thing (himself a constable!) threw him down some stone steps, 'breaking the said John his face, to the effusion of his blood and hazard of his lyfe'. In addition to paying heavy fines, all those involved had to limp before the magistrates to crave their pardon and that of poor John Hendrie, and to promise 'to live civilie and soberlie as becomes neigh-bours'.[56]

Assaults on town officers were taken very seriously. In 1405, the town decreed that anyone disobeying or insulting the provost or others in authority was to kiss the cuckstool; if the offence was repeated the delinquent was to be placed on the cuckstool and pelted with eggs, ashes and assorted noxious substances.[57] In 1666, Isobel Rutherford was thrown in prison for blurting out that 'if shee haid been ane man shee should have shot ane of the tounes officers thorrow the heid'.[58] Three years later, the town council went straight to the privy council and won a public apology from Francis Irvine of Hiltoun, brother of the laird of Drum, who had attacked a bailie with his dirk and boasted that 'he would cause his footmane take off the provests hatt [off] his heid at the croce and cause him kik him in the arse with his foott'.[59] In this, as in other less celebrated cases, the assault consisted of both blows and words: the courts applied the term 'injury' to physical and verbal assault equally. So, in 1561, Hector Dolloquhy was convicted of injuring Elspeth Irving, and ordered to come to the kirk to ask her forgiveness for the wounds that he had inflicted and the damaging words he had spoken. And in 1684, Elspeth Fraser, a tailor's wife, was convicted of 'injuring' Andrew Brown, tailor, in 'sayeing he wes the devills servant and in blooding and stricking him in the head'.[60]

Women were clearly capable of engaging in physical violence against each other and against men, but words were usually their first weapon of choice. With men, most insults precipitated a fight, but in the late seventeenth century 'only' 40 per cent of the slanders delivered by women were accompanied by punches.[61] Most slurs against women were of a sexual nature, while accusations of dishonesty predominated against men, but these gender lines were not firm and were regularly crossed in both directions. Personal honour and reputation were regarded as a kind of property, assets critical not only for social standing and self-image, but also for business, credit-worthiness, employability and marriageability. That was why people went to court and demanded restitution in the form of a public apology in addition to any fines imposed by the magistrates. In 1637, a couple convicted of slander were made 'to sit doun on thair kneis in face of the session and to crave God, the session, and [the] partie wronget pardon', and warned that a second offence would mean the pillory.[62] Apologies and fines were in order in 1684 when Anna Fraser was found to have called James Milne a 'base oyllie faced dog' and his wife a 'base yellow drabe', after one of their servants had defamed her with 'injurious words'. The same applied in 1664 when a slandering servant named Jean Baxter called Agnes Kempt, a married woman, 'ane wyle notorous houre', adding for good measure 'that if shee had not been so, shee wold not hav stayit sex quarters at Londone'.[63] Slander cases could backfire, however: when Janet Chisholm took Margaret Porter to court in 1540 for calling her a 'friar's whore' and a liar, this prompted Porter to show people where the tryst had taken place, as marked by the belt buckle Janet lost during the encounter.[64]

Families: natural and extended

The family household was meant to be a refuge from quarrelsome neighbours and the general irritations of community life. It was the fundamental unit of medieval and early modern society, the first line of defence against disorder. Rituals of birth, marriage and death were enacted in the household. From the fifteenth century, tax rolls suggest that between 10 and 20 per cent of Aberdonian households, including many of the poorest, were headed by women, mainly widows. A well-ordered household headed by an adult male, however, was regarded as the key to social stability and prosperity. In this ideal patriarchal household, father ruled, mother assisted, children obeyed, and servants acted with efficiency and discretion.

Needless to say, behaviour at home, like behaviour at church, often fell short of the ideal. The relationships at the heart of family life - husbands and wives, parents and children, masters and servants - normally left little or no trace in the public record unless, as sometimes happened, family dysfunction burst into violent or criminal behaviour that spilled outside the home. In 1664, a noisy couple was fined thirty shillings apiece for 'living turbulently togidder, not only to the disterbance of themselves but of their nichtbors round about'.[65] In 1543, Alexander Michelson went to court to show that he was 'grytly hurt and skaythit' by his wife, Margaret Rolland, who was giving all his goods away to the neighbours.[66] The cordiner David Lyall's treatment of his wife was so brutal that, in 1630, the kirk session sent him to the stocks in the 'bak vault' of the tolbooth with only bread and water for a week to atone for 'his wicked and prophain lyff [and] crewall stricking and dinging of Jeane Woode his spouse'.[67] And in 1562, George Burnatt, who had turned out his wife Marjory Mair when he suspected her of unfaithfulness, was ordered by the bailies to take her back, and not just into his house but into his 'hartlie favour, as it becumis ane mareit man to do to his wyf'.[68] Burnatt was being shamed here, for a responsible husband and father should not have needed to be reminded of his duties.

Emotional ties are the essence of family life, and that is precisely where the historical record tends to let us down. We know of many examples of husband and wife acting together in business affairs, but what did this mean for their personal relationship? Work could probably unite or divide a couple, and the same was true of religion. What, for example, were relations like in the Molleson household? Gilbert Molleson was a bailie of New Aberdeen throughout much of the 1660s and 1670s, years when the town council's persecution of Quakers was at its peak (see Chapter 13).[69] Yet Margaret Smith, his spouse, was an early convert to Quakerism.[70] Their son was apprenticed to an Edinburgh Quaker who had married one of their daughters.[71] The first Quaker wedding in Aberdeen was held in their house when another daughter, Christian, married the great Quaker leader, Robert Barclay of Urie.[72] Barclay later spent five months incarcerated in the tolbooth while his father-in-law was a magistrate. Was Bailie Molleson completely estranged from his family, or did they somehow manage to get along on other levels?

Another Quaker, Provost Alexander Jaffray of Kingswells, left a diary (really a memoir), written between 1657 and 1661. This offers a rare glimpse of family relations within an elite burgess household.[73] Jaffray was born in 1614 into a family of wealthy merchants. He grew up to be a prominent Covenanter and a key collaborator with the Cromwellian regime and, like his father, he served as provost of New Aberdeen. He was a man of deep, strict and restless faith: having been Presbyterian and Independent, he turned Quaker soon after completing his memoirs. Like many puritans, Jaffray was inclined to be critical of his own parents and of an upbringing he came to regard as insufficiently godly. He had a low opinion of his schoolmasters, who were at best 'not very capabell' and at worst 'openly Scandelous'.[74] He studied for a year at Marischal College (long enough to earn the right to be called 'Mr') but 'had no good example' from anyone there either.[75] He said little about his mother, except that his parents loved him and acted jointly in determining his future. His relationship with his cold, domineering father was troubled.

Jaffray is remembered as an effective provost and a courageous leader of the fledgling Quaker community in Scotland.[76] But he was something of a late bloomer: like many pre-modern people he had an extended youth, in so far as he did not have full independence, and a foreshortened adulthood. He did not come fully into his own until his father died in 1645, when he was thirty. Whatever psychological dynamic might have been in play, the elder Jaffray's control over his son was underpinned by his control over the family finances. When Jaffray was eighteen, his parents arranged for him to marry Jean Dun, daughter of Principal Patrick Dun of Marischal College and bearer of a large dowry. Arranged marriages were not uncommon among the rich, though the feelings of the couple were usually taken into account. Jaffray says the marriage was happy, but admits he entered into it blindly and that his parents' motives 'were not right, but carnal and worldly'.[77] Jaffray was still a minor when he married, and his father retained control of his finances, including Jean Dun's dowry. When he finally began to manage his own affairs, the diarist was stunned to find that his father had run his estate down by nearly £5,000, a huge sum.[78] This was a great crisis in Jaffray's life. Though furious, he never confronted his father and later thanked God for granting him the strength to remain submissive: 'if I head contended with him, he being a very passionate man, its lykli he might have disinherited me or have taken some suche coars'.[79] Like everyone else, Jaffray had been raised to respect his elders and obey his father, but here patriarchy was plainly reinforced by material considerations. The spectre of disinheritance meant that dealings with his father always had an anxious, tactical edge to them.

In a sense, Jaffray did talk back to his father, if only through his memoir, a cautionary tale directed to his children and grandchildren. In contrast to his own father, he became a much more attentive parent, reading scripture with his children, catechising them himself, and 'commending any virtue or reproving any vice, of which they may stand in need'.[80] It would be interesting to know how Jaffray's children regarded him as a parent. Perhaps his religious fervour was such that they found him as overbearing in his own way as his father had been. But there can be no doubt that he loved them. Jean Dun, a 'most kind and loving wife' said Jaffray, died after bearing ten children, nine of whom died young.[81] He remarried, and his second wife, Sarah Cant, bore eight more children, five of whom predeceased him.[82] Jaffray fretted when his loved ones were ill and mourned their deaths deeply – more deeply, he feared, than he really ought.[83] It was precisely because he loved his children so much that he worried that he might be insufficiently submissive to God's will in taking so many of them. So, he prayed that God 'would save [me] from letting these my dear children, or any thing else of my enjoyments, get too much room in my heart'.[84]

Jaffray tells us something about his relationships with his immediate family, but almost nothing of his dealings with servants. About half the households in seventeenth-century Aberdeen employed at least one female domestic to help with the labour-intensive routines of pre-modern life.[85] Many households hired more than one woman, and some employed male servants and apprentices as well.[86] Female domestics formed the largest single bloc of workers in the town, and about half of them came from the country (see Chapter 5).[87] Servants and apprentices lived in, and heads of household were responsible for their welfare and conduct. The authorities were particularly concerned that young women should not live on their own, and those who arrived in town without work were given just a few days to find a place in a respectable household or move on.[88] In the Middle Ages this injunction had applied to young men as well, but by the seventeenth century only women's domestic arrangements were at issue. There were those who spent their working lives in service, but most servants and apprentices were in their teens or twenties and were – eventually – destined to marry and set up independent households of their own. For them, leaving their parents in their early teens to live under the care and supervision of an employer (more likely a series of employers) was part of the normal process of growing up. They might occupy the lowest rung of their host household for the time being, but those born in town often came from roughly the same social rank as their employers. Many servants were the offspring of friends, neighbours or kin of the master or mistress, in which case their life prospects were probably comparable to those of the children of the house (who might themselves be working as servants in a nearby household).[89]

Servants have often been described as 'intimate strangers', a phrase that captures the ambiguity of their position well. Some servants and apprentices formed lasting ties of affection with the families they served, but masters were urged not to be too trusting. The baker's trade, for example, advised masters to watch out for apprentices baking and selling 'buns or pyes' on the side, while the weavers warned that apprentices and servants were not to collect payment from customers without the master's leave.[90] Everyone knew to lock their valuables in heavy chests so as to defeat light-fingered servants. But it was one thing to prevent servants from stealing household goods and quite another, amidst high rates of turnover, to prevent people who had shared your cramped quarters, emptied your chamber pots and laundered your bed linen from taking family secrets with them when they left.

Servants, of course, could have secrets of their own, especially if they had been having sex.[91] Servants and apprentices were not usually allowed to marry and were discouraged from forming attachments while contracted to a master, but living in crowded conditions amidst mixed company exposed them to both the risk of coercive sex and the opportunity for more consensual unions. Those who were discreet might be able to keep an affair quiet, or at least out of court, so long as the woman did not become pregnant. With no reliable forms of birth control available, that was a fairly faint hope. In the second half of the seventeenth century, an average of nearly twenty-five servants a year became pregnant out of wedlock in New Aberdeen, most often by a fellow servant (seldom of the same household), but sometimes by a married master (seldom their own). Accusations of rape were rare, and the records give few hints as to whether the sex tended to be coerced or consensual. The women in these cases almost never claimed that they had been seduced with promises of marriage, and the church authorities seem not to have pushed couples to marry. Once a woman's pregnancy became evident, she came under intense pressure from the authorities to name the father, which she almost always did. The magistrates promptly fined both parties: £10 each for fornication when both parties were single, and £40 each for adultery, which invariably meant a married man and a single woman. Female servants, who almost never earned more than £10 cash a year above room and board, had to dip into their savings or scramble to borrow the money. Men and women alike who failed to pay in full within the week could expect to be incarcerated for a few days and then subjected to a public whipping or banishment. Because female servants earned less cash than any man in regular employment, they were much more likely to face the full rigour of the law. Once the fine had been paid or the lash administered, the kirk session prescribed penance in the form of a series of shame-faced Sunday appearances before the congregation – as few as three for fornication, as many as twenty-six for adultery. Once the penance had been completed, the sinner was formally absolved of his or her sin and the matter was officially closed. There was no 'scarlet letter' in early modern Aberdeen.

Servants who became pregnant out of wedlock could expect to be dismissed by their employers. Many trudged back to their families in the country to give birth, returning to Aberdeen, if necessary, to complete their penance. Life was never simple, however, and the illicit pregnancy that brought a temporary end to one line of employment could open the door to another. Before about 1750, it was the custom in Aberdeen and all across Europe for well-to-do women not to breast-feed their own babies, but to pass the infants over to hired wet-nurses. In most places, wet-nurses were married mothers in rural villages who took urban children into their homes; only the very rich could afford the exclusive services of a live-in nurse. The high rates of illegitimacy in and around Aberdeen, however, and the careful fixing of wages by the town council, meant that there were always unemployed, unwed lactating women available to live-in at affordable rates. The wage for a wet-nurse in Aberdeen was fixed at £20 cash a year, double the best she could hope for as a regular domestic, plus generous tips from the godparents if the child survived to be weaned. The higher wage could help an unmarried wet-nurse repay her fine, though some of it might have to go to help support her own child, if it survived. Employers seem to have expected exclusive service from their wet-nurses, who had to arrange to leave their own babies with family or other nursing mothers.

Wet-nursing was one way for some of the single mothers in and around Aberdeen to cope with the difficulties of bearing and raising an illegitimate child, but it was at best a short-term solution to the problem of trying to earn a living. In a world of far greater insecurity than our own, the majority of people in Aberdeen lived close to the bone and could be tipped into destitution all too easily. Even the well-to-do could suddenly find themselves in dire straits should a business deal turn sour, a loan go bad, a ship go down, an inheritance evaporate, or a breadwinner die. A natural disaster like famine could bring ruination and starvation to hundreds (see Chapter 5). The spectre of poverty haunted medieval and early modern societies, and the problem probably grew worse as populations increased in the sixteenth and seventeenth centuries.

Family, friends and neighbours always formed the first line of defence against hardship. Those who were able could normally be counted on to lend a little money or food, invent a small job, deliver a hot meal or offer a dry bed, mind the children, assist in the care of the elderly or infirm, or pitch in wherever they were needed – all in the knowledge that the person they were helping would do the same for them if they could. But sometimes the need was too great, or too chronic, or the circle of family and friends too limited, or they were too pressed themselves to provide enough help. Where informal charity proved insufficient, townsfolk had to supplement their slender means with institutional relief provided by a guild or trade or, if they lacked such an affiliation, by the kirk. Aberdeen was never a rich burgh, and the demand for relief always seemed to outstrip the supply, but the community did what it could. Christian charity, after all, was a matter of Christian duty: as Bailie Skene put it, 'Scripture is so full and pungent to this purpose, that all that fear the Lord will find it more binding than any Act of Parliament, or any Humane Law whatsomever.'[92]

The poor and the poverty stricken: the corporate and common poor

In the rigorously hierarchical world of medieval and early modern Aberdeen, all poor people were not created equal. Among the established, permanent residents of the town, the needy fell into two main camps which may be called the 'corporate' and the 'common'. The corporate poor included distressed members of the burgess classes, the 30 per cent or so of urban families that belonged to an incorporated guild or trade.[93] When in need, corporation members, widows and children had access to hospitals, pensions, scholarships, loans, and funerals of a kind or on a scale quite distinct from anything available to the common poor. These facilities, funds and services were intended not just to provide for their physical needs, but to cushion them from downward mobility should disaster strike. For the urban upper classes, poverty was shameful as well as unpleasant, and corporate charity aimed at preserving the reputation and social standing of afflicted members and, indeed, of the corporation as a whole. In 1698, amidst the great famine (see Chapter 5), senior members of the incorporated trades were aghast to find one of their own, Alexander Idle, a former deacon-convener fallen on hard times, begging in the street and from door to door. They whisked the old man into their head-quarters in the old Trinity friary, but the Trades' Hospital was full and a room elsewhere had to be set up for him (but not his wife, since women were not allowed in the building) until more suitable arrangements could be made.[94]

The common poor who lacked a guild or trade affiliation had to rely on public charity, dispensed mainly by the kirk. As in every town, the full array of commercial and political rights adhered almost exclusively to adult male burgesses of guild or trade, but in Aberdeen all established residents were at least entitled to apply for public relief when they needed it. In fact, it was on the margins of Aberdonian society that simple membership of the community, being of rather than merely in the town, mattered most. To qualify as an insider, entitled to claim institutional charity in New Aberdeen, you were supposed to have been born of at least one Aberdonian parent, preferably in the town, or to have lived there continuously for seven years.[95] Old Aberdeen was a smaller community where it was easier to know who belonged, and entitlement there was left at a vaguer 'many yeires'.[96] However it was judged, the first principle of institutional charity was that the recipient be 'one of us', and eligibility for poor relief (whether or not one ever collected) was the single most fundamental mark of belonging to the town, of inclusion in the Eucharistic and civic community, in 'us'. Of course, poor relief was a privilege as well as an entitlement, and once residency requirements were met it could still be denied or revoked on moral grounds: criminals, people under church censure, 'sturdy beggars', vagabonds, layabouts and the other usual suspects need not apply. Like people everywhere, Aberdonians intended their scarce charitable resources for the 'deserving poor', the worthy and distressed widows, orphans, elderly, lame, sick, distracted and disabled of the town.

A considerable number of people in New and Old Aberdeen at any given point did not meet the residency requirement and were not eligible for public relief should some misfortune befall them. Some, such as the 'Egiptiens', or gypsies, who appeared in 1527, were passing through, some intended to stay and work a few months or years, others were hoping to settle.[97] Families, travellers, students, apprentices, sailors, labourers and beggars all flowed in and out of town, with single women arriving from the country to work as domestic servants forming by far the largest group.[98] These and other outsiders had no claim on institutional relief if they fell on hard times, and the authorities tried to discourage private almsgiving, for fear the town would be swamped with beggars. If visitors of quality, like Richard Franck, were always welcome, lesser strangers were generally regarded with suspicion. But there were always exceptions. Down-and-out sailors, like the five Englishmen who turned up in Aberdeen after French privateers cast them adrift in 1690, could expect help from the local shipmasters' association.[99] Destitute strangers on foot were less likely to be welcomed, but civic and church officials would arrange to bury those who died and, if not too pressed by their own poor, might provide a little something to others on condition that they leave. In times of famine and dearth, the town hired extra 'scurgers' to drive laid-off labourers and other refugees from the countryside back out of town.[100] They could not keep everyone out. From the sixteenth century, when the streets were thronged with importuning strangers, the deserving resident poor were issued with smooth lead tokens stamped with the year and 'ABD'.[101] A token was a licence to beg, but it was also a token of belonging, worthiness, entitlement and of the town's willingness to take responsibility for its own. Ideally, wearing it alerted fellow residents so that they might drop by with some food or a few coins before the token holder actually had to stoop to beg in the street (Plate 31).[102]

Outsiders in Aberdeen were much less likely to draw from public coffers than to contribute to them through the fines they paid for a variety of offences. Drunkenness, physical and verbal assault, breach of the Sabbath and commercial misdeeds all elicited fines that were turned over to charity. The resident deserving poor of Aberdeen benefited especially from the fines paid for fornication and adultery, which must have been inflated by the sheer size of the small army of female migrants in their midst. The fines of insiders and outsiders alike went to support the deserving poor of the town, but outsiders knew that they were being made to contribute to a welfare system on which they were never likely to draw.[103]

Money to support the common poor of Aberdeen came from a variety of sources, much of it raised and spent in the same year. In the Middle Ages, bequests to altars often included provision for the poor on the anniversary of the granter's death. After 1560, the net for alms was cast more widely through the community. By 1600, most English towns imposed a regular poor rate on taxpayers, but this was firmly resisted in Scotland. Like Edinburgh and Glasgow, Aberdeen resorted to temporary poor rates only in times of extreme crisis - as in 1595, 1619 and 1696 - and even then it was controversial.[104] In lieu of a compulsory poor rate, most of the money doled out to the common poor in Scottish towns was voluntary. Eighty per cent of it in Aberdeen came from three main sources: weekly voluntary offerings at the kirk door (the largest single source), special offerings at communion services held once or (at most) twice a year, and fines levied by the courts.[105]

Clothing: dressing up and dressing down

Public assistance to the common poor could take a variety of forms, including handouts of clothing, confiscated and spoiled food from the market, oatmeal, bibles and new testaments, winding sheets and coffins.[106] Left-over communion wine was intended for the bedridden poor, but it sometimes got into the hands of servants who were inclined to 'debauch themselves therwith to the great greif of all concerned'.[107] The clothing handed down to the poor reflected the Aberdeen climate. Aberdonians dressed for warmth. Most clothing was of wool, shorn from local sheep, woven and sewn into tunics and hose for men, petticoats, gowns, and aprons for women. On their heads most women wore kerchiefs, and men hoods and bonnets (Plates 6 and 7). Most cloth which has been found is fairly coarse and probably of local manufacture, although there is one fine woollen textile from the fourteenth or fifteenth century which may have been made from local wool but sent abroad for finishing, as was common in late medieval Scotland.[108] Aberdeen's merchants were actively involved in the cloth trade, and many of their customers would have lived in the two towns. The woollen plaid was a ubiquitous garment, although periodically the council tried to prohibit higher-status inhabitants from wearing it, as it tended to be associated with the poor. Men's blue bonnets similarly came under the council's disapproval in 1598 with the town ordering that no guild brother should wear them.[109] As these statutes show, differences in status were expressed visually in clothing; only the wealthiest could afford to follow changing fashions and wear fine imported fabrics, such as a silk ribbon from the late Middle Ages, probably worn in a fashionable woman's hair.

The concern of the Aberdeen council with proper dress reflected contemporary preoccupations - several sumptuary laws, regulating the types of dress different ranks of society could wear, were passed by the Scottish parliament from 1430 to 1701. Such legislation was common in late medieval and early modern Europe. An act of 1458 seemed to be aimed especially at the extravagance of ordinary people in towns and countryside. It also specifically defined the attire that wives and daughters could wear - an earlier act had merely stipulated that they dress according to their husbands' and fathers' estate, and some women undoubtedly made use of this loophole. Now their kerchiefs must be homemade and short with little hoods. Their gowns must not be made of rich furs nor were they to have long tails, except on holidays. Labourers must wear only grey and white on working days, although on holidays they could wear light blue, green and red. In 1471, parliament relaxed the restrictions on women somewhat. Although expensive imported silk was forbidden to men who had an income of less than £100, their wives were allowed to have silk in their collars and sleeves. However, in 1567 it was enacted that only prostitutes could dress above their station, perhaps in an attempt to shame 'respectable' women into dressing according to their rank. This was not terribly effective, however, as by 1575 the General Assembly was condemning the ostentatious dress of ministers and their wives. If ministers' wives would not conform, it seemed unlikely that other women would.[110]

On their feet, townspeople wore leather shoes, which survive in great quantity in excavations (Plate 8). Shoes were valuable and were patched over and over again before finally being discarded. Most were fairly simple and of a typical medieval turnshoe construction, being made inside out and then turned so that the grain was on the outside. For very wet weather, wooden pattens might be used to raise the wearer above the dirt and the mud. Finds of shoe leather from many Scottish towns including Aberdeen show evidence of changing patterns, and it is likely that fashionable Aberdonians followed the late medieval fashion for pointed shoes. Leather was also used for armour and for waterproof clothing.[111]

Clothing was held in place with belts and leather fastenings (Plate 8), although those who could afford to do so ornamented their clothing with fine metal objects, including silver girdles and the copper brooch with a double bird-head found in an excavation on Broad Street.[112] Wealthier Aberdonians wore gold and silver rings and beads, such as the coral ones mentioned in a court case of 1447.[113] These ornaments served a practical purpose as well, as they were convenient to pawn when money was needed. This is one of the most common reasons for them to appear in the town court records. Most men wore knives in their belts; the number of quarrels where knives were used showed that this particular practice was not conducive to the peace of the town.[114]

Pensions and doles

The kirk paid a doctor and schoolmaster to devote part of their time to the poor, and set a few young girls up in domestic service, a few young boys in apprentice-ships and scholarships, and helped a few unskilled men onto the public payroll.[115] The most common form of assistance comprised cash payments to support the poor at home. Those judged in chronic need were awarded regular pensions from the kirk. As in towns across early modern Europe, roughly 60 per cent of the Aberdeen pensioners were female, rising to 80 per cent or more in times of crisis.[116] About three-quarters of these women were widows, many with small children. In the late seventeenth century, a fairly steady 115 households a year drew pensions from the kirk, while a more variable number of people in temporary need drew occasional small cash handouts.[117] In the 1680s and 1690s, between 9 and 11 per cent of households in New Aberdeen received regular pensions from the kirk, year in and year out. These figures were toward the high end of the usual range of between 5 and 10 per cent, found for a broad spectrum of early modern towns from London to Lyon.[118] Adding those receiving occasional doles brings the total proportion of households drawing some measure of public assistance (that is, not including households drawing only corporate charity) to 15 per cent in a good year, and 25 per cent or more in a bad year.[119]

In the 1630s, the average kirk pension in New Aberdeen came to just under £15 a year, but by the final three decades of the seventeenth century it had fallen to less than £9. While the Aberdeen pension was being cut nearly in half, pensions in English towns rose steadily and often doubled.[120] In Edinburgh in the 1680s, kirk pensioners drew an average of £21 a year, more than double Aberdeen's pension.[121] Food and housing were probably cheaper in the somewhat depressed Aberdeen of the 1670s and 1680s than they had been in the relatively prosperous 1630s. Even so, it seems that the real value of the pension fell drastically, probably for the simple reason that more people needed to dip into a pot that had certainly not grown and may well have diminished slightly.[122]

The sum of £9 would not go far in Aberdeen.[123] You could not live on it if you tried: it was assumed that the common poor would continue to rely on neighbours, family and whatever resources they could scrape together. £9 would pay about half a year's rent on a very humble house.[124] A modest suit of clothes for a man on relief cost nearly £6 in 1680, for a woman nearly £8.[125] £9 compared to the £70 that an unskilled day labourer could expect to earn in an average year.[126] £9 a year worked out as 6d a day. In the 1680s, when grain was plentiful, 6d would buy nearly a pound of the coarse oat bread that was a staple of poor people's diets. In the famine years of the late 1690s, when there was very little bread at all, 6d would buy little more than half as much, if that.[127] By way of comparison, early modern armies calculated a soldier's daily ration of bread at one and a half pounds weight, whereas the elderly or others less robust could get by on one pound.[128]

People might not have been able to live on a kirk pension in Aberdeen, but if they were desperately poor they might not be able to live without it. Needless to say, there were strings attached. Pensioners were expected to be 'free of scandal', meaning that they had to have atoned for any convicted sins or crimes. They were to work if they could, and not to beg, except in dire emergencies, and then only when issued a token. In 1634, Katherine Leslie, a poor blind woman, was granted 4s weekly 'with this expres alwayes conditioun, [that if] she be found begging heireftir within the portis of the toune [she is] to be depryvit of hir pension'.[129] Pensioners were not to squander what little they had on hospitality. They were to attend church regularly, daily if possible, and sit in the back in seats set aside for the likes of them.[130] They were required to open their homes to kirk deacons twice a year, to present all children being supported, and to declare any that had died, gone into service, or turned sixteen so that the pension could be reduced accordingly.[131] Children at home were to be catechised monthly. In 1633, the St Nicholas kirk session warned that

> the poore boys that hes weeklie pensiones ... and yet beggis daylie [are] to be
> dischairgit of thair pensionnes And the deacones to tak particular notice of thair
> names and some utheris of thame that cannot say the Lords prayer and thairfore
> are dischairgit of thair pensioun till thay learne some grounds of religioun.[132]

By the middle of the seventeenth century, parents on relief were to ensure that their girls as well as boys attended an elementary school: in 1675 Janet Ross was warned that she would lose her pension 'if she doe not putt her daughter to the school'.[133]

Hospitals, correction houses and workhouses

Nearly everything done for the common poor of New Aberdeen came in the form of outdoor relief intended to assist them at home. In the seventeenth century, the only indoor facility open to the common poor was the mainly punitive and short-lived Correction House. It was established in the 1630s by puritan-minded merchants flush with money from the cloth trade and caught up in the latest English fashion for workhouses. The idea behind the workhouse, revolutionary at the time and destined to be in and out of vogue ever since, was that the poor be made to work for their own keep and for the profit of the town. The new facility was meant to house twenty people, ten indigent 'volunteers' and ten obstinate sinners, who would be set to soul-cleansing work, carding and spinning wool. The master of the house undertook to keep them inside, keep their friends outside, work them continually, provide 'such competent dyet as they sall deserve', read prayers to them on Sunday, and whip them on Monday when the authorities so ordered.[134] Some fathers and masters sent unruly sons or employees to the Correction House to teach them a lesson, but it seems that all of the prisoners sent there by the kirk session were women who had been unable to pay their fines for fornication or adultery.[135] Fines were the same for men and women, but women almost invariably earned less than men; the session did threaten to send one man to the Correction House, but a friend promptly stepped in to pay his fine.[136]

Almost as soon as the Correction House opened, the cloth market went off the boil. Far from generating profits, the town was stuck with a contract by which it paid the managers (Yorkshiremen who had helped establish Edinburgh's new workhouse) £240 a year of the kirk's money to maintain ten prisoners sent by the session.[137] Wartime looting and plague brought the whole costly exercise to a halt by 1647.[138] There was talk of reviving the facility in 1657, 1664, 1675 and again in 1683, as a manufactory specialising in knitted stockings, but these initiatives were stillborn or short-lived.[139] The workhouse ideal gained a fresh wind in England in the 1690s and in 1698, at the height of the famine, Aberdeen handed the building and its well-stocked coffers (from which hundreds of poor people had been deriving direct cash payments during the crisis) to a new consortium of investors.[140] Once again, the immediate needs of the real poor were being sacrificed in pursuit of a vision of the poor as they might be made. When it failed this time, in 1711, the Correction House shut for good.[141]

An altogether more agreeable form of indoor relief was available to the corporate poor in the form of hospitals funded primarily by 'mortifications' or legacies left by pious donors. These targeted donations of land, cash and promissory notes funded Aberdeen's colleges and schools as well as its hospitals, and even helped pay for its ministers and the upkeep of the church.[142] Of the mortifications directed to poor relief, the overwhelming majority benefited the corporate poor first and foremost. In addition to targeting guild and trade members, widows and children, most donors also inserted morality clauses to the effect that recipients be 'laufullie begottin', or 'nowayes given to wickedness nor vyce', or 'not inclined to poprie'.[143] Nearly every mortifier also inserted a clause favouring her or his needy relatives. Dr Patrick Sibbald, a long-time minister of New Aberdeen who had seen where this might lead, made the usual provision for kin in his mortification, but added that it applied only to relations 'not exceeding the fourth degree of consanguinity'.[144]

Hospitals were the flagships of Aberdeen's welfare system from the Middle Ages, when the two towns had five hospitals between them (see Chapter 3). By the seventeenth century at the latest, however, hospitals were open only to select members of the corporate poor. St Thomas' Hospital, for example, was New Aberdeen's most venerable and visible symbol not only of Christian charity, but of civic hierarchy and corporate wealth and power. During the boom years of the 1620s and 1630s it attracted a great many donations, to the point where it became the town's richest charitable institution and largest creditor. Originally founded in 1459 for 'poor and infirm men', that broad mandate proved insufficiently discriminating and by 1500 only burgesses of guild and trade were admitted.[145] In 1609, the merchant guild appropriated the dilapidated building and its valuable assets for itself and by 1631 the Guild Brethren's Hospital (as it was now known) had been rebuilt, in keeping with the guild's new power and prosperity.[146] The incorporated trades, having been pushed aside by the guild, gained a hospital of their own in 1632, when Dr William Guild, a minister of the town and son of a former trade deacon, ceded them the medieval ruin of the Trinity friary.[147] In 1633, the dowager Lady Drum gave £2,000 'of moneys from my self' to establish a hospital for guild widows and spinsters.[148] Her initiative helped fill a void in female society in Aberdeen, which had lacked any institutional focus since the nunneries closed after the Reformation. The hospital was eventually established in a house on the Gallowgate purchased in 1664, the delay due in part to the magistrates' decision in 1633 to use Lady Drum's money to kit themselves out in style for the belated Scottish coronation of Charles I (1625-49).[149] The litsters' trade, which was not part of the consortium of seven incorporated trades that shared the Trinity Hospital, opened a hospital for its distressed men and women in 1654. Little is known of this facility, which was probably very small.[150] The guild brethren's, trades', and guild women's hospitals were also small affairs, each of them accommodating just six inmates. In Old Aberdeen, Bishop Dunbar's relatively spacious hospital had room for twelve men.[151]

These hospitals were retirement homes rather than medical facilities, though medical care was provided when necessary. The only specialised medical facility before 1700 was the medieval leper house located in safe isolation in the Spital (see Chapter 3). Those such as Henry Voket, who was infected with leprosy in 1476, suffered a kind of social death, being forced to give up their possessions and live out the rest of their lives there.[152] Leprosy had receded by the seventeenth century, but in 1639 poor people with infectious diseases were still being supported with funds belonging to the 'seikhouse betwixt the Townes', though whether the building was still in use is not clear.[153] From their medieval origins, however, hospitals were intended to help the pious elderly to withdraw from the world and prepare themselves for death: inmates were known as 'bedesmen' or 'those who are bound to pray'.[154] The monastic ethos was retained long after the Reformation, though the bedesmen were now warned not to pray by rote, and not for the dead.[155]

When retired merchants were admitted to St Thomas' in the seventeenth century, they were still required to acknowledge themselves 'separat from the world and all worldly Imployments and relations, and that they ar enterit in that house as they profes to betack themselves to Godlivership'.[156] This entailed signing over to the guild all their worldly possessions. It also meant surrendering their burgess rights to vote in civic and guild elections, practise their trade, or participate in any corporate affairs.[157] On the plus side, admission to the hospital meant a furnished room to themselves, new shoes and clothes each year, peat for the fireplace, a warm gown in the distinctive russet colour the bedesmen wore outside the building, and a pension of £120.[158] By way of comparison, inmates at the Trades' Hospital had pensions of £50, while the guild women at Lady Drum's drew £27 a year.[159] Yet, even with £120, the guild bedesmen had to be warned not to beg except in dire emergencies – a warning that lends further perspective to the £9 kirk pension meted out to the common poor. The retired merchants were also required to stay sober, 'haunt not aill houses or tavernes', and avoid 'brawling stryffs' - again a reminder that such things were not beyond the realm of possibility. No female servants were allowed in the building, and no women visitors, except 'such as ar of Christian behaviour'. The bedesmen were to attend church daily, wearing their gowns, carrying their bibles, and arriving and sitting together near the front. They were to take all their meals together, and spend their days 'in prayer, reading, mortification, conference, and other suchlyke Christian exercises'. When they prayed, the magistrates, ministers, and council members who set the rules urged that they 'remember all ther Laufull Superiors – the magistrates, ministers, and counsell as also all ther Liveing benefactors'.[160]

The common poor were finally provided with a hospital of their own when the Poor's Hospital opened on 30 October 1741.[161] Great advances in the care of the common poor had come earlier in the eighteenth century, when an Infirmary and, later, a Dispensary were established (see Chapter 3). The Poor's Hospital, however, was not a medical facility but a workhouse, and at times it was referred to as such. On 31 December 1754, for example, a doctor seems to have had the final say in determining whether an applicant should be sent to recuperate in the Infirmary or work in the Hospital: 'Margaret Irvine was visited by Dr Livingstone and not being found a proper object of the Infirmary was recommended to the charity of the workhouse.'[162] The Poor's Hospital bore less resemblance to the hospitals established earlier for the corporate poor than it did to the old Correction House, which by 1741 had been defunct for thirty years.

The Poor's Hospital was originally located behind the tolbooth, on land that had at one time been the site of the town house of the Earl of Aberdeen. There were twenty-five beds and 'the vagabonds doe lye in the vaults on straw, with the covering of sacking'.[163] According to the town council's instructions, the people to be housed in the institution were the old, the weak and children under twelve.[164] Children over twelve were to work and often the Hospital found them apprenticeships or training. The Poor's Hospital may have been less frankly punitive than the original Correction House, but it was still freighted with moral judgements and still directed in part against the 'sturdy beggars' of earlier times. The authors of the *Statistical Account* in the 1790s described it as 'for the reception of such idle and strolling vagrants as should be found in town' as well as for 'the poor inhabitants , who had no visible means of earning their bread – also for boys and girls, the children of poor inhabitants and for destitute orphans, who had no relations to take care of them.'[165] The first overseers of the house, Mr James Kempt and his wife, were paid a joint salary but, after they left, the next incumbents, a Mr James Marr and Mrs Cruickshank, were paid separately. Mr Marr earned twice as much as his female colleague and he was also able to supplement his income by 'keeping accounts as distinct from the business as Master of the House'.[166] Other workers employed in the institution were a washing maid and a cooking maid; they were paid 13s 4d for every half-year.[167]

The town council was responsible for maintaining the institution with help from mortifications and bequests, as well as the income from the sale of the textile goods and rope made by the inmates. In 1742, the number of inmates greatly exceeded the original number of beds: there were forty old men and women, fifty-one boys and thirteen girls housed in the Hospital.[168] By the end of the eighteenth century, only twenty-five boys were in the Hospital and all the other poor were being maintained in their own homes.[169] A regular occurrence in the Ledger Books of the Hospital is a list of extraordinary payments to 'outpensioners' – those receiving money, but residing outside the building itself.[170] The norm was for the majority of in-patients to be male and for the majority of out-pensioners to be female. Most of the payments were to the old and bedridden and to widows with children. In the mid 1740s, there were also payments to women whose husbands were serving either willingly or unwillingly in the army. Children were received into the hospital on the death of a parent but it was not unusual for poor parents to abandon their children at the Poor's Hospital where they would remain until they were old enough to work. As in earlier centuries, demand for poor relief always outstripped supply, and eighteenth-century authorities followed their six-teenth- and seventeenth-century predecessors in drawing a sharp line between those whom they deemed 'deserving' and the 'undeserving' poor. The deserving poor received a modicum of support that might, if the system came under strain, become minimal. The wastrels, even though they were poverty stricken, were largely left to their own devices.

The Daily Task Books of the workhouse list the work that was assigned to the inmates each day. The women within the institution were involved in the day-to-day housekeeping of the building. In the 1740s, the main occupation was spinning and weaving. By the 1750s, it was rope and net making which was more profitable and was considered to be a purely male occupation. The workhouse records for Aberdeen are so complete that even the amount produced by each inmate has been recorded.[171] These records of actual practice in the Hospital offer a useful corrective to official policy and pronouncements. The council records, for example, complained of the women's lack of skill, stating that the men would need to train the women as only they had the expertise to work the 'muckle wheel'.[172] The workhouse records, however, reveal that it was the women who worked the 'muckle wheel' and also trained boys to work the wheels.[173]

Here the Poor's Hospital of the eighteenth century really does begin to resemble Aberdeen hospitals of earlier times, in that the official regulations contain idealised portraits of hospital life that turn out to be just as deceptive as other idealised descriptions of congregational decorum, neighbourly accord and familial bliss. It was not that these images were false, because there surely were church services that passed without serious incident, neighbours who did not squabble, families that got along, bedesmen that took easily to the neo-monastic life, and workhouse women who deferred to male instructors. But there were always those who could not, or would not, play the roles assigned to them.

In the case of the supposedly more genteel inmates of earlier hospitals, the gap between pious intentions and practical outcomes could be especially wide. Conflicts could easily be foreseen. Most guild hospital bedesmen, for example, had been married, some had known wealth and travelled abroad. They still had friends who would stand them a drink. Though they might plead their case eloquently to the admissions committee of town councillors, they were not necessarily cut out to be Christian role models and exemplars of mercantile piety. Thomas Beverley, a bedesman in Bishop Dunbar's hospital in the Old Town, was convicted in 1609 of giving Janet Lamb 'ane cuff'; and three inmates of St Thomas' were expelled in 1633, when their long hours in taverns were found to make them 'contentious leivares with thair nichtbors'. Patrick Stewart, admitted to St Thomas' in 1640 on account of his 'old aige, want of meanes, and inhabilitie of bodie', turned out to have a body capable enough to commit adultery with a sailor's wife before the year was out.[174] These stories may seem amusing several centuries later, but they might have seemed less amusing, or not amusing at all, if those involved had been our families and our neighbours. These countless exceptions to countless rules remind us of just how varied, colourful, flawed and fully human the lives of past generations were. And the fact that these stories were recorded at all testifies to the conviction that such conduct was not acceptable, that people could do better, and ought to be made to do so. It was that tension, between the rules and the unruly, that made Aberdeen go round.

3

Health in the Two Towns

E. PATRICIA DENNISON, GORDON DesBRISAY
and H. LESLEY DIACK

Dirt, disease and death

The living conditions of the people of New and Old Aberdeen varied considerably in the Middle Ages and later. Those who lived in the better quality houses (see Chapter 4), along streets such as Castlegate, did not have to be subjected to the same harsh conditions as the poorer members of society who, towards the end of the medieval period, huddled and squatted in the backlands. For the wealthier, luxuries such as bolsters and pillows, wall hangings, even very occasionally rugs on the floor and tiled or slated roofs, reduced the misery of draughts and leaking roofs. By contrast, wooden houses with thatched roofs and bedding and floor coverings of straw attracted vermin and disease, and were more susceptible to fire, a constant hazard in medieval and early modern towns.

As well as the standards of living within the home, exterior conditions also had a strong influence on the likelihood of good health. Congestion in the backlands, and the mixing of residential, agricultural and industrial premises, added to the risk of illness. So did the placing of water wells and midden pits in close proximity; the closeness of human beings to animals, such as pigs, free to roam the streets and root amongst the midden piles; and the medieval tendency to dump rubbish in the streets, ranging from human excrement to the remnants of slaughtered animals and gutted fish on market day.

All was not totally mindless squalor. Both archaeological and documentary evidence indicate that attempts were made to maintain a certain level of cleanliness. Cobbling made roads and alleys less likely to turn into quagmires.[1] Wooden battening placed in soggy areas, such as latrines, and the raising of interior floor levels above that of the muddy exterior also assisted attempts at cleanliness. Moss was used as lavatory paper. Wealthier homes might even be as sophisticated as to have an aquamanile, a pottery or metal jug in the shape of an animal for washing the hands between courses of a meal; at the table fingers were used, since forks were unknown as a utensil in the Middle Ages.

The burgh authorities also had a role to play. Numerous enactments from the town councils of the two burghs are clear indication of official efforts to try to keep the urban environment clean. The repetition of these rulings would suggest that they were often ignored. Middens were to be cleared once a year in New Aberdeen and in 1494 a town 'scaffyngir' was appointed, paid by a tax of one penny raised on every house and merchant and craftsman booth.[2] In 1506, it was agreed that four men should be appointed to clean the four quarters of the town; the filth they collected was then to be taken to the common midden, for which each household was to pay one penny a year.[3] Particularly serious attempts to clean up the town were made for the visit of Queen Margaret in 1511. All 'pynouris', labourers or 'porters',[4] who had horses were to clean the town of its accumulated middens; and no other work was to be undertaken until this was completed.[5] All swine, normally free to roam the streets, were to be removed, on pain of slaughter of the offending pig and the banishment of its owner. Even the kirkyard was not sacrosanct. The following year, the council decreed that fullers should not hang their cloth to dry over the kirk walls or within the kirkyard itself.[6]

Medieval and early modern societies were inevitably more susceptible to the vagaries of the weather: a poor harvest might bring with it famine or, at least, extreme hunger (see Chapter 5). Archaeological evidence has shown that the commonest meat eaten in Aberdeen was cow, but sheep, goat, pig, deer, fish, chickens, geese and wild birds also featured on the table. Meat was not readily available in winter. Rather than feed animals over the colder months, only animals retained for breeding were allowed to live through winter. The rest were slaughtered. Any meat kept for winter eating had to be heavily salted or spiced, to disguise the rankness of flesh that was no longer fresh.

The availability of fish was dependent on the success of a catch, but it is known that the Aberdeen people also ate shellfish; and oyster, limpet, winkle, cockle, mussel and razor-shells have all been excavated. Dairy produce and eggs came from the townspeople's own animals or were bought with other essential commodities at the weekly market. Vegetables were grown in the backlands. Though more limited in variety than in more modern times, they ranged from kale to leeks, syboes, fat hen (a nettle-type weed) and beans. Mushrooms and other fungi were eaten. Fruit and vegetables were supplemented by the gathering of soft fruit. Raspberries, blaeberries, brambles, wild cherries and rowans were all gathered in season.[7] Cereals, however, were the staple of the diet, the main crops being oats, rye, wheat and barley.[8] These were grown in the towns' crofts and common lands, although in times of dearth cereals had to be imported, often from the Baltic region. Wheat that was to be consumed solely at home, as a supplement to oatcakes, might be ground on domestic handmills and baked in private ovens. If, however, the wheat was processed for commercial purposes, it had to be ground at the towns' mills, for which a fee was charged. Only the craft guild of baxters, or bakers, was allowed to produce bread for sale.

Water was essential for cooking and drinking. Most homes probably had water-butts to collect rainwater. Water from wells and from the lochs and streams was of little use for drinking as the Middle Ages wore on, for it became increasingly polluted with industrial waste and seepage from midden and cess pits. Ale for the majority of people and wine for the wealthier sections of society were the normal drinks, though a sort of grain spirit might also have been produced.[9] On balance, the evidence does suggest that, as long as a sufficient supply of food and drink was available, although it may have lacked in variety, the medieval diet was adequately balanced and not unhealthy. The poorer members of society, inevitably, were the most vulnerable in times of dearth and high prices.

Several diseases were prevalent in medieval towns, some being endemic and chronic, such as leprosy. Leprosy was common throughout western Europe and the need for isolation of victims was understood. Before a firm diagnosis of leprosy was made, the potential victim was confined to home; but on a decision by the authorities that a member of the community was suffering from the disease, the 'patient' was forced out of the town to a leper hospital. What was not fully understood, however, was the exact nature of the disease, and many others were herded with the lepers, especially those unfortunates with disfiguring skin diseases. Aberdeen's leper house stood at Spitalhill, at a safe distance from both New and Old Aberdeen. It may have been founded by 1333, when Spitalhill is referred to as *mons hospitalis*, but it is more likely that this is an allusion to St Peter's Hospital which stood on the upper slopes of the hill.[10] It was certainly in existence by 1363, when the 'houses of the lepers' are documented.[11] From 1512, it was often called 'the sick house' and in 1526 *hospitale leprosum*.[12] Attached to the lepers' dwelling was a croft where they could grow the absolute basics for their solitary existence; and probably also a graveyard. Lepers were buried near to the house, it seems, again in order to avoid contamination.

The records give little hint of the quality of life of these poor, shunned souls. In most communities in western Europe, a number of the leprous group was permitted into the town to beg for money or provisions, as long as no physical contact was made with the healthy and the leprous individual stood down-wind. The leper was permitted to touch only with his stick and had always to carry a clapper or rattle to announce his arrival. Disfiguration, pain, the loss of toes and fingers and the twisting of limbs increased the sense of isolation and hopelessness. The forcible removal from family, home and normal companionship probably exacerbated the horror of the inevitable future for the leper. Death was the central theme of the church service that removed the leper from the healthy society. From the moment of certification as a leper, the victim literally entered into a 'living death'.[13]

Probably the most feared disease in medieval times was the plague or 'pest'. The translation into Scots of Sir John de Mandeville's Latin account of plague and its inclusion in the cartulary of the monastery of Kelso as 'Ane Tretyse Agayne the Pestilens' in the fourteenth century is clear indication of the fear that it held for all people.[14] No other disease evoked such terror, or elicited such a comprehensive, almost ritualised, set of responses.[15] Those reactions were complicated by the fact that contemporaries, who knew only what could be deduced through observation and experience, were uncertain exactly how it was spread and how to stop it. Not until 1894, long after it had retreated from north-west Europe, was the plague bacillus identified and its deadly path traced from infected black rats to fleas to humans.[16] The disease was kept virulent by these rats and other rodents. The black rat, *rattus rattus*, preferred indoor living to outdoors; wooden housing was readily gnawed; and soiled straw on the floors and inadequate sanitation encouraged the hordes to thrive. If the rodent was carrying infected fleas, such as *xenopsylla cheopis*, which then bit a human being, the disease was handed on.[17] Medieval and early modern people never understood this, but they knew full well that the plague was highly contagious and tended to move along trade routes, from town to town. News of plague spread fast: Aberdeen knew of outbreaks in Edinburgh and other places in Scotland within days, and merchants and mariners helped spread the alarm whenever the disease struck English or Dutch ports.

Plague was really several diseases. Bubonic plague was best known to contemporaries simply as 'the plague' or 'the pestilence' or 'the pest'. Historians now believe that plague epidemics often involved other diseases as well, including typhus, which manifested itself when resistance was low, as after famine.[18] But it seems clear that bubonic plague almost always played a central role in large-scale plague emergencies.[19] Many infectious diseases shared symptoms and were difficult to tell apart – hence the frequent use in the records of the generic term 'fever' – but people knew the bubonic plague when they saw it.[20] It was hard to miss. It struck faster and more lethally than almost any other disease. People tried countless treatments, but none worked.[21] Between 60 and 80 per cent of those infected died; few survived more than a month, and half died within eight days. Symptoms were horrific and unmistakable. The disease attacked the lymphatic system, provoking fever, headaches and vomiting, followed shortly by painful swelling of the lymph glands, especially in the groin. These swellings or 'bubos' (from which the disease was named) were accompanied by eruptions of the skin – blisters, carbuncles and tell-tale large spots in lurid colours that veered from orange to black. For the mortally infected, excruciating pain gave way to delirium, coma and death.[22]

Pneumonic plague also hit in the Middle Ages. The cold and rain of Aberdeen offered ideal conditions for this form of the disease, which might strike either as a secondary infection of the bubonic variety or as a primary illness. Flugge droplets travelled six feet merely by speaking and as much as nine to twelve feet by coughing and sneezing.[23]

The Black Death had a major impact on many towns in 1349; but lack of records makes it unclear how badly affected were New and Old Aberdeen. Thereafter, plague did hit on a regular basis – in 1401, 1498, 1500, 1514, 1530, 1538, 1545, 1546, 1608 and 1647. It was sufficiently virulent between August 1500 and January 1501 that no town records were kept. The explicit details which are available from Aberdeen's records of the 1640s, and which are detailed below, give a good indication of why plague was so feared.

Because there was no cure for bubonic plague, people in every town knew that their best hope lay in prevention. This required a collective response. The idea was to seal the town off from any people or goods that might be carrying the disease and, when that failed, to seal the sick off from the healthy. The council registers show that the authorities were intent on keeping the towns free of plague if at all possible. Measures such as setting aside special areas for washing clothes during the time of plague was one method of containment. The council enacted in February 1498 that all back dykes were to be built up and closed. Anyone failing to do so would be charged for the costs of this labour. Sections of the town had no protective walling at all, not even small 'heid dykes'. These were now to be walled; one section ran from the corner of the song school to the dyke of a burgess, another was set up in the Green and a third section ran from Shiprow. All the small gates in these 'heid dykes' were to be locked and the keys given to one responsible person in each quarter of the town. Outsiders were not to be harboured by the Aberdeen townspeople without special licence. Beggars not native to the town were to be removed and the town's own indigent were not permitted to enter the church for alms but were to wait for charity at the 'clock door'. All these rulings were announced throughout the town, residents being warned to take heed by the ringing of a hand bell.[24] The following June, the council levied either cash sums or labour from all the townspeople for upgrading of the main ports into the town.[25] Care to prevent the spread of plague resulted in two men being ordered to remain in a dwelling house and not leave until it had been firmly established that they had come from 'clean' places and that they themselves were clear of all sickness.[26] In October, a strong watch was placed on all town ports and the council ruled that no one should cross the Dee without the permission of the authorities.[27]

In 1499, the authorities forbade trading with 'north partis' until north-east Scotland was free of plague.[28] A year later, the council was equally vigilant. Travellers who had arrived by ship from Danzig (Gdansk) with a 'strange sickness' were ordered to stay within their lodgings for fifteen days, along with their servants, until it was certain exactly what the sickness was, on pain of forfeiture of all their goods. This was enacted on 15 August, but within six days it was decided that a further fifteen days of isolation was necessary; no one was to come out of the houses under pain of death; and the kists (wooden chests) brought off the ship were to be burned.[29]

In 1501, the potential danger was thought to be closer at hand - in Futty. No one from this little fishing settlement was allowed to enter New Aberdeen without licence. Offenders were to be branded on the cheek with a branding iron.[30] Five years later, it was ordered that anyone dwelling beyond Pitfodels was refused entry to Aberdeen, so creating a very tight cordon of exclusion.[31] Extensive preventative measures were taken again in 1506, and successfully so, as the plague did not hit either town.[32] Further enactments were made in 1528 to hold the plague at bay. In the next year, two responsible persons took daily watch, from six in the morning to six at night on the Bridge of Dee, the burgh's southern approach, to ensure that the town stayed free of plague. This was reinforced with the statute that no chapmen travelling from the south or unknown chapmen from outwith the town should be allowed to bring their packs to the market.[33]

Although populations might develop resistance to certain infections, increasing spatial mobility towards the end of the Middle Ages brought contact with new types of bacteria. Syphilis hit Scotland in epidemic proportions in the last years of the fifteenth century. Venereal disease had been well known, but a new strain of syphilis was apparently brought back from the New World with Christopher Columbus and his men in 1493. This spread like wildfire, mainly through ports. Aberdeen was one of the first towns in Scotland to succumb. The council records of 24 April 1497 indicate that 'gore' or 'grangore', as syphilis was then called, had become a major problem (Ill. 4).[34] Three days later, the authorities thought they had a solution. To rid the town of the 'infirmities coming out of France and strange places', all 'light' women were to desist from their vices and sins, their booths and houses were to be laid low and they were to take proper work for their own maintenance, on pain of a key of hot iron branding them on the cheek and their

Illustration 4
An outbreak of syphilis, 24 April 1497.

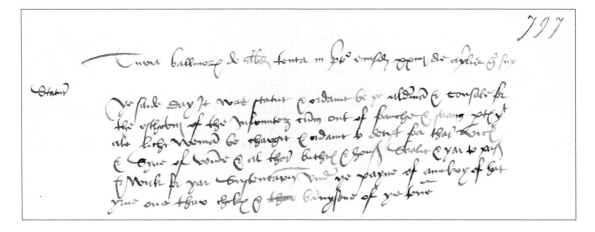

banishment from the town.[35] This may, to modern eyes, seem to be a misogynous solution to only part of the problem and to be a little harsh and unbalanced. By the time the infection hit Edinburgh in the following September, James IV (1488-1513) decided on firmer action - all suffering from the disease in Edinburgh were to be banished to the island of Inchkeith in the Firth of Forth.[36] Infections from overseas were probably the cause of great anxiety as they were unknown quantities. Generally, Scottish people, according to the records, considered syphilis to be of French origin, though the French, in turn, blamed the Italians for the disease. It is interesting, then, to read in the Aberdeen records that a close examination of all suffering from the 'strange sickness of Naples' was to be undertaken in 1507 (see Appendix 1). They were ordered to remain in their houses, and not to visit the fleshhouse, brewers or bakers, so as not to pass on the infection.[37]

Medieval townspeople were susceptible to many other diseases and debilitating conditions. Smallpox, cholera, tuberculosis, leukaemia and amoebic dysentry might strike at any time. And, in an age before antibiotics, a minor chest infection could quickly turn into a fatal condition, or an open cut become infected, with septicaemia and death setting in.[38] Skeletal evidence from Aberdeen has given greater insight into the health of the townspeople. They were smaller than modern people, men averaging five feet five inches and women five feet two inches. Skeletons give a good indication of health; for example, Harris lines, fine white lines on bones, indicate periods of stress, illness or malnutrition during the growing years of childhood. Other problems identified from bones are arthritis and *spina bifida* and it is now known that many medieval and early modern Aberdonians suffered from degenerative changes in the vertebral column, sometimes so extensively that two adjacent vertebrae might fuse together, causing considerable back pain (Plate 10). Schmorl's nodes, or lesions of the spine, are also evidenced. The high incidence and severity of this condition suggest that many of the population of Aberdeen were accustomed to hard physical labour from an early age. Spondylosis was another form of spinal lesion discovered, which might also have been associated with trauma, although it may have been developmental or genetic in origin. With this condition, the rear arch of the spine separates from the body of the vertebra on one or both sides. In some cases, the detached vertebral portion slipped forward and could cause obstetric problems in women.[39]

The condition of the teeth indicates that gingivitis was commonplace. This would lead to gum recession and ultimately to the teeth falling out. The fibrous medieval diet caused the white enamel of the teeth to wear away, particularly on the sides, and a build-up of calculus through poor oral hygiene could lead to decay. Where there was extreme wearing of the tooth surfaces, root abscesses developed; if not drained or extracted, the pressure might lead to open cavities around the root, causing excruciating pain.[40] Caries was also prevalent and it was discovered that there were more cavities than teeth, that is many teeth had multiple lesions (Plates 9a and 9b).[41]

Archaeological research into the samples taken from medieval cess and midden pits show clearly that townspeople suffered from internal parasites. Living closely with their animals, parasites were passed from them to humans. Many suffered from the nauseous and debilitating effects of ring-worm, as well as from parasitic worms, such as trichuris and ascaris, which might grow up to twenty inches in length. By travelling from the small intestine through the blood system to the liver, heart, lungs and trachea, worms produced obvious and immediate effects. Parasitic infection also reduced resistance to other diseases.[42]

Death was never far distant. Young children and women of child-bearing age were the most susceptible. Again, archaeological research has given an insight into the early years of a child's life. On teeth, disturbance in the development of the enamel on the crowns can result in enamel hypoplasia. Defects occurred most commonly from the second year through to the fourth of a child's life. There was evidence of fewer cases in the first year, which in modern populations is the peak time for enamel defects to occur. This lack of enamel hypoplasia in the first year of life has been explained by the fact that the diseases that were likely to cause enamel defects were probably fatal in the Middle Ages, and the baby did not survive. The majority of defects occurred after the age of about eighteen months. The reasons for this are thought to be that the infant lost much of the immunities from its mother's milk when weaned at about this time and also by the fact that at this age little ones were increasingly independently mobile and vulnerable to the dangers of midden heaps and the like.[43] Such a late weaning would have put physical pressure on the mother, particularly if she became pregnant while still breast-feeding, which was not a secure contraceptive. It has been estimated that only one third of women from Aberdeen survived this period of their lives. Women, however, once past this crucial stage, often lived longer than men, and widows formed a substantial group within urban society. To reach one's forties or fifties was considered a ripe old age.

Considerable effort went into combating sickness and disease. Lepers were isolated between the two towns, at a safe distance from both burghs. A little further north, on the upper slopes of Spitalhill, was St Peter's Hospital (Fig. 1.2). Founded between 1172 and 1199, it was to sustain 'infirm brethren', but a reference to 'sisters living there' in 1256 suggests that women were later included.[44] A further small hospital, founded in 1531–32, stood in the grounds of the Chanonry and cared for twelve poor men (Fig. 1.2). New Aberdeen had a hospital by 1459, dedicated to St Thomas the Martyr (Fig. 1.2). Founded by John Clat, its purpose was to care for the poor and infirm. A *maison dieu* is referred to in the cartulary of St Nicholas in September 1459, but this may be one and the same hospital. There was also a small hospital, dedicated to St Anne, in the fishing village of Futty. The four friaries in New Aberdeen (see Chapters 1 and 13) probably also offered advice and medication to the sick.

The reality, however, was that these hospitals were not genuinely open to all and could accommodate only very few. Their purpose was as much to give spiritual healing as physical, medical attention. Self-help was essential. Again, archaeological evidence has shown the types of medication taken. Figs were imported to Aberdeen and it is possible that they were used as a purgative. Seeds of the opium poppy suggest its use as a sedative. Poppyhead tea may also have been given to children during teething.[45] Hyoscyamus niger (henbane), which induced sleep and (if taken in large quantities) caused hallucinations, and Atropa belladonna (deadly night-shade), a muscle relaxant, were probably cultivated. And other species of plants would have been collected from the wild for their medicinal properties.[46] Grad-ually, over time, improved knowledge and natural resistance alleviated some of the debilitating conditions that afflicted Aberdeen's people. But many medieval diseases persisted into the seventeenth century and even later – some with more devastating effects than others.

Sevens and other venereal diseases

It may say something of the character of Aberdeen – as a port, a market town and a burgh with two universities – that the most stubborn of its afflictions was venereal disease. As has been seen, a particularly virulent form of syphilis had spread throughout Europe in the late fifteenth century. In Aberdeen, venereal disease persisted through the early modern period and beyond, although it took on a less deadly form by the end of the eighteenth century. The incidence of the disease is difficult to calculate with precision, for there was always a problem of potential misdiagnosis: the symptoms of syphilis (sores, pustules and a nose that in many cases was eaten away) could also be attributed to other diseases. And much mis-understanding continued: many doctors still believed that women's menstruation, considered to be 'a fluid of contagion', was a carrier of syphilis.[47] Treatments were many and varied, although it was never found necessary to open a Lock Hospital 'for the treatment and cure of venereal disease', as had been founded in London in 1746.[48]

There were three types of venereal disease mentioned in the Aberdeen records of the eighteenth century. They were lues venerea (L.V.), gonorrhoea and sevens (sivany or sibbens). It was not unusual, within months of a previous visit, for patients to be readmitted to the Infirmary with a venereal disease, despite pre-viously having been dismissed as 'cured'. Each time they returned, patients would often be diagnosed differently, as the disease progressed and symptoms changed.

This was especially true of female patients, in whom manifestations of the disease frequently took longer to appear. Of the three types of disease mentioned, sevens (and its other variants) is the most unusual. It appeared in Scotland in the mid seventeenth century but very little has been written about its nature or effects.[49] Even the origins of its name are obscure, medical sources providing contradictory meanings and derivations of the word.[50] Contemporary descriptions of sevens suggest two particular characteristics: firstly, spots which resembled raspberries; and secondly that the disease spread among families. According to one authority, it was probably a type of yaws, a contagious disease first mentioned in 1679, characterised by raspberry-like tubercles on the skin.[51] Most commentators suggest that sevens appeared in Scotland about the same time as the Cromwellian interregnum, in the 1650s. Many also suggest that Cromwell's troops brought the disease with them. Although it is not surprising that English troops were blamed for the problem, the equation of yaws and sevens is problematic, for the first mention of yaws occurred significantly later.

As already noted, one of the most distinctive symptoms of sevens was the raspberry-like tubercles on the skin. These could be easily distinguished. The argument that the disease was prevalent in families, and thus should be more properly called sibbens, to denote that it was passed among siblings, is partly substantiated in the Aberdeen records. The Ferrier family of Drumblade was admitted to the hospital in December 1761 and discharged in March 1762. Three children of the family were admitted, all with 'sivany'.[52] Medical sources at the time believed that the disease was conveyed through shared blankets and beds, rather than by sexual activity. This may be so, considering that one of the Ferrier children was aged only nine, though such a young age does not, unfortunately, preclude the other possibility for its transmission. Sibbens was found almost exclusively in the poorer areas of town, where the shared use of beds and bedclothes was likely to be more prevalent. Sevens eventually died out in Aberdeen during the last quarter of the nineteenth century.

The last plague

There were other diseases which died out earlier but had a far more devastating impact. Since the Black Death of the 1350s, the Scottish people contended with periodic outbreaks of bubonic plague for almost 300 years.[53] Towns tended to be hardest hit, and over that long period nearly every generation of Aberdonians was visited or threatened by the plague at least once. And then, suddenly and for reasons which have still not been fully explained, it was gone. Nobody knew it at the time, but the plague epidemic of the 1640s (which finally hit Aberdeen in 1647 and 1648) was Scotland's last.[54] Unlike leprosy, another great scourge of the Middle Ages and one that seems to have diminished gradually before finally dying out in the first half of the seventeenth century, bubonic plague went out with a bang: the final outbreak, almost certainly the worst of the century, killed roughly one of every five people in New Aberdeen.[55]

Aberdeen had worked out its basic quarantine procedures by the end of the fifteenth century, and successive generations revised and refined the procedures, consulting old men and old records to make sure that they had missed nothing. When plague struck in the 1640s only the middle-aged and older could recall the last time Aberdeen had been afflicted, in 1608. Plague entered war-torn Scotland from the south in 1644, carried by troops returning from infected regions of northern England. Edinburgh and Leith were badly hit in the spring and summer of 1645.[56] Aberdeen's officials watched these developments closely and, thanks to the careful work of the town clerks, the council's response to the crisis as it developed can be followed. The town council minutes record the official response to the disease from these earliest warnings to the height of the infection, at which point the records break off, resuming in time to describe the immediate aftermath and early recovery.

When the disease reached Angus in late June 1645, New Aberdeen went on alert.[57] The first step was to appoint a round-the-clock watch to monitor all movement in and out of the royal burgh, by land and by water. Four armed guards were posted at the Blockhouse, overlooking the harbour, and four more at the Bridge of Dee. Also, the ferry over the Dee was suspended. Two more guards were posted at each of the four ports and guards were soon added at Torry, across the Dee, and at Craibstone to the north. They were to monitor all comings and goings by day, and stop all movement by night. With two twelve-hour shifts, up to forty men a day were required for the watch. This burden was meant to be shared amongst the burgess elite: responsibility rested with the 600 male householders who were burgesses of guild and craft.[58] In time of plague, as in war, those who enjoyed the fullest rights and privileges were expected to take the lead in defending the town.

Measures against the plague were tightened in August 1645 when word came that Peterhead was infected.[59] With able-bodied burgesses stretched thin, elderly burgesses and the hundred or so burgess widows were invited to hire stand-ins for the watch at the rate of 10s a day – one-third above the standard daily wage for a labourer, and perhaps an indication that volunteers were hard to come by.[60] Although the urban economy was in tatters, it was reluctantly agreed that Aberdonians be forbidden to travel out to the annual St Bartholomew fair, the largest commercial gathering of the year. Merchants were not to receive any cloth from their rural outworkers for a month, 'until it please the Lord to cease the rage and fury of the said plague'.[61] But September brought no relief, and the magistrates reported that 'the continewall cair of our watches round about our towne for the plague' and the ongoing military threats and incursions 'makis our dayis very unpleasant'.[62] In October, when the plague had 'burst forth' from Peterhead and was 'both be-south and be-north this burgh,' back gates were ordered locked. All visitors currently in the town had to be reported to the magistrates. Tellingly, travellers at the burgh gates now had to present written testimonials from their minister stating 'upon his conscience' that they 'have not bein in any suspect pairt, nor suspect company'; for all the tough talk and strict regulation it still came down to a matter of faith and trust, because there was no way of being sure who might be a carrier.[63]

Perhaps these precautions had an effect, because Aberdeen remained clear of plague throughout 1645 and 1646.[64] The plague watch was eventually stood down and the restrictions relaxed, but fearsome outbreaks in Perth and Glasgow in 1646 and early 1647 offered no grounds for complacency.[65] In March 1647, the town council issued revised burial procedures. The old practice of burying the dead under the floor of St Nicholas Kirk had long offended Presbyterian sensibilities and was no longer practical or sanitary, given the increased demand for space occasioned by the wars (see Chapter 11). From now, everyone was to be buried in the churchyard; strangers and poor folk on the north side, honest townspeople tucked into the south.[66] There was far more room this way, but it would still not be enough when the plague breached Aberdeen's defences.

On 12 April 1647, Provost Patrick Leslie broke the dire news that 'the plague of pestilence wes raging' in Inverbervie, a mere twenty miles to the south.[67] A Covenanting regiment billeted in the burgh had withdrawn just two days before, presumably having received the same intelligence.[68] The burgess watch was reinstated and all the procedures of 1645 put back in place. It did not work this time. Two weeks later, the provost confirmed the worst: plague 'wes verilie instantlie expected to be neir our doore' and might already be amongst them.[69] This was no longer simply a plague alert but a full-blown emergency. Now the burgh's full array of plague responses was put in effect.

The first order of business was to lay blame. The plague, it was believed, was a manifestation of God's will, so the inhabitants of the burgh were to blame for the individual and collective sins that brought His divine and wholly unfavourable judgement upon them all.[70] Provost Leslie was more concerned with immediate causes and practical responses. He identified (though he did not name) a woman as having unwittingly set the impending disaster in motion. She had been allowed to move from the infected town of Brechin to Pettymuck, just outside Aberdeen. Two of her children had just died there of plague. Then, as now, children were efficient transmitters of infection, and one of those who died had been attending a junior school in Aberdeen and had 'had conversation with the children of many of the inhabitants of this burghe'.[71] This was every parent's nightmare. The provost could barely contain his famous temper. It could have happened, he raged, only because too many able-bodied burgesses had failed to do their civic duty: 'the watch wer not punctuallie keiped be the nichtbours and inhabitants on quhom it did fall', who 'disdainit to watche themselves' and sent 'thair servant or some weake nauchtie persone in thair stead'.[72] The assembled burgesses, some no doubt stung by the provost's rebuke, agreed to triple the watch to 120 men. The fine for absenteeism, previously unspecified, was now set at £100 (two-and-a-half times the already steep fine for adultery). The existing restrictions on people and goods moving in and out of the town were tightened, and contact with the people of Torry, or the parish of Nigg, or any other infected place was forbidden. Beggars from outside the town, barely tolerated at the best of times, were expelled.

An additional layer of regulation, backed by steep fines and corporal punishments, was now applied to life inside the royal burgh. These, too, accorded with long-established practice and with widely-held notions concerning the way the disease was spread through a 'miasma' of noxious air that adhered to infected people and the things and spaces around them.[73] It was believed that the miasma could be stored and transported in bolts of cloth, bed linens and clothing associated with infected people. So cloth imports were again banned (yet another blow to the town's industry, already reeling from wartime disruptions), linens and clothing from infected persons ordered burnt, and the sale of second-hand clothes by 'wedwyves' (female pawn-brokers) forbidden.[74] Equally reasonable was the association of stinking dung-heaps and middens with infection. These were to be carried well out of town and not used for fertilizer: 'fermorers' or market-gardeners were not to plough or harrow their urban or suburban plots until the middens were safely removed. Because domestic animals were suspected of carrying the disease from house to house, townsfolk were given forty-eight hours to round up and kill all dogs and cats. Mice and rats were to be poisoned as general threats to health and hygiene, though there is no evidence that people suspected the rats' role in hosting the plague bacillus.[75]

Because Aberdonians had a holistic view of disease, they were anxious to re-establish moral, as well as physical, hygiene. Moral contagion, too, was thought to originate with women: a day after the meeting on 27 April, the ministers warned the magistrates to clamp down on 'the many whooredomes and abominations in this city', especially among 'tapsters' or women who sold ale from cellars and door-to-door.[76] Isobel Kempt, a married tapster who had been cavorting with the drummer, Archibald Cullen, was singled out. There is no word on Archibald's fate, though he was probably fined. The magistrates, however, not only banished Isobel, but took the unusual step of threatening to drown her should she ever return.[77] She may not have appreciated it at the time, but being banished from Aberdeen as the plague set in was probably the best thing that ever happened to her for it may well have saved her life.

Isobel Kempt and other egregious sinners were banished in an effort to prevent their corrupt morals from infecting the rest of the urban population. Exporting moral lepers was one thing (every parish did it), but expelling townsfolk sick with the plague was quite another: to have done so would have amounted to a virtual declaration of war against the rest of Scotland. Yet separating the sick from the healthy offered the only hope of containing a plague epidemic. There were two ways to do this. The first was for the healthy to abandon the infected town for the relative safety of the countryside. Among the town's permanent residents, this was really only an option for the well-to-do. They could pursue their work outside the burgh and could afford to be absent from work and home for weeks or even months, perhaps retiring to a rural estate or to obliging relations who were willing to take them in (see Chapter 8). Some entire households decamped for the duration, but it was probably more common for the immediate family and the lucky servants who tended them to remove, leaving behind a skeleton force of servants to guard their properties and businesses. It seems to have been a simple matter for the burgh elite to gain permission to travel, at least in the less frantic early and late stages of the infection, but the authorities were loath to let servants abandon their posts. By this time, the watch was as intent on keeping people in, as before it had been on keeping them out.

Presumably, most people would have preferred to leave plague-infested Aberdeen, but the middling sort and the poor had no such option; a sixteenth-century bishop of Gloucester might have been speaking of seventeenth-century Aberdeen when he noted that in the face of plague 'there be certain persons that cannot flee although they would: as the poorer sort of people that have no friends nor place to flee unto, more than the poor house they dwell in.'[78] Among the majority who remained, separating the sick from the healthy was a necessity. This was no simple matter, because Aberdeen had no facilities that could cope with the hundreds of plague victims. People sick of other afflictions were normally cared for at home. The only purpose-built medical facility was the old leper house on the Spital. As leprosy abated, it had come to be known simply as the 'seikhouse', where people with infectious diseases were occasionally sent to die.[79] It was small and in a ruinous state by the mid 1640s and cannot have been much use.[80] In 1647, there were two private hospitals in the royal burgh, one for guild and one for craft burgesses (see Chapter 2). They were more like neo-monastic retirement homes than hospitals in the modern sense and they were very small, being intended for just six men each. In Old Aberdeen, Bishop Dunbar's ancient hospital could house twelve.[81] It is not known what role these facilities played in the epidemic, but it is likely that they served as isolation units for infected and dying male members of their respective constituencies. Rank-and-file plague victims were herded into emergency shelters, heavily guarded purpose-built huts located away from the main population at the Links and Woolmanhill.[82] The idea was to create a quarantined zone within the quarantined burgh. The effect was to establish transit camps where the diseased went through the last stages of their journey from life to death. Once the sick had been identified by the authorities, there was hard work to be done. The exact division of labour is unclear, but Aberdeen employed 'searchers' (all men) to locate, move, and bury victims, and 'cleangers' (men and women) to tend to the sick in the huts and clean up after them. The work was dangerous and required a robust immune system, a strong back and stomach, some courage and skill, and a willingness to take hard decisions and actions. Not many people were suited to it; most of Aberdeen's searchers and cleangers appear to have been hired from outside the town. Once an emergency was over, plague workers in some places were shunned, rather like hangmen, but in Aberdeen they were well paid and honoured for their efforts.[83] James Graham, one of the 'pryme and chief cleangeris', was hired from Leith, where he had apparently gained immunity and grim expertise during the plague of 1645. He was paid nearly £300 for his services to Aberdeen, and was made an honorary burgess as soon as the plague lifted.[84] A local woman named Janet Clerk, widow of a reader in the kirk (probably a plague victim himself), earned £50 for her work as a cleanger, more than double the top annual wage that a woman could normally earn, and in later years she was awarded a pension.[85] Yet, however efficiently and compassionately the plague workers went about their work, there was no hiding the fact that the dying comfort of individual sufferers was sacrificed for the collective good.

This was why the plague was so terrifying, because it threatened to rob its victims not only of their health, dignity, sanity and lives, but also of the family and friends who might comfort them through the ordeal. They could not even be assured of a decent burial. Many who died in 1647 had to be deposited in mass graves by the Links, where gravediggers cut 37,000 pieces of turf to cover them.[86] Sending a loved one to the huts (and the pits) was more than some people could bear, and experience had taught that the decision to do so could not be left to the victims and their families: the temptation to stay together was too strong, the disease too infectious, and the risk too great. It was in anticipation of the camps that the initial meeting of the burgesses concluded by instituting the plague regulation everyone feared most:

> that everie inhabitant give up the names of such persones as sall happin to fall seik in thair houssis immediatelie after the taking of thair sicknes, quhat seiknes soever it sall happin to be, with certification to these wha sall do in the contrair that thair houssis and haill familie sall be closit up.[87]

Later in the epidemic, when even the mortal risk of being locked up with an infectious person proved an insufficient deterrent, the town threatened to hang men or drown women for harbouring a stranger or failing to report a sick family member.[88] It was a threat seldom carried out, but a scaffold was erected for emphasis in 1647, and when one of the town's constables was found to have concealed a sick person in his own house he was sentenced to stand on it in shackles for two hours.[89]

By the end of May 1647, the plague was entrenched in New Aberdeen. Bubonic plague is a warm weather disease and it raged all summer and late into the autumn before abating in December, then erupting one last time in the following summer.[90] At its worst, the contagion was such that the town council, which normally met every week, held only two meetings, both of them outdoors, in a twenty-nine week period between May and December of 1647. One meeting was held at the Woolmanhill in early August, but by late September it was too dangerous to meet even there, and the council election had to be held just outside the burgh at Gilcomston.[91] The kirk session records for the 1640s have not survived, but they would probably show that the session, too, ceased to meet. Church services were not suspended until September (they resumed in January): it seems the obvious risk of infection had until then been outweighed by the pull to worship and the need for religious instruction and spiritual comfort amidst disaster.[92]

The disease was slower to reach Old Aberdeen and possibly less virulent when it got there. The magistrates watched developments in New Aberdeen closely, but they did not institute strict controls over movement in and out of their town until 23 May 1647, nearly six weeks after Provost Leslie had first raised the alarm in the royal burgh.[93] On 11 June, four 'visitors' [searchers] were appointed to check all sick persons for signs of the plague.[94] They were also ordered to visit every household and record the names of all the occupants, a precautionary step that would make it harder for people to hide infected family members. On 3 July, Old Aberdeen was finally put on a full plague footing: the watch was strengthened, people were ordered not to gather inside taverns, yarn and cloth imports were halted, and the public market was cancelled. Women and children were forbidden to go to New Aberdeen, though men could still go with the permission of a bailie. These precautions could not stop the disease spreading.[95] Just two weeks later, church services in Old Aberdeen were suspended 'for feare of the Infectione.' They did not resume until 26 December.[96]

In both burghs, the suspension of public meetings meant the suspension of public record, making it harder to know exactly what went on during the darkest days of the epidemic. It is clear, however, that the lack of formal meetings did not mean that burgh government ceased to function, or that ministers and elders ceased their labours. The diarist, Alexander Jaffray of Kingswells, was a bailie of New Aberdeen through the worst of the epidemic. 'All this time', he recalled, 'my family was preserved; which was the more observable, as I was every day among the sick people, being a magistrate.'[97] Jaffray was a rich man with an estate to which he could have fled, but while in office he took it for granted that it was his duty to remain in the infected town and do what he could to ease the suffering. He was not the only one. The burgh constitution mandated that only four of the nineteen council members could serve a second consecutive term.[98] Alexander Jaffray was not among the four who stayed on in September 1647, and he retired to Kingswells for a time. His brother, John, continued in office, as did Provost Leslie and two other magistrates. Remarkably, fifteen new men stepped forward to take on the burdens of office in the midst of the crisis.[99] The next year, amidst considerable political turmoil, Alexander Jaffray and four other prominent Covenanters refused to accept their election as magistrates, but agreed to carry out the functions of office for the time being, considering 'the dangerous conditioun of the toun be the infectioun daylie increasing'.[100] This degree of dedication was matched in Old Aberdeen, where the session clerk noted that, during the months when sermons were suspended, ministers contrived to hold smaller Sunday gatherings 'in the kirk, heir and ther throughe the paroch' and even 'at the huts'.[101] Aberdeen's most celebrated hero of the plague was Dr James Leslie, a physician who risked his life tending to the poor 'upone his awin charges'.[102] He was later rewarded (at his own suggestion – he was not a shy man) with a lifetime exemption from taxes.[103] Leslie's plague heroics not only boosted his own reputation – he went on to become principal of Marischal College – but they may have helped raise the profile of medical practitioners in Aberdeen: in 1657 the town council called upon him to establish its first guidelines for the medical profession.[104]

The plague placed a huge strain on the infrastructure and resources of the two Aberdeens. The royal burgh had been a prosperous place in the 1630s, but the civil wars of the 1640s brought economic ruin and mountainous debt even before the plague hit: 'this place', lamented the magistrates of New Aberdeen, 'is become so miserable that almost ther is non in it that can subsist and have any liveing.'[105] Towns traded to live, but the quarantine suffocated trade even more effectively than military blockades. Ever more, people were tipped into poverty as the plague wore on, but the suspension of church services cut off the weekly collections that formed the backbone of poor relief.[106] By the late summer of 1647, food stocks were dangerously low.[107] Just as in recent years hostile armies had had to be bought off, so money simply had to be found to bring high-priced grain into quarantined Aberdeen. When the bills were submitted, New Aberdeen claimed that plague-related public expenditure had totalled £30,000, much of it spent on food.[108] During the emergency, it was not always clear from where the money would come. The usual sources of credit were exhausted. The prospect of food riots conjured up in the minds of the burgh fathers the greatest of all early modern fears: chaos and disorder.[109] At their meeting in August 1647 atop the Woolmanhill, in language verging on the panic-stricken, the magistrates warned that the town 'cannot gudelie be manteined for lack of money', and that 'unles some speedie course be takin … the toun will be castin loose, and no ordour keipit at all'. The only solution they could think of was to empower council members to borrow money wherever, and at whatever rate, they could obtain for the 'distrest toun'.[110] In practice, the council ended up dipping into the remaining capital of the town's once abundant 'mortifications', legacies intended to fund various charitable ventures from the interest earned.[111] This was a drastic measure that, in effect, mortgaged the future: fifty years later, provision for the poor still did not match pre-plague levels and, well into the next century, Aberdonians would continue to pay inflated taxes simply to service the interest on these debts.[112] But there was nothing else that could be done.

By December 1647, the worst was over. It was still a capital offence to conceal a sick person but, as the weather turned cold, the disease grew less virulent. Two days before Christmas, Provost Leslie ordered householders to begin disinfecting their homes and belongings, to take all their 'uncleane, foull, or suspect guds' and see that they or their servants 'wash, cleange, purge, expose, and put the same furth to the frost air'.[113] Hard pressed as it was for money, the council made sure to pay the searchers and cleangers, who could not be allowed to leave town in case the disease returned with the warm weather.[114] But the spring was blessedly cool and wet and when the plague did flare up in the summer of 1648 – Old Aberdeen forbade all contact with New Aberdeen in August – it was much less deadly and did little to disrupt the recovery operations already underway.[115] By the end of 1648, Aberdeen was clear of the disease.[116] There were numerous plague scares in the years to come, especially in 1665 when London and other English cities suffered their final outbreaks, but the bubonic plague never returned to Aberdeen.[117]

The last plague took a terrible toll. New Aberdeen buried 1,600 people, roughly 20 per cent of the population. A further 140 died in the tiny communities of Torry and Futty. The parish of Old Machar, which included Old Aberdeen, is said to have suffered only twenty deaths, an implausibly low figure.[118] If the plague hit New Aberdeen harder than Old Aberdeen, it also hit some sectors of the population harder than others.[119] People with weak immune systems and less robust constitutions – the very young, the infirm, the very old – were at greater risk: when the plague was over, there were no elderly residents left in the Guild Hospital.[120] New Aberdeen's burial registers for the plague years, last seen in the nineteenth century, named sixty-five victims from about forty-five prominent households who were accorded burial in the privileged south side of the kirkyard.[121] That number seems low in relation to a total of 1,600 dead. It could be that less complete records were kept as the bodies piled up, but from studies of other towns it is to be expected that the well-to-do fared better than other people.[122] The extra money they spent on medication and treatment probably made little difference, but escaping to the country certainly improved their chances. There were children from these prominent households among the dead, but not servants. Servants would not have been buried with their masters, but some must have died with them. In fact, the plague probably killed a disproportionate share of children as well as teenagers and young adults (most of whom were servants or apprentices), partly because they tended to sleep several to a bed in cramped quarters that made the fleas' job easier.[123] Servants were also likely to be involved in the dangerous work of cleaning up after the sick, and some were left behind in the infected town when their masters retired to the country.

Servants and other unskilled workers, male and female, were easily replaced – there were always fresh immigrants from the country looking for work - but replacing skilled workers and masters of households was another matter. Within the burgess community, merchants outnumbered craftsmen by a considerable margin, but craftsmen seem to have been much harder hit by the plague, probably because their work kept them in the burgh. It is surely telling that, when the magistrates made their first moves to rebuild the urban economy (and tax base) in January 1648, they simply ordered merchants to move back into town, whereas they took steps to attract new craftsmen to replace those who had died.[124] There were, it was said, 'few number of craftismen within this burgh' because 'sindrie [sundry] ... ar dead of the plague of pestilence'.[125] When Provost Leslie attended parliament in March 1648, he was reminded by his colleagues to 'get craftismen' from Kilmarnock, Leith, Perth, Dundee, or wherever 'good craftismen may be haid'.[126] In August, the vacant Guild Hospital was commandeered for temporary use by newly arrived bonnetmakers and hose-weavers (probably refugees from Dundee, where the plague had just broken out).[127] The price of admission to craft burgess status was lowered for outsiders, but in return new craft masters were ordered to take on apprentices appointed by the town council - presumably those whose original masters had perished.[128] Of course, it was not just household businesses and workshops that had to be rebuilt in the wake of the plague, but families as well. As the disease and the shock of loss receded there was a predictable upsurge in marriages, as widows, widowers and orphans recombined into new families. The birth rate soon moved sharply upward, as couples old and new sought to replace the children who had died.[129]

Plague, it has been said, was 'both a personal affliction and a social calamity'.[130] As it raged, it devastated individuals, families and the community as a whole. But even after the last case in 1648, the effects of the epidemic continued to haunt the survivors and their children and grandchildren. Some communities recovered quickly, as Aberdeen had after its previous outbreak in 1608, but the epidemic of 1647 and 1648 was probably deadlier, and it came after almost a decade of civil war had already brought the royal burgh to the point of economic collapse. The last plague was Aberdeen's single worst disaster of the seventeenth century but, amidst the compound disasters of the 1640s, its specific long-term effects are difficult to distinguish from the general wreckage. It is certain, however, that long after the bubonic plague ceased to kill in Aberdeen, its bitter legacy lingered in grief and sorrow, dashed hopes and lost opportunities, debt and impoverishment, recrimination and survivors' guilt.

Plague may have been the most devastating of the diseases to hit in the seventeenth century but it was not to be the sole affliction. Smallpox was deadly, and it killed mainly children. Between September 1660 and April 1661, smallpox claimed 198 children in New Aberdeen, a level of mortality exceeded only by famine in the second half of the seventeenth century (see Chapter 5).[131] Yet no mention of the disaster is found in any civic or church records, leaving only the burial register

A C T

Anent Murthering of CHILDREN.

July 19th 1690.

OUR SOVERAIGN LORD and LADY, the King and Queens Majesties, Considering the frequent Murthers that have or may be commited upon innocent Infants, whose Mothers do conceal their being with Child, and do not call for necessary assistance in the Birth, whereby the new born Child may be easily stifled, or being left exposed in the condition it comes to the World, it must quickly perish. For preventing whereof, Their Majesties, with Advice and Consent of the Estates of Parliament, do Statute, Enact, and Declare, that if any Woman shall conceal her being with Child during the whole space, and shall not call for, and make use of help and assistance in the Birth, the Child being found dead, or amissing, the Mother shall be holden and repute the Murderer of her own Child : And Ordains all Criminal Judges to sustain such Process, and the Libel being remitted to the knowledge of an Inquest, it shall be sufficient ground for them to return their Verdict, finding the Libel proven, and the Mother guilty of Murther, tho' there be no appearance of Wound or Bruise upon the Body of the Child. And Ordains this Act to be Printed and Published at the Mercat-Crosses of the Head Burghs of the several Shires, and to be Read in all the Parish-Churches, by the Reader of the Parish.

Illustration 5
Act Anent
Murthering of
Children, 1690.

to tell the tale.[132] It was not that public officials were unmoved, but there was nothing to be done. Smallpox was a private, rather than a public, tragedy: the children who died left no jobs to be filled, no debts to be paid, no spouses to remarry, no dependants to burden the town.

Although the two most feared diseases - leprosy and plague - were to strike no more, the multiple scourges that afflicted the health of the townspeople in the Middle Ages endured into the seventeenth century and beyond. Cholera, *spina bifida*, osteo-arthritis, tuberculosis, leukaemia, amoebic dysentry, caries and the rest continued to lessen the quality of life. The increasing references to purgatives are also sure indication that Aberdonians were still susceptible to parasitic infections; personal hygiene was still not at the forefront of Aberdonian minds.

The chances of survival of new-born babies and toddlers remained hazardous. But, in spite of this, an extra mouth to feed might prove disastrous for a family. Mothers may sometimes have sought remedies by their own hands. In 1690, parliament passed an act 'anent murdering of children' (Ill. 5), claiming that there had been 'frequent' such cases; the mother was automatically to be found guilty if she had concealed the pregnancy and her child was still-born.[133] The act was passed in the midst of a torrent of other legislation consequent on the imposition of a Presbyterian settlement of the church. A virtual carbon copy of the English infanticide law of 1624, it is more likely that it was part of the reaction in 1690 of resurgent Presbyterian zealotry than the response to a real social problem. Although it is doubtful that infanticide was a common phenomenon, the act was ironic, given the devastation that would hit Aberdeen in the form of famine five years later, with its resultant deaths and female infertility (see Chapter 5). The four harsh years reduced the population of Aberdeenshire by 21 per cent; a loss that was made good only half a century later.[134]

Care of the poor in the eighteenth century

At the beginning of the eighteenth century, health and health care had not improved greatly from previous centuries. By 1750, however, there had been considerable change to medical provision for the poorer sections of the population. An infirmary was built to house the poor who fell sick (Ill. 6). The records of Aberdeen Infirmary, renamed the Royal Infirmary in 1772, are among the most complete and best preserved in the country; as well as the admission and discharge books, the doctors also kept casebooks in which each patient was recorded in detail, with the prescribed medicines and cures. In consequence, a great deal is known about this innovative venture.

In the 1740s, the charitably minded were encouraged to build both the Infirmary and a Poor's Hospital (see Chapter 2).[135] The Infirmary was built at Woolmanhill,

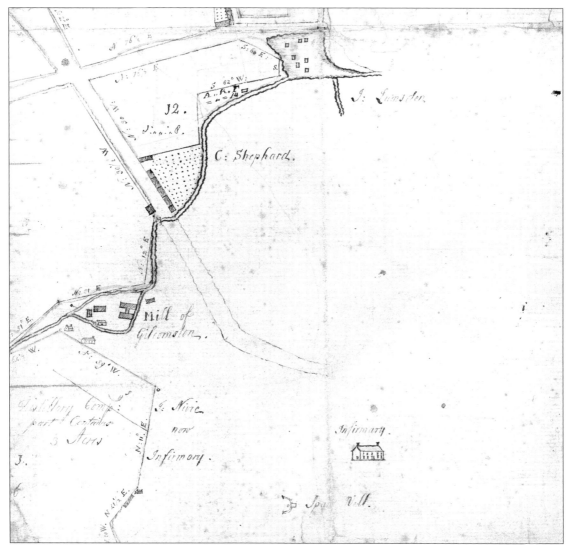

Illustration 6
The Infirmary, 1749.

on a green area in what was then the outskirts of the town, 'on account of the goodness of the air'. It would also be possible to graze a cow on the grass to provide milk.[136] It was intended to function 'for the benefit of the diseased poor in all the north parts of the Kingdom'.[137] On the completion of the building in 1741, the town council recorded:

> that the house intended by the Inhabitants of Aberdeen for ane Infirmary is now finished. That the objects to be entered therein are to be such poor persons who have Distempers upon their Bodys which are curable by Physicians, and such others that as meet with Misfortunes of Dislocations and broken bones,

they are to be taken in and to be cared for by Physicians and Nurses to attend them till cured, and then to be again sent to their houses, but if incureable to be sent out of the Infirmary and otherways to be taken proper care of by the parishes they belong to.[138]

On the same day, the council extended the use of the Infirmary to the 'three shires of Aberdeen, Banff and the Mearns' and sent a circular to that effect to the 'Noblemen, Gentlemen and Heritors' in the area.

To be admitted, patients had to be recommended by an individual or organisation that had donated money to the institution. If an individual donated over £5, the donor could then become a director 'to act in the management of the said Infirmary'.[139] The fourth article of the constitution stated that 'if any woman shall pay in the said sum, she shall have the liberty of naming a Director for life'.[140] There was never any question of the female donor becoming a director in her own right; and only two women donated over £5 – the countess of Erroll and the duchess dowager of Gordon. After recommendation, a physician examined patients, to ascertain whether they were 'proper' or 'improper objects' for treatment. Some might be more suited to the Poor's Hospital, or workhouse. In 1743, when Isobel Leslie applied for admission to the Infirmary, Dr Rose, the physician to the Infirmary, stated that she was not mad but 'obstinate, idle and drunk, a proper object for the workhouse not Bedlam'.[141] One of the other main criteria for admission was that patients were curable, as the Infirmary did not accept those who might die while in its care. Even following admission, patients could be asked to leave, if they did not progress as was expected, or if they did not behave in a seemly fashion. Many of the Infirmary's patients also spent time in the workhouse and the records are sufficiently full to track movements between the two.

At the nineteenth-century Huddersfield Dispensary, the majority of patients were young men needed to work in the factories; gender and age were the contributing factors in any admission to the Dispensary.[142] This pattern is replicated in eighteenth-century Aberdeen (Fig. 3.1). The first Sunday in January became known in Aberdeen as 'Hospital Sunday' and collections in the churches on that day were sent to the treasurer of the Infirmary. These donations were vital to its continuing existence. Associated with these payments was the privilege of the kirk session to recommend patients for the hospital. The two were so interconnected that the Infirmary checked which parishes had paid and which had not, to decide on the suitability of admittance of specific patients for treatment.

The Infirmary was such a success that, by the 1750s, plans were advanced for its extension. These included a ward for 'poor lying-in women'.[143] In the early 1760s, this came to fruition.[144] Before the decade was complete, however, the ward had been transformed into one for soldiers. This made economic sense, as far as the

Year	Men	Women	Total
1753	158	75	233
1754	171	86	257
1755	207	121	328
1770	602	256	858
1771	682	274	956
1772	671	283	954
1785	621	395	1016
1786	615	377	992
1787	685	428	1113
1788	589	451	1040
1791	611	434	1045
1792	613	446	1059
1793	672	476	1148
1794	619	384	1003

Source: NHSA, GRHB 1/1/2, 1/1/3, 1/3/1, 1/3/4, 1/3/5, 1/3/27, 1/3/28, 1/3/29, 1/4/1, 1/4/2.

Note: During the period of the Jacobite rebellions in 1745–6 Aberdeen Infirmary was used exclusively by the military for sick and wounded soldiers.

Figure 3.1 Infirmary admittance by gender, 1753-94.

directors of the Infirmary were concerned, since soldiers were paid for, at 6d per day, bringing much-needed capital.[145] As it happened, many women did not like having their children in the institution and few had made use of the facility. If the ward had continued to be used for the poor, the directors felt that it 'would have been financially disastrous'. The cost of running the Infirmary by the end of the century was £1,300 sterling per annum. The directors possessed fixed funds of £400, the remaining £900 raised from collections in parishes and donations from Scotland and abroad (see Chapter 17).

There was an element of paternalism involved in charitable donation and philanthropy often came from landowners. Landed gentry frequently appear in the list of sponsors of the Infirmary and the Poor's Hospital and also in the Mortification Accounts. Whenever there was a shortage of money for a specific capital project, the directors of the Infirmary produced an 'Abstract of the Statistics of the Infirmary', which was circulated widely to advertise the need for capital.[146] Another, more irregular, source of income was bequests. In 1740, John Rickart made his will, stating that, after other legacies had been paid, the remainder of his property should be 'devoted to the benefit of the Infirmary already founded, and the Workhouse about to be established'.[147] On his death in 1749, £4,172 was divided between the two institutions.

Later in the century, in 1781, a Dispensary was opened, to deal with the Infirmary's outpatients. As a consequence, more patients could be treated. By 1796-7, the Infirmary was dealing with 1,126 in-patients and the Dispensary with 2,500 out-

Disease	Number of patients	Number who died
Fevers, from infection	200	2
Fevers, with cough from cold	60	1
Scarlet fever, an epidemic	48	4
Smallpox, an epidemic	70	9
Chincough, an epidemic	20	2
Influenza, anepidemic	60	0
Malignant sore throat	10	2
Autumnal dysentery	30	0
Chicken pox	10	0
Cholera (prevalent at end of summer)	10	0
Pleurisy	11	1
Inflammatory sore throat	22	0
Rheumatism	30	0
Erysipelas	12	0
Inflammatory tumour	10	0
Consumption of the lungs	32	3
Marasmus/consumption, without cough	10	1
Cough, difficult breathing of aged persons	70	7
Asthma	10	0
Nervous and stomach complaints	88	0
Hysteric disorders	92	0
Stone and gravel	16	0
Difficult labour	12	0
Abortion/miscarriage	10	0
Accidents	50	0
Sexual complaints	40	0
Worms	10	0
Diarrhoea, or looseness	20	0
Inflammation of the eyes	21	0
Ulcers	25	0
Itch	35	0

Figure 3.2
Diseases of
dispensary patients,
March 1792-March
1793.

Source: NAS, GD 136/1194 (Sinclair of Freswick Papers), dated Aberdeen, 25 Mar. 1793 and including a 'Return of Dispensary Patients, who have been visited in their own houses by Dr Gordon, and who have had the benefit of advice and medicines.'

Note: Total figures in the source for each disease were miscalculated. The totals indicated here have been calculated on the basis of the individual entries.

patients.[148] Few of the Dispensary's early records survive, although there are several lists of the types of illnesses that were treated in the 1790s.[149] Figure 3.2 indicates the diseases, some of which were seasonal, that were dealt with by the Dispensary doctor.

In 1789, an epidemic of puerperal fever claimed the lives of at least three women.

The next year, twenty-three women were affected and eight of them died. The epidemic was getting worse. The Dispensary doctor who was mainly involved in the treatment of these women was Alexander Gordon.[150] Gordon, a native of the area and born in 1752, had been a naval surgeon before returning to take up his post at the Dispensary in the 1780s. He also discovered the link between midwives washing their hands inadequately and the spread of puerperal fever. Conducting a survey of women in Aberdeen who had caught the infection, Gordon was able to trace the source to a few midwives. His advocacy of hand washing before and after delivery was published as *A Treatise on the Epidemic Puerperal Fever of Aberdeen* (London, 1795). This was more than fifty years before the celebrated Austrian doctor Ignaz Philipp Semmelweis was credited with such findings. Gordon's discovery had a very dramatic effect on the incidence of the disease and the survival rates of mothers. By 1791, although twenty-eight patients were affected by puerperal fever, only one died.[151]

Middle-class health in the eighteenth century

Those who were able to afford treatment at home by their own doctor generally preferred not to run the risk of entering the Infirmary, where they feared infection. The case notes on the fee-paying patients of some doctors have survived. Some of the most comprehensive belonged to Dr David Skene, who maintained a private practice in the area from the mid 1750s until his death in 1771.[152] Writing to Lord Kames, he remarked that 'a decent coat and a life of drudgery in a very narrow circle is the genuine history of an Aberdeen Doctor'.[153] Skene's extant records relate to 111 female patients. Of these, twenty-nine suffered specific 'female disorders' – pregnancy, menstruation and associated problems. A further forty had contracted infectious diseases, such as typhus and smallpox. Several of those with smallpox were children, many of whom had just been inoculated by Skene and were suffering from after-effects. During the late 1760s, Skene had inoculated many families of petty lairds against smallpox. He also experimented with similar techniques to discover an inoculation against measles.[154] This was highly advanced for the time, for, although smallpox inoculations had been developed as early as the 1720s, vaccines against measles were not fully developed until the twentieth century.

Skene had also demonstrated an interest in women's health from early in his training. One of his first letters to his father dating from this period discussed female health problems.[155] His later interest in childbirth was perhaps an example of Enlightenment thinking, in his concern to encourage healthy children to become part of a loyal and educated workforce.[156] Skene appears, however, to have possessed a genuine interest in the health and welfare of his female patients. They clearly respected him and appreciated his efforts on their behalf, as several letters from grateful female patients indicate.[157] As for children, Skene was forward-thinking in his attitude to childbirth and was the prime motivator of classes for midwives in Aberdeen.[158] This was a controversial opinion, since some male doctors and mid-wives wished to push female midwives aside.

David Skene was a forerunner of more general developments. As medical knowl-edge and medical education improved in the course of the eighteenth century, so too did the treatment offered to the population at large. For the time, Aberdeen was well served, having its Infirmary, Dispensary and Poor's Hospital for the impoverished members of society. The presence of enlightened doctors slowly began to displace the misconceptions and misunderstandings of earlier centuries and authoritative good practice gradually took their place.

4

Housing in the Two Towns

GEOFFREY P. STELL

Centuries of documentary record-keeping and a steady commitment to urban archaeological excavation over more than a quarter of a century have meant that information on early houses and property in medieval and post-medieval Aberdeen is second to none among historic Scottish burghs.[1] In James Gordon of Rothiemay's 1661 topographical map and accompanying commentary on Old and New Aberdeen (Plate 38), the two towns possess a particularly rich and detailed early pictorial source, which, even with its recognised limitations, is the envy of most other Scottish burghs.[2]

Such relatively rich sources of information are not matched by an equal abundance of standing buildings, at least not in the central area of New Aberdeen, which was so ambitiously re-configured in the nineteenth century and further redeveloped in the latter half of the twentieth. The three oldest surviving houses in, or from, this area – Provost Skene's House (Ill. 7), Provost Ross's House and Benholm's Lodging or Wallace's Tower (bodily removed from Netherkirkgate to Seaton Park, Tillydrone, in 1964-5) – are very much a selective remnant, reflecting the highest standards of living among rich merchants and civic leaders in sixteenth- and seventeenth-century Aberdeen. And only one of the three, Provost Ross's House, conveys even the faintest impression of its original context and 'streetscape' surroundings.

The relatively sparse inventory of surviving domestic architecture in the city centre dating from before 1800 is rendered complete by three restored houses in Upperkirkgate (nos 6-8, Provost Robertson's House (1680), nos 24-6 (1694) and the gable-fronted mid seventeenth-century no. 42); by stepped terraces of solidly handsome Georgian houses lining Marischal Street, a hugely significant pioneering piece of urban planning and engineering laid out and developed from 1767; and by isolated survivors of this first era of urban improvement in modern Aberdeen in Schoolhill and Belmont Street.[3] Fortunately, a number of old houses, usually in run-down slum conditions, survived into the era of photography in the latter half of the nineteenth century, and photographic records of these architectural landmarks, particularly those emanating from the locally-based studios of George

Illustration 7
Provost Skene's
House.

Washington Wilson, add greatly to the corpus of historical and archaeological knowledge.[4]

The development of post-war Aberdeen is also charted indirectly by numerous photographs, drawings and descriptions of unloved streets of threatened (and subsequently demolished) buildings compiled by, or on behalf of, the Scottish National Buildings Record and its successor body, the National Monuments Record of Scotland (NMRS), administered by the Royal Commission on the Ancient and Historical Monuments of Scotland (RCAHMS).[5] The lost domestic architecture of Queen Street, Broad Street and Virginia Street can be re-visited through such records which, even though compiled merely a generation ago, now appear to be just another link in an increasingly remote chain of visual and recorded memory going back to the mid nineteenth century.

Meanwhile, a short distance to the north, the core of the burgh of Old Aberdeen has been subject to development pressures - in modern times mainly associated with the University of Aberdeen - that have been much more respectful in character and location. As a consequence, Old Aberdeen's architectural heritage has been more intensively conserved and managed over several decades. Thus, to this day, Old Aberdeen contains a proportionately greater number and range of traditional urban houses of seventeenth- and eighteenth-century date, including a few in the Chanonry which still bear physical witness to their medieval origins as residences of the canons and dignitaries of St Machar's Cathedral.[6]

Surviving houses of the post-Reformation period in Old Aberdeen include buildings which obviously derive from tower-house forms, such as the three-storeyed T-plan house at nos 20–22 Don Street. Dating from 1676, this building is known as the Bede House on account of its short-lived use after 1786 as a replacement for the Bishop's Hospital, when it accommodated eight bedesmen (see Chapter 3). More characteristically urban are those which stand end-on, or gabled, to the street, such as the two-storeyed row that was built as an investment by the Wrights' and Coopers' Societies in the early eighteenth century, and, just opposite them, also off the High Street, a gable-ended terrace of single-storeyed cottages at Grant's Place (1732). Other groups of low density housing include the court of single-storeyed almshouses known as Mitchell's Hospital in the Chanonry, which were designed and built in 1801 to house five widows and five unmarried daughters of merchant and trade burgesses of Old Aberdeen. In all these respects, the architectural contrast with the highly-developed city centre could not be more marked. Indeed, on a regional if not a national scale – and no doubt in the eyes of modern film directors – parts of Old Aberdeen certainly compete with streets in places such as Kirkcudbright, Dunkeld or Cromarty in conveying the general ambience, if not the precise domestic architectural detail, of a small urban community as it might have looked prior to 1800.

Taken together, the surviving or recorded evidence of domestic buildings in the two burghs is at least sufficient to permit a broad impression of their architectural character and social context. But, given that the overall picture is patchy and somewhat random, a general account of this kind can best proceed from the known and recognisable to the relatively unknown, that is, in reverse chronological order, moving backwards in time from the later Georgian era (when the population may have stood at around 17,000), downwards through the social hierarchy, and downwards, too, from visible, above-ground evidence to that which was once concealed below ground and has now been revealed by archaeological excavation.

Of the houses associated with the new developments in street-planning in the second half of the eighteenth century, the grandest and most expensive were those at the upper end of Marischal Street. This was a pioneering embanked thoroughfare which provided a direct route from the town centre to the quayside, as it was carried above the recently-created Virginia Street on Bannerman's Bridge (see Chapter 18). Laid out from 1766-7 by the architect William Law, the street was lined with stepped terraces of solidly handsome Georgian houses, in their regularity a match for any town in Scotland at that time, Edinburgh included. Built of Loanhead granite ashlar, they are of standard five-bay, three-storeyed design, each with central doorway, architraved openings and fine eaves cornices. Several had equally sumptuous panelled interiors; and the plan of each floor of the restored interior of no. 30, which dates from 1770, was possibly typical in consisting of two major and two minor rooms. Of the street itself, it has been said that:

> The east side, looking out to sea, was the more completely taken up ... The other sites were developed in 1799–1800 by the Aberdeen architect-builder William Dauney ... [while] ... the houses still remaining to be built on the east side were the work of the elder William Smith, active in the street from 1780. By that date the requirement to adhere to the regularity of the Law elevations had been given up; the later houses are easily identifiable by their lighter and greyer deeper-quarried Rubislaw granite and late eighteenth-century detailing.[7]

Nor was that regularity applied to any of the near-contemporary terraces of Georgian houses built on Schoolhill (where only one, no. 61, James Dun's House, 1769, still survives), Queen Street (all demolished) or the slightly later Belmont Street, developed on open ground on the edge of the Denburn valley in the 1780s. There, the five-bay, two-storeyed Menzies of Pitfodels house of 1788, once flanked by pavilions, remains a relatively handsome reminder of domestic life-style in what was then suburban Aberdeen, where long gardens ran down to the Denburn. Houses associated with the slightly earlier 'new' street developments – Virginia, Commerce and Littlejohn Streets – appear to have been of similarly varied and adventitious design, well represented by no. 23½ Virginia Street. Demolished in the 1970s, it was a compact, detached house probably dating from the 1760s, with applied classical details and curvilinear wallhead gablet and in general appearance and character an unmistakable product of north-eastern Scotland.[8]

Building habits at the upper end of the social hierarchy in post-Reformation Aberdeen were little different from those of other major regional centres. Like them, Aberdeen played host to what were, in effect, castellated country houses; their merchant, laird or noble builders from Aberdeen's vast rural hinterland made little or no concession to the urban environment in the construction and development of their town lodgings (see Chapter 8). Judging by its depiction on the Gordon of Rothiemay map, one of the most extensive of these 'town and country' houses was probably that of the Earl Marischal on the south side of Castlegate. It comprised a group of buildings ranged around a courtyard and had gardens which stretched southwards, to the line of what later became Virginia Street. The whole complex was removed on the building of Marischal Street after 1767.

The most substantial surviving house of this type is, of course, the restored pile of what has come to be known as Provost Skene's House, in the one-time fashionable residential quarter of the Guestrow or Ghaist Row.[9] Like other large town mansions such as Argyll's Lodging in Stirling, the architecture of Skene's House is the result of organic growth and alteration, in this instance originating in a three-storeyed rectangular tower with vaulted basement built in 1545 by Alexander Knollis (or Knowis). Aligned at right-angles to the street and occupying a courtyard site behind the street frontage, the building was evidently entered by a forestair. A generation later, in about 1570, the Knollis family added a three-storeyed extension on the same line, to which in 1626 a lower cross-wing or 'jamb' was added by Matthew Lumsden, owner of the property from 1622 to *c.* 1644. In 1669, the building finally came into the possession of its eponymous and wealthy merchant-owner, George Skene (1619–1707; provost of Aberdeen 1676–85; Plate 29), who heightened and regularised the appearance of the main block, very much in traditional Scots style, by replacing the original forestair with a large square stair tower. Panelling and plasterwork in what was already a thrice-remodelled interior were commissioned by Skene, and can still be appreciated to heightened effect in the re-furnished hall, chamber or parlour and (bed) room on the first floor. The most notable of the pre-Skene interiors, not fully re-discovered until 1951, is in the Long Gallery in the Lumsden west wing of 1626. There the coved ceiling bears a series of tempera-painted panels which depict the Life of Christ, including the Annunciation as well as representations of the *Arma Christi* – the Five Sacred Wounds and the Instruments of the Passion (Plate 22). Such religious emblems are generally found in association with the post-Reformation residences of Roman Catholic families, particularly in north-eastern Scotland.[10] The mansion remained a single unit in the ownership and occupancy of Skene's Aedie family relatives until 1732, when, for a century, it became sub-divided into separate east and west houses. For much of the subsequent period, however, it stood in its re-united form, until 1926, when it descended into use as a house of refuge and common lodging house.

The theme of *rus in urbe* was repeated on a lesser scale throughout New Aberdeen, where a number of urban buildings assumed contemporary tower-house forms or imitated their features to a greater or lesser degree. One such was the Keith of Benholm Lodging, also known as the 'Wallace Tower' (probably a corruption of 'Well-house Tower') which was a diminutive tower-house of characteristic north-eastern 'Z-plan' form, that is, with turrets, one of which retained a gunport of quatrefoil type, at diagonally opposite angles of the oblong main block.[11] Erected as his Aberdeen town house by Sir Robert Keith, brother of the fifth Earl Marischal (the founder of Marischal College), between about 1610 and his death in 1616, the tower and its garden occupied a conspicuous corner site in Netherkirkgate. From there, in 1964–5, it was removed and re-erected in Seaton Park, Tillydrone, where, not unexpectedly, the transplanted tower looks perfectly at home in semi-rural surroundings.

ABERDEEN BEFORE 1800

An even more elaborate specimen of the fortified house genre, again fully in keeping with the decorative regional style, was the lofty, four-storeyed house which stood on the north side of Schoolhill, until its demolition along with its terraced neighbours in the 1880s. Only after this was the identity of nos 16-26 Schoolhill recognised. It was established that 'Jamesone's House' had been built in 1586 by Andrew Jamesone, father of the celebrated portrait painter, George Jamesone (1588–1644) who was born there.[12] The most conspicuous feature of its south-facing street frontage was a projecting turret headed with a distinctive pair of corbelled angle-rounds, moulded window-surrounds and string-courses (Ill. 8). A corbelled stair-turret adjoined the main block in the west re-entrant angle and a wide arched entrance gave access to a pend through the lower but seemingly more elaborate eastern range. The overall form of the house is uncertain, but it appears, in part at least, to have developed out of an L- or T-plan tower and hall arrangement, examples of which then abounded in the Aberdeenshire countryside.

The nineteenth-century English scholar-architect, R. W. Billings, was particularly attracted to this building. He noted that 'Aberdeen is remarkable for the number of private dwellings ornamented by that light, graceful, angular turret which was adapted from the French château architecture ... [This house] is a very pleasing and picturesque specimen of this style. There are several others in the old parts of the town – as in the Gallowgate, the Castlegate, the Shiprow, and the Nether Kirkgate.'[13] The practice of ornamenting buildings with turrets was certainly widespread and may have persisted for some time, as it certainly did further north, around Inverness and Tain. Old photographs of the east side of Broad Street, for instance, show a corbelled and ogival-roofed angle-round associated with an otherwise relatively plain three-bay house (no. 68). Mistakenly identified in some sources as one of the Aberdeen childhood homes of Lord Byron,[14] this building was block-parapeted in characteristic local fashion and may have dated from as late as the last quarter of the seventeenth century.

Equally typical of their rural counterparts, other urban towers had projecting turrets which were similar to that of 'Jamesone's House' but were crowned instead with corbelled and gableted caphouses. 'Mar's Castle', reputedly a one-time town house of the earls of Mar, was of this form. Probably built in about 1594, it stood on the east side of the upper Gallowgate until 1897 and, like 'Jamesone's House', appears to have been of overall L- or T-plan layout with the remains of a corbelled stair-turret in one re-entrant angle.[15]

Closely comparable with 'Mar's Castle', both in external appearance and date, is 'Provost Ross's House', a surviving T-plan building set behind a small screened forecourt on the west side of Shiprow. Originally built in 1593, the house was acquired by Provost Ross of Arnage in 1702 and, together with its neighbour at no. 50 Shiprow, was salvaged and extensively repaired in 1954. The two buildings

Illustration 8
R. W. Billings, George Jamesone's House, Schoolhill.

have served as the Aberdeen Maritime Museum since 1984. The four-storeyed turret of Provost Ross's House, fronting Shiprow, contained a stack of small chambers. Judging from survey drawings of the 1950s, each floor of the three-storeyed main block appears to have comprised at least two main rooms (including a ground-floor kitchen) on each side of a central stair which was partly housed in a lateral outshot at the rear.[16] No. 50 Shiprow, which is likewise of three main storeys, is stepped downslope from Provost Ross's House, on a slightly angled alignment, and appears to be of seventeenth-century origin refaced and remodelled in 1710, possibly as part of a design incorporating ground-floor shops and upper-floor dwellings. Together, the two buildings now represent a last remnant of the terraced frontages, often made up of a medley of traditional and formal styles, which were once the hallmark of central Aberdeen. Such terracing, however exaggerated or stylised, was a particularly prominent feature of the Gordon of Rothiemay map of 1661.

Further down the hill, at nos 60–64 Shiprow, part of a surviving vaulted undercroft appears to pre-date the three-storeyed tenement-building of 1692 date which is known to have occupied this site until its demolition in 1876. An old photograph of this property at about the date of its demolition shows a pair of doorways, the larger entrance probably giving access to a common stair to the upper floors; this perhaps provides a pointer to the emergence of flatted dwellings in the royal burgh.[17] Houses of this type correspond well to Gordon of Rothiemay's general characterisation of the buildings of New Aberdeen as being 'of stone and lyme, rigged above, covered with slaits, mostly of thrie or four stories hight, some of them higher'.[18] But it is now difficult to establish just how many of these buildings, including the grander houses that have been described above, were designed with single or extended family ownership and occupancy in mind, and how many were flatted from the outset.

Gordon of Rothiemay goes on to provide one further significant clue: 'The dwelling houses are cleanlie and bewtifull and neat, both within and without, and the syde that looks to the street mostlie adorned with galleries of timber, which they call forestaires'. Such forestairs of stone or timber are generally associated either with flatted or 'stacked' cottages, or with houses set above shops or workshops, a basic building design, with several functional variations, that was common on the eastern seaboard of Scotland. The ancestry of this type of dwelling can be traced back to at least the last quarter of the sixteenth century, and extended geographically into Northumberland, where in the early eighteenth century Daniel Defoe noticed 'houses with the stairs to the second [that is, first] floor, going up on the outside of the house, so that one family may live below, and another above, without going in at the same door; which is the Scots way of living'.[19] In Aberdeen, such forestairs are now largely a matter of folk memory, but they are clearly in evidence in late nineteenth-century photographs of buildings that appear to be at least of eighteenth-century date. They are particularly prominent in a well-known view of the now-vanished community of the Hardweird in Gilcomston, and appear also in at least a couple of other views of the Upper Denburn (one at the foot of Mutton Brae, *c.* 1863), in Mitchell's Court, Guestrow, and in the fishing community of Old Torry.[20]

> In the 1780s, the fishing village of Futty (Ill. 9) on the opposite bank of the Dee estuary from Old Torry, and just to the south-east of New Aberdeen consisted of: several rows of low thatched cottages, running from east to west, between the high road and the Harbour .... Nothing could be apparently more comfortless than the exterior of those dwellings, each fronting the back of the opposite neighbour, and the narrow space between forming a line of dung hills crossed over with supporting spars from which hung lines, bladders and buoys, intermingled with dried skate and dog fish.[21]

Similar, low, single-storeyed cottages and bothies were doubtless scattered throughout and around Aberdeen in the seventeenth and eighteenth centuries, the 1732 cottages in 1–3 Grant Place, Old Aberdeen, simply representing a more solidly built, longer-lasting version of the type.

*Illustration 9
George Taylor's map
of Aberdeen, 1773.*

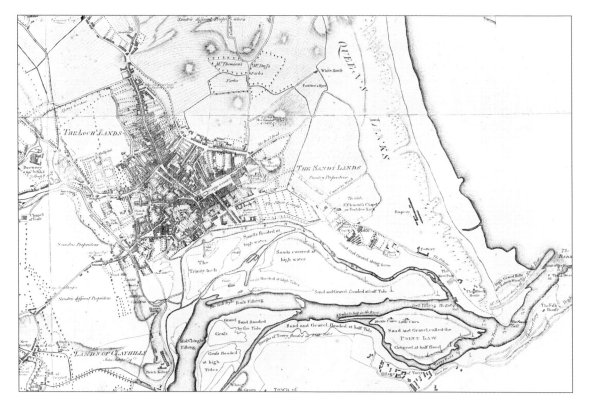

All surviving pre-1800 houses in Aberdeen are stone-built, most commonly of granite which came into more widespread use by the middle decades of the eighteenth century.[22] Although less easy to work than imported sandstone, granite became relatively cheap and readily available, and was laid as random or coursed rubble masonry and occasionally fine-jointed ashlar, mortared with clay or lime. Brick – local Seaton brick – also came into wider use by the beginning of the eighteenth century, mainly for details rather than for entire buildings. Pantiles, also often manufactured in the same local kilns, came to be used almost as widely as slates for roof covering.

Aberdeen before the seventeenth century

Information on house-types and building materials that can be drawn out from surviving or recorded above-ground evidence is for the most part related to the better-built houses of the wealthier townspeople. For a fuller appreciation of the buildings and physical conditions in which the majority of Aberdonians lived during the medieval and early modern periods, we must turn to the evidence presented by archaeology. Just as in Perth, Aberdeen has been well served over the past three decades by successive teams of professional urban archaeologists who have taken full advantage of the opportunities that have come their way. They have established an especially commendable record of making the results of their investigations known, not only for the benefit of their fellow-professionals, but also of their fellow-citizens.[23] Nonetheless, they themselves would be the first to acknowledge the limitations that have circumscribed their enquiries – and hence their conclusions. The archaeological evidence for domestic housing has been derived from a relatively small number of sites, mainly in Broad Street, Castle Street, Gallowgate, Netherkirkgate, Queen Street, St Paul Street and Upperkirkgate, and the total number of buildings excavated is proportionately small and, perforce, selective.[24] The evidence mainly reflects occupation and use of the backlands of the rigs (the linear medieval property plots), rather than of the prime sites on the street frontages, where the opportunities – and potential – for excavation have generally been more restricted. But such limitations are relatively minor in relation to the hugely significant and independent body of witness which archaeology has contributed – and continues to contribute – to all aspects of medieval and later Aberdeen.

Excavation has enlarged and substantiated our knowledge of lesser house-types and their detailed features in the later medieval and early modern periods. Excavation of Albion Court, behind Castlegate, for example, pointed to the existence in the seventeenth century of a two-storeyed terrace of houses, probably flatted and with separate access to the upper floors, rebuilt, together with the Castlegate frontage, in about 1760. Many such post-medieval buildings have been shown to have had either cobbled or beaten earth floors, plank floors not generally appearing until the early nineteenth century. The open hearths of the medieval houses were replaced, initially in some cases by smoke-hoods, subsequently by stone- or brick-built fireplaces and chimney-flues set against or within the walls. Window glazing was another unmistakable mark of domestic progress that was emerging by the middle of the seventeenth century; all of the excavated buildings appeared to have had glazed windows, the fairly small rectangular or lozenge-shaped panes having been set and fixed within leaded frames (Plate 11).

It is also likely that, in reality, the terraced street frontages which Gordon depicts in a regular, fairly stylised manner were of much more heterogeneous appearance and character, including many that were timber-framed, whilst the backlands are known to have contained a miscellany of structures, including many that have been identifiable as dwellings. Buildings of post-and-wattle construction have proved to have been a regular feature of the excavated sites in these backlands, particularly on the St Paul Street site where some well-preserved examples ranged in date from the later twelfth to the mid fourteenth century. All were built at right-angles to the street frontage, that is, on the same alignment as the rigs themselves, and at greatest extent a typical structure measured some eight metres in length by about four metres in width. The wattle walls, which were built around free-standing upright posts, may have been lined with clay or dung or may even have been turf-covered externally. Doorways would have been closed with a wattle or plank door, and what passed for windows was little more than a small lined opening in the wall, capable of being covered with boards or straw. The roofs would probably have been thatched, with or without a smoke-hole.

The floors were generally of clay or gravel, originally covered with straw. Differences in the flooring between the two ends of some buildings show that they had probably consisted of two rooms separated by an internal partition: at one end would have an all-purpose living-room and, at the other, a craft workshop or byre for animals such as pigs, sheep and hens, essentially an urbanised form of a typical rural long-house. Small stone hearths have been found in the middle of the floors of some of these buildings. Those that retained evidence of industrial slags and residues were presumably workshops, while the others were reasonably presumed to have been dwellings. Other buildings of this type may have housed animal stock, whilst many smaller ones were clearly little more than sheds. The rigs or plots in which all these buildings were set were clearly defined by boundary ditches and wattle fences. Many were further sub-divided into enclosures which were probably used for kitchen gardens and animal pens and most had small middens, where household and animal waste was accumulated (Plate 12). Most households would also have had access to a well sunk in a nearby close or would have had large open barrels set upright to collect rain water. The remains of a number of such barrels or water-butts have been found on the St Paul Street site.

In general, archaeological excavations in Aberdeen have convincingly demonstrated that in the medieval period stone-built houses would have been the exception rather than the rule, a point implicitly substantiated by the fact that a court case of 1317 mentions a stone house on the Gallowgate as if it was an unusual feature.[25] Most of the bigger houses would have been of timber-framed box construction, with panelled walling containing wattle-and-daub infill,[26] whilst smaller houses, as at the St Paul Street site, were of simple post construction with wattle walls.[27] Foundations of the larger structures comprised low stone walls or large wooden beams, examples of which have been found in excavations in the Gallowgate. Clearly, Gordon of Rothiemay's statement concerning the prevalence in 1661 of stone-built houses with slated roofs overlooks or minimises a very strong tradition of building in timber in Aberdeen. In the later Middle Ages, when the population may have stood at about 4,500–5,000, the majority of buildings in both burghs were probably of timber, and such houses continued to be built despite a ban on their construction in 1741. Some of the last examples were evidently still standing in the Gallowgate as late as 1840.

Slated roofs and even decoratively tiled roofs were certainly not unknown among the bigger buildings, but the great majority of medieval houses in both burghs would have been thatched with heather, rushes or straw, and some were possibly covered with timber shingles. Gordon may also have exaggerated with regard to slates, too, for thatch is known to have continued in widespread use, despite ineffectual bans in 1716 and 1741. Even as late as 1826, in the new 'improved' town centre, the source of a fire in King Street was identified as the heather-thatched roof of a cottage which had been built after 1802.

As opportunities permit, archaeology will add to this corpus of evidence on which most of our knowledge of the building and occupation of houses in medieval and post-medieval Aberdeen is based. But here, as elsewhere, the pattern and scope of such opportunities necessarily remain dependent upon other planning needs, and the results of the investigations may continue to be frustratingly uneven and fragmentary. Nevertheless, many of the clues that have already been unearthed – literally – give us a view of the development of housing in Aberdeen that is reasonably clear in its broad outlines, and certainly one that is sufficient to provide a viable research framework over the centuries in question. Nor does all the physical evidence remain buried and hidden from view. In Old Aberdeen particularly, and to a very much lesser extent in New Aberdeen, there is still much above ground that is readily accessible for continuing scrutiny and for increasing our understanding, not only of post-medieval house-types – essential links to their medieval predecessors – but also of their context in the overall morphology and street-pattern.

Part II

ECONOMY AND SOCIETY

5

People in the Two Towns

ROBERT E. TYSON

For much of the period under discussion, Aberdeen was known in Bruges as one of 'the four great towns of Scotland'. How great is not quantifiable. The first accurate estimate of the number of people who lived in Aberdeen is not known until Dr Alexander Webster's private census was conducted in 1755.[1] What is certain, however, is that before then growth was uneven and that there were lengthy periods when population declined. Starting from a very low number, growth was probably rapid in the twelfth and thirteenth centuries and by 1326 the town paid more tax than any other burgh except Berwick.[2] By that date, it had three friaries, a number exceeded only by Berwick, and the main streets were the same as those shown in Gordon of Rothiemay's map of 1661 (Plate 38).[3] There is no evidence to indicate what happened to Aberdeen's population in the fourteenth century. We do not even know if it was hit by the Black Death, a particularly lethal form of plague which arrived in Scotland in 1349 and reduced the population of Europe by perhaps a third (see Chapter 3). Nevertheless, it is possible that the level of population in *c.* 1300 was not reached again before the sixteenth century. Most of the estimates of Aberdeen's population in the fifteenth century are based on stent, or tax, rolls, and that of 3,000 inhabitants in 1408 is the most convincing.[4]

Demographic change

In the sixteenth century, a new phase of growth began. Despite periodic checks, this continued into the seventeenth century. When the first surviving Aberdeen baptismal register for an entire year begins, in 1574, it is clear that the population was growing rapidly.[5] Entry in the register was important for those seeking a testimonial, an apprenticeship or poor relief, so there was every incentive for parents to register the baptisms of their infants. Moreover, from 1647 the master of the music school kept the register on behalf of the council and seems to have included Catholic baptisms.[6] Until the end of the seventeenth century, the births likely to be missing, apart from those of a tiny number of Quakers (see Chapter 13), are those of babies who died in the few days before they could be baptised;

and those born out of wedlock, whose parents failed to satisfy the kirk session that they had truly repented. In 1693, however, it was discovered that the beadle of St Machar's Church was pocketing some of the fees for burials and baptisms in Old Machar parish and that these vital events did not appear in the registers, which commenced in 1641.[7] The re-establishment of Presbyterianism in place of Episcopalianism in 1690, together with the consequent growth of dissent, led some parents to have their infants baptised by ousted Episcopalian ministers, one of whom even had a meeting house in Old Aberdeen.[8] As Episcopalians became more tolerated, they opened their own chapels, while the established church itself began to fragment. By the middle of the eighteenth century, about a quarter of the population was dissenting, most of it Episcopalian, and less than half of all baptisms were entered into the baptismal register of Aberdeen's St Nicholas Church. In Old Machar parish, the equivalent figure for missing baptisms was at least a third.[9] This means that the baptismal register can be used to estimate population totals for little more than a century after 1574.

If we assume that one in ten of all births never appeared in the registers, and that until the early 1640s the crude birth rate (live births per 1,000 of population) was thirty-five, the population of Aberdeen rose from 5,500 in 1575-9 to 8,300 in 1640-44, when it was perhaps double that of 1500.[10] This compared with an estimated 26,000 inhabitants for Edinburgh (including Canongate), 12,000 for Glasgow and 10,000 for Dundee in 1639. Thereafter, Aberdeen and many other towns entered upon a period of decline and it is probable that by the early 1690s the population was not more than 7,000.[11] Some towns did manage to grow, among them Old Aberdeen. A unique census for this burgh of barony taken in 1636 gives a population of 831 but, as it omitted some of the poor and a number of leading burgesses, the true figure was probably at least 900. By 1695, this had doubled to over 1,800.[12]

By the 1740s, almost all towns were growing rapidly once more. According to Webster's census, Aberdeen (including Futty) had 10,785 inhabitants and Old Machar 4,945 in 1755. In 1801, when the first government census was taken, the comparable figures were 17,597 and 9,911.[13] Most of Old Machar's remarkable growth took place in Gilcomston, Windmillbrae, the Hardgate, Printfield and other suburbs of Aberdeen, but Old Aberdeen was no larger than a century earlier. In 1790, according to the *Old Statistical Account*, it had only 1,713 inhabitants. But even if Old Machar is included, Aberdeen's growth of 75 per cent between 1755 and 1801 was still less than that of Glasgow and Dundee.

In explaining these trends in population, pride of place is usually given to mortality, especially what are called crises of mortality - short but violent fluctuations in the death rate as a result of war, disease or famine, sometimes acting in combination - which might sweep away the growth of generations in a few short months. War was most likely to have had an impact in the earlier part of our period, as in 1336 when Aberdeen was sacked and burnt by the English.[14] In 1644, however, Montrose's 'Wilde Irishes' plundered the towns after the Battle of Justice Mill.[15] Spalding, in his *Memorialls of the Trubles*, gives a list of 118 townsmen who died, while the Council Register refers to 'near of eight score killed'.[16] Nevertheless, disease and famine were much more devastating.

Aberdonians were subject to a variety of epidemic diseases, the most feared and certainly the best documented of which was plague, a disease of rats which is transferred to human beings by fleas (see Chapter 3). The usual bubonic form killed 60–80 per cent of its victims, usually in the summer months.[17] Towns such as Aberdeen offered ideal conditions for the black rats, which lived between floors and in the roofs of houses, few of which were built of stone in the medieval period. Even in 1661, when, according to Gordon, there were numerous three- and four-storey houses with stone walls and slate roofs, many people still lived in old timber-built, thatched dwellings (see Chapter 4).[18] Aberdeen was also vulnerable because it was a port and a centre for internal trade. Plague was not endemic and the infected rats usually entered Scotland in ships from the continent and were then carried in sacks of grain, bales of cloth and other merchandise from one town to another.[19]

Nevertheless, Aberdeen probably had fewer visitations of the disease than any other large town in the British Isles. There appear to have been no major epidemics between the first outbreak of the Black Death in 1349 and 1499–1500; and only three – in 1514–16, 1547–8 and 1549 – between then and 1550. In 1603, the Council Register stated that 'it has plesit the gudness of God in his infinit mercie to with hauld the said plaig fra this burght this fifty-five yeris', despite epidemics nearby. It was not until 1647 that was there a major outbreak (see Chapter 3).[20] Aberdeen was helped by its distance from other major towns, but the main explanation for avoidance of the disease was probably the council regulations to prevent the plague from entering the town. The first decree was passed as early as December 1401 and from the end of the fifteenth century until 1664 regulations were passed whenever there appeared to be a threat. The town's gates were guarded, as were the ferry to Torry, the entrance to the harbour and, following its completion in 1527, the Bridge of Dee. No strangers were to be admitted without a licence, the non-native poor were expelled and ships suspected of carrying the plague were quarantined, their cargoes burnt. All cats and dogs were killed and in 1647 poison was laid for rats and mice, since it was believed that they carried the poison in their fur. At the same time, the council ordered local fairs to be closed and prohibited the import of cloth from the countryside, thus bringing the economic life of the town to a halt.[21]

The punishments for those breaking the regulations were severe, though there is no evidence that the gibbets, which were periodically erected, were ever used.

In most cases, the council relied on fines, brandings and banishment.[22] Nevertheless, from time to time plague entered the town. How it might do so can be seen most clearly in 1647. On 27 April, the provost told a meeting of townspeople that a woman from Brechin, where the disease was currently raging, had visited a family at Pitmuckston, just outside the burgh. Two of its members were now dead and, worse still, a child from the household had spoken to some of the pupils at the burgh's English school. The provost blamed those who were supposed to guard the town but had refused to do so and had sent their servants 'or some weake nauchtie persone in thair stead' (see Chapter 3).[23]

From 1514, when plague did break out, those suspected of infection were either shut up in their homes – usually the wealthy – or sent to huts on the Links and other sites on the edge of the town. Goods suspected of infection were burned and cleansers appointed to clean the houses and gear of victims, most of whom were buried in mass graves in the Links. Some townspeople fled but the majority were to all intents and purposes prisoners, which caused problems of how to feed them. During the 1647 crisis, which lasted seven months, no ships entered the harbour while town council meetings and church services were abandoned. In Old Machar, open-air services were held at Corsehill, the Carne Gulley, Cookstone, Persley, Scotstown and Grandholm, and money was given to provide food and drink for those members of the parish quarantined in huts.[24] Aberdeen town council estimated that total losses from the plague – through lost trade, hiring cleansers, burying the dead, building huts and a gibbet, and buying food for the poor – were £30,000 Scots. Between May and December 1647, 1,400 had died of the disease in Aberdeen, perhaps a fifth of the population. A further 140 perished in Futty and Torry, but only twenty in Old Machar (see Chapter 3).[25]

Epidemics of other diseases continued until the end of the eighteenth century and, indeed, beyond. Most are never mentioned in contemporary records but one that can be identified is smallpox or *variola major*. Although its case fatality of 15-20 per cent was much lower than for plague, it was much more contagious and in the long run it killed more people. One of the first references to the disease in Scotland is in the Aberdeen kirk session record for August 1610: 'There was at this time a great visitation of young children with the plague of the pocks'.[26] This was followed by outbreaks in 1635, 1641 (which is supposed to have killed 'twelve score of bairns') and probably 1661. Thereafter, epidemics, perhaps in an even deadlier form, became more frequent until the second half of the eighteenth century. By then, the pool of susceptibles – infants and young children born in the town and migrants from the countryside who had never been exposed to the disease and therefore had no immunity – was large enough for it to become endemic.[27] Between 1786 and 1794, 564 people were treated for smallpox by Aberdeen Dispensary of whom 119 (21.1 per cent) died. Inoculation was introduced into Scotland as early as 1726 but the general consensus is that it was practised in the countryside rather than in towns such as Aberdeen.[28]

Some diseases were chronic rather than epidemic in that they took much longer to kill their victims. One was tuberculosis which was firmly established by the end of the eighteenth century;[29] another was the offensive disease of leprosy, which was at its peak in the medieval period. There was a leper colony halfway between the Gallowgate and Old Aberdeen and by the sixteenth century the huts had been replaced with a 'hospitall' to which there was attached a croft. The last recorded admission was in 1612 and in 1662 it was described as a ruin.[30] Even more loathsome was a particularly virulent form of syphilis or great pox which arrived in Europe, probably from the New World, in 1493 and reached Aberdeen four years later. Gradually, it waned in severity and disappeared from the burgh records (see Chapter 3).[31]

Dearth or famine made regular visitations until the eighteenth century, usually when there were two or more bad harvests in a row. The first reference that we have is for 1356 when the provost was sent to England to purchase grain.[32] Harvest failure was probably most frequent in the second half of the sixteenth century, when grain prices rose sixfold and those of livestock fivefold, but continued into the seventeenth. There was a particularly severe crisis in 1622–3 and probably

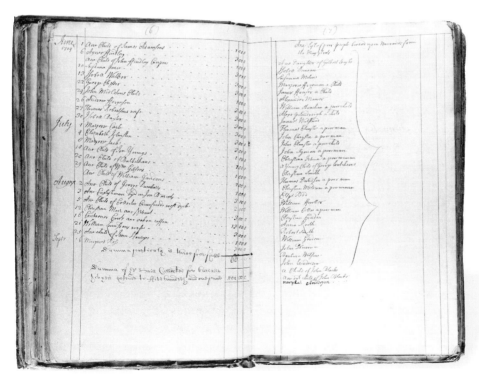

Illustration 10
Burials in Aberdeen,
1704. Burials paid
for appear on the
left-hand page, while
free burials were
recorded on the
right-hand page.

Harvest Year	Aberdeen	Old Machar
1690–94 (average)	178.4 (55.6)	125.4
1695	154 (44)	94
1696	349 (169)	182
1697	231 (107)	178
1698	377 (244)	242
1699	130 (46)	52
1700–04 (average)	113 (22.8)	76.2

Figure 5.1
Burials in Aberdeen
and Old Machar,
1690-1704.

Source: ACA, Kirk and Bridge Works Accounts, vols. i and ii; *Old Parish Registers*, parish of Old Machar, burial register, vol. i.

Note: Years cover 'harvest years', from October to September. Free burials are indicated in parentheses.

another in 1649-53. This, however, was followed by forty years of lower prices which ended with Aberdeen's last and certainly best documented famine, that of 1695-9.[33]

During these four years, the price of oatmeal, the staple food of most of the population, increased at least threefold and the meal market ceased to function. Those wanting food were forced to travel into the countryside. The main cause was a run of cold, wet summers and autumns which delayed harvesting so long that some farmers were attempting to salvage crops from the 1698 harvest as late as the following January. The situation was made worse by a severe depression in overseas trade, which hugely reduced incomes at the very time that needs were greatest.[34]

In the last and worst harvest year (October 1698 to September 1699), there were 327 burials in St Nicholas churchyard; 244 of them were paid by the town, which also provided 196 coffins. This compares with an average of 178 burials a year (56 free) between 1690 and 1694 (Fig. 5.1; Ill. 10). Yet this is almost certainly an under-estimate of the severity of the crisis as there were also some unrecorded burials in the Links. Mortality started to rise after the bad harvest of 1696 and the peak for those given free burials was the second quarter of 1699 when death from hunger was most acute. This was also the peak in Old Machar for all burials. For the remainder of Aberdeen burials, the peak came in the autumn of 1698, which suggests that most deaths were the result of famine-related disease, particularly typhoid and dysentery. 'Conceptions' (measured by date of baptism less nine months) declined early in 1696 and reached their lowest point in the second quarter of 1699, when there may have been spontaneous abortions and amenorrhea, or a temporary loss of female fertility. The result was three years of heavy mortality and four years of falling fertility, together with heavy migration; the non-native poor and anyone else who had not lived in town for more than seven years were expelled. The best estimate is that the population of Old Machar fell by a tenth, while that of Aberdeen fell by as much as a fifth during these years. This was despite the Aberdeen council's purchase of food from England (sold at a reduced price) and its acquisition of money from the wealthy to supplement the usual sources of poor relief which were quite inadequate to meet the demand made on them.[35] The famine of the 1690s was the last of a nation-wide proportion and the last to cause heavy loss of life in Aberdeen and Old Machar. This is despite subsequent harvest failures, notably in 1740-41 and 1782-3 (Ill. 11). None, however, lasted as long as 1695-9. In the eighteenth century, Aberdeen was a more prosperous community with a council better able to purchase and distribute supplies of food.[36]

Although crises of mortality were a major cause of death, particularly before the eighteenth century, 'normal' or non-crisis mortality was probably more important in the long run. Information about such deaths is scanty but the death rate was particularly high among infants and children, with perhaps as many as half of the young dying by their fourteenth birthday. A study of burials in St Nicholas churchyard in the second half of the seventeenth century shows that infant and child mortality peaked in the summer when intestinal diseases were most common, particularly among those being weaned. Once childhood was passed, a quite different seasonal pattern of mortality emerged. Those adults buried at the expense of the council, and who could therefore be classed as poor, were most likely to die in the spring and autumn, perhaps when diseases associated with malnutrition and squalor, notably typhoid, were most prevalent. Mortality for the remaining adults was at its highest during the winter months, as a result of respiratory disease such as pneumonia and bronchitis.

Further evidence is provided by the results of recent excavation of human skeletal remains at the site of the former Carmelite friary at the Green. The bodies were interred between the thirteenth and sixteenth centuries and include women and children, as well as men. Most diseases killed quickly and cannot be identified from skeletons but one man had both leprosy and tuberculosis and a number of children suffered from anaemia, scurvy and eye infections. Fractures and arthritis were commonplace and one man appears to have been struck with something like a meat cleaver. Dental hygiene was poor, with gum diseases and root abscesses widespread (Plates 9a and 9b). Periods of stunted growth can also be detected in the bones and teeth, as a result of either famine or serious illness (see Chapter 3).[37]

Far less information is available about fertility. It is generally assumed that in towns such as Aberdeen there were usually more deaths than births, but in some periods, usually ones of economic growth or following a major mortality crisis, the reverse

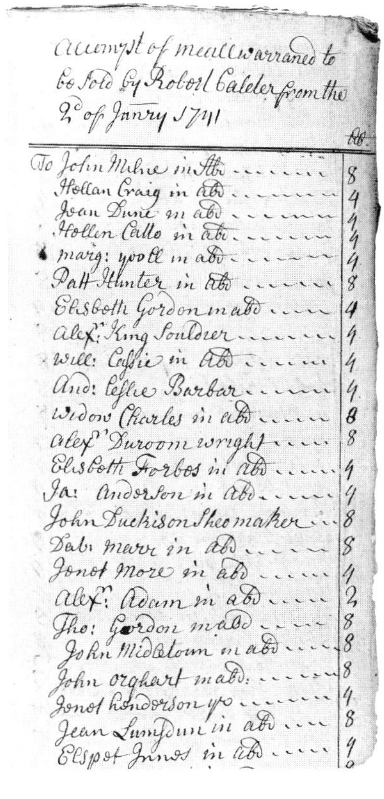
Accompt of meall warraned to be sold by Robert Calder from the 2d of Janry 1741

	bb.
To John Milne in Abd	8
Hellan Craig in abd	4
Jean Dune in abd	4
Hellen Callo in abd	4
marg: yooll in abd	4
Patt Hunter in abd	8
Elisbeth Gordon in abd	4
Alexr King Souldier	4
Will: Cassie in abd	4
And: Leslie Barbar	4
Widow Charles in abd	8
Alexr Duroom wright	8
Elisbeth Forbes in abd	4
Ja: Anderson in abd	4
John Duckison Sheomaker	8
Dab: marr in abd	8
Jonet More in abd	4
Alexr Adam in abd	2
Tho: Gordon in abd	8
John Middletoun in abd	8
John orghart in abd	8
Jonet henderson yo	4
Jean Lumsdun in abd	8
Elspet Innes in abd	4

Illustration 11
Famine relief in 1741.

was true. This was the result of young couples migrating from the countryside, as can be seen in the case of the 1650s. Following the plague of 1647 and the arrival in 1651 of a Cromwellian garrison of roughly 1,000 soldiers – one for every eight inhabitants – there was a marked rise in births. When the soldiers left in 1659, taking with them their wives and followers, baptisms fell by 29 per cent.[38]

The main determinant of fertility was nuptiality – the age at which women married for the first time – and the percentage of them that never married.[39] There are no data about the former, though it was probably 25–26 years, long after females had reached sexual maturity, but in *c.* 1800 just over one in five women never married at all. For men, the comparable figure for celibacy was only 6 per cent, a consequence of the exceptionally large imbalance between the sexes. In 1801, there were only sixty-seven men for every one hundred women, an astonishing figure which shows a greater difference than in Dundee, Edinburgh and Glasgow. Aberdeen and Old Aberdeen attracted very large numbers of young women from the countryside who became servants. In Old Aberdeen in 1636, for example, the ninety-six female servants made up 32 per cent of all adult women. Some would have left employment on marrying but many would have been unable to find husbands in the burgh.[40]

The interval between births, in most cases, was 24–36 months, mainly as a result of prolonged breast feeding (see Chapter 3), but a substantial minority of women appear in the baptismal register at much shorter intervals. These were usually the wives of the wealthier merchants, tradesmen and professional men, as is evident in 1695 from the records of the poll tax. The 180 Aberdeen couples (about 15 per cent of those in the burgh) who were worth 500 merks or more, had forty-six infants baptised in a twelve-month period, a ratio of one baptism for every 3.9 couples. But, for the 248 remaining couples who were worth less than 500 merks, the ratio was one to 7.3. In Old Aberdeen, the difference between the two ratios was even greater. For the rich (i.e. 500 merks and above) it was one to 2.8 couples and for the remaining couples one to 7.6. Wives with wealthy husbands could afford to employ wet nurses and regained their fertility soon after giving birth. Wet nurses were usually expensive to hire, but in Aberdeen some were mothers of illegitimate babies who used their fees to pay off fines levied by the Justice of the Peace Court, which had been set up in 1657, primarily to deal with sexual offences (see Chapter 2).[41]

Between 1572 and 1592, when a separate register was kept in Aberdeen, 16.3 per cent of all baptisms were of illegitimate children.[42] Despite the strenuous efforts of the reformed church (which imposed public humiliations on erring couples) and the Justice of the Peace Court (which fined, chastised and even banished them), between 9.7 and 14 per cent of all births in Aberdeen were illegitimate in the period 1661–87. This compared with between 6 and 8.4 per cent in rural Aberdeenshire, which was still well above the Scottish average. Pre-marital sex was clearly rife in

Aberdeen, for a quarter of babies were conceived out of wedlock. Thereafter, apart from in the 1720s, there was a steady fall in illegitimate births which by 1750 constituted only 3 per cent of births. In Old Machar, 10 per cent of all births were illegitimate in the late seventeenth century and 40 per cent of all mothers were pregnant on their wedding day, but by 1750 the ratio of illegitimate births was under 4 per cent. However, this reduction may be, in part, an illusion, since there was a decline in kirk discipline, while some mothers may have had their illegitimate children baptised in one of Aberdeen's Episcopalian churches, which had a more relaxed attitude to sexual offences than the established church.[43]

Ultimately, the growth of Aberdeen's population depended on its ability to attract migrants. The in-comers can be divided into two main groups: 'betterment migrants' who came mainly in response to economic opportunities; and 'subsistence migrants' who were compelled, for a variety of reasons, to leave the countryside. The former were most likely to be young individuals seeking apprenticeships or their female counterparts who became domestic servants. Opportunities were particularly great in the aftermath of one of the great outbreaks of plague. Following the plague year of 1647, the burgh council relaxed the regulations for the admission of apprentices. An act of January 1648 stated that the craftsmen admitted free since the previous Michaelmas were obliged to take any apprentice 'whom the counsell or session sale appoint .... Paying only to his maister ten merkis, and getting ane stand of cloth at his entrie.'[44] During the next few years, a number of men, including some from the countryside, were made burgesses because so many craftsmen had died during the epidemic. In the five-year period 1640-44, there were just over twenty entries a year in the burgess register but in 1647 there were seventy-eight and in 1648 thirty-nine.[45] The problem of maintaining numbers had been exacerbated even before the impact of plague by the civil war, particularly the sack of Aberdeen in 1644, which forced many townspeople to flee. Some of the wealthiest inhabitants departed for France, the Low Countries, Norway or Poland and others to towns to the north and south of Aberdeen.[46]

Where did the betterment migrants come from? Surnames in the fourteenth and early fifteenth centuries reveal that some burgesses or their forefathers came from as far away as Flanders (Fleming) and England (Inglis) and others from the Lothian (Dunbar, Haddington, Leith) and the Borders (Rutherford).[47] At the end of this period, it is likely that some of the skilled immigrants needed for new industries, such as Samuel Collins, a cotton manufacturer, came from the central belt or even England.[48] These, however, were not typical. The great majority of immigrants came from the north-east, particularly the environs of Aberdeen. Between 1625-49 and 1775-99, the proportion of apprentices who were natives of Aberdeen rose from a fifth to 40 per cent, but the mean distance travelled by the remainder was between fifteen and twenty miles.[49]

The best evidence, particularly for female servants, is provided by the marriage contracts for Aberdeen and Old Machar. These were usually signed just before the banns were called for the first time and included the place of residence of the future bride's and bridegroom's fathers. It cannot be assumed that the young couple were necessarily from the same place as their parents – though, in most cases, this was probable. Nor can it be assumed that couples stayed in Aberdeen or Old Machar once married. Nevertheless, the contracts make it possible to identify from where those who were apparently migrants came and the distance they had travelled.

Between 1704 and 1733, 1,188 marriage contracts survive for Aberdeen. Seven hundred and eighty-nine men (66.4 per cent of the total) and 670 women (56.4 per cent) had fathers living in Aberdeen. Of the remaining 399 men and 518 women, about a third came from within ten miles of Aberdeen and less than a fifth were from more than forty miles away. The catchment area for Old Machar was even smaller. There were 908 contracts between 1685 and 1714. No fewer than 743 (82 per cent) of the men and 716 (78 per cent) of the women came from that parish. Of the remainder, 116 men (71.1 per cent) came from within ten miles and forty-six men came from Aberdeen. The ninety-two women were even more likely to live nearby, for 168 (87.1 per cent) had fathers living less than ten miles away, and no fewer than 120 of them stayed in Aberdeen. This pattern of migration probably prevailed throughout the whole period covered by this chapter.[50]

No such evidence is available for subsistence migrants who were more likely to be older, married with children, travelling in groups, often from further away – although some were children who had lost their parents. These migrants were particularly likely to appear during years of harvest failure, in the hope of finding employment or charitable relief. Whenever there was plague, or, as in 1695-9, prolonged famine, the town authorities had no hesitation in expelling them. In the late sixteenth century and the first half of the seventeenth, there were periodic clearances of undesirables and those arriving without testimonials. In 1570, for example, fifty-two such people were expelled from Aberdeen while a further seventy-two had to find cautioners for their conduct. Another 102, including thirty-three vagrants, were expelled seventeen years later. In 1636, Old Aberdeen conducted a similar purge of 'all infamous persones all ydeleris, and those that have no certaine calling to live and wer not provyded of kaill are fewall and other necessaries of good neighbourheid and upoun recepteris of begeris ydeleris and vagaboundes or strangeris without licence'. At least forty such persons were identified and some, including entire families, were expelled; others had to find cautioners or were sent to work as servants.[51] By the eighteenth century, mass expulsions like this were a thing of the past. Such was the growth of the Aberdeen economy after 1750 that it was able to absorb large numbers of migrants from a countryside that, as a result of agricultural improvement, was shedding much of its population.

Occupations

How did the population of the two towns earn their living? The most important economic group in Aberdeen for most of our period was the merchant guild, which traced its origins back to 1222.[52] Membership gave a monopoly of overseas trade, at least in theory, not only in Aberdeen, but also in Aberdeenshire – until 1672, when an act of parliament allowed burghs of barony to export their own commodities and import all goods except wine, wax, silk, spices and wool.[53] At first, their numbers were modest; there were only sixty-three names on a list of the entire membership drawn up in 1445. In 1576, however, 318 members of the trade guildry paid taxes, in 1623 350 and in 1637 c. 370, though there was then a fall to 195 in 1655.[54] Some members were, in fact, lawyers, doctors of medicine and other professional men, but, even if these are omitted, the true number of merchants was undoubtedly higher because some were not wealthy enough to pay taxes. Although only about seventy-five merchants in the early seventeenth century traded overseas, there were numerous small men who earned a living trading with Aberdeen's hinterland. In the 1590s, there were complaints that too many of the latter had been admitted to the guild (see Chapter 8).[55]

A detailed study of a number of sources, including customs accounts, shows that there were at least 318 merchants in 1669, sixty-seven more than in the stent roll, and even this figure may be too low. Between 1530 and 1599, the number of men admitted to the guild averaged fourteen a year compared with only eleven between 1440 and 1530. There was a rise to thirty-one in the 1620s, though by the depressed 1660s the annual average was back to fourteen. Although there was some recovery to around twenty a year in the last three decades of the century, the peak of membership was clearly in the early seventeenth century.[56] At that time, an Edinburgh merchant could expect to live a further 21–23 years after being admitted to his guild. If an allowance of 10 per cent is made for those members who were not engaged in trade, this would give a membership of c. 350 in 1669, about 40 per cent more than appeared in the stent roll.[57]

The poll tax for 1695 gives the names of only 192 merchants, considerably fewer than could have been predicted from admissions, although there may have been a more rapid turnover because of depressed overseas trade, while the population was probably c. 500 fewer than in 1669.[58] More surprising is the figure of 247 merchants who paid the tax of £2 12s per £1,200 Scots on profits in the year beginning Martinmas 1748. The trade and population of Aberdeen had both risen since 1695 but it is possible that wealth was concentrated in fewer hands. Only forty-seven merchants, one in five, had profits of over £1,000 Scots, while in 1771 it was claimed that Aberdeen's most valuable trade, that in stockings, was in the hands of only twenty-two merchant houses. By the 1720s, however, men were joining the guild more for social and political reasons than for any commercial privileges.[59]

The other 'free' group in the town was the burgesses of crafts whose 'freedom' made it possible to practise their particular trade, sell their products in the town, and enjoy limited political rights. The emergence of the incorporated trades was not complete until the sixteenth century though the origins of the bakers date to 1398. Originally, there were nine such trades but these eventually fell to seven: the hammermen (who included crafts as different as cutlers, pewterers, glovers, saddlers, goldsmiths, blacksmiths and tinsmiths, glaziers, watchmakers and engineers); bakers; wrights and coopers; tailors; cordiners or shoemakers; weavers; and fleshers or butchers.[60]

Although apprentices to the trade included the sons of lairds and ministers, craftsmen, as a whole, were overshadowed economically, socially and politically by the merchants. There was little movement between the two; in the period 1399 to 1510 only 150 craftsmen became burgesses of guild.[61] Craftsmen also appeared to have been outnumbered by their more exalted brethren. In 1608, only eighty craft burgesses appear in the stent roll. In 1623, the figure was 114; and in 1637 it was 127. During the sixteenth century, only about four craftsmen a year became burgesses and even in the seventeenth the average was around ten, about half that for merchants. However, using the same method as for calculating the number of merchants, they were probably about 220 in 1669. Large numbers of craftsmen belonged not to the incorporated trade but to societies such as the litsters or dyers, the masons, the barbers and surgeons and the shipmasters, some members of whom were not freemen; not a single mason became a burgess between 1542 and 1700. Other tradesmen may not have belonged to any organisation at all for, in 1669, 313 craftsmen paid the stent, excluding forty-nine militiamen who were exempt but probably practised a trade.[62]

It is probable that, even before the eighteenth century, at least 60 per cent of Aberdeen's inhabitants were 'unfree' and had minimal privileges; newly arrived migrants had none. Tax rolls, even the record of the poll tax of 1695, tell us very little about such people, most of whom were probably unskilled or semi-skilled manual workers. Female employment is particularly difficult to determine. The poll tax lists the names of 745 female servants (as opposed to 192 males, some of whom were apprentices and journeymen) but not a single occupation is stated for the numerous female heads of household. It is clear from other sources, however, that women, particularly widows, played an important role in the economy. One woman recorded in the 1608 stent roll was a candlemaker, while other sources reveal that many were brewers, bakers and shopkeepers. One was even described as a merchant in the 1690–91 customs book.[63]

Indications of female employment in the seventeenth-century community appear in the census for Old Aberdeen of 1636, even though some of the poor were omitted. At the top were five lairds and gentlemen and twelve professional men, who included six lawyers and four professors and regents of King's College. Most of the remaining population earned their livelihoods by the sweat of their brows. They included fourteen farmers and gardeners but the economy was dominated by seventy-five tradesmen, most of whom belonged to the six incorporated trades. The most numerous were the twenty-two weavers and seventeen leatherworkers, though many of the ninety-six male servants were also employed in manufacturing. By the time of the poll tax, there were 138, with the biggest rise coming in the leatherworkers. But even more remarkable was the increase in the number of merchants from three in 1636 to thirty-six, and in 1680 they formed their own society (Fig. 5.2). The 1636 census also tells us about women's work. As well as 159 female servants, there were twenty-six female heads of households who had occupations assigned to them. Fourteen were employed in the preparation and sale of food and drink (including a 'puddin wricht') and ten in textiles. Three women were even admitted as trade burgesses in 1617 and another nine between 1640 and 1677.[64]

Categories	1636	1695
1. Lairds and gentlemen	5 (3.3)	9 (3.4)
2. Professions	12 (7.9)	13 (4.9)
3. Agriculture	14 (9.3)	9 (3.4)
4. Merchants	3 (2.0)	36 (13.7)
5. Tradesmen	78 (49.7)	138 (52.2)
6. Other occupations	8 (5.3)	12 (4.6)
7. No occupation given	34 (22.5)	46 (17.5)
Total	151 (100.0)	263 (100.0)

Sources: Old Aberdeen Recs, i, 347–55; List of pollable persons in the shire of Aberdeen, 1696, ed. J. Stuart (Aberdeen, 1844), ii, 583–632.

Note: Percentages are indicated in parentheses.

Figure 5.2
Male occupations in
Old Aberdeen, 1636
and 1695.

From the end of the seventeenth century, new occupations began to appear in Aberdeen. A tobacco spinner was noted in the poll tax record and it was claimed in 1790 that there were nearly 400 woolcombers who prepared wool for the merchant-hosiers to distribute to stocking knitters in the countryside (see Chapter 6). As the first textile mills appeared in and around Aberdeen, they provided employment in new occupations for the unskilled and semi-skilled, many of them women.[65] Between 1769 and 1800, 1,007 adult males were buried in St Peter's cemetery in the Spital which served both Aberdeen and Old Machar, of whom no fewer than 483 (48.0 per cent) were employed in manufacturing. Many were in traditional crafts, such as weaving and shoemaking, but 71 per cent of those in textiles were combers, bleachers, twist millers, cotton spinners and such like –

new trades, often semi-skilled and outside the control of any organisation. The incorporated trades, however, still defended their privileges. In 1772, the weavers, supported by the hammermen, tailors and shoemakers, presented a petition to the sheriff against encroachment by Old Aberdeen tradesmen, while as late as 1821 the tailors' incorporation won a judgement forcing James Mowat and Company to use only their tailors. In St Peter's cemetery, 24 per cent of all burials were of male labourers who accounted for 20 per cent of adult males in the valuation roll of Old Aberdeen, although they hardly figure in earlier lists.[66]

Incomes and wealth

Illustration 12
(opposite)
Stent roll, 1655.

These changes in occupations were accompanied by shifts in the distribution of wealth, though wealth was always concentrated in a few hands. The main evidence is found in the stent rolls (Fig. 5.3; Ill. 12) and other taxation records, but these can be supplemented by material in other sources. One study of Aberdeen in the late medieval period has revealed the existence of an élite of eleven merchant families who not only dominated the economic, social and political life of Aberdeen but sought to acquire estates in the countryside and marry into the landed class (see Chapter 8). Together, they accounted for over a third of all property transactions in the burgh, while their average payment of taxes between 1448 and 1472 was 25s, compared with 16s for all merchant burgesses. The average payment for a craftsman was 13s but only 147 of them paid taxes out of a total of 1,745 taxpayers. Overall, the top 6 per cent of taxpayers were responsible for between a third and a half of all taxes, though in 1408 they had contributed only about 15 per cent.[67]

Year of Tax	Percentage of taxpayers	Percentage of tax paid	Percentage of taxpayers	Percentage of tax paid
1408	5.4	14.4	45.4	25.7
1608	6.6	24.4	59.6	26.0
1655	5.0	24.7	61.7	24.5
1669	6.4	39.1	61.6	13.4
1695	6.7	29.1	57.3	20.0

Figure 5.3
Polarisation of
taxable wealth in
Aberdeen, 1408-1695.

Sources: *Abdn Chrs*, 312–17; *ACL*, i, 322–404; G. DesBrisay, 'Authority and Discipline in Aberdeen: 1650-1700' (University of St Andrews, unpublished Ph.D. thesis, 1989), 129.

In the first half of the seventeenth century the same proportion was responsible for about a quarter of the poll, significantly less than in 1448-72, while roughly the same proportion of tax was paid by the bottom 60 per cent of taxpayers (see Table 5.3). In 1669, however, the top 6 per cent now paid 40 per cent of the total and the bottom *c.* 60 per cent only 13 per cent. This apparent growth in inequality can be

	#	ß	g
Cristian wright huckster	1	4	0
Johne mollet messinger for broweing	4	0	0
and for the houss he dwellis in	1	10	0
Johne wobster merchant	33	6	8
George moorisones wyff	6	0	0
Robert off Johne porter for houss & bookes	3	0	0
and for dawghter to play for them			
Alex williamsone barber	8	0	0
and for the houss he dwellis in	2	8	0
James barnet burges	6	13	4
Johne middleton tailyor for houss broweing	8	0	0
and traid is			
Malces trayngeard craiggead houss and	0	16	0
Mr Robert barber to play it			
Alexander cook for traid & broweing	6	13	4
Gilbert thomsone for broweing & traid	4	10	0
James johnstone cobler	2	0	0
Alex colly cobler	3	0	0
Peotter hill barber for traid & broweing	5	6	8
Patrick murray cordoner for traid & broweing	17	0	0
Alex cockny tailyor	5	6	8
Hendrie pantone merchant	20	0	0
Johne connie barber for traid & broweing	16	0	0
Cummer frasser	3	0	0
Alex galloway elder	5	0	0
Robert berrie burges	3	0	0
Robert off alex hendrie	9	0	0
Archibald barber for his houss & traid	20	0	0
Robert gray merchant	16	0	0
George mylne for broweing	5	6	8
Robert abertrombie for broweing	1	0	0
and for the houss he dwellis in	2	8	0
William moore farrier	12	0	0
Patrick gollie myltis ferriers	10	0	0
Johne andersone torrie	30	0	0
towne of fittie			
Dawid nicolsone	4	0	0
Johne nicolsone	6	0	0
William freeman	1	0	0
George pim	4	0	0
Johne caddengead	1	10	0
Robert lepper bekper	3	0	0
Peotter lizie	6	0	0
Robert off adams farlie	1	10	0
Alex forrest for broweing	1	10	0
Summa lateris three hundreth and four	304	19	4
pundis nyntein schilling four pennis			

	#	ß	g
Peotter moore bekper	2	0	0
Johne huntiman timberman	2	0	0
Bessie watt brewer	1	0	0
Summa off the whole further quarter	134	13	4
pertheth to elleweven hundreth thurtie four pundis thrittein schilling four pennis			

Green quarter

	#	ß	g
Johne gilbert tobles	1	16	0
Andrew Job	0	12	0
Johne brabner wobster	1	4	0
Thomas hargie wobster	1	10	0
William tone merchand	14	0	0
George robertsone sladder	3	0	0
and for the wooll land ont in off Mr alex robertsone	2	8	0
Johne morland cowper	2	8	0
and for the houss he dwellis in	1	12	0
Dawid hutcheone wobster	1	0	0
Johne andersone yor bekper	20	0	0
Thomas boyas bekper	22	0	0
Laird bekper for his houss onlie	3	0	0
James andersone lapster	12	0	0
Dawid young for his broweing	4	0	0
Charles angus marinel	4	0	0
and for the wooll mael off Camboll messon his land	5	0	0
Johne harveye tailyor	4	0	0
Andrew burnet	2	0	0
Alex fargh merchand	30	0	0
George bompet gunner	3	0	0
and for the houss he dwellis in	2	8	0
Alexander burnet bailie	80	0	0
Andro gray chopman	1	10	0
and for hollin wmpgrad houss	1	10	0
William cheffar tailyor	6	0	0
Robert blew wrytt	3	0	0
Robert las wrytt	2	10	0
James andersone tailyor	1	4	0
James andersone bekper	5	0	0
Johne marr gardner	2	8	0
Alex jaffrey last probost	20	0	0
Summa lateris two hundreth threescoir three pundis	263	0	0

explained largely by the fact that, in the difficult period after the Wars of the Covenant, the council was forced to increase the number of taxpayers. During the first four decades of the century, the number was modest and relatively unchanging, despite the rise in population. It is probable that less than 40 per cent of household heads paid taxes in these years. Between 1637 and 1669, the number of taxpayers rose from 556 to 998, the equivalent of 60 per cent of all household heads, while the increase in tax paid was even more radical. Between 1608 and 1669, the average stent paid per person rose from £2 1s 0d to £9 13s 6d, an increase of 370 per cent, even though prices were actually lower in 1669.[68] Only about half paid the poll tax in 1695, though the bottom cohort were still contributing proportionally less than in 1608. The most intriguing change, however, is in the stent for 1748-9. This was paid by 1,547 heads of household, proportionally more than in 1669, but the average payment was only £4 6s 1d. Presumably, Aberdeen was a wealthier place and able to draw on a much larger number of taxpayers without resorting to the high average payments of 1669.[69]

The stent rolls also make it possible to observe changes over time in the geographic distribution of wealth. For administrative and taxation purposes, Aberdeen was divided into the four quarters of Futty, Green, Crooked (*Vicus Ecclesie* before 1449) and Even (Fig. 1.3). Futty stretched eastward from St Katherine's Hill and south along the sea as far as the fishing village of Futty, while Green lay to the west and included not only the Green, but the area south of Schoolhill, including the Netherkirkgate. Crooked lay to the north of the Castlegate and east of Guestrow, while Even lay to the west of Crooked and north of Green. A detailed examination of the 1669 stent roll reveals that three-quarters of Green taxpayers paid less than £5, 15-20 per cent more than the other quarters, but the burgh's very top cohort (those paying £5 1s 8d) was evenly distributed through all four quarters. The rich were most likely to live in and around the Castlegate, where the quarters met. The Green also had proportionally fewer moderately wealthy taxpayers (£15–40), while Futty had the lowest percentage in the bottom level. Crooked with 33 per cent of all taxpayers was the largest quarter, followed by Even with 25 per cent, Green with 23 per cent and Futty with 19 per cent.[70]

Crooked was always the largest quarter between 1408 and 1755, followed by Even, while Futty and Green vied for third place. However, the average amount paid by each quarter on a percentage of the average from all quarters varied considerably over time, presumably in response to change in the geographic distribution of wealth. Crooked and Even never held premier position in any of the rolls between 1408 and 1748-9, while Futty was first in 1669 and 1712 and Green in 1408, 1608 and 1755. By this time, Futty had rather quickly sunk to fourth (Fig. 5.4).

Although the stent rolls are an invaluable source, none provides anything like the amount of information found in the poll tax for 1695, which was levied to pay

Quarter	1408	1608	1669	1712	1755
Futty	100.0	103.6	124.2	118.9	77.8
Green	110.4	107.1	77.2	92.5	109.9
Crooked	100.0	95.1	99.7	89.2	106.7
Even	98.5	97.6	103.0	111.1	105.9
All	100.0	100.0	100.0	100.0	100.0

Sources: *Abdn Recs*, 312–17; *ACL*, 372–406; ACA, Stent Rolls, 1655-1669; Valuation Roll of the Town of Aberdeen, 1712; AUL, MS 57 (Taxation Book of Aberdeen, Martinmas 1748 to Martinmas 1749).

Note: Figures are shown as a percentage of the mean for the four quarters in 1408.

Figure 5.4
Average tax collected per quarter in Aberdeen.

for the armed forces in Scotland. Unlike the stent rolls, the poll tax was supposed to include everybody, except the very poorest and children under the age of sixteen in households where the head had a personal poll of less than 30 shillings (which meant he or she had less than 500 merks of stock). The basic rate for those with no trade, including women and children aged sixteen and under, was six shillings, and for servants and tradesmen with less than 500 merks of stock twelve shillings. For richer merchants and tradesmen, how much was paid depended upon wealth. The highest band was above 10,000 merks. Those claiming to be gentlemen - and twenty-eight did so in Aberdeen and nine in Old Aberdeen - paid £3 and the professions paid specific sums - notaries, for example, paid £4, but ministers and doctors £12. Although fewer than half of households paid the tax, the records reveal an enormous amount about how wealth was distributed in both Aberdeen and Old Aberdeen.

Of the 999 households in Aberdeen and the freedom lands who did pay, 491 (57.3 per cent) had stock worth less than 500 merks and contributed only a fifth of the £2,419 16s 10d raised. The fifty-two who were valued at over 10,000 merks, the elite of the burgh, paid no less than 27.1 per cent. Old Aberdeen was not only much smaller - only 297 paid, though this was proportionally much larger than for Aberdeen - but slightly less wealthy, for they raised only £475 6s 2d, though the population was about a quarter in size. No fewer than 253 (85.2 per cent) were in the lowest level and between them they raised 44 per cent of the total amount. Only two were valued at over 10,000 merks but they raised 6.3 per cent of the tax.[71]

Aberdeen at the end of the eighteenth century was clearly a very different place from 1695, let alone 1408. The town was no longer hit by violent crises of mortality and the crude death rate was lower than in 1750, for reasons that are not clearly understood. It was a much larger town, thanks mainly to heavy migration. Its economy was growing rapidly, at least compared to the standards of the past. Between 1748-9 and 1807, merchant profits rose nearly sixfold and casual profits, mainly those of tradesmen and shopkeepers, eightfold. This increase was well above those for population growth and inflation. Even more importantly, new forms of industrial organisation culminating in factories, led to new, unskilled and semi-skilled types of labour which came to rival, or even surpass, traditional forms of employment.[72] Whether the gap between rich and poor, or between the middling sort and those either side of them, was greater than in it had been 1408 remains a matter for speculation.

6

The Economy: Town and Country

IAN BLANCHARD, ELIZABETH GEMMILL,
NICHOLAS MAYHEW *and* IAN D. WHYTE

Part 1: the economic context, c. 1124-1540

Throughout the period between *c.* 1124 and 1540, economic activity in Aberdeen, the north-east and the lands of Moray assumed a largely passive and marginal role in relation to the great changes which transformed the economy of Lothian and southern Scotia. The first such transformation in the lands lying to the south of Moray occurred during the years 1125-57. Against the background of a major silver production boom in Scottish-controlled Cumbria, a new feudal order was imposed within a little more than twenty-five years upon the lands of the Scottish king in Lothian and in his 'English empire' beyond the Tweed and Solway.[1] The changes so wrought fully justified the statement of Ailred of Rievaulx that the kingdom over which David I (1124-53) ruled was now 'no longer a beggar from other countries, but of her abundance relieving the wants of her neighbours – adorned with castles and cities, her ports filled with foreign merchandise and the riches of distant nations'.[2]

The material resources available to David I were also transformed. As the mining bonanza ran its course, he was able, on occasion, to make direct grants from mine revenues to would-be followers.[3] Far more important to him, however, were the indirect effects of the boom. As its inflationary effects were diffused through the economy of Lothian and the Scottish lands south of the Tweed and Solway, property values within the supply network of the mines increased rapidly, making such land an ideal gift for either ecclesiastical supplicants or would-be knightly followers. Such gifts David dispensed with both liberality and political judgement, creating a new and powerful feudal state in the north.

At each of the seven principal nodes of the commercial network (Fig. 6.1), which reached its greatest extent during the years between *c.* 1140 and 1146, a mint was established to fabricate the silver. Local merchants obtained this silver in exchange for the provisions and manufactures they carried to the Cumberland mines. The large quantities of coin obtained by the merchants were then distributed through a carefully regulated regional trade network to local artisans and members of rural society as the merchants acquired new wares for their trade. Cash incomes were

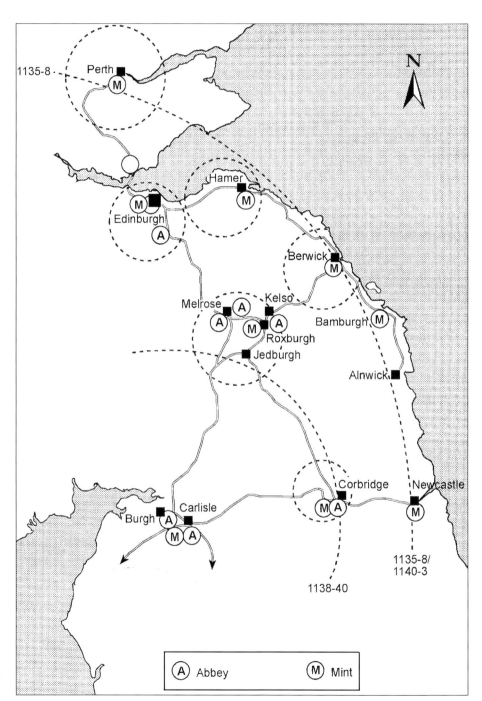

Figure 6.1
The seven principal
nodes of the
commercial network,
c. 1140–46.

enhanced and a demand created amongst the local population for manufactures, which the merchants satisfied, from either local sources or 'abroad', through the same carefully regulated trade systems. In the absence of productivity changes, as inflationary pressures were diffused through the economy of Lothian, Cumbria and Northumbria, denizens of the regional economies enjoyed enhanced monetary incomes obtained in coin, which had a markedly enhanced purchasing power elsewhere. To protect and stimulate this trade, whilst maintaining a stable, ordered form of society, David actively intervened into the economy employing both traditional and contemporary means to achieve his ends. 'Foreign' merchants, who threatened to swamp the Scottish economy with their wares, were largely confined to those coastal settlements which were encompassed within a *portus*-system, where local burgesses had first option of buying wares from the ships which could land only at these places appointed by the crown.[4] Such produce as escaped these pre-emptive practices and was carried up-country by the aliens was further disadvantaged in being subject to the king's internal tolls, from which denizens of the royal burghs engaged in inter-regional trade were exempt.[5] The prices at which alien wares were sold by foreign and denizen merchants to Scottish consumers were thus equilibrated, the latter group thereby being afforded protection from foreign competition. In the acquisition of raw materials (particularly wool and hides or cloth for finishing), craftsmen in the Scottish burghs enjoyed similar pre-emptive rights which again allowed them to sell their wares at prices which were competitive with those of their alien rivals.[6] As the silver boom ran its course and inflationary pressures enhanced incomes, David thus ensured price equilibration between foreign and domestic wares. He also, by channelling trade exclusively through burgh markets, where transactions were validated before witnesses, ensured that bargains (made in accord with the prevalent rights of pre-emption and the payment of taxes) would be honoured. Disruptive 'free market' practices, which threatened his artfully contrived price structure, were thus kept at bay. By his interventionist commercial policies, David ensured that rising incomes would not be associated with social disorder, and that each member of society would benefit from the inflationary effects of the mining boom in conditions of peace and tranquillity.

That society itself was also changing, as the inflationary effects of the mining boom, which were diffused through the economy of Lothian, Cumbria and Northumbria, caused land values within the supply network of the mines to increase rapidly. David found he was possessed, in the royal demesne, of an asset which he could grant to others without diminishing royal revenues. In such a manner, were the royal burghs created. Equally, he now possessed the means to create knights' fees and baronies characteristic of the new 'feudal order'. A knight could now be sustained on a fraction of the land which had once been required for a royal thegn.

Thus, at the nodes of the new commercial system such land, encompassed within the royal demesne, became an ideal gift which David liberally dispensed to either ecclesiastical supplicants or to would-be knightly followers. At each of the seven principal nodes of the extended commercial network formed in the early 1140s, David showed his intent. He surrounded his fortified royal residence with mercantile and ecclesiastical satellites and a ring of close friends and supporters, bound to him and his heirs by feudal obligation, and capable of rendering him military and administrative service of the most up-to-date kind.

It was to this new, well ordered 'feudal society', embracing Lothian, Cumbria and Northumbria, that the lords of the north and north-east, utilising the services of their household merchants, dispatched, via the Aberdeen *portus*, the produce – furs, skins, wools, salmon – of their estates. Each year, between 1125 and 1157, these merchants, attached to lordly households, travelled south, joining the communities of Gaels who transiently settled at this time in Dundee and the Fife ports.[7] Here, like the Flemings and Franks, they sold their wares for high prices, receiving in exchange the new, highly prized Scottish silver coins, which they carried home at the end of the trading season, thereby providing the basis for a new monetary system in the northern lands.[8]

This northward flow of Scottish silver coins collapsed, however, with the decline of production at the 'Carlisle mine' during the years between about 1146 and 1157.[9] Moreover, in 1157 the new English king, Henry II (1154–89), regained possession of Cumbria and Northumberland. This, coupled with the English king's monetary policies, ensured that the impact upon Scottish monetary systems of the English mining booms, which in 1165 and 1195 pushed silver production up to unheard-of levels, was both slight and ephemeral. Only at the peaks of these periods of intense English mining activity did sufficient silver pass north to generate significant activity at the Scottish border mints and, even then, the quantities of specie involved were increasingly diminutive. Aristocrats and knights who had obtained large cash incomes from their small estates in Lothian during the inflationary age of the first great mining bonanza (1125–55) now, as the Scottish monetary stock dwindled and prices fell, saw their incomes decline.[10] They responded to their difficult predicament, in part, by creating that dangerous myth of a former 'golden age'. This myth became entangled with other political considerations, and led to disastrous military ventures. In 1173–4, and again in 1215–16, King William I 'the Lion' (1165–1214), and then King Alexander II (1214–49), sought to regain the lands and silver mines lost by the Scots in 1157. Thus, during the years 1157–1215 successive Scottish kings and their followers continued to sustain themselves in a difficult age in part on a diet of nostalgia, recalling former glories. More realistic were their attempts to come to terms with their new situation by transforming the existing pattern of small-scale landholdings into one of large estates where a greater volume of produce, though returning less cash per marketed item, allowed the maintenance of high levels of cash income. By such means, from the very onset of the monetary crisis in the 1150s, they established a new epoch in Scottish history – the 'Age of Colonisation'.

The great families of Lothian now began to push hard on the frontiers of that realm – into northern England, Galloway, the West, Fife and the Mearns and Moray.[11] In the wake of such families came the knights intent on the same objective. Indeed, it was this latter group which was at the cutting edge of the movement of colonisation, constantly extending the frontier in not always congenial circumstances.[12] In such a manner, aristocrat and knight sought to alleviate the impact of the contemporary monetary crisis. As prices fell, they might earn less for each item of their produce, but, by gaining control over greater amounts of land that yielded a greater volume of produce to sell, they could maintain their incomes and position. Before the death of William the Lion in 1214, vast tracts of the Scottish countryside had been engrossed and given over to sheep runs, leaving a dispossessed peasantry in its wake and engendering real royal concern about their fate. It was proclaimed that:

> Earls, barons and freeholders of the realm should preserve the peace and do justice by their serfs. They should live as lords upon their lands, rents in kind and money rents, not as farmers, not as shepherds, devastating their domains and patrimony with a multitude of sheep and other beasts; bringing penury, poverty and destruction to God's people.[13]

Subject to acute deflationary pressures, during the years 1153-1215, the aristocratic and knightly families of Lothian had sought by a process of 'internal colonisation' to create large estates in order to augment their diminutive existing landholdings. By such means, they could avoid the effects of the acute fall in prices. Because of this fall, they might earn less for each item of estate produce they sold but, by acquiring more land and by producing and selling more commodities, they were able to sustain their incomes. Nor did these aristocratic and knightly producers find any difficulty in disposing of the products of their herds and flocks. During these years, as domestic prices fell and the exchange value of the currency collapsed, reducing the foreign exchange price of Scottish goods in continental markets, these wares, previously over-priced, became once more highly competitive on international markets. Foreign and particularly Flemish merchants flocked to the Scottish ports, stimulating a major export boom. Estate produce was transported in increasing quantities to the havens, which now became the focal points of a completely new commercial network, which at the close of the twelfth century was given a new jurisdictional identity.[14]

In the west,[15] but even more predominantly along the eastern seaboard, new burghs were created to service the needs of the new commercial system. These encompassed, during the years 1153-1214, a series of regional trade systems in Lothian,[16] Scotia [17] and Moray, which were classified in a schedule of customs duties on ships, current at Berwick in the early thirteenth century.[18] In these regional trade systems, the same patterns of colonisation as elsewhere may be discerned. In the north, however, they evolved much later than elsewhere, coming only after King William's defeat of the rebel Donald MacWilliam in 1187. Nevertheless, from 1187 the Scottish crown made vast new territorial gains in the lands to the south of the Moray Firth, which opened up the area for outside settlement. At Aberdeen, a diminutive estuarine settlement south of St Nicholas Kirk, endowed with burghal and other rights by David I, had sufficed to service the commercial requirements of local communities during that monarch's reign and perhaps also during that of his grandson and successor, Malcolm IV (1153-65).[19] Only during William I's reign, and perhaps as late as c. 1190, does this community seem to have felt the full effects of the export-led trade boom. As a result, there was a gradual move in the focus of the settlement to the more defensible land to the west, on the higher ground near the castle, where, by the time of King William's death, all of the main streets within the burgh gates were in existence. Settlement within these bounds was still highly restricted at this time, comprising a small number of tenements between Upper-kirkgate and Netherkirkgate, situated to the west and north of the Broad Street market. It was only during the subsequent years of the thirteenth century that the Gallowgate and eastern Broad Street areas were developed, providing the burgh with its late medieval aspect.

By the closing decade of the twelfth century, Aberdeen had begun on that path which would make it a major trading centre and the focal point of commerce in the north-east. Symbolic of these latter changes was the creation, by King William's brother (Earl David of Huntingdon), of a new burgh at Inverurie in c. 1190. This served as a bridge between Aberdeen and the existing trading complex (based on Inverness, Forres and Elgin) of the Moray Firth. It also acted as a collection point for the produce gathered at Nairn, Banff and Cullen (all founded during the decade 1189-98) from the contemporaneously settled lands of Strathbogie and the coastal plain beyond. At that time, William granted to the burgesses of the new port-towns exclusive rights to trade in wool, hides and pelts, restricting rural producers to dealing only with these privileged burgesses. Alien merchants, similarly, might deal only wholesale with burgesses, except at fair-time, when inter-regional trade was most active.[20] In such a manner, the king recognised the existence of the new trading network and brought it within the framework of the prevailing system for collection of royal dues (or *cain* of ships) on maritime commerce.

The debasements underpinning the growth of the export trades during these years also added an extra element to the economy of these port-towns, which would provide a further cause for royal interest in these centres. As has been shown, by engendering a fall in the exchange value of the currency and reducing foreign exchange prices of Scots produce in conditions of continental inflation from *c.* 1170, debasement had led to a major growth in exports. It had also resulted in an overpricing of imports and, thereby, had created an active balance of trade. Accordingly, the overseas trade boom had been associated with inflows of specie to the realm which had caused a reorientation of mint activity during the years 1153-1214, as English silver coined at the border mints was replaced by German metal imported and minted at the east coast ports.[21] Thus, progressively, as the colonisation process and associated export-led trade boom maintained their momentum during the years *c.* 1171-88 and *c.* 1195-1210, bringing a countervailing import of continental European silver, a growing proportion of the population experienced the impact of monetary and commercial growth and associated changes in the 'real' economy. Subsequently, however, during the years *c.* 1198/1210-42, they also experienced the 'real' effects of monetary and commercial contraction. The new Scottish economic order, which had finally been realised during the closing years of the twelfth century, moved to a new rhythm which was dictated by those forces contemporaneously at work in the international economy. The boom of 1152-1215 was followed by a slump, as Scotland was drawn into the general economic crisis of 1215-40, before successive changes in Scottish overseas commercial activity occasioned boom conditions in 1240-1390, 'crises' in 1390-1425 and 1445-60, and a further and final medieval boom of 1470-1540.[22]

For some half a century prior to 1240, Aberdeen merchants, in common with other Scottish traders, had experienced a new pattern of commercial activity. From that date, however, as economic activity in Aberdeenshire and the lands of Moray yet again assumed a largely passive and marginal role in relation to the great changes, which were contemporaneously transforming the economy of Lothian and southern Scotia, the north-east was eclipsed. Trade continued as before, but the Aberdeen traders were now forced to assume a smaller share of a rapidly expanding Scottish overseas trade. The diffusion of new intensive agricultural technologies from Northumbria to the shores of the Forth in the years after 1240 completely transformed the economy of Lothian.[23] Rising land productivity again allowed Alexander III (1249-86) and his successors to recreate that 'feudal order', which for a century past had existed only in the minds of lawyers and legal forms of a bygone age.[24] In Lothian, lord and peasant alike again enjoyed incomes comparable with those of their forebears in David I's reign.[25] Unlike the incomes of their forebears, however, their incomes were 'real' and not the product of a 'monetary illusion'. Enhanced agricultural yields in reducing unit production costs and 'real' prices of indigenous wares not only permitted denizens of the region to enjoy a higher level of self-consumption, but also afforded them an increased volume of marketable goods. Thereby the intra/extra-Scottish competitive position of Lothian was enhanced in both domestic and international trade. The ports servicing the resultant expansion of overseas trade - Berwick between 1240 and *c.* 1320;[26] and, after the political fragmentation of the region occasioned by the Wars of Independence, in *c.* 1320–1540, Edinburgh/Haddington, to the north of the Anglo-Scottish frontier;[27] and Newcastle to its south [28] - prospered mightily. For some 300 years, from *c.* 1240 to *c.* 1540, on the other hand, the north-east was eclipsed. The merchants of Aberdeen and the lords of Moray continued to trade in much the same commodities - wool, hides and pelts - as before. Commercial activity in the port continued to move to established rhythms, but from *c.* 1240 to *c.* 1540 both port and region played only a diminutive role in total Scottish overseas trade.

Different levels of commercial intensity made for a marked divergence in the forms of business practice prevailing in, on the one hand, Lothian and southern Scotia and, on the other hand, Aberdeen and the north-east. Since at least the late thirteenth and early fourteenth centuries, and possibly earlier, an intricate trading system had existed in Lothian, well known in international mercantile circles.[29] Within this trade system, greater or lesser lords could dispose of their estate produce to a group of alien and denizen merchants, who operated through a dense network of trading centres.[30] This group of merchants, operating on the basis of retained trade profits and credits extended them by their lordly suppliers, enjoyed an independence and prosperity unknown amongst their counterparts further north. During successive trade 'booms' - in 1240-*c.* 1310, after the dislocations of the Wars of Independence in *c.* 1360–90, in 1425–45 and in 1470–1540 - they pursued an active commerce, exporting in their own name Scottish staple wares - wool, woolfells, hides and, from the Forth ports, small amounts of coal and salt. Returning from the Netherlands or Dieppe,[31] they carried an assortment of spices, silks, linens and household wares, bought out of the profits of their export trade. These they placed for sale on the shelves of their shops, and the goods became a prominent feature of the great merchant-owned houses, which were located in prime sites amidst the houses of the nobility, in the centre of towns like Edinburgh.[32] It was at these shops, moreover, that lord and commoner alike could acquire the exotica, which adorned their well-built and elaborately accoutred houses.

By contrast, as late as 1500 the denizens of Aberdeen, the north-east and Moray continued to employ older, and very different, forms of business practice from those prevailing in Edinburgh and Lothian. As some 350 years before, great lords, like the bishop of Aberdeen, continued to maintain a direct interest in the disposal of the products of their estates - wool, woolfells, hides and salmon.[33] In the case of salmon, most was disposed of at Aberdeen to English merchants who brought luxury wares from London to tease the appetites of the great northern lords.

Meanwhile, wool, woolfells and hides (and small quantities of salmon too), placed in the care of Dutch or Scots skippers or factors who were usually Aberdeen merchants acting on their lord's behalf, were dispatched to Netherlands markets. By such means, large cash balances were realised in the Netherlands when the commodities were sold. Some of these balances were then deployed by putting them out on the exchange to meet obligations outstanding elsewhere in Europe, such as payments due to the papal court. Others were spent on a wide range of consumer goods, which were then shipped home to accoutre the richly adorned great houses of the northern lords (Plates 13 and 14).[34] The fees they obtained for their services to the great lords were invested in small quantities of salt and iron which, on returning to Aberdeen, they could sell to the low-income denizens of the northern town.[35] But the merchants and skippers who transported these wares from Aberdeen remained essentially satellites of an estate-orientated commercial system - and the denizens of Aberdeen thereby preserved an older, still medieval way of life.

Part 2: The medieval market, c. 1400–1550[36]

The records that tell us most about the domestic economy of medieval Aberdeen are the registers containing the proceedings of its council and of its head, bailie and guild courts. These are, essentially, the records of the burgh's judiciary and government, and they are a jewel in the crown of Aberdeen's, and indeed, Scotland's medieval archives. They survive in an almost uninterrupted series beginning in 1398, and they contain a wealth of information about the economic life of the town, as well as about its social and political circumstances and developments. It seems that the main elements of the trading framework that can be observed in such a detailed way from the fifteenth century onwards were well established by that time. In particular, the town had enjoyed a weekly market and an annual fair since the thirteenth century (Ill. 13).[37] The economic evidence contained in the registers is mostly in the form of burghal ordinances governing trade and commerce, of proceedings against those who infringed the rules which had been made, and of civil lawsuits which sometimes resulted when buying and selling - especially the trade between merchants - went wrong. Because the records are those of the local government and courts of law, they can give the impression that things were always going wrong - that the craftsman constantly needed to be instructed and reprimanded because he was, by his very nature, greedy and delinquent; that the merchant was always at law because he was by nature greedy and quarrelsome. Of course, things were not always so; trade and commerce were supposed to be peaceable and co-operative activities. Nevertheless, they were controlled and regulated in a much more direct and intricate way than would be expected today,

*Illustration 13
Charter of Alexander
III, granting
Aberdeen an annual
fair.*

and we need to understand the nature of the supervision in order to see how the market itself worked.

As the opening lines of extracts from the guild court of October 1507 demonstrate, the town certainly sought to exercise a thorough control over the work of its craftsmen and women (see Appendix 1). The basis of many of the regulations published by the provost, bailies and council were the rules and conventions set out in earlier collections of laws relating to burgh government.[38] The town authorities periodically (typically in the guild court following the Michaelmas head court, which marked the beginning of the new burghal year) issued series of ordinances such as this, which were addressed to a range of craftsmen and others and were intended to ratify and to strengthen the established customs. In addition, particular circumstances would prompt the authorities to issue special reminders of their duties to craftsmen and women. For example, the issue of 'black' (copper) money in the early 1480s, which was intended to supply the need for small change in retail transactions, caused problems for retailers who did not want to receive payment for their goods in the base coin. An ordinance made on 11 July 1482 told Aberdeen's fleshers, brewsters and bakers that, if they did not set to and supply the community, they would be expelled from their craft for a year and a day.[39]

By far the largest part of the regulations concerning crafts relates to those involving provision of household necessities, most obviously foodstuffs.[40] But the authorities' control was by no means limited to these. Indeed, as time went on, the scope of the rules widened. We then find prescriptions about the cost and quality of shoes,[41] gloves,[42] horseshoes,[43] and salmon barrels.[44] The detailed mechanisms for this control varied from craft to craft. A loaf of bread had to be of a certain weight to sell for a penny and twice that to sell for two pence. Candle was also sold by weight (usually a pound of made candle for three pence in the later fifteenth century, rising to six pence per pound by the early 1530s) and had to be available in different sizes. Provision was made to deal with things that varied in quality, such as meat and ale, by setting several different prices. Special appraisers were also appointed to examine carcasses or taste ale before it was sold. They then scored the price on the carcass or on the alewife's board for all to see.[45] The sale of cleaned fish was controlled differently again, certainly from the mid fifteenth century. Instead of the flesher actually selling the fish, he was allowed to charge a fee - a penny per shilling's worth of fish - for cutting up and cleaning the larger varieties.[46]

The detailed requirements for goods manufactured by town craftsmen and women varied, of course, according to the product. The overall principles were that those who exercised the privilege of trading in the town had to make their finished products available to all townspeople when they needed them. Craftsmanship had to be of good quality; and the price had to be no more than that of the raw materials, plus an allowance for a reasonable profit. There were a variety of penalties for failure to keep to the rules, some of them monetary, some involving escheat of the manufactured goods or destruction of equipment. Beyond doubt, however, the worst punishment was to be excluded from the craft - denied the privilege of making a living by it.

The notion of a reasonable profit is fundamental in any concept of fair trade, and the authorities in medieval Aberdeen were quick to take action when they found people charging what were thought to be entirely unreasonable prices for their goods. In March 1473, for example, three hucksters were fined for selling figs and raisins for enormous prices, although we are not told how huge these actually were.[47] In April 1482, fleshers were fined for buying fish before the proper time and for taking an unreasonable profit ('wynning') for breaking fish.[48] By and large, however, it was not so much a question of extortion, as one of finding the balance between the craftsman's need to make money in return for his work, and of the customer's ability and willingness to pay for it. Put another way, it was how much the craftsman's work was worth, especially when some kinds of work could, in practice, be done by the consumer. Crafts such as candlemaking, brewing ale, and baking oatcakes were not exclusive to those who made a living by them, for they required a minimum of equipment. The raw materials required to make them - tallow, malt, and oatmeal - were readily available in the market place.[49] Indeed, in many cases these simpler crafts were carried on by women baking or brewing or candlemaking for their own household and then selling the surplus. In times of scarcity, this sort of trading was forbidden because it was felt unfair to allow a few people to purchase scarce raw materials which everyone needed and then to sell the finished article at a profit.[50]

By contrast, when there was a boost in demand, even humble traders were enjoined to ply their craft. Prior to the arrival of James IV (1488-1513) for the Christmas festivities of 1497, the alderman, bailies and council gave anxious instructions to bakers, brewsters, fleshers, fishers, stablers, candlemakers, cordiners (shoemakers), tailors, skinners and suppliers of fuel to be well-prepared to meet the needs of the king and his entourage for twenty days or more – in case the king stayed longer. Merchants were told to have wax, wine, and spices and other merchandise ready.[51] The royal visit certainly stimulated added business – sellers of elding (fuel) were told, in particular, to bring their supplies daily, indeed hourly, to the market. (It was, after all, winter.) Even so, the royal visit may not have been welcomed unequivocally by the craftsmen. Quite apart from the pressure they were under to supply the royal entourage, they may well have had worries about how generously or promptly they were to be paid for their goods. This point was not explicitly covered in the instructions given to them and the medieval royal custom of taking prises and of purveyance was a perennial source of grievance for the subjects of Scottish, as well as English, kings.[52] Interestingly, money (£40) was set aside from the town's anticipated income from its fishing 'grassums' (entry fines). This was to pay for the wine, spices and wax which the town was to offer to the king by way of a propine, the term used for a gift in kind made to the king or to a noble. But these were the items supplied by the merchants rather than the town's craftsmen.[53]

Local craftsmen and the whole town depended on a supply of raw materials, particularly food, coming from the countryside.[54] Medieval towns were more rural in character than their modern counterparts. Townspeople had their own back yards in which to grow vegetables, and many owned their own pigs, as we know from the town authorities' repeated attempts to prevent animals from wandering unchecked.[55] In addition, corn was grown in the vicinity of the burgh, and there was common land for grazing.[56] In May 1490, a town herdsman was appointed to keep the whole town's cattle until All Saints' Day, at about which time they would have been slaughtered to avoid the cost of winter fodder. (Cattle are very often referred to as 'marts' because their destiny was sometimes to be slaughtered at the feast of Martinmas, on 11 November.) The herdsman's fee per cow was to be 6d and per stirk 2d.[57] But small-scale urban husbandry cannot have been on a scale sufficient to support the town's needs for food and it would have been only the wealthier burgesses who owned much land or many beasts.

The town depended to a considerable extent on foreign imports of food.[58] Inventories of the cargoes of ships entering Aberdeen in the mid 1460s, mainly from various ports in the Low Countries, show that large quantities of grain were being imported, although, of course, this is not to say that all of it was consumed in the burgh itself.[59] By the sixteenth century, the reliance on supplies from abroad is evidenced by the large consignments of grain bought up by the authorities for distribution within the town.[60] As well as grain, fruit and vegetables were imported for the local market and were much in demand. Impatient hucksters sometimes hurried down to meet incoming vessels to buy apples, onions, figs and raisins straight from the mariners, even before they reached the quay and the customs were paid.[61]

Nonetheless, the reliance of the town on supplies from the Scottish countryside was, without doubt, considerable. When setting the assize of bread in January 1517, the provost, bailies and council took into consideration the price of locally grown wheat, the weight of the 2d loaf in Edinburgh, Dundee, Perth and other parts of Lothian and Angus, and the quality of Lothian and Angus wheat compared with that grown in the countryside around Aberdeen.[62] The price and quality of local (as opposed to imported) wheat was seemingly the determining factor, suggesting that local wheat was the main source of supply. If this was so, then the preponderance of local supplies of oats, oatmeal, bere (barley) and malt (generally referred to as victual), which were more obviously traditional Scottish cereals, must have been at least as great.

The goods which came to town from the countryside were supposed to come first to the market on the Castlegate, the symbol of the burgh's privileged trading position in the region. The burgh and burgesses of Aberdeen had been granted a weekly market by charter of Alexander II (of c. 1214x1222) and its merchants were given exclusive trading privileges.[63] Alexander III granted the burgesses a yearly fair in 1273.[64] In the first place, all goods produced in the sheriffdom which were intended for export - most obviously wool, woolfells, hides and fish - had to be channelled through Aberdeen and customs paid on them.[65] Moreover, all goods intended for consumption within the burgh which had come from the countryside - most obviously grain, fish, dairy produce and eggs - also had to come first to the market where dues were collected. Once these things had been done, the 'landmen' - the people who came from the country to sell their wares in the market place - and townspeople could trade with one another. For many townspeople, the most important thing on sale in the market was victual - the commonly used term for grain - meal which they made into oatcakes and porridge and malt which they brewed into ale. Detailed rules controlled the conduct of transactions in the market. It was not permitted to buy at a higher price than the going rate, or to offer more for a particular set of goods than other inhabitants had already agreed to give. Offering generous measures of grain in order to secure a sale was forbidden. Towns-people were ordered to commit themselves to the purchase of the particular item once they had gave their earnest-money, and they were supposed to take their goods away as soon as they had been bought.[66]

The apparent need to force people to leave the market place once their shopping was done - their poke had been filled with meal or malt, their keling (cod) had been cut and cleaned, and their eggs and apples or pears chosen - suggests that it was natural for them to linger. Of course, people did not go to market only to spend their money - they went to meet their fellows and to gossip and to see the spectacle of the town about its business. We may imagine that Bruegel drew inspiration for his paintings, such as *Netherlandish Proverbs* or *The Fight between Carnival and Lent*, from the colour and variety he saw in the Flemish market places of his day. And because the market was a recognised public place - a forum to which people were known to visit, as well as being the focus for buying and selling - it made sense for it to be where royal and burghal proclamations were made. Here, too, offenders against the burgh laws were humiliated in front of the community, while goods which had been distrained for debt, such as horses, plate, jewellery or cloth, were publicly valued. Cakes and ale, pies and sweetmeats were sold and the town's common minstrels doubtless provided additional entertainment.[67] So, the market was a most interesting and exciting event - the townsman's equivalent of the social gatherings of the tournament or the pilgrimage - even though the actual purchases were often limited and the market place itself was frequently bleak and its provisions meagre.

The town provided modest commercial facilities in the market place. The tolbooth was maintained and repaired at the town's expense,[68] and standard grain measures were available for general use.[69] In bad weather, grain was supposed to be measured either underneath stairs, or in the tolbooth.[70] Providing trustworthy measures, especially for grain, was important if arguments between traders were to be avoided. The town also sought to guard against unreliable townspeople who failed to pay their debts. In January 1532, the bailies were told to hold an inquiry into irresponsible women who bought victuals 'in great' (that is, wholesale) in the market place, without the means to pay for them. The bailies were instructed to make a list of such women and read the names aloud at the market cross and forewarn the landmen. The proclamation was also to make clear that any man who sold victuals to these women in future did so at his own risk and that purchasers should expect no help from the provost and bailies.[71]

Because the market was in a fixed place - the Castlegate - and was held at fixed times, the urban community knew when and where to come. To draw particular attention to what was on sale, the town's handbell man would walk through the town ringing the common handbell to advertise what was there (Plate 30). Of course, it was important that the man possessed accurate information. In February 1513, the bell man, Philip Clerk, did not have the facts right. He was fined and had to beg the owners' forgiveness for having gone through the town without authority, telling all and sundry to come and buy oysters at 4d the hundred - when the boatmen who had brought them to town were selling them at 6d.[72]

The market was the place where families went to buy their food and other supplies, and where craftsmen bought their raw materials. Craftsmen were not given preferential treatment, nor any exemption from the rules about forestalling, just because they were in business.[73] Hucksters - petty retailers - were expected to wait to make their purchases until the townspeople as a whole had had their turn.[74] In times of scarcity, the authorities restricted the amount of victual which individuals were allowed to buy, allowing them only so much as was needed for their own households. The idea behind this decree was to prevent people, and particularly the unfree, from retailing victual or brewing and baking for sale.[75] Women were prominent as purchasers of malt and meal for their families' needs. Often they also made ale and cakes for sale. In October 1522, for example, eight townswomen (two from each of the town's quarters) were given the exclusive task of agreeing victual prices with the landmen before anyone else was allowed to go to market. Some of the women were to go to the malt market and some to the meal market, suggesting that the sale of each was located in a different place.[76]

There is little evidence about the landmen - the people who came from the country to sell their wares in the market place. Some were humble farmers acting on their own account, trudging to market with a sack of meal slung on their back; and some were probably estate officers, representing local lairds or religious houses. There is much more information to be gleaned about local nobles and other landed men and the town seems to have had rather ambivalent relations with them (see Chapters 8, 9 and 10). On the one hand, it was naturally concerned to stay on good terms with them. We know, for example, that the town often gave presents of wine to people of rank, because these are included as items in the occasional surviving accounts of the deans of the guild or as propines recorded in the council registers.[77] In addition, goods for export were allowed a higher purchase price when the vendors were persons of rank. In a ruling of 1400 or 1409 (the year is not certain), the council and the majority of the burgh merchants ordained that no one was to buy Buchan wool for more than 2s (or 24d) per stone, except that of lords and free tenants who might be offered up to 30d for theirs, the same price as was permitted for the wool of Mar and Garioch.[78] By the same token, lairds and townspeople who bought salt or iron in bulk were to be given concessionary rates.[79] On the other hand, the town was clearly concerned lest nobles should exercise too great an influence in its affairs or corner the supply of export goods. A statute of the guild court in 1467 forbade merchants from encouraging lords to take wool from their tenants in part-exchange for their rents, thereby undercutting the market price.[80] Another ordinance, made in October 1411, decreed that no one was to procure the help of lairds against their neighbours or the inhabitants of the town. People were to help officials and their neighbours when they saw them in need of assistance, especially against outsiders.[81] The kind of anti-social behaviour they anticipated may have been the sort of crimes with which Margaret Balcromy was charged much later. She was convicted of a number of offences against the rules for buying and selling victual in January 1493, harbouring an unlawful person, and 'for conspiracioun in the inbrynging off gentill men be senistir informacion upoun the officiaris off the toun' and 'for the lychlyng (slandering) off the offyciaris'.[82]

The issue of the town's highly distinctive economic relationship with local nobles is related to the more general question of the extent of its reliance on the surrounding countryside for essential goods, and most obviously foodstuffs. It is possible, when we are looking at a medieval town, to think of it as a sort of enclave, separate from its environs. This is partly because the records, as well as quite naturally dealing with the town's own affairs, tend also to be preoccupied with defining the town's privileges and, by definition, excluding those outside from enjoying these rights. Yet there was, in practice, a regular and steady flow of traffic into the town from the country. There is increasing evidence by the sixteenth century of chapmen - pedlars carrying their wares on their backs - who were allowed to pass through the burgh on their way.[83] Also by the sixteenth century, the local government was encouraging landmen to come into town to augment the supply of food.[84]

The existence of this interchange is evident, paradoxically, from what had to be done to prevent movement in times of insecurity and danger. Fear of epidemic disease spreading from outside made the town shut its gates, even against commercial traffic. The guild court in 1507 was worried by the strange 'sickness of Naples' (see Appendix 1);[85] and more sustained evidence of a severe episode of plague blights the records in the years 1513-15. The town did everything it could to protect itself against this contagion (see Chapter 3). In October 1513, there had been reports of a plague which had struck various burghs and other parts of Scotland and a statute forbade anyone in the burgh to receive, without permission, strangers and vagrants from beyond the Mounth or elsewhere where the plague was suspected to be.[86] In January 1514, a further measure forbade those without licence to receive anyone or any cloths or other goods from suspect places. No landmen from suspect places were to come into the burgh.[87] The efforts seem to have been in vain. Despite repeated further measures, many townspeople seem to have perished in this period. Yet, the town persisted. In July 1515, the four gates of the town were to be guarded against persons suspected of having the disease, and especially people from Old Aberdeen, where plague was evidently suspected.[88]

The records do not tell us very much about the provenance within the region of goods sold in the market place, although in a few cases a dispute between purchaser and vendor reveals where one of them came from. In October 1509, for example, Thomas Lammyntoun was ordered to pay twelve shillings to Andrew Criste in Cottown ('Corcoftoun'), which the former owed for a cow.[89] There is also a case in August 1400 in which one Lord Robert, a monk of the abbey of Old Deer, was a claimant for debt.[90] In addition, the entries in the records about forestallers – those who infringed the town's trading privileges and customs by buying up goods before they came to market – show such persons operating at a variety of locations within the sheriffdom and sometimes at a considerable distance from Aberdeen.[91] Highly valued goods largely intended for export, such as wool, skins and hides, were the most common feature of forestalling.[92] Less valuable goods, most obviously foodstuffs for the town's consumption which would not keep, probably travelled much shorter distances. Indeed, the authorities even had trouble ensuring that fish caught locally at Futty, Cove Bay, and Findon were brought to market. White fish was a particularly important source of food, especially for the poorer people in the town who needed to be able to buy it for themselves in small quantities. Measures were repeatedly taken to ensure that fish was not sold at the shore or to landmen, or in large quantities to retailers, but that it came to market and was available to everyone.[93]

These regulations were designed to make sure that the townspeople had enough food and other necessities. Of course, the availability of food varied and there were certainly times when supplies were scarce. Yet, the expectations that people had are surely an important indication of what was generally available, and those of townspeople in medieval Aberdeen were, in many ways, rather high. The evidence suggests that the commons expected to eat white fish on a regular basis, and we also know that ordinary people commonly ate meat.[94] This leads on to a further question, whether ordinary people in Aberdeen were relatively well-off. The evidence on this point is highly equivocal. We know that the wives of craftsmen often worked to supplement their husband's income. The guild court record of 1507 shows that the wives of dyers and cordiners were sometimes brewsters: the ordinance instructed that they must have one vat to brew in and another for their (husband's) craft.[95] The rules thus prevented the wives of cordiners and dyers from engaging in the cost-cutting exercise of using their husband's equipment. In their case, it was probably on grounds of hygiene but, when fleshers' wives were forbidden to make candles to sell in 1506, it seems likely that this was to stop them from having an unfair advantage in terms of a free supply of tallow.[96]

Despite restrictions such as these, it does seem clear that in many households there were two breadwinners. A further question is whether married women merely supplemented an adequate income earned by their husband, or if their activities were absolutely necessary in order to make ends meet. And, if that was the case, what of women who were the sole breadwinners in the household, as many

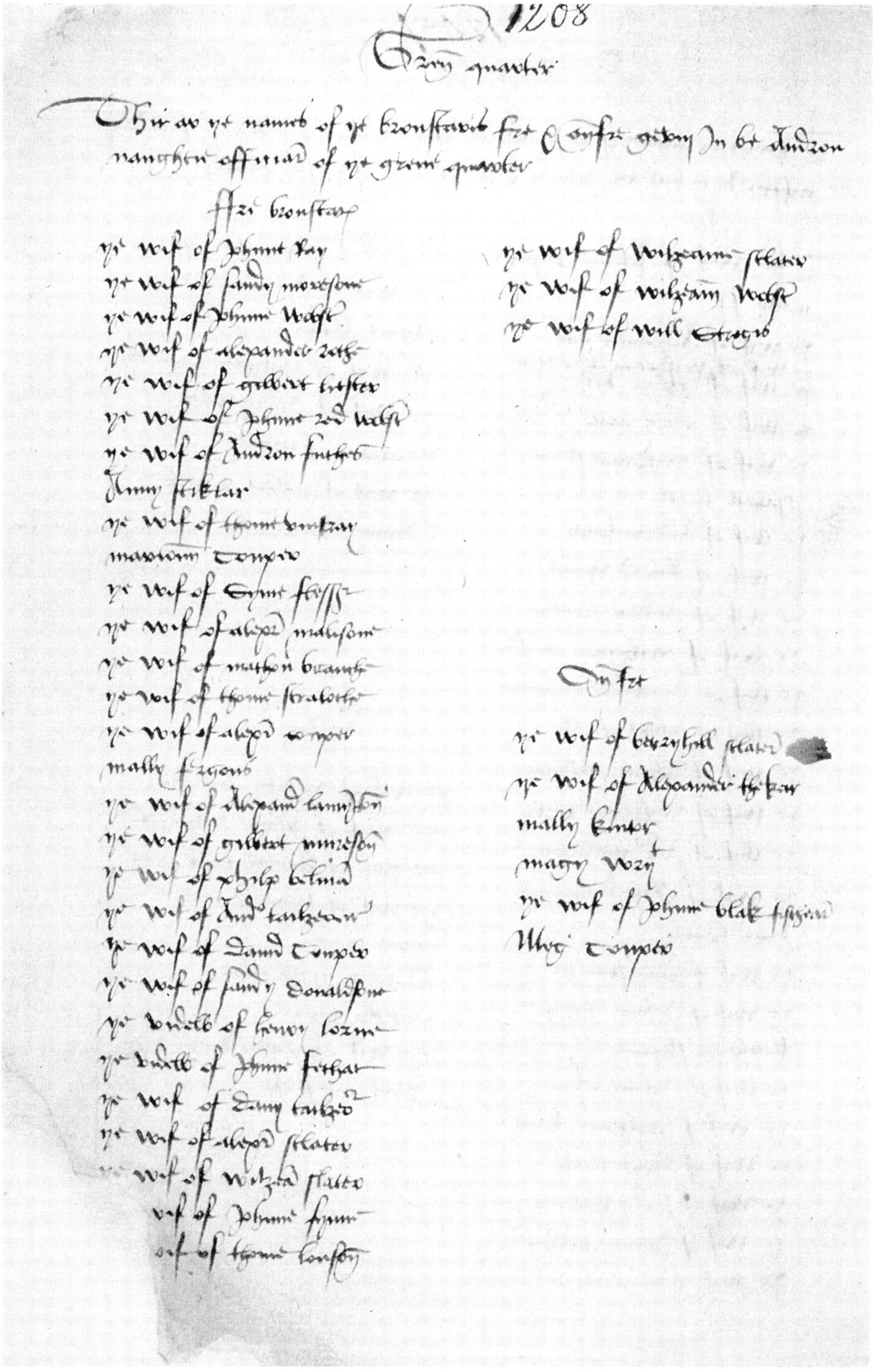

Illustration 14
A list of female
brewers in the
Green, 1509.

| ABERDEEN BEFORE 1800

undoubtedly were? There is evidence from other towns that about one house-holder in every five was a single or widowed woman.[97] The vast bulk of brewsters in Aberdeen were women and they often fell foul of the regulations. But it is not clear whether they did so because it was, more often than not, impossible to trade within the rules, or because breaking the rules, in order to make a little extra profit, was not greatly feared. No fewer than eighty-eight women were fined in 1472, and a further fifty were amerced in 1520, for breaking the assize of ale.[98] Both cases represented a large proportion of the total number of brewsters in Aberdeen for a list of 1509 included just over 150 names (Ill. 14).[99]

Of course, not all the brewsters brewed only for sale, nor relied solely on brewing for their livelihood. The numbers of brewsters are much larger than those involved in any other single occupation in medieval Aberdeen. In particular, the numbers of bakers and fleshers are very small by comparison, for these were exclusive crafts, confined to free, male burgesses. In their case, of course, the master baker or flesher also had servants and apprentices working under him. The point that applies to the domestic 'crafts' taken as a whole, however, is that they do seem to have had a substantial market of customers – the poor, their fellow artisans, merchants and visiting grandees. The authorities took the view that their work had to be super-vised, to ensure that those who relied upon them would not be let down. The close regulation of trade can be contrasted with the contemporary practice of allowing the market to determine supply. But, because of the detailed rules and their enforcement, we know a great deal more than we otherwise might about the daily working lives of very ordinary people in medieval Aberdeen.

Part 3: Town and country, c. 1550–1800

Pre-industrial Scottish burghs have been described as communities which were organised around a market, emphasising the degree to which the market place and the activities which went on within it were central to the functioning and well-being of the burgh community.[100] This section considers the market economy of Aberdeen in terms of the town's economic relationships with its hinterland in the early modern period and the processes of regulating the markets through which these relationships were maintained. Throughout the period between c. 1550 and 1800 Aberdeen was one of Scotland's major regional centres, the third or fourth town measured in contributions to royal burgh taxation, volume of trade or population.[101] The population of the town, possibly around 6,000 at the start of the seventeenth century, may have risen to about 8,300 by 1640, to which can be added approximately another 900 in Old Aberdeen. The impact of the Covenanting Wars and the ravages of plague in 1647-8 may have reduced this to between 7,000 and 7,500 in the second half of the seventeenth century.[102] The famines of the later

1690s may have cut population to under 6,000 by 1700, but in the eighteenth century there was steady renewed growth to a population of about 10,785 in 1755, and 17,597 by 1801.[103] In relation to the population of its hinterland, the demographic and economic significance of Aberdeen increased during the early modern era. In 1695, the town accounted for under 6 per cent of the population of Aberdeenshire but this rose to 9.3 per cent in 1755 and to 14.4 per cent in 1801. Even in the 1790s, when many smaller centres were experiencing steady growth, Aberdeen still accounted for nearly 70 per cent of the population of Aberdeenshire and Banffshire living in settlements with more than 400 inhabitants. Its importance as *the* regional market centre of the north-east thus grew during the seventeenth and eighteenth century.

The High Cross in Aberdeen's market place remained the symbolic heart of the community throughout the early modern period. It was still here that offenders were punished, proclamations read and celebrations held.[104] And it was also a symbol of its influence far beyond the boundaries of the burgh. The importance of Aberdeen's markets is emphasised by the degree of regulation to which the buying and selling of basic commodities and many luxury items were subject. The price, weight and quality of staple commodities were strictly controlled for the dual purpose of protecting the producers against competition from 'unfreemen' both within and outside the burgh, giving them a fair return for their costs and labour, as well as protecting consumers against exploitation.

The merchant guild had a monopoly of trade within the liberty of Aberdeen, but craftsmen could trade in the raw materials and products of their particular crafts, while people from outside the burgh were allowed to sell their own produce in local markets or within the town. Aberdeen's merchants, in turn, bought goods from country people at local markets, in Aberdeen's own market place, and from other merchants acting as middlemen.[105]

The burgesses of Aberdeen protected their trading monopolies by controlling the operation of markets and fairs elsewhere within the sheriffdom. Even rural fairs were important, as Aberdeen merchants conducted so much of their trade through them, buying up commodities such as cloth and stockings. In 1587, a group of merchants travelling from Aberdeen to the Trinity Fair, near Banchory, were attacked and robbed by the son of a local laird and his henchmen. The merchants each claimed for losses of up to 1,000 merks in money and as much in the value of merchandise. Even allowing for some exaggeration, this emphasises how urban wealth spread into the countryside.[106] Trading at a smaller scale was handled by itinerant chapmen. In the early seventeenth century, one chapman is recorded trading at Tarves in flax, iron, alum, tobacco, aniseed and liquorice; perhaps he had a booth as well as a pack.[107] The poll tax book lists a number of small-scale traders, while rurally-based 'merchants' in the poll lists of the 1690s were probably also chapmen.[108] By the later eighteenth century, some chapmen, at least, were wealthier than most of the farmers to whose families they sold their wares.[109]

In the early seventeenth century the burgh council lobbied the Convention of Royal Burghs unsuccessfully for action against three local landowners - Leith of Harthill, Gordon of Newtown and Lord Forbes - who had arbitrarily raised the custom charged at fairs on their land, an action which was threatening to disrupt trade.[110] Attempts by upstart baronial burghs, such as Fraserburgh, Newburgh and Peterhead, to encroach upon the town's trading rights were strenuously opposed.[111] Competition from Fraserburgh proved especially troublesome. In 1616, the council raised a special tax for funds to pursue an action against the trading activities of the inhabitants of Fraserburgh.[112] Rural markets and fairs were also monitored. In 1596, payment was delivered to Gilbert Guthrie, who had visited markets and fairs throughout the sheriffdom in order to prevent illegal trading by unfreemen.[113]

There was, too, periodic friction between New and Old Aberdeen over trading activities. This reached a peak during the last forty years of the seventeenth century, when the bishops of Aberdeen, as superiors of Old Aberdeen, and the town's burgesses, vigorously promoted Old Aberdeen as a trading centre, at a period when New Aberdeen was in financial and economic difficulties (see Chapter 11).[114] In 1662, when Old Aberdeen tried to change its market day from Monday to Thursday, this was opposed by New Aberdeen which perceived a threat to its Friday market. Old Aberdeen's market day was moved to Tuesday as a result.[115] Fairs were important, too, for Old Aberdeen. Specific locations were assigned to traders in particular commodities. The town's bailies were on hand to ensure fair trading, while an armed watch was also present to try and prevent disorder.[116] In 1665, St Luke's Fair generated customs of £34 13s 7d - or the equivalent of the sale of about 700 cattle at the rates which were charged. In fact, a wide range of commodities was sold, including cattle, horses, sheep, linen and woollen cloth, stockings, timber, leather and shoes.[117]

In the royal burgh, the system of price controls was one of the most comprehensive in Scotland.[118] The fixing of maximum prices of commodities such as bread, meat and ale was done in the interests of the burgh community as a whole, rather than to the benefit of the producers. The regulation of the price of basic foodstuffs was particularly important to ensure adequate supplies at prices that even the poor could afford. The larger Scottish burghs in the later sixteenth century opted for pegging the price of staple commodities at a relatively low level.[119] In Aberdeen this led to periodic clashes between the burgh authorities and the baxters and fleshers.[120] In times of dearth, more stringent measures were taken to ensure that food supplies were available for the town's population by, for example, banning the export of victual.[121] Other commodities where the price was fixed included beef, mutton, wine and even exotic imports like raisins and figs,[122] while the price of shoes, various grades of woollen cloth and even the cost of shoeing a horse were regulated.[123] In Old Aberdeen, too, the accuracy of weights and measures, as well as prices, was periodically checked, as was the quality of ale.[124] The price of some commodities, particularly ale, produced by the unfree inhabitants of New Aberdeen was also regulated.[125]

Most trading contraventions, apart from infringements of decrees concerning price and quality, still in 1600 or in 1700 as much as in 1400, usually related to forestalling and regrating. Forestalling involved buying up goods before they came to market, so as to corner the market, preventing the operation of an open trading system. Regrating involved reselling at a profit.[126] If anything, the language used in council legislation had become even more highly emotive. In 1598, forestallers, rather than bad weather conditions and a poor harvest, were blamed for the shortage of food supplies. Those who bought grain direct from farmers and evaded sale in Aberdeen's market were described as 'devourers and suckers of the blood and substance of the poor'.[127] Regulation also fell with a heavy hand on the inhabitants of Old Aberdeen. They were required by their own authorities to exhibit produce for sale within the town itself rather than taking it to New Aberdeen, whose authorities, it was claimed in 1672, often detained Old Aberdonians for forestalling (Ill. 15).[128] Even within the town, every effort was made to confine dealing to the market place where it could be supervised; goods for sale had to be displayed at the cross on market days for a minimum period, even if they were subsequently sold elsewhere.[129] While action against forestalling and regrating was particularly important, as has been seen, in the case of both basic foodstuffs and high-value export commodities, the authorities in the royal burgh were continually trying to extend their controls to include new commodities, such as bark and timber.[130] Even the charges levied by those who hired horses to enable inhabitants to bring home peats were controlled.[131]

Although Aberdeen's official trading liberty was the sheriffdom, the town's effective trading hinterland extended further, from Montrose in the south to Elgin in the north.[132] Aberdeen was unusual in that the region it dominated was the most lightly urbanised of those around any major Scottish town. The hinterlands of Edinburgh, Dundee and Glasgow contained other sizeable towns, which often played important roles as satellite trading and manufacturing centres.[133] In Aberdeenshire, however, Old Aberdeen, Peterhead and Fraserburgh were the only settlements which could be considered as true towns. Ancient royal burghs, such as Inverurie and Kintore, had populations of only around 300 and were so impoverished that they were regularly excused from sending representatives to attend the meetings of the Convention of Royal Burghs.[134] In 1692, Kintore claimed to have no markets or trade, while the income from Inverurie's markets was a mere £4

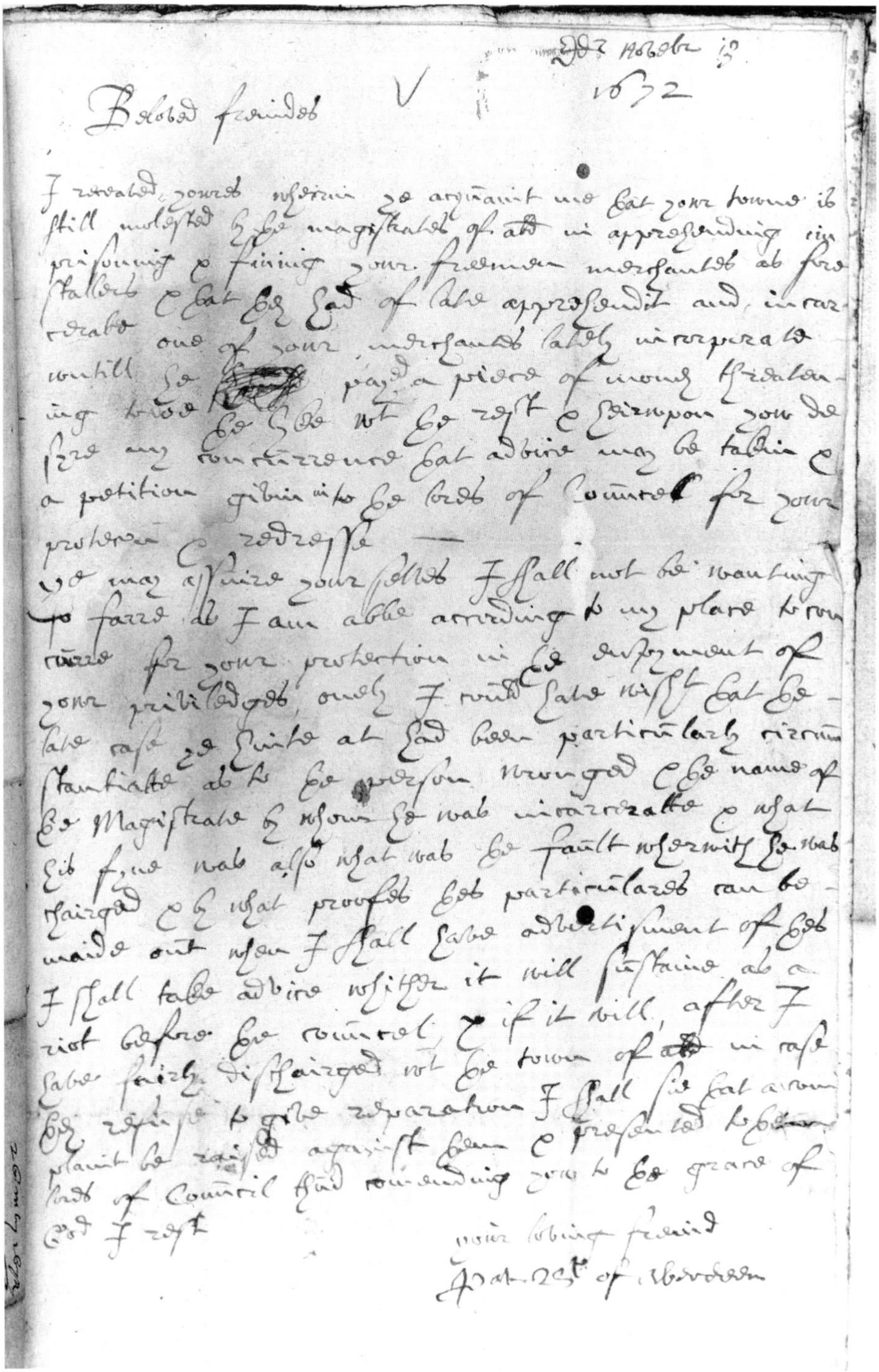

Abd Novebr 13
1672

Beloved freindes

I receaved yours wherein ye acquaint me that your towne is still molested by the magistrates of abd in apprehending imprisoning & fining your freemen merchants as forestallers That they had of late apprehendit and incarcerate one of your merchants lately incorporate untill he payed a peece of money threatening to use the like wt the rest & thereupon you desire my concurrence that advice may be taken & a petition given into the lords of Councel for your protection & redresse —
ye may assure your selves I shall not be wanting so farre as I am able according to my place to concurre for your protection in the enjoyment of your priviledges, onely I could have wisht that the case ye write of had been particularly circumstantiate as to the person wronged the name of the Magistrate by whom he was incarcerate & what his fine was also what was the fault wherwith he was chairged & by what proofes thes particulars can be maide out when I shall have advertisment of thes I shall take advice whither it will sustaine as a riot before the councel, & if it will, after I have fairly discharged wt the town of abd in case they refuse to give reparation I shall see that a complaint be raised against them & presented to the lords of Councill thus recommending you to the grace of God I rest

your loving freind
Patr: Bp of Aberdeen

Illustration 15
Letter from Patrick Scougall, bishop of Aberdeen, to the bailies of Old Aberdeen (November 1672), relating to forestalling.

Scots.[135] In the north-east more widely, only Elgin (with possibly 3,000 to 4,000 inhabitants in 1639), had a significant regional role, and its population seems to have been declining during the seventeenth century.[136] Banff had a population which probably never exceeded 2,000 during the seventeenth century and was probably closer to 1,500. Cullen (with under 1,000 inhabitants in 1639, and less than 500 in 1691) was another royal burgh whose trading activities and corporate organisation were so low-key that, in the early seventeenth century, the Convention had to mount what was virtually a rescue package to keep it functioning.[137] Outside these centres, population within the north-east was scattered in rural settlements. Some of these had acquired the right to hold markets and fairs as burghs of barony and regality. Others were licensed to hold markets and/or fairs, but were not granted burghal status. Of the 'seatouns', or fishing settlements, located along the coast, only a few – such as Rosehearty, Newburgh and Ellon – maintained a significant coastal trade.

Aberdeen was the focus for a hinterland in which economic activity was dominated by agriculture and fishing. Aberdeenshire, with around 10 per cent of the population of Scotland, had the greatest area of arable land of any Scottish county in the later eighteenth century, but relatively little of this was on first-class soils.[138] Despite its size, Aberdeen was not a major industrial centre before the later eighteenth century. In the sixteenth and seventeenth centuries it was a trading, rather than a craft, town.[139] It may be significant that in 1616, during a period of prosperity and growth, when the burgh council sought the construction of an extension to the tolbooth, the contract was given to a rural or 'landward' mason in Old Rayne, rather than to a burgess.[140] In 1637, merchants accounted for 370 of the 569 taxpayers – 65 per cent. In 1669, the stent roll listed *c.* 600 burgesses, around 350 of whom were merchants and 250 craftsmen.[141] Aberdeen had proportionally more merchants and fewer craftsmen than Edinburgh and relatively few large-scale manufacturing industries.[142] As a result, Aberdeen depended much more than other major Scottish burghs upon trade with its rural hinterland in order to maintain the prosperity of urban merchants, professional groups, and crafts.[143] In the early seventeenth century, out of about 350 merchants, only around seventy-five were involved in overseas trade; the rest operated mainly within the north-east.[144] Aberdeen maintained close social links with its rural hinterland. From the fourteenth and fifteenth centuries, many of the élite merchant families married into north-eastern landed families and also acquired estates of their own (see Chapter 8). Equally, it became a status symbol for noble and lairdly families to maintain a town house within the town.[145] In turn, given the overwhelmingly rural nature of settlement within the north-east, the region depended to a significant degree for its prosperity on the trade generated by Aberdeen as a centre of consumption and as an entrepôt. Aberdeen's concentration on trading and the finishing of goods and raw materials, rather than on their production, meant that its relationship with its hinterland was symbiotic, rather than parasitic. The region depended upon the town as a market centre, as a port, and as a focal point from which rural industrial production could be organised. In addition, the town was a social centre and provider of professional services.[146]

Internal trade within north-eastern Scotland was channelled towards Aberdeen through a network of market centres. Most of these were purely rural in character. Only a handful, as we have seen, had any pretensions to considering themselves urban. Figure 6.2 shows the market centres which had been authorised by the early eighteenth century. The problem is to decide which ones were active and which had failed or declined. Burghal rights could remain dormant for long periods, but might be revived by an enthusiastic proprietor. Clatt received its charter as a burgh of barony in 1501, though by the late seventeenth century it was only an ordinary parish centre. In the early eighteenth century, however, attempts were being made to re-establish its rights as a burgh of barony to hold markets and fairs.[147] Late seventeenth- and early eighteenth-century topographical descriptions which mention functioning markets and fairs, or the existence of facilities such as tolbooths (in places like Ellon, Kincardine o' Neil and Old Meldrum) or victual houses (as in Tarland), indicate that some centres were certainly functioning.[148] Unfortunately, absence of reference to thriving markets and fairs in such sources cannot necessarily be taken as proof that no trade was occurring. Surprisingly, some of the smallest

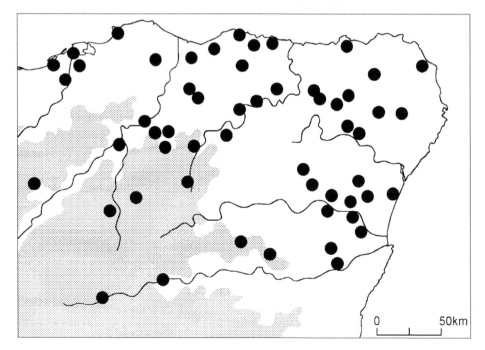

Figure 6.2
Authorised market centres in north-east Scotland by the early eighteenth century.

0   50km

centres, mere rural kirktouns, hosted some of the most prominent and widely-known fairs in the north-east. St Lawrence Fair at Old Rayne, one of the largest in northern Scotland, St Serf's Fair at Culsalmond, St Bartholomew's fair at Kincardine o' Neil and those at Keith, Old Deer and Kinkell were frequented by people from all over the region. The Aiky Fair at Old Deer was described as being the largest in northern Scotland in the later eighteenth century, with up to 10,000 people attending it, spread over fifty or sixty acres.[149] The markets, and especially the fairs held in these rural locations, were frequented by Aberdeen merchants who bought cloth, stockings and other commodities, often acting as middlemen for the wealthier merchants who actually exported the goods.

The poor state of roads in the north-east, before the belated introduction of turnpikes at the end of the eighteenth century, is emphasised by various commentators.[150] However, it is easy to make the mistake of assuming that there had been no improvements in communications before the advent of the turnpikes. In fact, a number of ministers who contributed to the *Statistical Account* in the 1790s commented that the statute labour system was able to maintain the roads in reasonable condition.[151] The town council had been concerned to repair the coastal road to the south since the seventeenth century.[152] And even the road over the Cairn o' Mount was in good shape at this time.[153] In the later seventeenth and early eighteenth centuries, there is evidence that a number of local landowners provided finances for the construction of bridges to serve specific market centres, such as Edinglassie, or to aid local and regional communications more generally.[154] By the end of the eighteenth century, the distances over which agricultural produce and raw materials were being carried to and from Aberdeen suggests a considerable improvement in road conditions from the seventeenth century. Parishes as remote as Tarland and Leochel (twenty-six and twenty-eight miles respectively from Aberdeen) were sending grain to Aberdeen and bringing back lime.[155] The rapid growth of Aberdeen during the later eighteenth century is likely to have stimulated agricultural improvement over an ever-widening area of the north-east.

One of the most important sets of connections between burgh and landward area concerned food supply. A certain amount of Aberdeen's food supply was drawn from the town's own arable lands, which extended up to four miles to the west. Gordon's bird's eye views from the 1660s and Slezer's views from the 1680s show both Old and New Aberdeen as being surrounded by corn fields (Ill. 16).[156] In Old Aberdeen oats, bere, kale, carrots, turnips, onions and orchard fruits were produced from yards and gardens within the town's limits, while livestock were also housed. A population listing for Old Aberdeen, dating from 1636, includes eight husbandmen and four gardeners.[157] The 'freedom lands' belonging to Aberdeen were unusually extensive. In his map of Lower Deeside drawn probably in the 1580s, Timothy Pont inscribed the word 'Free-dome' in large italic letters stretching from

Facies Civitatis Novæ ABERDONIÆ ut a propugnaculo Blockhous dicto aspicitur   New ABERDENE from the Block-house

Reduced from the plate in
Slezer's Theatrum Scotiæ 1693

Illustration 16
John Slezer, View of
New Aberdeen from
Torry, 1693.

Pitfodels and 'Hasilheid' in the west, past Rubislaw and crossing the Denburn, to the line of the River Don (see Plate 25).[158] In fact, the freedom lands were much more extensive than that. Their boundary ran up the Dee valley towards Peterculter, then curved northwards through Ord and over Brimmond Hill, before returning eastward through Bucksburn and Kittybrewster to the coast.[159] The availability of large quantities of manure meant that the fields close to the town gave relatively high yields of oats and bere, though some land close to the town remained unimproved moorland until the later eighteenth century.[160] One reason for this was the need to maintain areas of grazing for livestock being brought to the town for sale and for slaughter, another resource whose use was carefully regulated by the burgh council.[161]

It has been estimated that the basic food consumption of the town's population was around 16,000 bolls of meal a year in the later seventeenth century, though by the second half of the eighteenth century potatoes were making a significant contribution to the diet of ordinary people.[162] If one works on the assumption that a boll of meal was produced from one boll of oats, that the basic yield of oats was around three times the quantity of seed sown, and that tenants needed about two thirds of this for seed and to meet their rents, then this would have represented the surplus from *c.* 16,000 acres of arable land.[163] In addition, large quantities of malt would have been consumed in the form of ale. In various sample diets for the seventeenth and eighteenth centuries, it has been shown that ale contributed up to 19 per cent of total calories.[164] The scale of grain consumption is indicated by the town's eight public mills in the later seventeenth century. Five were water-powered, two were tide mills and there was one windmill.[165]

The Aberdeen shore work accounts provide a good deal of detail concerning the coastal traffic in grain and other commodities in the north-east.[166] The town drew regular grain supplies from Buchan, via Fraserburgh and Peterhead, as well as from further north, in Moray, Ross and Caithness. Much of the traffic was in small quantities, often carried in open boats, sometimes fishing vessels, presumably carrying cargo during slack periods in the fishing year. Much of the malt brought from Montrose was probably consumed by Aberdeen's brewers. In addition to meeting the needs of the resident population, ale was required to slake the thirst of those who visited the town on business, especially those attending markets and fairs. Brewing remained an important industry in Aberdeen in the early modern period. In 1509, over 150 brewers were listed in the town, around 80 per cent of them the wives of burgesses (Ill. 14). Brewing was a common occupation for widows as well as burgess wives.[167] Little wheat was produced in Aberdeen's hinterland, and it is probable that the cargoes of wheat which came along the coast from Montrose and Arbroath were used by the town's baxters for baking wheaten bread. The significance of the coastal grain trade in the seventeenth century is shown by the fact that Sir Robert Farquhar of Mounie, one of the town's most prominent merchants during the 1640s and 1650s, made his fortune in this particular branch of trade.[168]

The shore work accounts show that in no year between 1596 and 1670 did imports of grain from either Scotland or abroad amount to more than 3,350 bolls of victual. Usually they were much less.[169] The accounts, however, do not provide a complete picture of Aberdeen's seaborne trade. The origins of vessels are not always given, particularly for smaller cargoes, many of which would have been carried by local boats operating through small harbours within the north-east. This means that, while contacts with ports such as Montrose, Peterhead and Fraserburgh are prominent in the accounts, the numbers of vessels using smaller ports, such as Newburgh, may be under-represented. However, unless the accounts under-record the amount of victual brought into the town on a major scale, which seems unlikely, the implication is that, except in years of dearth, most of the grain required by Aberdeen's population and not produced on the burgh's own lands was imported overland, rather than by sea. Legislation against forestalling of the town's grain market was specifically framed in terms of grain coming overland.[170] Twelve miles was the approximate distance over which grain could be transported overland in bulk, either by cart or by packhorse, during the seventeenth century.[171] This covers an arc from Newburgh to Stonehaven, through Inverurie, and includes ample areas of good quality arable land to produce a surplus of the quantity required. The shore work accounts highlight other sea-borne links between Aberdeen and her hinterland. Millstones from the quarries at Auchmedden, on the north coast of Buchan, were shipped southwards from Pennan, as was bark for tanning from Inverness and slates (probably in some cases flagstones, rather than roofing slates) from Caithness.[172] On the other hand, few shiploads of peat are recorded; most of the town's fuel supplies probably came overland in creels and carts. High-value, but low-bulk, commodities, such as plaiding, were also transported, predominantly by packhorse while cattle and other livestock travelled on the hoof. Aberdeen was also an important centre for livestock and meat trading. Much of this was designed to furnish the needs of the town itself, although by the second half of the eighteenth century many cattle sold at Aberdeenshire fairs were destined for the English market, travelling over hill routes, such as the Cairn o' Mount, and by-passing the town entirely.[173]

Many facets of Aberdeen's townscape and economy reflected the town's rural setting. Thatched roofs remained common until well into the eighteenth century, while pottery and pantiles were fashioned from local clay.[174] Another local resource consumed by the inhabitants in considerable quantity was peat. Aberdeen remained a peat-, rather than a coal-burning, town into the later eighteenth century.[175] Old Aberdeen faced problems throughout the seventeenth century in regulating the cutting of peat in its own peat moss, and trying to prevent those with rights to cut peat for their own use from selling it.[176] Aberdeen itself required so much peat that it had to be brought in from further afield. In the late seventeenth and early eighteenth centuries, substantial quantities of peat came into the city from the parishes of Banchory Devenick, Newhills, New Machar and even Fetteresso.[177]

Aberdeen's close ties with its hinterland are highlighted in particular by the growth of the plaiding industry, a manufacture which, more than any other, determined the town's prosperity in the seventeenth century. The export of coarse woollen plaiding seems to have begun around 1580 and it expanded dramatically from c. 1610. Between 1610 and 1614, average annual exports were about 13,000 ells. By the early 1630s, this had reached 93,000 ells, with a peak of 121,000 ells in 1639. In the 1650s and 1660s, exports dropped to 60–70,000 ells and there was a further serious decline from c. 1680 as foreign markets contracted. The employment provided by plaiding manufacture was considerable. In 1624, it was estimated that c. 20,000 people in the north-east earned their living from this industry. The figure should not be taken as accurate, but it provides a rough indication of scale. In addition, it must be remembered that the work of every weaver was supported by women and children who undertook spinning and carding. Very little of the plaiding was woven in the town itself. The poll tax records for 1695 list fewer than sixty weavers in both Old and New Aberdeen. By contrast, in some Buchan parishes, a fifth of the pollable male population was described as weavers. Nearly 1,200 weavers were listed throughout the county, outside Old and New Aberdeen.[178]

Much of the plaiding industry seems to have operated on the basis of the 'kauf-system', with independent weavers selling individual webs of cloth to merchants in local markets and fairs. Putting-out systems, where a merchant entrepreneur controlled production by giving out the raw materials and then buying back the finished products at agreed rates, did exist in the seventeenth century, but were frowned upon by the burgh authorities.[179] Old Aberdeen specifically banned the distribution of yarn to weavers in New Aberdeen or the surrounding countryside, in order to protect the town's own weavers, always provided that they wove their cloth as well, and as cheaply as their rural competitors.

Woollen stockings were exported from the area in the seventeenth century, but the main growth of the industry was during the eighteenth century. Some 219,360 pairs were exported in 1743 and 910,320 in 1793.[180] The industry had originally been based on local wool, with individual women selling their products to merchants in local markets and in Aberdeen itself. From the mid eighteenth century, however, Aberdeen merchants organised putting-out systems using better-quality imported wool. By 1795, there were an estimated 30,000 knitters in Aberdeenshire and adjoining parts of Kincardineshire, most of them part-time women workers.[181] The story of the textile trades is the best example of the continuing, mutual dependence of Aberdeen and its vast rural hinterland. The Industrial Revolution would come late to the 'Granite City'. In 1800, as in 1700, much of the industry on which a large part of its wealth rested was domestic or cottage based, located outwith and often far removed from Aberdeen itself.[182]

7

The Economy: Aberdeen and the Sea

GORDON JACKSON

Medieval origins

An island ruled by invaders has a desperate need for ports.[1] They are the route to the world left behind, the source of luxuries in an inhospitable land. For all but the wildest living, it paid to be near the coast. Although archaeologists have detected signs of early trade, it was King David I (1124–53) who introduced 'feudalism' to help unify the state and extract value from the peasantry. He also introduced burghs where mercantile initiatives might realise that value and turn it into wealth and thereby into royal power. Whether David's burghs created trade, or simply regularised for the benefit of the crown places whose comparative advantages had already marked their trading potential, is debatable (see Chapter 6). But at least they encouraged and protected the complex search for maritime contacts, markets, suppliers and shipping that started most ports on their way. Success and merchants bred together. They may not have been gamblers, but they qualified as risk takers in a world where simple agriculture was the economic base and social caution was the norm.

The granting of a royal charter did not 'create' the port of Aberdeen, as its wording implies (see Introduction and Chapter 1). It prohibited foreign merchants from trading in the sheriffdom of Aberdeen 'except in my burgh of Aberdeen', and from retailing in Aberdeen market except between Ascension Day and the Feast of St Peter in Chains (1 August), when they could deal 'in common with my burgesses'. Moreover, to tighten Aberdeen's hold over the cloth trade, nobody could make dyed or shorn cloth except in the burgh. Unfortunately, a real economic purpose did not automatically provide access to continental commerce. Many medieval ports were served by foreign merchants attracted from European centres where Scots had little experience. Talk of wool-wealthy abbeys exaggerates their mercantile status. Neither wool nor skins nor fish actually offered much 'added value'. By contrast, the import schedule shows a lack of the simplest foundations of economic life: timber and iron. Indeed, for a king more outward looking than his people, David's royal burghs were a way of protecting the foreign merchants who for the next three centuries frequented the eastern ports, where they made an important contribution to the development of the urban network.[2] Who better to know the potential of northern Europe than the man from the Hanse, the commercial association of north German towns and merchants? And the burghers of Bruges, who rated Aberdeen among the four 'great towns of Scotland' in the fourteenth century, knew the rest (see Chapter 17).

For a century or more after its foundation, Aberdeen's trade expanded on the basis of wool, hides, skins, and leather and fish, exchanged for timber and iron in Scandinavia and the Baltic, manufactures and superior cloth in the Netherlands, and wine from France and the Rhineland. If we add miscellaneous luxuries, medieval trade begins to look exciting. A French source of *c.* 1270 ranked the Scottish wool ports as Aberdeen, Berwick, Montrose and Perth, and the years 1328–31 were a peak, when cargoes from Aberdeen were dispatched on thirty-six vessels with 1,400 sacks of wool, compared with Dundee's 755 sacks and Perth's 240.[3] Moreover, growth was increasingly based on local efforts as Aberdonians explored the Baltic and used the Scottish Staple in the Netherlands. Located at Bruges and Middelburg and then, from 1508, at Veere, all Scottish wool and hide exports were legally directed to the Staple.[4] However, when European-wide commerce expanded as merchants exchanged more actively the products of regional specialisation, the richest were those at the centre of things, and the poorest were those, like the Scots, on the edge of the world. Their best seaborne trade was the shortest: coastwise with England, with ports that increasingly, from the fifteenth century, welcomed Scottish connections, as they had before 1296 and the onset of the Anglo-Scottish wars.

If medieval history is a mystery it is largely because the economic pot went off the boil, and evidence is consequently scarce. European-wide stagnation ran from the early fourteenth century to the mid fifteenth century, a turbulent period as kingdoms and provinces struggled to emerge, or survive, not least Scotland during the Wars of Independence from 1296. Aberdeen was hard hit when burned by the English in 1336, though the direct consequences of recurring war for Scottish-English trade may be exaggerated.[5] There were also exogenous traumas such as the long Anglo-French wars (1337–1453), while Anglo-Hanseatic disputes were probably as upsetting as Scoto-Hanseatic ones. A general maritime turmoil encouraged the curse of piracy. Aberdeen lost vessels, wealth was dissipated, risks were avoided. But Aberdeen also joined in when exports were falling behind those of Dundee and Perth from the 1390s. Despite their denials to the contrary, Provost Robert Davidson, with the earl of Mar (see Chapter 9), organised attacks on foreign shipping. Gains included a bad name. The Dutch objected, and the Hanseatic League proscribed trade with Scotland from 1415 to 1436. Profits could be more than balanced by costs, and it is not clear whether declining trade encouraged merchants to turn pirate, or piracy ruined trade.[6] Not until the sixteenth century were European rulers strong enough to end piracy in home waters and lift a great burden from commerce.

The damage done by man was as nothing compared with the onslaughts of mother nature. There was no precedent for the demographic catastrophe following the arrival of Black Death in 1349. Everywhere in western Europe commercial activity was hampered by fear and falling demand, prolonged by recurrent epidemics of plague until the fifteenth century.[7] There were also problems with climate, wetter and colder winters, leaving Scotland prone to famine and, on such occasions, dependent upon England and Prussia for emergency supplies of grain. Still, survivors withdrawing from marginal land raised *per capita* output and offered exportable grain to encourage reviving trade.[8]

Finally, there was competition. Safety in convoy and access to shipping, finance and market intelligence sucked foreign trade to Edinburgh, increasingly the chief market and centre of coastwise distribution. Between the early fourteenth and late fifteenth centuries, Edinburgh's customs receipts grew from £439 to £1,528, and Aberdeen's from £349 to £366. The disparity reflects Edinburgh's superiority in woollens, rising strongly between 1450 and 1600, compared with persistent contraction in overall wool exports from 1450 to 1600 and Edinburgh's growing share of the export trade in hides.[9] To make matters worse, imports of woollens were restricted in the Netherlands and the English market was erratic.[10] Meanwhile, local disputes with visiting Danzigers in the late fifteenth century may have been the reason for their vessels by-passing Aberdeen for neighbouring ports, to the council's great annoyance, and perhaps also explain why few Aberdeen vessels entered the Baltic between 1500 and 1550.[11] This was, beyond doubt, a long period of depression in Aberdeen, though not much different from the experience of many 'British' ports.

Fish and fishermen

There was, however, one area in which Aberdeen continued to prosper. Although there were no fishing ports in the modern sense of the term until the early nineteenth century, there were three branches of the fish trade in which Aberdeen engaged: salmon, herring and white fish. It owed its huge success with salmon to the bountiful Dee which had formed its harbour. From earliest times, there were fishing stations on the islands round which the river ran, especially the southern edge of the Inch. These 'stells' - nets supported by wooden stakes, or with one end hauled by boat - caught salmon which was less frequently eaten fresh than salted and barrelled in dry or wet pickle by local coopers for export merchants. They shipped to London at least from the mid fourteenth century, and in the fifteenth century vessels from Aberdeen frequented Grimsby - and other places - where the absence of customs officers encouraged imports in which London fishmongers showed interest.[12] Accurate trends in volume and value are hidden by volatile taxation and irregular counting of ships. For instance, a massive increase in duty in

1481 may have inhibited export volume while creating a substantial upward trend in revenue; we do not know what tax the market could bear. Moreover, a reduction in barrel size, by 14 per cent in 1573 and 20 per cent in 1625, meant their number rose faster than the volume of fish. One thing is clear. Whatever the measures, Aberdeen was by far the leading exporter of salmon, with over 40 per cent of national trade in the years 1460-1599,[13] though the council may have exaggerated when telling the privy council in 1580 that without salmon there could be no burgh or inhabitants, only 'desert solitude' – and that would not pay the taxes![14] During the years 1596-1670, foreign exports fluctuated greatly, but trending upwards from *c.* 400-600 barrels around 1600 to *c.* 1,100 in the 1620s and *c.* 1,600 in the 1630s.[15] It was somewhat lower in the 1650s, and no higher in 1712. The market was chiefly in Holland, Zeeland and France (notably Veere and Dieppe) with some lesser interest in the Baltic, Germany and Iberia. What cannot easily be quantified is the amount sent to Leith or London. Nor is it clear how much came from the Dee and how much arrived coastwise, from Findhorn, Banff, Peterhead, Newburgh and Montrose. Some was exported in the same vessel, as in 'a ship of Montrose … with some salmon for France being to take in the rest of her loading here'.[16]

Protection from foreign competition in production enjoyed by riverine salmon fishing did not extend to other fish. Codfish were also popular because their size allowed the split fish to be lightly salted at sea and then dried and barrelled on land. There are signs that this was once a lucrative trade: in thirteenth-century Flanders cod was known as *aberdaan*.[17] But cod were usually caught with lines in cold waters, a capitalist operation facing stiff competition from northern Europeans who were nearer the fisheries. Early voyages to Iceland, Norway and even White-Sea Russia usually involved salted or dried cod, some caught by Scots, but often bought fully processed from local fishermen. It was, however, a small trade, and did not progress much in Scotland following the development in the fifteenth century of the Newfoundland fishery where most 'British' codfish were subsequently caught. Of course, there was some inshore catching of white fish for consumption, starting, perhaps, in Aberdeen to feed a concentrated and relatively wealth population. Futty housed both salmon and inshore fishermen from before 1500, but here, as elsewhere, the pattern was for fishermen to migrate to fishertouns along the coast from which catches might be taken easily to the commercial ports. Important suppliers such as Findhorn, Banff and Peterhead date from the fifteenth century, while six fishertouns were established along the coast south of Aberdeen in the seventeenth century.[18]

By comparison with salmon and cod, herring was the 'Great Fishery', a source of protein for urban Europe and wealth for the Dutch, whose 'Golden Age' was based on this humblest of fish. Although herring were easily netted from small boats for local consumption, the demand was international, especially after the

Baltic fishery collapsed. While Scottish fishermen answered the first call, they failed at the second. An appeal by parliament in 1492 for all ports to build fishing vessels to secure foreign trade to stop the drain of bullion, was not without some effect.[19] In January 1587, a record hundred Scottish sail arrived in Aberdeen roads with fish for processing.[20] But in the long run the great gainers were the Dutch whose carrying trades gave access to superior Biscay salt and northern European markets. They turned peasant livelihood into capitalist industry, with factory ships ('busses', with large crews who caught and lightly salted the herring ready for further processing back home), quality control and careful marketing. They invaded Scottish waters with vast fleets, supported by men o' war, out-fishing the Scots, ensuring that their diverse inadequacies were not overcome. James VI (1567–1625) tried to control these 'bloodsuckers on my realm';[21] Charles I (1625–49) tried to tax them; and attempts to drive them from 'British' waters helped to cause three wars, all to no avail. Protection was replaced by potential profit when the fishery was handed over to company speculators, but intermittent royal fishery companies (with Scottish sub-sets) also failed through lack of drive and knowledge. The only known effect in Aberdeen was negative, when, in 1669, 'aine ship of the kings ... bound north for fishing payd no ancorage beeing exemted by his majesty'.[22]

Of course, relatively small quantities of herring continued to be imported to Aberdeen from neighbouring fishertouns, for local consumption or exportation, but by the end of the seventeenth century Glaswegians rejoiced that the west-coast cure was preferred in the Baltic. Visiting inshore and deep-sea boats were indirectly valuable to Aberdeen because they paid anchorage dues on their voyage north or south between England and the Shetlands. There was even, in 1653, a previously unknown whaler, 'the English ship that came from Greenland'.[23]

The harbour

It may not be true that a harbour ideal for landing salmon is bound to be poor for trade, but it is true that developing commerce cannot easily reconcile the demands of both fish and ships.

With trade struggling out of the doldrums, it is no surprise that Aberdeen suffered the physical drawbacks facing most 'British' ports in the late fifteenth century. The harbour of Dee was too big for its mouth. It followed a typical pattern: a meandering, slow-moving river fought powerful seas in the debris of sand hills, shingle and bars. It coped with medieval cockleshells that sailed, as a common name implied, by *The Grace of God*, and gratefully bottomed in mud. But the fifteenth-century revolution in ship-design produced ocean-going vessels for which silty harbours of great size and no depth were adapted satisfactorily only with large expenditure and new engineering.[24]

On the eastern side, the harbour was sheltered from the sea by the 'Futty links' ending at the river mouth at 'Sand Ness', in the south-east corner.[25] The town and its quays stood at its north-west corner, while in the fifteenth century the deep-water channel hugged the southern side extremity, and between it and the town were channels and islands that came and went with the tide, only one – the Inch – topping high water. Small vessels sailed up the eastern side of the harbour to the town quays, but larger ones kept to the 'Gawpuill'[26] on the southern side of the harbour mouth, opposite Torry, from whence imports were ferried to the town in small boats. Nor were the approaches to the harbour satisfactory. The southern route skirted the rocks of Girdle Ness, while vessels approaching from the north without careful assessment of the tide risked grounding on the Bar, which at low water in the 1650s registered barely two feet of water.[27] The nature of the Dee determined that Aberdonians could not afford to improve it effectively before the railways changed their world. Or, looked at from the other side, the harbour served its traffic because it was largely a progression of small, shallow-draught vessels.

There was a quay of sorts from earliest times, but the start of modern facilities was its extension eastwards from the town centre around 1450.[28] Needless to say, it was ruinous by 1484: early physical structures rarely withstood the action of water for long. Further repairs around 1527 and 1562 were necessary, now supported by levies on imports and exports in 1543 and salmon in 1571. The fact that taxes were on goods rather than ships indicates the nature of the works: they were for goods, not ships. The first serious attempt to tackle the shortcomings of the harbour occurred in 1596, when a royal charter was obtained to levy dues on goods *and* ships, that is, to make the traffic bear the cost of appropriate 'shore works'.

Large harbours like Aberdeen's were a nuisance because, before modern dredging, maintaining depth was monstrously hard work. The best assistance was often 'natural', that is using training walls to divert water to increase scour, especially at harbour mouths. So the shore works following the 1596 charter were in two parts. In the north of the harbour, the quay was again extended towards Futty, though not completed until 1659 and then only consisting of dry-stone walls filled with sand. To the south, the harbour mouth was trained by the building of a bulwark between the Torry shore and the sea, opposite Sand Ness (Plate 35). Beyond this, and periodic repairs, there was no major attempt to improve the harbour until the pressure of trade increased rapidly towards the end of the eighteenth century.

It is difficult to assess the effectiveness of these works but Thomas Tucker, in his report on Scottish ports in 1655, noted that vessels still tied up in the Gawpool adjacent to Futty and Torry. This gave 'opportunity of much fraud, in landing goods privately, but prevented of late by appointing the waiters by turns, to watch those two places narrowly, *when there is any shipping in harbour.*'[29] The sting was in the tail. So far as shipowning was concerned, the situation was dismal. In 1626, only ten vessels, of between thirty and sixty tons, had belonged to Aberdeen. Of these, one was leaky and fit for only the Norwegian wood trade, and two were out of commission and lacked crews. The town had only forty mariners and hired ten elsewhere.[30] Thirty years later, Tucker reported nine vessels (see Fig. 7.1) and, though both number and individual size were derisory by later standards, he credited Leith with only 'some twelve or fourteen' of which two or three were 200 or 300 tons, and the rest 'small vessels'. Dundee had only ten but their size reflects, to some extent, its superior trade by that time. Montrose had twelve, but the largest was some forty tons, six were under thirty tons, and five were under twelve.[31]

Aberdeen		Dundee	
No.	Tons	No.	Tons
1	80	2	100
1	70	1	90
1	60	1	60
3	50	1	55
2	30	1	50
1	20	1	40
		1	30
		1	25

Figure 7.1
Number and size of vessels belonging to Aberdeen and Dundee in 1655.

It is unnecessary to reconcile such figures with meaningful trade, since volatility was the norm in seventeenth-century commerce. Scottish ports suffered disproportionately during the Wars of the Covenant, when English ports were on the winning side. Dundee, Tucker acknowledged, had been 'a prey to the soldier'. Aberdeen, he could have said, was devastated in the 1640s by military occupations and its sacking by Montrose in 1644 (see Chapter 11). Recovery was hampered by plague in 1647 (see Chapter 3). A third of the people and thirty-two ships disappeared in the war and its aftermath.[32] How many ships were replaced is unknown, but too much should not be made of small numbers. Aberdeen's short-haul vessels could accumulate more ton/miles than larger vessels making a couple of long trips in the year. Moreover, for centuries Aberdonians had employed exogenous vessels as a way of apportioning scarce capital between vessels and goods: they could hire the former but not the latter.

Imports and exports

Nor was it simply the wars of the 1640s and 1650s that caused trouble. Doubtless the banning of wool, hide and skin exports by the republican government between 1652 and 1660 was some justification for the council's claim in 1654 that 'none can subsist or have any living',[33] but this was part of on-going fluctuations in trade.

There was a serious depression in the 1630s, before the Revolution, a rise in local activity in the Cromwellian period, and contraction in the 1660s, after the Restoration.

The overwhelming impression is that seventeenth-century Aberdeen was an importing rather than an exporting port, and this would tie in with the small number of locally-owned vessels. European imports, well into the eighteenth century, tended to arrive in foreign bottoms. These imports were chiefly bulk items on which town and hinterland depended, brought from foreign or British ports. The most indispensable item was grain, of which Aberdeen was a net importer between 1596 and 1670. Initially, regular Danzig vessels filled the granaries, while in times of dearth it was all decks on hand, from near and far: 'Hanes Widerman dwelland in Stralsound for ane shippes ladining of beir';[34] 'a frenche barks lodning of 24 chalders beir';[35] and, not forgetting the coastal trade, 'meill in 3 fische boitts from Peterhead'.[36] However, Scottish and English cargoes increased in the 1620s and sufficed in normal years from c. 1650. Montrose was always the major source. Roughly 260 cargoes went one way or the other between 1596 and 1670 and about half of them brought grainstuffs.[37] The coastwise route was usually preferred. A descendant of Grant of Monymusk, whose estate sent beir and meil coastwise to Aberdeen in the early seventeenth century, was still complaining a century later of the lack of decent roads north of the Tay and the impossibility of getting a carriage to Aberdeen.[38] Traffic went not with the crow, but by tracks which skirted mountains, rivers and bog.[39] At the other end of the scale, wine was 'essential' for all but the poor. Chiefly of French origin, its volume was unexpectedly low, perhaps because landowners shipping produce to Aberdeen from neighbouring 'creeks' also landed their wine nearer home. Direct imports rarely exceeded one hundred tuns and were often less than fifty tons by c. 1650; coastal imports were also small.

The bulk raw materials list should, perhaps, be headed by salt, the mainstay of fish curing. Biscay salt was by far the most prized and voluminous in 1596–1636, reaching ten times the Scottish salt from the Forth and only sinking under the most dire international tensions. It also came from third parties such as Amsterdam, otherwise noted for onions. Only after c. 1650 did larger supplies arrive from Scottish sources. Forth ports also supplied coal in small quantities, never exceeding one hundred chalders between 1649 and 1670. It was useful in nascent industry, but houses were still burning peat (see Chapter 6).

Of even greater importance for industrialisation was imported bar iron, a few dozen tons in the early seventeenth century, rising in the second half. Though doubtless Scandinavian, only sixteen known shipments arrived directly . The rest came from Danzig, Holland and sometimes Bruges and Ostend, as part of their entrepôt service. Further evidence of underdeveloped foreign trading (or highly organised coastal trading?) is the greater number of shipments via other Scottish ports (Fig. 7.2).[40]

Bruges	1	Anstruther	2
Danzig	3	Dundee	21
'Holland'	13	Dysart	1
Ostend	1	Leith	13
'Scandinavia'	16	Montrose	14
		Newburgh	1
		Pittenweem	1
Total Foreign	**34**	**Total Scottish**	**53**
Unidentified	16		

Source: *Shore Work Accounts*, index.

Figure 7.2
Sources of iron
cargoes, 1596-1670.

The timber trade was different. Direct cargoes predominated: usually mixtures of deals for building a growing town; staves and hoops for the universal containers; and miscellaneous wood for multifarious purposes, including shipbuilding. Despite their importance, Aberdeen required only around ten cargoes per annum – never more than twenty – between 1596 and 1670 (Fig. 7.3). Nor were they always in Aberdeen vessels, as a record entry in 1619 reveals: 'Ressavit from 3 flemynges for thair 3 schippes full of tymber about 3500 dales and treis.'[41] Norwegian masters often brought wood to be sold 'at the mast', reflected perhaps in 'ane passant Norroway man' in 1644, and Scottish vessels sometimes called at several ports: 'for 160 dales in Frances Sewardes bark of Kirkcaldye [which were] left of his barks ladning unsauld in the Newburghe.'[42] Backing up the deals were an average 30,000 slates per annum, together with lime, from Scottish sources.

Most interesting as evidence of trades old and new was the vast miscellany from Zeeland, mainly from Veere. Tobacco, iron, wood and tar were obviously re-exports, and some of the flax, hemp, linen yarn, madder and woad may have originated in the Baltic. Cheese, sugar, fruit, seeds and, above all, onions were presumably Dutch. Manufactures came from Holland itself or from down the Rhine, Maas and Scheldt. Their range was remarkable, denoting civilised living at all levels: soap, fine candles and oils; paper, books, bibles, printer's type, ink, pens, candlesticks and spectacles; copper, brass and pewter goods, tin-plates, bells, clocks and instruments; spinning wheels and needles; fine woollens and linens, ribbons and corsets; paint and paint-ings; and, for the rich, tulip bulbs. The schedule was further swelled by products of the Dutch East Indies: tobacco, nutmegs, pepper, spice. Unfortunately the Shore Accounts recorded many such things as 'goods', measured by tun or by last. Some 'goods' also arrived coastwise, especially from Leith. Though the Forth was slowly industrialising and Edinburgh was manufacturing 'luxuries', they doubtless in-cluded many re-exports. In 1561-71, for example, Leith sent 225 vessels to Zeeland,

Dundee sent seventy-nine, Aberdeen forty-five and Montrose thirteen.[43] It was easier to find vessels and credit in Leith than Aberdeen.

Exports from Aberdeen changed little in the early modern period. Skins and hides were always in demand but grain exports, substantial in some years in the early seventeenth century, depended on the climate and local demand; they would not last. Exports, however, now included increasing amounts of plaiding and stockings, whose cost advantage (through cheap materials and labour) opened a market among the continent's poorer classes. To encourage plaiding exports, Aberdeen council imposed maximum prices on local weavers in 1584, though they thought it vulgar stuff, forbidding women to wear it in 1580 (unless they were harlots), and merchants were not to compromise their dignity by wearing it outside the town.[44] However the export trade did not prosper, with cargoes rarely more than thirty tons and declining before rising in the 1650s (Fig. 7.3).

Figure 7.3
Import and export cargoes at Aberdeen, 1596-1670.

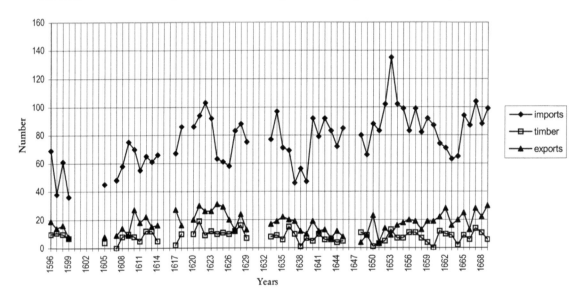

The disparity between vessels entering and clearing Aberdeen in foreign trade was occasioned by the greater demands of imported raw materials and by extensive Forth coal exports which offered vessels (often Dutch) for return cargoes direct to Aberdeen or via Leith.[45] Aberdeen merchants still lacked the mercantile intelligence or connections implied in the 1531 rule that Scots could not unload in the Dutch Staple without consulting the Conservator – the chief official of the Staple, appointed by the crown.[46] They were perhaps a little better off than when burghal law required Aberdonians to accompany their exports, for in 1603 the council reduced the absurd nineteen merchants who should have travelled on the forty-ton *John of Aberdeen* – to eleven![47]

ABERDEEN BEFORE 1800

The seventeenth and eighteenth centuries: a new economy?

A notable increase of European economic activity towards the end the seventeenth century barely stretched to Aberdeen. It was to do with oceanic, imperial trade, while, in Smout's phrase, 'the poor Scot hardly began to move outside the medieval trading area where he had always been at home.'[48] Yet Aberdeen, while needing foreign goods, was (except perhaps for salmon) peripheral to European consumption. The number of vessels clearing rose only slightly from about twenty per annum in the 1660s (Fig. 7.3) to about twenty-three in 1680-86 (Fig. 7.4),[49] and they may not be strictly comparable. The former apply to Aberdeen, while the latter include the sub-ports, and the irregular inclusion of coasters further complicates the issue and implies little advance. But the same applies to other ports, and Figure 7.4 shows clearly that Aberdeen (including her sub-ports) was no longer the leading northern port. Total clearances were fewer than at Dundee (and Inverness) and only half those at Montrose. Shipments from the coal and general exporters of the Forth were from three to six times those of Aberdeen. Arrivals were no better than at Dundee and considerably fewer than at Montrose. Neither the Baltic nor the Norway trade had kept pace with neighbouring headports, and this is reflected in the importation of the two most economically significant raw materials: deals and iron were half those of Dundee.[50] The poor standing in English trade may be a function of distance,[51] but the falling share of royal burgh taxes, from 8 per cent in 1612 to 6 per cent in 1683, and 4.5 per cent in 1697, was not determined solely by Aberdeen's performance. The proportion declined because Edinburgh and Glasgow made remarkable strides and, to illustrate the point, Dundee actually 'fell' more than Aberdeen.

Aberdeen's lost primacy was not through the failure of merchants or harbour. No amount of enterprise can overcome unfavourable factors. Nor was inter-port rivalry always meaningful: the coal ports would always be ahead. Aberdeen's problem was a hinterland offering little new (beyond grain), offset to some extent by plaiding, of which it was the chief manufacturer. Regrettably, the continental market was constrained by hostilities with the Dutch (1652-4, 1665-7, 1672-4) and the French (1688-97, 1701-14). Apart from the obvious features of invasion, the wars *against* England until the sixteenth century were probably less damaging to Aber-

Figure 7.4
Directon of trade and shipping: total vessels arriving from, and clearing to, specific places, 1680-86.

	England		Baltic		Norway		Germany		Holland		Flanders		France		Spain		America		Total	
	From	To	From	To	From	To	From	To	From	To	From	To	From	To	From	To	From	To	From	To
Aberdeen	11	10	22	21	68	39	4	7	41	43	2	0	36	13	0	2	0	3	184	138
Montrose	20	28	20	15	138	140	1	1	31	56	0	0	13	14	0	0	0	2	223	256
Dundee	12	17	32	27	101	70	0	0	40	42	0	1	0	16	1	2	0	0	186	175

Source: Smout, *Scottish Trade on the Eve of the Union*, Appendix I, Table III.

deen's trade than the wars *for* England in the seventeenth century.[52] After stagnating during the wars of the 1640s and 1650s, exports of plaid had been running at some 138,000-168,000 ells per annum, peaking, it is said, around 1670, but markets contracted with import substitution in Sweden, prohibition in France in the 1690s and rising prices associated with increasing wool exports.[53]

The encouragement of stocking manufacture, which was admirably suited to small-scale production, was an initiative taken by merchants when opportunities offered, and show that Aberdonians could respond to – or even encourage – demands for which they had supplies, capital organisation and market knowledge (see Chapter 6). While stockings could not balance the losses in the plaid trade, they did at least offer hope for the future. Little, however, was to be gained from the growth in linen production, perhaps the most important influence in the industrial emergence of Dundee, Perth and Glasgow.

One reason for Aberdeen's relative decline from the seventeenth century was its excessive dependence on European trade, when Glasgow (and indirectly Bo'ness and Leith) were enjoying the first fruits of the American connection. Interestingly, a vessel arrived in Aberdeen from Virginia in June 1666, though its ownership and cargo are unknown. A connection, however, was established, not for imported tobacco, but for exported 'settler goods' – the necessities of everyday life carried in three vessels in 1680-86.[54] These may not have been local initiatives. In 1685, for instance, Newcastle's *Henry & Francis* was advertised as calling at Leith, Montrose, Aberdeen and Kirkwall for goods or passengers before crossing to New Jersey.[55] It was a sensible way to fill vessels.

Figure 7.5
Vessels belonging to leading Scottish precincts in 1707 and to head- and sub-ports in 1712.

The formal inclusion of Scotland within the English mercantilist system, which was one of the objects of the Union in 1707, required listing of all British vessels in a Register-General of Trading Ships, later analysed to show improvement in the first five years of Union (Fig. 7.5).[56] In 1707, 215 vessels grossing *c.* 14,500 tons were registered, of which twenty-two grossing 941 tons belonged to Aberdeen, fourth-

| | 1707 | | 1712 | | 1712 | | | | | |
| | Precinct | | Precinct | | Headport | | | Sub-ports | | |
Port	No.	Tons	No.	Tons	No.	tons	ave. tons	No.	Tons	ave. tons
Aberdeen	22	942	88	3408	39	2155	55	49	1253	26
Bo'ness	26	2451	104	6913	37	3844	104	67	3069	46
Dundee	25	1315	57	2922	57	2922	51	0	0	0
Kirkcaldy	18	1690	69	3867	31	2778	90	38	1089	29
Leith	39	3354	106	8202	103	7982	77	3	220	73
Montrose	6	584	72	2669	41	2040	50	31	629	20
'Glasgow'	22	1274	140	5384	105	4881	46	32	503	16

Source: BL, Harleian MS 6269, courtesy of Dr Eric Graham

ABERDEEN BEFORE 1800

equal by number but only sixth by tonnage. After five years Aberdeen had grown roughly four-fold, ranking fourth by number and fifth by tonnage, a feat of mercantile perspicacity or clerical assiduity.[57]

The fact that over half the vessels within Aberdeen's precinct were owned in the sub-ports was not unusual. It spread the cost of shipping, relieved pressure for laying-up space in winter, and eased the recruitment of labour which traditionally moved along coastlines in search of work or moved with the vessels.[58] What is surprising by this time is how few of Aberdeen's vessels were 'sizeable' for foreign trade; only three exceeded one hundred tons in 1712. This was enough for the Baltic, and almost certainly the advance between 1707 and 1712 served the rising share of Scottish vessels in Baltic trade, peaking at 64 per cent in 1708.[59] Scottish vessels passing the Sound in the 1720s were approximately double the number of 1707.

Given the extent of recent warfare and privateering, it is surprising that there was any economic development in the early eighteenth century. Yet contemporaries inured to endemic strife detected signs of progress. Daniel Defoe, a great mercantile publicist, wrote of 'a very great manufacture of linen' in Aberdeen, and stressed the importance of worsted stockings sent to England, Holland and the Baltic. He also mentioned the growing quantity of victuals sent chiefly to Holland for both East Indiamen and men-of-war: 'Aberdeen pork having the reputation of being the best cured, for keeping on very long voyages, of any in Europe.'[60] He was writing at a time of peace, when things were looking up, and he could be positive about recent progress, with an ebullience not entirely aimed at selling his *Tour* to the merchants whom he praised. 'The people of Aberdeen', he wrote in his summary,

> are universal merchants, so far as the trade of the northern part of the world will extend. They drive a very great trade to Holland, to France, to Hambrough, to Norway, to Gottenburgh, and to the Baltick; and it may, in a word, be esteemed as the third city in Scotland, that is to say, next after Edinburgh and Glasgow.

Aberdeen's universality was indeed confined to northern Europe. Given the limited hinterland, there could be little change. The two or three vessels a year to North America with 'settler' goods was a tiny share of the most dynamic trade of all. Not surprisingly, there was little share in the growing trades in Russian and Prussian wood, iron and flax, which went chiefly to the expanding industries of the central belt. The obverse of this was the absence of abundant manufactures such as swelled the trade of Leith and Bo'ness, and of coal to excite foreign interest. Nor was Aberdeen suitably placed to share the western ports' Irish bonanza. Finally, there was no significant change in the fisheries. Only 1,687 barrels of salmon were exported in 1712, though more went to London, and eventually curers such as G. & W. Davidson, founded in 1770, improved their methods and were poised for a notable break-through. It was a good time. John Richardson, the great Tay fishmonger, commented in 1766 on the high regard for Aberdeen salmon in Paris, 'where they give any price when scarce since they buy no other salmon'.[61] The local white fishery was less successful. The inhabitants of Futty were notoriously poor and their boats were little better than their hovels (see Chapter 4). Compared with fishing, regular pilotage fees were attractive, and became the chief support of Futty Fishers Provident Society (1761). Since they exhibited little interest or expertise, the council endeavoured to attract fishermen from Hartlepool in 1771; they would not stay.[62] If anything, the local herring fishery was worse, failing to respond more than marginally to subsidy acts in 1718, 1747, 1750 and 1756; other conditions were still not favourable.

That Aberdeen could respond to economic incentives is shown by the alacrity with which it took up the subsidy on whale fishing. Whale oil was a vital raw material usually secured from the American colonies, where production costs were low enough to undermine a subsidy of 1733 aimed at encouraging larger British ships and more potential sailors. However, a doubling of bounty in 1750 following a similar price rise in the late 1740s induced the first flush of a widespread industry.[63] Aberdeen followed other Scottish ports in 1753 with Aberdeen Whale Fishery Company, an amalgam - as such speculations usually were - of regional landowners (led by Sir Archibald Grant of Monymusk) and local officials and merchants led by the provost. The fishery failed for lack of experience in masters and officers. Returns were a matter of faith that did not cover costs. *St Anne* was withdrawn in 1757, but any cost-reduction was offset by *City of Aberdeen*'s appalling performance until she was sold to Newcastle in 1763. Yet the company was not unsuccessful. The Bounty made up for the losses, and individual members made money out of supplying the whalers' needs. Many people benefited directly or indirectly from the state's desire to nurture this 'nursery of the navy'.[64]

Many British ports enjoyed enormous growth after each of the eighteenth-century wars, but Aberdeen's foreign trade was almost static between 1763 and the early 1780s. By contrast, coastal tonnage entering rose tremendously between 1759 and 1776, when it was eight times as great as foreign tonnage (Fig. 7.6). Thereafter, coastal activity fell during the American Revolutionary War (which also involved the French, Spanish and Dutch). This once again illustrates the intimate relationship between the two branches of trade, and the fact that arrivals rose more quickly than clearances fits into the pattern of miscellaneous foreign goods and coal arriving coastwise while bulky exports went directly abroad.

The American Revolution also had a devastating effect on Aberdeen shipowning. Vessels 'belonging', that is 'home' vessels that entered the port in foreign *or* coastal

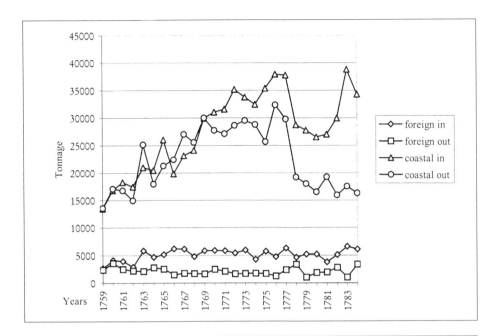

*Figure 7.6
Tonnage of vessels
entering and
clearing Aberdeen,
1759-84.*

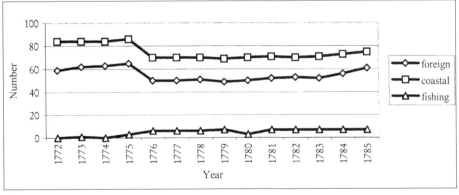

*Figure 7.7
Number of vessels
belonging to
Aberdeen, 1772-85.*

trade, had reached about sixty by the early 1770s, but fell drastically in 1776. In both foreign and coastal vessels, expansion began when peace came in 1783 (Fig. 7.7). The appearance of fewer than ten 'fishing' vessels has, of course, little to do with a 'fishing port': they were almost entirely large whalers and small herring busses.

Aberdeen in the 1790s

What, then, was the state of Aberdeen's trade in the early stages of the industrial revolution that changed the face of Scotland, and, more immediately, of the French Revolution of 1789 which brought disruption to French and Dutch markets and general warfare from 1793 to 1815? The first impression is how little had changed since the seventeenth century. The Netherlands, Scandinavia and the Baltic still predominated as trading partners; the warm south came a very poor second. The American trade seemed promising but was relatively insignificant, and well into the nineteenth century ships were best filled by sharing voyages with Dundee; both ports also used the Forth & Clyde Canal to trade via the Clyde.[65]

Nevertheless, by 1790 Aberdeen was exhibiting more clearly the characteristics of a major port. While the range of contacts remained small, the schedule of goods was expanding. Sweden was now the usual source of iron, and Aberdeen was the third largest importer of it. Norway still supplied all manner of semi-processed wood such as oak knees for ships, staves, laths, bits of carts and handles for everything, the principal change being the decline of sawn deals and a huge increase in rough-sawn 'timber' for further processing in local sawmills. (Supplies of timber and naval stores from the eastern Baltic were severely disrupted by the Napoleonic War.) But, unexpectedly, in 1790 Holland (doubtless as entrepôt) also supplied iron, linseed, hemp, wood-ash, processed wood (especially wainscot boards) and almost all the flax, of which Aberdeen was the third largest importer. The regular vessels were crammed with fruit, vegetables, bacon, dairy products, plants and seeds (especially clover), as well as such manufactures as books and paper, pens and pencils, spectacles and mirrors, chemicals and dyestuffs. But eastern luxuries were now more likely to arrive coastwise from the East India Company's depot in London. The American trade sounds exciting, but the apples, some flax and ashes, seeds, plants, staves, rosin, tar and turpentine could doubtless have been got more easily and cheaply from nearby Europe; they were little more than saleable ballast, balancing the value-added exports.

Transatlantic exports were now more exciting for being the products of rising local industries; and Aberdeen was one of six ports whose industries were identified by Henry Melville, the great political manipulator, as 'flourishing to a degree beyond conception'.[66] The West Indies took an assortment of furniture and cabinetware, haberdashery, clothes, shoes, linen and diverse cloth, hardware, cutlery, steel watch chains, Jews' harps, hats, dolls, perfumery, combs and hair powder, French, Spanish and Portuguese wine, and at least one 'tea kitchin'. These were for the use of the colonial elite and contrast sharply with 'slave linen' exported from Dundee. Cargoes for New York and Halifax were aimed at a lower market: footwear, stockings, soap, candles and books, some cottons and linens but no silks and little haberdashery. Coal, rather than bricks, stiffened the ships.

Exports to northern Europe were chiefly foodstuffs as Scottish agricultural improvements took off. Scandinavia required large quantities of barley, oatmeal and potatoes, with some re-exports of wine and sugar, and assorted cloths and haberdashery. Riga took only bricks. The rest of Europe was quite different. The wool trade was long dead, and worsted stockings were the chief exports, some 680,000 pairs in 1789. Roughly 98 per cent followed the old route to Veere, accompanied now by nascent 'industrial' manufactures such as wood and metal household goods, until recently imported from Holland. Rotterdam, by contrast, took only barley. Ostend took chiefly salmon, and some stockings. One thing is worthy of comment. The foreign plaidings trade had gone completely, leaving locally produced linens and cottons going chiefly to America, and a miscellany of calimancoes, camblets, corduroy, duffle, dyed woollen cloth, lastings and velveret – all exported to Gothenburg in Sweden.

So far as salmon was concerned, the last quarter of the eighteenth century was a period of novelty and excitement, though not particularly of larger catches. The use of river nets and traps was theoretically the only legal fishing, but those without access to river rights were beginning to fish outside the harbour with encouraging results, so much so that the burgh claimed, and received by charter in 1804, the ownership of fishings in Nigg Bay. More importantly, there was a significant change in curing methods which fitted in well with declining continental market opportunities. The traditional method of salting and barrelling, varying with the proposed market and sometimes involving par-boiling the fish, gave way in the 1770s to the 'kitting' process which used less salt in a vinegar pickle. This was favoured in the London market and drew larger amounts into the regular fast coasters (some of which worked in both directions, bringing fresh salmon from northern fishertouns and taking the processed fish to London). Finally, the fresh trade bloomed. Salmon boxed in straw had little chance of exciting the palates of the genteel set, but partial freezing did. Its origins are vague but, probably around 1780, a Mr Dempster of Dunnichen replaced the straw with ice and a superior trade was born. Salmon was diverted increasingly to London on the eve of the longest modern war against France.

This same war was to intensify national and local government interest in herring. An Act of 1787 offered 20s per ton for large boats plus 4s per barrel which seems to have encouraged busses, but they had disappeared by 1800. Nor was there much response to the 1s per barrel for small boats, increased to 2s in 1796. In a desperate attempt to increase the food supply, and raise foreign exchange, the 1808 Act 'for the further encouragement and better regulation of the British white herring fishery' offered £3 per ton for busses over sixty tons plus 2s per barrel. What Adam Smith would have said about this largesse may be guessed from his scathing remark that with earlier subsidies 'it has ... been too common for vessels to fill out for the sole purpose of catching, not the fish, but the bounty'.[67] Not, alas, in Aberdeen in the early nineteenth century. Both wet fish and herring awaited the coming of steam. Whaling, however, revived with declining foreign competition and rising bounty and prices after 1783, and the Aberdeen Whaling Company (led by James Gibbon and Thomas Bannerman) enjoyed reasonable success in the 1780s and 1790s.

Starting with the *Hercules*, in 1783, the Company employed two or three whalers until the end of the century, when there were four: *Hercules, Latona, Robert* and *Jane* (owned by the newly formed Union Whale Fishing Company). By the end of the Napoleonic War there were five companies and thirteen or fourteen vessels, yet another example of the transformation of the Aberdeen economy taking place between 1780 and 1830.

Foreign trade in 1789 was handled by a community differing widely in its interests and importance. Errors accepted, 154 importers declared 927 entries of goods.[68] Of these, only two made more than fifty entries, six more than twenty entries, and twenty-two more than ten, while 101 made fewer than five, and forty made only one. This pattern resulted partly from 'small' men importing one or two items from Veere or Rotterdam, but there were important exceptions. Flax importers often imported nothing else while some linen manufacturers and putting-out merchants imported a few large shipments, ranging from Leys Masterson's 1,500 cwt, Alexander Bruce and Young & Walker each with 1,098 cwt and Andrew Paterson with 698, to sixteen men with single shipments between 373 and 1 cwt, chiefly below 50 cwt. Although Dutch traders were usually 'general' merchants, they sometimes shipped a small amount of flax along with other goods. A single shipment of flax does not necessarily indicate a 'small' dealer in flax, nor does a small parcel necessarily constitute the whole of a merchant's activity.

Vessels on the Dutch run were also specialists, advertised by masters, owners or the emerging shipping agents as 'ships laid on' for roughly time-tabled voyages. It was easier now for small merchants to secure cargo space, and for the new manufacturers or landowners to indulge in overseas or coastal trade. But these were not typical vessels. In other trades, individuals took the initiative, chartering vessels for private or shared use. An analysis of the number of merchants per vessel (Fig. 7.8) shows that Aberdeen was clearly not dominated by 'small men'. Of eighty-one arrivals in 1789, fifty involved only one importer; Scandinavian and Baltic specialists usually filled a whole vessel with assorted wood and fibres. They were substantial men in the port. The same is true of transatlantic importers and those from Iberia.

Finally, excluding masters, shippers tended to specialise in importing or exporting. Of seventy exporters in 1789, only twenty-four were also importers. Of these, eighteen made fewer than four shipments, usually smallish parcels to their foreign suppliers. Moreover, exporters mostly specialised by product or region. Thomas Bannerman shipped wine (and one stiffening of bricks) to Grenada; many shipped only foodstuffs; William Dalmahoy shipped only boots and shoes; George Davidson shipped only salmon, not surprisingly since he was a curer. Manufacturers shipped only cloth or stockings. In fact, if Defoe sought his 'universal merchants' he would probably have praised only William Forbes, for a variety of goods sent to Bilbao,

Importers per vessel	1	2	3	4	5	6	7	8	9	11	12	18	21	23	25	36	Total
Vessels from																	
Iceland	–	1	–	–	–	–	–	–	–	–	–	–	–	–	–	–	1
Bergen	10	–	–	–	–	–	–	–	–	–	–	–	–	–	–	–	10
Kristiansund	13	4	1	–	–	–	–	–	–	–	–	–	–	–	–	–	18
Kragero	1	–	–	–	–	–	–	–	–	–	–	–	–	–	–	–	1
Gothenburg	7	2	2	1	–	–	–	–	–	–	–	–	–	–	–	–	12
St Petersburg	1	–	–	–	–	–	–	1	–	1	–	–	–	–	–	–	3
'Easter Tsar'	3	–	–	–	–	–	–	–	–	–	–	–	–	–	–	–	3
Riga	–	–	–	–	–	–	–	–	–	–	1	–	–	–	–	–	1
Memel	4	–	1	–	–	–	–	–	–	–	–	–	–	–	–	–	5
Danzig	1	–	2	–	–	–	–	–	–	–	–	–	–	–	–	–	3
Hamburg	–	1	–	–	–	–	–	–	–	–	–	–	–	–	–	–	1
Rotterdam	1	–	–	–	–	–	–	–	2	–	–	–	–	1	–	–	4
Veere	–	–	–	–	–	1	2	–	–	–	–	1	1	–	1	1	7
Ostend	1	–	–	–	–	–	–	–	–	–	–	–	–	–	–	–	1
Dunkirk	1	–	–	–	–	–	–	–	–	–	–	–	–	–	–	–	1
Bordeaux	1	–	–	–	–	–	–	–	–	–	–	–	–	–	–	–	1
Oporto	1	1	–	–	–	–	–	–	–	–	–	–	–	–	–	–	2
New York	1	1	–	–	1	–	–	–	–	–	–	–	–	–	–	–	3
Whale fishery	4	–	–	–	–	–	–	–	–	–	–	–	–	–	–	–	4
Total vessels	50	10	6	1	1	1	2	1	2	1	1	1	1	1	1	1	81

Source: NAS, E 540 (Aberdeen Customs Quarterly Accounts, 1789)

Note: 'Easter Tsar' is unidentified; goods imported suggest the south-eastern Baltic, no further north than Estonia.

Figure 7.8 Number of vessels from foreign ports, with specified number of importers, 1789.

Veere, Drunton, Halifax, Ostend and Rouen, and for various imports from Memel, 'Easter Tsar', Gothenburg, Riga, St Petersburg and New York.

There was another consideration in assessing Aberdeen's performance in foreign trade. Ultimately, great ports must acquire appropriate fleets. Reliance on outside shipping was dangerous when vessels began to increase in size and regularity of movement. Before the Registration Act of 1786, a port was credited with vessels 'belonging' counting each once in the year at master's declaration of 'tons burthen', that is carrying capacity. This figure was obviously volatile, depending on shipping activity, but with safeguards it is a reasonable guide to Aberdeen's fleet and its comparative standing. In 1772, it consisted of fifty-nine foreign-going vessels (totalling 3,990 tons) and eighty-four coasters (4,440 tons), the fifth largest 'fleet' in Scotland behind Leith, Bo'ness, Port Glasgow and Greenock, and way ahead of Dundee. In the number of coasters, Aberdeen was second – by one – to Bo'ness, and in tonnage it was first (Fig. 7.9). This obviously ties in with the spectacular performance in coastal trade (Fig. 7.6), though it is less easy to square it with the foreign trade figures. The effect of war is obvious in 1776, and (at 143 vessels and 7,941 tons) Aberdeen had not quite recovered its earlier totals when the modern registry was

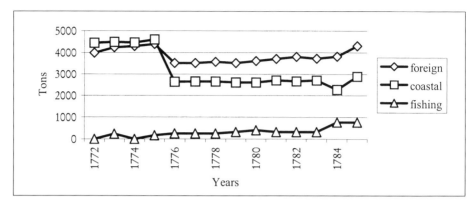

introduced in 1786. All vessels were measured over the next two years, and a sudden rise in tonnage reflects this rather than sudden trade growth. Nevertheless, at the count in September 1788, Aberdeen had 158 vessels totalling 11,677 tons, the second largest number after 'Glasgow' and the third largest tonnage after Glasgow and Leith. Only three were over 200 tons, and 80 per cent were under a hundred tons, reflecting the short-haul pattern of most Aberdeen traffic.[69]

We have noted that Aberdeen's foreign and coastal trade was advancing along with the agricultural and industrial developments around the city, with an aggregate of approximately 75,000 measured tons of shipping entering the port and 34,000 tons clearing. How much this was within the port and how much in the sub-ports is difficult to assess, but the precinct as a whole supported this trade with a huge increase in shipowning. The port was not only on the move but equipping itself with the necessary vessels, though in 1789 Aberdeen's import trade (Fig. 7.10) still relied on forty-four vessels belonging to Banff, Charlestown, Fraserburgh, Gardenstoun, Macduff, Montrose, North Shields and Peterhead, as well as Norway and Sweden. More positively, this means that Aberdeen could cope with over half her trade. In this regard, it is necessary to stress the intimate coastal contacts in shipping that allowed rather than hindered the sensible investment of scarce resources of capital and market intelligence. In the early 1790s, the fleet was rising slowly, to 198 vessels and 14,516 tons in 1795; by 1800 it had reached 281 vessels and 23,235 tons and by 1804 comprised 295 vessels and 30,464 tons, half as much again as Leith.[70]

This spectacular rise of trade and shipowning towards the end of the century naturally increased the demand for ships. Scotland was not a particularly enthusiastic shipbuilder for most of the eighteenth century, preferring to make use of large plantation-built vessels and small foreign-built ones. The catalyst for change was, as noted above, the American Revolution and the rush of information about shipbuilding after 1786 in response to the government's urgent demand for hard information about shipowning and shipbuilding to replace the 'guesstimates' that

| | 1789 | | | | 1790 | | | |
| | Inwards | | Outwards | | Inwards | | Outwards | |
From	No.	Tons	No.	Tons	No.	Tons	No.	Tons
Denmark/Norway	31	2,033	24	1,482	36	2,416	10	576
Sweden	12	657	2	126	14	723	–	–
Russia	2	256	1	106	6	789	–	–
Poland	4	361	–	–	6	583	–	–
Prussia	8	1,319	–	–	–	–	–	–
Germany	1	48	1	58	–	–	–	–
Holland	10	988	8	723	21	1,783	3	363
Austrian Flanders	–	–	4	236	–	–	2	104
France	2	184	4	285	2	154	2	111
Spain	2	167	3	239	–	–	–	–
Portugal	1	154	–	–	2	224	–	–
Italy	–	–	–	–	1	151	–	–
Ireland	1	100	–	–	–	–	–	–
Guernsey	–	–	1	110	–	–	–	–
Greenland	4	916	4	916	4	916	4	916
New York	5	278	1	102	1	150	1	150
Brit. N. America	–	–	1	88	–	–	–	–
Brit. West Indies	–	–	3	595	–	–	1	241
Total foreign trade	83	7,461	57	5,066	93	7,889	23	2,461
Coastal trade	1,004	66,704	662	27,938	817	45,224	814	31,086

Source: PRO, Customs 17/11, 12, *passim*.

Note: There is a mathematical error in the source of this table for 1789; the number from New York should be three, there were two vessels from Portugal, and one from Austrian Flanders.

Figure 7.10
Vessels in foreign and coastal trade entering and clearing Aberdeen, 1789-90.

previously sufficed. There was a sudden rise in national shipbuilding following the Registration Act of 1786, and in 1787 Aberdeen's official total made her the third largest shipbuilder in Scotland (Fig. 7.11). During the slump, Aberdeen's totals fell more than some, to fourth place in 1791. The founding of Alexander Hall's yard in 1790 doubtless helped to reverse the depression and, in short, Aberdeen (plus her sub-ports) was the nation's leading shipbuilder by 1800, with 20 per cent of the vessels and 22 per cent of the tonnage.[71] In the early days output had mostly been coasters and short-haul vessels, but certainly in the 1790s 100-tonners and bigger were coming off the stocks, encouraged, perhaps, by the availability of Scottish wood for shipbuilding. The Rothiemurchus forest, for instance, was being developed as an alternative to Russian shipbuilding timber from c. 1796. This was not a flash in the pan; in the decade after Waterloo, Aberdeen was the leading port in every year but one, with 23 per cent of national tonnage.[72]

There were two noticeable aspects of this overall growth in trade and shipping. Firstly, it represented a large growth in coastal sailing, which was partly related to

Year	No.	Tons	Year	No.	Tons	Year	No.	Tons
			1791	10	671	1801	42	3461
1787	20	1262	1792	na.	na.	1802	27	3571
1788	17	1373	1793	13	953	1803	22	2204
1789	9	485	1794	2	842	1804	24	3595
1790	9	810	1795	9	609	t805	20	2103
Average	13.75	982.5	Average	8.5	768.75	Average	23	2986.8

Figure 7.11
Ships built in
Aberdeen and its
sub-ports, 1787-1805.

Source: PRO, Customs 17/12–17, 22–27.

the growing trade in kitted and fresh/chilled salmon carried to London in 'express' smacks. This cut transit times and led to more traffic in fresh foods and to the emergence in Aberdeen and Dundee of coastal shipping lines that played an important part in the early nineteenth-century development of the north-east, especially when converted to steam. Secondly, the coal trade burgeoned, with approximately 35,000 tons arriving from England (largely Sunderland) in 1789, and 4,000 tons from Scotland (Alloa, Bo'ness, Inverkeithing and Kirkcaldy). Many of the 111 coal importers were concerned only with coal, some as consumers and some as manufacturers; only fourteen in the English trade and eight in the Scottish imported anything else. So far as coal vessels were concerned, they made up a large proportion of the vessels entering the port.

All this rather exciting activity put pressure on port facilities. Concern about the entrance had led to a report by John Smeaton in 1770 recommending a new impounded scouring system inside the harbour (as in Dover and Ramsgate), recognising that the town could not afford it and that salmon fishers would object. Eight years later, he tried again, recommending training the entrance with an extended north pier and new south pier, which did indeed deepen the water inside the harbour mouth. Nevertheless, the harbour was still inadequate. It remained so after the rejection of a major scheme in 1797, by John Rennie, the greatest British ports engineer, in favour of another scheme by Thomas Telford which preserved the salmon and deepened some of the water, but in the end was neither cheap nor cheerful. Aberdeen was still arguing the relative importance of cost and demand for space in the 1830s. There was nothing unusual in this. Large dock schemes were hugely expensive. Small ports could rarely afford them, and rich ports thought long and often about their adverse effect on port dues and profits. Not until shipowning rose as an independent profession was there a greater interest in spending money on facilities for handling shipping.

ABERDEEN BEFORE 1800

8

Elite Society in Town and Country

MICHAEL LYNCH *and* HELEN M. DINGWALL

In 1685, Alexander Skene, a bailie, landowner and son of a former provost, wrote *A Succinct Survey of the Famous City of Aberdeen.*[1] It is of interest as being the first significant history of a royal burgh published in Scotland. In an age which was profoundly conscious of rank and lineage, when various groups of titled and landed *arrivistes* were engaged in seeking out new ways to give expression to their status, it is the counterpart of the armorial, genealogical table and family history. It repeated and embellished the story to be found in the *Chronicle* of Hector Boece, first rector of the new University, that Aberdeen was created a royal burgh by Gregorius, legendary 73rd king of Scotland. Skene also claimed that the town had been in 'special favour' with successive kings of Scots from Alexander II (1214-49). The volume also recorded another act of self-aggrandisement - the commissioning of a new coat of arms for the burgh by the polymath, Sir George Mackenzie of Rosehaugh, historian, herald, novelist and hanging judge (Plate 23). Skene's *Succinct Survey* and his *Memorialls*, also published in 1685, were, on the one hand, an extended defence of the time-hallowed rights and privileges of a burgh establishment against the 'inferior sort of people' within the town in a 'polemick age'. They were also the prototype of a later, Enlightened age, when civic ideals permeated society. Skene recommended regular visits being made to the town's schools so that magistrates could examine both the curriculum and individual pupils. He envisaged a public library - but of 'books suitable for magistrates' and the dean of guild, such as the printed acts of parliament and *Regiam Majestatem* and commercial maps, some available only in London (see Chapter 16).

A new burgh community?

In the course of the seventeenth century, Aberdeen's élite was transforming itself effortlessly from the medieval ideal of a hierarchical, closed society run by an overarching concept of the 'community of the burgh', in which the 'good' were naturally respected and obeyed, into a civic state in which gentility and a new notion of authority were grafted on to old ideas of order and place. The

Reformation had been propelled by a longer-term replacement of the seven deadly sins by the Ten Commandments, each of which was reinforced by both kirk session and the civil power (see Chapter 13). The new magistrates, however, needed novel, blunt instruments to reinforce their powers. As well as kirk session elders and deacons, who (it was feared) might intrude on the jurisdiction of the town council, Aberdeen set up a Justice of the Peace Court, which employed constables - 'well qualified, sober and discreet men' drawn from the lower ranks of the burgess class - to root out 'whoredom, drunkenness and swearing'. On the spot fines were levied on 'country people' guilty of swearing on market days.[2] New means were being found to reinvent 'the myth of the burgh community'[3] - a sense of belonging and engagement by all burgesses, who amounted to some 30 per cent of the male inhabitants of the town as a whole. Excluded from real power, seventeenth-century constables, most of them craftsmen or small booth-owners, became the moral traffic wardens of urban society. As part of the same process, the provost became a 'lord provost', the bailies became both 'Christian magistrates' *and* 'civil magistrates' and merchandising, it was urged, should be acknowledged to be 'as gentlemanly an activity as tillage of the land'.[4] Aberdeen's town council and its merchants, like rural lairds, feuars and heritors before them, had joined the scramble for a new status and respectability in a new kind of Scotland.

In death as in life, it was important for status to be seen and acknowledged. Society was officially stratified in a variety of different ways - even in fees set for marriage and simple burial. 'Honest [i.e. worthy] and rich folks' paid 18d; 'sober folks' were charged 12d; but the rites of passage for the 'poor and indigent', who made up the bulk of the population, were free.[5] But simple burial was not enough for the élite in burgh society; family monuments and sepulchres littered the parish church of St Nicholas before and after the Reformation. Although the reformed church officially tried hard to discourage burials within churches, old and cherished practices were difficult to root out, especially where kin or status were involved. The lucrative practice of charging for 'lair silver', which allowed kin to be buried together in virtual family vaults, continued for a considerable time after 1560 and charges were doubled in 1585, at £3 for adults and £1 for children. One means of assessing the numbers of the privileged few who could afford to pay for a lair within St Nicholas is the fact that the fund realised just £105 in the two-year period of 1584-6.[6] Money was a passport to such privileges. A surer means was lineage and inheritance; the rights of those whose forefathers had endowed foundations or masses before 1560 entitling them to free burial within St Nicholas were upheld in a ruling of March 1585. One beneficiary was Elizabeth Forbes, widow of the former, long-serving provost Thomas Menzies of Pitfodels.[7] In effect, the pre-Reformation chantry was replaced by the family sepulchre.[8]

Civic ceremony, which had rapidly developed in the century after 1450, was another means of enacting power and privilege. The emergence of a variety of processions and ceremonies, secular as well as religious, can be traced to this period, ranging from the annual Corpus Christi procession, first recorded in 1440,[9] to various rites of misrule associated with May games or with the feast of St Nicholas, which featured a 'boy bishop'. In the Corpus Christi festivities, which were the highpoint and most solemn of the new civic ceremonies, the merchant guildry and craft guilds processed in strict order of rank through the streets. Those closest to the blessed sacrament were the élite, who also enjoyed regular access in the burgh church beyond the rood screen, which was the physical barrier for all others in society. Behind them in the procession came the craft guilds (who also had their own altars in the burgh church but in less auspicious positions) in order of seniority and precedence. After the Holy Blood banner, emblem of the merchant guild, came the banners of St Eloi of the hammermen, St Crispin of the skinners and St Obert of the bakers.[10] Collectively, this was the *corpus christianum* or community of burgesses. The festivities celebrated the doctrine of the real presence in the eucharist but also 'the great chain of being', which had put the great and the 'good' in charge of the community.[11] The 'unfree' - those without the privileges of burgess-ship who made up the bulk of the inhabitants - were mere spectators in civic ceremony.[12]

The rites of misrule, despite appearances, served much the same purpose (see Chapter 16). Throughout Europe, they acted as a safety valve in a society which remained both hierarchical and deeply stratified.[13] What was sometimes known as the 'abbot of unreason' or the 'lord of inobedience' in other Scottish burghs such as Peebles and Edinburgh, was in Aberdeen called the 'prior' or 'lord of Bonacord'.[14] In Aberdeen, they featured in festivities linked to both Corpus Christi and the feast day of St Nicholas of Myra (6 December) and these revels were organised and paid for by the burgh authorities. By the early sixteenth century, the cult of Robin Hood seems to have taken over from that of Bon Accord (see Chapter 16). In May 1508, the town council ordered a parade of all able men between the ages of sixteen and sixty to process behind Robin Hood and Little John 'with their arraynment made in green and yellow, bows, arrows and all other convenient things'.[15] What was common to both cults was the ordinance that the lords of misrule and their retinues should *ride* through the town. A further clue to the origin and significance of this custom may lie in the early description in 1442 of the religious tableaux associated with Candlemas; in them, the merchant guild took the role of the 'knyghtes in harnace'.[16] The natural rulers of the town were mounted on horseback. Those who enacted other roles did so on foot.

Although these celebrations were periodically condemned for their excesses by the town council and eventually banned by parliament in 1555, they would return in different forms a generation after the Reformation. Although there was no longer a lord of misrule controlled by the rulers of the town - whether in the shape of the lord of Bon Accord, a boy bishop or Robin Hood – another old ceremony was adapted to provide the same message underpinning the authority of the magistrates. The regular inspection of the burgh marches and freedom lands was first recorded in 1398. Here, the bailies were referred to as *lineatores*, literally meaning liners. By the first decade of the sixteenth century, the duty had become a ceremony – a 'riding' of the marches. In 1504, the participants were ordered to 'ride to decoir and honor the toun in their array' in company with the Abbot and Prior of Bon Accord. In 1508, the statute was repeated, but by now the focal point of the ceremony had become Robin Hood and Little John. In 1535, 'all young abill men' were ordered to attend. In 1546, it involved the 'haill nichtbouris of the toune'.[17] And by 1594, the riding was also linked to a wappinschaw, in effect a muster of all able-bodied men in the town. Each bailie became a 'commander' of his own quarter of the town.[18] The riding had become a ritual enactment of the royal burgh's privileges and independence as a 'chief vassal' of the crown. It was, in effect, a local version of the new ceremony of the 'riding of parliament' which also became more formal and ritualised in the 1580s and 1590s.[19]

Another device was used to ram home the same message. In 1595, the council ordered that a fast – the new austere, Calvinist rendition of a Catholic feast day – be accompanied by another full-scale wappinschaw, with a muster roll of 400 men.[20] Religious and secular ceremony was, once again, conjoined and the authority of the burgh magistrates underpinned by both. By 1661, the burgh's standard had been incorporated into the ceremony and the standard bearer, invariably the son of one of the élite, led the procession on a 'stately steed', in what was a newly invented 'ancient fashion'.[21] The wappinschaw became a surrogate for the civic ceremony which had to be jettisoned after the Reformation. It was a new device used to reiterate an old message. By 1599, the council ordered that musters be held each Monday and by 1607 they included both free and unfree. In 1619, a remarkable total of 550 inhabitants took part.[22] The burgh community was in process of being re-ordered and the authority of burgh magistrates being reinforced. Other, perhaps more tangible, symbols of burgh authority came with the building in 1626 of a new tolbooth, still encased within the present-day Town House, and the construction in front of it of an elaborate market cross.[23] Fashioned with twelve elaborate panels depicting Stewart kings from James I (1406–37), as well as with armorial bearings, it was an urban equivalent of a triumphal arch – and a formidable, three-dimensional reminder of the privileges not just of the burgh community but of the rulers of that community.

Burgesses, merchants and 'merchant men'

The 'free' in burgh society were those who enjoyed privilege of burgess-ship, of being an acknowledged member of a privileged caste. The size of the burgess community is difficult to calculate with much precision at any one point in time but, in practice, it can roughly be equated to that of the taxable population (see Chapter 5). A series of thirteen stent, or tax, rolls exists for the period 1448–68. They are the earliest surviving for any burgh and they reveal an average of some 320 taxpayers.[24] By the early seventeenth century, the number of taxpayers had risen to over 500; there were 553 in 1608 and 569 in 1637.[25] This was not only the result of population increase for new categories of those liable for tax had been widened so as to increase revenue in an age when burgh government was becoming more intrusive and more expensive.[26] These figures, as a result, equate favourably with those for Edinburgh, which had 1,152 taxpayers in 1608 and 1,548 in 1637.[27] In other words, bearing in mind that Edinburgh was probably more than three times the size of Aberdeen, proportionately more inhabitants paid tax in Aberdeen than in the capital.

Does this mean that the burgh community was larger and more representative in Aberdeen? That would be a leap of faith that is likely to have little substance in reality. In every town, there was 'a community within the burgh community'[28] – a smaller group in which real as opposed to notional power resided. In Aberdeen, there are various indicators of the size of this élite group, which was mostly made up of merchants: it was somewhere between sixty and eighty-five. There were some sixty-three members of the merchant guild in 1445; and in 1446, eighty-three *mercatores* met in the tolbooth to choose commissioners to be sent to England. Yet these figures are surprisingly low for a town of Aberdeen's size. The much smaller burgh of Dunfermline had about fifty in its merchant guild in the same period and Perth had over a hundred in its guild in the 1450s.[29] All of this would suggest that there are oddities about the social make-up of Aberdeen society. The number of overseas merchants was less than what one might expect in a town of its population and so was the size of its ruling élite. It is certainly the case that Aberdeen had fewer craftsmen than most other equivalent towns; its merchants outnumbered tradesmen by almost three to one: in 1637, there were only 127 craftsmen and over 350 merchants paying tax.[30]

Aberdeen had a highly distinctive social structure. It had proportionately fewer overseas merchants than Edinburgh; it had, for its size, considerably fewer craftsmen than either Edinburgh or the manufacturing centre of Perth; but it also had many more small merchants who depended for their livelihood on inland trade in Aberdeen's vast hinterland, with its network of market centres and other small towns.[31] At times, the record makes explicit this basic distinction between 'merchandis' and 'merchant men'[32] – in other words between overseas merchants and inland traders. It was a social profile guaranteed to preserve and protect a small, tight-knit hierarchy.

Yet, there is a puzzle to unravel here. It has been estimated that by the early seventeenth century the merchant guild numbered somewhere between 300 and 350. Of this number, an educated guess is that only seventy-five regularly traded overseas.[33] In other words, the numbers of overseas traders had not changed much in the course of 150 years. Yet the size of the merchant guild had increased enormously over the same period. Does this mean that the intervening period had seen a dramatic extension and widening of the burgh élite? The answer is a distinctively Aberdonian one. The burgh had increasingly struggled to meet its tax bills as the sixteenth century went on. There were repeated complaints of difficulties in raising taxation; burgesses were frequently pursued for non-payment; and claims were regularly made that Aberdeen merchants had to pay more in tax than their equivalents in other burghs.[34] These problems reached a crescendo amidst the increased pressures of national taxation which came with the crisis of war and invasion triggered by the 'Rough wooing' of the 1540s; in 1544, the burgh complained that it was unable to meet the demands made on it by the crown because it was 'decayit and puir'. In 1551-2, it was forced to take the drastic step of alienating its salmon fishings and common lands by feuing them to 'particular persons'.[35] This short-term 'fix', designed to raise revenue, became a long-term burden, as price inflation steadily eroded the flat-rate annual fee paid by the feuar.

Another solution to the burgh's fiscal crisis was to increase the categories of those liable for taxation. In 1558, Aberdeen lowered the tax threshold of every inhabitant to the 'value of £40 Scots in goods and land', a figure which was well below the usual standard of £100 rent or 2,000 merks of moveable property which was later set by parliament at the end of the century.[36] The inevitable result was that more were drawn into the tax net in Aberdeen than elsewhere and certainly more than ever before in the burgh itself. Another device was sharply to increase the numbers admitted to the merchant guild, so as to raise income from entry fees; in the period 1623-6 an average of twenty-seven a year were admitted.[37] This was a dangerous tactic for there were complaints in the 1590s that the wholesale admittance of too many burgesses of guild was the reason for 'great poverty of many of them'.[38] The result is a curious one: as time went on, Aberdeen had fewer and fewer entrants as simple burgesses and more and more entered as members of the more prestigious guildry. Yet, in practice, that status was illusory. The increasing size of the taxable population and the rising numbers in the merchant guild had little to do with either population increase or increasing social mobility; both were devices for raising revenue.

A paradox operated in many early modern towns, and Aberdeen is a classic example of it. The more the burgh increased in size, the tighter became the grip exercised by its hierarchy – an élite within an élite. Who made up this small coterie? Unusually, the answer is not readily discernible from the tax rolls. In Edinburgh, the top 10 per cent of taxpayers, who were almost invariably overseas merchants, owned a formidable 56 per cent of the burgh's wealth at the turn of the sixteenth century. In Aberdeen, the equivalent figure was only 38 per cent.[39] And increasingly as the sixteenth century went on, Aberdeen's council had complained that many of its overseas merchants were spending much of their time in Leith and Dundee, leaving their home port a 'dry pond'.[40] Wealth and position on the town council and elsewhere belonged, not to overseas merchants, but to an urban patriciate whose income depended not on the export and import trades, but on rural land-holding. Like the nobility as a whole, who relied on the outdated so-called 'auld extent' which dated back to the thirteenth century in order to avoid paying a fair share of national taxation, the Aberdeen patriciate remained undertaxed. This was because taxation was levied on trade and stock *within the burgh*. As a result, wealthy merchant lairds do not figure amongst the highest taxpayers in any of the stent rolls. Yet they dominated the town council and especially the magistracy.

The urban patriciate: merchant lairds and 'gentillmen'

Every medieval town had close links with its rural hinterland. In the case of Aberdeen, the two are sometimes difficult to disentangle. The patriciate of merchant lairds needs to be distinguished from the ordinary 'landmen', small traders, chapmen and farmers from the country who thronged the town on market days (see Chapter 6). Over the course of centuries, it had laid down roots in Aberdeen's rural hinterland, both by intermarriage with the gentry and by investment in landed estates. It has been estimated that one in ten burgesses married into the families of landed gentry in the century after 1424.[41] Its numbers are difficult to pin down with certainty. In 1317, a list of thirty-seven burgesses living *rure manentes*, in the countryside, was drawn up.[42] It has been estimated that in the early seventeenth century, the 'merchant lairds' numbered somewhere between forty-five and fifty.[43] Their intrusion into burgh politics was gradual, but relentless. By 1500, the pattern of the council being dominated by a small group of families had set firm: 46 per cent of the council and 53 per cent of its officeholders were drawn from eleven families in the period 1434–1524. In 1661, Gordon of Rothiemay, who drew the well-known map of both New and Old Aberdeen, pointed to the eight families which by then virtually monopolised burgh office – the Chalmers, Menzies, Cullens, Collisons, Lawsons, Grays, Rutherfords and Leslies. At least half of that group would also be in a list of the patriciate families of two centuries before.[44]

Another map which is revealing of the power structure that operated in and around Aberdeen is that of Lower Deeside drawn by Timothy Pont, probably sometime in the 1590s, as part of his survey of Scotland (Plate 25).[45] What is unusual about the map is the number of placenames detailed on it – no fewer than 389 – which is a good indicator of an active land market and fairly intensive settlement.[46] Clearly drawn on the map, at the edge of the burgh's 'freedom lands', is the estate of Pifodels, finally acquired by the Menzies family in 1521 through marriage, after a process of acquisition which had lasted the better part of a century.[47] Pont drew what was in effect a 'landscape of power', in which baronies, rural estates, tower-houses and other prestigious buildings were all carefully depicted.[48] Standing out on this landscape of Deeside, near Peterculter, was the tower at Drum, depicted with five storeys and three bays, set in extensive parkland and policies.[49] The family of Irvine of Drum would be one of the main external influences operating on the royal burgh in the fifteenth century, and perhaps before that (see Chapter 9).

The visible presence of landed power – nobles and 'gentillmen' – was also obvious for all to see within the town itself. The fact that the royal burgh was the seat of a sheriffdom and the collection point for the great customs levied on exports inevitably meant that noble holders of royal offices such as these would reside in the town for at least a part of the year. The earl of Crawford, who became hereditary sheriff of the shire sometime in the early part of the fifteenth century, and Lord Forbes, his deputy, were two such regular visitors (see Chapter 9). The royal office of Constable of the Castle, despite the destruction of the fortress in 1308, continued and it was retained in the family of Kennedy of Carmuc until the end of the sixteenth century. Although it is known that this family had long owned property in the area of St Katherine's Hill, they had an anonymous presence in the town for much of this period.[50] In addition, however, regional crises would from time to time bring other magnates and powerbrokers to the burgh (see Chapter 9). Alexander Stewart, earl of Mar, as the chief agent in the north for Governor Albany during the minority and exile of James I, became a familiar figure in the town between 1406 and 1420. He pursued his royal duties alongside a lucrative sideline in piracy, in partnership with the provost of Aberdeen, Robert Davidson.[51] In the later 1470s, Earl John, youngest brother of James III (1460–88), spent a good deal of time in Aberdeen, in a vain attempt to consolidate the earldom of Mar in his own hands and to counter the Gordon influence in both the region and the burgh.[52] These episodes brought a noble or quasi-royal household to the burgh, with its attendant demands on the burgh's economy and food supply, but they also had a habit of turning the town into a cockpit of regional, or even national, magnate struggles (see Chapter 9).

In the fifteenth century, the Castlegate was flanked by the town houses of gentry such as Sir Alexander Irvine of Drum, local nobles such as the third Lord Forbes and the Earl Marischal, and by those who were not so local, including the earls of Buchan and Erroll.[53] This in itself was testimony to the sheer extent of Aberdeen's rural hinterland and how much the burgh dominated it. Yet there was a price to pay for such a large noble presence. The town could at times be the flash-point for noble violence. In 1527, Seton of Meldrum was killed by the Master of Forbes in the house of the burgh's provost, Gilbert Menzies.[54] More often, the cost of living alongside nobles is to be measured not so much in terms of violence, which was relatively unusual in the fifteenth century at least, but in pensions. In 1494, almost 50 per cent of the burgh's income amounting to £150 was spent on noble pensions.[55] Some of this was to meet the bill for royal offices and largesse, such as the pension paid to the earl of Crawford as hereditary sheriff and the £100 paid to Lord Erskine out of the customs in 1494.[56]

Other gifts or arrangements involving nobles were to buy off trouble (see Chapter 9). In the century from 1440, the town entered into extraordinary deals with various magnates during political crises. In 1440, it appointed Alexander Irvine of Drum as 'captain and governor' of the burgh, but the understanding quickly fell apart. By 1442, the council vowed that in the future 'na gentillman of the cuntreth sal haue watteris or takis [tacks or leases] of this toune'.[57] If the attempt to find one protector failed, the memory of it did not inhibit the town from entering into a ten-year bond of manrent with the earl of Huntly in 1463. If the town guaranteed the earl's personal safety while within its precincts, he undertook to protect its investments and holdings which lay beyond the burgh boundaries.[58] Such arrangements were distinctly unusual and in breach of various acts of parliament, but Aberdeen's repeated efforts to find a 'minder' probably reflected two things: the burgh's lucrative, but vulnerable, fishings and freedom lands; and the glasshouse effect of being a regional capital with a significant landed presence within it. Both points are illustrated by the town's long history of friction with the house of Forbes. In 1463, Lord Forbes accused the council of conspiring in attacks made on his retainers and property. In 1482, it in turn accused him of plundering a burgh fishing. Eventually, in 1526, Forbes was granted an annual tun of wine in return for 'protecting' the burgh's fishings or, more realistically, in order to stop him plundering them himself. Yet by 1530, when Forbes invaded the town as part of a wider dispute between his family and the rival network of Gordons and Leslies, this arrangement had broken down (see Chapter 10).[59]

Nestling amongst the noble town houses, on the south side of Castlegate, was the imposing timber-built residence, complete with gallery and forestair, of Menzies of Pitfodels. The family first gained the provostship in 1433 and near-monopolised it for the better part of a century after 1493 (see Chapter 10). After that building was destroyed in a fire, in or around 1529, it was replaced by a stone-built house, said to be the first in the burgh. The only surviving remnant of it is an elaborate heraldic panel, displaying the arms of Thomas Menzies of Pitfodels, provost of the burgh for a long period until his death in 1576, still to be seen built into a property in Belmont Street.[60] Yet as late as 1661, Gordon of Rothiemay described it and the house of the Earl Marischal as the two 'most remarkable' in the Castlegate.[61]

For ambitious burgh families such as the Menzies, the issue of the intrusion of landed power into burgh politics, which was a common feature of successive reigns from James II (1437-60) to that of James V (1513-42), provoked recurrent crises but also offered various opportunities. One result, it has been suggested, was an intense rivalry between 'town' and 'county' factions in burgh politics. Prominent burgesses, such as Sir John Rutherford, twice married to the daughter of a local laird, nine times provost between 1485 and 1500 and continuously on the council between 1501 and 1527, became a client of a landed magnate, to the extent of entering into a bond of manrent with the future third earl of Huntly in 1490.[62] This was the scenario for the coup effected in 1493 against Rutherford's 'maisterful oppressioun' of the burgh which brought an alternative regime into place, with the Menzies family holding the office of provost. Yet this was not so much a 'town' faction brought to power as a rival oligarchy with different links to an alternative landed network. The wheel came full circle a century later, in 1593, when the ending of a 'race of Menzies' provosts was accompanied by accusations that they had acted like a 'landward baron', treating Aberdeen as if it were a personal 'burgh of barony'. Again ironically, the Menzies, for long clients of the earls of Huntly, were replaced by a provost, John Cheyne, who was the client of a rival noble, the Earl Marischal (see Chapter 10).[63]

At times, the rivalries of competing burgh factions, each linked to outside power brokers, resulted in outright crisis. There was a violent clash between town and country at elections in 1486 and 1525, followed in each case by royal intervention.[64] In 1525, the armed invasion of the burgh by a consortium of Setons and Leslies with eighty of their retainers had an unusual feature: these local lairds went so far as to demand a vote in burgh elections. This novel claim, it was alleged, was part of an attempt orchestrated by a rival burgh faction, led by John Collison, to prevent the office of provost passing from Menzies father to son - from Gilbert Menzies of Findon to Thomas Menzies of Pitfodels. Unsurprisingly, Collison belonged to another prominent burgess family which itself had extensive connections with local 'gentillmen', including the Leslies. So serious was the crisis, which was exacerbated by the lack of a powerful alternative noble protector because of the recent death of the third earl of Huntly, that it needed the intervention of the crown two years later to stop the rivalries of the opposing networks of Leslies and Forbeses from swamping Aberdeen politics (see Chapter 10).[65] But each had its own *parti pris* within the burgh itself, amongst its merchant lairds.

Acts of parliament of 1491 and 1503 tried to keep town and country apart, by forbidding the purchase of rural lordships by burgesses and by prohibiting the holding of burgh office by rural landowners.[66] The first of these processes did not particularly figure in Aberdeen, except for a few obvious exceptions, but the second was unstoppable. The burgh was at times virtually taken over by landed influence. About thirty barons and lairds were admitted to the merchant guild in the period 1399-1530. And in 1584, forty-one landed clients of the earl of Huntly were made burgesses of guild in a single enactment.[67] The influence of landed interests or outright interference were, of course, not unusual in sixteenth-century burghs: Lord Ruthven held the provostship of Perth for almost forty years until 1584 and exercised day-to-day control over the town through the appointment of two cadet families as bailies.[68] Yet the process of gentrification of burgh government probably came earlier in Aberdeen than elsewhere and it was more intensive. The Reformation brought little change to any of these processes. The kirk session, when first set up in 1562, replicated the same pattern as already existed within the town council. The faction grouped around Thomas Menzies of Pitfodels, who had been provost for almost twenty years, dominated the new, Protestant assembly, despite the fact that it was distinctly conservative, if not outright Catholic, in religion (see Chapters 10 and 13).

Although the Menzies family would later come to be seen as the classic example of a landed family seeking to expand its influence by virtually annexing the burgh, this judgement probably puts the phenomenon the wrong way round. Both it and the Rutherfords came to power through a process of gentrification: a long march towards acquiring influence in burgh government and a slow, parallel process of acquiring property outside the town. Owning land – both within the burgh and furth of it – and acquiring fishings were more reliable and lucrative businesses than the often hazardous ventures of actual trade, overseas or with other burghs in Scotland. Preferential arrangements – for evading full payment both of customs and burgh taxation – were regularly struck, for the benefit of both local nobles and these urban-based lairds.

The 'merchant lairds' who controlled Aberdeen for most of the two centuries after c. 1450 were more lairdly than merchandising. Their successors, in the seventeenth century, were not necessarily drawn so overtly from the landed classes. John Cheyne, provost in 1623–4, for example, was a lawyer. But the close-knit patriarchy remained although its composition was subtly changing. Which represents the age better: the fact that Alexander Jaffray, grandson of a baker, was appointed provost in 1636 or the acerbic reminder made to him of his humble origins when he took office – a bacon pie pointedly left on the provost's chair? Aping the gentry remained the best way to succeed in burgh life: Jaffray would also became a wealthy rural landowner, with an extensive estate at Kingswells.[69]

Professionals in Aberdeen before 1800

One of the major features of the larger Scottish burghs was their more complex socio-economic profile, and a significant factor in this was the presence of professionals, or individuals following careers that would nowadays be regarded as professional. In the period before 1800, members of four main groups came into this category: clergymen, teachers, lawyers and medics. All of these groups originated in the medieval church. Clergymen, of course, were present from the burgh's earliest days, and by the close of the Middle Ages a small number of teachers, notaries and medics were also active in the town.[70] Once three of the four groups had been secularised, and the fourth had been changed radically by the Reformation, professionals became an even more significant group in Aberdeen society. Of course, as in most burghs, government remained largely in the hands of merchants, in name if not always in practice. By contrast, although several professionals came to play a role in political and governmental affairs in Aberdeen, most were primarily important because of the services which they provided. They were vital, too, to the progress and development of the town's intellectual environment. The Edinburgh *literati* may have dominated the Enlightenment, but there was enlightenment in Aberdeen also, and this was influenced by the presence of the professionals in the two university towns.[71]

Numbers of professionals

Reliable information regarding the number of professionals is difficult to acquire in the pre-census period, but Aberdeen is blessed with better sources than many places and a number of taxation rolls have survived, yielding occupational information. The detailed and comprehensive biographical list of members of the Society of Advocates provides further evidence of the legal establishment at least.[72] Data regarding lawyers and other professionals, drawn from a series of local taxation rolls dating from the seventeenth and eighteenth centuries, is indicated in Figure 8.1.

These figures, however tentative and incomplete, reveal that the numbers of professionals remained relatively static until the middle of the eighteenth century, after which numbers grew, particularly in the legal community. The high number recorded in the education category in 1696 reflects a number of teachers, mostly single individuals running small local schools, who were not represented on the taxation rolls (see Chapter 14).[73] It is debatable whether they should be included as professionals, but their work was of a professional nature, however humble the level at which they operated. As indicated in Figure 8.2, the general trends indicated in Figure 8.1 are mirrored by data from the Burgess Registers for the period. The steady increase in professional occupations is confirmed in all areas, but particularly

Date	Church	Law	Education	Medicine	Surgery	Other	Total
1604	1	9	1	1	–	–	12
1639	–	14	–	2	7	–	23
1655	–	12	3	2	4	–	21
1696	7	16	15	4	7	1	50
1712	1	10	5	3	2	–	21
1727	3	14	4	4	14	–	39
1759	7	26	17	8	15	2	75
1795	13	45	22	22	15	13	130

Source: ACA, Stent Roll Bundles (1604); Press 18/Bundle 12, Band of Relief, 1639; Press 18/Bundle 59, Suit Roll, 1727, List of men aged over sixteen, 1759; Police Commissioners' Rent Roll, 1795.

Note: Education figures include those teaching in universities and schools; surgery figures include surgeons, barbers, barber/wigmakers and apothecaries.

Figure 8.1 Professionals listed in Aberdeen taxation rolls, 1600-1800.

Date	Church	Law	Education	Medicine	Surgery	Other	Total
1450–99	–	–	–	2	1	–	3
1500–99	–	5	2	3	2	–	12
1600–99	14	69	21	24	31	–	159
1700–99	18	72	17	19	52	11	189

Source: Abdn Burgs, 1–161; ACA, MS Register of Burgesses, 1700–1800.

Note: An attempt has been made to exclude admissions of burgesses not likely to have been resident in the burgh, such as group awards to military companies and other dignitaries.

Figure 8.2 Burgess admissions of professionals in Aberdeen, 1450-1800.

in the categories of law and surgery. Growing occupational specialisation is also evident in the variety of 'other' designations, which included five architects, two musicians, an organist, two surveyors and a 'history painter'. The cultural aspirations of at least some Aberdonians are reflected in the presence of at least two dancing masters, noted in the manuscript Burgess Register as *chorodidasculi*. The large numbers of burgesses in the surgery category after 1700 may be explained by the requirement that surgeons and barbers become burgesses and by the obligation that they obtain permission to practise from the town council.

It is clear, then, that Aberdeen contained a significant number of professionals. They were not numerous enough to affect the merchant dominance of the burgh, but their presence reflects the more complex socio-economic composition of the burgh and hints at the influence of these professionals in the surrounding area, as well as in the town itself.[74] Surgeons in the period are not normally classified as professionals by historians or sociologists but, despite their craft status, and particularly in Aberdeen where physicians were much less regulated than in many places, they were in some senses rather more professional than their medical colleagues. The legal and medical professions are considered in detail here; the church and education are dealt with fully in other chapters (see Chapters 13, 14, 15 and 16).

The legal profession

By the sixteenth century, Edinburgh had become the heart of the Scottish legal system and the location of the central law courts. However, the late development of Scotland's central courts of justice, and the importance before the Reformation of canon law (specialists in which tended to be based in diocesan centres) meant that Aberdeen was an established centre of legal expertise from the Middle Ages. The cathedral library in Old Aberdeen was well stocked with tomes of canon law and several members of the cathedral clergy were trained in the discipline (see Chapter 17). By at least the early sixteenth century, the bishop also exercised a supervisory role over notaries who performed legal services for clients throughout the diocese: in 1540 he summoned local notaries to renew their authorisation to practise.[75] It was probably not long afterwards that the Society of Advocates was established, its membership embracing most branches of the legal profession, including advocates, writers, notaries, procurators, sheriff clerks and commissary agents.

The Society's membership list demonstrates broadly the extent of recruitment to the legal profession. In the sixteenth century there were fifty-one members,

Illustration 17
Detail from notarial instrument by Thomas Mollisone, town clerk from c. 1589 to his death in 1622, showing his manual.

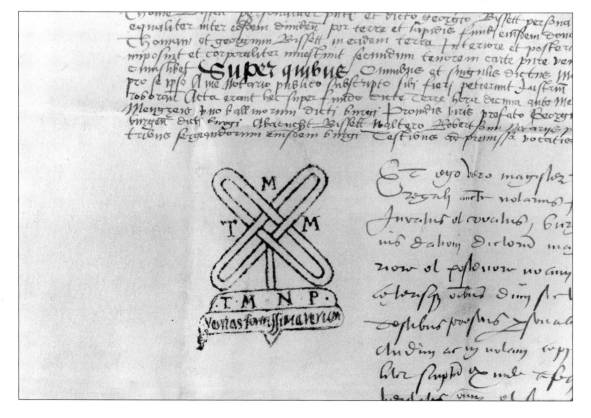

rising to sixty-one in the seventeenth century and 108 in the eighteenth century. This confirms the major expansion in the size of the legal profession during the eighteenth century, suggested by Figures 8.1 and 8.2. As demonstrated in both tables, lawyers had come to form the largest group of taxed and burgess professionals, in the latter case despite the requirement that surgeons obtain burgess status. Numerical growth was paralleled by an increase, for some at least, in political power. The notary Thomas Mollisone, for instance, acted as town clerk from *c.*1589 until his death in 1622 (Ill. 17), while several members of the Society of Advocates served as burgh magistrates and provosts. John Cheyne, who became a member of the Society in 1576, was elected as provost in 1593-4, and in the same year he was also nominated a burgh commissioner to parliament.[76] James Scougal had an even more varied career, serving as civilist and rector of King's College during the 1680s, as well as provost of Old Aberdeen from 1680 to 1689, before being appointed as a Senator of the College of Justice in 1696.[77]

It is clear from perusal of the *curricula vitae* of the Society's members that their influence in wider society was significant, and grew over the centuries. Of the fifty-one individuals who joined the Society in the sixteenth century, sixteen held a range of public offices, including magistrate, clerk to the town council, sheriff clerk, commissary, procurator fiscal and burgh agent. During the seventeenth century, of the sixty-one new admissions to the Society, twenty-seven held a range of similar offices, while the eighteenth century saw sixty-nine out of 108 new members taking on an increasing variety of posts. By this time, in addition to the range of sheriffs, commissaries and academics, the list included a number of directors of the Aberdeen Banking Company and other business initiatives, and a number who were listed as being 'substantial property owners'. Typical of the top echelons of the eighteenth-century legal professional was Duncan Davidson. He was admitted to the Society in 1794, and his responsibilities included joint procurator fiscal of Aberdeen, clerk to Robert Gordon's Hospital, director of the Aberdeen Banking Company and the Aberdeen Savings' Bank, fiars juror, JP for Aberdeenshire, dean of the Faculty of Marischal College, and lieutenant of the Aberdeen Volunteers. He also served as both treasurer and president of the Society, which by then had secured storage space in a loft of the West Kirk (Ill. 18).[78] As well as catering for the routine legal needs of the people of Aberdeen and the surrounding area, lawyers were able to exercise both direct and indirect influence in many aspects of society and, increasingly, in the economy. Judicious marriages to the daughters of landed gentry meant that, by the turn of the nineteenth century, the legal profession was firmly established as part of Aberdeen's social élite.

A number of legal practitioners also held university appointments and, although some of these may have been sinecures, legal links with the academic community were strong. As with many institutions of the time, Aberdeen's two university

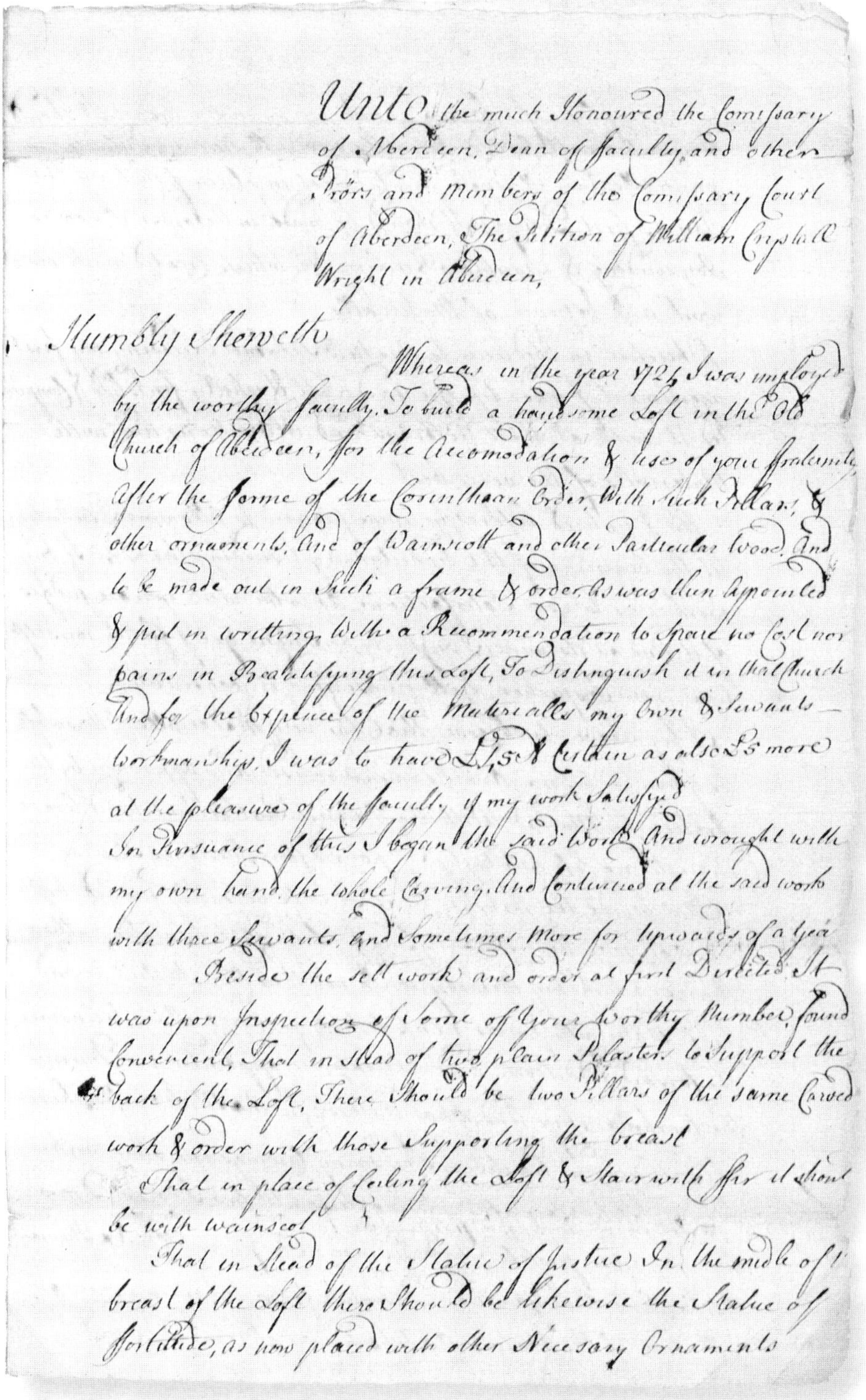

Unto the much Honoured the Comissary of Aberdeen, Dean of faculty, and other Priors and Members of the Comissary Court of Aberdeen, The Petition of William Crystall Wright in Aberdeen,

Humbly Sheweth

Whereas in the year 1724 I was imployed by the worthy faculty, To build a handsome Loft in the Old Church of Aberdeen, for the Accomodation & uses of your fraternity After the forme of the Corinthean Order, With such Pillars, & other ornaments, And of Wainscott and other Particular Wood, And to be made out in Such a frame & order, As was then appointed & put in writting, With a Recommendation to Spare no Cost nor pains in Beautifying this Loft, To Distinguish it in that Church And for the Expence of the Materialls my own & Servants workmanship, I was to have £15 Sterline as also £5 more at the pleasure of the faculty, if my work Satisfyd

In Persuance of this I began the said Work And wrought with my own hand the whole Carving, And Continued at the said work with three Servants, and Sometimes More for upwards of a year

Beside the sett work and order at first Directed It was upon Inspection of Some of your worthy Number found Convenient, That in Stead of two plain Pilasters to Support the back of the Loft, There Should be two Pillars of the same Carved work & order with those Supporting the breast

That in place of Ceiling the Loft & Stair with fir it should be with wainscot

That in Stead of the Statue of Justice In the midle of the breast of the Loft there Should be likewise the Statue of Fortitude, as now placed with other Necessary Ornaments

*Illustration 18
Letter of William
Crystall, requesting
payment for
building work
conducted on behalf
of the Society of
Advocates.*

colleges were influenced heavily by dynastic factors. Prominent academic families included the Gordons, who were also well represented in the legal profession. John Gordon of Seaton, commissary clerk, gained the chair of civil law at King's in 1696, and found himself surrounded by other academic Gordons.[79] Similar links between the Society of Advocates and the colleges extended the networks of both family and profession. Acquisition and retention of posts was, of course, closely linked to local and national politics, especially during sensitive or potentially problematic periods, such as the purges which followed the Reformation of 1560 and the Restoration of 1660 and the lengthy Jacobite threat in the late seventeenth and eighteenth centuries (see Chapter 15).

The medical profession

As with practitioners in most professional groups, physicians and surgeons found their early origins in the medieval church. Priests offered medical care as well as hospitality to travellers, and there were establishments in Aberdeen to care for the resident poor. Once medicine became secularised from around the twelfth century, treatment passed from the hands of the religious to physicians trained at universities and surgeons who undertook local apprenticeships, though, of course, lay practice of all sorts continued. One of the earliest offices created in King's College was the post of mediciner, but Aberdeen was nonetheless slow to contribute to the professionalisation of medicine. Indeed, the Aberdeen M.D. degree was regarded by many with disdain until well into the nineteenth century, since it could be obtained on the basis of little medical training or demonstration of knowledge. The town's surgeons and barbers appear not to have had any lasting formal organisation either, at least from the middle of the seventeenth century. Nevertheless, a number of individuals, if not organisations, were influential in the progress and delivery of medicine in Aberdeen. Friction between the two university colleges meant that a reputable medical school did not come fully into being until the nineteenth century, though an agreement between the two colleges in 1818 may be taken as the first step towards that end.[80]

Because medicine was a field in which lay and professional alike could practise almost unchecked, it was more difficult for qualified practitioners to gain the sort of exclusivity that was enjoyed by members of the legal profession. Patients exercised their rights to consult all sorts of practitioner, and this diluted the dominance of those who considered themselves to be the legitimate practitioners. This was not helped by the poor state of medical training in Scotland before 1726, and in Aberdeen for much longer thereafter.[81] The first medical practitioner to appear on the Aberdeen Burgess Roll was Mr Walter Prendergest, admitted in 1444 as *medicus, ex gratia*. He was followed a few years later by Archibald Tulach, 'leiche'.

Later burgess admissions included Mathew McKaill, 'professor of medicine',[82] in 1717, and William Chalmers in 1771.[83] Nevertheless, it is clear from Figures 8.1 and 8.2 that physicians were few in number before the eighteenth century.[84] The post of mediciner at King's College (the first such post in Britain) was, in the early centuries, occupied by individuals who mostly regarded the post as a sinecure and did little in the way of medical teaching. They included James Cumyne, appointed in 1522, at a fee paid by the burgh of ten merks yearly and half of the fishings at the fords of Dee, in return for which he treated the sick of the burgh, in addition to attending to his university duties.[85] The most notable early holder of the post, and the first to make a contribution to academic medicine, was Gilbert Skene, appointed in 1556, who is credited with the first medical publication in Scots, a treatise on the plague entitled *Ane Breve Description of the Pest*, published two years later (see Chapter 3). He was also a regent in arts, indicating that medical teaching was part of the general education programme and not geared particularly to the practice of medicine.[86] Skene managed to survive the university purge of 1569, probably because his subject was not deemed politically contentious, though a re-grant of his office in 1571 suggests that he had not been fully operational for some time.[87] The post of mediciner subsequently lapsed, but was reinstated by James VI in 1619, the first new appointee being Patrick Dun, who was already regent at Marischal College when appointed to King's.[88] Dun resigned the medicinership in 1632, but was evidently still involved in anatomical teaching, as he petitioned the privy council in 1636 for 'two bodies of men, being notable malifactors', for the purposes of dissection.[89]

In the first half of the eighteenth century the post of mediciner was dominated by members of the Gregory family, a medical dynasty comparable with the Monro family in Edinburgh (see Chapter 16). James, son of James Gregory, professor of mathematics in St Andrews and Edinburgh, gained the King's College post of mediciner in 1725, and was succeeded in 1732 by his son of the same name, the latter followed by his brother John in 1755. John had studied medicine at Leiden, the most popular destination of Scottish medical students in the years before 1726, and eventually gained a chair of medicine in Edinburgh in 1766.[90] Nevertheless, the prominence which the Gregorys bestowed on medical teaching proved brief. Following the Gregory era, the mediciner's post once again carried relatively little status. Progress in medical teaching required more regular and organised teaching, within a medical school, and even the foundation of a chair of medicine at Marischal College in 1700 did little to enhance medical studies in Aberdeen. Attempts to foster greater collaboration between the two Aberdeen colleges in the eighteenth century failed, and the colleges tried to develop their own medical schools. By this time, Marischal College was better placed than King's to develop the subject, particularly after the foundation of the near-by Infirmary in 1740.[91]

The main catalyst of progress, however, came not from the professionals themselves, but from their students. The Aberdeen Medical Society, founded in 1798,
became an influential body, and by the early years of the nineteenth century it
was organising formal classes on medical subjects under the patronage of a number
of incumbent professors.[92] This gradually brought about a degree of co-operation
between the colleges, though a union of the colleges did not take place until 1860,
and only thereafter did medical education and training flourish in Aberdeen.[93]

Until more co-ordinated medical education was achieved, it was left to individuals to influence medicine, among them Alexander Gordon, physician to the
Aberdeen Dispensary, who made a significant contribution to the knowledge of
puerperal fevers with his publication of *Treatise on the Epidemic Puerperal Fever of
Aberdeen* in 1795. This book outlined for the first time the contagious nature of the
disease.[94] It would take another half-century before the work of Semmelweiss
confirmed Gordon's theories, though had Gordon enjoyed the benefits of a stronger
medical establishment, or had he moved to Edinburgh, he may well have gained
a much greater reputation.

The other groups of medical practitioners – surgeons, barbers and apothecaries
– are not often considered as professional occupations, though some were apparently wealthy. In 1444, the wife of the barber Patrick White had lost a gold ring
worth 40s.[95] The activities of surgeons and apothecaries, in particular, were crucial
to the delivery of medical care in Aberdeen, and apprenticeship training may well
have equipped surgeons for their role much more appropriately than a university
degree. The surgeons and barbers did not constitute one of Aberdeen's seven
incorporated trades, but they did form a separate society, receiving a seal of cause
from the town council in 1537. Further confirmation of the privileges of barbers,
surgeons and periwigmakers came in 1647, but thereafter the group apparently
included only the barbers and wigmakers, the surgeons having no real formal
organisation.[96] In terms of numbers, the burgess registers reveal the admission of
seventeen surgeons, forty-one barbers, six barber/periwigmakers (designated in the
manuscript register *as tonsor et capulletarius*) and twenty apothecaries before 1800.
The discrepancy in the numbers of surgeons noted in Figures 8.1 and 8.2 may be
explained in part by economic factors, for some surgeons may have been exempt
from paying certain taxes. Gilbert Quhite appeared in the burgess register as a barber
in 1479, while in 1554 William Urquhart, surgeon, was admitted without charge,
'for his gratuitous service made to the town'. It may well be that a number of the
barbers listed were in fact surgeons, and it may also be that a number of those
designated barbers were actually barber-surgeons, rather than barber/wigmakers.[97]
Apothecaries were even more shadowy than their colleagues. They had no organisation and little evidence survives regarding their training or activities, although
their dispensing services were probably important to the overall function of the

medical profession. A hint that they were not numerous comes from the award of burgess status to Hew McGie in 1649 'in respect of the few numbers of his trade within this burgh'.

The professionals in Aberdeen before 1800 were, with the exception of the lawyers, poorly organised. Their influence stemmed from talented individuals rather than strong corporations. The legal profession alone possessed a long-standing professional body, and individual lawyers were able to function in many other areas of society, and particularly in its policing and economy. Medical men, by contrast, were sometimes influential individually, but their corporate organisation and professional progress were hampered considerably by the ongoing friction between the Aberdeen colleges and duplication of academic posts and services. The surgeons and barbers did what surgeons and barbers did everywhere. They formed no enduring organisation, and were controlled by the town council which granted individuals permission to practise. Yet, it is clear that professionals, in combination with churchmen and the university professoriate, were a significant factor in the profile of the socio-economic élite of a burgh which was not a simple merchants' town, but a complex and important centre for the whole of the north-east of Scotland.

Part III

POLITICS AND POWER

9

The Burgh and the Realm: Medieval Politics, c. 1100-1500

STEPHEN BOARDMAN

What role did the burgh of Aberdeen play in the political history of the Scottish kingdom in the medieval period? One problem in producing a coherent answer to this question is the lack of any significant contemporary chronicle that was centred on the burgh and its hinterland. The surviving Scottish chronicles of the late medieval period were almost all maintained and compiled in religious houses in Fife, and they tended to concentrate on the affairs of the diocese of St Andrews, embracing Fife and Lothian.[1] Hector Boece's early sixteenth-century *Historia* and his *Lives of the Bishops of Aberdeen and Mortlach* are the first narratives that contain more than bare and fragmentary descriptions of the events and affairs of the north-east.[2] In Boece's case, moreover, local knowledge has to be set against his distance in time from the events he described. At best, his works serve as witness to the way in which the history of medieval Aberdeen was understood and interpreted early in the sixteenth century. Boece, and the later popular accounts which he inspired, tended to stress the loyalty of the burgh and its inhabitants to the Scottish crown and their positive contribution to the great events and personalities that were held to have shaped the kingdom's history. The notion of the burgh and its hinterland as a bastion of 'conservative' social and political values has been reinforced by some later academic studies too. In the 1970s, it was suggested that the key feature of the political culture of Aberdeen and the north-east in the sixteenth and seventeenth centuries was the conservatism manifest in both religious affiliation and loyalty to the crown.[3] The same study discerned medieval roots and evidence for 'northern conservatism' in the continued support shown by Aberdeenshire lords for the inept and unpopular James III (1460-88) long after others had abandoned him. The notion of steadfast north-eastern loyalty to the king and kingdom has been pushed back to even earlier periods. The burgh of Aberdeen's critical role in maintaining the Bruce cause in the dynastic and civil conflicts now known as the Wars of Independence has been heavily emphasised. Similarly, the great battle of 'Red Harlaw' in 1411 has been seen as a conflict fought to protect not only the burgh, but also the political and territorial integrity of the late medieval kingdom, from the 'wild' host of Donald of the Isles.

While not deliberately avoiding discussion of spectacular and well-known historical incidents, this chapter seeks to outline the more mundane ways in which the burgh fitted into the political and governmental structures of the kingdom in the medieval period. What follows is a survey outlining certain key characteristics of the burgh's role in the governance of the realm, with a few episodes examined in more detail. The emphasis on events and developments in the fifteenth century reflects the greater volume and diversity of sources generated during this period by the increasing activity of burghal and royal government.

The burgh and the crown to 1329

Aberdeen was one of the major economic and administrative centres of late medieval Scotland. Between the thirteenth and fifteenth centuries, a royal mint occasionally produced coinage (Plate 15) and some exchequer audits, during which the crown's financial officers presented their accounts, were held in the town.[4] Except in unusual circumstances, however, Aberdeen was never significant as a royal residence or as a location for assemblies of the kingdom's political elites.[5] The pattern of royal progresses varied from reign to reign, depending on the personal inclinations and circumstances of individual monarchs, but direct and sustained royal lordship, in the shape of a monarch resident for prolonged periods in the vicinity of the burgh and its hinterland, was relatively rare. Despite this, Aberdeen did feature as a regular stop on the itineraries of almost all medieval kings from the reign of David I (1124-53).[6] These occasional visits fulfilled a number of functions. At a general level, they meant that, for a while, the burden of supporting the royal household was borne by a burgh and region that otherwise was not greatly inconvenienced by the direct demands of the royal court.[7] Particularly contentious or disruptive political issues affecting the locality might also demand the personal presence of the king to exercise direct royal lordship.[8] Most importantly, however, Aberdeen lay on the edge of a huge and complex administrative, political and economic hinterland that stretched far into the upland zones lying to the west and north of the burgh (see Chapter 6). In this sense, it was a natural centre through which the crown attempted to govern much of northern Scotland. In the fourteenth and fifteenth centuries, royal visits to Aberdeen were often described in terms of the king or his representatives arranging for the business of the 'northern parts' of the realm.[9] The burgh and its inhabitants, meanwhile, formed political and social relationships with the magnates who operated in, and dominated, this extensive hinterland - most notably with a succession of great regional overlords who acted as royal representatives in an area that extended from Aberdeen deep into the central Highlands and sometimes beyond (see Chapter 8). One common feature of these magnates was their involvement with the affairs of Gaelic Scotland. And for the chronicler Jean Froissart, visiting Aberdeen in the company of David II (1329-71) in 1365, one of the striking aspects of the burgh was that it lay on the frontier of 'la sauvage ecosse'; 'a city which lies on the sea and is at the entrance to wild Scotland'.[10]

The identification of Aberdeen as a 'frontier' burgh and as an important staging post for the projection of royal power into areas where the king's authority was far from secure was probably established long before the fourteenth century. In the thirteenth century, the inhabitants of the province of Moray were demonised in Scottish chronicles as persistent and pernicious rebels against the rule of kings Alexander II (1214-49) and Alexander III (1249-86). On one of the few occasions that Alexander III is known to have visited Aberdeen, his presence was explicitly explained by the fact that he was on his way to deal with the affairs of Moray.[11] A sense of the 'natural' Highland hinterland of the burgh, and at the same time the social and cultural 'otherness' of that hinterland, surfaced more than two centuries later in the 1495 foundation charter of Aberdeen University. The charter claimed that, amongst other goals, the new institution was designed to civilise the inhabitants of the north and west of the kingdom (see Chapters 15 and 17).[12] The laudable pedagogical aims of the bishops of Aberdeen were echoed in geographical scope, if not necessarily sentiment and approach, by the ambitions of the contemporary Gordon earls of Huntly. The dominant force in north-eastern politics in the 1490s, the Gordon earls were also the crown's principal lieutenants in the north and the chief prosecutors of the forfeiture of the MacDonald lordship of the Isles after 1492.

Something resembling a coherent political narrative of the burgh and its relationship to surrounding aristocratic interests can begin to be constructed only from around the end of the thirteenth century. At this point, the lordships around Aberdeen were dominated by the Comyn earls of Buchan and their kinsmen, the lords of Badenoch and Lochaber.[13] The Comyn hegemony in the region, however, was effectively destroyed in the aftermath of Robert Bruce's seizure of the Scottish throne in 1306. Robert I (1306-29) pursued his struggle against the Comyns and their supporters, who had been allied to Bruce's dynastic rival John Balliol (1292-6), with a ruthless efficiency.[14] The defeat of the Comyn earl of Buchan by Robert and his followers at Inverurie on 22 May 1308 opened the way for the systematic harrying or 'herschip' of the earldom of Buchan. The immediate destruction of the earldom's agricultural wealth was followed by a more permanent dismemberment of Buchan as a unified territorial lordship, as parcels of territory were granted out to Robert's supporters.[15] Meanwhile, the victory at Inverurie allowed Robert to besiege, capture and then destroy the royal castle at Aberdeen.[16] In the sixteenth century, Hector Boece suggested that the burgesses of Aberdeen had played a decisive role both in Robert's triumph at Inverurie and the assault on the English garrison holding Aberdeen Castle.[17] Later tales elaborated on the account, adding picturesque details, such as Robert's permission for the burgh to use the royal tressure in the burghal coat of arms as a reward for the loyalty of its inhabitants in 1308 (Plate 23). Similarly, the origin of the burgh motto was also traced to the events of 1308, with the phrase 'Bon Accord' claimed as the secret password used by the urban community, as it co-ordinated the assault on the English garrison. In fact, the burghal motto and the double tressure, which was usually reserved for noble families descended from daughters of the royal house, do not appear on the burgh's arms until sometime after 22 October 1408. Indeed, the production of new seal matrices for the town in 1430 may well mark the point at which they were first introduced.[18] Their authorisation was presumably inspired by some signal service performed by the town's inhabitants. If the royal concession was made just before the new matrices were produced, then it might relate to James I's military campaigns against the lordship of the Isles in 1429, in which Aberdeen burgesses, such as Thomas Chalmers, were active.[19] If, however, the grant was of an earlier date, then the widely advertised sacrifice of the Aberdeen townsmen at Harlaw might have been what motivated the change. Whatever the case, there are no other examples from the medieval period of such a grant to a corporate body.[20]

There is, however, some substance to the subsequent notion that Aberdeen received lands and privileges as a reward for supporting the hero king. In at least two cases, lands or annuities granted by Robert I in the aftermath of victory became the subject of legal disputes or challenge in the late medieval period. John Bellenden, one of Boece's vernacular translators and adaptors, reported that on the day of Bannockburn in 1314 St Magnus of Orkney had appeared as a knight in shining armour to the inhabitants of Aberdeen, informing them of the Scottish victory. Bellenden linked the saint's appearance with a gift of five pounds from the customs of Aberdeen for bread, wine and wax, donated by Robert I to the cathedral church of St Magnus in Kirkwall.[21] A five-pound annuity to the bishop of Orkney payable from the customs of Aberdeen had, indeed, been established during Robert's reign. However, in the reign of Robert III (1390-1406), the annuity appears to have been revoked and diverted to the monastery of Scone. The bishop of Orkney was eventually reinstated as the beneficiary of the annuity during the governorship of Robert, duke of Albany (1406-20).[22] It may be that the story outlining the origins of the grant was, at least partly, designed to give the bishop's threatened annuity a moral-historical justification that took it beyond the struggle over legal right. Similarly, the much celebrated grant of the forest of Stocket to the burgh by Robert I (Ill. 19) required to be defended in the 1490s, when the minority regime of James IV (1488-1513) granted various rights in and around the burgh to the

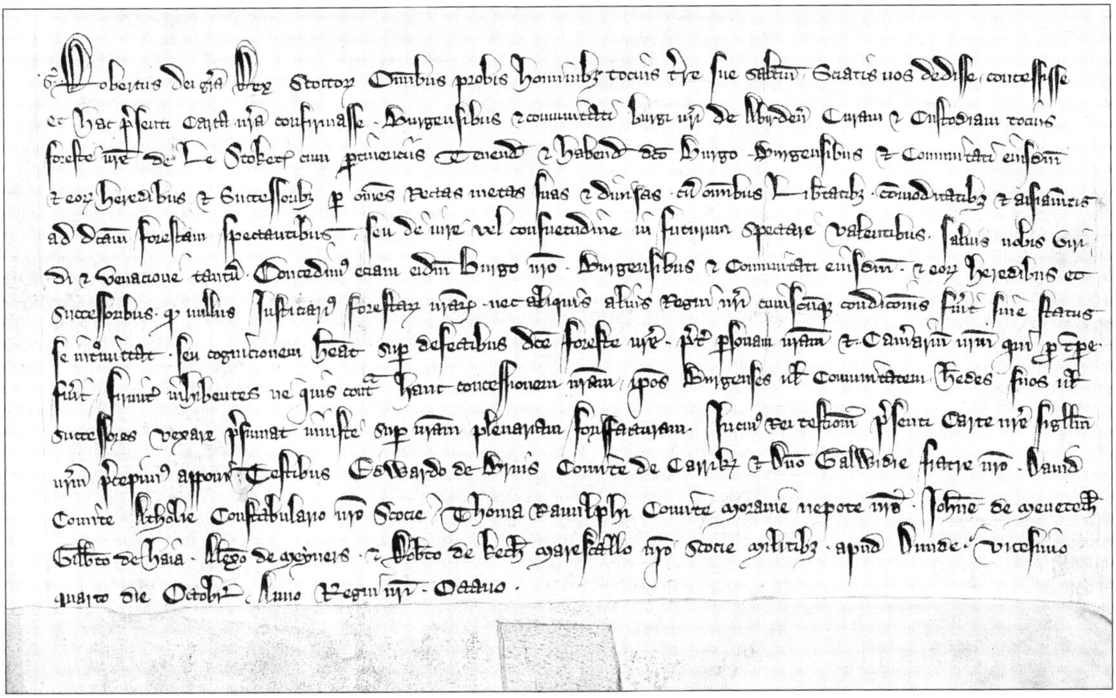

*Illustration 19
Charter of Robert I
(24 October 1313),
granting the burgh
custody of the forest
of Stocket.*

redoubtable sea captain, Andrew Wood. In 1494, the burgh representatives clearly made great play of the fact that the original grant had been 'maid to the said toune be King Robert Broiss, of maist nobell mynde'.[23]

Nevertheless, the town's subsequent protestations of loyalty to the Bruce regime should not be taken at face value. Initially at least, the sudden Bruce ascendancy established in 1308 was probably regarded with fear and suspicion by many in Aberdeen. Like most other regions of Scotland, the inhabitants of the burgh seem to have been thoroughly divided in terms of their allegiance to the Bruce and Balliol causes. Several prominent local figures - such as Bishop Henry Cheyne of Aberdeen, whose family estates in Buchan may well have been put to the flames in 1308 - were hardly likely to welcome Robert's kingship. Cheyne spent much of the remainder of the reign in exile before securing a belated reconciliation with the Bruce regime.[24] Similarly, the king's own nephew, Donald, earl of Mar, spent most of the decade after 1306 in the service of the English king Edward II (1307-27).[25] Even the loyalty of some of those who remained and exercised power in the north-east is likely to have been equivocal. Sir Walter de Berclay, sheriff of Aberdeen, was amongst those implicated in the Soules conspiracy of 1320 to assassinate Robert I.[26]

Despite justifiable caution about the burgh's sixteenth century self-image as a bastion of precocious 'patriotic' sentiment, there is little doubt that strategic factors gave Aberdeen a highly significant role in the Anglo-Scottish conflicts that dominated the first half of the fourteenth century. The town played a critical role in the maintenance of the Bruce dynasty's war effort in the reigns of Robert I and David II, acting as the main port through which Flemish and French supplies and manpower reached Scotland.[27] It was no doubt this function that encouraged both Bruce kings to grant a series of economic and jurisdictional concessions to the burgh, including Robert I's much lauded grant of the forest of Stocket (Ill.19). Although Aberdeen was one of the few major urban centres that remained in the relatively uncontested control of the Bruce partisans, this did not render the town immune from attack. On at least two occasions, it seems to have been put to the flames by English forces. The burgh was apparently burnt in the summer of 1326, although whether by accident or hostile action remains unclear.[28] In the summer of 1336, Aberdeen was subject to a much better recorded assault personally led by the English king Edward III (1327-77), who 'levelled the town of Aberdeen to the ground'.[29] It was probably fearful anticipation of events such as this which had prompted some of the town's inhabitants to bury their wealth for safe-keeping (Plate 16).

New patterns of regional lordship, 1329-1435

In many ways, the direct effects of Anglo-Scottish warfare were less significant for Aberdeen's long-term interests than the changes in local power structures brought about by the eclipse of the Comyns and their allies. The dislocation of the early fourteenth century, and the effective disappearance of many of the families that had dominated the region prior to 1306, had the effect of freeing the town's extensive hinterland from the political control of magnates based in the north-eastern lowlands.[30] No new regional overlord emerged from the wreck of the shattered earldom of Buchan, although by the end of the fifteenth century two of the families brought into the earldom by Bruce - the Keiths and the Hays - had attained comital status as Earls Marischal and Erroll respectively.[31] Meanwhile, the other great regional lordship adjacent to Aberdeen - the earldom of Mar - was weakened firstly by periods of comital exile in England, and then by a series of failures in the male line of the various families which held the title in the second half of the fourteenth century. In 1377, on the death of the childless Thomas, earl of Mar, the earldom passed into the hands of the late earl's brother-in-law, William, earl of Douglas, a magnate whose main interest was in the affairs of southern Scotland.[32] William's son and successor James, second earl of Douglas and Mar, was killed at the battle of Otterburn in August 1388, and Mar then came into the possession of Sir Malcolm Drummond, the husband of James' sister and heir, Isabella. Drummond maintained links with a number of prominent Aberdeen burgesses, most notably the future provost, Robert Davidson, his 'procurator'.[33] Nevertheless, Drummond was hardly an imposing figure, and his attempts to build a local lordship in the north-east were in any case curtailed by his early death (again childless) in 1402.[34] In the absence of leadership based in the north-east, the power vacuum in the central Highlands was filled by a number of families that extended their authority from other regions.

From their Hebridean heartland, the Clan Donald lords of the Isles acquired control of Lochaber and steadily advanced their interests through the Great Glen to the area around Inverness. In the last decade of the fourteenth century, Donald, lord of the Isles, concluded a marriage with Mary Leslie, sister of the earl of Ross, which eventually gave Donald and his successors a strong claim to the vast Ross inheritance.[35] A less spectacular, but nevertheless significant, development centred on the Angus lowlands, where the Lindsay lords of Glen Esk emerged as the dominant political, social and military force during the fourteenth century. By the 1390s, David Lindsay was clearly an active figure in the governance of the central Highlands and his elevation to the title earl of Crawford in 1398 reflected and confirmed the family's new status as a regional power.[36]

For Aberdeen, however, the most important developments of the fourteenth century centred on the growth of Stewart power in the Highlands. Under the guiding hand of Robert the Steward – the nephew, heir and chief political rival of David II, whom he succeeded, as Robert II (1371–90), in 1371 – the Stewarts acquired a formidable collection of Highland or semi-Highland earldoms and lordships.[37] By the time of Robert II's accession to the throne, Robert and his sons controlled the earldoms of Strathearn, Atholl and Menteith and the former Comyn lordship of Badenoch, the last held by the new king's son Alexander, also known to history as the 'Wolf of Badenoch'. After 1371 Alexander became the chief representative of royal authority in the north of Scotland, acting as lieutenant for a huge area stretching from the earldom of Atholl to the Pentland Firth.[38] His marriage, in 1382, to the widowed Euphemia, countess of Ross, also brought Alexander effective control over the earldom of Ross and a number of associated lordships around the Black Isle and Inverness. Alexander's lordship, however, did not represent a return to the type of integrated regional power that embraced both the central Highlands and the north-eastern lowlands. The earldom of Mar remained in the hands of men indifferent, or openly hostile, to the king's lieutenant, while his relationship with major ecclesiastical figures such as the bishops of Aberdeen and Moray was spectacularly bad. Eventually, Alexander's many enemies were given political leadership by his elder brother, Robert, earl of Fife and Menteith (and later duke of Albany). They managed to revoke his lieutenancy (in 1388–9) and to wreck his control of Ross by engineering his divorce from Countess Euphemia.[39] Alexander's infamous assaults on the burghs of Forres and Elgin and his burning of Elgin

Cathedral in the summer of 1390 were clearly the desperate acts of a man whose political career was in free fall. Stripped of their royal offices and driven back into their central Highland strongholds, the Badenoch Stewarts appeared to be a spent force in the 1390s.

The fortunes of Alexander and his family were transformed by the death of Malcolm Drummond, lord of Mar, in 1402. Drummond's marriage to the countess of Mar, Isabella Douglas, had produced no children and the nearest heir to the aged Isabella was Sir Thomas Erskine, the descendant of a marriage made by a daughter of the old comital line earlier in the fourteenth century. The Erskine claim had the support of Albany and Crawford, but it was swept aside by the sudden seizure of Countess Isabella and her subsequent forced marriage to Alexander Stewart, the eldest son of the lord of Badenoch.[40] A significant feature of the Stewart seizure of Mar in 1404 was the support he received from the lesser lords of Mar and at least some of the burgesses of Aberdeen, particularly William Chalmers, the custumar of the burgh, and his colleague, Drummond's erstwhile procurator, Robert David-son. Stewart's close relationship with Davidson blossomed as the two men launched lucrative piratical ventures, in a notable fusion of aristocratic military muscle and mercantile expertise which operated to their mutual advantage in the opening decade of the fifteenth century (Ill.20).[41] Chalmers, meanwhile, was instrumental in protecting the earl's ill-gotten gains, during negotiations with the aggrieved parties held at Bruges in 1416.[42] But Chalmers had other interests too. Like many Aberdeen burgesses, he had invested in land outwith the burgh (see Chapter 8), possessing estates at Findon, Methlick and Murtle, and other rural families from the north-east, in Mar and elsewhere, such as the Forbes and the Irvines of Drum, were also attracted into Stewart's service. This local support eventually persuaded Albany, Crawford, Erskine and their allies to accept Stewart's occupation of Mar for his lifetime. For the first time in almost a century, Mar was held by a man who could also wield considerable influence in the central Highland lordships lying to the west of the earldom. And for the next thirty years Alexander Stewart, earl of Mar, was the dominant lord in the north-east.

Mar's regional power had another increasingly important function for those exercising royal authority in the early fifteenth century. In 1406, the young heir to the Scottish throne, the future James I (1406–37), was captured at sea by English privateers and began an eighteen-year imprisonment in the custody of the English king. When, later that year, James's father, Robert III, died, effective control of the royal administration passed to the deceased king's brother, Robert, duke of Albany, who was appointed governor of the realm. Albany was already embroiled in an increasingly bitter dispute with Donald, lord of the Isles, over the earldom of Ross. After 1406, the governor came to rely more and more on Mar as his chief agent in the north. Earl Alexander became a royal lieutenant whose activities across the

*Illustration 20
Letter from the
bailies and council
of Aberdeen to their
counterparts in
Danzig/Gdansk (1
December 1410), in
which the former
deny accusations of
piracy made against
Aberdonians.*

north of Scotland were subsidised by the revenues of the burgh of Aberdeen.[43] Mar's role as the chief upholder of the governor's interests and policies against those of Donald of the Isles in and around Ross and Inverness underlies the famous confrontation between the forces of the Lordship of the Isles and an army under the command of Mar, at Harlaw in 1411.

The battle of Red Harlaw has entered traditional accounts as a defining moment of not just local, but national, significance. The armies involved have been presented as far more than simply the adherents of two powerful regional lords, but as emblematic of a deep-seated clash of cultures between Highland and Lowland Scotland.[44] It has long since been pointed out that, in reality, the cultural contrast between the forces involved can hardly have been this stark, given the extensive following that Stewart commanded from the Gaelic-speaking west of Mar, Badenoch and elsewhere.[45] Much, of course, depends on identifying what Donald of the Isles intended to do as his forces marched into Aberdeenshire. The most extreme view is that Donald, the grandson of Robert II, was engaged in an attempt to contest Albany's right to govern the kingdom, if only to justify the annexation of much of Scotland north of the Mounth to his own lordship.[46] Most are inclined to accept that Donald's aim was an assault on Aberdeen - the foremost urban symbol of Mar's lordship. This is possible, for the Clan Donald was certainly not averse to full scale attacks on royal burghs, as the inhabitants of Elgin found to their cost in 1402.[47] Yet, in this, Donald could hardly be distinguished from Alexander of Mar, the defender of Aberdeen in 1411, who may well have been involved in his father's burning of Forres and Elgin in the summer of 1390.[48]

The idea that Harlaw was a battle fought to save Aberdeen, and by implication much of the north-eastern lowlands, from the depredations of wild Hebrideans depends on the account provided in the 1440s by Abbot Walter Bower. According to Bower,

> In 1411, on the eve of St James the Apostle, there was a battle at Harlaw in Mar, when Donald of the Isles with 10,000 men from the Isles and his men of Ross entered the district, crushing and pillaging everything and reducing it to waste. His aim on that expedition was to sack the royal town of Aberdeen and then to subject to his authority the country down to the River Tay.[49]

Bower was notoriously hostile in his depiction of Gaelic Scotland, re-writing or amending several passages from his main source, John of Fordun's *Chronica Gentis Scotorum*, in order to show Gaelic society and its leaders in the worst possible light. He was also, given the tumultuous nature of the political situation in the 1440s, during the minority of James II (1437-60), exceptionally keen to highlight and condemn examples of flagrant magnate disorder and defiance of royal authority.[50] Even if the motivation behind Bower's narrative can be questioned, there is little doubt that the picture of Harlaw as a clash between a wildly destructive and alien Highland host and the representatives of royal authority was widely disseminated in the fifteenth century. In February 1478, the English man of letters, William Worcestre, received various brief snippets of information about the history, topography and saints of the Scottish kingdom from an anonymous Scot.[51] Worcestre collected an entertainingly garbled account of the battle of Harlaw - 'Bellum apud Herlawe in Scocia' - which misidentified the chief protagonists and placed Harlaw 'on the west of Scotland in Galloway'. Like Bower, the tale preserved by Worcestre saw the Highland force, a great army of caterans ('lez Keteryns'), as an overt danger. Curiously, the Aberdeen burgesses in Bower's own time seem to have forgotten that they were supposed to be engaged in a life and death struggle with the MacDonald lord of the Isles for the destiny of the kingdom. Writing to Donald's son, Alexander, earl of Ross and lord of the Isles, in April 1444, in an attempt to secure the release of English merchants taken into custody by Alexander's men in Inverness, the provost and burgh council provided an interesting, and no doubt exaggerated, summary of Alexander's career:

> For sen, loved be God, heddirtillie [until now] yhe hau al tyme obeit the king alsweil as ony lord of Scotland, and kepit ane hale part til him, for the quhilkis, God will, and yhe sal sone haue grete loving and reward; God forbid that yhe suld, for a litil monee that thir Inglismen has promissit yhou, warpiss your gude name, and the reward and thank yhe have deservide and wonnyn of the king.[52]

Even if the significance of Harlaw was exaggerated in the retelling, there is little doubt that the events of 1411 reinforced Mar's dominance of the region and his relationship with Aberdeen. Earl Alexander's principal burghal partner in crime and business, Robert Davidson, had perished under the axes of Donald's army at Harlaw, along with 'many burgesses' (Plate 17).[53] However, Mar's role as a royal lieutenant in the north for the Albany governors, his military leadership of the entire north-east, and his continuing career as a maritime adventurer ensured that his links with the burgh remained strong. In particular, a number of prominent Aberdeen burgesses appeared as witnesses to the earl's charters, including Gilbert Menzies, who served as provost of the burgh in the 1420s. Mar's official standing within the burgh was such that in 1412, the year after Harlaw, the burgh council passed a statute insisting that no burgess should 'have lord or lordship other than the king, the duke (of Albany) and the earl of Mar'.[54] And in a quite extraordinary appointment for an early fifteenth-century magnate, Mar was named as a member of the Aberdeen town council in in the same year.[55]

New lords and new rivalries, 1435–1500

Alexander continued to fulfil the role of regional overlord until his death in July 1435.[56] However, hopes of a smooth transition of lordship after Alexander's demise were dashed by the early death of his son and designated successor, Thomas. After Mar's death, James I annexed the earldom to the royal demesne under the terms of a royal confirmation of the lordship to Alexander in 1426.[57] In 1435, Mar thus became a royal lordship, a fact that was to have a profound influence on the way in which the regional politics of the north-east reflected and affected the affairs of the Stewart court for the remainder of the century. The assassination of James I in February 1437 left a young king, James II, on the throne and the earldom of Mar with no active overlord. The burgh once again had to deal with a situation in which competing magnate affinities fought for control of Mar and wider lordship in the north-east. Medieval politics were notoriously fluid, and alliances could often be redrawn with bewildering speed but, in the absence of a decisive royal intervention, two affinities contested the succession to Earl Alexander's role in the region: the Seton lords of Gordon and Strathbogie and the Lindsay earls of Crawford.

The spectacular rise of the lords of Gordon in the fifteenth century is a tale that undoubtedly deserves closer investigation. Despite the prolonged association of the Gordon earls with Aberdeen, in the early fifteenth century the family's main area of operation and interest lay further to the north and west. The Seton presence in the region, in fact, dated only to the reign of Robert III, when a younger son of the lord of Seton in East Lothian acquired the lordship of Strathbogie through marriage to the heiress of Sir John Gordon. Strathbogie was a lordship that occupied a strategic position on one of the main routes between the Moray coastal plain and Aberdeenshire.[58] Far distant from their Seton kinsmen, the lords of Strathbogie identified themselves more and more firmly with the family of the Gordon heiress who had brought them Strathbogie. Eventually, Alexander Seton's son, George, second earl of Huntly, dispensed with the surname Seton altogether, and reverted to his grandmother's name of Gordon.[59] In a sense, the Seton/Gordons, like the Stewarts of Badenoch/Mar before them, were a family that came to dominate Aberdeenshire after first establishing military power on the frontiers of the lowland north-east and in the testing grounds of the central Highlands. Throughout his career George, earl of Huntly, was most commonly attended by retainers drawn from Moray, rather than Aberdeenshire, and he chose to be buried, like Alexander Stewart, earl of Mar, in Inverness, rather than in Aberdeen.[60]

Ranged against the intrusion of Seton/Gordon influence into Mar and Aberdeenshire after 1437 were a variety of Mar families linked in various ways to the major regional power south of the Mounth, the earls of Crawford. Before the emergence of Alexander Stewart, earl of Mar, David Lindsay, first earl of Crawford, had been highly influential north of the Mounth. In fact, Lindsay's death in c. 1407 and the minority of his son Alexander may well have been critical factors in allowing Stewart to establish his wide-ranging lordship. At some point between 1392 and 1432, the earls of Crawford acquired the hereditary sheriffship of Aberdeenshire and they were regular visitors to the burgh in that capacity. From May 1432, Crawford's sheriff-depute was a powerful local lord, Alexander Forbes of that Ilk, who had also served as bailie of Mar for Alexander Stewart.[61] In terms of the succession to Mar after 1435, both Crawford and Forbes were supporters of Sir Robert Erskine, as the latter attempted to resurrect his family's long-dormant claim to the earldom.[62] Frustrated by James I's annexation of the earldom, Erskine's ambitions were rekindled by that king's death, and in 1438-9 Erskine received title to the various components of Mar and its associated lordship of Garioch through processes conducted by Forbes as sheriff-depute of Aberdeen.[63] The Aberdeen burgh council seems to have swung its support behind Robert Erskine's claims. In 1439, it bestowed the status of burgess on Erskine, styling him earl of Mar.[64]

Robert Erskine's ambitions in Mar were opposed by a powerful combination of men with local and national influence. In the years after 1437, these men portrayed themselves as upholding the royal interest in the earldom which had, after all, been explicitly claimed for the crown by James I in 1435. In 1436, the king had made plain his long-term interest in the lordship by visiting the earldom and beginning new construction work at Kildrummy.[65] Crucially, the last account rendered to the crown for Mar in 1438 confirmed that Kildrummy, the chief castle of the earldom, was being held by Alexander Seton of Gordon.[66] Despite Erskine receiving formal title in 1438-9, it was clear that Seton simply refused to surrender the castle to the new earl.[67] At the royal court Seton could rely on the support of his father-in-law, the Chancellor, William Crichton, who was particularly active in obstructing Erskine's attempts to have his title formally ratified.[68] Possession of Kildrummy was just one of the issues souring the relationship between Seton and the families supporting Erskine. The Seton family held claims to extensive estates in Aberdeenshire, most notably the baronies of Aboyne and Cluny, as the result of earlier marriages to heiresses. In these baronies, the Seton/Gordon titles seem to have been resisted by Erskine's principal supporter, Alexander Forbes.[69] In 1442, the stand-off between Erskine and his allies, on the one hand, and Seton and Chancellor Crichton on the other, developed into a rather more vigorous contest. It would seem that sometime during that year the would-be Erskine earl of Mar seized Kildrummy by force.[70] If Seton lost Kildrummy in 1442, he had by no means abandoned the struggle with his Aberdeenshire foes. In April 1443, David, third earl of Crawford, wrote to his beleaguered sheriff-depute, Alexander Forbes, telling him that the young king had been informed of the 'hereschip' made by Seton on Forbes and his allies.[71] In September or October of the following year, the Seton/Forbes dispute was temporarily resolved in a settlement concluded in Aberdeen. Alexander Seton confirmed Alexander Forbes' son and heir in various estates in Cluny and received James' bond of manrent in return.[72] Seton had vindicated his claim to lordship in Cluny and Aboyne, but the Forbes family had managed to secure title to the estates it possessed in the barony of Cluny. A similar dispute between Alexander Seton and the Keiths had also ended, shortly before August 1442, with Seton receiving 'letters of retinue' from Sir Robert Keith.[73]

In the absence of a full-scale analysis of the internal burgh politics, the affiliation of the Aberdeen townspeople to the various magnates contesting power in the north-east during James II's minority remains uncertain. Still, a majority of the political elite was perhaps wary of Huntly. His interest in the burgh's fishing rights prompted the town to decree in 1441 and again in 1447 that 'na gentilmen of the cuntreth sal haue watteres or takis of this toune'.[74] Indeed, the political turbulence of James II's minority, at both the local and national level, evidently persuaded the burgesses of Aberdeen that they required the formal protection of a powerful local magnate. At some point before 3 October 1440, Sir Alexander Irvine of Drum was appointed to the office of 'captain and governor' of the burgh.[75] Irvine was already heavily involved in burghal affairs and, as the son of the Alexander Irvine who had been killed at Harlaw in 1411, he had excellent credentials as a man committed to upholding the burgh's interests in times of crisis. There is no indication that the office of captain and governor was in any sense a permanent or continuous feature of burghal government. On the whole, burgh councils tended to be extremely wary of allowing non-burgesses to exercise authority over any aspect of the urban community. It seems that the role of captain, with its strong military connotations, was invoked only in times of notable political instability to provide muscular protection of the town and its interests. Irvine was re-appointed to his office in October 1441 but, although the sense of crisis had clearly not abated by September 1442 - when the council issued detailed regulations for the town's defence - Irvine's term of office was not renewed the following month.[76] In October 1445, in a *volte face*, Aberdeen's council declared that henceforth no lord should be chosen as captain of the burgh.[77]

Whatever the immediate reasons for the termination of the office of captain, there must be some doubt as to whether Irvine, even with the full backing of the burgh, had the power and prestige to protect urban interests against the new powers emerging in the north-east. In particular, Seton of Gordon, who was created earl of Huntly in 1445, was clearly outstripping his rivals in the region. By 1446, Huntly was also flexing his muscles south of the Mounth, in the heartland of David Lindsay, third earl of Crawford. Crawford had been associated, at a distance, with the coalition that had resisted Seton's claims in Kildrummy, Aboyne and Cluny. In January 1446, Huntly replied in kind, appearing in support of the Ogilvy family in a dispute with the Master of Crawford over the office of bailie of Arbroath Abbey. In the armed confrontation that followed, the so-called battle of Arbroath, Huntly and his allies were defeated, but Crawford suffered fatal injuries. Alexander, the new, fourth earl of Crawford - known as 'earl beardie' or the 'Tiger Earl' - followed up his victory by ruthlessly harrying those in Angus who had challenged his family's authority.[78] Nevertheless, the confrontation at Arbroath pointed towards the shifting balance of power in the north. Within six years, Huntly would be back in Angus leading an army against Crawford to much greater effect. In Aberdeen-shire, meanwhile, families such as the Forbes had little choice but to accept Huntly's lordship. In 1446, a disputed inheritance in the Forbes of Kinnaldie family was put to the arbitration of Huntly and a panel that included Alexander, Lord Forbes, and the Aberdeen burgess Gilbert Menzies.[79] In the period 1447–8, the disputes over Mar and possession of Kildrummy seem to have been resolved in favour of the young James II, although a final resolution of the contesting claims would not occur until 1457. In June 1448, Erskine agreed to surrender Kildrummy to the king's appointee before 3 July of the same year. The young king travelled north to Aberdeen during the following month, probably to enforce the terms of the indenture, and by 21 July Kildrummy was in the hands of Archibald of Dundas, brother-in-law of the royal councillor Sir Alexander Livingstone of Callendar.[80]

While the disputes in Mar gradually fell into abeyance, new political tensions were growing in the north that would soon also affect Aberdeen. The real front-line for Huntly's political ambitions lay in the central Highlands, Moray and around Inverness where he contested for regional dominance with John, earl of Ross and lord of the Isles. In 1451, James II made a series of provocative grants of the lordships of Badenoch and Lochaber, passing control of the associated 'royal castles' to Huntly. Ross, who was in effective possession of these lordships and castles, re-sponded with a devastating attack on Badenoch and the Great Glen that saw the castles of Ruthven and Urquhart destroyed.[81] These actions precipitated the major political crisis of James II's reign. In February 1452, the king summoned William, eighth earl of Douglas, to a meeting at Stirling Castle. The two men were not on the best of terms for a number of reasons, but the specific issue at stake in 1452 was Douglas' refusal to break a tripartite bond involving himself, Ross and Craw-ford. Much ink has been spilt on the nature and purpose of the bond and its potentially treasonable intent.[82] On the regional level, however, it looks like a coalition of men whose interests were threatened by Huntly and his Crichton representatives at court. If the bond also included Earl William's younger brothers, the earls of Ormond and Moray and the lord of Avandale, then it meant that Huntly's lordship was effectively surrounded by a group of magnates pledged to render mutual support. Whatever its aim, Douglas's refusal to annul the bond resulted in his violent death at the hands of the king and his courtiers.

Douglas's demise sparked a major civil confrontation that affected all areas of the kingdom, including the north-east. Two months after his death, on 21 April 1452, the burgh council was preparing for war and put the burgh into a state of readiness for physical attack: 'because of perile apperand, the toune salbe strygthnit and fortifiit with walles and strynthes in all gudeli haste'.[83] The source of the 'peril' may have been localised fighting between pro- and anti-Douglas elements within Aberdeenshire, or the council may have anticipated a more co-ordinated assault on Huntly interests from the Douglas earls and Ross to the north, or from Crawford to the south. As it was, the decisive battle in the northern civil war of 1452 was fought on 18 May, when Huntly defeated Crawford in a bloody encounter at Brechin.[84] Huntly's great victory did not bring the rewards that he might have anticipated. After finally defeating the Douglas earls in 1455, James II seems to have viewed Huntly as a man with dangerous regional ambitions. Thus, in both Moray and Mar after 1455, it was the king's agenda, rather than Huntly's, that was pursued. On 5 November 1457, in Aberdeen's tolbooth, the claims of Thomas, Lord Erskine, to the earldom of Mar were finally rejected and the crown's rights vindicated.[85] The inquest was conducted in the personal presence of the king who had come north on a justice ayre in October, and who seems to have spent almost forty days in the region to enforce the message that royal rights were now paramount.[86] Huntly, who had been acting as custodian of Kildrummy, was relieved of his office and the castle given over to the care of Patrick, Lord Glamis.[87]

The royal annexation of Mar and James's decision to grant it to his younger son, John, raised the possibility that a strong royal lordship would emerge in the north-east. This possibility was forestalled by King James's premature death in 1460, at the siege of Roxburgh. With an under-age monarch (James III) and an even younger earl of Mar, effective control of the north-east gravitated once again towards Huntly. In 1462, George, master of Huntly, recovered control of Kildrummy from the royal custodian, Lord Glamis. Thereafter, the Gordons seem to have acted as effective overlords of Mar.[88] On 13 January 1463, the alderman, bailies, council and community of the burgh of Aberdeen bound themselves in something akin to manrent for ten years to Alexander, earl of Huntly.[89] In return for Earl Alexander's obligation to defend the burgh's 'freedoms and infeftments', the burgh community bound itself to be 'lele and trew' to Huntly. Moreover, when the earl came to Aberdeen, the burgesses were to 'conserve and keep' him and his company within the burgh and to take part with him in his defence as they would defend themselves, excepting only the king's rights and the freedoms of the burgh. Whether there was any reason for Huntly to feel anxious about his safety in Aberdeen is unclear, though there are indications of problems between Earl Alexander and the earl of Erroll in 1461–2. At any rate, as in the minority of James II, the burgh was prepared to suspend full autonomy in political and military affairs and to compromise its status as a corporation directly answerable to the crown and its officers, in order to protect its local interests. The terms of the agreement clearly flouted various pieces of parliamentary legislation designed to stop burgesses entering the service of magnates or employing aristocratic support in burghal affairs. As recently as March 1458, James II's parliament had proclaimed that no burgess:

should make leagues or bands nor any convocation or riding of the commons in despite of the common law but at the command of their head officer. No man dwelling in a burgh should be bound in manrent na Ride na Rout in fere of were with na man bot with the King or with his officiars. And als that no indweller purchase na outlordship na mastership to landward to Rout na Rid.[90]

Shortly before 18 July 1463, Earl Alexander and other unnamed lords attempted to make use of the burgh's pledge of loyalty by summoning the alderman and burgesses to a muster at the Cabrach, in Alford parish.[91] Cabrach, lying on the border of Banffshire and Aberdeenshire, may have been a traditional muster point for the communities of Mar and Aberdeenshire when they were required to defend their 'country'. It was certainly used as the mustering point for the north-eastern earls before the Battle of Glenlivet in 1594. The burgesses of Aberdeen, however, excused themselves from the hosting of 1463. They could not, so they claimed, obtain horses because of the general response to the earl's summons in the town's neighbourhood, besides which they had been told by the royal administration to guard the burgh against possible English attack.[92] The object of Huntly's muster at Cabrach is unclear, but if the burgesses largely avoided involvement with events there, then their detachment from military affairs was not complete. In the following month, the community had to respond to complaints from Lord Forbes that unnamed persons from the burgh, including men from the provost's own household, had approached the Forbes lordship in a warlike manner.[93] But the correspondence of 1463 also raises more general questions about the involvement of the burghal community in military endeavours. The stress on towns as essentially commercial and financial enterprises perhaps obscures their role as major concentrations of manpower. Given the restricted size of most magnate affinities, the Aberdeen burgh levy was probably regarded as a significant military force that had the added advantage of relatively rapid assembly.[94]

At any rate, unease about the propriety of a royal burgh pledging itself to the service of a major regional magnate may be reflected in the bond given by the burgh council to Huntly, which was intended to endure for a decade. In 1472 - when it was due to expire - James III would reach maturity at the age of twenty-one, and the burgh council may well have anticipated that its arrangement with Huntly could not continue in the reign of an adult monarch. In fact, James III's assumption of the reins of government came earlier than his twenty-first year, and in 1468-9 the master of Huntly was replaced as custodian of Kildrummy by the royal retainer Henry Kinghorn.[95] In 1472, the revenues of Mar were not accounted for at the royal exchequer, presumably because the king's youngest brother, John, had assumed personal control of the earldom. By May 1476, however, it became clear that Earl John was struggling to assert his lordship in the area. In that month, James III wrote to Aberdeen burgh council requesting that it offer the young lord its support in his affairs.[96] It seems likely that Earl John's chief obstacle was the continuing influence of the Gordon earls in both the burgh of Aberdeen and the earldom of Mar. For the remainder of the century, the politics of the north-east would be dominated by the tension between the established influence of the Huntly earls, and a succession of royal representatives wielding titular authority in Mar. As it was, John's career was to be short and ineffective. The familial support evident in the king's letter to Aberdeen of 1476 was soon withdrawn, as he quarrelled spectacularly with both his younger brothers, Alexander, duke of Albany, and Earl John. As a result of this estrangement, John was arrested by the king and died, in highly mysterious circumstances, in 1479.[97]

With John's forfeiture, Mar was returned to direct royal control and the problems of administering an absentee royal lordship resurfaced. Tensions between royal assignees and local lords who sought to dominate the offices and lands at the crown's disposal were obvious. In 1480-82, for example, James III's appointment of his retainer Thomas Cochrane as the custodian of Kildrummy Castle was clearly resented by Huntly and his followers.[98] Huntly's involvement in the notorious hanging of James III's associates, including Cochrane, at Lauder Bridge in 1482, was a product of this dissatisfaction. Indeed, Huntly's behaviour throughout the national political crises of 1482-3 seems to have been dictated by the issue of control over the 'royal' lands and offices in Mar. First, Huntly was involved in the coup against James III in 1482 and the demise of the keeper of Kildrummy. Then, when the coup was hijacked by the king's younger brother, Albany, who obtained the earldom of Mar and Garioch in October 1482, Huntly rediscovered his loyalty to the king and helped bring down the Albany regime. The earl and his family finally received their rewards in the form of the keepership of Kildrummy Castle and leases of the lands of Strathdon and Strathdee.[99]

There is little in Huntly's behaviour during the early 1480s, save in the respect of defending established regional power, to support the suggestion that the north-eastern lords were distinctively 'conservative' - though the final political conflict of James III's reign, the great rebellion of 1488 in which the king lost his life, would seem to offer more convincing evidence for the thesis. In 1489, Alexander, master of Huntly, and a number of other north-eastern lords, with the express backing of the burgh of Aberdeen, rose in rebellion against the regime established by regicide. The terminology and symbolism employed by the north-eastern rebels was certainly overtly royalist, and it would be wrong to dismiss this as empty rhetoric. Yet, the events of 1488-9 were shaped by the same resentment against arbitrary interference in the running of the locality evident in the 1470s and 1480s, albeit that this time the interference came from a regime of distinctly dubious legitimacy.

The burgh of Aberdeen undoubtedly played a major role in the unfolding drama of 1488-9. In the spring of 1488, faced by a large rebel coalition under the nominal leadership of his own son (the future James IV), James III attempted to rally support for his cause in the north-east. He visited Old Aberdeen for the consecration of his new Chancellor, Bishop William Elphinstone (Plate 18), and then issued a number of charters from Aberdeen in April 1488.[100] At some point in April or May 1488, James and the supporters of his son reached a provisional settlement of their differences in Aberdeen.[101] The agreement, however, failed to halt the conflict and James III's death at the battle of Sauchieburn in June 1488 led to the establishment of a new political regime that operated in the name of the young James IV. The victors of 1488 began a campaign against those who had remained loyal to the dead king, summoning many to face charges of treason, removing James III's adherents (including Chancellor Elphinstone) from office and cancelling grants made in their favour by the deceased monarch. Elphinstone soon made his peace with the new regime, but a number of north-eastern lords, most notably Alexander Gordon, master of Huntly, and Alexander, Lord Forbes, were prominent in resisting it.

By 1489, a growing outrage at the act of regicide that had brought James IV's supporters to power, combined with political and financial persecution of men associated with James III, provoked a major rebellion. Alexander, Lord Gordon, and James, earl of Buchan (the late king's half-brother), had been plotting insurrection as early as January 1489, but a separate revolt broke out in April 1489. This was led by the earl of Lennox and Lord Lyle, who were swiftly besieged in Dumbarton by forces loyal to James IV. A parliament held in July 1489 made arrangements for lords from various regions to support the siege of Dumbarton for a period of twenty days.[102] According to the parliamentary timetable, the earls and lords of the north-east were due to appear at Dumbarton on or around 26 August. Instead, assembling the northern forces had the effect of precipitating a regional revolt. Shortly before 12 September 1489, the northern rebels drew up a formal protest against the new regime. The first complaint was the government's failure to punish those who had been responsible for James III's death. Thereafter, the document dealt with the supposed misgovernance of the new king's treasury, lands and offices by the leading figures of the minority administration, and their partisan use of royal courts.[103] Having issued their declaration, the Master of Huntly, the Earl Marischal and Lord Forbes marched south to support the rebels in Dumbarton, raiding the estates of prominent supporters of James IV in Perthshire as they passed. On 12 September 1489, the alderman, bailies and community of Aberdeen gathered to approve the declaration signed by the northern lords.[104]

The willingness of Aberdeen's burgesses to support the rebellion may well have reflected the local influence of Forbes, Marischal and Gordon, but it was probably also influenced by the arbitrary treatment meted out by the new regime to the provost of Aberdeen, Sir John Rutherford of Tarland. Rutherford had enjoyed the favour of James III, despite indications that he did not possess the full support of the burgh community itself. His position as provost had been under assault in 1487 and in November of that year he had required specific royal support to counter claims made against him by David Menzies.[105] From 1485, Sir John had been allowed the fermes (rents) of the lands of Easttown and Tarland in Cromar by James III. After the king's death, the new financial officers of the crown refused to recognise Sir John's rights and began proceedings to recover the rents uplifted quite legally by Rutherford between 1485 and 1488.[106] In 1489, Sir John thus faced the prospect of his lands and goods being distrained to pay his debt to the crown. His position was paralleled by that of the Master of Huntly, who found the new regime unwilling to honour James III's gift of a fee of one hundred merks per annum for the custody of Kildrummy Castle.[107] The rebel complaints about the misgovernance of royal lands and strengths embraced local, as well as national, issues.

After combining with the western rebels in Dumbarton, the northern lords were involved in an indecisive skirmish with royal forces near Gartloaning, before retreating to Dumbarton. Eventually, the government was forced to conclude a negotiated surrender of the rebels in Dumbarton. The terms of the surrender included one major concession, the calling of a parliament that was to meet in February 1490. This assembly produced a settlement that addressed many of the concerns raised by the rebels' proclamation, which had been supported by the burgesses of Aberdeen and by presumably many others. By 1494, the minority regime had backed down over the issue of the Gordons' fee for Kildrummy. The Gordons of Huntly reigned supreme once more in Mar. Despite his shared animosity to James IV's new councillors, Sir John Rutherford fared less well. He does not appear to have enjoyed the favour of the Gordon earls and was never restored to his Cromar estates, which went instead to Huntly's brother. He resigned as provost of Aberdeen in 1492, to be replaced by Alexander Rede.[108] Meanwhile, the royal burgh did not emerge from the crisis of 1489 with its interests unscathed. On 26 December 1489, about a fortnight after the surrender of Dumbarton, near-by Old Aberdeen was erected into a burgh of barony – the price, perhaps, for Elphinstone's loyalty to a troubled regime.[109]

By the early sixteenth century, new political configurations were beginning to take shape (see Chapter 10). The burgh of Aberdeen was tied to the political overlordship of the earls of Huntly, who increasingly dominated not just the burgh's regional hinterland but also exerted influence on burghal politics directly through their links to prominent burgess families, most notably the Menzies. In a sense, though, this was nothing new. Throughout the medieval period, the burgh had been an essential component of lordships that operated over a much wider area than Aberdeenshire itself. At the same time, however, the relentless expansion of the royal patrimony in the fifteenth century meant that the bases of local power and influence in the north-east, like many other areas of the kingdom, now had to be defended in the royal court, as well as in the locality.

10

The Menzies Era:
Sixteenth-century Politics

ALLAN WHITE

The rise of the Menzies family

In Aberdeen the sixteenth century both began and ended with a power struggle. The key actors in the drama were members of the Menzies family. At the outset of the century they were fighting for supremacy in town politics. As it drew to a close they were waging a losing campaign to preserve their political influence. The family which dominated sixteenth-century Aberdeen politics - providing the burgh's provost for all but twelve of the first eighty years of the sixteenth century - had originally come to Aberdeen at the beginning of the fifteenth century from Perthshire. Wealth and astute marriage enabled them to increase their standing, entering the burgess elite of about a dozen families. It was this group which dominated the political, economic and religious fortunes of the burgh (see Chapter 8). Ostensibly, the public programme championed by the Menzies family was simple, but clear: the defence of the rights and liberties of the burgh community. This was to be achieved through containing the predatory ambitions of powerful local gentry families, a prudent loyalty to those who acted in the name of the crown and a sensible and pragmatic conservatism in the matter of religion. The family was determined to preserve exclusive control of the town's governmental machinery, with the extensive access to patronage which it afforded.

The interest of local magnates in burgh affairs arose from the town's wealth. Aberdeen was a regional capital and the sea was its window on the world. The proper functioning of the town's economy was of vital importance for the prosperity of the region (see Chapters 6 and 7). Wool, hides, fish, raw materials of every kind, many of them owned by landed families, found their way to Aberdeen for export. Several rural landlords also owned property in the town.[1] The cupidity of the lairds, however, was often aroused by the prospect of acquiring lands and fishings that formed part of the burgh's patrimony. Attempts to appropriate these resources were made by a compact of local lairds. By 1521, John, sixth Lord Forbes, was involved in a long-running, occasionally violent dispute with the burgh, ostensibly over fishing rights.[2] He was bought off by an annual gift of wine, in exchange for his protection but, when the council reneged on the deal in 1530, there was a renewed outburst of violence that was quelled only after royal intervention.[3] The Forbes family was not unique. In 1525, the town was assaulted by the Setons of Meldrum and the Leslie family (enemies of the Forbes kindred) who were attempting to prevent the election of Thomas Menzies of Pitfodels (*d.* 1576) as provost, in succession to his father, Gilbert Menzies of Findon (*d.* 1543).[4] The Leslies were related by marriage to another prominent burgess, John Collison (*d. c.* 1535). Collison's father had entered the inner circle of burgesses by marriage into the guildry in 1448. He acquired an extensive urban estate and his son, John, married Elizabeth, the only daughter of Leslie of Wardis.[5] Collison was perhaps using his connections with neighbouring lairds in an attempt to prevent the development of an effectively hereditary Menzies provostship. The Leslie faction was probably also taking advantage of the recent death of the third earl of Huntly, and the minority of the fourth earl, to extend its own influence over the power vacuum which had appeared in Aberdeenshire. And it is this underlying factor which probably also explains the violent conduct of the Forbes family in the 1520s.

Ironically, in light of later developments, the Menzies family had begun its rise to power as the defender of the rights and privileges of the burgh against a narrowly oligarchical government with close ties to the landed families of the hinterland. The object of its attack was Sir John Rutherford of Tarland (1467-1528), who served eleven times as provost and who was an associate of landed families such as the Gordon earls of Huntly, the Leslies of Balquhain and the Cumyns of Culter (see Chapter 9). The opposition to Rutherford was led by David Menzies, who was unable to depose Rutherford until 1488, in the aftermath of the battle of Sauchieburn. By then, Rutherford's commendation by the late James III (1460-88) and his links with the earls of Huntly seemed more of a liability than a political advantage.[6] Rutherford attempted to save his position by signing a bond of manrent with the earl of Huntly in 1490.[7] Diverse town and country interests on the town council were usually kept in check. But they tended to flare during royal minorities, when the drift of national policy was unclear, or when the position of the earl of Huntly, as chief magnate and guarantor of peace and order in the region, appeared threatened.[8]

Aberdeen attempted to keep on good terms with local nobles and their gentry clientage, but the burgh was reluctant to accept full-scale dependence on any one of them, save when general political instability rendered desirable the protection which rural aristocrats could offer. Four major crises affected the burgh during the course of the sixteenth century. Religion was the leitmotiv of all four. The death of James V (1513-42) precipitated the inconstant earl of Arran, next in line of succession to the infant Queen Mary (1542-67), to power as governor of the realm. Arran's power was concentrated south of the Forth, and he was unsure as to how long his authority would last.[9] He attempted to consolidate his influence in other parts of the country by building alliances with those who already exercised regional power. Nevertheless, by intruding his own candidates as provosts in seven of the country's chief burghs, he also managed to bypass strictly local interests.[10] In Aberdeen the Menzies family was drawn to Arran's interest, and in 1543 Thomas Menzies, the provost, was appointed as the government's comptroller.[11] Menzies served on Arran's council and was one of the witnesses to the Treaty of Greenwich, which was ratified at Holyrood in August 1543.[12] Arran's dangerous and seemingly capricious disregard of the equilibrium of political forces in the regions earned him a rebuke from his opponents during a convocation held at Perth in July 1543. He was asked to follow the counsel of the magnates and the churchmen and to refrain from following the advice of 'private persons'.

Menzies's tenure of office as comptroller was short-lived. Having encouraged Aberdeen to refuse support to the fourth earl of Huntly and his ally Cardinal Beaton, against the governor and his pro-English policy in August 1543, Menzies found himself isolated in September, when Arran abandoned the English match and his 'godly fit' by professing his religious orthodoxy. Arran's previous sympathy for an association with England had, in part, been motivated by an element of reformist religious sentiment. In Aberdeen, as in other burghs, an evangelical preaching campaign was mounted, without much success. Two renegade Dominican friars, John Roger and Walter Thomson, were supported by the town in their work of preaching and teaching 'the true word of God' and praying for the good estate of the governor.[13] Both belonged to Arran's stable of reformed preachers. Thomson eventually disappeared from view, but in 1544 Roger was found with his neck broken at the foot of the walls of St Andrews Castle, possibly dispatched by order of Cardinal Beaton. The preachers may not have met with much success. But Thomas Menzies, later a discreet defender of the Catholic cause in the Reformation, was given a remission in 1544, along with prominent members of the emergent Protestant party, for contravening the acts of parliament 'about those who dispute about Holy Scripture, or hold any opinions, or read any books against the said acts'.[14]

Menzies managed to retain the provostship, despite the existence of an opposition party in the burgh, until January 1545. Arran and Huntly reached an accommodation in December 1544 and following an extraordinary election, in January 1545, Huntly was elected provost of Aberdeen, with Menzies acting as his depute.[15] In September, Arran finally abandoned his former client, and in the normal October election Huntly was once more elected provost, while the Menzies family was evicted from office.[16] Defeat at the battle of Pinkie in September 1547 saw Huntly carried off to prison in England and the death of two of his main supporters in Aberdeen, Master John Gordon and William Rolland.[17] The Menzies family mobilised its supporters, took advantage of the power vacuum and swept back to power. Huntly was forced to rely for his government on the disaffected country party amongst the burgesses, as well as on a group of isolated and disaffected merchants and lawyers, who found themselves excluded from the Menzies clique. Protests were lodged by the Menzies family against Huntly's intrusion into government, as well as by the deacon of the powerful hammermen's craft. In the end, Huntly's victory in 1545 was a hollow triumph. It represented the extension of Gordon power into the heart of the burgh administration, but it also proclaimed the failure of the use of executive power by the nobles and gentry through the agency of client burgess families. Huntly was forced to take control of the town himself, as there was no other way his writ could run there. He effectively polarised burgess opinion and alienated those on whom he should have been relying for the exercise of power.

The crisis of 1543-7 brought into play various themes that were to feature regularly in the history of the burgh during the second half of the century. Dissenting religious opinion does not seem to have featured very strongly until after the establishment of Protestantism in 1560. In 1521, John Marshall, the master of the town's grammar school, was summoned to answer before the council for his anti-papal views. The case was obviously not that serious, since he was prepared to recant in 1523.[18] Nevertheless, other indications of religious dissent followed. In 1525, James V wrote to the sheriff of Aberdeen, ordering that heretical books be seized at the port. In 1527, the English ambassador reported that Scottish merchants were importing copies of Tyndale's vernacular translation of the New Testament into the east-coast harbours – and Aberdeen may have been among them.[19] In 1535, a prohibition on the import of Lutheran books by way of the east-coast burghs was promulgated, although there is no evidence that Aberdeen sheltered a Protestant congregation at the time.[20] Still, in 1544 warning had been given that Beaton's proceedings against heretics might be extended to Aberdeen. The earl of Huntly gave orders to his lieutenant depute in the town that proceedings were to be initiated against two burgesses for the 'hinging of an image of St Francis'.[21]

One of those responsible for this minor act of religious vandalism was Thomas Branche, a minor burgess who subscribed to the Congregation in 1559 at St Andrews and who was appointed a deacon of the Aberdeen kirk session when it was first established in 1562.[22] Apart from that, he features rarely in the town's records and never in connection with religious dissent. The existence of a small community of Protestants before 1560 can be surmised only by references to John Brabaner, a burgess of Aberdeen, who took up the ministry of the Word at some time before 1560. In October of that year, the council ordered the town's treasurer to give him a gown and suit of clothes for all of his labours in preaching, teaching and administration of the sacraments 'without any recompense'.[23] He does not appear in the town records before this date, save in connection with a dispute over livestock and with the town's Dominican friars, who refused to bring their corn to his mills to be ground.[24] Significantly, Brabaner was not appointed as Protestant minister of the new kirk in Aberdeen, perhaps because he was known as 'ane vehement man for inculcating the Law and pain thereof'.[25] Apart from these isolated cases, there are no substantial traces of Protestant opinion until the Reformation exploded on to the Aberdeen scene in 1559, shattering the pattern of unadventurous orthodoxy which had previously characterised the religious practice of the town (see Chapter 13).

The advent of reform

The political instability engendered by the Lords of the Congregation and the anti-French reaction of the latter half of 1559 were observed with studied neutrality by the burgesses of Aberdeen. The council, mindful of the uncertainties of the mid-1540s, was unwilling to be caught on the wrong foot again. A deep-rooted reluctance to move against legitimately constituted authority, together with a determination not to alienate the earl of Huntly and his powerful affinity, was the keynote of the town's public policy for the next two decades. News of iconoclastic rioting in Perth, Dundee, Stirling and elsewhere prompted many of the clerics and religious orders in the town to take the precaution of depositing their charters and valuables with sympathetic supporters or with the town council itself. From May 1559, the Dominican and Franciscan friars salted away their properties and endowments.[26] In June, the chaplains of St Nicholas Church gave their vestments and altar plate into the town's custody until the threat of violence had ended.[27] And in July, the bishop, remembering the fate of treasure belonging to his predecessor, William Stewart – which had been stolen by Forbes of Corsindae in 1544, as the bishop was trying to protect it from a threatened English invasion – divided his valuables amongst the canons of the cathedral and his relative, the earl of Huntly.[28] Years later, Alexander Anderson, the principal of King's College, was accused of doing the same with the resources of the college in order to prevent them from falling into Protestant hands.[29] The chaplains of the parish church presumed that the danger had passed in October 1559, since they asked for the return of their altar plate so that they could resume divine service.[30] At that point, the Congregation was on the verge of evacuating Edinburgh, and in November Catholic worship was to be restored there. It was with a keen sense of anxiety that Thomas Menzies announced to the council on 19 December 1559 that an imminent attack was to be made on the religious houses of the town by an iconoclastic mob drawn from Protestant sympathisers in Angus and the Mearns.[31]

The mob arrived on 4 January. A meeting of the council was convened by David

Plate 1. Dubford standing stone (courtesy of City of Aberdeen, Archaeology Unit). *See Introduction.*

Plate 2. Cults Cairn (courtesy of City of Aberdeen, Archaeology Unit). See Introduction.

Plate 3. Bronze Age cist burial from Scotstown, Aberdeen (courtesy of City of Aberdeen, Archaeology Unit). See Introduction.

Plate 4. Prehistorical pottery remains (courtesy of City of Aberdeen, Archaeology Unit). *See Introduction.*

Plate 5. Tillydrone motte (courtesy of City of Aberdeen, Archaeology Unit). *See Introduction.*

Plate 6. Artefacts relating to the manufacture of cloth (courtesy of City of Aberdeen, Archaeology Unit).
See Chapter 6.

Plate 7. Man with a bonnet (detail from ACA, Council Register, ii, 102; courtesy of ACA). See Chapter 2.

Plate 8. Artefacts relating to trade and industry (courtesy of City of Aberdeen, Archaeology Unit). See Chapter 2.

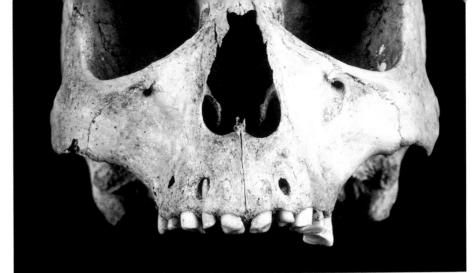

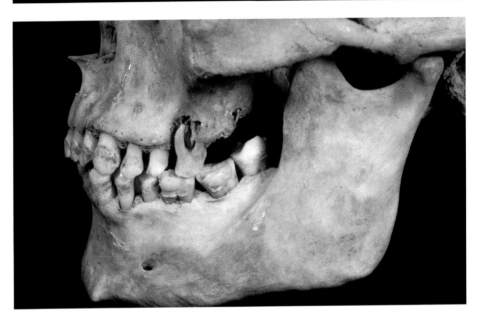

Plates 9a and 9b. Medieval dental decay (courtesy of City of Aberdeen, Archaeology Unit). See Chapters 3 and 5.

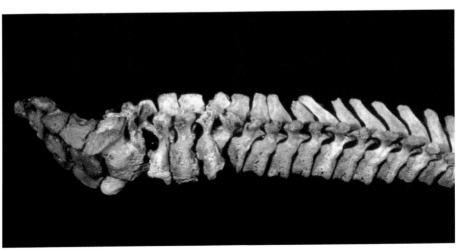

Plate 10. Spinal column of a child, showing healed tuberculosis of the spine (courtesy of City of Aberdeen, Archaeology Unit). See Chapter 3.

Plate 11. Artefacts relating to trade and industry (courtesy of City of Aberdeen, Archaeology Unit). *See Chapter 4.*

Plate 12. Reconstruction of backlands (courtesy of City of Aberdeen, Archaeology Unit). *See Chapter 4.*

Plate 13. Goods imported in the thirteenth and fourteenth centuries (courtesy of City of Aberdeen, Archaeology Unit). *See Chapter 6.*

Plate 14. Goods imported between the thirteenth and eighteenth centuries (courtesy of City of Aberdeen, Archaeology Unit). *See Chapter 6.*

Plate 15. A silver half groat minted in Aberdeen in the reign of David II, 1329-71 (courtesy of City of Aberdeen, Archaeology Unit). *See Chapter 9.*

Plate 16. Coin hoards found in Aberdeen (courtesy of City of Aberdeen, Archaeology Unit). *See Chapter 9.*

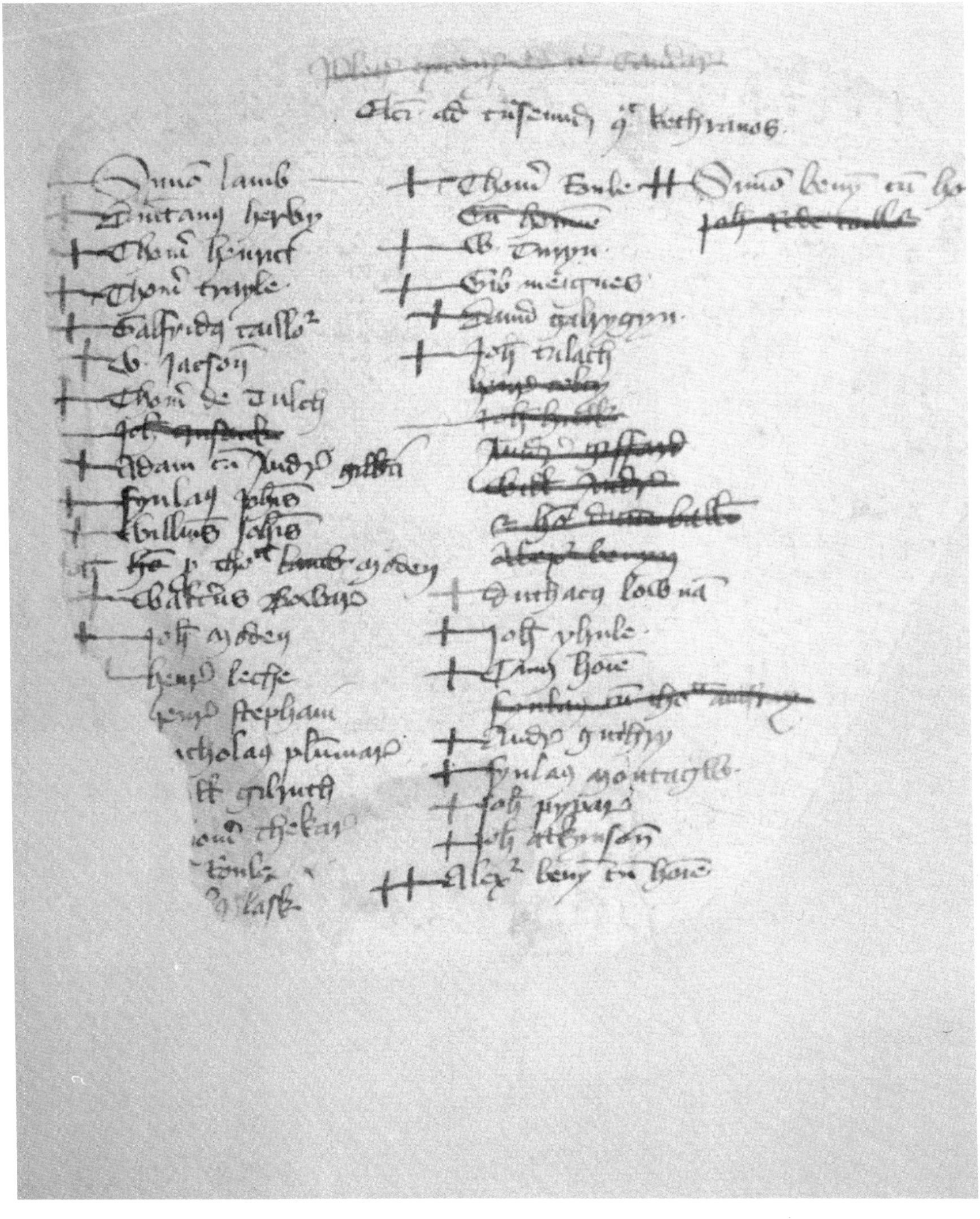

Plate 17. A list, dating from c. 1411, of Aberdonians deployed to fight 'caterans', probably at the battle of Harlaw, 1411 (ACA, Council Register, i, 291; courtesy of ACA). See Chapter 9.

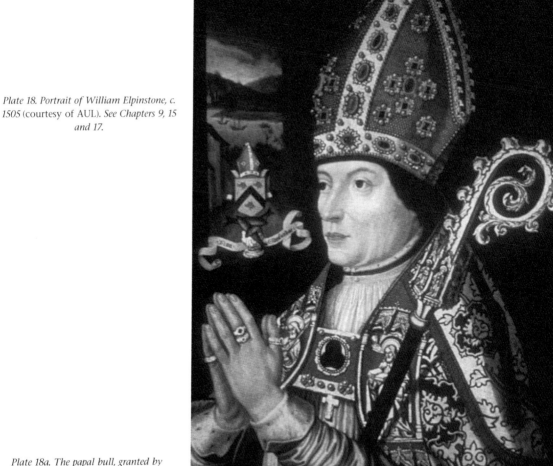

Plate 18. Portrait of William Elpinstone, c. 1505 (courtesy of AUL). See Chapters 9, 15 and 17.

Plate 18a. The papal bull, granted by Alexander VI on 10 February 1495, founding Aberdeen's first university (courtesy of AUL). See Chapter 15.

Plate 19. Book of Hours, commissioned by Bishop Gavin Dunbar in 1527 (AUL, MS 22; courtesy of AUL).
See Chapter 17.

Plate 20. The burgh seal of Aberdeen, depicting St Nicholas (courtesy of ACA).
See Chapter 13.

Plate 21. Sasine Register, volume v (1), The Protocol Book of David Nicholson, 1521-35 (courtesy of ACA).
See Chapter 1.

Plate 24. Portrait of George Keith, 4th Earl Marischal (courtesy of AUL). *See Chapters 10 and 15.*

Plate 25. Timothy Pont, detail of map of Lower Deeside, c. 1590s (reproduced by permission of the Trustees of the National Library of Scotland). *See Chapter 8.*

This part of the coast
besrd: Aberdem is all amisses

Item the Myles are too little.

S: Mattraesnesse

K: of Nigg
Bi: of nigg
Cokhorse

Torry
Kirkhill
Binnapast
guer Torry
Tullos
Faichmches
o: Coldhen
Coldhem
Lorrstoun
Loch Lorrstoun
Looes foun
Larritou
Kinkorn
Karnroin
of Lacart
Coues.

Muchtelle in th

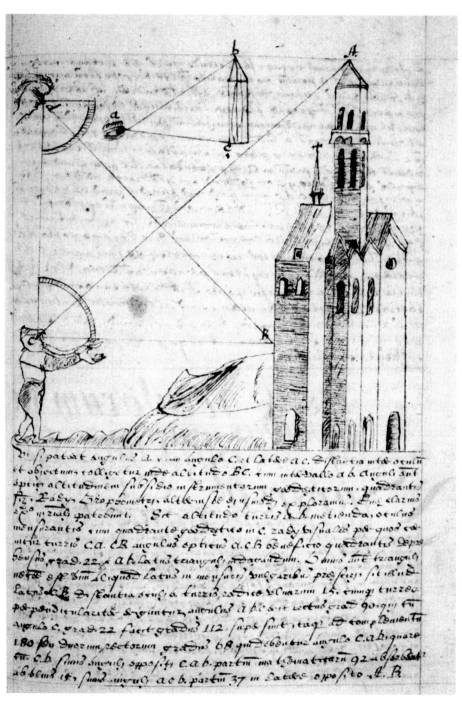

Plate 26. Notes on trigonometry: from James Downie's copy of the dictates of William Johnston, 1633–4 (courtesy of AUL). See Chapter 15.

Plate 27. Notice of mortification by Catherine Forbes, Lady Rothiemay, in 1642 (courtesy of ACA). *See Chapters 14 and 16.*

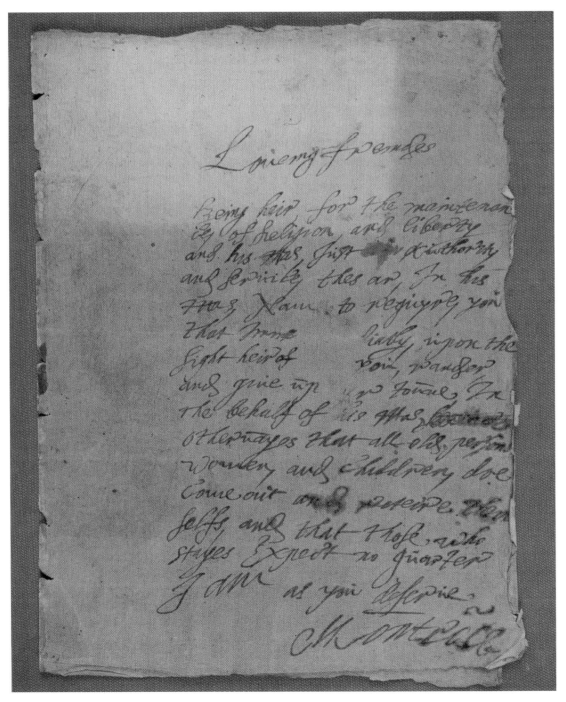

Plate 28. Autograph letter from the Marquis of Montrose, 1644 (ACA, Town Correspondence, Letters Supplementary, no. 306a; courtesy of ACA). See Chapter 11.

Plate 29. Portrait of George Skene, provost from 1676 to 1685 (courtesy of ACA). *See Chapters 2 and 4.*

Plate 30. The town bell of Old Aberdeen, 1742 (courtesy of ACA). *See Chapter 6.*

Plate 31. An eighteenth-century beggar's badge (Marischal Museum, ABDUA: 18709; courtesy of Marischal Museum, University of Aberdeen). See Chapter 2.

Plate 32. Badge of the provost of Aberdeen, 1760 (courtesy of ACA).

Plate 33. King's College, Old Aberdeen, c. 1785 (courtesy of AUL). *See Chapter 15.*

S COLLEGE OLD ABERDEE N

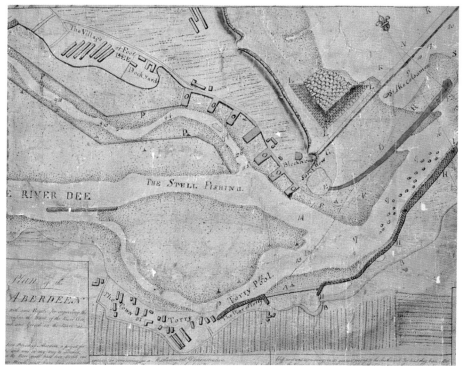

THE
ABERDEEN's JOURNAL

From TUESDAY December 29 1747, to TUESDAY January 5 1748.

From the London Gazette, December 22.

Hamburgh, December 19. N. S.

HE Accounts which we receive of the late Hurricane are full of many difastrous Effects; of 30 Sail of Ships, which were lying in the Road of Cuxhaven, two only escaped either persisting, or being driven a shure. It was feared that the Boat belonging to His Britannick Majesty's Ship the Sheerness was lost, and the Men in her; but she was driven some Miles up a Creek, and received no Damage. A Dutch Officer is arrived here to inlist Volunteers for the Land-Service of the States-General; and their Minister in this Circle has applied for, and obtained Leave of the Magistrates for that Purpose.

Hague, Decr. 22. N. S. We are now informed from Zealand, that two Dutch Armed Vessels, of 20 Guns each, were lost near Flushing in the Storm of the 12th inst. and that not one of the Men were saved. The Dutch Officers, who were taken Prisoners of War by the French and have had Leave to come home upon their Parole, are greatly alarmed with a Declaration of M. Chiquet, that his Court intends shortly to order them all back again to France. The new Council of War has wrote circular Letters to all the General Officers in the Service of the State, who were employed at Bergen-op-Zoom, or in the Neighbourhood of that Place, to desire they would give in Writing whatever they know with any Certainty relating to the Defence of that Fortress. M. d'Envie, Major-General of the Bavarian Troops in this Country, arrived here three Days ago, in order to enter as Lieutenant-General into the Dutch Service.

Hague, Decr. 26. N. S. The Prince of Orange received last Saturday the solemn Deputation from the States of Overyssel, with the Diploma of his Election as Hereditary Stadtholder of that Province, and at the same Time His Highness took the Oaths proper upon that Occasion. The same Day it was publickly declared, that her Royal Highness the Princess of Orange was seven Months gone with Child. And Prayers have accordingly been ordered in all the Churches for her happy Delivery. The States of Holland, who have been constantly assembled for several Months, separated last Saturday for the Holidays, and are to resume the Assembly on the 10th of next Month. Before they separated, they resolved upon raising Four Millions Three hundred Thousand Florins by Way of Lottery, which is to be opened the 2d of next Month. Their High Mightinesses have lately published a Placart for the Encouragement of Privateers, by which they are not only to be exempted from the Obligation of giving up one Man out of Three for the Use the Fleet, but are likewise promised, upon taking any of the French Men of War or Privateers, a Reward of 150 Florins for every Man alive before the Engagement, and likewise the same Reward for every Pound Weight of Bill, computing together the Weight of Metal that each Gun carries on board the said Ships And as farther Encouragement, all Men of War, Privateers and other Ships thus taken, are to belong absolutely to the Captors, without any Deduction whatsoever. We hear from Paris that the Dragoons of Puygnyon, who have been for two Years past in Brittany, have received Orders to march the Beginning of Spring for Flanders. Letters from Brussels of 20th mention, that Marshal Saxe set out for Paris the Sunday before, and Marshal Lowendahl at the same Time for Namur; and that the Marquis of Contades, Governor of that City, commands there in the Absence of Marshal Saxe.

Admiralty-Office, Decr. 22.
Commodore Mostyn has sent into Plymouth the Grand St. Juan of St. Sebastian, a Privateer of 20 Guns, and 220 Men, which he took on the 7th inst. And also the Thetis of Bayonne, of 18 Guns, and 345 Men which he took on the 9th inst.

From the London Evening Post, December 24.

Genoa, Dec. 9. The 2d Instant four Vessels arriv'd in our Harbour with some Corsican and and French Recruits; They sail'd from Calvi in Corsica the 26th of last Month in Company with 36 Ships more, which had on Board 1500 French and Spanish Troops, and steer'd for the Gulph of Spezzia. We have since receiv'd Advice that they are all safely landed at Porto-Fino, Sestri, and other Ports in this State.

Paris, Dec. 22. Marshal Saxe reckons to spend a Fortnight or three Weeks at Court, during which he is to assist at the Councils to be held on the new Measures that are to be pursued with respect to Military Operations in the Netherlands. As it is resolv'd that the War shall be carried on there with the utmost Vigour, the Court is making the necessary Dispositions for employing three Armies in that Country, viz. one of 60,000 Men is to assemble on the Meuse as soon as the Weather permits; another of the same Force will rendezvous near Bergen-op-Zoom; and the third Army is to be formed in the Neighbourhood of Louvain, in order to serve to reinforce either of the other two, as Occasion may require. Besides which, there is to be a Flying Camp, consisting of the light-arm'd Troops, which will be posted nearer to the Enemy's Frontiers. For the Execution of these Measures a Train of Artillery is getting ready in the Neighbourhood of Namur, which is to consist of 120 Pieces of Battering Cannon, and 40 Mortars, and we are to have another Train at Mechlin. Marshal Lowendahl is charged with the Direction of such Operations as are to precede the Opening of the Campaign in Form. Such are our Preparations for the Land Service, in the Midst of which we do not neglect the Marine. We are told the King has granted the Privateers of St. Malo the Exemption from the Admiralty Fees and Duties which they had been soliciting for some Time past; In Consideration of which they engage to send out a

greater Number of Ships than they have ever yet done. The Jews in this Kingdom have offer'd his Majesty to arm one hundred Ships of Force at their own Charge, if he will but give them Leave to build a Synagogue in this Metropolis: And Letters from Brest advise that the Jews are actually building there, as also at Rochefort, and some other adjacent Ports, twelve Men of War, which are to be ready against the Spring; and that the King is to pay them the Interest of their Money, 'till he can reimburse them the whole Expence of this Armament.

Paris, Dec. 25 The Comptroller of the Finances sent not long ago for the Farmers General, and told them his Majesty expected they should pay the Prizes in the present Lottery as fast as they were drawn: Upon this they expressed some Reluctance, and desired to have some Time to draw up their Remonstrances. The Comptroller told them, That as for Time it was precious; and as for Remonstrances, they would be vain; the King had already considered the Point, and would be obeyed; but added, That the King did not desire to constrain them, since there were others content to take their Farm upon themselves, and who, to obtain it, would do this and more.

Hague, Dece. 19. We have some private Letters from Hamburgh, which say, That the Great Mogul has entred Persia with an Army of 300,000 Men.

As the Publick may be alarmed with the Report that ran so currently Yesterday upon the Exchange, that a Contract is negociating for the Delivery of 400,000 Quarters of Wheat to our mortal Enemy the French, we hope every *Englishman* will judge so tenderly of his Neighbour, as not to believe it possible any Merchant can entertain so pernicious a Thought, or be such a Traitor to his Country, at a Time when our Allies the Dutch have totally prohibited all Commerce with that perfidious Nation under the severest Penalties.

However the Report Yesterday might arise, of a *particular Contract* for sending 400,000 *Quarters of Wheat* to France, it is certain that an Article from Bourdeaux, in a late Dutch Mail, mentions that a *large Number of English Ships*, laden with Corn, had put in there, and caused a sudden Plenty in the Midst of Scarcity; adding, that those Ships had sailed under a *Pretence* of being bound for the *Mediterranean*. If these were *private Traders* only, who ventured thus to risk their Fortunes, in contempt of their *Duty* and *Allegiance*, the Affair deserves to be particularly *enquired into*, that the Delinquents, if taken, may be *punished*. But if their Voyage was in Virtue of a *Contract*, that is a JOBB, the Business is the more *iniquitous*, as it must be a Transaction among Persons of *no small Distinction*. We will not pretend to guess who the JOBBERS may be; but it was very imprudent of the *French*, who were to be *essentially served*, to blab a *Secret* that may prevent their *Friends* here from making a little *more Profit* of our *present Plenty*.

We hear that it having been affirmed, in a certain H——— *Assembly*, that the Practice of Sm———g would never have arisen to its late Pitch but for the Encouragement of some R—

Plate 37. Matthew Paris, Map of Britain, c. 1250 (courtesy of the British Library). *See Chapter 17.*

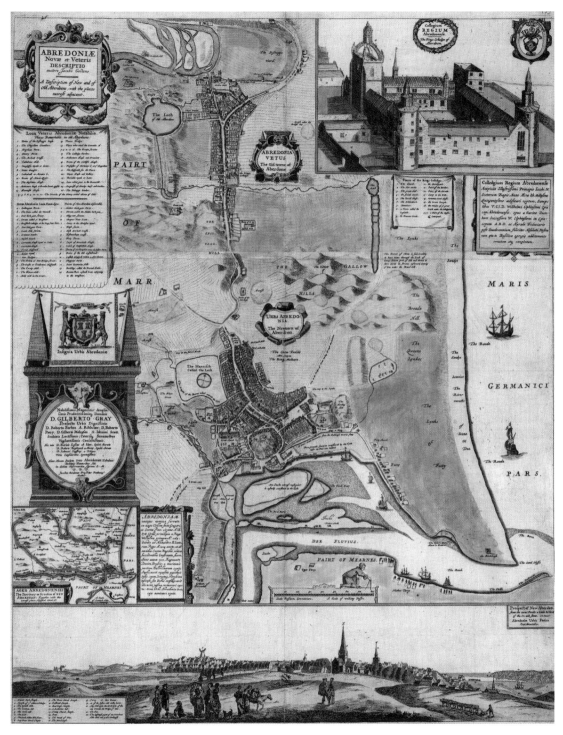

Plate 38. James Gordon of Rothiemay, View of Aberdeen and Old Aberdeen, 1661 (reproduced by permission of the Trustees of the National Library of Scotland). *See Chapters 1, 2, 4, 5 and 18.*

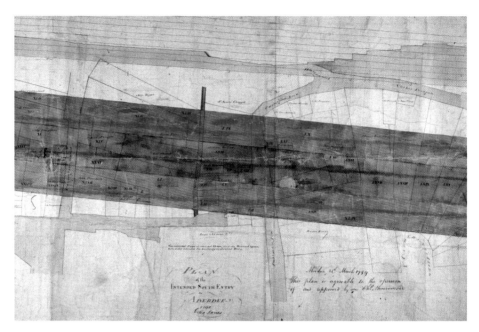

Plate 39. Plans for the new southern entry into Aberdeen, 1798 (courtesy of ACA). *See Chapter 18.*

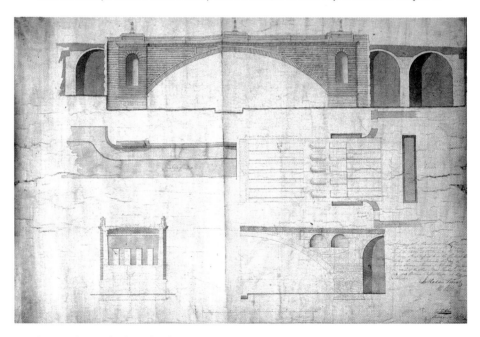

Plate 40. Thomas Fletcher, Plan for Union Bridge, 28 October 1802 (courtesy of ACA). *See Chapter 18.*

Mar, the treasurer of the town, while the friaries were being sacked. Mar may have chosen his moment well, since the provost and at least six other members of the council were not present, perhaps seeing to the defence of their rural estates. In their absence, the council approved a comprehensive programme of religious reform. The revenues of the friaries were diverted to the support of Protestant preachers and the military endeavours of the Congregation. The only councillor to dissent vocally from the proceedings was Gilbert Collison, the master of the kirk work.[32] Four days later, on 8 January, the burgh's head court met, again in the absence of the provost. Mar again took charge and pressed on with reformation. The singers in St Nicholas Kirk were dismissed and the unnamed preachers in the town were ordered to be paid an honest wage. On this occasion, further opposition was expressed by the provost's son, as well as by prominent craftsmen and burgesses associated with the clerical party of Bishop Gordon, who was still resident in Old Aberdeen. Mar, sensing that the tide might be turning against him, ordered those burgesses who were custodians of the treasures of the parish church to produce them in the dean of guild's court.[33] On 12 January the commissioners refused to hand over their charge until the whole council should be present. Thomas Menzies, the provost, returned to the burgh once a truce had been concluded between the regent, Mary of Guise, and the Lords of Congregation, as the restorer of order. Half of the council gathered behind him in opposition to Mar and his supporters, who included 'extranears' to the burgh. These were joined by six others who took instruments on their opposition to the reformed proceedings including three notaries who practised in the burgh, two burgesses with kinsmen amongst the chaplains in St Nicholas and a leading craftsman, Alexander Chalmer.[34] This force of opinion was strong enough to prevent any further steps towards the establishment of a Protestant policy. But it was insufficiently powerful to reverse entirely the prevailing course of events. The Protestant party may have been in a minority, but it was a significant minority and too powerful to be ignored.

Protestant nation, conservative north-east

The next ten years saw the town treading a wary path between obedience to a gradually Protestantising central government and an increasingly conservative Gordon affinity. In the years 1560-69, twenty-seven men served on the council. Those who died in office were succeeded immediately by their sons. The twenty-seven councillors were drawn from the ranks of just thirteen Aberdeen families. Fourteen of the twenty-seven served continuously. Whereas there had been some degree of mobility in the council's ranks before 1560, this now ceased. From 1563 to 1569, only five men held the office of bailie, two of them sons of the provost, two sons-in-law of the provost and the other a strong opponent of the Reformation.

The Reformation prompted the Menzies family to tighten, not slacken, its grip on the town. And its power was invariably exercised in favour of delaying or inhibiting the progress of the Reformation.

The patterns and practices of Catholicism were to prove difficult to dismantle. A short distance outside the town, a fully-fledged Catholic establishment was maintained in Old Aberdeen with its bishop, cathedral and academic establishment, based at King's College. It was from here that many of the defenders of Catholicism in the initial phases of the Reformation were to be drawn. The university itself had provided some of the resources which had fuelled the attempts at Catholic reform associated with Archbishop John Hamilton of St Andrews and the provincial councils of the old church held in the 1540s and 1550s. The burgh commonwealth was also a religious community. Civic ceremonial was marked by religious observance (see Chapters 8 and 13). Of the major religious orders present in the town, the Dominicans and Franciscans had issued from reform movements in the Low Countries and enjoyed a high reputation in the town (see Chapter 17). The Franciscan church had been newly built with financial support from the town in 1521. The parish church, lavishly adorned with altars, paintings and sculpture, was served by a large body of chaplains who performed various services in the town in the shape of education, the law and medicine. Many of these chaplains were members of prominent burgess families, serving chapels which had been endowed by their forebears. The rhythms of the year were marked by Catholic periods of feast and fast. The chief festival was Corpus Christi, when the population of the whole town marched in procession behind the Blessed Sacrament, displaying in its order of proceeding the hierarchy which prevailed within the town, making it into an image of the city of God. The abrupt cessation of all of these observances and markers of the parameters of community life in the burgh left a vacuum which the reformed kirk found an initial difficulty in supplying. It was only as the century drew to a close, when memories had faded and the clergy who sustained these memories disappeared, that the possibility of an alternative religious civic identity developed. Until that time, the reformed Church remained chronically under-resourced and struggling to maintain its position in burgh life.

The town received its first official minister in the second half of 1560. Adam Heriot was a former Augustinian canon of St Andrews and claimed his former prior, Lord James, the future earl of Moray, as a patron.[35] Aberdeen was showing a fine political sense in accepting Heriot as its pastor. He was moderate in his opinions and seemed an ideal candidate for the post: learned, quiet and a scholastic theologian, Heriot was slow to obey the instructions of the General Assembly to take order with the survival of Catholicism in the area. The new minister arrived shortly after the Reformation parliament of August 1560. But it was not until Queen Mary's demonstration of impartiality - in bringing down her most powerful Catholic subject, the earl of Huntly, following the battle of Corrichie in September 1562 - that the town council was prodded into establishing a kirk session and the machinery of Protestant discipline. It was determined that the session should not become a focus for opposition to the council, an eventuality that was to occur in the prolonged dispute with the craftsmen in 1587. In November 1562, the session was chosen behind closed doors by the ruling group on the council, which effectively constituted itself as the session. It was to take almost a decade for this pattern to be broken. Until then, the affairs of the reformed kirk in Aberdeen were effectively governed by a minority of those of Protestant pedigree, with a large representation of conservatives and crypto-Catholics. The new session forbade any 'disputation nor ressonying of the Scriptures be at dennar or supper or oppin table, quairthrow arrysis gryte contentioun and debate'. Neither was the preacher to 'publeish nor speak of na speciall mater, to the rebuking of ony notable or particular persoune, without the consent and avisament of the Assemblie had thairto, and gif he do he sall onderly the correctioun of the Assemblie' (see Chapter 13).[36] There were to be no private conventicles in burgesses' houses, no cells of zealots existing as a challenge to the official expression of burgh religion. The inhabitants of Aberdeen found that they had exchanged one jurisdiction for a sterner and tighter form of discipline. The Reformation increased the power of the council, rather than diminished it.

It is only in the tangled web of events following the deposition of Queen Mary in 1567 that a clearer picture emerges of the political and religious complexities of the burgh. A more dynamic minister might have tackled the survival of Catholicism in his parish with greater energy. Adam Heriot was faced with the survival of much of the structure and personnel of the Catholic Church. The former chaplains of the parish church were still prominent members of urban society and were connected to many of its leading families. Even the parish church was not ordered for Protestant worship until 1574, and then only with great reluctance.[37] After 1560, the Catholic church in the town became a privy kirk. The Menzies family bought up the treasures of the parish church and kept a priest at home, the former prior of the Carmelites, John Failford, who was still receiving books from the continent in 1574.[38] Another Carmelite was ordered to be dined by the members of the council on successive nights during the week, so that he might be supported and presumably continue to exercise his priestly functions privately. Another chaplain was given the sinecure of keeper of the town's lighthouse.[39] Some of the town's inhabitants managed to combine membership of both the 'privy' Catholic kirk and the public Protestant kirk with little sense of contradiction. There was a dual ecclesiastical establishment whose membership overlapped. This was also true of many clergymen. John Collison, a chaplain of St Nicholas, refused to support the ministers of the kirk for many years, but agreed to lead the psalm singing in the kirk on Sundays.[40]

The years 1568 to 1573 were hard years for Aberdeen. Civil war and its aftermath presented the town's constitution with a major threat from which it never really recovered. The burgh tried hard to stay neutral in the increasingly bitter conflict, despite its strong Catholic party and conservative instincts. The fifth earl of Huntly, although nominally Protestant, jealously guarded his family's traditional rights and prerogatives in the north. As one of the deposed Queen's principal supporters, he was associated with a Catholic and conservative interest. In the unfolding civil war, Aberdeen found itself dragooned into acting as a regional capital for Huntly's Marian administration. In August 1568, Huntly had besieged the town and attacked the provost's house with a force of 1,500 men. When forced to make peace with Moray in May 1569, Huntly's coercion of Aberdeen into supporting him was recognised. While the earl was forced to pay vast fines, the town was discharged from complicity. The Catholic party in the town was left undisturbed, although the Regent Moray took the opportunity to purge King's College of its largely Catholic staff and began the process of turning it into a respectable Protestant institution under a new principal, Alexander Arbuthnot.[41]

The death of Moray in 1570, and the regency of the earl of Lennox which followed, inflamed the north once more. Lennox's dependence on English support, his determination not to take counsel from those who were 'wys and substantious' and his threat to territorial power blocks prompted Huntly to take the field against him. Aberdeen had given a strong demonstration of where its loyalties lay in June 1569, when it ordered the king's arms to be carved on the façade of the tolbooth. It was very reluctant to replay the events of the mid 1540s and to ally itself too closely with the Gordon party in the north. The acceptance of any other lordship than the crown's would effectively ensure the dissolution of the community of free men, which was how the burgesses saw themselves.[42] Huntly could not afford to leave a strategic port at his back whilst he was involved in military adventures in the south. Aberdeen was the port of entry for subsidies from Europe for the Queen's party, as well as being a useful point from which to engage in the illicit carriage of men and money to and from the continent. Aberdeen was the only suitable centre of administration from which Huntly could exercise his vice-regal authority, the holding of courts and the collection and control of revenue. Only Aberdeen could provide the resources of trained lawyers and clerks to ensure the proper conduct of this administration. His courts were often more attractive to litigants than those of the king. The alarm of the earl of Lennox at Huntly's judicial activity underlines its effectiveness. The courts were absolutely essential to Huntly, if his jurisdiction and commission as the queen's lieutenant in the north-east were to be taken seriously, but they demanded considerable legal and administrative resources in order to be effective. The burgesses clearly hoped that their policy of coerced co-operation with Huntly would win them gentle treatment, should the

Queen's party lose the civil war. They followed a masterly policy of public distance and private accommodation. It was certainly the case that the shipping interests of the Menzies family benefited from the strategic needs of the earl of Huntly.

The Pacification of Perth, a private agreement made in February 1573 amongst the leading warring nobles in the civil war, made it clear that Aberdeen was to be left to its fate at the hands of the earl of Morton, who had succeeded as regent in November 1572. Once more it was to be ground between the twin millstones of local and national politics. Morton's chief interest in Aberdeen was in raising money from fines to support his administration.[43] His second objective was to eradicate the nest of crypto-Catholic sympathisers operating near the heart of the burgh's administration. But Morton, as others before him, was to find that the town could not be effectively governed without the Menzies network. A significant body of opinion had retained Catholic habits, but was at a loss as to how to express them. The regent ordered the inhibition of feast days in the town. The craft guilds, with their strongly religious origins, maintained an attachment to the celebration of Christmas.[44] The grammar school pupils also petitioned to be allowed to enjoy their usual Christmas holidays.[45] Their enthusiasm may have been encouraged by the master of the grammar school, the committed Catholic John Henderson, who eventually fled to exile in France.[46] The regent ordered the removal of the organ from the kirk, the dismantling of some of the altars that remained and the demolition of the choir screen.[47] Most of these orders were obeyed, but the screen was still intact in the 1590s and one of the altars remained in 1584 – despite the increasing Protestant intensity following the arrival of John Craig as minister in 1573.[48]

The regent also launched an attack on the Catholic households in the town. Two of the bailies were ordered to ensure that their wives conformed to the Protestant settlement. Gilbert Menzies was imprisoned in Edinburgh and released only on his promise to conform.[49] Whilst Janet Knowles, the bishop's concubine and the daughter of a prominent burgess family, was ordered, but refused, to renounce the mass, she expressed her willingness to renounce the authority of the bishop of Rome.[50] The subversion of the machinery of Protestant church government and its exploitation by conservative opinion had hitherto ensured the relative powerlessness of the minister unless his authority was bolstered by external support. The chief aim of the Protestant party, once Morton's power was assured, was to break the grip of the Catholic household and its stranglehold on the life of the new Kirk. John Craig used his office as a fulcrum to ensure a gradual application of the principles of Protestant polity to his charge. The central government assisted him by making life more and more difficult for such prominent Catholic clerics and academics that remained in and around the burgh, including the remaining former Catholic staff of King's College. The net was tightening around Old Aberdeen and its nest of unabashed Catholics, centred on the bishop's palace and the diocesan chancellor's house.[51]

During the last decades of the sixteenth century the boundaries of the burgh community were changing dramatically. For most of the century the burgh had formed a close society, jealous of its privileges and zealous in its attempts to exclude local nobles and lairds from interference in its internal affairs (see Chapter 8). As the century progressed long-established loyalties were tested, and positions of power and influence were challenged. This ensured an alteration in patterns of patronage and association. Each representative group in the town was looking for some kind of catalyst or rallying point during these years, a spokesman or issue which could co-ordinate opposition and increase its corporate effectiveness. Protestantism certainly provided a platform, but many were reluctant to embrace its tenets, since they shared in the general conservatism of the region. Eventually, discontent and division focused around the question of the craftsmen's rights to representation on the council. The underlying issue, however, was the coherence of the community and the loyalty of those who governed it to traditional values.

The principal target of the craft assault was the 'abominable race of Menzies', with their kinship network, local landed colleagues and burgess associates.[52] These accusations have a familiar refrain - they had been levelled by David Menzies against Sir John Rutherford, as provost, as long ago as 1487. As the Menzies were at the head of opposition in 1487, so they were the target of it in the 1580s and 1590s. Like many other families, the Menzies family had undergone a process of 'gentrification' through its determined acquisition of lands outside the burgh. In 1590, their chief opponent, Master John Cheyne, described Thomas Menzies as a 'landward baron, na merchant nor trafecker, only brought from landward, for the maintenance of his friends'. The distinction between town and country was further eroded with economic consequences for the ordinary inhabitants of the burgh. The amount of merchandise passing through the port had fallen drastically. Many merchants had deserted it altogether and were trading through Leith and Dundee, leaving Aberdeen, according to the complaint of the guild court, a 'dry pond'.[53]

By the end of the 1580s, the Menzies faction was finding it more difficult to exercise patronage. The limitations on its power were particularly evident in its failure to install William Kinloch as master of the song school in 1586. Kinloch was a Catholic sympathiser, and a minority on the council objected to his appointment on religious grounds.[54] A similar scenario emerged in 1588, when the clerkship of the council, which had been in the hands of the Menzies family and exercised by a depute since 1505, fell vacant.[55] Objections were raised to a new Menzies appointment and further complaints were made that council meetings were not regularly announced, councillors were not summoned in good time, business was manipulated and no record of attendance was kept. The register of meetings was not available for inspection and a large part of the town's documents had been impounded by the Menzies, who were not persuaded to release them until 1592.[56] No investigations could be made into the proper administration of the town's finances and patronage or how it had been administered over the previous century. Moreover, the Menzies had opened the council to their own associates amongst the Gordons and their supporters in the locality. Formerly, political conflict had been restricted to the council chamber and tensions had been resolved within its confines. By the end of the century, the council chamber could no longer contain such differences of view and the ranks of the burgesses had been swelled by those whose interests were not always those of the common good of the burgh.

In 1587, there was a disputed election for the provostship. Alexander Rutherford was elected by the head court. Afterwards, Huntly persuaded the council that Gilbert Menzies should serve as provost for that year. The Menzies, learning from the previous year's election that their authority was under threat, brought in their allies from the surrounding countryside in an effort to capitalise on the support they had been building up so assiduously over the previous years.[57] Their triumph was temporary and marked the beginning of their fall. The price of Huntly's support was heavy. In June 1588, Gilbert Menzies and his brother Thomas signed a bond of manrent with the earl for themselves and their kin.[58] The provost of Aberdeen was now in Huntly's pocket. The compliance of the provost was absolutely essential should the earl's negotiations with Spain come within the bounds of possibility. In 1590, Huntly wrote to Edinburgh, referring to the provost and his family as 'my dependaris'.[59]

Huntly was generally recognised as the mainstay of Catholicism in the northeast. He had a rival for influence in the region in the person of the Earl Marischal, a convinced Protestant (Plate 24). Marischal had already been involved in Aberdeen as a member of a commission authorised by the General Assembly to visit King's College to investigate the possibility of its reform.[60] The discovery of the earl of Huntly's links with Spain, and the regular comings and goings of Jesuits and other Catholic priests through Aberdeen, fuelled pressure for further reformation in the region. The Earl Marischal was a likely replacement figure for Huntly and promised to be an effective instrument for reform, but he had no party through whom he could work in the burgh and its environs. A possible, if unlikely, alliance was offered in the shape of the leader of the opposition to the Menzies family, in the shape of Master John Cheyne, a Louvain-educated lawyer, at the head of a burgess-craftsman alliance.[61]

In 1587, an attempt was made, in the Common Indenture, to settle the points at issue between the craftsmen and the merchant patriciate of Aberdeen. To their dismay, however, the crafts discovered that the Indenture consolidated the control that the council already exercised over the crafts. They were not granted representation on the council, they could not admit candidates to their own craft, and even the two auditors of the town's accounts were to be chosen for them by the council from a leet of six. It may have seemed a valuable recognition of the identity and contribution of the crafts to burgh life, but its interpretation, which was largely left to the council, went against the crafts. The trouble came to a head once more in 1590.[62]

By 1590, the flight of richer merchants from the burgh was threatening the economic survival of lesser merchants who had sheltered under their umbrella. They were more inclined to listen to Master John Cheyne, representing the new men of the burgh. Cheyne complained to the Convention of Royal Burghs that Master Thomas Menzies, the provost, and Alexander Rutherford were not constituted representatives of the burgh, since they had not been appointed with the consent of the entire community.[63] Deep factionalism was revealed even in the ranks of the council. The majority of the craft complainants came from the wealthier craftsmen, some of whom had served on the kirk session, while others had been deacons of their trades. This opposition party represented a fusion of two distinct interest groups whose ambitions were related, but not identical. The succeeding years saw the strategic retreat of the merchant oligarchy from its domination of burgh affairs. What forced this was the acknowledgement that it was impossible to govern the burgh without the support of the consensus of its population.

In 1592, the Court of Session removed the political stalemate in Aberdeen by ordering that acts of parliament relating to burgh elections should be followed in every respect.[64] This prepared the way for craft representation on the council and for craftmen to participate in elections. The decision introduced the principle of mobility into the static structure of burgh government. It now became possible for the council to be renewed within two years. In 1593, John Cheyne was elected provost. His first action was to ask the community for a vote of confidence; all present held up their hands signifying that the consensus the Menzies had once commanded had now swung behind their chief opponent.[65] The notion of community had been reconstructed on alternative lines to those that had prevailed for the previous half century.

Throughout 1593, the spectre of Spanish invasion and the suspected treachery of the earl of Huntly dominated events, both nationally and locally. The discovery of the 'Spanish blanks' pushed the king to bridle Huntly's power. One of the victims was his Menzies clientage. The Earl Marischal, Huntly's rival, was promoted to lieutenant of the north. He already enjoyed some support in the anti-Menzies lobby. John Cheyne had been an associate and had acted occasionally as his agent in the burgh.[66] The new regime in the burgh was willing to co-operate with the impeccably Protestant Marischal, and encouraged the foundation of Marischal College, located in the buildings of the former Franciscan friary (see Chapter 15). As a seminary for the provision of the Protestant preachers the region so desperately needed, godliness and reformed learning were to prosper there.

The waning of the Menzies era, however, did not inaugurate a new age of burgh politics. There had been no fundamental constitutional revolution in Aberdeen. The system which had spawned Menzies power remained broadly intact after 1593 (see Chapters 8 and 12). The leading actors were, however, different and the script was to be moderately Protestant, rather than conservatively Catholic. The Cheyne regime was soon to discover that it too could not govern the burgh without the consensus of its inhabitants. The reform of the Church, the radicalisation of the crafts and the breaking open of the oligarchy were to prove a mixed blessing to the burgh and compound a potent and unpredictable blend of religion and ambition.

11

'The civill warrs did overrun all':
Aberdeen, 1630–1690

GORDON DesBRISAY

O Eternal and ever liveing God
Who hes created mankind to societie
In the which thow that is the God
of order and hates confusion
hes appoyntit some to rule and governe
and others to be governed ...[1]

These terse lines are from a prayer recited each year in the council chamber of New Aberdeen on the last Wednesday before Michaelmas (29 September), when members of the outgoing town council gathered to elect their successors.[2] They neatly encapsulate seventeenth-century views of society and authority, in which the social world, no less than the natural world, was God's creation, the existing social order was more or less as He wished it, and the powers-that-be at every level were sanctioned by His mandate. This was comforting so far as Aberdeen's burgh fathers were concerned, but any sense of self-congratulation was tempered by a note of menace, a stark reminder that they were accountable to 'the God of order' who 'hates confusion'. Confusion was the opposite of everything a godly community and its town council stood for. Urban life generated enough disorder to keep the council and its allied agencies busy at the best of times, but when external forces brought added confusion the burgh could come close to being overwhelmed. Throughout the seventeenth century, there were periodic crises sparked by crop failure, outbreaks of deadly disease, or the loss of vital overseas markets. When two or more of these crises overlapped, as when the final collapse of the plaiding trade coincided with harvest failures and famine in the 1690s (see Chapters 5 and 6), disaster could ensue. At its most extreme, confusion could tip into chaos, the nightmare scenario of a total breakdown of society that haunted the early modern imagination. Chaos was most often associated with war, especially civil war, which many seventeenth-century commentators considered the greatest evil that could befall society.[3] Seventeenth-century Aberdonians would not have disagreed. The Covenanting era of mid-century marked a profound watershed in the fortunes of both burghs. These were among the most miserable years in Aberdeen's recorded history; as James Gordon wrote in 1660, whilst 'the civill warrs did overrun all, ther wes no citie in Scotland which did suffer more hurt then Aberdeen did, nor oftener.'[4]

Aberdeen before the Troubles

Aberdeen's seventeenth century can be divided into three distinct periods: before, during, and after the Troubles. Early modern life was never entirely easy or secure, but on the whole Aberdeen did well in the first four decades of the seventeenth century. No one could have known it at the time, but in New Aberdeen the 1630s witnessed a peak of population and prosperity that was not to be matched for the better part of a century. The population of the two towns together touched almost 10,000 in that decade: probably between 8,000 and 8,500 in New Aberdeen and some 900 in Old Aberdeen (see Chapter 5). The prosperity that fuelled this growth was driven by merchants who controlled the manufacture (mainly in the country-side) and export (mainly to the Netherlands) of plaiding, a coarse cloth made of carded wool that was a speciality of the north-east. By the 1630s exports were fifteen times greater than at the start of the century, and they reached an all-time peak in 1639.[5] Prices remained high as volumes increased, and merchants made fortunes.

The new money trickled through the north-east economy, and a good deal of it pooled in Aberdeen. In the 1630s, the royal burgh was not only richer than at any other point in the century, but possessed of a more expansive and generous spirit. There was an unprecedented outpouring of charitable legacies or 'mortifica-tions', so many that in 1632 the town council had to create the new office of master of mortifications to manage all the accounts.[6] For a time, anything seemed possible. The town council initiated or approved a wide array of projects. New private homes were built and old ones remodelled.[7] Semi-private hospitals (really retirement homes) were built or refurbished for the most favoured of the town's poor, while a public workhouse, the Correction House, was erected for those whose lives had less happy trajectories (see Chapter 2). There was investment in infrastructure, including the water supply and (most expensively) the roads. In 1632, the council decided to build a bridge at Bucksburn, because 'sundrie poore people hes lostit thair lyiffis' trying to cross the burn in winter to reach the market in Aberdeen.[8] At the harbour, work started on extending the quay, though vital repairs still had to be done throughout the century, even at times of grave crisis (see Chapter 7). A new crane was built, and a large packhouse for folding and measuring plaiding.[9] The north aisle of St Nicholas Church gained a new lead roof. A new butchers' shambles (the 'fleshous') was built behind the tolbooth in 1631. The tolbooth itself was completely rebuilt between 1616 and 1630 (see Chapter 4). New Aberdeen even gained its first park in 1635, when the council accepted the artist George Jamesone's offer to create a public pleasure garden at his own expense, on ground gone to waste beside the Well of Spa.[10]

The project that best captured the expansive spirit of the day, however, was the refurbishment of Greyfriars Kirk. A 'pleasant and magnifick edifice lyand in the hart of the toune', it fell into decay after the Reformation and 'throw laik of glass wyndoes, hes lyen waist without ony divyne worship' for many years.[11] Earlier campaigns to raise money for repairs had failed, but in 1633 Dr William Guild, minister of New Aberdeen and one of its greatest benefactors, offered to pay for the costly work.[12] After new windows were installed in 1635, the town council invested £700 to buy and immediately demolish a large house next door, so that 'the beautie of the said kirk (whilk hes beine so long obscurit)' could be seen to better advantage, 'for the decoratioun of that pairt of the toune'.[13] In the more straitened years ahead, public projects of this sort were carried out on a strictly utilitarian basis: there were fewer private donors able to underwrite such work and town councils could not afford to spend money on aesthetic improvements.

Aberdeen and the National Covenant

Aberdeen in the 1630s seemed a secure bastion of conservative and Episcopalian preferences. It was the unofficial capital of a 'conservative north'[14] led by conservative (sometimes Catholic) nobles, capable bishops, and a generation of Episcopalian divines – the celebrated 'Aberdeen Doctors' – whose willingness to tolerate both the king's intervention in the kirk and a relatively broad range of ecclesiastical preferences among Protestants set them apart from their more doctrinaire Presbyterian colleagues.[15] Up close, however, things appeared less settled. Even Old Aberdeen, by far the more quiescent of the two burghs (where there was as yet no merchant guild to contend for authority with the college or the kirk, and where the three magistrates were appointed by the bishop, rather than elected), witnessed 'fratricidal strife' amongst the King's College staff as soon as the reforming Bishop Patrick Forbes died in 1635.[16] In New Aberdeen, the relatively broad-based political establishment was already divided by the mid 1630s into two main camps that subsequently formed the cores of local royalist and Covenanting parties.[17]

The coronation parliament of Charles I (1625-49), held in Edinburgh in 1633 during the king's first visit to his northern realm, was a watershed for both the political nation and the royal burgh. Strained relations between the monarch and his Scottish subjects could barely be papered over. New Aberdeen was represented by Provost Paul Menzies and Bailie Patrick Leslie, who probably went to Edinburgh as heads of rival factions on the council, and certainly returned as such.[18] Menzies, the senior representative, was absent on the critical last day of the parliament, when the king had demanded that the entire legislative agenda of 168 measures be voted on as a package, with little or no discussion.[19] Anyone tempted to vote against innovations in religion or taxation would also have to vote against bills which they favoured.[20] Menzies was happy to back the king, but in his absence Leslie sided with the incipient opposition minority and voted against the package. The king took note of his name, and Leslie returned to Aberdeen under a cloud. Menzies, by contrast, returned with a knighthood.[21]

Back in Aberdeen, Menzies (now Sir Paul) was elected to a tenth consecutive term as provost but, in the following council year (1634-5), Patrick Leslie was chosen. The king, by now given to intervening in burgh elections, ordered that Leslie step down and Menzies be reinstated.[22] Both men complied. The nineteen-man town council, however, still featured ten Leslie supporters and nine Menzies men. Since the councillors chose their own successors from a long shortlist of their own devising, and since the split clearly extended beyond the incumbent council, there was little hope of their choosing non-partisans at the next election, and considerable risk that Leslie would be returned, making Aberdeen the first burgh to defy the king's electoral wishes.[23] The Archbishop of St Andrews (also Chancellor of Scotland) wrote ahead to warn that if Leslie was elected or even allowed to vote 'it culd not but come to your trouble', and the Bishop of Aberdeen (also a privy councillor) and the Sheriff of Aberdeen sat in to monitor the proceedings.[24] After much delay, the Leslie faction walked out and the Menzies party elected a council in its own image. This proved unworkable and in February 1636 the privy council, noting the 'factions and hearts-burning among the neichbouris', overturned that election and appointed a new, compromise council based mainly on the previous, deadlocked body of 1634-5.[25] Patrick Leslie agreed to step aside for a year rather than 'breed some new matter of offence to his majestie'. In an effort to effect an acceptable compromise, the conservative Gilbert Menzies of Pitfodels, whose ancestors had dominated Aberdeen councils in the previous century and had done so much to reduce the influence of landed men in urban affairs (see Chapter 10), was removed because he was a 'kingis barone' rather than a practising merchant, as the Aberdeen constitution required. For provost, the privy council reached outside the poisoned circle of incumbents to appoint Alexander Jaffray (father of the diarist and more famous provost of the same name). The recommendation of Jaffray apparently came from the king himself, on the advice of the Earl of Traquair, who followed developments in Aberdeen closely, but the appointment of the grandson of a baker was not welcomed in all quarters. A bacon pie was left to greet him on the provost's ceremonial chair (see Chapter 8).[26]

The bishops who intervened in Aberdeen politics in 1635 did so in their (controversial) capacities as agents of the crown, rather than of the church. As concerned as the government was to restore calm in the townhouse, it saw no immediate threat to the local religious establishment. Indeed, in 1636 the authorities in Edinburgh were so confident of Aberdeen's essential conservatism and Episcopalianism that they sentenced Samuel Rutherford, Scotland's most outspoken radical Presbyterian, to exile in the royal burgh.[27] The idea was that Rutherford, far from his base in the radical south-west, would find scant support in the conservative north-east, while exposure to the Aberdeen Doctors might have a softening effect. The minister, of course, was not for turning. Rutherford was forbidden to preach, but he was free to argue with ministers and mix with local people.[28] He made infrequent reference to Aberdeen in his 219 surviving letters from there, and these mostly scathing: 'all are corrupt here' and 'I see God in few', he grumbled, claiming that the population consisted of Catholics, Arminians (anti-Calvinist Episcopalians) and 'men of Gallio's naughty faith', by which he meant magistrates indifferent to religion.[29] Rutherford exaggerated: Catholics were a tiny (if entrenched) proportion of the urban population; Arminians were a minority even among the clergy; and nowhere in Scotland did magistrates, ministers, elders and deacons wage the distinctively Calvinist crusade for 'godly discipline' with more rigour than in Aberdeen.[30] Like many Covenanters (and not a few Episcopalians) to follow, Rutherford was happier stressing the divisions between Presbyterians and Episcopalians while passing over fundamental continuities in theory and practice. He made Aberdeen seem more distinctive (or aberrant, in his view) than it really was.[31]

Samuel Rutherford was cooling his heels in Aberdeen on 23 July 1637, when the famous riots attending the introduction of the new Scottish Prayer Book in Edinburgh touched off the Covenanting revolution. Since the parliament of 1633, Charles I's high-handed ways in matters of church and state had aroused mounting concern in all sectors of Scottish society. The new Prayer Book, produced with minimal consultation and little regard for Scottish religious sensibilities, only confirmed the 'absolutist anglicising' of this absentee king.[32] A wide coalition of nobles, lairds and ministers formed to pressure the king to address their grievances. The royal burghs, which tended to act cautiously and as a bloc, hung back at first, but by October 1637 most town councils had declared for the opposition.[33] Aberdeen was not among them.

In February 1638, King Charles issued a proclamation that heightened the tension in Scotland. He gave no ground on any issue of concern, but offered to pardon those in opposition for their actions to date, if they would desist. Subsequent opposition would be regarded as treason.[34] With none of their concerns addressed, however, those in opposition felt they had no option but to push ahead, and the king's new threat required that they act in solidarity. In a matter of days, the

National Covenant was drawn up. First subscribed in Edinburgh on 28 February 1638, it was a cleverly bland but ambiguous document meant to be acceptable to a broad spectrum of people.[35] There was no explicit denunciation of royal power over the kirk, nor of bishops, nor of contentious civil policies. It expressed loyalty to the king, but it also (and this was the key to its revolutionary potential) bound signatories to defend the very kirk, laws and liberties of Scotland that the king was thought to be undermining.

On 16 March 1638, two commissioners from the Convention of Royal Burghs and three Covenanting lairds brought a copy of the National Covenant to New Aberdeen to be subscribed by the town council. Had it been a matter of money, a 'head court' of the 600-odd burgesses of guild and trade would have been called; recent head courts had twice resisted royal interference by denying the king's direct request that they increase the salaries of Aberdeen ministers as part of his wider campaign to raise the 'dignitie' of the clergy.[36] But with no fiscal issue at stake the matter stayed in chambers, with the current council, as was customary with weighty matters, joined by members of the previous council. After much discussion, the twenty-eight current and past councillors declared that they could not endorse the National Covenant, because it fell 'within the compass of contempt of his majesties royal authoritie'. The councillors were divided almost evenly between the Menzies and Leslie factions, but 'all in ane voice planelie and absolutelie refused to subscryve'.[37] At this point, Aberdeen was one of a handful of royal burghs that had not accepted the Covenant; by May 1638 it was the only one. 'All the rest of the burrowis', lamented John Spalding, the contemporary royalist and Episcopalian chronicler, 'subscrivit this covenant and leivit in peace'.[38]

Loyalty to the king was the reason that the council gave for its famous refusal of the Covenant. That is not a claim to be taken lightly, but almost everyone on both sides claimed to be loyal, and many on the council had done their share of protesting, resisting, and even thwarting the king's wishes in recent years. Commentators at the time all identified two additional factors. One was the persuasive influence of the Aberdeen Doctors, whose preaching and writing posed Scotland's most rigorous intellectual challenge to the Covenanters. A more direct sort of influence was exercised by George Gordon, second marquis of Huntly, the greatest nobleman in the north-east and one of the king's staunchest supporters. Huntly was aloof and diffident. But when the Forbes, Frasers and others amongst his traditional enemies in the region came out for the Covenant (described at the time as 'a new ranckling of an old ill curd wound'), he was provoked into taking a stance.[39] With his Gordon followers and their associates, he could field a large army at short notice and he could bring considerable pressure to bear on the two burghs.

By the summer of 1638, both the Covenanters and the king were preparing for war. Aberdeen was the target of intense political and diplomatic pressure from both sides. In April the king had written to commend the council and ministers for refusing the Covenant, a service 'more considerable in regard of the neglect of otheris'. As a further sign of favour, he renewed and extended the royal burgh's ancient commercial and legal privileges, in what came to be known as the 'Great Charter'. The king's letter may have encouraged Professor John Forbes, the most distinguished of the Aberdeen Doctors, to write the first of his anti-Covenanting tracts. Huntly gleefully circulated it among his Covenanting neighbours, who were mortally offended by what they took to be slights upon their honour. The un-worldly Forbes was shocked by the threats directed his way: 'This is an unchristiane answere to turne a theologicall dispute into a criminall process', he complained, but it was an early sign of how things would go.[40] The Aberdeen Doctors are generally held to have bested the Covenanters in the ensuing pamphlet war, but the latter had little interest in debate, and the former lacked the political will and experience needed to turn their writings to tangible effect (see Chapter 13).[41]

Aberdeen was given a second chance to subscribe the National Covenant in July 1638, when a team of eight Covenanting luminaries arrived to win the council, ministers and now also 'the bodie of the toune' over to their cause.[42] The delegation consisted of three prominent ministers, including Andrew Cant, 'ane superexcellent preacher' who would later serve in Aberdeen; and five nobles or lairds, including James Graham, earl (later marquis) of Montrose, who would take Aberdeen by force on two occasions, once for each side.[43] In 1638, Montrose was a Covenanter, and he came in peace. The visit began badly when the Covenanters arrived to find that the council had already reiterated its rejection of the National Covenant. Irked, the visitors refused to drink from the ceremonial cup of Bon-Accord, a slight that prompted officials to lock the Covenanting preachers out of the burgh's churches. One result was that the two sets of ministers never debated face to face the issues which separated them. However, Lady Pitsligo, sister of the Earl Marischal (and 'ane rank puritane' according to Spalding), offered the visitors the spacious forecourt of her brother's house on the Castlegate. The Covenanting ministers preached from Marischal's balcony on Sunday 21 July, being careful to avoid the times of regular services that might have reduced their audience. They extolled the virtues of the Covenant to a large crowd and tried to counter the printed objections raised by the Aberdeen Doctors. About fifty people from in and around the two burghs subscribed the Covenant: a disappointing result for such a high-profile diplomatic mission.[44] Some of the signatories, sneered James Gordon, were 'poor mechanickes or those of the faeminine gender', but others were less easily dis-missed.[45] In Old Aberdeen, John Lundie, the grammarian of King's College, shocked his colleagues by signing.[46] In New Aberdeen, Patrick Leslie was joined by several members of the current town council, and by two of the town's four ministers –

William Robertson at Futtie and, beyond 'all manis expectatioun', William Guild, philanthropist and Aberdeen Doctor.[47]

The fact that a majority of Aberdonians declined the opportunity to subscribe the National Covenant on this occasion has always been taken as a defining moment in the town's history, but in fact nothing was definitively settled and support for the Covenant increased immediately after the visitors left. Attention again focused on the town council, where the old factions reasserted themselves with a vengeance. In the weeks leading up to the annual council elections in late September, support for the Covenanters widened to include not just signatories but others leaning that way. In a letter of 16 August 1638, the royalist Provost Robert Johnston warned the Marquis of Huntly that:

> some few of our councell, to the number of sex or sevin or thairby hes sub-scryved the covenant, Yett we find that the most pairt of our presente councell, ar that way Inclyned, as being upon that faction. And so it is to be feared that at the approching election of our magistrattis and councell at Michaelmes nixt, They sall carie the same be pluralitie of voytes to thair covenanting faction.

If the Covenanters should prevail, warned Johnston, they would 'draw the most pairt of our towne upon that course with thame'.[48] The Covenanters (almost literally) smelled blood: Montrose feared that if 'some too busy people' convinced the king to ban Covenanters from the Aberdeen election, it would cause such an uproar there 'that every one wil be rady to thrust his sworde in his nighbours side'.[49]

It nearly came to that. Huntly, indeed, procured a letter from the king, which Provost Johnston gamely read out at the election, but it did not explicitly ban Covenanters, and (despite the silence in the printed record) a Covenanting majority was elected, capturing no fewer than five of the seven main offices.[50] The new provost was Alexander Jaffray the elder, ironically the nominee of the privy council in 1636. Since then, however, he had signalled his serious commitment to the anti-royalist faction by being one of the original signatories of the Covenant in Aberdeen.[51] Ex-provost Johnston walked out in protest: 'ryising up frome his plaice and standing befoir the Counsell tabill [he] protestit as of befoir saying he would not stay nor be any longer present at the electioun, becaus thair was so many covenanteris chosin'.[52] In his post-mortem report to Huntly, Johnston claimed that anti-Covenanter supporters were waiting for him at the market cross, 'with swords redie to have made a tumult and comotion be reason of chusing of covenanters' had he not stayed their hands.[53]

Huntly was furious, and probably embarrassed, by the election results, but he soon had an opportunity to reassert his authority when the king's privy council issued an alternative covenant in September 1638. It attracted little support elsewhere, but Huntly was determined to see it endorsed in his own sphere of influence.[54] On 5 October, a large crowd gathered at the market cross of New Aberdeen to hear him read out the so-called King's Covenant. Huntly's large band of retainers cleared his way to the cross, and the town's royalist-leaning militia stood at the ready in the background. When he was done, Huntly shouted 'God Saif the King!' and retired across the Castlegate to the laird of Pitfodels' balcony, amidst what he claimed to be 'almost universal applause'.[55] From there, he could see that the Master of Forbes and other Covenanting barons were not so well received. He might have been equally pleased to note that the newly-elected magistrates could barely restrain the militia from attacking the Covenanters, and that it took a sudden downpour to cool tempers.[56]

Huntly ordered that 'the whole bodie' of the town meet to subscribe the King's Covenant. The magistrates, having taken the precaution of ordering the militia to stand down, held the meeting on 8 October. Huntly had not instructed them to debate the King's Covenant, just sign it, but Provost Jaffray asked two of the Aberdeen Doctors, Robert Baron and James Sibbald, to help remove 'all scrupill out of the mynds of the people'.[57] This they did by appending to the document a list of their own scruples, mainly to do with preserving episcopacy.[58] It was not what Huntly had in mind, but he admitted backstage to being 'not muche averse from theyr opinion', and so 'the most pairt' of the people signed, in effect, their own modified version of the King's Covenant.[59] Some leading members of the civic establishment, including Provost Jaffray and several others on the council, had now subscribed both covenants.[60]

Aberdonians soon faced another tricky decision. The king had agreed that a General Assembly of the kirk be held in Glasgow in November 1638. As matters spun further from his control, however, it became clear that the Assembly would be hijacked by Presbyterians intent on abolishing episcopacy. No bishops planned to attend, so the Aberdeen Doctors were the Episcopalians' last hope. But they were not cut out to be heroes, nor martyrs, and begged Huntly to explain to the king that 'by that journey appearintly we can doe litle or no good, and may receave much evill'.[61] In the end, none went but Dr Guild, the surprise Covenanter.[62]

As a royal burgh, New Aberdeen had been expected to send lay representatives as well as ministers to the Glasgow Assembly, but on 5 November the town council received a petition from 'a great number' of anti-Covenanter residents, asking that no one be sent: the king had not issued a summons; the local version of the King's Covenant rejected the abolition of episcopacy; and it would cost money. Besides these partisan arguments, however, the petitioners expressed misgivings any Aberdonian could appreciate:

the commissioner that sal happin to be chosin (if any be) … must neids ather displease his Majestie (as God forbid) ... or oure neighbour burrowes, or sall wrong the trust committit to him be this burghe, or utherwayes wrong his awin conscience in assenting or disassenting, protesting or not protesting.[63]

This was Aberdeen's great dilemma. In a world built on deference and hierarchy, just what were people to do when the chain of command broke? To whom were they responsible amidst the confusion of divided loyalties and conflicting demands? If they could not agree among themselves, how were they to deal with the contending parties in the coming war? Even if they wished to dispense with principle and follow a pragmatic line, which way was safest?

Aberdeen and the Wars of the Covenant

More than any other burgh, Aberdeen lay on the contested frontier between the Covenanting south and the royalist north. The fault-line ran right through it. Not, perhaps, down the middle, as there were probably more anti-Covenanters than Covenanters in the burgh, but without opinion polls, open elections, or neutral observers as guides, it is hard to gauge the proportions of people on either side of that line (or attempting to straddle it). Popular and scholarly tradition, which has played up evidence of royalist and Episcopalian influence and all but buried evidence of support for the National Covenant, is unreliable in this regard. On the eve of civil war, Aberdeen was already deeply divided and this political confusion was a source not just of tension but of real vulnerability.

Complete unanimity was not to be expected, but Aberdeen was divided in a particularly unfortunate way. Opposition to the Covenanters was strong enough to keep it from fully endorsing the National Covenant. That, in turn, made it an immediate target of Covenanting armies. At the same time, however, support for the Covenanters was strong enough to undermine the already slim prospects for a royalist counter-offensive. Whatever the balance of opinion at any given moment, there were always enough royalists and enough Covenanters in Aberdeen to ensure that it could almost never fully commit to, or (more to the point) be fully trusted by, either side. That lack of trust meant that both parties would apply an extra measure of restraining force in the form of crippling exactions of money and material, and repeated and sustained military occupations.

The Glasgow Assembly had ended in December 1638 with episcopacy abolished, bishops deposed, and war all but declared. Charles I planned an invasion from England to reassert his authority, and the Covenanters prepared to fight. The First Bishops' War of 1639, the opening round of the Scottish wars, was a generally tepid affair that grew very tense in and around Aberdeen. The royal burgh, in particular, was too important and strategically vital for its own good: neither side could afford to leave it to the other. Unwalled and awkwardly sited for defence, Aberdeen changed hands five times in four months, and its people were the first to experience the comings, stoppings and goings of rival armies.[64] In what amounted to a dress rehearsal for the Troubles of the mid 1640s, the events of 1639 revealed patterns of wartime behaviour which would become all too familiar to Aberdonians in the years which followed.

Early in 1639, the two burghs were under Huntly's protection, so they had to prepare to defend themselves against Covenanters from the south and north. The town council of New Aberdeen, however, was dominated by home-grown Covenanters who hesitated to put the burgh in a defensive posture that any opposing army would consider a provocation. The magistrates had to be prompted to take action by royalists and others, but after a slow start they moved quickly to have the town's ports reinforced, back gates sealed, and 'catbands' (iron bars or chains) set across streets to stop horses. Grain and gunpowder were hoarded, and strangers queried. A council of war was appointed, a nightly watch posted, and cannon hauled into position. To the north-west, along the edge of the marshy loch, planks were installed as cover for musketeers. To the north-east, men and women (for not even widows, ministers or magistrates were exempt) frantically dug a perimeter ditch from the Gallowgate Port to the Castle Hill. When not digging, men aged sixteen to sixty practised military drill.[65]

There was only so much that Aberdeen could do for itself; it had to rely on Huntly's forces to hold off the Covenanters, who were expected in numbers. But Huntly, too, was feeling the pressure. There were rumours of plots against him, and he was advised in January 1640 to move out of his house in Old Aberdeen and 'go duell in New Abirdein', where his friends could more easily protect him. Huntly moved his family into the laird of Pitfodels' mansion on the Castlegate, and posted eight of his own men to stand guard all night; when every other household doused its fires and candles at curfew, Huntly's stayed lit.[66] The great lord's obvious concern for his own safety sent a discouraging signal to the townsfolk; some already doubted Huntly's stomach for a fight, much as he in turn had grounds for suspecting the resolve of their Covenanting leaders.[67]

The closer the Covenanters came, the less tenable Aberdeen's and Huntly's position seemed. On 20 March, New Aberdeen's town council took steps to secure vital deeds and charters from capture. Two days later, the bishop and chief bailie of Old Aberdeen reviewed the militia there and found most of the 160 men 'waik, febill and unarmed'.[68] Much the same situation pertained in towns across Britain, but none of them as yet faced imminent attack.[69] Before the day was over, King's College was locked up and its staff and students scattered, and the bishop (a marked man) had abandoned his palace in Old Aberdeen.[70] Prominent royalists fled both burghs, some to estates or relatives in the country, others to England or the continent.

Huntly, recently appointed king's lieutenant for the north of Scotland, was not the man to rally dispirited troops. On 25 March he 'haistellie resolves to leave Abirdein in the midst of thair distressis', ordering royalist forces to meet him at Inverurie. Aberdonians 'knew not whome to obey, whidder the Kingis proclamatiouns and his lieutennandis charges, or the covenanteris commandment'. The Marquis soon made their choice easier. Five thousand men gathered at Inverurie but, with news of twice as many Covenanters approaching, Huntly sent them home and retired to Strathbogie.[71] Two days later, on 28 March, New Aberdeen's militia captains resigned, acknowledging that they could not 'withstand the great power and armie approching to this burgh, a great many of the inhabitantis having alreddie deserted and left the toune, and thay having no help nor supplie of men frome the cuntrie to resist the invasioun of the said armie'. Swords were set aside, the watch stood down, cannon removed, catbands lowered and the town's gates opened.[72]

In the evening of Friday 29 March 1639, Old Aberdeen became the first town in the Scottish wars to come under military occupation, when 2,000 north-east Covenanters led by Lord Fraser and the Master of Forbes 'cam in order of battell' and camped in and about the burgh. Next morning, Montrose led 9,000 southern Covenanters into New Aberdeen. His cavalry wore blue sashes (his pointed response to the red of Huntly's men), and the infantry blue ribbons in their bonnets. The 'blue bonnets' would become a familiar image amongst the armies of the Covenant. In the Upperkirkgate Port and along the Broadgate and Castlegate they clattered, then out of the Justice Port to the Links, where the north-east Covenanters joined them for inspection and a late breakfast. Most men sat where they were and ate their provisions but others went to buy food in town, returning to report that they 'war not maid welcum and payit deir for sic as thay gat'. Montrose, already irritated at the money and effort Aberdeen had wasted trying to thwart his army, called over Provost Jaffray and ordered the new ditches filled immediately, and his men catered for 'without extortioun'.[73]

Extortion was a fact of life under military occupation, but the hoarding of black-marketeers and exorbitant demands of individual soldiers were nothing compared to the extortionate demands of successive military regimes.[74] During that first incursion, Montrose took the bulk of his forces off in pursuit of Huntly, leaving the Earl of Kinghorn and his 1,800 men of Angus and Fife to occupy New Aberdeen. Kinghorn's were the first of thousands of soldiers to billet in Aberdonian homes. For eight days' quartering he charged the town nearly £4,800, which he (like most commanding officers to follow, and with as dim prospects) promised would be repaid. Unused, perhaps, to giving peremptory orders, he assembled the townsfolk in the Greyfriars Kirk and asked their opinion of his demands. The remarkably plain-spoken response was that they would obey because 'they ar under bondage and thraldome for the present, and nowayes habill to resist'.[75] There was more blunt talk on 9 April, when Provost Jaffray informed the townsfolk that Covenanting nobles had imposed a massive fine of 100,000 merks (£66,667) for putting them to the trouble of bringing an army north. This was an impossible sum and grossly unfair: if the nobles insisted, said the townsfolk, they asked for one month's grace to remove their families and personal effects, 'and thaireftir lat the nobillmen dispose of the toune at thair pleasure'.[76]

The threatened fine served its purpose because the next day, 10 April 1639, 'the most pairt' of the people of New Aberdeen finally subscribed the National Covenant, much as the 'kingless, helples, freindles' people of Old Aberdeen, under similar pressure, had done the week before. By now, 'the most pairt' of both burghs had subscribed both the National Covenant and the King's Covenant, amidst varying degrees of sincerity, insincerity and duress. On 11 April, Montrose rescinded the fine, but he insisted that his new allies surrender the names of royalist neighbours who had fled, 'that we may plunder thair goodis at our plesour'.[77]

Targeted plunder, quartering, taxation and fines were weapons that most armies of occupation indulged in, not caring that they risked unleashing an endless cycle of retribution upon their departure. All it took was one reversal of fortune for Aberdonians to see the need to resist these tactics. Montrose's forces, having brought Aberdeen into the Covenanter camp and captured Huntly, withdrew south in mid April. As soon as they were gone, a representative of Aberdeen's 'first subscriveris' of the National Covenant proposed that he and his colleagues should not bear any of the costs of the occupation, since 'thay wer not the occasioun' of them.[78] Then the tables turned. On 15 May 1639, royalist forces led by Sir George Ogilvy of Banff scored a surprise victory over north-east Covenanters at the 'Trot of Turriff', and that evening entered New Aberdeen unopposed.[79] Covenanters now ran for their lives. Their homes were immediately plundered, and the royalist commanders proposed making these 'auld' or original Covenanters bear the entire burden of the new occupation. The majority of householders stood to benefit this time but, perhaps expecting further reversals, they answered:

> all in ane voice that thay wold not separat nor divyde thameselffis from the auld covenanteris, since they ar all memberis of on bodie and incorporatioun with thame, bot wald willinglie contribute and bear burding with the saids auld covenanteris for thair greater ease of suche ane heavie burding, and for eschewing the plundering of thair houssis and gudes whairwith thay war threatned.[80]

Solidarity cut both ways, and the Covenanters had to agree to drop their earlier claims. Even so, this was a courageous defence of the old civic values of the burgh community in the face of mounting incivility.

In addition to money, supplies, room and board, Aberdeen was often called upon to contribute soldiers or weapons to one army or another, which it was seldom willing to do except for its own immediate defence. Before the Trot of Turriff, New Aberdeen had refused the Earl Marischal's request for soldiers and cannon, and when Ogilvy captured the town and made the same request three days later, he got the same answer.[81] But even-handedness won no friends in the increasingly acrimonious and partisan climate of civil war. Aberdonians found it virtually impossible to appease either side. Compliance could be almost as dangerous as defiance, and compulsion was no excuse. Too often, the town was compelled to concede something to one side, only to be punished for it when the other side returned. Aberdonians had been in no position to resist Ogilvy's royalists on 15 May, but still stood up for Covenanting neighbours and refused to supply men and guns. Yet when the Covenanters returned on 23 May, the townsfolk were treated as collaborators. Montrose gave them twenty-four hours to pay a fine of nearly £7,000. He commandeered their cannon and all the weapons he could find, actions intended to shame as well as disarm.[82] The Covenanters also threatened to scuttle ships in the mouth of the Dee to block a threatened English invasion, but a petition signed by leading north-east Covenanters successfully argued against that, saying it would mean the 'perpetuall wrack' of the urban and regional economy, and the 'overthrown of thair toune for ever'. All this, said Montrose, was because Aberdonians, having signed the National Covenant, had then 'wilfullie and willinglie' received 'enemies of the good causs': 'the toune of Abirdein wes not to be trustit nor beleivit (for the most pairt) to be good covenanteris'.[83]

The heavy-handedness of the Covenanters might have driven some townsfolk more firmly into the royalist camp, but the royalists were unsteady allies unlikely to prevail, and almost as overbearing. In early June 1639, several of the king's ships appeared off Aberdeen, and the Covenanting army, fearing a co-ordinated attack that never materialised, withdrew south.[84] The royalists occupied the two burghs once again, now under the command of Lord Aboyne, Huntly's nineteen-year-old son. He brought arms, ammunition and letters from the king pardoning those who signed the National Covenant against their will, and offering to accept half as much loot as the Covenanters.[85] Local Covenanters had predictably fled, but royalists did not flock to Aboyne. Amidst the shifting fortunes of war, 'the greatest pairt of the nightboures' had abandoned Aberdeen, and others were keeping a low profile.[86]

Those who remained acted with commendable courage and solidarity, as when they set aside partisan politics to stand behind their Covenanting provost. Aboyne's men had captured Alexander Jaffray the elder in the countryside, and, at an extra-ordinary meeting of all available townsmen, the prisoner Jaffray looked on while Robert Johnston, the royalist provost whom he had replaced, asked if anyone had any 'accusation, challenge, or grevance', or charge of 'disloyalty or miscarriage', to level against Jaffray. Although there cannot have been many Covenanters present, the crowd offered its unanimous support. Not only were there no accusations, 'thay give him thair approbatioun and applause'. The provost was freed and immediately joined in the latest oath of allegiance to the king.[87] Not everyone was convinced: later that day Robert Johnston's son sent the Marquis of Hamilton damning information about Jaffray for future reference.[88]

Word soon arrived that Montrose and Marischal were leading their armies back north. Aboyne decided to hold Aberdeen for the king, putting the townsfolk in grave danger.[89] It was one thing to surrender to an advancing army (Aberdeen had already done so four times) but to resist and fail, according to the accepted code of warfare, was to risk unrestrained plunder or worse, as many towns had experienced in the course of the Thirty Years' War (1618–48) which was still wreaking havoc and atrocities across northern Europe. Aboyne ordered every able-bodied man to join in the defence of Aberdeen on pain of death. Despite that threat and despite their recent oath to the king, the two burghs supplied just one hundred musketeers between them — a significant, but hardly overwhelming, show of support for the royalists.[90]

Before dawn on 18 June 1639, Aboyne led his forces out to the Bridge of Dee to make their stand.[91] Aberdeen men occupied the bridge itself and did most of the fighting, while the royalist cavalry and, a little further off, nervous townsfolk watched from the north bank. Wives and servants crept onto the bridge to deliver food and drink. A townsman named John Forbes was the first Aberdonian to die in the wars, shot through the head on the first day of battle. His friends said he had been singled out, and they shot a man on the other side 'out of indignatione': in this early stage of the wars citizen soldiers still frowned on the deliberate killing of an opponent.[92] The next day, the Covenanters successfully stormed the bridge, killing three more townsmen and wounding dozens more. From there, they marched into town unopposed as Aboyne's cavalry retreated in confusion. Local Covenanters in both burghs emerged from hiding and 'proudlie' lined the streets to welcome Montrose's men, while royalists fled again.[93] Further evidence that this was still a limited war came when Montrose, under pressure from his officers to allow their men to sack Aberdeen, insisted that they wait until morning in the hope of cooling passions and maintaining control.[94] Early next day, however, a ship arrived bearing news of a peace treaty ending the war.[95] Aberdeen was spared, but the sense of relief was tempered by the knowledge that the treaty had been concluded at Berwick on 18 June, ironically just as battle had commenced at the Bridge of Dee.

Aberdeen was left to pick up the pieces and learn what lessons it could from this opening round of hostilities. There had been relatively little bloodshed, but there were few households in either burgh that had not suffered. Bishop Adam Bellenden, whose palace at Old Aberdeen had been vandalised by Covenanter troops shortly after he had left for England, wrote to the Marquis of Hamilton 'to shew you [how] in this tumultuarie and barbarous late sturris, my house wes plunderit and demolished, my rentis withholden, and I my self persewit, and forcit to flee'. Thus far, he could have spoken for many Aberdonians. Few who stayed and endured the rival occupations would have endorsed his claim, however, that 'no man in the kingdome hath a harder pairt in the loss then I', a point he emphasised by complaining of the high cost of living in Berwick ('we live heir at a deir rate').[96] Back in Aberdeen, it was understood that those hardest hit, as ever, were those who began with the least to lose. In New Aberdeen, the town council made emergency funds available to help the poorest residents, and Provost Jaffray proposed (albeit in vain) a new tax to support the 'meaner sort' brought to 'extreme povertie' by multiple quarterings of troops.[97]

As individual Aberdonians struggled to rebuild homes and businesses, or simply survive, the town council set about trying to restore civic finances. Ten years earlier, New Aberdeen had been flourishing and the books had balanced, but by 1637, with so many expensive projects underway, the newly-acquired debt stood at £10,000, all of it contracted, so the council claimed, within the previous five years.[98] That was an alarming figure at the time, but the brief war of 1639 plunged the royal burgh a further £20,000 into arrears.[99] As it became clear that the truce was merely a lull in the hostilities, the burgh fathers faced the likelihood that the current debt, bad as it was, might get much worse. They had survived the financial emergencies of the First Bishops' War by borrowing at interest from local lairds and merchants (especially Robert Farquhar, one of Scotland's richest men), and from the mortifications in their trust. On 27 November 1639, they made the fateful decision to rely more heavily on the mortifications, which were awash with money from the recent boom. Mortified funds on loan were called in and the money used to pay off outsiders. In-house financing was an elegant (if partial) solution to the looming problem of wartime borrowing, one which promised to simplify and therefore speed arrangements, and deny any hostile creditors the opportunity to 'chairge the toune for payment of thair dettis when the toune ar not prepared nor furnished with moneys to pay the same'.[100] It also, however, mortgaged the future to an extent no one in 1639 could have imagined.

For the present, the main problem facing Aberdeen was not credit, but credibility. The decisive defeat of the royalists at the Bridge of Dee and the uneasy peace that followed gave local Covenanters a chance to consolidate their authority in the town and convince the Covenanting regime of their loyalty. They failed, but not for want of trying. In September 1639, Patrick Leslie was finally elected provost, and an increased majority of Covenanters joined him on the town council. Over the next few months, Aberdeen agreed – not just in council but in a series of assemblies of burgesses – to a whole array of financial and political demands imposed by the Covenanting regime.[101] This counted for something, but Aberdeen's credibility with outside Covenanters depended on their pursuit of religious reform. Complying with the outward forms demanded by the Covenanters was not difficult, since religious practice in Aberdeen had never been as far out of line as some supposed. Godly discipline resumed with a zeal that more than met Covenanting standards: fornicators and other miscreants were punished as harshly as ever, and in much the same numbers. A crackdown on Catholics was also demanded and readily effected.[102] Even where Covenanting principles required real change, it was carried off with some aplomb. Covenanters famously forbade the celebration of Christmas, an unpopular device in a place full of students. It was soon agreed, however, that pupils would be at their desks on 25 December in return for an additional three 'play days' at the start of each quarter.[103] Even on the bitterly contentious issue of communion, Aberdeen conformed at the earliest opportunity: in November 1639, communicants in both burghs received the Lord's Supper sitting, Presbyterian-style, rather than kneeling, Episcopalian-style. Spalding reported some grumbling, but no scenes.[104]

Ironically, the smooth introduction of Covenanting practices owed something to the return from exile of the Aberdeen Doctors, ministers known and trusted by the townsfolk. In Old Aberdeen, the new-fangled communion was administered by Dr Alexander Scroggie; in New Aberdeen by Dr William Guild and Dr James Sibbald, with Dr John Forbes contributing a preparatory sermon.[105] The problem was that only Guild had subscribed the National Covenant. In May 1640, a letter to the magistrates of New Aberdeen from Covenanting officials in Edinburgh expressed disbelief that 'those ministeris compleaned of long since (and we were informed from the Synod, should ather have been removed or silenced) are keiped amongst yow and suffered to vent thair old rotten dregis of superstitioun and divisioun'. This was not altogether fair, but the message was clear: no one to the south was going to believe that Aberdeen had sincerely embraced the Covenant so long as the uncovenanted Doctors remained in place. Not even the invitation made by the council of New Aberdeen, sitting pointedly on Christmas day, to Alexander Henderson, co-author of the National Covenant, to be minister in place of the late Dr Alexander Ross cut much ice. Henderson was the first of a series of prominent Covenanters who refused to serve in Aberdeen: 'cast your eyes on another', wrote George Gillespie, for 'I will leave no lawfull means unessayed to hinder your purpose concerning me'.[106]

The price of Aberdeen's suspect loyalty was made plain later that month, when Major General Robert Munro and the Earl Marischal led a Covenanting army north to pre-empt a royalist rising – the opening move in what became known as the Second Bishops' War. On 28 May, at Marischal's request, a guard of honour of over 800 townsmen wearing bonnet ribbons of Covenanter blue escorted the two regiments from the Bridge of Dee into the town.[107] Once there, the southern Covenanters treated their hosts as vanquished enemies rather than allies, insisting that they sign the insulting 'Articles of Bonaccord'. These denounced all who had not subscribed the National Covenant as 'evill patriotts' (nine townsmen were arrested and sent to Edinburgh on this count), and ordered that no uncovenanted minister be allowed to preach on pain of banishment of 'both preacheris and heareris'.[108] The town was ordered to have 12,000 pounds of bread ready in four days, along with 1,000 gallons of ale, 3,000 ells of tent cloth, 1,200 pairs of shoes and 50 cart horses.[109] The document ended with threats and a sneering demand for an immediate answer of 'Bonaccord or malaccord'.

By late July 1640, Marischal and Munro had so thoroughly subdued the town and surrounding region that it was safe to hold a General Assembly in Aberdeen, although the town had to make an emergency appeal to local presbyteries for provisions to feed those who attended.[110] Righteous Covenanters quickly purged Aberdonian pulpits of those deemed 'malignant'. Dr Scroggie in Old Aberdeen was deposed and replaced by William Strachan, who quickly established an 'extra-ordinary love and correspondence' with the people there. In New Aberdeen, Andrew Cant was nominated in place of the deposed Dr Sibbald. Cant was joined the next year by two other Covenanting ministers: John Row, hired to replace the late Dr Alexander Ross, and John Oswald, who replaced Dr Guild, now principal of King's College.[111] By the end of 1641, Aberdeen's ministers were all Covenanters.[112]

In July 1640, Marischal was commissioned to raise a new regiment of foot in Aberdeenshire; he ordered the two burghs to supply a company under his brother's command, and wrote back in August to say that he meant it. If the issue of trust was a legacy from the First Bishops' War, so was Aberdonians' reluctance to bear arms other than for their own defence - particularly if it meant serving under the dictatorial Marischal. As fencible men slipped away in droves, the magistrates threatened to revoke the burgess rights of any who failed to muster. The merchant guild suggested that the incorporated trades supply most of the recruits, since their members had more servants and apprentices to spare.[113] In the end, twenty men from Old Aberdeen and 120 from New Aberdeen marched south to join the Army of the Covenant gathering on the Borders. They arrived too late to participate in the triumphant invasion of England, but joined in the occupation of Newcastle in September. By then, a staggering 60 per cent of Marischal's men had deserted, including a good many Aberdonians.[114]

The mood of Aberdeen's reluctant conscripts cannot have been helped by knowing that a notoriously ill-behaved Covenanting regiment was moving into town just as they left. The magistrates had argued that Munro's brutal thoroughness had 'left this pairt of the cuntrie in peace', but Aberdeen remained under garrison for a further eighteen months.[115] The Aberdeenshire regiment of the Master of

Forbes terrorised people in both burghs: when a man went out after curfew to fetch medicine for his wife, who had just delivered a still-born child, he was severely beaten; when a woman refused, at gunpoint, to a loan of one of her horses, a drunken officer shot the animal through the head.[116] Lord Sinclair's 500 Caithness men did little from October 1640 to February 1642 but eat, drink, and sin: they impregnated sixty-five servants.[117] The Aberdeen authorities treated these women more harshly than those who 'fell' with civilians: Spalding describes a dozen women fined £40 (four times the usual fine for fornication), tied together, and whipped out of town by the hangman.[118] Whether the sex was consensual was a question seldom raised. Many convicted servants were 'tapsters' who sold ale from cellars and door-to-door.[119] Working unsupervised around alcohol and soldiers greatly increased their sexual vulnerability (or sexual availability, said many contemporaries). Pregnant tapsters were usually expelled from town, but only after settling their accounts with the female brewers – usually burgess wives or widows – for whom they worked (see Chapters 2 and 6).[120]

Sinclair's regiment departed on 9 February 1642, and Aberdeen was free of soldiers for two years. Aspects of normal life returned: a man was licensed to manufacture golf balls, suggesting play had resumed (if it had ever stopped).[121] But the royal burgh was now £40,000 in debt, and the entire 'common good' did not even cover payments of the interest due on the debt.[122] As it pursued various financial expedients, the town council joined its new ministers in further Covenanting reforms: funeral services were simplified and the evening prayer services which had been held ever since the Reformation were converted to thrice-weekly lectures, a hallmark of radical Presbyterianism (see Chapter 13).[123] To counter one effect of prolonged exposure to soldiers, a 1642 act against swearing put a fine box for adults and a punishment stick for children into every home.[124]

The peaceful interlude ended in August 1643. England had drifted into civil war the year before, and the king had since scored a series of victories. Covenanters knew that if Charles prevailed in England, he would crush them next. To save their revolution, they entered into the Solemn League and Covenant with English parliamentarians. The fateful decision to intervene militarily in England divided Covenanters and revived royalist hopes. As tensions in the north-east grew, Aberdeen was made to supply another 131 men for service in England. There were difficulties in finding volunteers: twenty-eight men, drawn from the lower ranks of burgh society, were forcibly impressed to make up the quota. Two weeks after they left, the magistrates reinstated the nightly watch in fear of a royalist attack.[125]

Huntly was as cautious as ever, but some of his followers decided not to wait. On 19 March 1644, before dawn but after the watch had retired, Sir John Gordon of Haddo and one hundred mounted men raced into New Aberdeen and dragged from their homes Provost Patrick Leslie, Robert Farquhar, and the brothers John and Alexander Jaffray the younger. Haddo had a grudge against the Jaffrays, lending this action, like so many in the wars, a personal edge. The Covenanter prisoners were paraded in the Gallowgate and then spirited away to Huntly's castle at Strathbogie.[126] The raid was brilliantly executed but counter-productive. The violent kidnap of fellow burgesses, even Covenanters, was no way to encourage Aberdonian royalists to rise up. Haddo should have known better: he had attacked the Jaffrays before in the course of their personal feud, only to find the council 'take it done as to the toun of Aberdene'.[127]

Huntly ran into that same wall of civic solidarity. His hand forced, he elected to occupy Aberdeen in advance of a Covenanter response and, less realistically, in anticipation of a royalist rising.[128] But when he and his force of 600 arrived at Aberdeen on 25 March, they found the gates locked and the people in a 'warlike posture'. The gates opened only after Huntly promised that no one would be 'troublit' in their persons, goods or consciences. Covenanters were plundered regardless, but when Huntly tried to seize the burgh's stent rolls so that his men could exact forced taxation, the 'haill inhabitants' reminded him of his promise, bluntly adding that such treatment was no more than they expected of him and 'they behovit to suffer till it pleas God to send relief'. The burgh also refused to sell him arms, claiming that it had none to sell, least of all to him or any others 'wha ar opposit to the Church and estatis'.[129] Relief came on 2 May in the form of the Marquis of Argyll, the Earl Marischal and an army 6,000-strong. Huntly retired from Aberdeen and released his prisoners. Haddo was captured and soon executed as a criminal and a rebel.[130]

The occupation of May 1644 was the first time that an incoming Covenanter army reclaimed Aberdeen without imposing punitive terms. The Earl Marischal, party to the infamous Articles of Bonaccord in 1640, now promised there would be no violence and all would be done 'in a legal way'. He asked only that his men and horses be received 'cheirfullie'.[131] This change of tone, more redolent of a liberation than a conquest, signalled that Aberdeen had, for the moment, regained some credibility with the Covenanting leadership.[132] The balance of opinion in the town was probably as divided as ever, but the balance of power had swung decisively to the Covenanters. Indeed, the period from May to September 1644 marked the high tide for Covenanters in Aberdeen and the low ebb for royalists. There were other signs. In April 1644, Dr John Forbes, royalist and Aberdeen Doctor, went into voluntary exile in Holland. Since being deposed from the chair of divinity at King's in 1641, he had lived in Old Aberdeen on his private income, attending church and even sitting for communion, but the radical turn of events provoked by the Solemn League and Covenant and the tightening grip of local Covenanters convinced him to go.[133] Meanwhile, in May, Provost Patrick Leslie told the assembled townsfolk that Argyll and other nobles had agreed, 'seing this toun hade not in any sort transgrest', that Aberdeen pay only the same amount of tax as Dundee, a Covenanter stronghold.[134] This was a breakthrough, but there was more. Leslie asked that the town approve the council's nominees for the vacant chair of divinity at Marischal College; their first choice was Samuel Rutherford! The 'haill inhabitants' consented to what once would have been unthinkable, though many must have calculated, correctly, that Rutherford would never come.[135]

As Aberdonian Covenanters enjoyed their high summer, a committee of estates settled into the burgh to oversee mopping-up operations against royalists. Politically and militarily, the burgh was at last a secure Covenanter base – and that proved fatal when the royalist cause suddenly revived. Montrose was now the king's man and a marquis, and in August he linked up with 2,000 Irish troops sent over by the Earl of Antrim and commanded by the Celtic general Alasdair Mac-Colla. Montrose was a leader in need of an army; the Irish needed a Scottish (preferably Protestant) noble to give them credibility with Highland royalists. On 1 September, they defeated a larger but inexperienced Covenanter army at Tippermuir (Tibbermore) near Perth, killing hundreds. The north-east was still the key to royalist aspirations. Huntly, who despised Montrose, would be no help, but his dispirited followers might be won over if the Covenanter base at Aberdeen could be neutralised.[136]

On 4 September, Aberdonians learned the Irish were coming.[137] With a committee of estates and a regiment in town, the townsfolk were denied their usual option of a negotiated surrender preceded by the prudent flight of those on the wrong side. They would have to fight, but given it was Montrose and the hated Irish, five times as many townsmen turned out as had served at the Battle of the Bridge of Dee. As in 1639, when Aberdeen faced Montrose in the company of Huntly and then Aboyne, its security depended on its allies – who were again found wanting. The Forbes, Frasers and other north-east Covenanters refused to serve beside Lord Gordon (Huntly's eldest son, a Covenanter) or the 3,000 Gordons he brought with him, so the Gordons withdrew, reducing the Covenanting army by more than half.[138] Lord Burleigh assumed command, as president of the local Covenanting committee of estates; but, like Huntly and Aboyne before him, he was not the calibre of general that Aberdeen needed.[139]

Montrose had 1,500 men with him when he approached Aberdeen on the morning of Friday 13 September 1644, distinctly less than he had commanded at Tippermuir, just twelve days earlier.[140] Burleigh had a force of 2,500, including 500 from both burghs. Confident because of his numerical advantage, Burleigh elected for open battle, rather than remain in town to force a siege, as had happened at Dundee, where Montrose had lacked the men and time to persevere. Aberdeen lacked Dundee's fortifications but there were probably enough natural and man-made obstacles to warrant taking a stand inside the burgh given their superior numbers.[141] Instead, the defenders marched out to block the Hardgate, the western route into town, from atop the steep hill by the Justice Mills.[142] Montrose sent a commissioner, accompanied by a drummer, to demand surrender. Anticipating the answer, he advised women, children and the elderly to leave, and warned those who remained to 'expect no quarter'. The Covenanters duly replied that they would 'spend the last drope of our blood' to defend the town. Then the unexpected happened: while returning to royalist lines, the unarmed drummer was shot dead, 'aganes the law of nationis', by a trooper of the Fife regiment.[143] It was 11 a.m. The Battle of Justice Mills, sometimes called the 'Fecht of Aberdeen', was on.

The defenders fought bravely but were disorganised and no match for the Irish, some of whom were veterans of the Spanish Army of Flanders and 'so well trained as the world could afford no better'.[144] After two hours, the Covenanters broke and ran. John Spalding was an eye-witness: 'There was littill slauchter in the fight, bot horrible wes the slauchter in the flight.'[145] Wealthy burgesses on horseback had the best chance of escape, but three members of the town council were killed and others barely got away.[146] Men on foot had less chance, and a high proportion of the dead from the town were tradesmen and men of humble means.[147] Those who fled into town were the most likely to die, the Irish 'hewing and cutting doun all maner of man thay could overtak within the toune, upone the streites, or in thair houssis, and round about the toune, as oure men wes fleeing'. The terror tactic of rape was systematically applied: 'Sum wemen thay preissit to defloir, and uther sum thay took perforce to serve thame in camp'. Men were forced to strip before being killed, to spare their clothing. Corpses lay naked where they fell, burial forbidden: 'The wyf durst not cry nor weip at her husbandis slaughter befoir hir eyes, nor the mother for the sone, nor dochter for the father; whiche, if thay war hard, then thay war presentlie slayne.'[148] The ritual violence continued for three full days. By 16 September, 160 men and an unknown number of women and children were dead.[149] 'And nothing hard bot pitifull howling, crying, weiping, murning, throw all the streittis.'[150]

Montrose had been no friend to Aberdeen as a Covenanter, but when he had taken the town by force in 1639 he had restrained his men. Now that seemed like a lost world. The troops Montrose commanded in 1644 had seen and perhaps done terrible things in Germany and Ireland, and in their treatment of civilians they took the Scottish wars to a new level of ferocity. No Scottish burgh had suffered like Aberdeen, and none would again until the English sack of Dundee in 1651. Montrose stayed out of town on Friday night, the worst of it, but he was there on both Saturday and Sunday. He saw the bodies, he heard the screams and he did not try to stop it: on the contrary, he adopted Irish dress in solidarity with his men.[151] By the international codes of war, a town that refused surrender was fair game and the murder of the drummer was further incitement. But contemporaries also understood that 'not everything which is lawfull is honourable', and what happened at Aberdeen was regarded by Covenanters and royalists alike as an atrocity.[152] That it was perpetrated mainly by Irish Catholics in the name of the king only confirmed the darkest fears and prejudices of Scottish Protestants.

Montrose proceeded to win four more victories over the Covenanters before his army was crushed at Philiphaugh, near Selkirk, one year to the day after the Battle of Justice Mills. In the process, he had destroyed much of the Covenanter's military power in Scotland, destabilised their regime, and undermined their war effort in England. But Aberdeen ended any real hope of his conquering Scotland for the king. The sack of a major royal burgh may have put the fear of God into his enemies, but it cost him any hope of winning over Lowland royalists.[153] After Aberdeen, he could only destroy, never unite. But destroy he did, and so did the Covenanting armies chasing him. Montrose and the Irish returned to the vicinity of Aberdeen on four more occasions. On 14 October 1644, one month after the sack, terrified survivors fled at their approach, men refusing Marischal's call to arms, women carrying young children away on their backs through an early snowstorm.[154] Montrose did not occupy the burgh on this occasion, and when he returned to the area briefly in March, May and July of 1645 he kept most of his forces outside the town.[155] Delicate negotiations ensued each time, as the magistrates tried to fend off his demands amidst expressions of gratitude made through gritted teeth for 'your lenitie and many singular favors vochsafed hitherto on this poore distressed toune'.[156] But there was steel behind the pleasantries. In July 1645, fresh from his victory at Alford, the Marquis commanded that Aberdeen supply a company of soldiers. He added a bone-chilling warning that upon refusal 'all the just and severe resentment shall be useit againis the toune that can be useit againis the greatest enemies to the Kings Majestie', but the council sent three brave men out to tell him of 'thair innabilitie and impossibilitie to obey'.[157] The defeat of Montrose and the Irish at Philiphaugh did not end the royalist threat, and Aberdeen continued to suffer brief incursions into 1646. Throughout most of the period between 1644 and 1647, the royal burgh was occupied by a series of Covenanting forces which did not always offer much by way of protection but, like soldiers before them on either side, behaved badly, ran up huge bills and consumed resources 'lyk grashopperis'.[158]

It was perhaps fitting that the Marquis of Huntly launched the last armed assault against Aberdeen in the Wars of the Covenant. Provoked by Covenanter raids, he and 2,000 men stormed and set fire to the royal burgh on 14 May 1646. A depleted garrison repulsed two assaults but succumbed to the third. No Aberdonian died, but many in the garrison were killed or captured.[159] Huntly's men were beginning to plunder when the return of the rest of the Covenanter army put them to flight.

The residents emerged from hiding to put out the fires, but many houses were lost.[160] As in 1639 and 1644, albeit with more harm done, Huntly had asserted his mastery over Aberdeen to no good end, and with no clear sense of what he intended to do next.[161]

By April 1647, with the war winding down, the last occupying force, a Covenanting regiment of foot, had left. Any celebration that the exhausted townsfolk allowed themselves cannot have lasted long, because two days later Provost Patrick Leslie announced that the bubonic plague had reached Inverbervie. Civic defences as tight as any directed against armies were put in place, but by the end of the month this deadliest of invaders was among them (see Chapter 3).

After the Wars of the Covenant

Aberdonians, especially after the horrors of September 1644, must have asked why their 'God of Order' had seemingly abandoned them to such confusion and chaos. The answers they settled on helped crystallise political and religious positions that had been forming for some time, and would take a generation to play out. For radical Covenanters, revolution (or 'reformation' as they called it) had not gone far enough, and must be purified and advanced. Refusing to co-operate with royalists and lukewarm Covenanters was a first step towards appeasing God. For ardent royalists, the fact that Montrose and the Irish were on the king's side was irrelevant. All the horrors, said John Spalding, stemmed from the 'mother syn' of altering religion and opposing the king.[162] Between these extremes stood a broad swathe of people, sympathetic to either the royalist or Covenanting cause but anxious to pull community, kirk, king and nation back from the brink.

This last group had its chance with the Engagement of 1648, by which moderate Covenanters attempted to restore the king's authority in England in return for the preservation of Presbyterianism at home and its promotion in England. The Engagement split the Covenanter movement. In New Aberdeen, where the start of the Engager crisis overlapped with the plague, Provost Patrick Leslie (who had been Aberdeen's lay representative at the General Assembly of 1648), most of the town council and a majority of the kirk session supported it. All three ministers – Andrew Cant (who was incensed by Leslie's actions), John Row, and the newly appointed John Menzies – opposed it, as did Alexander Jaffray the younger (whose father, the elder, had died in January 1645).[163] When the Engager movement collapsed on the battlefield at Preston in August 1648, political and religious authority passed to a radical minority in both the nation and the burgh: Patrick Leslie was deposed, not by the king this time but by Covenanters.[164] Alexander Jaffray, meanwhile, rose to some prominence in the new regime, becoming one of four Covenanters sent to negotiate the return of Charles II (1651/1660-85) from Holland.[165] Jaffray accompanied the king (a virtual prisoner of the Covenanters) to Aberdeen in June 1650, when Charles saw one of the limbs of the late Marquis of Montrose suspended from the tolbooth. A further insult followed, when he was subjected to a sermon by John Menzies, based on the text of 1 Samuel 16:1: 'How long wilt thou mourn for Saul, seeing I have rejected him from reigning over Israel?' [166] On the king's next visit, in February 1651, he exacted modest revenge on the extremists by knighting Patrick Leslie for his belated efforts on behalf of the crown.[167]

The watchword of the radicals was separation, keeping the ungodly at bay while making the world safe for the godly to do His work. In 1648, Alexander Jaffray and his friends fenced in the common land atop St Katherine's Hill to keep out 'whoores, shankwyvers [female stocking knitters] and horssis', so as to provide a place of solitude for 'the use of themselves' and the godly.[168] Other, more important initiatives proved self-defeating but had long-term effects. In the aftermath of September 1644, the ministers had suspended the annual kirk session elections and cut the session's ties with the town council. From the mid 1640s until the mid 1650s, kirk and council were effectively estranged. In 1646, the council bitterly complained that its members were debarred from the session, in defiance of long-established custom.[169] Session elections were held only when the ministers felt confident of radicals sweeping the board. In 1648, in the middle of the controversy over the Engagement, matters had deteriorated to such an extent that the council made pointed inquiries as to the legality of holding meetings of the session without a minister present.[170] Purifying the kirk session, however, crippled the war on sin. The kirk's moral persuasions and shaming rituals were far less effective without the fines and corporal punishments which only magistrates could administer. Against the background of an English garrison which occupied the town from 1651–9, Andrew Cant railed against the rising tide of fornication that he feared would bring the judgement of God down upon them all.[171]

The problem was finally solved in 1656 with the establishment of a Justice of the Peace Court that allowed the magistrates to return to their customary role in godly discipline ('menacing their persons and exacting on their purses') without compromising the independence of the kirk session. The separatist impulse behind the 'justice court' generated a new degree of inclusion in civic affairs, providing places for thirty-six elected constables a year, many of them men from further down the social scale than the elders and deacons on the session, whose work they complemented rather than rivalled. The partnership functioned smoothly for decades. The justice court was Aberdeen's most successful institutional innovation of the seventeenth century (see Chapter 2).[172]

The separatist tendencies of the radicals in Aberdeen threatened schism, a situation avoided elsewhere in Scotland. The charismatic Jaffray converted to Independency after being captured by the English at the Battle of Dunbar in

September 1650. When he returned in 1652, he convinced John Menzies and John Row to join him in establishing an Independent congregation that would consist only of the godly, unburdened by the Kirk's obligation to tend to all of God's wayward sheep.[173] This left Andrew Cant, elderly and irascible, as the only minister for the rest of New Aberdeen. The experiment in Independency soon fizzled out, but it had two lasting effects. The first was to deal a blow to the Covenanter movement in Aberdeen from which it never recovered: by the mid 1650s the town council and the burgh kirk were clearly drifting back to more moderate positions.[174] The second was to pave the way for Quakerism, the first sustained schismatic movement among Scottish Protestants. From 1663 onwards, it attracted a small but dedicated following of former radical Covenanters who demanded novel and seemingly subversive notions of community and citizenship (see Chapter 13).

As for the moderate majority in Aberdeen, they celebrated the miraculously bloodless Restoration of 1660 in fine style. The Troubles were over. The English garrison was long gone, having pulled out of the town in December 1659. On hearing news of the restoration of Charles II, the men of the town assembled in the churchyard of St Nicholas at 7 a.m., laid down their arms, and went inside to hear sermons by the new Episcopalian minister John Paterson and the newly moderate Covenanter, John Menzies. Then it was off to the market cross, where there was music and confections and two casks of wine, 'the on[e] claret and the other whyte'. Toasts were drunk, glasses smashed. Bells rang all day and there were bonfires and celebratory gunfire all night.[175] When people sobered up, there were details needing attention: Samuel Rutherford's *Lex Rex*, a defence of the Covenanting revolution, was publicly burned (one of Andrew Cant's last public actions was to object to this), and the Marquis of Montrose's stray limb was returned, with straight-faced solemnity, to his heir.[176]

For all the heart-felt celebration, however, Aberdeen had come too far to go all the way back to the way things had been. The royal burgh did not settle smoothly into the second period of episcopacy. The writings of the Aberdeen Doctors of blessed memory were reprinted, but did not sell. The four ministers of 1660 were soon two: Cant was sent packing and Paterson left for a bishopric. The two who remained, Menzies and George Meldrum, had come of age under the Covenants and would clearly have preferred a Presbyterian settlement. They were slow to conform to episcopacy, but successive town councils stood by them. Replacing Cant and Paterson proved difficult. Between 1662 and 1665, no fewer than eight Episcopalian nominees turned down the call to Aberdeen: it proved harder to lure Episcopalian clergy to Aberdeen in the 1660s than to attract their Presbyterian counterparts in the 1640s. Only with the hiring of William Blair in 1680 and George Garden in 1682, both of whom came of age after 1660, did the royal burgh acquire

Episcopalian ministers of real distinction – not, in other words, until the Covenanting generation had passed.[177]

The material consequences of the Wars of the Covenant were profound and long-lasting. Hundreds of people – the exact number cannot ever be known – perished or left the town forever (see Chapter 5). Personal loss and suffering rippled through the community. People with broken bodies and minds had to be provided for. A detail of Gordon of Rothiemay's map of 1661 shows a man with no legs using his arms to pole himself towards Aberdeen – a veteran returning home? The dead left families and friends to mourn, businesses to run, debts to pay and dependants to support.

The survivors picked up the pieces amidst a shattered economy. Even allowing for exaggeration and early modern accounting practices, the material losses of New Aberdeen were astounding. Charles I was executed on 30 January 1649. Earlier that month, Aberdeen informed the Scottish parliament that its losses in the wars that had brought down the king came to £1,582,910, of which parliament agreed to repay £631,700.[178] In 1637, the town council had fretted over a public debt of £10,000; by 1646 the debt was ten times that. Some £77,000 was owed to the mortifications alone: 'the haill moneyes mortified to our colledge and schooles … and to our hospitallis, wedowes, orphanes, and common poore, manufactories and other pious uses are taken up by us and spent.' Individual lenders were 'nevir lyke to get ane pennie' owed to them. Twenty-six merchants who once had paid a large part of burgh taxation now resided in France, Poland or the Netherlands, paying nothing, and many more had absented themselves for months or years. The plaiding trade on which so much depended was at a virtual standstill by 1646. Successive armies had destroyed all the local sheep flocks, and there was no wool from the south while the plague raged there. Exports fell to nearly nil, and by 1648 prices were also falling.[179] Things got worse before they got better. The plague of 1647-8 was accompanied by harvest failure and high prices (not matched until the deadly 1690s) that lasted until 1652. An English naval blockade strangled east-coast shipping in 1651 and 1652 and, for some, this was the last straw: the English, they said, had 'neirby extinguishit the spunk, and cutt off any poor remainder of hopes we haid of recovery'.[180]

Aberdeen did recover from the wars, but to what extent? The English army imposed a degree of stability on the north-east in the 1650s which had not been seen in years; crop yields improved and shipping lanes re-opened. The period from 1653 onwards clearly witnessed considerable recovery.[181] But New Aberdeen had a long way to go to restore its pre-war prosperity. Many of the exuberant projects of the 1630s failed or languished in the post-war era. Fewer new houses were built and churches and other public buildings received only the most basic maintenance. Fitful efforts to revive the Correction House failed (see Chapter 2). It proved difficult to find anyone willing to take on the once-profitable packhouse.[182] The quay needed rebuilding and the roads fell into disrepair. By 1645, George Jamesone's pleasure garden was ruined.[183] And there were fewer new charitable mortifications in the second half of the century than in the decade of the 1630s alone.[184] As for plaiding, from an average of 93,000 ells just before the wars, post-war exports peaked at around 75,000 ells in the 1670s, but at much lower prices.[185] Volumes and prices tumbled in the 1680s (see Chapter 6). Bailie Alexander Skene noted glumly in 1685 that 'Our trade is much decayed by what it hath been forty or fifty years ago, before our late intestin troubles began.' Aberdeen's difficulties, however, did not stem, in his view, only from the Troubles. There were other factors at work, well beyond its control: they included the Portuguese re-conquest of Brazil from the Dutch which had been completed in 1654, 'for it was the Dutch Plantations in Brasile (which the Portuguyes now possess) that were furnished with our Plaiding and Fingrams'.[186]

Where the wars had had a more direct effect was with regard to the public debt. Year after year, the lion's share of civic taxes went to servicing the debt owed to the mortifications: in 1669, two-thirds of an £8,000 levy went on interest payments alone.[187] In 1678, Charles II granted New Aberdeen the right to collect heavy excise duties to help clear debts from 'the late disastrous time of tumults and rebellion … the annual interest of which debts exceeds and exhausts their public revenue, so that if their creditors were to put the laws in execution against them, in addition to the ruin of the commerce and the destitution of the citizens, the said burgh and our government would be almost destroyed.'[188] Even so, on the eve of famine in 1695, the royal burgh still owed £92,392 to its charitable trusts.[189] The exhaustion of those trusts and the ongoing burden of wartime debt was surely a factor in Aberdeen's inability to meet the demands of this last great crisis of the century.

The heavy taxes occasioned by the wars made New Aberdeen a much less competitive place to do business, especially after 1672 when royal burghs lost many of their exclusive trading privileges.[190] Merchants were freer to live in towns that were not taxed so heavily. The effect on the two burghs of Aberdeen was very different. Old Aberdeen had borne its share of suffering but, in comparison with New Aberdeen, it escaped relatively lightly from both the wars and the plague, and it carried nothing like the same burden of public debt into the post-war era.[191] Alexander Skene reported that merchants were leaving royal burghs because of heavy taxes, to the point where it was cheaper to buy a 'great large Lodging with all accommodations' in a royal burgh than a 'common thack house' in a burgh of barony like Old Aberdeen.[192] As post-war New Aberdeen slumped, Old Aberdeen prospered. A thriving merchant community developed there, mainly after 1672, where there had been none before.[193] Old Aberdeen's population more than doubled between 1635 and 1695, whereas New Aberdeen's fell: many people appear simply to have shifted from one town to the other to avoid taxes.[194]

In 1661, James Gordon surveyed Aberdeen's experience of the wars, and he concluded that even the most horrific individual event paled next to the cumulative effect of the Troubles: 'neither the disaster inflicted by Montrose nor the burning of the place by Huntly did so much injury to the town: these were light evils if they be compared with the daily misfortunes of twenty-three years, under which now borne down it has sunk.'[195] That statement rang even truer thirty years later. By then there were few witnesses left to either the pitched terrors or the daily traumas of the 1640s. Stories of valour and villainy remained but were trimmed to suit current realities: the local Covenanting tradition quickly faded from sight. The wartime debt, on the other hand, remained all too vivid to future generations. Amidst the great struggle of order and confusion, it was not just a reminder of wartime confusion, but an ongoing source of confusion in the sense of dashed hopes, lowered expectations and limited opportunities. If Aberdeen did not quite sink from the wars, neither did it regain its former buoyancy until well into the next century.

12

Revolution to Reform: Eighteenth-century Politics, c. 1690-1800

DAVID FINDLAY *and* ALEXANDER MURDOCH

'Glorious' Revolution and Union

It is impossible to understand the political history of eighteenth-century Aberdeen without assessing the significance of the so-called 'Glorious' Revolution of 1688-9. The two most turbulent events for Aberdeen during the first half of the eighteenth century, the Jacobite uprisings of 1715 and 1745, were directly connected to the Revolution, which had resulted in the removal of James VII (1685-9) and his replacement by William of Orange (1689-1702). During the winter of 1688-9, a Williamite army under the command of Hugh Mackay of Scourie was quartered in Aberdeen. The following July over half of Mackay's forces were slaughtered by a Jacobite army at Killiecrankie, near Pitlochry in Perthshire, but Mackay's presence in Aberdeen immediately before this murderous encounter is probably an indication that the new regime was unsure of Aberdeen's allegiance. The town council was certainly unhappy about the expenses which it had incurred as a result of the military occupation.[1] It was probably also unconvinced by the general's politics. In January 1689, it decided to send George Garden (1649-1733), minister of the East Kirk and Second Charge of Aberdeen, to the new king, in order to represent its political and ecclesiastical concerns. Garden was, in some ways, a strange choice. In 1692, the privy council deprived him of his ministry, on account of his failure to pray for King William and Queen Mary (1689-94) – a clear indication of Garden's Jacobite sympathies and, given that he was entrusted with official council business, of the council's political inclinations too.[2] Not surprisingly, considering the weakness of Presbyterianism in the north-east, Garden continued to minister in Aberdeen until he was deposed by the General Assembly in 1701, ostensibly for his expression of Bourignonism, a heresy that the kirk was keen to stamp out. But if the town wished its representative to inform William of its broadly Episcopalian sympathies, then Garden was its man. The new king offered hope to Episcopalians – for many, initially at least, religious interests may well have tempered their innate sympathy for the Stewart dynasty. Nevertheless, two councillors (James Reid, master of the hospital, and James Milne) protested against

Garden's appointment in 1689, which strongly suggests that Aberdeen was politically divided at this important moment in the nation's history.[3]

Signs of this division were apparent in 1688, the year in which the Revolution began. On 20 November, William Hay wrote to the countess of Errol that 'your ladyship has heard of the new election of the magistrates heir [in Aberdeen], quhich as I am informed was done by a list sent from Edinburgh to the old Councill by their dictator Bailyie [David] Adie'.[4] The exact purpose of this intervention in local affairs from the south remains uncertain, but more was to follow. In September 1690, the privy council devised a list of acceptable burgesses, from whom a new council might be elected to replace those who 'wer imposed upon the towne and keept in place by letters impetrrat from the Court by priests and popish recommendations'.[5] On 23 June 1691, it issued a warrant ordering a new election for the office of provost.[6] John Sandilands of Countesswells had been on the privy council's blacklist, but had nonetheless served as provost from 1690 to June 1691. That he was deposed at the new election implies that he was still not well affected to the new Williamite order.[7] Indeed, much of the local political establishment probably was, and remained, Jacobite in sympathy. In 1696, the council elections were quashed by the privy council 'as there were only nine counsellors present at the former election and the new one'.[8] The inquorate meeting suggests that there was still far from overwhelming support for the new Williamite council in the 1690s. And if the attitude of John Allardyce, Aberdeen's representative to the Convention of Royal Burghs from 1692 to 1714, its provost from 1702 to 1707 and its parliamentary commissioner from 1703 to 1707, was at all typical, then Jacobite sympathies lingered even longer at the uppermost levels of political society. During the parliamentary divisions on the Treaty of Union (1707), Allardyce failed to vote in favour of articles two and three – the crucial sections of the treaty which paved the way for the Hanoverian succession and the Anglo-Scottish parliamentary union.[9]

The Jacobite rising of 1715

Early eighteenth-century governments possessed various stratagems for inculcating loyalty among doubtful subjects. In 1709, for instance, a royal proclamation giving thanks for the duke of Marlborough's victories over the French at Ghent and Lille, during the War of Spanish Succession (1702-13), was read from the pulpit in Old Aberdeen.[10] A semblance of resignation had descended over both Aberdeen towns and, although it has been argued that 'Aberdeen was always loyal to the House of Stuart', the authorities in both towns were committed, in public at least, to the House of Hanover.[11] Mercantile wealth and prosperity depended upon public loyalty to the existing establishment, whatever its complexion. Yet, the façade of acceptance soon dropped when news circulated of the death of Queen Anne (1702-14). Many superficially united Britons embraced the imminent Protestant Hanoverian succession. In Old Aberdeen, the kirk session arranged for the bells of St Machar's to be rung in celebration of the arrival of George I (1714-29) in London.[12] But most Aberdonians (and most others north of Forth) preferred the (still Catholic) Stewart alternative, the Old Pretender, James VIII (d. 1766). For them, for the moment at least, 'religion mattered less than sovereignty' – and the bells of St Machar's remained silent while those of King's College chimed and an effigy of the Hanoverian king was burned in the old town.[13]

As early as August 1715, the New Aberdeen council considered a report that 'the Highlanders were in some motion and lyke to ryse and might perhaps attack the toune'.[14] During both the '15 and the '45, the Jacobite threat was perceived to be a Highland problem. This perception was at odds with the reality, especially during the '15, when lowland Aberdeenshire was a centre of Jacobitism too. Jacobite sympathies were also evident in the town itself. In August 1714, the council corresponded with the Secretary of State regarding 'that dysorder that fell out here the tenth instant'.[15] Some young men 'attended by women went thrrow the streets with two viollers playing to them'. But the intent of these people was clear enough, as they 'drank [to] the pretender King James his health', after singing Jacobite songs that expressed the hope that the 'King enjoy his own again'.[16] As the Jacobite threat intensified, Aberdeen was ordered to deliver to Edinburgh the armaments stored for its defence, which included large amounts of gunpowder. Clearly, and with good reason given that James VIII had been proclaimed king at the market cross in both Aberdeen towns on 20 September 1715, the Hanoverian authorities feared that Aberdeen's armoury might be used against the government. The same day, furthermore, the Jacobite Earl Marischal had entered the towns unopposed and was then entertained by the Incorporated Trades in New Aberdeen.[17] The universities in both New and Old Aberdeen were also supportive of the Jacobite cause.[18] And ninety-four of the New Aberdeen burgesses were apparently Jacobite in sympathy – or so it was claimed by those councillors still in office in 1716.[19] One of the Jacobites was probably Alexander Gray, minister of St Clement's at Futty, who had been ordained in 1683 and who had been a burgess of Aberdeen since 1695. Gray was deposed by the General Assembly in 1716 for praying for the Chevalier St. George (the Old Pretender) during the rising.[20]

In New Aberdeen, the key development in the uprising was the removal of council members and their replacement by others of a Jacobite persuasion. On 29 September 1715 Patrick Bannerman was elected provost, 'the greater part of the burgers of Gild and tradesmen of the burgh having met together'.[21] Bannerman had, as the council minutes indicate, been elected on a popular mandate, representing the majority of Aberdeen's burgesses and tradesmen, the 'greater part' of whom were present during the election itself. The new Jacobite council was effectively a war cabinet, and it used its political power to advance Jacobite interests beyond Aberdeen. The town's store of Lochaber axes was sent to the Jacobite camp at Perth, together with a printing press, types and utensils, for use in the production of propaganda. Meanwhile, the council resolved to exact substantial taxation to pay for the Jacobite campaign, and it ordered the town's ministers to pray for King James.[22] The impact of its actions, however, was limited. Little more than four month's after Bannerman's election, the Old Pretender was sailing back to France, crownless.

Between the Jacobite risings

The failure of the '15 left the government with the problem of reasserting its credibility. The experience of the rebellion had fostered insecurity in the very heart of the growing commercial town in New Aberdeen. Although the popular Jacobitism evident in 1715 appears to have ebbed, an application made by Colonel John Middleton of Seaton (1678-1739) to extend the house at Castle Hill, in order to accommodate a troop of horses, suggests that magistrates loyal to the Hanoverian regime found their position vulnerable without a substantial military presence in the town. Other measures were also taken to bolster the Hanoverian regime. Both King's and Marischal were purged of Jacobite staff, and in the craft institutions of New Aberdeen efforts were made to ensure that Jacobite sympathisers were excluded from office. In 1726, in anticipation of the election of the Deacon of the Hammermen, it was stipulated that candidates 'should Qualifie by Swearing the Oath of Allegiance and Subscribing the same with the Assurance to His Majesty King George'. The practical effect of excluding Jacobites, as in the 1690s, was electoral apathy. During elections for the post of deacon following 'the year of the unnatural rebellion', not more than about six members of the trade were present, leaving the meetings inquorate.[23] Yet, whatever the political inclinations of its inhabitants, the town's communal interests once again encouraged interaction with the Hanoverian government.

In 1728, the provost (George Fordyce) and bailies used the offices of Andrew Fletcher, Lord Milton (1692-1766), 'a sincere and real friend to the Town of Aberdeen',[24] to secure the appointment of James Chalmers as principal of Marischal College - the Earl Marischal's patronage rights having passed to the crown following his involvement in the '15 (see Chapter 15).[25] Similarly, in the early 1730s, the provost urged Milton to use his parliamentary influence 'for having our gift on ale [and] wines received or prorogat because our public debts are swelling to such a hight, that unless the said gift be renewed ... the town must in a few years inevitably go to ruin'.[26]

Even internal squabbles were referred to Milton. A major rupture within the Aberdeen magistrates occurred in 1735, caused by a mixture of competing political factions, a struggle between landed heritors and urban-based merchants, and their respective tax bills. In 1736, the Dean of Guild (James Strachan), the Convener of the Incorporated Trades (Alexander Forbes) and several merchants protested at the council meeting 'against the heritors and others therein mentioned, in relation to the proportioning of the cess of the said Burgh betwixt the Merchants, Traders and Heritors of Land, Fishing and Houses'.[27] The proportion of tax to be assigned to commercial and to landed interests was in dispute, with Patrick Duff of Premnay (a close associate of Milton) leading the heritors, and the council itself unable to resolve the matter. The provost, William Cruickshank, wrote to Milton informing him of 'a great division [that] has lately happened in this place ... a party of those in the late administration have still opposed such as were for the interest of your Lordship and your friends, especially since the late election'.[28] It is no surprise, on these and other occasions, to find the council seeking the assistance of Milton, the Edinburgh-based 'chief executive' of Scottish politics until 1764.[29] Milton could deliver favours, but through Duff, and latterly Cruickshank, he was also bonding local interests to his wider network of clients. Pen and the patronage of leading establishment figures were becoming the hallmarks of local political management.

At a national level too, politics was becoming synonymous with the art of patronage. After the Anglo-Scottish union of 1707, Aberdeen lost its independent parliamentary representation. Instead, together with the burghs of Arbroath, Brechin, Inverbervie and Montrose, it constituted the new Aberdeen Burghs constituency, which had an electorate of eighty-five voters. In 1715, the Tory James Erskine won the seat, though his election was subsequently overruled.[30] Erskine would have been unpopular with the loyal core of Aberdeen magistrates who wished to align themselves with the second duke of Argyll, one of the architects of the Anglo-Scottish union and still an influential figure in government. Erskine's successor, Colonel Middleton (who represented Aberdeen Burghs between 1715 and 1739, but only after appealing successfully against the results of the 1715 and 1722 elections) was, in this respect, more suitable. The son of a principal of King's College, he was a warm supporter of the duke's party.[31] Nevertheless, there was a price to pay for securing Aberdeen's vote. Middleton negotiated a reduction in the town's contribution to royal burgh taxation in 1727 and parliamentary approval for the local ale tax (noted above) to fund civic improvements in 1731.[32]

Argyll's links with Old Aberdeen were also close. His secretary, William Smith, was made an honorary burgess of the town in 1741, though by then the duke had cut his links with Sir Robert Walpole's government, and his star had begun to wane. When news subsequently circulated of Argyll's brief triumph in the 1741 election, eleven bottles of claret were uncorked at King's College in celebration; but by 1742 the duke was again in opposition, and he died a year later.[33] Nevertheless, Campbell influence in government remained strong and Middleton's successor as MP for Aberdeen Burghs, John Maule (1706-81), was secretary to Argyll's brother, Archibald Campbell, Lord Islay. Islay had remained in government after his brother's departure from Walpole's camp in 1739 and, collaborating closely with Milton, he continued to serve as the London-based manager of Scottish affairs until 1743, and again from 1746 until his death in 1761. It is no coincidence that Marischal College also looked to Islay, who succeeded his brother as third duke in 1743, as its unofficial patron following the Earl Marischal's exile. Indeed, the Argyll interest in Marischal continued after Islay's death, with his nephew, Lord Bute (1713-92), prime minister from 1762 to 1763, serving as the university's chancellor from 1761 until 1792.[34]

Patronage, however, did not feed people. The town's dependence upon the quality and quantity of the harvest was especially exposed in 1740, when a poor harvest made for high prices. The council, 'considering the great scarcity of victual in this burgh, and the extraordinary high prices given therefore, by reason most of the meal in the countrey was already bought up for exportation [decided that] it was absolutely necessary to buy a sufficient quantity of meal for the servicing of the inhabitants who are not able to provide for themselves'.[35] Particular concern was expressed for 'the poor [who] have been great sufferers'.[36] While the council recognised a responsibility to use its resources to prevent starvation (a kind of early form of social security), its concerns were probably dictated as much by considerations of public order as by compassion (see Chapter 2). The mob was not as prominent a feature of eighteenth-century Scottish or Aberdonian politics as in other parts of Europe. Nevertheless, in 1731 the council had banned the public playing of the pipes for fear of the 'tumults' with which they were associated, which suggests a keen awareness of the connection between popular culture and popular disorder. It was similarly aware that economic privation, which stemmed both from the immediate impact of the Anglo-Scottish Union and food shortages, was apt to lead to disturbance, as it did on several occasions between the 1720s and 1740s. Yet, ultimately the council's only sanction against popular agitation was military force, and as late as 1783 the provost was lobbying other burghs against disbanding the military. The army was essential 'in order to keep the necessary Peace in Towns when an uncommon Scarcity prevails'.[37]

The Jacobite rising of 1745

The new politics of patronage was rudely interrupted during the late summer of 1745 when the council put the town into a posture of defence in response to 'ane insurrection in the Highlands'. Fencible men were divided into twelve companies.[38]

Between September 1745 and February 1746, Aberdeen was again under Jacobite control. The Aberdeen minister John Bisset noted the arrival of 'thirty Macgregors [in] the town this night [12 December 1745]', again connecting Jacobitism and the Highland clans, and ten days later it was reported that the sermon in Old Aberdeen had been cancelled following a disturbance. The church treasurer had been 'harassed' by rebels and money had been extorted from him by threat.[39] During the Jacobite occupation, both Aberdeen burghs were again politically divided. In Old Aberdeen, despite the signs of warmth noted above to the Argyll and Hanoverian interests, enthusiastic Jacobite supporters, such as John Gordon of Glenbucket, had been made honorary burgesses.[40] When the New Aberdeen magistrates prepared to defend the town against the Jacobite army, 'a considerable number of burghers came up in a body to the Council House' to protest, arguing that the 'Highlanders must be irritate at such a procedure'. Any attempt to put the inhabitants of the town under arms was in 'vain' because 'the town is so divided'.[41] A list of suspected Jacobites drawn up in 1746 indicates both the extent of Jacobite support within Aberdeen and the broad social basis of its appeal: those identified included Robert Montgomery, an Old Aberdeen beggar, as well as affluent merchants, tradesmen and surgeons in New Aberdeen.[42] According to the latter's council, reconvened after the arrival of the duke of Cumberland and government troops, some of the magistrates had not acted 'with that zeal and affection to your Majesty's person and Government'.[43]

In 1746, the second Jacobite threat to the Hanoverian regime disappeared on the battlefield of Culloden. In Old Aberdeen, a day of thanksgiving was proclaimed by the kirk session. The inhabitants were instructed to 'spend the day in a religious manner' and subsequently a bonfire was lit to mark Cumberland's birthday.[44] But celebrations soon gave way to reprisals. In the late summer of 1746, a major riot took place in New Aberdeen, causing considerable damage to property. One of its targets was the seat of the civil magistracy, the Town House; its grand windows were broken during the disturbance. There is little evidence in the council minutes as to who exactly was to blame for the riot. But subsequently, James Morison, the provost, and three bailies wrote to the earl of Albemarle (one of Cumberland's commanders at Culloden), 'heartily regrat[ing] that our compliments of congratulation to your lordship should be attended with an account of a notorious ryot and breach of the peace committed in this city, Friday night last'. The culprits were among 'brigadier Fleming['s] regiment lying here and that even some of the officers have been concerned therein'.[45] The riot had occurred on the anniversary of the Hanoverian succession, some of the soldiers perhaps using the celebrations to express their triumphalism on a still unimpressed town. Indeed, in a contemporary 'Memorial for the Magistrates of Aberdeen', there is a complaint that the commemorative solemnities 'put the poorer sort of inhabitants at considerable expense' –

exactly the section of Aberdeen society most likely to evince political disaffection to the triumphant British establishment.[46]

The magistrates did not, and politically could not, let the matter rest: 'elections are nigh at hand [and] our inhabitants are insisting to have their damages repaired and such satisfaction given to the town as the insult done deserves.'[47] Many of the town's poorest inhabitants had suffered disproportionately during the riot, so that they had 'not wherewith to repair their damage'. Yet, the officers involved in the disturbance remained unrepentant and unwilling to recompense the citizens. In the words of the provost, the 'principall officers are full of resentment against us [the council]'.[48] The civil magistracy, it would seem, remained impotent in the face of military occupation. Meanwhile, Albemarle promised nothing in his reply to the magistrates, but wrote immediately to Lord Ancram, who was responsible for the troops at Aberdeen, informing him 'of how bad consequence it must be to His Majesty's service when differences arise between the civil magistrate and the gentlemen of the army, especially officers of high rank'.[49]

Other tensions between the council and the military, whose occupation lasted for several months after Culloden, also surfaced. The army had usurped the council's power of imprisoning suspected criminals in the tolbooth (Ill. 21). The provost and three bailies wrote to Albemarle concerning two Aberdeen merchants, Andrew Walker and Walter Nicol, 'who were committed prisoners to the Main Guard on Wednesday last … for what crimes we know not'.[50] The magistrates complained that the responsibility granted to them by the army's judge advocate to make enquiries about all Aberdeen inhabitants who were absent at the time of Cumberland's entry into the town had been overturned. It was an important point, not only about the relative powers of town council and military but also, in effect, about who defined loyalty and disployalty to the government. After enquiring about these men, the council was satisfied that they had been absent on legitimate business. In the bitter atmosphere of post-Culloden Scotland, the regular activities of merchants (and many others) were curbed by an army keen to exact some reprisals on a town suspected of Jacobite sympathies. Albemarle sympathised with the town's plight, and wrote to Ancram that 'trading merchants of a Royal Burgh should not be detained in your main Guard'.[51] Suspicion continued into the winter of 1746-7, when a proclamation was issued 'against inhabitants [of Aberdeen] receiving strangers into their houses, or letting houses to strangers'.[52]

Despite the tensions, the turmoil of military occupation actually placed the loyal core of magistrates in a powerful position. After the rising of 1715, George I permitted the provost and four bailies to elect a new magistracy and council, thereby circumventing the normal electoral process.[53] In a 'Petition from the Governours of the City of Aberdeen appointed by the Duke of Cumberland' to the Lord Justice Clerk, the provost and three of his bailies petitioned that the same procedures of

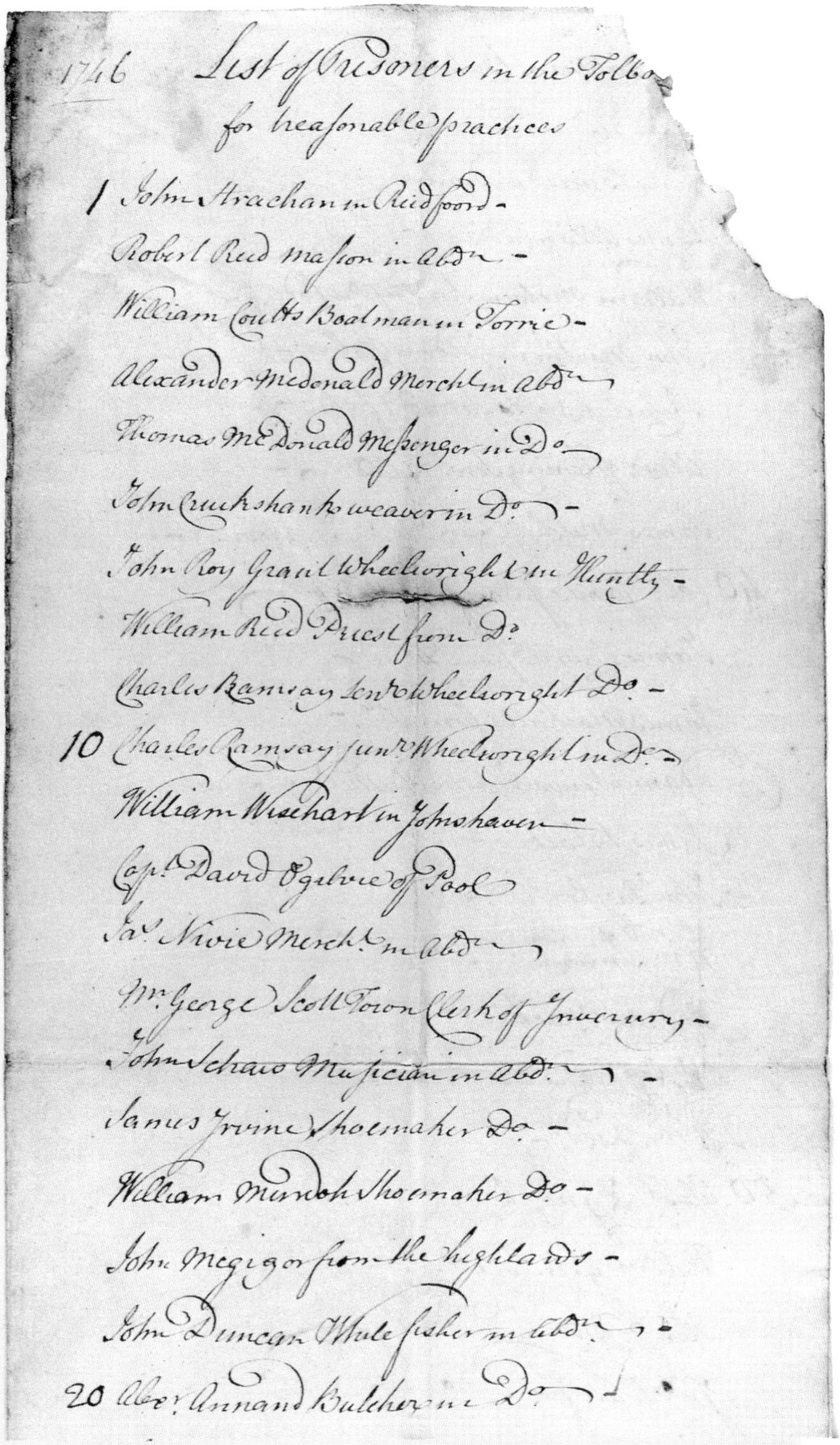

1746   *List of Prisoners in the Tolbo...*
         for treasonable practices

1 John Strachan in Reidford –
   Robert Reid mason in Abd –
   William Coutts Boatman in Torrie –
   Alexander Mcdonald Merchl in Abd
   Thomas McDonald Messenger in Do
   John Cruickshank weaver in Do –
   John Roy Grant Wheelwright in Huntly –
   William Reid Priest from Do
   Charles Ramsay senr Wheelwright Do –
10 Charles Ramsay junr Wheelwright in Do
   William Wishart in Johnshaven –
   Capt David Ogilvie of Pool
   Jas Nivie Merchl in Abd
   Mr George Scott Town Clerk of Inverury –
   John Schaw Musician in Abd –
   James Irvine Shoemaker Do –
   William Murdoch Shoemaker Do –
   John Mcgrigor from the highlands –
   John Duncan Whale fisher in Abd –
20 Alexr Annand Butcher in Do

Illustration 21
A list of prisoners
held in the tolbooth,
1746.

appointment should be used again in 1746. No doubt this was to avoid messy questions being asked about who was, and who was not, entitled to vote in the election. During the first half of the eighteenth century, there was frequently a disparity between the loyal public stance of the town, as represented by its council, and a more elusive reality. Like all royal burghs, Aberdeen frequently expressed its loyalty to the establishment – and no doubt many of the magistrates and others were strong adherents of the established government. But, in reality, the town was divided in its loyalties, and throughout the early eighteenth century Jacobite sympathies simmered just below the surface.

Parliamentary politics after 1745

In the aftermath of the Jacobite defeat at Culloden, the patterns of post-Union politics and political management slowly re-emerged. At Westminster, Aberdeen remained part of the 'district' of burghs which was represented by a single MP.[54] As its MP was elected by a majority vote of the burghs, Aberdeen's increasing size and importance did not translate into parliamentary influence. The key contest over the seat usually occurred in the smaller burghs which formed part of the constituency. The third duke of Argyll, who was still advising the ministry on parliamentary elections, wrote that 'Mr [Charles] Maitland, the great favourite [for election], appeared there as delegate from the town of Lord Arbuthnott [Inverbervie], a non-juror. I am informed that this Mr. Maitland did lately give a most false account of the late poll election at Brechin to the Earl of Morton', which implied that the Jacobite vote in the smaller towns in the district could still swing the election.[55] Maitland (c. 1708–51), an honorary burgess of Old Aberdeen since 1739, lost at the general election in 1747, but won a by-election in 1748, despite the government's efforts to thwart him.[56] On Maitland's death in 1751 his earlier opponent, David Scott (1689-1766), a relative of the important English lawyer William Murray (later Lord Mansfield), was elected, and in 1753 Argyll wrote to the ministry that the Aberdeen council had asked him to recommend a candidate for MP. In his opinion, 'their present Member has behaved himself very well, with some little touch upon the merit of his relation' [Mansfield].[57]

Representation of the constituency continued to be decided in the other burghs, rather than Aberdeen alone. In 1768, Scott was succeeded by Thomas Lyon (1741-96), who had purchased the castle at Inverbervie, though he successfully attracted the vote of Aberdeen too. When Lyon retired in 1778, he arranged for the election of the banker Adam Drummond (1713-86).[58] In 1784, the opposition Whig Sir David Carnegie (1753-1805), with a large estate in Angus and the support of the three Angus burghs, took the seat, but in 1790 government intervention secured the election of the wealthy former East India Company merchant Alexander Callander

(1741-92), who was backed by Aberdeen.[59] After Callander's death, he was replaced by the first Aberdonian to hold the seat since the Union, Alexander Allardyce (?1743-1801). Allardyce, the grandson of a former Aberdeen provost, had been admitted as burgess in 1745 while still an infant, and subsequently made a fortune in Jamaica as a slaver.[60] His biography in the *History of Parliament* records that 'It was later said of him that he had "sold about as many blackmen as there are white in his native city"', indicating that admiration for his achievements in his native town outside the town council itself was somewhat limited. He spoke in parliament on 28 April 1794, in favour of the Aberdeen Police Bill, and his importance as a major East India Company and Bank of England shareholder ensured that for the first time since 1707 Aberdeen had some influence in parliamentary affairs. The Police Bill was duly passed in 1795, followed in 1800 by an Improvement Act, which paved the way for urban expansion. After Allardyce's death in 1801, his brother-in-law, James Farquhar, a proctor in Doctors' Commons in London, succeeded as MP, with the support of the government's new Scottish manager, Henry Dundas.[61] By the end of the century, the town council had thus been successful in increasing Aberdeen's voice in parliamentary affairs at Westminster, which was particularly useful when it sought the expansion and development of the town. Nevertheless, its success necessitated close co-operation with the government and the capital interests of wealthy Aberdonians, such as Allardyce, who could offer the council patronage and influence in London.

Urban politics from the 1780s

The cosy bonds of patronage which linked both local and parliamentary politics were seriously challenged towards the end of the eighteenth century, in the era of the American Wars of Independence (1776-83) and the French Revolution (1789-92). When news broke of the colonial revolt in America, many of the élite in Aberdeen took a predictable line. In 1776, Alexander Gerard, the professor of divinity at King's, used the Old Aberdeen pulpit to denounce the 'opposition of the colonies to the government of Britain [which] has been raised under a false pretence of liberty, and has proceeded to maliciousness'.[62] Gerard failed to understand the colonial argument of 'no taxation, without representation'. For him, the system of Scottish political patronage and clientage *did* provide representation. By that standard, the colonists, too, already possessed 'representation', though, as soon became clear, not everyone in Aberdeen shared Gerard's conception of representation.

During the 1780s, substantial public opinion manifested itself in favour of local government reform. Aberdeen reformers were in no doubt as to the origins of their discontent. At a public meeting of burgesses, held in opposition to town council government, the town's Jacobite legacy was identified as the source of a governmental system which exercised the will of 'the people above' (as the moral philosopher Adam Ferguson had once put it in relation to another issue) rather than that of the burgesses or the population at large. The need to demonstrate loyalty to the government had come above all else, and Hanoverian loyalists continued to come under less scrutiny in other aspects of their public life until the changes which swept British politics from 1783, in the aftermath of the American War of Independence. In 1787, the author of *Farther Proceedings of the Burgesses of Aberdeen* (Ill. 22) argued that:

> The rebellion in 1715 contributed not a little to strengthen the hands of those who were in office at that period. The state of public matters from thence till some time after the succeeding rebellion in 1745 had a very sensible influence upon the privileges of the burgesses. From this last period till a considerable time after, the general suspicion which lay against many of the citizens, who were supposed to be warmly attached to the Stuart family, gave those who were then in the council a very exclusive power, and a large share of uncontrouled authority; because the instant a man suggested an idea interfering with public management, he was particularly pointed at, as disaffected to the Hanoverian succession, and a Jacobite.[63]

These developments had been possible because of the peculiarities of burgh government, which allowed councillors to elect their successors without reference to the burgesses as a whole. Oligarchy flourished, subject to periodic bouts of popular displeasure. In 1783, John Ewen, one of the first to become prominent in demands for change, claimed that a return to past practice would vindicate the rights of the community as a whole. 'In past periods,' he wrote, 'your representatives in the council of the burgh were chosen by the community; not self-elected, as they now are. Even at a more arbitrary, and less remote period, every matter of importance was determined in the head courts or general assembly of the burgesses, when the utmost decorum was observed, and every transaction determined by vote.'[64] Another of Ewen's pamphlets answered those who defended the existing burgh constitution on the grounds that it was associated with contemporary expansion in trade and manufacturing (see Chapter 6). 'With equal truth,' he observed, 'might he have ascribed their prosperity and commercial advantages to the government of Turkey'. Ewen continued by offering an alternative explanation for the 'progress of improvement', which had 'been more rapid in the last thirty years, than for centuries before':

> To what has this been owing? To the almost total annihilation of feudalism, by the act for abolishing heritable jurisdictions; the more extensive influence of mild and equal laws; and, in spite of the most deep rooted prejudices, that happy

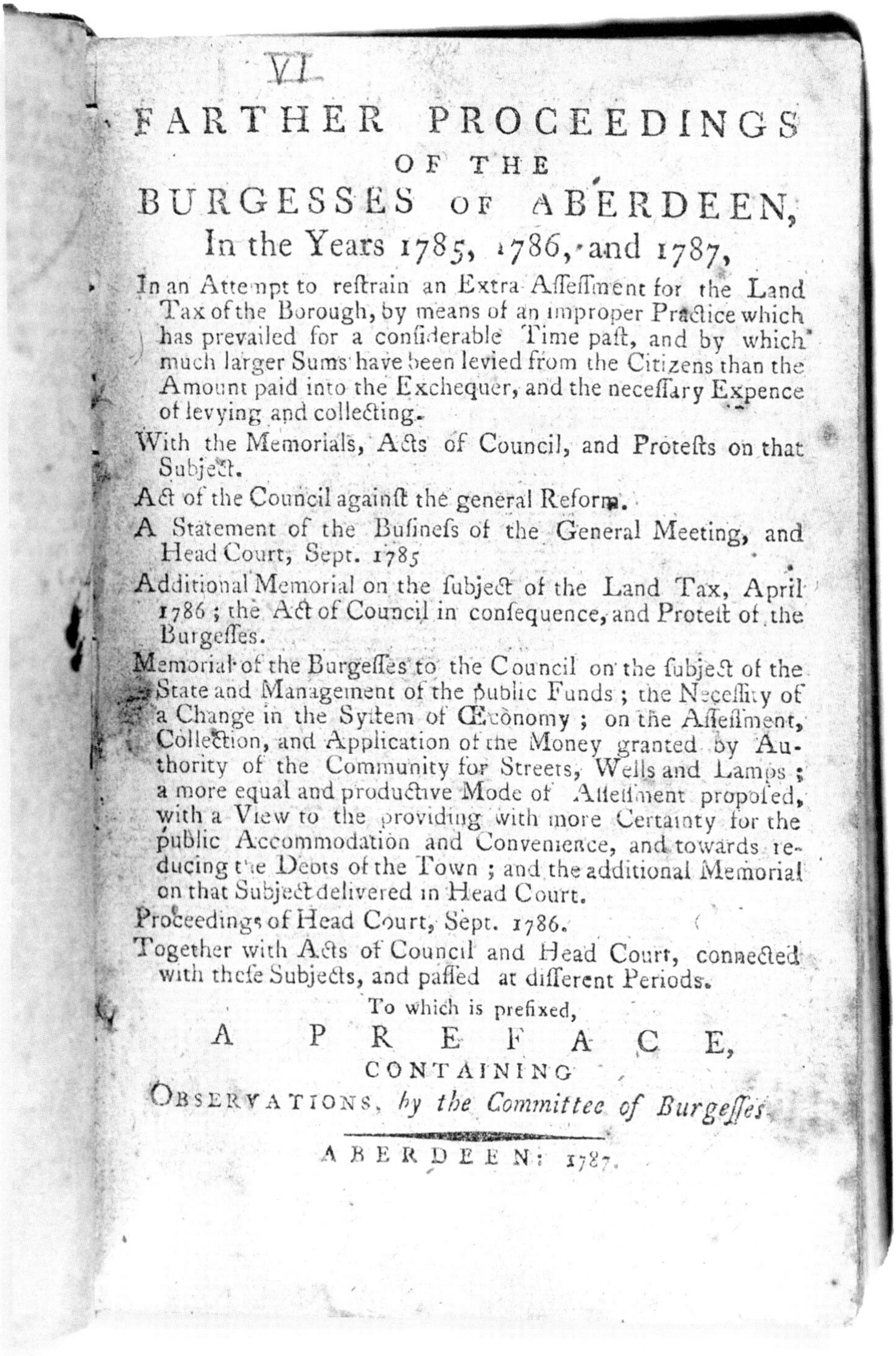

VI

FARTHER PROCEEDINGS
OF THE
BURGESSES OF ABERDEEN,
In the Years 1785, 1786, and 1787,

In an Attempt to reſtrain an Extra Aſſeſſment for the Land Tax of the Borough, by means of an improper Practice which has prevailed for a conſiderable Time paſt, and by which much larger Sums have been levied from the Citizens than the Amount paid into the Exchequer, and the neceſſary Expence of levying and collecting.

With the Memorials, Acts of Council, and Proteſts on that Subject.

Act of the Council againſt the general Reform.

A Statement of the Buſineſs of the General Meeting, and Head Court, Sept. 1785

Additional Memorial on the ſubject of the Land Tax, April 1786 ; the Act of Council in conſequence, and Proteſt of the Burgeſſes.

Memorial of the Burgeſſes to the Council on the ſubject of the State and Management of the public Funds ; the Neceſſity of a Change in the Syſtem of Œconomy ; on the Aſſeſſment, Collection, and Application of the Money granted by Authority of the Community for Streets, Wells and Lamps ; a more equal and productive Mode of Aſſeſſment propoſed, with a View to the providing with more Certainty for the public Accommodation and Convenience, and towards reducing the Debts of the Town ; and the additional Memorial on that Subject delivered in Head Court.

Proceedings of Head Court, Sept. 1786.

Together with Acts of Council and Head Court, connected with theſe Subjects, and paſſed at different Periods.

To which is prefixed,

A P R E F A C E,
CONTAINING
OBSERVATIONS, *by the Committee of Burgeſſes.*

ABERDEEN: 1787.

Illustration 22 Farther Proceedings of the Burgesses of Aberdeen in the Years 1785, 1786 and 1787, with a preface of observations by the Committee of Burgesses (Aberdeen, 1787).

intercourse which has been opened and maintained with our fellow subjects in the southern parts of the island. To these, with a nameless train of salutary consequences, and not to a system the most arbitrary and wretched that can be conceived, are we to ascribe 'that prosperity and commercial importance' [quoting his opponent], to which till then we were utter strangers.[65]

The council which came under such criticism comprised the magistrates (the provost, the bailies who served in the burgh court, the treasurer and the dean of guild), ordinary merchant councillors, from whom the magistrates were elected, and the deacons of the Incorporated Trades, who could not serve as magistrates. By the late eighteenth century, members of the Incorporated Trades were seldom individual craftsmen who worked with their hands, and deacons were always drawn from the wealthier members of the incorporations, who were in effect running businesses as tailors, in the building trades or in other traditional areas of craft activity. The issues that emerged as dominant during the debates on burgh politics reflected the oligarchic nature of Scottish burgh constitutions. They included the 'set' (or constitution) and the growing resentment amongst merchant burgesses and members of trades incorporations at being taxed, even although they had no effective say in burgh government. There was also growing pressure for political involvement from those who were not burgesses or members of incorporations, and for an extension of political rights to a broader band of the town's population. This political debate was carried out against the background of that extension of 'improvement' on which John Ewen and his opponents agreed, in spite of their differences, and which marked the physical expansion of the town and the growth of its population. The real issue, in this context, was governmental response to the problems of economic expansion - 'police', as it was still quaintly termed in Scotland - although the public debate from 1783 to 1793 focused more on the constitution and political accountability than on urban expansion.

Reform in the age of revolution

Aberdeen was in the forefront of the movement for burgh reform during the 1780s. Although letters calling for reform of burgh government by 'Zeno' (an Edinburgh burgess named Thomas Macgrugor) were published in the *Caledonian Mercury* in Edinburgh at the end of the American War of Independence, John Ewen rapidly followed these with his letters in the *Aberdeen Journal*, published as 'a CITIZEN of Aberdeen'.[66] There had been concern over the defence of the town during the war for American privateers had attacked the Scottish coast but, despite the comments of Alexander Gerard in 1776, there was considerable sympathy for the American rebellion. James Mackintosh, the author of *Vindiciae Gallicae*, had as a schoolboy in Scotland conducted debates in the classroom on the American War, based on reports in the *Aberdeen Journal*. He recorded that one of his professors at Aberdeen, James Dunbar, marked the dismissal of Lord North's government in 1782, 'in his pompous way', by telling Mackintosh, on meeting him in the street, that 'I congratulate you, the Augean stable is cleansed'.[67] Critics of the British political system, such as Dunbar and Mackintosh, attributed failure in the American War to the shortcomings of the constitution, and the fall of North's pro-war ministry opened the way for reformers throughout Britain to seek support for constitutional change.

Reformers in Aberdeen who sympathised with Ewen's letters in the *Aberdeen Journal* formed themselves into a committee, which corresponded with a similar body based in Edinburgh, designed to promote a Burgh Reform Act. The Aberdeen committee, which sent representatives to the annual conventions held in Edinburgh, was one of the most active in Scotland and, in some senses, the most successful. It pressurised the existing magistracy to call a burgh head court of all the burgesses, by beat of the town drum, in September 1784.[68] Reformers in Aberdeen were not acting in isolation. The movement for burgh reform was national. Yet, perhaps Aberdeen typified the idea that burgh reform represented what historians of Scotland writing in the Liberal tradition once called its political 'awakening'. The transition from Jacobitism to a Whig regime had involved so much state intervention that after the fall of the wartime North government pressure for political reform in Scotland seemed to appear quite suddenly.[69] 'Our situation is so different now,' wrote John Ewen early in 1783, 'that we are amazed at the change; and awake, as from a dream, to find ourselves so fallen.'[70]

The power of the idea of awakening, from a 'feudal Jacobite' past into a modern age where personal liberty guaranteed the security of property from excessive taxation, had particular impact in Aberdeen. Under the leadership of local merchants, such as Ewen and Patrick Barron of Woodside, and with sympathetic support from the *Aberdeen Journal*, considerable pressure was exerted on the existing magistracy, even if the aim of reforming the burgh constitution was thwarted for more than a generation by the outbreak of the French Revolution in 1789 and Britain's war with France from 1793. Just how extensive support was for the reform movement cannot be determined from the council minutes or from the publications of the reformers themselves, although some lists of supporters included names of as many as 215 burgesses. The Committee of Burgesses at Aberdeen sent, and later published, a letter to all the 'boroughs' in Scotland who had declared for reform and contacted 'neutral boroughs' as well.[71] In Aberdeen itself, it petitioned the council in 1784 to be allowed to nominate members to inspect the burgh accounts and later the town records, requests which the council approved, under threat of litigation at the Court of Session in Edinburgh. The issue which emerged specific to Aberdeen was that the council, by setting the level of cess to meet the town's assessment for the national Land Tax, was building up a revenue surplus for which it could not properly account. Subsequently, the debate extended to the council's management of burgh investments, including purchases of land and other assets, without proper accountability to the burgesses as a whole. Meetings of the burgesses were called, with or without council approval, to discuss these issues, so that public debate of the town's future development became a political issue which, to a certain extent, politicised the community.[72]

Even before revolutionary events in France transformed the situation, there was considerable debate in Aberdeen over whether this activity represented reform or agitation undermining public stability. In 1786, James Chalmers, printer and publisher of the *Aberdeen Journal*, published a leaflet which defended his editorial policy. In it, he claimed:

> It is but justice to myself, to answer that ever since the rise of the proposal for a reform in burgh elections, I have uniformly inserted such papers, on both sides, as contained the argument; and as to those in particular, which were written against the projected system of reform, I not only inserted such as were sent to the Journal, but, that my readers might have the fullest view of the debate, I took in such as appeared in other papers.[73]

Clearly, there were many still opposed to reform, and their number included George Forbes, an advocate and procurator fiscal of the burgh courts. Forbes issued a series of letters and pamphlets which became increasingly critical of the Committee of Burgesses, and it was their circulation which eventually provoked Chalmers into justifying his publication policy at the *Aberdeen Journal*. In September 1784, under the pen name 'Vindex', Forbes had advocated appeal to the Court of Session to obtain legal recognition of the authority of a head court of burgesses. By 1786, he was publishing pamphlets against the burgesses under the *nom de plume* 'Anti-Covenanter'. A satire published in Edinburgh, purportedly the composition of a burgh reformer using another highly significant pseudonym ('Oliver'), suggests that some at least of those in public life in Aberdeen remembered the legacy of Covenanting enthusiasm and Cromwellian occupation.[74] One of Forbes's leaflets mentions the convenor of the Incorporated Trades in 1786. Forbes accused this 'meddling Tailor' of using Incorporated Trades funds to defend 'rioters'. He also identified an apprentice at the *Aberdeen Journal*, named Ramsay, as one of those imprisoned following disturbances, 'as he had often been'.[75] In the council minutes for 28 July 1786, an act was recorded by the provost and bailies, as sheriffs and justices of the peace, 'prohibiting and discharging all apprentices, journeymen and servants of every kind within this city from being concerned in illegal or tumultuous meetings or processions, therein mentioned under several penalties contained in the said Act, particularly that if any person or persons shall contraveen any part of the said prohibition ... he shall not only be liable in a penalty of ten pounds Scots but also shall on such conviction be rendered incapable of ever [being] admitted a freeman of this city and if he is an apprentice that he shall lose the benefit of his indenture.'[76] Clearly, there had been crowd trouble of some sort which had raised political tension in the burgh in 1786, well before news from revolutionary France encouraged further popular action.

One of the first public expressions of sympathy for events in France occurred when the Committee of Burgesses, at their annual dinner on 4 June 1789, pledged a toast to the French Estates General.[77] It may be wondered how far the disturbances of 1786 reflected an established tradition of popular action. As already noted, altercations arising from both political and economic issues were common in the first half of the eighteenth century. More followed. In 1768, journeymen tailors had organised a strike and wool combers (who had organised themselves into a 'society' by 1755) had resisted the attempts of manufacturers (merchants) to introduce English labour to train apprentices after the combers had refused to do so themselves.[78] It was a time of dearth and there had been mobbing in the town over shortage of meal and high prices, but no overt challenge to the council's authority. The implication of the publications of 1786 is that at least some hoped, or feared, that direct popular action and pressure for constitutional reform would become linked. By 1792, they had – with riots in favour of reform occurring in Aberdeen, as well as in Edinburgh and many other burghs. In December 1792, a 'Tree of Liberty' appeared on the streets of Aberdeen, a potent symbol of the revival of past rights, decorated as it was with apples and lit by lanterns symbolising renewal. In the same month, sailors in the harbour boarded ships, unrigged those ready to sail, and stopped the loading and unloading of cargoes. Although the commander-in-chief for Scotland sent companies of the Black Watch to maintain order, the magistrates accepted a proposal for arbitration of wages by a committee of three merchants before the troops arrived.[79] Three years later, in 1795, crowds gathered in Schoolhill, Netherkirkgate and Shiprow after two ships with cargoes of grain had been boarded and unloaded in the harbour. They attacked the cellar of the merchant William Rae and destroyed 16 bolls of oatmeal, 40 lbs of soap, 8 lbs of snuff, furniture and a complete set of meal weights.[80] The 'Tree of Liberty', however, was not in evidence on this occasion, since the country was at war with France and the Treason Acts had come into effect. Had repressive government legislation inhibited the linkage of political and economic grievances which had previously occurred in Aberdeen, or were these separate spheres of public life?

Political, if not class, conflict became overt in 1793 over two related issues. The council proposed to finance a scheme to expand the urban water supply and enactment of a Police Act, both of which would provide increased municipal services under authority of a private act of parliament.[81] Both would also result in increased taxation for the burgesses, and both met with opposition. A general meeting of the 'citizens, burgesses and inhabitants', called by handbills and an advertisement in the *Aberdeen Journal* on 11 March, met to express opposition, and Patrick Barron of Woodside, the veteran of the burgh reform committee's activities of the previous decade, was called unanimously to the chair. The council's water scheme would bring water into the homes of those who could afford it, while an alternative plan, published by Alexander Anderson, to increase the number of town wells, had been ignored. The published account of the meeting declared 'that an attempt to give a supply of water into the houses of the upper ranks of the citizens, by a fund drawn by assessment from the pockets of the inhabitants at large, is founded on a principle as unjust, as the proposal itself is unexampled'. It was further claimed that the bill 'would in its general tendency prove very hard and extremely oppressive upon the lower and middling ranks of tradesmen, manufacturers, and shop-keepers, who collectively form the great body of the inhabitants and by whose industry a great part of all public burdens is supported'.[82] Meanwhile, the Police Act was opposed because it would involve new taxes when 'the Treasury Funds and common good of the burgh' (the financial assets of the corporation) were not being used to provide the 'police' which the citizens of the town had a right to expect.

The council nonetheless obtained its Police Act in 1795 (Ill. 23), for a term of twenty-seven years, but at the price of conceding a wider degree of representation on the board which was established to administer the act. The board comprised thirteen commissioners, rather than the town council, and the commissioners were to be elected. Echoes of the old Scots system of self-election remained, however. Eight commissioners were elected every two years, and they completed their number by voting to retain five of their eight predecessors. The principle of indirect election as a means of limiting popular faction was a notion influential among liberals in France and the United States, as well as Britain, at the time. The encomium on the election, published in Thom's *History of Aberdeen* (1811), resonates with the issues of the 1780s in its explanation of the election of police commissioners for the burgh: 'the whole occupiers and possessors of dwelling-houses, &c of the rent of five pounds sterling or upwards' residing in the burgh had the vote. Thom praised the 'manner of conducting the election' as 'worthy of imitation, wherever it is necessary to collect the voice of the people.' Voters sent lists to the burgh court for counting and 'there is neither noise, bustle, nor confusion.' The duty of the Police Commissioners related to the economy of the town, Thom recorded in 1811, 'without trenching on the rights or jurisdictions of the magistrates as a corporation, or on the rights and properties of individuals.'[83] Nevertheless, the commissioners quickly exhausted the willingness of the ratepayers to pay for more services. Within five years, the creation of Aberdeen's new West End began, with

ANNO TRICESIMO QUINTO

Georgii III. Regis.

****

CAP. LXXVI.

An Act for the better paving, lighting, cleanfing, and otherwife improving the Streets, Lanes, and other Publick Paffages, of the City of *Aberdeen*, and the Roads and Avenues within the Royalty thereof; for the better fupplying the Inhabitants with Frefh Water; and for the removing and preventing all Obftructions and Annoyances within the faid City and Royalty. [19th *May* 1795.]

HEREAS the City of *Aberdeen* has of late Years greatly Preamble. increafed in Buildings and Inhabitants, and the Roads, Avenues, Streets, Lanes, and other Publick Paffages, within the faid City and Royalty thereof, are at prefent too narrow, indirect, and incommodious, and are not properly paved, lighted, and cleanfed; nor are the Inhabitants fufficiently fupplied with Frefh Water: And whereas it would be greatly for the Safety and Accommodation of the Inhabitants of the faid City, and of all Perfons reforting to the fame, that the faid Roads, Avenues, Streets, Lanes, and other Publick Paffages, were enlarged and altered, and that they were more fufficiently paved, lighted, and cleanfed, and the faid City better fupplied with Frefh Water; that all Incroachments, Annoyances, and Obftructions of every Kind upon the faid Roads, Streets, Avenues, Lanes, and other Paffages, were removed and prevented; and that all Perfons dealing in Gunpowder within the faid City were prohibited from keeping at any One Time in their Houfes, Shops, or Warehoufes, more than a certain Quantity of Gunpowder: But as thefe ufeful and falutary Purpofes, for Want of proper Powers and a fufficient Fund to pay the Expence thereof, cannot be accomplifhed without the Authority of Parliament: May it therefore pleafe Your Majefty that it may be enacted; and be it enacted by the King's moft Excellent Majefty, by and with the Advice and Confent of the Lords Spiritual and Temporal, and Commons, in this prefent Parliament af-

I   12 U 2   fembled.

Illustration 23
The Police Act, 1795.

the passage of the first of a series of acts of parliament permitting the council to invest heavily in the town's expansion. The act of 1800 enabled the construction of Union Street and King Street, which 'were to form the crucial axis for expansion'; an 'imaginative and bold strategy' that 'reflected the confidence and adventurousness of the city fathers'.[84] The same act also began the process by which the old politics of Aberdeen became literally, as well as politically, bankrupt, hastening the process by which the reforms first projected in the 1780s came to fruition. A 'new town' was built on the foundation of a new urban oligarchy and burgh politics, wider than before, if as yet only marginally so.

Part IV
SHAPING MENTALITIES

13

The Faith of the People

MICHAEL LYNCH *and* GORDON DesBRISAY
with MURRAY G.H. PITTOCK

Aberdeen and its hinterland has long been a region that went its own way. It has been dubbed the 'conservative north' in the sixteenth and seventeenth centuries, to reflect its cautious reaction to the Reformation, its suspicion of radical Presbyterianism and its outright hostility to the Covenanting revolution of the late 1630s and 1640s (see also Chapters 9, 10 and 11).[1] This chapter does not attempt a comprehensive analysis of the religious beliefs of Aberdonians from the foundations of the burgh of New Aberdeen in the twelfth century to the eve of the Enlightenment for that could well be the subject of a large volume in itself. Rather, it focuses on three phases in that story. Each showed a distinctive Aberdonian religious temperament as well as a characteristic thrawnness. Aberdeen was usually determined that the burgh itself and not outsiders - whether royal government or the General Assembly - should take control of its own faith as well as deciding for itself how to combat the forces or ideas which threatened it.

Medieval Catholics and new-found Protestants

The two burghs of Old and New Aberdeen had a formidable number and range of churches, chapels, friaries and hospitals.[2] It has been estimated that about eighty, or one adult in four, in the bishop's burgh was a cleric.[3] There were almost as many clergy, of different sorts, in New Aberdeen. Even here, with a population of some 4,500 in 1500, more than one adult male in twenty would have been a priest, chaplain or friar. The old town was dominated by its cathedral of St Machar (Ill. 24), which had almost sixty secular clergy attached to it and had long functioned as the parish church. The royal burgh had its parish church of St Nicholas, which by 1500 was the largest burgh church in Scotland. But, in addition, Old Aberdeen had a further church - the Snow Kirk, or St Maria ad Nives, founded in 1498 and intended to serve as the parish church.[4] There was another church at the tiny fishing port of Futty. Although the first documented references to it belong to the later fifteenth century, its dedication to St Clement - typical of tenth- or eleventh-

*Illustration 24
Cathedral of St
Machar, Old
Aberdeen, 1790.*

century dedications in ports on the other side of the North Sea, in Denmark and Scandinavia – suggest that it may have been the earliest church in either burgh.[5]

The royal burgh had no fewer than four friaries, the largest concentration of mendicant orders in any Scottish burgh – the Trinitarians (or Red Friars), reputedly founded in Aberdeen, close to the harbour, as early as 1211; the Dominicans (or Black Friars), whose house in the burgh was established near Schoolhill sometime between 1222 and 1249; the Carmelites (or White Friars), another thirteenth-century foundation, in the Green, who also served as chaplains of St Ninian's Chapel on Castle Hill; and the Observant Franciscans, a stricter, reformed version of the Franciscan friars, who founded their house in the Gallowgate as late as 1469 (Ill. 25). It is likely that each order attracted and served different groups in society. The proximity of the Red Friars to the docks suggests a special duty towards seamen. Both Dominicans (the Order of Friars Preachers) and Carmelites saw preaching to the faithful, rather than a life of solitary contemplation, as part of their spiritual mission. And the Observant Franciscans, in common with the Black Friars, were licensed to hear confessions (including deathbed confessions) and to bury within their own graveyards the lay brothers of their order. Each of the four friaries, as a result, enjoyed a steady series of benefactions and obits from the burgesses of the town over the course of the Middle Ages.[6] They were, in their different ways, an integral part of the Church's provision for the souls of the faithful. For preaching, it is likely that burgesses would have gone to the churches of either the Black or White Friars, rather than St Nicholas.[7] Apart from an isolated incident in 1544, when two burgesses were imprisoned for hanging an image of St Francis, perhaps a copy-cat gesture following a similar anticlerical protest in Perth, Aberdeen's friaries seem to have avoided the resentment which afflicted mendicant orders in other Scottish burghs.[8]

The focus of faith and devotion for most Aberdonians, however, was the burgh church dedicated to St Nicholas, who was also depicted on the burgh's seal (Plate 20). By the end of the reign of James IV (1488–1513) and after the recent completion of its new choir, the church extended to some 256 feet in length and 103 feet across

Illustration 25
Reconstruction of
the friary of the
Observant
Franciscans,
Gallowgate.

its transepts.[9] Within it, there were some thirty altars, founded over the course of three centuries or more and dedicated to different saints; and more than fifty chantries, located at these altars, had also been endowed.[10] Expenditure on devotions is easier to trace than faith or piety; the records yield substantial investment in both the fabric of the burgh church and in chaplainries, obits and dedicated Masses within it almost from its foundation until the eve of the Reformation. Some dedications, such as those to St John the Evangelist, the Blessed Virgin and the Holy Rood can be traced to the last quarter of the thirteenth century.[11] Others, such as the Holy Blood altar or that dedicated to Our Lady of Pity, were the product of the new fashions in piety of the fifteenth century, which saw an increasing preoccupation with the Passion of Christ or with the Virgin and the Holy Family (see Chapter 17). Still newer was the Holy Name of Jesus, founded in 1520,[12] reflecting a more personal linkage to Christ than before. A few, such as those of St Anne and St Lawrence the Martyr, had noble or lairdly patrons, but most foundations were the work of pious individual burgesses, usually drawn from the upper reaches of society. A few were the saints of particular craft guilds: St Eloi of the hammermen or metalworkers; St Crispin of the skinners; and St John the Baptist of the coopers, wrights and masons. Yet Aberdeen's burgh church had less craft altars than its counterparts in either Perth or Edinburgh, where all fourteen incorporated crafts had their own altar and chaplain. Instead, almost a third of the altars were under the direct patronage of the burgh council.[13] In addition, specific Masses, often reflecting changes in patterns of piety, were endowed at existing altars. By 1542, a cycle of different Masses was said each day at the altar of St Anne, founded sometime before 1358. They included the Mass of the Five Wounds of Christ, one of the most popular of the devotions belonging to the cult of the Passion which typified the later fifteenth century.[14]

Within this huge church, the shape and dimensions of which can only be guessed at from the present structure, there was no heating. The focus of light would have been the high altar at its eastern end. One practical expression of piety by burgesses was the regular donation of candles and wax. The sheer length and acoustics of St Nicholas must have posed formidable problems to the first Protestant ministers after the Reformation. Its design, with its cruciform structure and aisled nave and a ribbed timber wagon ceiling over the choir and eastern apse constructed probably between *c.* 1483 and 1515, was more suited to sung High Mass or plain chant than the voice of a preacher, even if the pulpit was placed centrally after the Reformation.[15] This was a problem shared by all the large pre-Reformation burgh churches in Scotland, which were designed both for the faith of the living and the succour of the souls of past generations. In the *Scotichronicon,* written by Walter Bower, abbot of Inchcolm, in the 1440s, the Mass was described as being for 'the salvation of the living and the redemption of the dead'.[16] The design of the church provided for both kinds of piety – the prayers of the living and prayers for the dead. The attention of the congregation as a whole – or *corpus christianum* – was naturally drawn to the large-scale spectacle focused on the great altar. According to regulations set out in 1491, a minimum of twelve choristers had to be in attendance there during sung High Mass.[17] On the great feast days of the year, and perhaps at other times too, it is likely that the congregation saw the spectacle of all thirty-odd priests connected to the church – thirty-four choir stalls were ordered in 1507[18] – co-celebrating sung High Mass. By contrast, the private chantry chapels and altars scattered around the perimeter of the church were where individual chaplains said the votive Mass for the dead on behalf of the ancestors of their patrons or deceased members of their guild. But the regulations drawn up in 1519 insisted that no private masses were to be said while the 'great Mass' was being celebrated at the high altar.[19]

It was difficult within such a sprawling structure for the new Protestant faith, focused on the sermon, to operate effectively. One resort was the division of the church in two or more separate congregations, as happened in Edinburgh's St Giles' in 1562. Another solution, which came much later, was the building of new churches specifically designed as preaching boxes: the first was that at Burntisland (1600); another was Christ's Church at the Tron in Edinburgh (1647).[20] In Aberdeen, the device of division of the burgh church was not employed until 1596, when a wall was built to create the East and West Kirk; the specific reason given at the time was to make each a 'preaching kirk'.[21] Before that, it is difficult to imagine how effective a single Protestant minister, such as Adam Heriot, a former Augustinian canon of St Andrews hired in 1560 and bought a Genevan gown, could have been in a structure designed for the sung High Mass, rather than the spoken sermon. In St Andrews, where in the overnight reformation on 10/11 June 1559 the altars, rood screen and altar rails were removed, statues and stained glass windows depicting the saints smashed and the walls whitewashed, the change was sudden and dramatic: a transformation as dramatic as the replacement of a technicolour architectural landscape picture by a black-and-white negative.[22] In Aberdeen St Nicholas, much of the internal fittings of a Catholic church remained for some time after the Reformation: in 1574 the Regent Morton, on a visit to the burgh, was appalled to find the carved timber choir screen, choir stalls, reredos and even the organ still in place. The explanation given to him, that they were there to keep out the draughts in what was an unheated building, has an appeal to anyone brought up in Aberdeen, but it does help illustrate how slow and cautious the business of religious reform must have been in a conservative society.[23]

There were a number of reasons for this. The century and a quarter before 1560 had seen enormous investment by the burgess community in the extension of its burgh church. Its full extent can only be guessed at, but went far beyond the capacity of individual benefactors. From 1442, the council made regular payments to the masters of the 'kirk wark' from various sources, including the town's revenue from fishings on the Dee and Don, and a series of taxes and other dues were levied by it on both merchants and the town as a whole.[24] Hidden from sight for the most part, however, is the formidable cost of kirk silver and increasingly expensive imported liturgical vestments and artefacts; a five-year levy on the burgh's main exports to the Low Countries was imposed in 1514 to pay for Mass books and altar gear.[25] There were more than thirty prebends to be attired. Some of the new Masses (such as the four said at the altar of St Michael and the six weekday Masses attributed to the altar of St Anne) could be associated with an existing altar but would also have demanded additional vestments.[26] The church itself – like the elaborate processions on the great feast days of St Nicholas (6 December), Candlemas or the Purification of Our Lady (2 February), the Annunciation of the Blessed Virgin Mary (25 March), Corpus Christi (in June), the Assumption of the Virgin Mary (15 August) – was a reflection in three dimensions of the ordered hierarchy of the town.

The growth and expansion of the burgh church increased the patronage of the town council. And the clergy themselves, like the brethren of the four friaries in the town, were almost invariably local in origin: council statutes proclaimed the desirability of appointing 'burges sonnys and native menne borne of the toune before ale utheris'.[27] It was unthinkable, in such a close-knit society, to dismiss local men wholesale, depriving them of both occupation and pension, as the radicals within the new Protestant General Assembly, such as John Knox, demanded. Even more unpalatable was the thought of excommunicating brother, cousin or neighbour for following the old faith since excommunication meant that the sinner would have been unable to collect debts or rents. Had this happened, the burgh economy would quickly have ground to a halt. Money, privilege, power and kin all underpinned the burgh church, both as a building and as a temple of the soul.

In such a society, where change was instinctively feared, religious reform would have to take the form of a 'magistrates' reformation'; it should be cautious, controlled and top-down, designed to foster the values and also enhance the power of the élite. And, by and large, this is what happened. The new kirk session, the disciplinary arm of the new faith, was set up in 1562, just before the visit to the town of the distinctly Protestant privy council which accompanied Mary, Queen of Scots (1542-67), on her visit to the north-east to suppress the fourth earl of Huntly. The first pages of its records laboriously recited the Ten Commandments and proclaimed penalties against their infraction. But who were the newly appointed session elders who were the new civic guardians of the Ten Commandments? They were, in effect, the town council in a novel guise and probably a majority of the new Protestant elders were closet Catholics. The session clerk, an ex-priest, began its record with a recitation of the sign of the cross and occasionally scribbled 'pro

Jesu et Maria' in the margin of the volume. The new minister, so the session's ordinances carefully enacted, was not allowed to preach on any sensitive subject or to issue a public rebuke to any 'notable or particular person' without the prior consent of the session; the élite had drawn up an insurance policy for its own preservation. The record also carefully drew up a list of penalties and fines for those who presumed to challenge or criticise 'prowest, baillie or magistrate, the precheour or elder'. The Seven Deadly Sins of the Middle Ages had given way, it is true, to a new preoccupation – with the Ten Commandments. Yet the avowed aim of Aberdeen's new session, 'that gud lyfe, conversatioun, and maneris may scheyne, and the rottin, poysinit and filthy flouer of vyce … may be wed out and pluckit up be the rutis', was echoed by magistrates in towns throughout both Protestant and Catholic Europe in the age of the Counter-Reformation.[28] The vernacular catechism sanctioned by the provincial council of the pre-Reformation church in 1552, issued in the name of Archbishop John Hamilton, had included 'a true and faithful interpretation' of the Commandments and there was little difference between it and the gloss of Aberdeen's new kirk session elders of 1562.[29] Nor, in the pursuit of a reformation of manners, was there much distance between the old Catholic church and the new Protestant one: for both churches, the second half of the sixteenth century was the age of the catechism.[30]

One of the most frequent concerns of the Aberdeen session in the 1570s, when its record becomes a little fuller, was irregular marriage, which accounted for almost 20 per cent of all offenders. The old custom of handfasting without benefit of clergy was one target. Another was the habit of couples stretching the trial marriage which followed a formal calling of the banns in church beyond the customary twelve months; in some cases, it was claimed, the 'trial' had lasted six or seven years. Most offenders were given a deadline to marry formally. By the mid 1570s, the session had begun to interpret the law more strictly: couples had to find caution that they would remain celibate *until* marriage. But how novel was this new morality? It could be said to reflect both the ordinances of the pre-Reformation church council of 1552 and the edicts of the Counter-Reformation Council of Trent as well as the Protestant *First Book of Discipline* of 1560-61.[31] The attention given to irregular marriage and other sexual offences, amounting in total to some 85 per cent of all cases,[32] is a good illustration of the extra mechanism of social control which the kirk session provided. In these respects, the events of the first generation after 1560 are more easily explained as an urban hierarchy seizing the opportunity to effect its long-term aim of a reformation of manners amongst both privileged burgesses and underprivileged ordinary Aberdonians than as the desire of born-again godly magistrates to effect a Calvinist reformation.

The success and failure of any reformation is not easily pinned down. Conformity to the new faith, where it was required – amongst office-holders and ex- Catholic clergy who wanted either to hold on to their pensions or to their new jobs as readers in the new Protestant church – was probably effected readily enough, although it was not until 1573 that it became a legal requirement, enforced by act of parliament.[33] Genuine conversion was much more difficult to effect and may have taken generations for some parts of Aberdeen society. The concerns of the Aberdeen establishment to consolidate its own position, economic as well as social, were as much a barrier to rapid progress of the new faith as was the burgh's religious conservatism. The true faith was to be inculcated amongst the populace, but not without regard for the social order or profit. The kirk session, amongst its first ordinances made in 1562, ordered servants to attend preaching only every second Sunday, and then only if their master granted them permission to do so.[34] God had to wait until the chores were done.

The harrying of Catholics was not conspicuous amongst the session's activities, despite appearances to the contrary in its occasional mission statements or flurries of activity just before or after the town welcomed official, godly visitations from Edinburgh, as happened in 1562 and 1574. Recusants made up less than 10 per cent of transgressors who appeared before the session in the 1570s.[35] In November 1562, the session was hurriedly set up just before the visit of Queen Mary, accompanied by her largely Protestant privy council. An earlier rumour of their imminent arrival, ten months before, was probably what triggered the town to sell off part of its church plate and other ecclesiastical valuables by public auction – a full fifteen months after Edinburgh had done the same.[36] This episode has consistently been misinterpreted.[37] Eight chalices from side altars within St Nicholas and two from elsewhere (including the well-known chalice and statue of Our Lady of Pity from the chapel at the Bridge of Dee which ended up in Brussels)[38] were sold off for a sum little more than £18. This was tokenism on a very limited scale: there were over thirty side altars and more than fifty chantries in St Nicholas. Some clerical vestments were also disposed of at the same time but from their description it seems unlikely that they amounted to those of more than a handful of priests.[39] And in 1574, the minor flurry of activity targeting superstitious practices amongst craftsmen and pupils of the song school and the imposition of a Calvinist-style fast was not enough to persuade Regent Morton of the progress of the Reformation in the town. He seems to have been particularly offended by two things: the remaining trappings of Catholic worship within the burgh church and the survival of images in private hands. The undertakings given by the council at the time of his visit to remove the organ and choir stalls from the church had to be followed up by assurances a few months later that it had also confiscated and burned a haul of statues and crucifixes. It was also only at this point that a stool of repentance was built for the public humiliation of offenders.[40]

Some pre-Reformation fittings and decoration seem to have survived the purge of 1574. In 1584, the back of an altar was taken down and a series of payments were made between 1588 and 1592 for the whitewashing of various pillars and aisles within the church, including that formerly belonging to the cordiners. The images which were removed then were not recorded but they were replaced by the lettering of wholesome parts of Scripture and the 'Belief', the Protestant version of the old 'Confiteor'.[41] In the parish church of St Andrews, the replacement of Catholic imagery, whether on walls or windows (what has sometimes been called by historians the 'books of the humble'), had taken place literally overnight in 1559. In Aberdeen, the same process took a generation. The new devotion, like the new print culture, also demanded the ability to read, which was almost certainly still confined to a minority of the population - probably about a third of adult males, but rather less of women.[42] In some churches, scenes from the Old Testament seem to have been used to decorate and instruct from about the 1590s onwards. The first record of any wall decoration in St Nicholas is not to be found before the 1660s when four tapestries, including the Finding of Moses and the Tale of Esther, adorned the walls of what by then was St Nicholas West.[43]

It is unlikely that Aberdeen's kirk session operated in anything more than fits and starts for over thirty years after its setting-up in 1562. There is little in its record to reflect its activities, or even its formal existence, from then until a burst of activity in 1568, after the deposing of Queen Mary. But that was followed by another lull until the autumn of 1573 and the end of the civil war between supporters of the Queen and the King's party, backing the infant James VI (1567-1625). A regular programme of reform was not instituted until the mid 1570s but it overwhelmingly focused on sexual misdemeanours. It is likely that a campaign enforcing ecclesiastical discipline in a broad sense - targeting slackers rather than fornicators - was not embarked upon before the 1590s.[44]

Godly magistrates and dissidents

It is a commonplace to think of the Reformation as a decisive event, which enacted change both swiftly and radically. Yet, in a town such as Aberdeen, it was trying to plant roots in a society which was by instinct conservative and resistant to change. As a result, the Reformation tended to succeed most where it changed least. There were some clear elements of continuity. The *First Book of Discipline* prescribed daily prayers in the 'great towns'. In Aberdeen, at the insistence of the council, there were both morning and evening prayers (the latter accompanied by the singing of the Psalms); it was an arrangement that mirrored the old matins and evensong.[45] The 'Chronicle of Aberdeen' was a kind of diary compiled by Walter Cullen, the product of an old, established burgh family, who became a reader in the new church. This Calvinist clergyman railed, in one page of his chronicle, against the Massacre of St Bartholomew in France (1572) as the work of papistry and the decrees of the Council of Trent, while on adjoining pages he recorded the deaths of various local Catholic chaplains and clerical officials. This was hardly surprising. His uncle was the pre-Reformation vicar of Aberdeen and in 1577 Cullen accepted collation to the vicarage from the old Catholic bishop, William Gordon, in a traditional ceremony.[46] Cullen, however, did have to work beside a series of outsiders appointed as minister of the burgh.

Here, the Reformation did bring about a change, with the arrival of the salaried professional in place of the chaplain who almost invariably had been drawn from the local community. Cullen's relationship with at least one of the newcomers seems to have been strained: the 'Chronicle' records that John Craig, appointed minister in 1574, left his 'floik unprowyditt' when he was appointed chaplain to the king in 1579.[47] By the 1590s, New Aberdeen had three ministers as well as its reader. This, again, suggests, a pro-active policy by the council. Both Perth and Dundee, by contrast, still had only two ministers at this period. The reason is obvious. The population was increasing, probably fairly sharply. The quarterly celebration of Communion had by now to be extended over two Sundays. In a real sense, the *corpus christianum* – the old idea of a single burgh community at prayer [48] – was already a relic of the past before the decision was taken to split the burgh church and its congregation into two parishes in 1596. Old habits, however, are slow to die, and especially so in Aberdeen; worshippers seem to have resented being directed to one or other of the new churches (see Chapter 2).[49]

Aberdeen's reformation was top-down in two senses. Its pace was directed by the town council and kirk session acting in concert; and it aimed to bring the élite and the burgess classes into conformity before seriously tackling the more intractable problem of the 'unfree' – labourers, servants and the poor who made up about seventy per cent of the population. The different sectors of urban society were treated very differently. All who were able to read were ordered to acquire their own bible and psalm book and bring them to church. The remainder – potentially the majority of the population – presumably followed the service as best they could. All women 'of honest reputation' were allowed to have stools to sit on during prayers and preaching.[50] The rest had to stand and some of the poorest ranks of society may well have been excluded, as in other towns.[51]

It is generally well nigh impossible for historians to reach the beliefs of the common folk or 'unfree', below the level of the privileged burgess class which made up about 30 per cent of the inhabitants (see Chapter 8). One exception comes in an unusual form, with the records of a major witch-hunt in and around Aberdeen in 1597. The causes of this witch panic are obscure and in dispute.[52] What is certain is that the burgh authorities and a sheriff depute (acting on behalf of the sixth earl of Huntly) applied for and received from the crown two commissions of justiciary.

The hunt began within the town itself but quickly extended outwards to encompass a series of rural parishes in Aberdeenshire, ranging from nearby Dyce and Fintray to Deer and Methlick, further away to the north. The trials were held in the tolbooth, before varied assizes including local farmers and landholders as well as Aberdeen burgesses, and they resulted in the execution by burning on the Castle Hill of twenty-seven alleged witches and the acquittal of a further eight. It is tempting, when offered an insight into the mind of the lower levels of society, to seize it and to accept the proposition that the sixteenth- or seventeenth-century peasant knew more about the Devil than God. How else are we to treat the testimony of a Hallowe'en dance or 'sabbat' at the fish cross in the Castlegate, with the witches 'transfformit in uthier lyknesse, sum in haris, sum in cattis, and sum in uther similitudes'?[53] It is, however, much more likely that these records of what was the largest urban witch panic in Scotland reveal the thought processes of the accusers – principally the magistrates of Aberdeen – rather than those of the accused victims. The sabbat became more crowded and exotic as one confession, almost certainly extracted by means of systematically depriving the accused of sleep, followed another. The full motives for the involvement of the earl of Huntly, sheriff of the shire and a Catholic magnate who had recently apostasised very publicly in a ritual cleansing of his soul conducted by the presbytery in the burgh church and streets of Aberdeen, are difficult to unravel.[54] It easier to understand why Aberdeen's own magistrates took such a prominent part in this witch-hunt.

It is hardly surprising that a reformation of religion took decades or even generations to take effect. In 1604, the session ordered that the 'common ignorant people and servants' attend a primitive Sunday school at which two boys from the 'Inglische' or vernacular school read out extracts from the catechism and the hapless, captive audience repeated them, parrot fashion. By the 1630s, presumably because this device had not worked sufficiently well, catechists and victims sang their responses, in a process known as 'lining'.[55] Plain chant, abolished at the Reformation, had returned in a novel guise, as a blunt instrument of catechising the underclasses. If effecting conversion to the new faith was difficult enough, a reformation of manners was usually still more problematic. Again, it was only in 1604, following a murderous brawl amongst apprentices, that the session insisted that craft masters bring their servants and apprentices to church on Sundays. Whether this mechanism, designed to curb 'ovr mekill libertie' which encouraged 'folie and huirdome', worked is doubtful.[56] At best, such youths would have had a minimal education; they would probably have attended the vernacular or 'Inglis' school, intended to give basic reading skills, but like other children of the non-burgess classes would have left school at the age of seven or eight. It was only the children of burgesses who would have continued their education for another five years or so at the grammar school (see Chapter 14). In St Nicholas, the pupils of the grammar school (generally the children of the upper ranks of burgh society) were given seats close to the pulpit to make sure they benefited from the Word of God.[57] Others had to make do as they could and there can be no certainty that attendance at church was anything more than occasional or perfunctory amongst the 'unfree'. By contrast, the impression given by an English visitor, Richard Franck, who visited the burgh in 1656, was one of hierarchy and orderliness: 'The magistrates sit under the soveraignty of the mace, and every merchant in his peculiar pew; where every society of mechanicks have their particular seats, distinguished by escutcheons, suitable to their profession.'[58] Franck, of course, recorded only what he saw - the seemly ranks of the 'free' burgess classes - for he would not have seen many of the 'unfree' or poor in the burgh church. And ironically, by the 1650s, decorative art was used, not for the glory of God, but for the badges of rank which adorned the pews of the élite and reinforced social distinctions amongst them.[59]

Religious conservatives: schoolmen, recusants and crypto-Catholics

Theologically, both Aberdeen and its hinterland remained conservative. Although the strength of Episcopalian adherence in the area is well-known, it is sometimes alleged that the Episcopalians of that day were hardly more than Presbyterians with bishops, and that it is fundamentally anachronistic to associate Scottish Episcopalianism with Tractarianism or any such movement. This is, in fact, far from clear as a general rule. There were many Episcopalians in the seventeenth and eighteenth centuries who held proto-Tractarian views, as the different responses in different areas to the 'Usages' controversy (concerning the reintroduction of Catholic practices into the liturgy) showed in the 1720s.[60] In the seventeenth century, figures such as William Forbes (1585-1634), minister at Monymusk and St Nicholas from 1616, principal of Marischal College and subsequently bishop of Edinburgh, held that 'many of the differences between the Church of Rome and the Protestants were merely superficial' and that 'Purgatory, Praying for the Dead, the Intercession and Invocation of Angels and Saints' were all practices which could be derived from Scripture.[61] King's College, still umbilically linked to the bishopric that began it, was a core zone for this conservative practice. The image of Our Lady on the cross by the Town House was not removed until the 1790s, while the 'portrait of our Blessed Virgin Mary and her dear Son Baby Jesus in her arms' at the Bishop's Palace did not disappear till 1640.[62] John Forbes of Corse (1593-1648), Henry Scougall (1650-78) and James Garden (1647-1726), who all held the chair of divinity at King's, were at the forefront of Aberdeen's conservative theology. Opposition, however, came at a cost: two of this trio of divinity professors were deprived of their posts by the General Assembly, while the other died young.

The reports of contemporaries show that these views were by no means eccentric representations of the temper of the town. On 31 July 1684, an agent of the Episcopalian administration in Edinburgh described Aberdeen as 'the onlie toune in Scotland most conforme to the government both in principle and practice'.[63] In the 1690s, Episcopalians 'did what they could apparently to obstruct the inquiries of Presbyteries as to the movements and actions of the "trafficking priests" of Rome'. Later, the Quietist mysticism of the Episcopalian gentry developed much common ground with pre-Reformation Christianity, setting up 'a correspondence with certain Roman Catholic mystics, especially the celebrated Madame Guyon'.[64] The fourth Lord Forbes of Pitsligo (1678-1762), a friend of Archbishop Fénelon, set up an ecumenical religious retreat at Rosehearty for the Episcopalian Jacobite Dr George Garden (1649-1733), after the latter had been expelled from his Aberdeen living in 1701, 'where persons of different religious persuasions lived together in the love of God and the practice of self-abnegation'. Among early enthusiasts for this community was Chevalier Andrew Ramsay, the religious universalist who was subsequently to become tutor to Prince Charles Edward Stuart. Christian universalism, strong among both Freemasons and Jacobites in the early eighteenth century, had thus a degree of support in the north-east. Forbes of Pitsligo himself, out in the '15, was to be General of Horse to Charles Edward in the rising of 1745, as well as a notable moral and political philosopher, whose essays on government foreshadowed Hutchesonian utilitarianism.[65]

Episcopalian conservatism was succoured by the examples of prominent recusant nobles, such as the earls of Huntly and Erroll, as well as the long-standing influence of a powerful group of Catholic burgesses, centring on the family of Menzies of Pitfodels.[66] Catholic missionaries were active in the rural areas in the 1630s, while popery remained the main problem facing local presbyteries in the 1640s.[67] Praying for the dead in the consecrated ground of the churchyard of the old Snow Kirk, which had been abandoned as the parish church of Old Aberdeen in 1583, was a persistent practice. Indeed, Roman Catholics used it as a burial ground until the nineteenth century. Problematic, too, were the repeated contacts with Catholics by staff of King's and other inhabitants of the burgh.[68] In the royal burgh, the celebrated crypto-Catholicism of the 1620s chapel ceiling in Provost Skene's house, which may refer to the 'Mysteries of the Rosary' (Plate 22), is evidence of similar crypto-Catholicism among the well-to-do.[69]

Significant and restrictive control, however, was exercised over traditional and superstitious practices by Episcopalian and Presbyterian authorities alike. Yet, even in serious cases, the canniness traditional to the region was maintained. At Inverurie in 1657 'John Mill and Isabel Mackie confessed the sin of charming', but 'she had to wait till he was through [with his repentance], in order to get the sackcloth, of which there had been but one in stock'.[70] Town regulations increasingly took on a puritanical tone: in 1626 Aberdeen banned 'superfluous and costlie banqueting' at christenings, set a maximum of six men and six women at parties, and forbade 'suggoures, droiges, or confectiounes brocht from forane cuntras'. In 1642, 'swearing of any oath' became liable to an 8d fine for the use of the poor, and 'ane box' was 'to be in everie familie for this effect'.[71]

Aberdeen's distinctiveness from the rest of Scotland was nonetheless borne witness to during the long troubles of the Covenanting years and their aftermath. The Aberdeen Doctors, a group of six ministers who had graduated in divinity from King's in the 1620s, played a major role in Aberdeen's resistance to the National Covenant of 1638. The controversy, waged with their Covenanting adversaries in an increasingly elaborate exchange of printed pamphlets, took the form of an academic, theological discourse on obedience to lawful authority. It is usually claimed, with some justice, that the disputation discomfited Covenanting advocates of resistance.[72] Yet the Aberdeen Doctors probably had a wider impact than this learned minor *cause célèbre*, which was virtually over by the end of 1638. University teachers also had a perceptible effect on their pupils: between 60 and 75 per cent of the ministers who graduated from the Presbyterian hothouses of Edinburgh, Glasgow and St Andrews between 1616 and 1638 were to be found in the ranks of the Covenanters. Over half of the graduates from King's and Marischal, by contrast, opposed the Covenant.[73] The confused period of the Cromwellian occupation in the 1650s, however, saw the emergence of a new phenomenon, which was viewed with great suspicion by both the burgh and church authorities – Quakerism. The two threats to uniformity and order, Quakers and Catholics, dominated much of the second half of the seventeenth century (see Chapter 11).

After the Restoration, conversions to Catholicism became more frequent, a situation which appears (perhaps unusually) to have continued after 1688. The regime of Charles II (1651/60–85) gave some support to folk practices on both sides of the Border: 6,325 maypoles were allegedly erected in England in the years after the Restoration.[74] In Scotland, St Andrew's Day was apparently celebrated for the first time since the Reformation, and in 1665 the 'Game of the Royal Oak', a celebration of the providential escape of Charles II from capture in 1651, was being supported and played in Aberdeen.[75] In such circumstances of official backing for folk revival, it was little wonder that Catholicism, still deeply rooted in the burgh's hinterland, gathered strength. In both 1669 and 1675, the burgh, perhaps under pressure from central government,[76] moved to ban Catholics from becoming burgesses; here, the very repetition of such regulations underlined the persistence of the problem.[77]

In the 1690s, Catholic estimates suggested that 70 per cent (almost certainly an overestimate) of Scotland's Catholics lived in Banffshire; it was in this area that the Scalan seminary in Glenlivet opened in 1717.[78] In 1714, it was reported that Catholic priests in Strathbogie 'are very insolent', living 'as openly and avowedly as any minister ... and the papists in that countrey do repair to their Idolatrous Mass as publickly as Protestants do to the Church'. In Dunbrennan and Fochabers, Catholics were accused of setting up schools run by 'popish women' and sending a quota of thirty Gaelic-speaking ordinands to Rome, while in Crathie and Kindrochit 'within these few years there are two hundred ... apostatised to popery'.[79] By 1736, it was estimated in the parishes of Crathie and Kindrochit/Braemar that one-third of the population were Catholics.[80] Similar concerns had been expressed at Kincardine o' Neil in 1706, where 200 Catholics were alleged to have been received in a single day.[81] Local Catholics continued to be prominent on the Continent and elsewhere, George Conn (1598–1640) becoming papal nuncio to the court of St James in 1636, and dying just before he could receive his cardinal's hat.[82] As was the case elsewhere, Catholicism grew in strength after the Union of 1707. As an Aberdeen schoolmaster wrote in December 1706: 'Here lies, entombed in her own ashes, yet with the hope of a blessed resurrection, the famous nation of the Scots ... she, full of years, though yet in undiminished vigour of limbs, losing control of her mind, yielded helpless to fate. Pray for her!'[83] Such an invitation to pray for the dead was in itself, of course, the stuff of north-east religious conservatism.

New 'Friends' and a new threat

In Aberdeen, the first Quakers, or 'Friends' as they preferred to be called, were English missionaries visiting the Cromwellian garrison which occupied the town from 1651 onwards. When Principal John Row of King's College found them insulting ministers, teaching human perfectibility, and referring to the college as 'a cage of unclean birds' in 1657, he complained to the local commander, who promptly banned Quakers from the burgh.[84] Problem solved. Beginning in 1663, however, a handful of local people, some of them prominent burgesses, turned Quaker.[85] Because they were local they could not simply be expelled and the authorities were unclear how best to respond to the dissenters in their midst. They opted, on the whole, for hostility, with full government backing. Restoration Scotland witnessed state-sponsored persecution of various religious minorities and dissenters, and in Aberdeen Quakers bore the brunt: conventicling Presbyterians were not much in evidence in the area, and Catholics were usually protected by their powerful allies and deep roots in the community.[86]

Years of periodic crackdowns and sporadic arrests tipped into outright persecution in the late 1670s, when virtually every adult male Quaker in the vicinity was imprisoned in the tolbooth. No Friends died for their faith in Aberdeen, but long incarcerations and crippling fines took a heavy physical, emotional and financial toll. Far from being deterred, however, the Aberdeen Quakers made this their finest hour. Indeed, the experience of persecution in and around Aberdeen helped inspire

Robert Barclay of Urie to write his *Apology for the True Christian Divinity*, which remains the classic statement of Quaker principles.[87] Barclay described Aberdeen as 'the place where our fiercest oppressors are judged to be', which was true in Scotland.[88] In 1679 the Lord Advocate, Sir George Mackenzie of Rosehaugh ('Bluidy Mackenzie' of Covenanter lore), advised the provost of Aberdeen to show leniency to Friends, to 'keep your toune from being spoke of as more than ordinary violent'.[89] By then, it was over twenty years since John Row's intervention and the very idea of solving Aberdeen's Quaker problem so easily was a subject for black humour. When Quaker prisoners inadvertently started a small fire in the tolbooth, a magistrate remarked that it would be best to store barrels of gunpowder in the vault below so that next time 'they might be quit of the Quakers'.[90]

Why did Quakers cause such a stir? In Restoration England there were tens of thousands of Friends, but in Scotland only a few hundred.[91] Aberdeen was Scotland's main Quaker centre, and there were smaller gatherings close by at Urie, near Stonehaven, and at Kinmuck, but there were never more than a few dozen Friends in the area: in 1672, the adult Quaker population of New Aberdeen stood at fourteen women and ten men.[92] Not only were Quakers few in number, but they were pacifists who, apart from lobbying for religious toleration, did not meddle in politics. They were clean-living Protestants who read their bibles, chided their children, disciplined their wayward members, and looked after their own poor. They opened a school.[93] They paid their taxes. Nevertheless, most contemporaries regarded Quakers as scandalous, if not dangerous, people.

The root of the problem lay in the central Quaker belief that God's light was in everyone – a simple idea which Quakers pushed to revolutionary lengths. The democratic implications of the doctrine of the 'light within' inspired Friends to reject Calvinist ideas of predestination and total depravity, to dispense with a professional ministry, and to worship in silence. It also encouraged them to ignore the conventions of social hierarchy: Quakers used the deliberately egalitarian and anachronistic 'ye' and 'thee' when they spoke, refused to doff their hats or curtsy to their betters, and adopted a distinctly sombre style of dress.[94] Non-Quakers regarded all of these things as offences against propriety, good order, good taste, and God. Indeed, early Friends worshipped in silence but were otherwise inclined to make noisy spectacles of themselves. They interrupted sermons and harangued ministers. In 1677, an English visitor reported that 'we saw a mountebank on the stage near the Tolbooth, wherein are several Quakers ... these Quakers never ceased preaching to people, and loudly reprehended the folk and the fool on the stage, whilst he made them a return with a whining and grinning face'.[95] Even when Quakers were trying to be decorous, they attracted trouble. At a celebrated open-air debate between Quakers and divinity students, held before a boisterous crowd of 'some hundreds' in 1675, theology gave way when a gun was fired and turds were thrown and both sides fled the stage claiming victory.[96] Most outrageous of all, perhaps, was the way that Friends' egalitarian impulses extended to Quaker women, who took on public roles as preachers, prophets, missionaries, and writers: the Aberdeen poet Lilias Skene, once the very model of Presbyterian female piety, took on all these roles after she turned Quaker.[97] 'Our giddy people', sniffed Henry Scougal, professor of divinity at King's between 1674-8, 'go over to that sect and party, where all ranks, and both sexes, are allowed the satisfaction to hear themselves talk in publick.'[98]

Quakers were arguably the first Protestants to break permanently from the Church of Scotland: Episcopalians and various factions of Presbyterians had struggled for control of the Kirk, but Quakers wanted no part of it. Unlike Catholics raised in a rival faith, first-generation Quakers were apostates. Breaking from the Kirk challenged venerable and still-potent notions of civic and religious unity. Burgh fathers were accustomed to speaking for 'the haill toun', and, however notional such unity was in practice (having already been stretched to the limits of credibility to accommodate Aberdeen's entrenched Catholic minority), the idea of unity to most was still dear. It was partly a matter of insecurity: early modern people believed that God was always watching and judging and that a community that tolerated sin and error would be made to suffer collectively. Already nervous about the possible consequences of their tip-toeing around Catholics, Aberdonians were not about to tolerate new-fangled Protestant dissenters out to overturn the ideological and institutional foundations of their community.[99]

In 1671, the full extent of the Quaker challenge to civic and religious unity became apparent. Friends that year purchased their first property in Aberdeen, a kale yard on the east side of the Gallowgate where they intended to bury their dead.[100] Behind 'great dycks of stone and morter' they dug their first grave for a child of the shoemaker Thomas Milne.[101] Everyone except suicides and executed criminals was expected to be interred in a churchyard, but Quakers rejected the idea of consecrated ground and knew there was no law requiring churchyard burial.[102] Legal or not, their new burial yard was seen as an affront to decency and good order. Three days after the burial, Provost Robert Forbes and two bailies supervised the exhumation and removal of the corpse to the burial ground of the Futty kirk. The magistrates ordered the walls of the Quaker graveyard pulled down, and Thomas Milne was fined and made to pay the gravediggers' wages and the kirk's standard burial fee. Over the next five years, however, the walls were rebuilt and torn down six times as one adult and five more children (including another of Milne's) were buried and exhumed.[103]

Every community has deeply held customs and traditions surrounding death. In this, as in other areas of religious and social life, Friends were making a radical break - 'schisme and divisione', the authorities called it, an affront to 'the former good old order', an effort not only to rob the kirk of burial dues but 'to separat themselves and to macke ane uther incorporatione'.[104] In fact, the Quakers sought only a limited, religious, separation. By building their new burial ground in the heart of the burgh, they signalled their intention to have it both ways, to remain permanently apart from the mainstream congregation while still claiming the privileges of full membership in the 'incorporation' of the royal burgh – an incorporation traditionally held to be inextricably bound with a single congregation of believers. In setting themselves up as a distinct society within Aberdeen, Quakers were trying to redefine what it meant to be Aberdonian. The authorities understood this, and countered in 1675 by amending the burgess oath to exclude Quakers and Catholics from full burgess rights.[105]

Quakers were not strangers in Aberdeen, and that was part of the problem. Alexander Jaffray of Kingswells, Aberdeen's first Quaker, had been provost, and Alexander Skene of Newtyle had been a bailie and ruling elder of the kirk session, but even less illustrious Friends were bound to the urban community by a whole web of family, neighbourhood, and business ties. Familiarity could breed contempt.[106] John Menzies, professor of divinity at Marischal College, had been a close ally of Jaffray's in their Covenanting days and had even helped him establish a short-lived Independent congregation in the 1650s. But after 1660, Menzies conformed to Episcopacy and became an implacable enemy of Quakers: in 1671 he gave circuit court judges in town to try witches such 'bloody and cruel' advice regarding Quakers that 'even the Bishop drew down his hatt, and the Judges ... sate silent'.[107] Conflicts over Quakerism could divide families as well as old friends. Nearly two-thirds of the early Quaker converts were women – hardly surprising given Friends' enlightened views on gender – and several of them converted independently of, and presumably in defiance of, their husbands.[108] Margaret Smith was married to Bailie Gilbert Molleson, who never converted and continued to serve on town councils throughout the era of persecution.[109] Their children followed their mother's faith. The first Quaker wedding in Aberdeen was held in the Molleson house when Robert Barclay of Urie married their daughter in 1669, and in the 1670s their son was apprenticed to a Quaker merchant in Edinburgh – partly, we might surmise, so that his father would not have to arrest him in Aberdeen.[110]

In 1676 the Scottish government reaffirmed the Conventicle Act of 1670, directed mainly against dissenting Presbyterians in the south-west, which made it illegal to preach without a bishop's permission or to hold or attend unsanctioned services.[111] Quakers refused to comply, prompting the magistrates to raid their meetings and arrest any men present. The prisoners responded with passive resistance, choosing to remain in prison rather than acknowledge any fault by paying their fines. This principled stand was possible because Quaker women kept the community

ABERDEEN BEFORE 1800

together by managing businesses, keeping meetings, delivering meals to the prisoners, and lobbying for their release.[112] Between March 1676 and November 1679, virtually every Quaker man in the north-east, about forty in all, spent weeks or months in the tolbooth. They were packed, as one bailie put it, 'as salmond in a barrel', and lacked adequate light, heat, air and sanitation.[113] A doctor testified that they were 'not only in manifest hazard of their health, but in a manner of indangering a plague'.[114] Despite these conditions, several prisoners, most notably Robert Barclay and George Keith, wrote books and tracts and letters from prison, all to convince influential people throughout Britain and as far afield as Germany that Friends deserved toleration.[115] On the outside, Lilias Skene assumed the mantle of an Old Testament prophet to demand that the Aberdeen authorities let her people go. Wife, mother and mother-in-law of prisoners, her jeremiad included a very personal appeal to the Scottish tradition of 'guid nichtberheid' in which she turned tables on the authorities by invoking the very community values which Friends were accused of undermining:

> So at this season I ame moved in this same Zeal for truth and compassion upon your Soules, Magistrats preachers and people, to bear ane open testimony against the spirit of persecution ... for assuredly the Lord will not hold you guiltless.... And for my part your severityes and crueltys are a confirmation unto me that truth is not on your side ... neither would ye unnecessarily throng in honest men that had families wives and children deeply suffering with them & in them in those cold nasty stinking holes where ye have shutt them up, who have been as neatly handled and tenderly educated & as speciall in their generation as any amongst you.[116]

As the stalemate dragged on, there were signs that the Aberdeen public may have felt some sympathy for the Friends: when the captain of the militia, ordered by the privy council to seize Quaker property in lieu of their fines, tried to auction off Friends' goods, there were few bidders.[117] In the end, it was outside pressure that broke the deadlock. Barclay's friends in high places won his release in 1677 and he travelled to London for a series of audiences with the duke of York, later James VII & II (1685–88/89).[118] Nothing changed at first, but late in 1679 the Duke moved to Edinburgh and in November the Quaker prisoners were set free: 'His Influence upon the Government', reported Barclay, 'opened our prison doors, wheir many of us had lyen severall years in most noisom holes'.[119]

Quakers left prison unbowed and with much of their property intact. But persecution had taken a heavy toll. Having won their great fight for toleration, Friends largely withdrew from the public arena. Under persecution, Friends had all but ceased to attract new members and, once it was over, they preferred to keep their own company: in 1682 Aberdeen Quakers forbade marriage outside the group.[120] Natural increase, however, allowed for slow growth, and by 1700 there were about one hundred Friends in and around Aberdeen.[121] Debts incurred during the crisis made it difficult to carry on as before: Alexander and Lilias Skene sold Newtyle in 1680, probably to pay creditors, and in 1682 their son John emigrated to America after his business failed.[122] Robert Barclay accepted the governorship of East New Jersey that same year (on condition he did not have to go there) and devoted the rest of his short life to encouraging Friends and other north-east Scots to emigrate. When Barclay died in 1690, aged forty-one, emigration slowed.[123] By then, many older first-generation Quakers had also died, and so too had their fiercest opponents. By the early eighteenth century, Quakers had become a settled part of Aberdeen life. In 1710, the sons of Robert Barclay and Alexander Jaffray petitioned the town council to repeal the act of 1675 that denied both Quakers and Catholics burgess rights. The council refused, being reluctant to overturn a by-now venerable tradition. But in a telling response it claimed there was no need for repeal: 'its notourly knowne that all Quakers children whose parents were burgers, are allowed liberty to trade, alse freely as any other burgers, though they be not actually admitted burgers.'[124] Like the Catholic minority before them, Quakers had become – in practice if not in theory – a familiar and acknowledged part of the burgh community. They had, after all, helped to change what it meant to be Aberdonian.

14

Schooling the People

SHONA VANCE

From the twelfth until the end of the eighteenth century, schooling in Aberdeen developed in response to the evolving needs of the society it served. This evolution encompassed changes in funding, control, curricula and particularly in ideas as to *who* should be educated. At the outset of the period formal education was largely a clerical preserve. Clergymen required schooling since performance of the ecclesiastical liturgy depended on a degree of literacy, as well as on vocal and musical ability. Gradually, however, secular society also required educated and articulate men. As faith in memory came to be superseded by trust in written words, powerful laymen began to recruit literate clergymen whose skills enabled them to maintain a written record of official transactions.

In Aberdeen, the foundations of the educational practices that would meet both ecclesiastical and secular needs are evident in the arrangements for schooling made by the church authorities in the mid thirteenth century. In Old Aberdeen, the constitution of St Machar's Cathedral, drawn up for Bishop Peter de Ramsay in 1256, outlined the duties of individual members of the chapter. The cantor was to give choral instruction to the boys in the choir and to oversee their discipline.[1] Effectively, he was master of the cathedral's song school. Meanwhile, it was the chancellor's duty to provide a master who would preside over the 'scholars of Aberdeen' and educate them in grammar and logic. In other words, he was to choose a teacher for the cathedral's grammar school – and what are sometimes described as burgh schools were actually schools of this sort which were originally attached to churches.[2] References in the 1256 statutes to the 'scolarum de Aberdon' in the plural may also imply the existence of a grammar school attached to St Nicholas, the parish church of New Aberdeen. This church dates from at least 1157, although there is no certain record of an associated school until 1418, when John Homyll was appointed 'master of the schools', in succession to Andrew de Syves.[3] Similarly, in 1483 Richard Boyle was appointed master to the song school of St Nicholas, succeeding a previous teacher. It seems likely the school was well-established by the fifteenth century.

Religious trends in late medieval Scotland placed increased emphasis on the sung liturgy (see Chapter 13). Privately endowed altars were founded in St Nicholas from 1278. The multiplication of endowed altars, chantries, chaplainries and obits was accelerated by the increasing incidence of collegiate churches, which created many endowed positions for musically trained clergy. The story of the re-foundation of St Nicholas as a collegiate church is a protracted and complicated one, which began in 1456 and ended only in 1540. Soon after 1480, which was when it was first termed a 'college', St Nicholas, like other burgh collegiate churches, had an attached song school.[4] Not only did these various foundations and endowments create increased demand for vocally trained clerics; they also provided a means of support for those who would train the attendant clerics. As with the chapter of St Machar's in Old Aberdeen, the schools of New Aberdeen in the early period were staffed by the chaplains of the burgh church. For instance, in 1479, when Mr Thomas Strachan was appointed master of the grammar school, he was awarded a stipend of £5 Scots by the burgh council, 'ay and quhil he be promovit til a service within the Kirk of Sanct Nicholess of Abirdene'.[5] Similarly, pupils at both New Aberdeen schools could find means of support during their period of study in the various clerkships funded by the townspeople for the service of the many altars of St Nicholas.[6]

Curricula in the medieval period

Reference to what was actually taught in the schools of Aberdeen prior to the Reformation is scarce. The 1256 statutes stipulated that no vicar should be admitted to the choir unless he was able to read and to sing. It is likely that the cantor was expected to teach the boys of the choir to read and to write, as well as to sing. Certainly, after the Reformation, this duality of function of the Old Town school-master was explicit. Meanwhile, a master appointed to the song school of St Nicholas in 1485 was expected to teach the children to sing and play the organs.[7] More detail is available with regard to grammar schooling. The statutes of 1256 stipulated that this type of school provide tuition in grammar and logic and by 1544 the master of the grammar school was expected to instruct children 'baith in sciens, moners, vrytings and sic uder vertewis concerning thaim'.[8] This suggests a social, as well as an academic, role for the school in the community. The only extant sixteenth-century curriculum shows that teaching in the burgh had also developed in response to the humanistic influences which had begun to affect Scotland earlier in that century.[9] The *Statuta et Leges Ludi Literarii Grammaticorum Aberdonensium*, printed in Paris in 1553, offer an insight into what was then understood by 'sciens, moners, vrytings and … sic uder vertewis'.[10] The boys were introduced to elementary arithmetic, and were expected to converse only in Latin, Greek, Hebrew, French or Gaelic, but never the vernacular. There is no evidence that either French or Hebrew was taught in Aberdeen at this time, but Greek may have been. During a visit to Aberdeen in 1540, James V (1513–42) was said to have been entertained by scholars giving orations in Latin and Greek.[11] Whether taught or not, it was clearly felt desirable, well in advance of the triumph of Protestantism, that school pupils in Aberdeen should have a knowledge of the biblical languages.

The school day ran from seven o'clock in the morning until six o'clock in the evening, starting with a prayer and ending with divine service, with two breaks when the boys might go home or into town for breakfast and lunch. What might nowadays seem an unreasonably long school day was well in accord with the practices of the time and would not change significantly with the Reformation.[12] Every morning the boys were tested on grammar, and those who did not perform adequately were punished. After the reading of a lesson by the master and individual class teaching by the under-masters – or doctors as they were known – the younger boys could go into town. Those of the master's class had lessons on Terence, Virgil and Cicero until noon, when they too were released for lunch. The master inspected the work of all three classes between three o'clock and five o'clock and disputations in Latin were heard between five o'clock and six o'clock, when all would proceed to evening service.

Other features of schooling in Aberdeen also underwent significant changes prior to the Reformation. By the early fifteenth century, while masters were still churchmen, the secular authorities of the burgh were taking an active interest in their appointment and function. In 1418, while the chancellor of the diocese of Aberdeen admitted the master of the grammar school to office, the master was presented to the chancellor by the town council for formal approval.[13] Appointments to the mastership of the music school made it clear that the school's primary function was to meet the requirements of the burgess community. At the end of the fifteenth century, the master was enjoined to teach the children, particularly those of burgesses, to sing and to play the organs.[14] From the 1520s, as was happening elsewhere in Scotland, disputes between the ecclesiastical and secular authorities as to the patronage of the grammar school began to emerge.[15] In 1529, Mr John Byssat was accorded a pension of ten merks by the town, 'for the weill of *thair* grammar skuill and *thair* barnis'.[16] The civic authorities of Aberdeen were taking an increasingly proprietorial attitude towards schooling – and secular interference in schooling preceded, and did not result from, the Reformation.

The desire of the civic authorities to control schooling may have been part of a wider-ranging determination to regulate urban life, but it was also rooted in an increasing awareness amongst both churchmen and humanists of the desirability of educating the laity in a Christian society.[17] Similarly, Bishop Elphinstone's foundation of King's College in 1495 had been motivated by a desire to educate both clerics and laymen in accordance with developments in other European states.[18] For such an enterprise, the classical education in Latin offered by a grammar school was a pre-requisite. In addition, communities dependent on trade demanded a certain level of literacy and numeracy in their members, since these skills were required to understand contracts and to maintain account books. It was in the interest of burgesses to ensure a suitable education for their sons.

Little has been said so far of basic literacy, numeracy or of the education of the poor and women. Only after the Reformation do these issues emerge from the records. That is not to argue against the existence of less formal means of education for these groups. It is possible that a basic instruction in letters could be obtained from the friars of one of the regular orders that had settled in Aberdeen from the thirteenth century.[19] For boys, a basic schooling lasted only until about the age of seven or eight. For those who went to the grammar school, it continued until the age of twelve. Schooling for girls may have been available, as it was, for instance, in Edinburgh in 1499.[20] If this was the case in Aberdeen too, it seems not to have infringed the privileges of the masters of the established song and grammar schools, which of course catered solely for boys. There is, at least, no evidence of rivalry between official and unofficial schools before the Reformation, whereas after the Reformation, when official teachers in both Aberdeen burghs felt their livelihoods to be threatened, they drew attention to the activities of unregulated, independent teachers. The one reference to the existence of independent schooling opportunities prior to 1560 dates from 1521, when John Marshal asserted his right to pursue other grammar teachers in the burgh before the burgh courts.[21] These unidentified teachers may have been offering instruction in reading and writing in the vernacular, as well as in Latin, and to girls as well as to boys.

The age of Reformation

By the mid sixteenth century, reformers - humanist, Catholic and Protestant - had already embraced both the idea of the need for an educated Christian commonwealth and the specifics of the contents of much of the curricula needed to effect this ideal. Education was a cornerstone of the Catholic Council of Trent which first met in 1545 as well as of the *Book of Discipline*, the blueprint for the new society drawn up by Protestant ministers in 1560. Even so, religious reform had profound consequences for schooling in both Aberdeen burghs. The *Book* of 1560 outlined an education plan that would prepare everyone according to their ability to serve the commonwealth according to its needs. The reformers wished to establish a school in every parish. They also envisaged the presence of a grammar school in towns, while in the countryside they hoped for at least an arrangement by which a minister or reader could instruct children in the rudiments of reading, writing and knowledge of the catechism.[22] The aims of the programme were made quite explicit: to keep the young on the straight and narrow; to help their elders through public examination and the repetition of the catechism; to provide the universities with able students; and to profit the commonwealth.[23]

Although the plans of those who wrote the *Book of Discipline* foundered on inadequate finance, alternative means of achieving their aims evolved over time. The example of Aberdeen shows that at least in towns existing structures were amended efficiently, but not necessarily dramatically, and resources re-deployed. The chaplainries that had previously supported masters, and sometimes also scholars, at the burgh's schools were ostensibly abolished following the iconoclasm of 1559-60. But the chaplains of St Nicholas resigned their property into the town's common good, and it was out of this fund that schoolmasters were paid.[24] Efforts were made by central government to accelerate this type of transaction: in February 1562 the privy council assigned the buildings and revenues of friaries to town councils, specifying those of Aberdeen, Elgin, Inverness and Glasgow, for the maintenance of 'hospitalis, scolis and utheris godlie usis'.[25] In reality, however, there were delays and difficulties in using windfall profits from the sale of friary lands. In some towns, the actual grants were not made until 1567. And in the case of Aberdeen, some of the revenues seem to have been alienated into other hands, not all of them Aberdonian.[26]

The immediate effects of the Reformation on schooling in Aberdeen were more dramatic in New Aberdeen than in Old, where the university remained under Catholic control until 1569 (see Chapter 15).[27] They were also more dramatic for the song school than for the grammar school. Sacked in the iconoclasm of 1559-60 and its master having fled to France, the song school remained moribund for almost a decade.[28] Association with the discredited medieval Church (and its ideas regarding salvation, singing of the Catholic liturgy and performance of Masses for the souls of the dead) meant that there was little obvious role for a song school in a reformed burgh. It was only in 1570, when Andrew Kempt petitioned the town council for appointment as master, that regular teaching recommenced.[29]

In the early days of the revived school, a wary eye was kept on the religious soundness of the master. In 1574, the kirk session reminded Kempt that he was not 'to give any play to his scholars on the days dedicated to superstition and papistrie'.[30] Nevertheless, it soon became apparent that the song school could be utilised to sustain and support new, Protestant, beliefs. The master of the school was precentor in St Nicholas Church, and with the church's division into two charges – the Old Kirk and the New or West Kirk – in 1596, the town decreed that the schoolmaster and a school doctor, or a sufficiently competent pupil, should take up the psalms in both churches.[31] In addition, the pupils of the song school, for whom a double seat in the church had been ordered in 1592, were expected to attend morning and evening prayers and to sing psalms with the congregation.[32] The aims of the *Book of Discipline* could thus be met by utilising the resources of the old church in efforts to secure the new.

The grammar school also had a role in moulding the inhabitants of the godly commonwealth. This function was highlighted by a petition from the grammar schoolmaster to the council in 1603. It included complaints that:

> in tymes bypast the scholeris of the said schooll, quho suld hawe bene edifeit in godlines be the hering of the word, hes bene, aganis conscience, neglectit in that poynt, be reasoun thay sitt in sic a place quhair thay can not heir the voce of the minister; desyring thairfor, seing thay are the seminarie of the kirk and commoun weill, to prouid sic a place for thame as thay may heir and may be instructed.[33]

The minister of Old Aberdeen was even more explicit on the role of children as the 'seminarie of the kirk' and disseminators of doctrine in the community. In 1650, he 'required all parents of chyldren both within the towne and paroch to put ther chyldren to scooles that they might bee instructed to read that the familie worshipe might be promowed both in towne and paroch and that everie familie might have one at least within it that might read.'[34] A few months later, the Old Aberdeen kirk session decreed that the scholars were to say the catechism each Sunday before the church service, and that the parishioners were to come early to church 'for the hearing and learning of the samen that they may be the perfyter quhen they are examined'.[35] The function of children as catechisers for the wider community envisaged by the first *Book of Discipline* was still being promoted in 1700, when two scholars were instructed to repeat on the Sabbath a portion of the catechism before the congregations of St Nicholas and Greyfriars Kirks.[36]

If the schools of Aberdeen had a positive function to perform within reformed society, they also demonstrated the kind of difficulties which civic and ecclesiastical authorities faced in imposing a reformed discipline on the community (see Chapter 13). The greatest problem concerned holidays and the town council's attempts to put an end to the manifestation of 'popery', which it saw in the traditional celebration of Christmas. From the 1560s to the 1640s, the council intermittently sought to put a stop to a holiday at Christmas. The scholars reacted adversely, and even violently, to the potential loss of this privilege. In 1569, the grammar school pupils contented themselves with a written complaint.[37] By 1580, they were accused of committing 'enormities' around Christmas time, having 'taken the school, meaning to have the old privilege at Yule'.[38] Various concessions were granted until 1612, when the scholars of the grammar, song and writing schools of Aberdeen were accused of forcibly occupying the song school, bearing and using arms, rioting, and generally terrorising the burgh community.[39]

Ultimately, the recalcitrants were arrested, warded in the tolbooth, and twenty-seven of them expelled.[40] These were hardly the ideal members of a godly commonwealth.

Post-Reformation curricular development

Teaching and learning in the town nevertheless continued and developed in accordance with the perceived needs of society. Religious practices apart, the curriculum of the grammar school does not appear to have changed very markedly between 1553 (and the stipulations of the *Leges Ludi Literarii*) and 1700, when a set of laws for the grammar school of New Aberdeen was laid down by the council. Even then, the new regulations bore a close relationship to a Glasgow curriculum dating from 1573.[41] After spending the first term becoming accustomed to reading Latin, scholars proceeded to more advanced levels of grammar and vocabulary. As these studies progressed, pupils encountered the poetry of Ovid, Virgil and Terence, the prose of Erasmus, Cicero and Caesar, and the political and historical works of George Buchanan. They were then to practise composition according to the 'dictats of Rhetorick and rules of Elegancie'. Public disputation, regular questioning on the *Shorter Catechism* and the repetition of rules and authors reinforced what was learned in the classroom. Provision was also made for those in the grammar school who were learning to write, but nothing was said of basic reading ability or numeracy. Clearly, these were not envisaged as the prime responsibility of the grammar school. Where, then, were these skills attained?

In New Aberdeen, it seems unlikely that reading and writing were taught in the music school. When Andrew Kempt was appointed as its master in 1570, he was charged with teaching the children in 'musick, manners and vertew'.[42] When Andrew Melville became master in 1636, his duties were specified as 'instructing the youth in the airt of musick, singing, and playing'.[43] Although there was no mention of Melville being expected to teach manners and virtue, the contents of his commonplace book suggest that this may nonetheless have been understood as part of his duties. Among items noted are an 'ABC', which comprised an alphabetical set of moral exhortations, and 'Ane godlie instructione for old and young'.[44] It seems reasonable to suppose that in Melville's time a moral and 'social' education still formed part of the curriculum. Meanwhile, in Old Aberdeen the master of the song school, as well as being reader and precentor in St Machar's, also taught children to read and write. In 1641, the tuition fees which Alexander Wilguis asked of the scholars of the Old Aberdeen music school were set according to whether children were learning only to read, to read and to write, to read, write and sing, or to read, write, sing and play a musical instrument.[45] Five years later, his successor had the additional responsibility of teaching arithmetic.[46] The reason for the notable differences in the curricula of the two song schools is that one served a major town and the other provided for what was, in effect, a rural parish. The curricula of rural song schools were akin to those of 'little' or 'English' schools in towns.[47] By contrast, the song school of New Aberdeen could concentrate on music because other schools in the town concerned themselves with numeracy and literacy. In New Aberdeen, as a result, complaints about independent teachers were confined to those who taught music.[48] In Old Aberdeen, complaints were numerous about independent teachers of reading and writing.[49]

The earliest record of an independent English school in New Aberdeen dates from 1583, when John Phinevin, 'teacher of the younge childrene', was granted a contribution from the council for the rent of a house in which he held his school.[50] This was probably the forerunner of the town's official English school.[51] Certainly, the authorities eventually recognised and provided for two English schools, al-though, in doing so, they reiterated that the council was obliged to fund and provide only the town's grammar and song schools. The location of these English schools - at 'the north-west end of the kirk yard' - was identical to that where Phinevin taught, and close to both the song and grammar schools.[52] By 1612, one of the English schools had become known as the writing school.[53] Both were taught by the readers in the Old and New Kirks, although it was only in their capacity of reader that the town paid them. Any additional income these poorly paid quasi-clergy made came from the tuition fees demanded from pupils - so their ability to charge such fees was jealously protected from any 'adventurers' who might organise private tuition in English.

From the 1580s, independent 'adventure schools' were tolerated, but only so long as they did not infringe upon the activities of the masters of the official English school. For instance, when, in 1607, Edward Diggens sought permission to set up as a teacher of English and arithmetic, he was granted permission on condition that he confined himself to instruction in these subjects. He was also only to teach children over the age of ten, by which time pupils would have left the official English school.[54] The subject restrictions were probably to protect the grammar school's monopoly of teaching Latin, and the age restrictions to protect the mon-opoly of the English schoolmaster.

Towards a more utilitarian curriculum

The Covenanting troubles of the 1640s did much to disrupt everyday life in the burgh, and the English school suffered notably. In 1644, the dean of gild was ordained to give 'to Alexander Gray reidar twenty merkis money quhilk sall be allowit ... because the said Alexander hes few scolars in his schoole these trouble-some tymes'.[55] It was only in the 1660s, after the uncertainties of the Covenanting era and the period of the Cromwellian occupation were past, that the authorities began to regulate the various schools teaching English in the town more systematically. Instead of *ad hoc* arrangements for licensing teachers and schools, something like a policy began to emerge. An awareness of a need for a more sophisticated and utilitarian form of schooling can be detected in the permission granted to Robert Webster in 1661 to hold a school specialising:

> for the good of the youth to teach and instruct such thereof as he suld have occasion in reading as also in writing both Roman and currant hand and in arithmetik naturall practice logarithms and algebraicall the true and perfyte maner of keeping books of merchants accompts efter the Italian order as also the airt and study of navigatione.[56]

Conscious efforts were now being made to find teachers suited to meeting the town's educational needs. In 1662, the council set out its policy regarding elementary education. It concluded that too many unqualified persons with little ability had been setting up English schools. As a consequence, a specialist teacher of reading and writing had been recruited from Edinburgh, who 'to the effect the scoolls may be better regulat and the youth instructit in tyme comeing' was to be the sole licensed English teacher in the town, except for the young children of Futty and the Castlegate, who already had another teacher. The council also permitted some women to carry on teaching elementary reading.[57]

It is clear that the council was beginning to recognise the need for quality control in the provision of teaching, bringing teachers in from outside if necessary. It was also providing teaching which met the varying demands of the urban populace, accepting the need for establishing schools in more than one quarter of the town and conceding that women were capable of teaching children at an elementary level. In 1674, an additional two men and three women were permitted to continue teaching 'in respect of the distance from severall parts of the toune to the said [principal] school and of the inconvenience and hazard young children might incur thereby', an interesting indication of the council's concern for the welfare of the burgh's children.[58] Yet it was also from the 1660s that complaints about unlicensed teachers in Old Aberdeen became most insistent.[59] What is clear from the litany of such complaint in both burghs is that there was a market for tuition in literacy, and no shortage of men and women able and willing to supply it.

Complaints about the infringement of the grammar schoolmaster's privilege of teaching grammar disappear from the records after 1620, to be replaced in the 1660s by specific complaints about the activities of independent English and arithmetic teachers.[60] One interpretation would be that a classical education was becoming less important to the burgesses of both towns, while a utilitarian education became more so. This is perhaps also implied by the decision of the master of the grammar school in the early seventeenth century to hire Andrew Howat to instruct the scholars in writing and arithmetic.[61] Prior to this, the only mention of teaching arithmetic appears in the licence granted to Edward Diggens to teach in 1607. The *Leges Ludi Literarii* had specified that the scholars were 'to have a slight taste of arithmetic', and the burgh fathers of the 1620s do not seem to have viewed the subject with much greater urgency. Howat was contracted merely to 'schaw thame some principles of arithmetick'.[62] By the second half of the seventeenth century, however, numerical skills, particularly those with a commercial bent, were becoming increasingly desirable. In 1655, John Brown's petition for licence to hold a school professed his ability to 'educat young children in reiding, wreiting, and laying of compts'.[63] Two years later, James Duncan successfully petitioned for financial support for 'training up and instructing the youth in reiding, wreiting, and arithmetic'.[64] As has been seen, the curriculum devised by Robert Webster in May 1661 was very clearly intended to equip the burgh's youth for engagement in trade.

Yet there were limits to the scope of such learning. The only contemporary foreign language to be taught in seventeenth-century Aberdeen, and even then only intermittently, was French, which Mr Andrew Cameron was allowed to teach in 1622.[65] In 1635, Alexander Rolland also secured the right to advertise and teach 'ane Frensche schoole' to all who might wish to learn the language.[66] And over fifty years later, in 1687, a French Protestant was given a hundred pounds 'for his supply' and given permission to teach French to whomsoever might be interested, the council promising to try to provide him with premises for his school.[67] Despite these opportunities for learning French, much of the town's trade was destined for elsewhere in continental Europe. Knowledge of Dutch, German or Norwegian might have been of greater use, since the Netherlands, the Baltic and Scandinavia were the town's most significant trading partners in the seventeenth century.[68] How, or indeed whether, these languages were taught is not clear.

The education of girls

The General Assembly of the Kirk was suspicious of sewing and other girls' schools.[69] Aberdeen's council was more concerned with restricting women from teaching boys and with preventing unlicensed teachers from infringing the privileges of their licensed colleagues. From as early as 1598, complaints frequently circulated about independent, female teachers. The first concerned a school run by John Thomson, his wife Margaret Forbes, and another woman, Marion Cheyne, who were warned to teach only girls.[70] In 1636, two women were discharged from keeping schools.[71] A rhyme noted in the commonplace book of the master of the music school shows that women were thought by some to be as apt for education as men:

The weaknes of a womanis witt
Is not to natures fault
Bot laike of educatione fitt
Makes nature quhylls to halt.[72]

The first instance of an officially regulated school for girls in Aberdeen came in 1642 with the mortification of £1,000 Scots by Catherine Forbes, Lady Rothiemay (Plate 27). Her bequest was intended for the support of a schoolmistress to teach young women to 'write and so and any other art or science whairof they can be capable'.[73] Yet, Lady Rothiemay stated that Aberdeen was the town 'wherin I was educat and bred the most pairt of my youth' – clearly implying that earlier opportunities for female education existed.[74] Subsequently, other benefactresses also concerned themselves with the education of girls. Jean Guild included girls as well as boys in her 1649 mortification for the maintenance and education of ten orphans.[75] While boys were to be supported until the age of eighteen, girls were thought to have received an adequate education and preparation for adult life by the time they were fifteen. Although discriminatory, both sets of provision were remarkably enlightened in an age when basic education ended at the age of seven or eight. It was instructed that, during their tenure of the pension, the orphans, 'both male and female, how soone through aige they sall be fund capable, be educat and trayned up in the knowledge of the ground of Christian religione, and also in reading, wreiting, schewing, and all such as may fitt them for anie vertuous calling or trade of lyfe, according to ther sex'.[76] Underlying these provisions were the same concerns that had informed the educational schemes of the first *Book of Discipline*, allied to a fear of unemployment, particularly among women, which dominated the social thinking of early modern urban society.[77] Catherine Rolland left means for the education of the daughters of decayed burgesses of guild. From the age of eight until the age of fifteen, they were to be tutored in 'sewing, and reading, and other vertue' by a suitable spinster or widow.[78] Often, independent female teachers were tolerated, on condition that they restricted themselves to teaching elementary literacy.[79]

Poor scholars

These mortifications were part of a series of charitable donations for the support of education in Aberdeen.[80] After the Reformation, particularly in New Aberdeen, charitable foundations tended to take the form of mortifications entrusted to the town council. Bursaries for education replaced chantries and obits (see Chapter 13). Even so, many of these benefactions were as characteristically explicit in their nepotism as pre-Reformation benefactions: poverty was a less important criterion for charitable support than relationship to the benefactor.[81] Some donors, such as George Robertson and William Guild, sought to extend educational opportunity for the sons of craftsmen. A very significant mortification was that of Patrick Dun for the support of a principal teacher and three under-masters at the grammar school of New Aberdeen. This gift ought to have relieved the town from its financial support of the grammar school, as well as ensuring a free education of quality for poor children who were capable of studying there. Problems, however, with the investment of the fund meant that it was not until 1666 that Dun's wishes could be implemented. Even then, the proceeds from his bequest paid for three masters rather than four.[82]

Despite such ineptitude, the civic authorities also helped in the provision of education for the poor, although they tended to react to requests rather than initiating charitable contributions. Independent teachers, such as Edward Diggens in 1607, made a virtue out of their intention to teach the poor for nothing - or 'for godis sake' - in their petitions to obtain a licence to hold a school.[83] In 1657, James Duncan claimed to have been teaching writing, reading and arithmetic for nine years. He petitioned the council for the use of an empty schoolhouse, on the grounds that 'he had many poor ones and pensioners that had nothing to pey for ther instruction and housmails great and tymes hard and difficult'.[84] In 1658, the collector of the kirk session was ordained to pay Duncan twenty pounds yearly for teaching poor scholars.[85] Meanwhile, poor boys not suited to academic life were sometimes helped to learn a trade. In 1657, the son of Robert Spence was given twenty pounds for his education and 'training up at ane traid', as his father, who had fallen on hard times, was heir to a generous benefactor of the burgh.[86]

But how many of these children of the poor could read at all? The extent to which literacy rates of the past can be measured or determined is highly questionable.[87] In the absence of quantifiable evidence, reliance has instead to be placed on indirect indicators of literacy. One of these is the growing number of schools established in the seventeenth century, which perhaps suggests that literacy and numeracy were increasing amongst the general population. The arrival of a printer and bookseller in Aberdeen also indicates a reading market beyond the academic élite. While many of the printer's duties were connected with serving the academic community - he was, for instance, instructed to publish a list of books required for use in the burgh's schools - others seem to have anticipated a wider audience.[88] The printer was responsible for producing public notices of employment opportunities and for affixing notices of bursary competitions to the church door. The logical extension of the practice came in 1657 when the council instructed him to publish 'ane weekly diurnal to be sellit for the use of the inhabitants'.[89] While far from an indication that everyone in Aberdeen could read, this at least suggests that literacy was fairly widespread within the burgh by the middle of the seventeenth century.

The demands of polite society

The subtle, but nonetheless significant, changes in schooling priorities which had begun to take place in Aberdeen in the Restoration period drove educational policy in the following century as well. These changes signalled a shift in the cultural priorities and tastes of the townspeople. Increasing attention was given to the concerns of 'polite' society. From the late seventeenth century, Aberdeen possessed a licensed dancing master. He was first mentioned in 1695, when the council forbade him from holding public balls.[90] While the authorities were not, even then, altogether comfortable with public displays of enjoyment, by 1721 the dancing master was able to present himself as an asset to the burgh. Claiming that for almost twenty years he had been instructing 'the youth of this place in all the principles of manners and good breeding', James Hunter petitioned the council to receive the same encouragement given to others in the town who sought to inculcate the young with a liberal education and good manners.[91] In June 1742, in response to an 'application made by many of the principal inhabitants setting forth that the town was at a great loss for want of a right dancing master to educate their children', it was agreed to place an advertisement in public newspapers, inviting applicants to come for a trial.[92] While 'a great number of Gentlemen and Ladys' of the burgh attended the dancing master's trial, the successful applicant was warned not to enlist apprentices as pupils without their master's knowledge.[93]

In their pursuit of social graces, Aberdonians also became interested in music, or at least music of a different sort from in the past (see Chapter 16). Ironically, this spelt the death knell of the music - previously song - school of St Nicholas, which became defunct in 1758.[94] One factor explaining the decline in its fortunes may have been the proliferation of independent music teachers. As late as 1698, it had still been necessary for the council of Old Aberdeen to ban private teachers, male or female, from teaching vocal or instrumental music.[95] Another contributory factor was probably the formation of the Aberdeen Musical Society in 1748. This group of amateurs and professionals performed public concerts, while congregations participated in hymn singing, thereby dispensing with the need for a trained choir. The teaching of French, on the other hand, continued to thrive in the town, and became another branch of schooling for which the council took responsibility. In 1789, it granted John Nicholson, who claimed to have been teaching the language in the burgh for nineteen years, an annual salary of £100 Scots.[96]

Constructive benefaction

Despite the educational demands of polite society, the schooling of the poor continued to be a concern in the eighteenth century (see Chapter 2). Large benefactions by private individuals approached the problem in ways aimed at educating individuals with a view to the perceived requirements of the society. These benefactions were aimed most particularly at the elementary education of impoverished children. In 1737, John Kemp, an apothecary in London, left the residue of his estate, amounting to £1,077 3s. sterling, towards the schooling of the Aberdeen poor in reading, writing, and accounts.[97] In 1766, Andrew Gerard, an Episcopalian minister and later bishop, left £190 7s 10d sterling for the endowment of a school for the poor, where a schoolmistress would teach no more than thirty children at a time 'to read the Bible and any plain English book'.[98] Another English school for the poor was founded by Mr James Thain in 1788.[99]

The largest and most significant private eighteenth-century benefaction was made in 1729 by Robert Gordon, who donated £10,000 sterling for a school to maintain, educate and apprentice boys, especially the sons and grandsons of merchant and craft burgesses of Aberdeen, whose parents were too poor to provide for them themselves.[100] Robert Gordon's Hospital was to be built between Schoolhill and Blackfriars, where it still stands. The first duty of the master of the school was to oversee both the catechising of the boys and their regular attendance at religious worship. No boy was to enter the hospital below the age of eight years or above eleven, though boys could remain there until the age of sixteen. Applicants were required to produce a certificate testifying to their poverty. The boys were to have board, lodging, clothing and washing in the hospital (Ill. 26). Ideally, schoolmasters were to be found who could teach the boys to read English and Latin 'in so far as the Governors shall think fit they should be taught within the Hospital', but more particularly to provide instruction in writing, arithmetic, book-keeping and vocal music. The priority was that the boys should be given an education useful in burgess society. Similarly, on leaving the Hospital, the boys were to be feed as apprentices to merchant or craft burgesses. Those who successfully completed their apprenticeships were to receive £200 Scots, if they had been feed to a merchant, or £100 if their training had been in a trade. Most interestingly, the governors were exhorted to be:

Illustration 26 Clothing expenses for boys at Robert Gordon's Hospital (detail from ACA, Quarterly accounts of Robert Gordon's Hospital, May-August 1750.

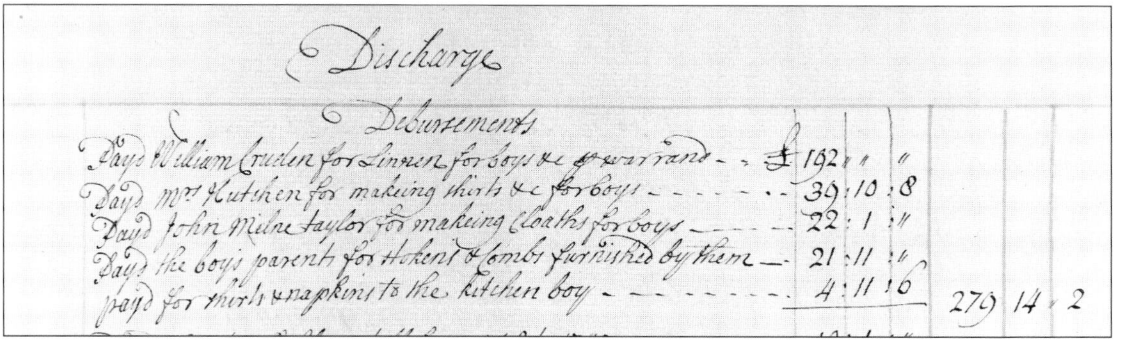
Discharge
Debursements
Payd William Cruden for Linnen for boys &c p warrand .. £ 192 : " : "
Payd Mrs Hutchen for makeing shirts &c for boys ...... 39 : 10 : 8
Payd John Milne taylor for makeing Cloaths for boys ...... 22 : 1 : "
Payd the boys parents for Hosens & Combs furnished by them ... 21 : 11 : "
payd for shirts & napkins to the kitchen boy .... 4 : 11 : 6 279 14 2

at pains to know the Capacity and Genius of the Boys, two or three years before they go out of the Hospital, that they may be able to judge what Business or Trade they will be fittest for, so that their education in the Hospital may be adapted to their Genius, to fit and qualify them for the Employments they are to follow.[101]

The first boys were admitted on 10 July 1750.[102] In spite of the good intentions behind the foundation, and the opportunities for social and economic advancement afforded by its provisions, the Hospital does not seem to have been a particularly happy place for those who lived and learned within its walls. In the early decades of its existence, there were problems with discipline, the boys frequently being a nuisance in town, and there were several instances of boys running away – usually with the intention of going to sea.[103] An early historian of the school stated that 'the only creditable feature of the period thus dealt with was the institution of what may be called the "College boy" system'.[104] This was an initiative which allowed selected boys from the Hospital to attend lectures in mathematics and natural philosophy at Marischal College, without having to pay. Things improved in the last decade of the eighteenth century with the appointment of Rev. Alexander Thom as master of Robert Gordon's in 1790. Thom held his post for thirty-six years, to general approbation.[105]

Educating girls in the eighteenth century

By the eighteenth century, schooling for girls was probably widely available in Aberdeen. In 1705, the burgh council rejected a mortification by Charles Carden, largely intended for the schooling of his own progeny. Even so, its discriminatory terms are revealing. While boys were to be educated in reading, writing, music and grammar, and supported in university study, girls were to study only reading, writing, music and sewing.[106] In 1734, Mrs Helen Duff of Braco gifted 2,000 merks Scots for the maintenance and education of 'a virtuous sober young woman of good character and reputation whose parents are not sufficiently able to educate her'. The recipient was to be at least thirteen years of age, and was to apply the benefaction to 'her education and maintenance in Learning, sueing, and all Millinars work, Pastrie, and such other such useful Eduacation, fit for a Gentlewoman, within the town of Aberdeen that may enable her to gain her bread honestlie and in a lawfull way'. Economic considerations and concerns of public morality still seem to have been the motivation behind educational provision for women. Nevertheless, it was understood that a respectable young woman should be literate: before she took up the bursary, she was to be 'fully taught to spin, wive stockings, Reiding, wreiting, and arithmetick, so as the same may not hinder her from her other Learning'.[107] Spinning and weaving schools had been the only educational establishments exempt from a ban on independent schools in Old Aberdeen in 1695, and there may have been several institutions of this sort in both burghs.[108] Applications to set up private sewing schools were common.[109] The council of New Aberdeen took steps to provide for skilled tuition in spinning. In 1745, the daughter of an Aberdeen merchant was awarded £3 sterling 'for her maintenance at Edinburgh during the time of her education as a spinning mistress'.[110]

The council looked beyond the north-east for the best tuition in other subjects too. In 1706, one of the town's bailies was instructed to approach Mr Whitingdaill, writing master in Glasgow, in order to entice him, on fairly generous terms, to Aberdeen 'to teach such persons in the arte of navigatione as shall be recommended to him by the magistrats as poor'. It is significant of the changing direction of Scotland's trading aspirations that Aberdeen should look to Glasgow for a 'saileing master'.[111] In 1744, enquiries were made at Edinburgh for 'a fitt person for teaching English in the Publick schools of this Burgh and to converse with such persons and to know what they would demand for salary and fees'.[112] Things had come a long way since the council had only grudgingly tolerated the existence of an English school in Aberdeen. Independent schools, however, were not always of a very high standard. Writing of his early schooling in Aberdeen, Lord Byron recalled having his ears boxed at home, when it was discovered that all he had learned at the mixed-sex school of one 'Bodsy Bowers' was to repeat 'God made man, let us love him' and that he could read not a syllable.[113]

The grammar school in the eighteenth century

Despite the growing variety of educational establishments in eighteenth-century Aberdeen, the council's main concern remained the grammar school. In 1750, the decision was taken to rebuild the school, not simply because the old building was in a state of decay, but also because it was not big enough.[114] This new school was designed to accommodate a maximum of 160 pupils.[115] The grammar school was not, it would seem, threatened by the proliferation of other types of school and it retained a distinctive niche in the instruction of Latin. While it was originally mooted that the language would be taught at Robert Gordon's Hospital, its instruction was not compulsory. Indeed, the aspirations instilled into boys in the two schools were different – at Gordon's education was intended to lead to apprenticeship, while at the grammar school it was supposed to lead to university education and public life.

Life for an eighteenth-century grammar school pupil was not markedly different to that encountered by a sixteenth-century scholar. In 1710, it was decided that no boy below the age of nine years should be admitted to the school unless he was particularly gifted, and that all boys enrolling should already be fluent readers of English, with an ability to write well, and have 'somewhat of arithmetic and music'.[116] Equipped with these elementary skills, it was envisaged that pupils could immediately commence their classical education. Facility in public speaking remained an aim of the grammar school education, in order to give boys 'vivacity in the Latine tongue, with some boldness and confidence'. A theatre was erected in a public space, at the council's expense, so pupils could display their oratorical skills.[117] Although these public performances were soon abandoned, the boys of the grammar school still followed an entirely classical curriculum throughout the eighteenth century.[118] There is no indication that arithmetic, mathematics or navigation were taught within its precincts. Indeed, an overview of statutes and official curricula might suggest that the school remained untouched by the fervour of Enlightenment enquiry that affected members of the two local universities in the later eighteenth century (see Chapters 15 and 16). This, however, seems unlikely, given that James Beattie (1735-1803), a poet and an author of several respected philosophical tracts, served as an under-master at the school from 1758 to 1760.[119] A member of the Aberdeen Philosophical Society, he presented papers on epistemology, criticism and taste, poetry, reason and morality – though it remains tantalisingly uncertain as to how much of his erudition was communicated to his pupils.[120]

In 1706, a book of morals was commissioned for the use of the boys of the grammar school, even although their riotous behaviour, which had been so marked a feature of the late sixteenth and early seventeenth centuries, does not seem to have been a particular feature of the eighteenth century.[121] The most colourful incident took place mid-century in the course of the annual visitation of the school by the magistrates, ministers and professors of Marischal College. A boy judged one of the best scholars in the school was incensed when an much inferior scholar who was closely connected to the school visitors was given a much more valuable book than he himself had won. Ripping apart his book with a penknife, he threw it at the man who had given it to him and ran from the school.[122] Discipline towards the end of the century was giving cause for concern, due principally to the great age of the incumbent rector. Ultimately, the council appointed a younger, though still experienced, co-rector to run the school with him.[123] Meanwhile, it approached the disciplinary problem in a traditional fashion. Like many of their predecessors, eighteenth-century town councillors believed that, if only boys could be made to attend church and to pay attention while they were there, all would be well. The masters and doctors of the grammar school were to have their pupils rehearse the *Shorter Catechism* by heart on Sundays. Immediately after divine worship, they were give an account of what they had heard in the sermons 'as having a very great tendency to cultivate and improve the morals of the scholars'.[124] Even in the Age of Reason, old orthodoxies died hard.

Conclusions

Throughout the centuries, Aberdeen's schools had been re-orientated time and time again to meet the perceived needs of the society they served. The pattern, approach and aim of schooling developed in accordance with broader developments in society, initially religious, but ultimately commercial. Initially, it was the church that had required appropriately trained functionaries, but gradually urban society recognised the importance of the instructors of literacy and numeracy within its bounds. The economic imperative at the heart of Aberdeen meant that, in addition to education in music, the classics and basic literacy, the town provided tuition at a relatively early period in arithmetic, book-keeping, navigation and French, as well as ensuring regulated provision of training in textile crafts. Pious benefaction, motivated by concern for social stability, sought to ensure the education of the poor. The logical extension of these moves was the eighteenth-century foundation of Robert Gordon's Hospital, whose founder envisaged the education of individuals for an active and utilitarian life. That same desire for social stability, coupled with an acceptance of the concept of female intellectual ability, did much to provide for the education of girls. But probably most intriguing and most revealing of the belief in the power of education, and the desire, regardless of means, to obtain it for one's children, is the evidence of the existence of independent schools. These could not have existed had there not been a genuine desire in Aberdeen, beyond what could officially be sanctioned and provided, for schooling the people.

15

Educating the Elite: Aberdeen and its Universities

DAVID DITCHBURN

Founders and feuds

It was that most unholy of popes, Alexander VI (1492-1503), who granted Aberdeen its first university on 10 February 1495. Less than a century later - on 2 April 1593 - a second college of higher education was established barely two miles from the first. Institutions such as the College of St Mary in the Nativity in Old Aberdeen (soon to become known as King's College) and Marischal College in New Aberdeen are rarely, however, the simple product of bureaucratic fiat. Particularly if they are to prove successful, they require elaborate and advanced planning. Both King's and Marischal were, in this respect, quite typical. Both have foundation dates, but neither was simply created on those days.

The principal architect of King's was William Elphinstone (Plate 18), bishop of Aberdeen since 1483, and Elphinstone's arduous journey to Rome, in order to obtain approval for the university in Old Aberdeen, was but one step on a long path.[1] Its beginning - the original idea of founding a university - remains obscure, though, if not actually Elphinstone's conception, he certainly possessed the experience, means and vision to ensure its achievement. Its end, even in 1495, lay some way off. Meticulous financial planning and targeted staff recruitment took time, as did the construction of the college buildings. In 1498, three years after the papal charter had been issued, Elphinstone was purchasing gunpowder, wheelbarrows and carts in Middelburg - presumably to facilitate building work on the new college.[2] The start of teaching in some subjects was understandably delayed until 1505 and Elphinstone was still revising his plans and provisions for the college in 1514 - the year of his death.

At Marischal matters progressed more swiftly. Elphinstone's counterpart in the development of Aberdeen's college was George Keith, fourth Earl Marischal (*d.* 1623) (Plate 24). Keith's journey was less spectacular and lengthy than that of Elphinstone. The Reformation had done away with the need for papal permission for a new university. Instead, approval for the new college was obtained from the General Assembly of the Church of Scotland (in April 1593) and from parliament (in the following July). Teaching began in the next autumn and the new college, financed from the earl's secularised church lands in Inverbervie and Cowie, was housed in the former Franciscan friary on Broad Street, bequeathed by the town council. These arrangements were simple and straightforward and the earl was spared the scrabbling for resources which the bishop had undertaken a century earlier. Nevertheless, in some ways Keith's plans were even more audacious than those of Elphinstone. Old Aberdeen, by then, already possessed a university: did Aberdeen (or for that matter Scotland) really need another, similar institution? The foundation of Marischal meant that Scotland, with 3.3 institutions per million of population, had a far higher proportion of universities than any other European country.[3] At first sight, the notion of yet another university seemed preposterous. But then so too had the plan to establish the earlier college. By 1495, Scotland already possessed two universities – St Andrews (founded by papal bull in 1413) and Glasgow (similarly established in 1451).

There is a similar argument against the wisdom of founding both King's and Marischal. Proliferation made for weakness. St Andrews, Glasgow and (it turned out) King's were all inadequately resourced. Student numbers at the existing institutions were limited and none had succeeded, by virtue of its academic reputation, in stopping the long-established drain of students to the more prestigious continental universities. The negative attitude towards Scottish universities was summed up by Adam Bothwell, bishop of Orkney, who as late as 1560 considered that his nephew ought to be sent to France or the Low Countries because 'he can leyr na guid at hame'.[4] The academic record of both Elphinstone and Keith suggests similar attitudes. Although commencing his own studies at Glasgow, the bishop had progressed to the universities of Paris and Orléans. The earl, on the other hand, was a product of the Calvinist academy in Geneva. Dynamic new institutions of learning, as envisaged by Elphinstone and Keith, might have overcome the unappealing nature of the existing Scottish universities. But had Elphinstone and Keith invested their resources in those institutions already established, they might have done more, and more quickly, to strengthen university provision in Scotland as a whole.

In seeking papal approval for King's, the bishop advanced several counter arguments to the notion of concentrating university provision in St Andrews and Glasgow. Aberdeen, he claimed, was located amidst a population which was 'rude and ignorant of letters, and almost barbarous'.[5] A new institution was required to rectify this lack of civility since, Elphinstone claimed, existing universities were inaccessible from the north-east of Scotland. His argument is hardly credible. There is no evidence that Aberdeen was the cultural wasteland depicted by Elphinstone to the pope. Its cathedral had long since possessed a well-stocked library, as did other religious institutions in the town.[6] Among those who had leafed through the locally available tomes had been John Barbour, arguably the most accomplished of all medieval Scottish authors. Barbour, of course, was a cleric and Elphinstone's new college was intended for laymen as well as clerics. Still, there is ample evidence to suggest that secular society, too, had its *literati* – men who were familiar not only with the best of contemporary Scottish poetry (that of William Dunbar was transcribed in the town's Sasine Register), but also more esoteric foreign works.[7] These literary interests had been pursued notwithstanding the lack of a local university, though many who did so (like Barbour) were graduates.[8] Indeed, the bishop's own academic record, as well that of many of his senior colleagues in the diocese, belies the notion that existing universities were inaccessible.

While some of his arguments as to why a university was required in Old Aberdeen were patently spurious, Elphinstone also claimed that suitable men could not be found 'for preaching the word of God' or 'for administering the sacraments of the church'.[9] There is no evidence of a shortage of priests in Scotland, but Elphinstone clearly envisaged an institution which would educate clergymen to a higher standard than had been customary. But his college was to have another purpose too. As a leading figure in the Scottish government, the bishop was acutely aware of the shortage of lawyers and so it was planned that the new institution would also foster legal studies. Yet in sponsoring the education of what would become known as middle-class professions (see Chapter 8), Elphinstone's plans were hardly innovative. St Andrews and Glasgow had initially entertained similar notions, even though the study of law had failed to develop strong roots at either. Why, then, did the bishop not devote his resources to bolstering the shaky foundations of these institutions?

Practicalities played a part. Elphinstone was able to second teachers from his own diocese. As at St Andrews earlier in the century, the existence of a tightly-knit, educated circle of graduate clergymen in the vicinity of the proposed college is likely to have provided not just a pool of potential staff, but also an intellectual impetus to the university's very foundation.[10] Meanwhile, Elphinstone was able to finance his university in no small part because, as bishop, he was able to sequester ecclesiastical revenues from his diocese for the new college. It would have been much more difficult, though perhaps not impossible, to assign these revenues to either of the two existing universities. Locals who contributed to the venture – and these included ecclesiastical colleagues, relations and Aberdeen burgesses – might also have been less willing to fund a more distant institution. This, of course, suggests that a degree of local pride was also important to the venture.

Here it is perhaps relevant to digress in the direction of Scottish ecclesiastical politics. Originally the Scottish bishops had all been of technically equal status, since none had been accorded the rank of archbishop and most had only one direct superior – the pope. This changed in 1472, when St Andrews was elevated to archepiscopal status. Glasgow was to follow in 1492. These promotions were resented by other bishops – including Aberdeen's – who now found themselves directly answerable to one of their erstwhile colleagues. Episcopal pride had been dented. Many won temporary exemption from archepiscopal oversight, but there was little possibility that other bishops might acquire similar status to that of St Andrews and Glasgow. Still, the foundation of a university would at least place the bishop of Aberdeen on a par with St Andrews and Glasgow, whose archbishops were patrons of their local universities. The reasoning here is speculative, but the possibility remains that King's College was partly a piece of vanity, masterminded by a bishop anxious to regain status for both his diocese and himself. Whatever the balance of Elphinstone's true motives, his plans were supported enthusiastically by a king – James IV (1488-1513) – who dabbled eagerly, if inconsequentially, in the excitement of Renaissance ideas. Learning in the Middle Ages was worthy of respect, and both bishops and princes who sponsored intellectual developments acquired personal repute.

Vanity, then, may have played a part in the foundation of King's, as it almost certainly also did in the foundation of Marischal.[11] Traditionally, the origins of Aberdeen's second college were regarded as the initiative of a convinced Protestant – and of that there can be no doubt – who despaired of the supposed crypto-Catholicism which riddled King's and who had abandoned hope of reforming the university in Old Aberdeen. Keith's overriding aim, according to this view, was to provide a college which trained committed Protestant ministers. There is some merit to the argument. Marischal was certainly a Protestant institution. Its constitution was modelled on that of Glasgow, as designed in 1577 by Andrew Melville, the leading figure in the second generation of Protestants reformers, and its first principal was Robert Howie, a man steeped in the Calvinist education of Swiss and German universities. There remained, too, a pressing need for Protestant ministers, especially in the north-east, where Catholicism lingered longer than in most parts of Scotland. Unfortunately, the other side of the equation is predicated upon a fallacy – that King's was a crypto-Catholic institution. True, reformed notions had been as slow to penetrate King's as they had the north-east as a whole. The teachers at King's, unlike those of the other Scottish universities, had been prepared to stand up for their Catholicism. This impertinence had, however, attracted the intervention of both state and church and in 1569 the college had been purged of its Catholic staff.[12] Henceforth, King's was resolutely Protestant and, although its production of ministers remained limited, this was rather more a consequence of having become a Protestant oasis in a still largely Catholic landscape than it was of lingering Catholicism in the college itself.

The great debate at King's, as Keith established his rival institution, was concerned neither with function nor with religious ideology, but rather with constitutional matters. Radical Protestants placed great importance in providing each of the Scottish universities with new constitutions. Although those for St Mary's College at St Andrews and Glasgow had been completed swiftly, royal approval of that for King's had been delayed – even though its provisions were probably being enacted, at least in part. The controversy surrounding the 'New Foundation' – which raged from 1575 until its final rejection in 1617 – was largely symbolic of a larger tussle for power between radical churchmen, led by Andrew Melville, and a more cautious king, James VI (1567-1625).[13] Reformers such as Keith had been personally involved in the debates over the New Foundation. The ensuing stalemate perhaps convinced the Earl Marischal that it would be simpler to establish a new college with a new constitution than it would be to win James VI's approval for the New Foundation of King's. Indeed, this may explain the lack of clarity as to what exactly Keith was founding – a new, independent academy, a new college in the existing university, or a new college in a new university. Keith himself was perhaps uncertain, preferring to leave his options open until the wrangle over the New Foundation was resolved.[14] What, however, is beyond dispute is that Keith, in close collaboration with the Aberdeen town council, founded an institution which closely resembled King's in both functions and purpose.

In accounting for this duplication, the quest for prestige emerges as a credible contributory motive. Keith was the champion of north-eastern Protestantism, but his dominance in the region was not unquestioned. Traditionally, political leadership in the area had been the preserve of the (still Catholic) earls of Huntly. The foundation of a college which bore Keith's comital name provided not only a durable and public monument to Keith munificence. It cocked a snook at his rival. There was, too, a perhaps delicious irony in the prospect of ministers trained in the Earl Marischal's college converting Huntly's Catholic adherents. Meanwhile, the earl's partner, the town council of Aberdeen (recently purged of its succession of Menzies provosts (see Chapter 10)), also viewed the initiative as a project in prestige. And Old Aberdeen, it is worth remembering, was still an entirely separate entity. The two burghs shared a name, but not a university.

While a combination of immediate motives – some altruistic, some personal, most associated with religious interests – explains the foundation of both Aberdeen colleges, their appearance ought also to be examined in a wider context. In this respect, King's and Marischal have fared rather differently from their respective historians. While a brilliant analysis of how the bishop's college related to academic developments elsewhere in Europe has been published, the earl's college has received no such treatment, even though more universities were founded in the 1590s than in the 1490s.[15] This historiographical oversight is itself revealing of the wider context in which both colleges were established. King's was both part of,

The Sapient Septemviri.

Illustration 27
John Kay's depiction
of the 'Seven Wise
Men', the King's
College
establishment which
opposed union with
Marischal College in
1786.

*Illustration 27
John Kay's depiction
of the 'Seven Wise
Men', the King's
College
establishment which
opposed union with
Marischal College in
1786.*

and a product of, an international world of learning in a still overwhelmingly Catholic Europe. Local and national support were vital to its development, but its emergence was also integral to a wider trend which witnessed the expansion of higher education throughout northern Europe – with the opening of the first Netherlandish, Swedish and Danish universities (at Leuven or Louvain in 1425, Upsala in 1477 and Copenhagen in 1478), as well as many others in northern Germany.

Ironically, of course, this international process was also the beginnings of the nationalisation of the universities. King's stood on the cusp of a new learning environment. Marischal, despite the cosmopolitan educational experiences of both its founder and first principal, was a product of that new environment. Its emergence, amid the national rivalries of the crown and an effectively nationalised church and the local jealousies of two ambitious magnates, defined Marischal more firmly than King's as the product of Scottish, rather than European, developments.

Local rivalries were important in explaining the failure to effect a merger between the two colleges before 1860. Amalgamation was discussed frequently, especially in the later eighteenth century, when the notion received support at Marischal, but implacable hostility from the majority of the lacklustre staff at King's (Ill. 27).[16] Union had, in fact, briefly been effected in the mid seventeenth century. In 1641, the two colleges were united by decree of Charles I (1625-49), to form the 'King Charles University of Aberdeen'. Given the king's name and pretensions, and his sister's marital connections, this was surely a deliberate echo of the first imperial

ABERDEEN BEFORE 1800

university in the (then) German-speaking world, the Caroline University at Prague, founded by the Emperor Charles IV in 1347. The Scottish Caroline, however, was not a success. Staff at Marischal were suspicious that it was a take-over by its older rival and during the Cromwellian period the two colleges were already drifting in separate directions.[17] The arranged marriage was formally annulled after the Restoration, by the Act Recissory of 1661. Yet in many ways amalgamation made sense, since it offered the prospect of economising on both ruinously expensive (and increasingly ruinous) buildings and overt duplication in arts teaching. Savings might have been used to fund teaching in law and medicine, which neither college had the means to undertake effectively on its own, while at least one professor thought that professorial salaries could also be increased.[18] Academic rationale counted for little, however, by comparison with older rivalries, both between the two colleges and between the two burghs. Disputes over the location of a united university remained a perennial stumbling block.[19]

The failure to achieve union exacerbated rivalries. The two colleges remained in competition for students, only now their institutional identities had been sharpened by discussion of amalgamation. This factionalism percolated the student community too. In December 1659, between thirty and forty Marischal students, replete with dirks, cudgels, iron clubs, batons and pistols, perpetrated a riot in Old Aberdeen, suspecting that four of their peers had been pressurised into defecting to King's. Students of King's, agitated by the alleged poaching of students in the other direction, were to cause an equally vicious affray in the Castlegate in December 1668.[20] These were only the most notorious of a number of violent incidents between rival students, which erupted even on the most sombre of occasions. A fracas at a funeral in 1667 prompted the Aberdeen council to instruct that students should no longer be invited to burials.[21]

Academic staff, as befitted their age and increasingly middle-class status, were expected to deport themselves in a more gentlemanly fashion (see Chapter 8). Yet, if not rivalry, then certainly detachment from 'the other place' is evident among staff too. In response to an innocuous request for information regarding tuition in Aberdeen, James Beattie, professor of moral philosophy at Marischal from 1760 to 1803, noted that Marischal professors did not take student lodgers. He did not know, one way or the other, whether those at King's did. Boarding in Aberdeen cost about £20. He professed to having no idea of similar costs in Old Aberdeen. Neither could he offer a judgement as to whether the cost of tuition was more expensive at King's than at Marischal, since he knew nothing (apparently) about conditions two miles away.[22] Beattie was perhaps deliberately concealing information about King's in order to secure the student recruit for Marischal. But, if we accept Beattie's professions of ignorance at face value, they reveal an astonishing ignorance of conditions in the old town.

Curricula and cut-backs

Elphinstone's original plans for King's curriculum were ambitiously broad ranging. The college was to have five faculties covering arts, canon law, civil law, medicine and theology. The inclusion of medicine is especially striking, for even at the most famous medieval universities, save Salerno, Montpellier, Bologna and Paris, its teaching was intermittent. Law, too, was a subject which not all of the older European universities sponsored. Although legal studies were becoming increasingly fashionable in the new universities of the fifteenth century, in England budding lawyers were trained at the Inns of Court, rather than at Oxford or Cambridge, while civil law had been excised from the Parisian curriculum by a papal fiat of 1219.[23] Nevertheless, while Elphinstone's plans for King's seem modern, the breadth of his curricular conception is deceptive. In common with other universities, new students were expected to matriculate in the arts faculty. The other subjects were for postgraduate study and then, as now, comparatively few students proceeded to this more advanced level.

That, from the outset, only minimal numbers were expected in the medical faculty is strongly suggested by the limited resources put at the disposal of James Cumming, the first lecturer in the subject. Cumming supplemented his annual salary of £12 6s by moonlighting as a physician in the neighbouring royal burgh.[24] Although in 1568 one of his successors, Gilbert Skene, achieved the distinction of publishing the first Scottish medical treatise (on the subject of plague - see Chapter 3), King's mediciners were largely untroubled by students.[25] Under the terms of the New Foundation, medical teaching was to be abandoned. This made financial sense, but the ultimate triumph of those who rejected the New Foundation (in 1617) meant that medical appointments continued to be made thereafter. A few doctors graduated in the seventeenth century and a more regular trickle of on average about five per year emerged between 1715 and 1799, a significant number of them Englishmen.[26] To an extent, however, King's contented itself with preparing medical students for more detailed studies in Edinburgh. Marischal, meanwhile, had no pretensions of fostering such study in its early years. It was not until 1700 that a chair of medicine was established, though its early holders regarded it as little more than a sinecure. Cumming's appointment was thus something of a false start and only in the eighteenth century did medical teaching in Aberdeen revive, and then only modestly and almost as much by accident as design. The bequest of relevant texts - notably by Lord Bute and Sir William Forsyth, whose libraries were donated to Marischal in 1782 and 1790 respectively - and the growing opportunities for doctors, especially in the colonies, stimulated student interest in the subject. The foundation of the Aberdeen Medical Society in 1789 provided a forum for lectures and further demonstrated the market for medical studies, to which both colleges responded belatedly. At Marischal, regular medical teaching began following the appointment of William Livingston in 1793.[27]

Legal studies proved equally difficult to sustain, though Elphinstone (himself a lawyer) seemed to lay greater emphasis on this subject than medicine. The canonist, in 1505, was to be paid £23 6s 8d (almost double the mediciner's salary), while the civilist was to receive a more modest £20 per annum.[28] Still, even although canon law - that is the law of the Catholic church - somewhat incongruously survived the Reformation, the impetus behind its study was fatally weakened by the advent of Protestantism. The days of a legal system which 'smellit of poperie' and whose foremost judge was the bishop of Rome were clearly numbered, though as late as 1639 the canonist James Sandilands persuaded the kirk's General Assembly that canon law instruction should be limited rather than abandoned.[29] He had a point, for its precepts remained the basis of marital and testatory law. Canon law was not therefore choked, but instead allowed to wither. Meanwhile, its civil counterpart was also neglected by a Protestant establishment much more interested in theology. At King's, study of both laws, like medicine, had been earmarked for abandonment under the terms of the New Foundation. This perhaps was merely formal recognition that these subjects were moribund and the late sixteenth-century civilist, Nicholas Hay, had certainly spent most of his time as a judge in the new commissary court, rather than as a teacher in the classroom.[30] A successor, Alexander Dauney, professor of civil law from 1793, was cheerfully to admit in 1826 that until two years previously 'I have never been called upon, nor have I given, any lectures.'[31] The re-appointment of a civilist from 1619 evidently failed to translate into effective teaching. At Marischal, meanwhile, though civil law was taught in the eighteenth century, there remained doubt as to whether the college could confer degrees in the subject. Many at King's argued that it could not. In 1745, the House of Lords decided otherwise, incidentally clarifying that Marischal was, indeed, a university, something which had remained doubtful ever since the college's foundation.[32]

Retrenchment in medicine and law - partly a result of financial cutbacks and partly a consequence of Protestant indifference - left King's to concentrate on the rather more limited areas of arts and theology, which had in any case probably been its true strengths even before the Reformation. Theology, both Catholics and Protestants could agree, was a vital tool for would-be priests and ministers, though they differed, of course, in their interpretations of the subject. The pre-Reformation syllabus involved study of the Bible and Peter Lombard's twelfth-century *Sentences*, the starting point for all Biblical criticism in the Middle Ages.[33] By good fortune, a series of lectures delivered to theology students by William Hay between 1533 and 1535 has survived and exemplifies the means by which the subject was taught at King's. In lecturing on unction, order and marriage, Hay followed the comments of Peter Lombard, digressing to cite and consider other authorities and to ponder occasionally the significance of appropriate examples. On marriage, for instance, he alluded to the 'divorce' of the English king Henry VIII (1509-47) and Catherine of Aragon.[34] Theology, it is worth remembering, encompassed ideas of acute political, as well as religious, significance in the sixteenth century. It still did in the seventeenth century, when the theological establishment at King's was peddling a Protestant irenicism that found no favour with the uncompromising Calvinism of the Covenanting regime in the 1630s. The so-called 'Aberdeen Doctors' (see Chapters 11 and 13) envisaged Protestant Europe setting aside its disagreements in order to defeat the Catholic powers, but many, including the most eminent doctor of them all, John Forbes, were forced, or felt obliged, to demit office under Covenanting pressure (see Chapter 16).[35] This was the high point of interaction between politics and theology at King's. Yet, important though the issue was to contemporaries, it has served to overshadow the more routine, but also more profound, purpose of the theological and philosophical instruction - the attempt to reconcile faith and reason. It was this issue which had taxed the great medieval theologians - whose conclusions Protestants so despised - but whose agenda reformers continued to follow.

Theological study did not begin at the postgraduate level. The focus of the arts degree for most of the period was also fundamentally religious in nature. In this respect, too, the Protestant *coup d'état* of 1560 changed little. Before the Reformation, the arts curriculum was modelled closely on that of Paris, with a particular emphasis on the study of Aristotelean texts and the 'transferable skills' of grammar, logic and rhetoric.[36] Since Aristotle's works had been translated into Latin (especially during the twelfth and thirteenth centuries) and copious commentaries on them had been subsequently penned in Latin, it was (naturally enough) the language of instruction, save for first-year students learning the rudiments of (Latin) grammar. There was, of course, a philosophical dimension to such study and, as a means rather than an end, it sharpened linguistic and argumentative competence. Yet, the real interest in Aristotle lay in the insights which he, and commentators on him, offered to religious understanding. Not that Aristotle was accepted uncritically. The great fourteenth-century scholar Pierre d'Ailly encapsulated the view of many in declaring Aristotelean texts as 'opinion rather than knowledge'.[37] Nevertheless, love him or loathe him, Aristotle remained central to the ongoing debate regarding the balance to be struck between reason and faith.

Protestants, too, regarded Aristotle as pivotal to their concerns and his work retained a dominant position in the revised arts curriculum set out in the New Foundation for King's and subsequently at Marischal. At both colleges, first-year students were introduced to Latin and Greek texts. The following year, still using these media, they developed their skills of 'invention, disposition and elocution' –

that is, the collection of data, its formulation into an argument and its articulation. Third-year students were trained in the rudiments of arithmetic, geometry and trigonometry (Plate 26), while their Latin and Greek were advanced through a study of Cicero's *On Duties* ('for the better shaping of morals') and various Aristotelean texts. Aristotle again featured prominently in the curriculum pursued by fourth-year students, in order to introduce them to physiology and natural history, though they also found time for geography, astronomy, cosmography and, towards the end of the year, 'the rules of the sacred tongue' – Hebrew.[38]

The extent to which all the elements of this model curriculum were actually taught remains uncertain. Its execution optimistically presupposed an adequately qualified teaching establishment. Hebrew specialists, in particular, were scarce. At Marischal, Hebrew was introduced in 1642 and taught by John Row, who, the following year, received 400 merks from the council for compiling a Hebrew dictionary dedicated to the council.[39] Throughout the period before 1800 language teaching, however, was stronger at King's. Hebrew was probably taught there by James Lawson, appointed sub-principal in 1569, though its instruction may not have survived Lawson's departure for the Edinburgh ministry in 1572.[40] Neither did it survive the deposition of John Row as principal in 1662, Row having previously transferred from Marischal. The foundation of a chair of oriental languages eleven years later afforded a greater measure of security to Hebrew's presence in the King's teaching schedule, though it was not until 1727 that a similar post was established at Marischal.[41]

The similarities between the pre- and post-Reformation curricula are striking. The main difference lay in the increasing emphasis which reformers placed on Greek and Hebrew, though even this reveals more about Elphinstone's conservatism than it does about Protestant innovation. Greek was being taught in many of the fifteenth-century Italian universities and, though the study of Hebrew was slower to develop, it had already sparked the interest of John Vaus, an early King's graduate, who, after study in Paris, had been appointed grammarian at King's by 1516.[42] Nevertheless, the special place accorded by the reformers to Greek and Hebrew reveals their true intent. They were not interested, any more than their medieval predecessors, in linguistic skills *per se*. Instead, proficiency in Greek and Hebrew permitted students to study Aristotelean and Biblical texts in their original language, devoid of erroneous Latin translations and without recourse to (what they saw as) flawed interpretations of medieval Catholic scholars.

Radical as the changes seemed in the context of the arts curriculum, there was little novel, or distinctly Protestant, to such an approach. Pre-Reformation humanists, such as the famous Netherlandish scholar Erasmus, had attempted to do much the same and the early Protestants themselves recognised that there was little innovative about their teaching programme. As the reformer George Hay announced to the final-year students of 1569, 'novelty is rightly detested by all men of wisdom'.[43] It was not innovation that Protestants sought to foster, but rather a 'back-to-basics' approach that entailed different insights into an established curriculum. It is, then, hardly surprising that, despite minor modifications to the curriculum (such as the addition of Homer and Pliny to the reading list of Marischal students in the early seventeenth century), the essence of the curriculum remained the same throughout that century. Latin, Greek, Hebrew; grammar, rhetoric, logic and ethics; Biblical and Aristotelean study remained the staple of the educational diet, with occasional diversity provided by geography, astronomy, physics and mathematics.[44]

This is not to argue that students of the pre- and post-Reformation eras would have noticed no difference in their tuition. Although the fundamentals of the curriculum remained similar, new analytical tools and interpretations were applied to its content. Some were of only temporary popularity – notably Ramism, the philosophical approach pioneered by the French Huguenot Pierre de la Ramée (1515-72), which was used by many to find flaws in Aristotelean logic. As already noted, however, Pierre d'Ailly had observed over a century earlier that much of Aristotle's work was opinion, not knowledge. A more recent commentator has noted that 'the craze for Ramism was out of all proportion to the insights Ram[ée] had to offer'.[45] Still, fad-of-the-moment it was and Ramist approaches were probably influencing tuition at both King's and Marischal from the early seventeenth century. Aristotle's credibility, however, was only temporarily dented and by the 1620s both Aberdeen colleges were once again unavowedly Aristotelean in outlook. Aristotle proved hard to dislodge from the pedestal upon which so many academics had placed him. As late as 1692, lecture notes reveal that his outlook continued to dominate much teaching at King's. Indeed, although the more modern ideas advanced by Descartes, Locke and Newton were increasingly adopted in the later seventeenth and early eighteenth centuries, especially in scientific studies, many teachers, of philosophy in particular, remained sceptical of new approaches.[46]

Despite the cautious welcome afforded by some teachers to some new ideas, neither King's nor Marischal were especially innovative in their approach to teaching. The curriculum, and the line taken on it, bore striking similarities to those followed in the pre-Reformation continental universities and then those developed elsewhere in Protestant Europe and North America. Latterly, indeed, ideas and influences were transmitted along an east–west axis which meant that the Aberdeen colleges had far more in common with the schools of Danzig and Harvard than they had with Cambridge or Oxford.[47] Nevertheless, conformity with accepted fads of the reformed world, rather than pioneering individualism or debate, was the norm. It is telling that around 1700 exactly the same lectures in logic were delivered at both King's and Marischal.[48] Not surprisingly, in such a staid environment, students developed a cross-generational trade in lecture notes and outsiders considered it realistic in the seventeenth century to standardise teaching in all of the Scottish universities.[49] These plans ultimately failed, but the fact that they could be contemplated at all reveals the extent of conservatism in the world of Scottish learning before Enlightenment ideas took root.

If we view matters in a longer context, two great intellectual movements of the period covered by this volume did have a profound effect on study in Aberdeen – humanism from the fifteenth century and Enlightenment from the eighteenth century. Humanism, which pioneered the rediscovery and study of classical authors largely forgotten in the Middle Ages, was already influencing academic institutions and outlooks before the foundation of King's. There are signs that it influenced Elphinstone's intentions for Old Aberdeen too, notably in the emphasis placed from the outset on the study of Latin texts and in the high status accorded to the (Latin) grammarian. Its precepts continued to influence the curriculum for long afterwards, not least in the ongoing use of Latin as the language of instruction. Only in the 1730s did English become the medium of teaching at King's and, probably at about the same time, at Marischal – though as late as the 1770s examinations were still conducted in Latin. Humanism, however, was not simply a philological exercise. Humanists studied humanity as opposed to divinity. In this respect, too, we can see humanistic notions influencing the curriculum at King's, for instance in the study of poetry, philosophy and history, though the pace at which these subjects were incorporated within the teaching schedule varied. History was slow to gain prominence, but poetry was studied from the outset and philosophical concerns increasingly displaced spiritual ones as the mainstay of the curriculum.

The second of the great intellectual developments to affect Aberdeen was the Enlightenment. While some branches of teaching were slow to respond to the new learning, Enlightenment ideas were adopted quickly in others and, in their pioneering advocacy of 'Common Sense' philosophy, scholars such as Thomas Reid and James Beattie made a vital contribution to both the Scottish Enlightenment and international learning.[50] New approaches to particular subjects also stimulated debate regarding the entire curriculum. George Turnbull, who taught at Marischal from 1721 to 1727, was an early proponent of abandoning what he regarded as the uselessness of existing patterns of study. Instead, he sought its replacement by an overriding focus on mathematics, science, history and politics, which he regarded as more relevant to the maintenance of moral well-being among his students. Mathematics, it is worth remembering, was still regarded by many as a moral tool because it imbued the competencies of rationalism and discipline.

In a Scottish context, Turnbull's ideas were comparatively novel, though it was only after similar changes were implemented at other Scottish universities that many were adopted at Marischal in 1753. This constituted the most radical overhaul of the curriculum since the college's foundation and in the same year King's followed suit. Henceforth, at both colleges the second and third years of undergraduate study were transformed by the new concentration on mathematics, science, geography and history. And it was to support the greater emphasis on scientific enquiry that plans were devised to construct museums, laboratories, botanical gardens and a new observatory - the last erected on Castle Hill in 1781. Nevertheless, the overhaul was not absolute. Classical languages remained the core of first-year teaching and philosophy retained its domination of final-year studies, while the new initiatives for the intervening years were blighted (especially at King's) by failure to realise all of the envisaged plans. Old Aberdeen had to wait for its chemical laboratory and museum, while the commitment of King's to mathematics was undermined by the failure to appoint a salaried professor in the subject for most of the eighteenth century.[51]

Segregation and integration

Eighteenth-century endeavours to introduce a more 'useful' curriculum were matched by growing numbers of bequests to fund professorial appointments and also bursaries to subsidise students from less well-to-do backgrounds. In 1762, John Paterson bequeathed £100 in East India Company annuities to augment the salary of the professor of medicine at Marischal, while in 1817 Sir John Macpherson (a King's graduate of 1764 and subsequent governor general of India) left £2,500 in stocks and shares to finance a bursary for Gaelic-speaking students.[52] Despite such provision - which had existed ever since the foundation of King's - it proved difficult to attract students. In the first decade of the seventeenth century, matriculations at King's were running at an average of only 19.1 per annum, while those at Marischal, at an average of 22 per year, were only marginally greater. Many students dropped out before completing degrees, ensuring even fewer graduates.

Both Aberdeen colleges were small by comparison with other institutions. Glasgow managed to attract an average of 27.4 per year in the same period, though this, too, paled into insignificance with matriculations at many continental universities. In the Middle Ages, several hundred new students enrolled annually at Bologna, Cambridge, Ferrara, Oxford, Padua and Paris, and by the seventeenth century about 200 new students matriculated each year at Calvinist Heidelberg. Even Frankfurt-an-der-Oder (founded in the same decade as King's, but in the later 1630s in the middle of a war zone) attracted about one hundred new students each year.[53] Although numbers in Aberdeen increased in the later seventeenth and eighteenth centuries, King's and Marischal still reached only a roughly equally shared total of 300 students by 1750 and numbers were subsequently to decline again, albeit only slightly.[54]

Recruitment rates were impaired by several factors. Although there were few formal entrance requirements at any university, the prohibition on women (in Aberdeen and everywhere else) was absolute. They, it would seem, were more dangerous than Protestants, whom the pope did not ban from Catholic universities until 1564. Under the terms of the New Foundation, retaliation was planned by conducting 'careful inquiry' of the religious inclination of students, lest they lurk in 'the shadows of popery'.[55] Prospective students were thus male and Protestant, and also unmarried. Most men, however, busied themselves with more practical and immediately profitable matters than higher education, and with wives. Even lairds and nobles who could afford to send their sons to college largely chose not to before the seventeenth century, unless they were intended for a clerical career. The secularisation of university life, despite Elphinstone's hopes, was achieved only slowly.

Some students were attracted from abroad – arts graduates at King's included two Englishmen in 1608 and 1661 and an Irishman in 1638, while William from Bern in Switzerland graduated from Marischal in the 1790s. By then, those from south Britain were joined by the sons of colonial emigrants from America and the Caribbean.[56] Nevertheless, both King's and Marischal remained essentially regional institutions, with complementary catchment areas. Students from the Highlands and the north tended to enrol at King's, while Marischal drew more heavily on students from Aberdeen, Aberdeenshire, Kincardineshire and the Northern Isles.[57] It was a predominantly regional élite that attended the Aberdeen colleges.

The exclusivity of the student body was emphasised in a raft of regulations regarding conduct.[58] Most important, in underlining that students inhabited a world apart from the rest of society, were the orders which governed language, dress and accommodation. Students were expected to converse in Latin or Greek. At King's, Hebrew was added to the list of acceptable languages for discourse, at the instigation of the principal, John Row, in the mid seventeenth century, though by then Elphinstone's notion of permitting French too had been abandoned. Those who reverted to the vernacular encountered a beating.

Linguistic exclusivity (which did much to sharpen linguistic skills) was matched by a distinctive dress code. Modelled on clerical garb, students wore academic gowns, an enduringly ostentatious legacy of the religious mission of early universities. There were other reminders of this too, most obviously the importance accorded to prayer. The original religious focal point of King's was the chapel, constructed on the north side of the college. Before the Reformation services were held frequently throughout the day, every day. The academic community was not required to attend every one of these occasions – though it would assemble on a daily basis for compline, before supper, and more frequently on Sundays and feast days. Attendance at religious services remained an important element of post-Reformation student life too, though in Old Aberdeen the focus for such occasions was largely shifted to St Machar's Cathedral and the public school on the east side of the college. The chapel, meanwhile, was relegated to housing *ad hoc* functions, including graduation ceremonies.[59] Marischal students attended the burgh kirk of St Nicholas – but they did so not as individuals, but as a community, processing according to elaborately defined rules.

The academic year lasted from October to April, with graduations moved in the later seventeenth century from July to May. During term, the quasi-monastic nature of student life was particularly apparent with regard to accommodation arrangements. Students were prohibited from receiving visitors after dusk and those students who absconded for a nocturnal tryst elsewhere were punished – at Marischal by a public flogging. College laws reflected a wider concern for moral rectitude too. Drunkenness, gambling and fornication were especially frowned upon and those who indulged in such practices faced expulsion – to the hissing of their peers at King's. More innocuous exploits – such as swearing, slopping out from windows and, that eternal bugbear of the middle-aged, noisiness – were met with reprimands too. A regime of this nature relied upon policing and this was the responsibility of the college hebdomadar, assisted by trusted student censors. But it also relied upon students continuing to live on campus, in easily policed environs.

In 1505, Elphinstone had provided bursaries for five theology students and thirteen arts students, who were to reside on campus.[60] By the 1530s, this accommodation was located adjacent to the staff quarters, on the south side of King's, in seven rooms named after the signs of the Zodiac. Furniture was spartan. According to an inventory of 1542, 'Aries' included only a bed and a kist. Some rooms had two or more beds and others a cupboard, trestle table, desk and chair as well – though by 1753 only bedsteads, tables and chimney grates were provided.[61] Lighting was provided by candle and oil, an annual supply of candles costing King's £2 in 1712-13, with another £3 due for oil.[62] Meals were consumed in a hall located on the eastern side of the college. Much of the food and drink was prepared in the college kitchen or brewhouse, though as early as 1504 ale was also being bought from Gilbert Piot, a local brewer. By the 1540s, most ale and bread were bought in, while local women who made oat-bread and ale seem (despite ordinances to the contrary) to have routinely wandered into the college precincts to sell their wares. The content of more substantial meals – breakfast, dinner and supper were served in college – depended on seasonal availability, though the purchase of various types of meat and fish and, above all, expensive spices such as saffron, suggests that college residents ate well by comparison with other sections of society. There was, however, variation in the amounts that they consumed. In 1753, poorer students were normally served bread and ale for supper, while the wealthier adorned their plates with an additional selection of eggs, pancakes, meat or fish.[63]

The areas on the east and south of King's were to remain the focus of on-site domestic life throughout the period, though by the 1730s the lodgings on the south side had been demolished and replaced by a three-storey building, in which staff and students resided above new classrooms (Plate 33).[64] The on-campus accommodation, however, was not large enough to house all students, especially with the modest increase in numbers evident from the seventeenth century. Even in the sixteenth century, the New Foundation for King's had recognised that some might live externally, though this was a trend which staff periodically viewed with dismay. Their views were no doubt partly motivated by the financial consideration of lost rents, though to this must be added a genuine, if snobbish, concern that residence outwith college encouraged idleness and immorality, through interaction with 'many temptations from low or bad company'.[65] The eighteenth century witnessed a number of attempts to curtail external residence, save in 1753 for those who had found lodgings with staff. One eminent teacher, the philosopher Thomas Reid, noted the restrictions with evident approval: 'We need not but look out of our windows to see when they rise and when they go to bed,' he recorded.[66] Nevertheless, such intrusive oversight was not welcomed universally. Students voted with their feet and numbers at King's declined, forcing the authorities to renege on their attempt to monopolise the daily life of their charges.[67]

Lodgings outwith college were readily found and often cheaper than those on campus. William Grant, a Marischal student, paid his landlady, Mrs Shand, £3 10s a quarter in 1768-9, with an additional £1 per annum for laundry. Mrs Shand evidently provided a home for several students, for she was simultaneously receiving rent from Charles Ogilvie, another Marischal student.[68] Indeed, it was not unusual for several students, often from the same part of the country, to lodge jointly. Those who housed them clearly earned a substantial part of their income from such arrangements, though for many landlords student lodgers merely augmented other earnings. In 1769, Alexander Bain resided with a merchant in Old Aberdeen, while in 1783 William Elliott, an English student at Marischal, lodged with a local printer.[69] University staff often made similar arrangements. George Colman, another Englishman, initially stayed with Lucky Lowe, probably the economist (or housekeeper) at King's, though academics offered additional perquisites. Private tuition and moral direction were among those advertised by the King's humanist (or Latin teacher) Thomas Gordon, who, in 1744, resided in Humanity Manse, now the Research Institute for Irish and Scottish Studies.[70]

The gradual migration of students from on-campus accommodation to external lodgings made it ever more difficult to enforce codes of conduct. Indeed, even before the eighteenth century there is ample evidence that many students failed to abide by what their elders expected. The riots of the mid seventeenth century which left Old Aberdeen looking 'lyke a hospitalle' have already been noted.[71]

Individual students who infringed the codes were dealt with by the kirk session. They included several accused of fornication and several more whose sexual liaisons had resulted in paternity.[72]

The attempt to segregate students from the wider community clearly failed. To some extent the expectations of the college authorities were unrealistic, though the experience of Aberdeen was not unusual. Since the Middle Ages students everywhere had an notorious reputation for bawling, brawling, drinking and whoring - which was why many towns refused to house a university. Yet, if by medieval and early modern standards, students constituted an unsavoury community, by modern standards their teachers were hardly paragons. External factors played a part in this, since innovative ideas often caused political offence. Such a climate was hardly conducive to advancing new ideas. Aside from the purging of both Catholic teachers in 1577 and the 'Aberdeen Doctors' in the 1630s, John Row was deposed as principal of King's after the Restoration and James Garden, professor of theology at King's, was removed for failing to subscribe the Confession of Faith in 1697. Even greater purges (of Jacobite-inclined staff) were conducted at both King's and Marischal, following the failure of the 1715 rebellion.[73] Throughout the period, church and state vied to meddle in university affairs and, while the pretensions of the former had been overcome by the eighteenth century, those of government remained deeply entrenched, at Marischal especially. Of the seven professorial chairs established by 1690, five were in the gift of the hereditary chancellor, the Earl Marischal, while appointments to the remaining two (of divinity and mathematics) were made by the town council. Following the earl's forfeiture, in the aftermath of the Jacobite rebellion of 1715, comital patronage was superseded by that of the state.

Nevertheless, external interventions were not the sole barrier towards effective teaching and learning and - given the comparatively dynamic environs of eighteenth-century Marischal - perhaps not a barrier at all. But there were undoubtedly other problems. While Elphinstone had scoured the academic world for suitably qualified appointments, enticing Hector Boece from Paris to become the first principal of King's, in the seventeenth and eighteenth centuries nepotism was rife. By 1690, the King's teaching staff 'was virtually two extended families'.[74] At Marischal, political appointments at least made for a good number of outsiders, who brought fresh ideas with them. At King's, the appointment of a disproportionate number of men from the north-east who had been educated in Aberdeen made for a staid intellectual environment.[75] As we have also seen, several academics regarded their posts as sinecures. Many immersed themselves in institutional wrangles. Despite sixteenth-century prohibitions at both colleges, many devoted their energies to outside bodies, such as the kirk sessions and town councils.[76] Yet others, such as the eminent mathematician Colin Maclauren, who taught at

Marischal between 1717 and 1727, were absent for lengthy periods and frequently distracted by their ambitions of securing more favourable posts elsewhere – in Maclauren's case in Edinburgh.[77]

Success or failure?

Maclauren's brief career in (or rather away from) Aberdeen highlights a number of more general problems which the Aberdeen colleges faced in this period. Many staff lacked either commitment or endeavour. They often had very few students and resources at their disposal rarely matched the requirements of a stimulating academic environment, despite occasional financial assistance from the state. These were not new problems. The dispute regarding the New Foundation may be regarded, partly at least, as a squabble between ideals and reality – between those who wished to maintain the broad range of teaching envisaged by Elphinstone and those who believed that law and medicine could not properly be financed given existing resources. Proponents of the former line of argument emerged victorious, but without ever adequately addressing the criticisms of their opponents. The limited ability of the colleges to replace out-dated instruments and inadequate experimental hardware continued to impair mathematical, scientific and medical studies until 1800.[78]

Solvency remains one criterion by which modern universities are judged. Others include performance in research and teaching. Had the staff of early modern King's and Marischal been subjected to the government sponsored audits of research which their modern successors periodically experience, my co-editor (an assessor) would probably have despaired of his *alma mater*. Internationally renowned scholars, such as the 'Aberdeen doctors' and the philosophers Thomas Reid and James Beattie, were the exception. Less than half of the seventeenth- and eighteenth-century staff are known to have published the results of their research, compared with over three-quarters of those at Edinburgh.[79] It is more difficult to judge the teaching standards since limited publications did not necessarily make for poor teaching. There are signs of curricular innovation to help graduate prospects, such as Marischal's introduction of Arabic and Persian in the later eighteenth century, with a few students taking up career opportunities with the East India Company.[80] Signs of innovation, however, are limited and belated, while indications of conservatism, especially at King's, are strong. In 1799, King's, significantly, was the last of the Scottish universities to abandon regenting, the system whereby one teacher took arts students through the full four years of their course. Marischal had been the second last – in 1753. Aberdeen's universities, we may conclude, were small and undistinguished in European terms.

Viewed from another perspective, however, the history of the two colleges may be regarded far more positively. Although neither King's nor Marischal were at the forefront of consistently trail-blazing teaching and research, their founders had never entertained such ambitions. Elphinstone and Keith had planned to establish centres of learning with a strong regional focus. By this criterion, the colleges were surely a success. They attracted the vast majority of their students from those barbarous parts which Elphinstone had hoped to educate. The loyalty of students and the wider community of northern Scotland to both colleges was expressed in successful public appeals (such as that of 1658 to finance new buildings at King's) and regular bequests for bursaries.[81] This is not to suggest that King's and Marischal were parochial backwaters. In the early sixteenth century, the King's curriculum was modelled closely on that of Paris and the other great international centres of learning in medieval Europe. In the seventeenth century, both colleges were integral components of a network of small, reformed schools, colleges and universities, which stretched from the Baltic to North America, with ideas and influences passing back and forth among them. And in the eighteenth century, the horizons of Aberdeen academia shifted, as Scotland's horizons shifted, towards an engagement with Enlightened ideas, developments in English institutions, and imperial aspirations. The Aberdeen colleges blended their strong regional roots with a wider world vision, thereby providing a fitting environment for a local élite to take advantage of wider opportunities.

16

Contrasting Cultures: Town and Country

MURRAY G. H. PITTOCK

The aim of this chapter is to establish the richness of the north-east's culture. 'Culture' is understood as the totality of the means of human communication and display, with an emphasis on that which transcends the simply functional. In a chapter of this scope, what follows serves chiefly as a descriptive account, reflecting the depth, resource and variety of north-east culture, but there is also an emphasis on a number of underlying conditions, which illustrate the unique qualities of Aberdeen's social, intellectual and geographical environment. One of these is the idea of space, and the special conditions of experience dependent on a compact city deeply interwoven with its hinterland; another is the *mentalité* of what has been dubbed 'the conservative north' (see also Chapters 9, 10 and 11).[1] The third is the special intellectual environment of a city top-heavy with universities and collegiate churches. For the purpose of exploring these themes, Old Aberdeen and New Aberdeen will be treated together, but the distinctive identities of the miniature cathedral city and flourishing trading town will retain a certain heterogeneity.

Ceremonial and civic culture, c. 1300–1560

Aberdeen's origins are outlined in the first two chapters; but from the perspective of this chapter it is important to be aware of the effect of space on human behaviour and cultural relations. At the beginning of this period, most of the inhabitants lived in small post and wattle buildings. By 1317, there was at least one stone house in the Gallowgate, but until the sixteenth century these remained scarce, outside the Chanonry in Old Aberdeen at least (see Chapter 4).[2] Technology was at a low ebb everywhere; and Aberdeen's isolated geographical position led to a tardy adoption of the limited amount available: the town clock on the tolbooth which appeared in 1450 apparently lacked skilled personnel to service it.[3] Prominent water reserves in the lochs and burns drove the town's corn mills. Prosperity and breadth of contacts are indicated by the number of imports from north-east England, the Low Countries, the Rhineland and France (see Chapter 17), while the odd artefact of elephant tusk bespeaks trade from yet further afield.[4] By land, Aberdeen was isolated: it was relatively large as the capital of a rich region but many days' journey from other major centres. (As late as 1740, the journey from Inverness to Edinburgh took Lord Lovat twelve days by coach.[5]) By sea, however, the town was exposed to international contacts on a pronounced scale, and the presence of a cultural interchange which was significantly to shape Aberdeen's experience over the ages (see Chapter 17). By 1348, New Aberdeen was said in Bruges to keep company with Edinburgh, Dundee and Perth as one of the 'four great towns of Scotland'. And by the early fifteenth century, the population of the trading burgh was perhaps in the range of 3,000 to 4,000.[6]

Aberdeen's status as the major northern Scottish town was reflected in the number of royal visits it received. There were five between 1450 and 1500 alone.[7] Preparations for such visits were costly and extensive: middens were cleared from the streets, swine were removed for a fortnight, and the town was decked with branches, herbs, flowers and greenery brought in by the inhabitants. There was a repeated concern to provide a 'reception … as honourable as any Burgh of Scotland, except Edinburgh allenarly, and at as great expence'.[8] The 1511 visit of Queen Margaret could be seen 'as the culmination of the burgh's century-long efforts to achieve pre-eminence among all the Scottish burghs save Edinburgh alone'.[9] Propines of wine, wax and spices were frequently presented, while on the occasion of James IV's (1488-1513) marriage in 1503, a delegation bearing the burgh coat of arms in silver and accompanied by the town minstrels journeyed to Edinburgh. James IV visited the burgh for the first time after his marriage in 1507, when a poem to Aberdeen apparently written by his scribe, the poet William Dunbar (uncle of the future Bishop of Aberdeen), was entered in the town's protocol book, along with some other verse: perhaps the town clerk felt inspired (Ill. 28)![10]

When Queen Margaret visited in 1511, she was presented with a gift of £200, and 'while she remained … the streets were daily decorated with arras work and tapestry', no doubt many of which hung on the 'fore-houses' of the more prestigious dwellings, which offered 'a fine view' from the 'wooden gallery or balcony' which 'frequently embellished' the house-fronts.[11] The processions and pageants which greeted her included the Salutation of the Virgin, the Three Kings of Cologne, the Expulsion of Adam and Eve from Paradise, a representation of Robert the Bruce (1306-29), and a family tree of the Stewart kings, together with 'four-and-twenty maidens all clad in green, of marvellous beauty, with flaming hair, playing on timbrels, singing, and saluting the queen'.[12]

William Dunbar provided 'the sole account of the pageantry' in a poem possibly 'designed for recitation' as a climax to the proceedings. Its apostrophes to the burgh and its queen offer a compliment to both, captured in the rhetoric of some of the most elegant lines ever penned on Aberdeen:

*Illustration 28
Poetry by William
Dunbar.*

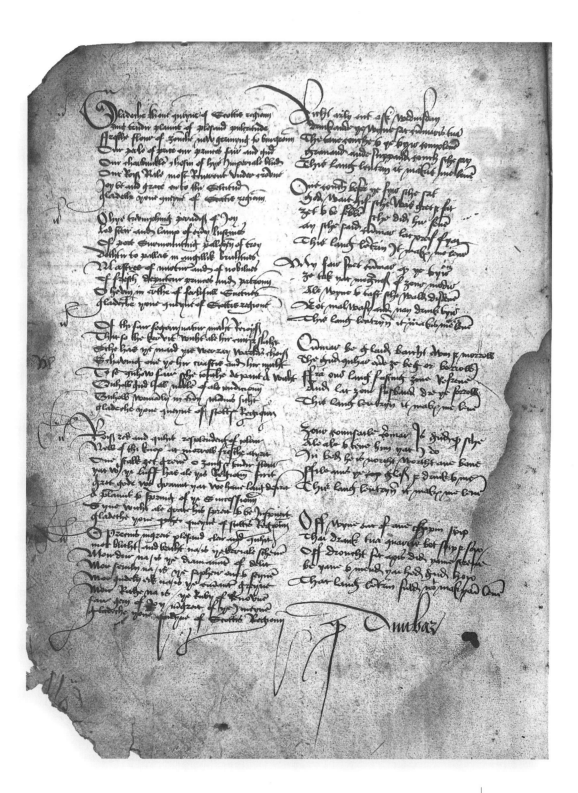

Blythe Aberdeane, thow beriall of all tounis,
The lamp of bewtie, bountie, and blythnes;
Unto the heaven [ascendit] thy renoun is
Of vertew, wisdome and of worthines
He nottit is thy name of nobilnes.
Into the coming of oure lustie quein,
The wall of welth, guid cheir and mirrines,
Be blyth and blisfull, burgh of Aberdein.

And first her mett the burges of the toun,
Richelie arrayit, as become thame to be;
Of quhom they cheset four men of renoun,
In gounes of velvot, young, abill and lustie,
To beir the paill of velves cramase
Abone hir heid, as the custome hes bein.
Gryt was the sound of the artelyie:
Be blyth and blisfull, burgh of Aberdein.[13]

If this was in some ways the culmination of Stewart visits, made at the peak of the power and prestige of James IV's Scotland, subsequent visits remained lavish: in 1527, 'two tuns of the best of new wines' (504 imperial gallons, 2,293 litres) were reserved for James V (1513-42), while in 1562, the sum of 2,000 merks was dedicated to the 'preparatioun and decoration of the town' for the entry of Mary, Queen of Scots (1542-67). The Reformation seems to have made little immediate difference to the level or nature of royal visits, as 3,000 merks were raised to stage 'plays, histories, antiques and such other decorations' for the visit of James VI (1567-1625) in 1579, though sadly he turned back after reaching Dunottar.[14]

Amusement, however, did not require the presence of kings. Aberdeen possessed a strong sense of burghal pride and traditions of public recreation on a significant scale in the period. Dice and gaming counters, discovered by archaeologists, were probably used for gambling purposes, and it is likely that cards were too.[15] More active sporting pursuits included golf and perhaps football - despite several parliamentary attempts in the fifteenth century to outlaw both games in favour of archery.[16] Mystery plays and pageants were also favourite amusements. Indeed, Aberdeen was possibly the first royal burgh in Scotland to mount a stage production, when in 1440 *Haliblude* was produced on Windmill Hill, on the eastern side of the Gallowgate; staging expenses were five merks.[17] On the level of popular celebration, the annual reign of the Abbot of Bon-Accord gave vent to a season of misrule common to much of European culture at this time. The Abbot and Prior, 'Lords of Bon-Accord', headed the craftsmen's procession to St Nicholas Kirk on Candlemas Day, and remained 'masters during their term of office' of revels 'such as the festivals of St Nicholas the patron saint of the town, the first day of May, and Corpus Christi day'.[18] From 1508, the cult of Robin Hood and Little John became intermingled with the Abbot of Bon-Accord in Aberdeen. The cult of Robin Hood was well known in Scotland from at least the early fifteenth century and traces of Robin Hood can be found in the May games of many towns.[19] There are telling clues that perhaps belie the traditional view of the May revels as totally one of 'upturned order'. Significantly, the occasion had the blessing of the authorities: in Aberdeen the town paid the Abbot to fulfil his role (see Chapter 8). The choice of man to lead the common people in their day of dominance is also interesting. In 1445, it was decided in Aberdeen that, due to 'diverssin enormyties in tyme bigane be the Abbitis of this burgh callit Bone Accord', there should be 'nae sic Abbotis'. The position was to be held in future only by the alderman or a worthy bailie.[20] Although the May revels served to release tensions within urban society, they were monitored by the ruling group (see Chapter 8). In spite of this, each successive celebration 'did aye pretent to surmount thair predecessouris in thair ryteous and sumpteous banketings', with a resultant impact on civil order which led to the games being restricted in 1552 and prohibited in 1565 (the Reformation being no doubt influential), though sporadic attempts were made to continue the May amusements.[21]

Cross-dressing and riot continued at Christmas and New Year until at least the end of the sixteenth century, despite a determined and prolonged effort to ban the Yule holiday, resisted by the boys of the grammar school, who held their school by force in order to stop Christmas lessons.[22] Many other customs disappeared under the eye of reform, including the weekly Monday prayers for the dead, announced publicly by a priest 'by ringing a bell through the streets'.[23] From the fifteenth century at least, gravestones might bear the name of the deceased's trade, but dates appeared later, as did 'the custom of attending funerals in black clothes'. The kirkyard at St Nicholas remains rich in early dated stones.[24]

Well-supplied with popular amusements, New Aberdeen also benefited from the presence of major civic institutions as cultural repositories: the kirk of St Nicholas and the grammar school. Only two miles away, Old Aberdeen boasted both a cathedral and from 1495 a university at King's College. These institutions ensured the continuous presence of a cadre of professional men, with a vested interest in the propagation of high cultural levels of education and display, many of whom lived in close proximity in the Chanonry in Old Aberdeen. By 1445, there were almost thirty canons or prebendaries attached to the cathedral, and the foundation of King's College further expanded the numbers of the intelligentsia.[25] In a remarkably persisting tradition, the Chanonry remained a King's College residential precinct until the 1980s. In an era dominated by canon law (see Chapter 17), Old Aberdeen's multiplicity of cathedral appointments offered a major career route to clerical lawyers, many educated in France, the Low Countries or Italy. Just as the closes of old Edinburgh gave birth to the Enlightenment, operating in a confined space, this group produced over time men of extraordinary talent, such as Archdeacon John Barbour, author of *The Brus*, and the humanist Hector Boece, the first principal of King's (1494-1536). Aberdeen, as the seat of a bishop, provided a greater variety of career paths for the clergy, and may even have served to confer on the city's solicitors the historic title of advocate.[26]

The bishopric of Aberdeen had been moved from Mortlach to Old Aberdeen in 1131,[27] and the ensuing development of the city as a diocesan capital was in the long run to benefit both sacred and secular cultural achievement. A palace was built near the cathedral, eventually to be complete with 'a summer house three storeys high, from which a magnificent view of the sea could be obtained'.[28] Bishop Elphinstone's own tomb, probably derived from Antonio Pollulaiolo's tomb of Sixtus IV, erected in 1493 in St Peter's, Rome, is in itself a fitting monument to the enormous impact this gifted pastor had on the culture of his adoptive city, heart of the third richest diocese in Scotland.[29] Not only did Elphinstone found a university; his researches also led to the compilation of a Scots liturgy, the *Breviarum Aberdoniense*, published in 1509-10 with the support of James IV. Hector Boece was probably a member of the 'research team' that made this possible, and it was thus in a sense Aberdeen University's first major research project. Elphinstone's concern for the liturgy was also reflected in the daily singing of Divine Office from 1506 by the twenty vicars choral and six other singers under John Malison as precentor.[30] The bishop's fascination with the story of Santa Maria Maggiore's foundation on the site of a summer snowfall in Rome led him to establish a new parish church of St Maria ad Nives (the Snow Kirk) beside what is now Humanity Manse; the kirkyard still survives.[31]

Within King's College itself, the Gothic woodwork is a tribute not only to local joinery, but perhaps also to Aberdeen's long-standing contacts with Flanders.[32] The intellectual culture surrounding the new university was to reflect the quality of its material equivalent. Elphinstone himself had shown some interest in developing a distinctive curriculum, possibly including 'the exciting possibility of developing Celtic and Udal customary law'. Thus King's was closely linked to, and rose from, the scholarly background of church culture, which had already produced John of Fordun's *Scotichronicon*, subsequently completed by Walter Bower, itself a contemporary prose patriot text which complemented the substantial achievements of John Barbour in verse.[33]

Barbour was born around 1325, and served as precentor at Dunkeld Cathedral before becoming archdeacon of Aberdeen in the late 1350s. His masterpiece (though not his only poem), *The Brus*, was written in 1375-7. It is the first considerable poem in Scots, and a majestic tribute to the patriotism of the Wars of Independence:

A, fredome is a noble thing,
Fredome mays man to haiff liking,
Fredome all solace to man giffis,
He levys at es that frely levys.[34]

Given the considerable role played by the church in Bruce's cause, it was fitting that a priest should write the king's patriot epic, and frame its nationalism in eschatological terms: 'he that deis for his cuntre/Sall herbryit in till hewyn be' (*Brus* II: 343-4). The signs are that the poem did not go unappreciated by Robert II (1371-90), who granted Barbour 'a charter of twenty shillings' on 29 August 1378; a Requiem Mass was held for the author till the close of the fifteenth century.[35]

Barbour's poem is both an epic and a romance, emphasising the qualities of 'chewalry', 'leaute', 'pite' and 'curtesy' as the 'high' virtues of the Scottish knights, and Bruce himself above all. This reinforces the epic scale of their achievement, for, speaking in the voice of great genres recognisable in the west for both their prestige and universality, the poem forestalls any English attributions of disloyalty, treachery, meanness or simple good fortune to the success of Scottish arms: *The Brus* claims Scotland's place in the ranks of fitting subjects for elevated literary treatment on a European scale. At the same time, Barbour hints that the 'high' qualities of Scottish chivalry and courtesy are not the sole preserves of the nobility, for in war the 'symple yumanry' can be as good as a knight.[36] Just as Bruce is the epitome of the virtue of pity, so Edward I (1272-1307) is merciless: as he nears his end, his servants come to him to ask what is to be done with the captured Scots from Kildrummy, and the King replies 'grynnand, "Hyngis & drawis"', the hideous punishment for treason. Edward's lack of mercy is the counterpart of his base assault on the 'noble' virtue of freedom. In his oppression, Edward is unmindful of the state of his own soul: Barbour observes 'How nycht he traist on Hym to cry ... To haiff mercy' when he shows so little himself (*Brus* IV: 313 ff.). Such patterning underpins the moral seriousness of the Scots' intentions, and the triumph of their virtue: but Barbour intends his poem to be a pleasure as well as an exemplar. Right from the start, *The Brus* promises to be a 'delitabill' story in the manner of romance, but one of more value than those which are 'nocht bot fabill', being 'suthfast': the very first verse paragraph making a triple insistence on the 'suthfast' quality of what is being related, and thus the 'doubill plesance' of the truth of Bruce's victory (*Brus* I: i ff). The veracity of texts and authorities was of great importance in Barbour's age, especially to those such as he who were entrusted with the authority of the most sacred text of all, and historians continue to believe that there is good reason for relying on Barbour as a source, albeit one by no means infallible.

Popular and rural culture, c. 1300–1800

The defining role of space in cultural interchange was as important in the case of the rural north-east as it was for the town. If the latter was a concentrated and relatively cosmopolite local capital, with an unusually large and geographically isolated urban professional elite, the former was sizeable, remote (Dee, Don and Ythan isolated east Aberdeenshire from the south, prior to the building of the Bridge of Balgownie) and populated with a strong intermingling of Scots and Gaelic speakers.[37] It was also thickly strewn with folk traditions. Nowhere is this clearer than in the massive contribution made by the north-east to the supposedly 'Border' ballad tradition: 'Buchan … has probably produced at least 50 per cent of all traditional song lore collected in Scotland', while over 30 per cent of Childe's Scots ballads and 'almost one-third of his A-texts come from Aberdeenshire'.[38] The Greig-Duncan folksong collection tells a similar story. The long-standing transmission of such material from the fifteenth, sixteenth and seventeenth centuries can be paralleled more recently in the case of Jacobite songs, many of which appear to have been 'never heard except in the bothies and farm-kitchens of the north-east'.[39] Mar, Garioch, Formartine and Buchan were themselves areas where Gaelic persisted until a relatively late date (it was still spoken in six parishes in the 1730s), and because of the political and ecclesiological outlook of these areas, with Jacobite and Episcopalian sympathies, they were often conflated with the Highlands by eighteenth-century propagandists and later historians. But although most of the Aberdeen hinterland did not lie in the Highlands or, latterly at any rate, speak Gaelic, it was a strongly delineated region, with a distinctive speech from an early date. What is arguably the strongest regional variant of Scots, evident as early as the appearance of 'phippit' for 'whipped' in 'the session records of Elgin' in 1592, was guyed a century later by Dr Archibald Pitcairne: 'Fat ha' they deen? If that be true, we are bout a beik of bees without stangs', while Robert Forbes translated Ovid into Aberdeenshire dialect and authored the oft-reprinted *Ajax's Speech to the Gracian Knabbs. In Broad Buchans* (1748).[40] The marked qualities of local speech and the deep seaming of local traditions were both features which set the north-east apart. Local tales could have a very long life; one possible example of this is the still current story of the sandstorm which buried Forvie, near Newburgh, under a 1,700-acre mini-desert, an event which at least one source has dated to 18 August 1413.[41] Sometimes the stories hint at much older continuities of consciousness, such as the endurance of pre-Christian custom in the practices of the Christian era.

Perhaps the most peculiar and distinctive example of this is to be found in the cultural role of the north-east's especially numerous standing stones and stone circles (see Introduction). These continued to be 'associated in historic times with the administration of justice and other public business'; they were also connected with the 'disposal of the dead whether by burial or incineration'.[42] One of the most curious examples of their use for business is at Old Rayne. Facing on to Bennachie is a stone circle, only a quarter of a mile from the old bishops' summer palace beside which the cross now stands. It is one of the ancient monuments which rings Mither Tap on the mountain's summit, a heartland of military and no doubt religious antiquity; even today a huge Green Man, decked with wildcat and badger, greets tourists at the visitor centre under Bennachie. As late as 1349, the bishop's court was held, in the presence of the earl of Ross, the king's justiciar, 'at the Standing Stones of Rayne'.[43] Stone monuments of this kind (many of which ring Bennachie) were popularly attributed to the Druids; but they were also referred to in more contemporary religious terms, as in the 'Auld Kirk o' Alford', 'Sunken Kirk' on Tofthills Farm in Clatt parish, and 'Chapel o' Sink' on Westerton Farm, Fetternear (in these latter cases it was believed that 'spirits have caused the circle to sink underground'). Other stones were attributed to saints: 'St Brennan's [Brandan's] stanes' at Bankhead near Tillynaught; 'St Marnan's Chair', a standing stone at Banff which is 'all that remains of a circle which stood on the site of the present parish church of Marnoch', and 'St Walloch's Stone', 'close against the outside of the wall of the old church of Logie-Coldstone'.[44] As these examples suggest, both prehistoric and historic standing stones were integrated into the continuing religious culture of the north-east. Other examples include 'the parish church of Midmar, which ... occupies part of the area of a stone circle' and the Pictish stones 'inside the ruined St Fergus Church' (see Introduction).[45] The removal of such stones was reputed to bring ill-luck. There were also other (perhaps connected) superstitious set-asides, such as the 'Goodman's Acre' and 'Halyman's Rig', left uncultivated on farmland as a propitiatory offering of a pagan kind. In November 1646, two men in Strath-bogie were 'accused of sorcery, in alloting some land to the Old Goodman'. Offerings of salt and meal were placed for the 'Goodman'. Notwithstanding this and similar superstitions, many stone circles were removed, though this was apparently a dangerous practice. Horses were reputed to decline going between two gateposts formed of stones removed from Mains of Hatton Circle, Auchterless, while near Auchleven a farmer lost his cattle and was ruined after removing the stones. The 'Devil's Hoofmarks' at Cothiemuir Circle are further indicators of the superstitious side of reverence for these sites, which were on occasion supposed to conceal treasure. They also served as landscape markers, such as the 'Doupin Stane' at Wynford Farm on the marches of Aberdeen where new burgesses were painfully bounced. Flint arrowheads were called 'elf shots' or 'elf bolts', while as late as 1876 a Neolithic mace-head was used as a witch stone to protect cattle in a byre near Stonehaven.

Throughout the north-east there were many examples of the survival of a strongly Celtic religious tradition. As late as 1649, fires were still being lit in Old

Aberdeen on Midsummer Eve, while sacred wells were also in continuing use. 'Hallow Fires' were still being 'kindled on the eve of All Saints' in Buchan up to the 1850s.[46] Visitors to St Fithac's Well in the Bay of Nigg irritated the kirk session in 1630, while 'in 1652, the synod gave injunctions to the presbytery of Turriff, that they should take special notice of all superstitious persons frequenting the Well of Seggat'.[47] Placed under suspicion by the Reformation, even in the seventeenth century however, traditional wells could evade religious scrutiny under the guise of 'taking the waters'. This happened at St Peter's Well at Peterhead after 1636 and at the Spa Well in George Jamesone's 'Four-neukit-Garden' at Aberdeen, which had a reputation stretching back to the Middle Ages.[48] Saints' fairs, such as that at Fordyce (held on 30 October from 1499) and on All Hallows (1 November) from 1592, could be associated with wells or other similar surviving religious practices.[49] They were occasions of major celebration and entertainment, and could go on for days (eight in the case of St Luke's in Old Aberdeen).[50] For those unwell or unlucky enough not to go, the 'fairin' was the term used to describe 'the gifts which a householder would bring home with him for the enjoyment of those who had not shared in the fun of the fair'. There were some real peculiarities among fair customs. 'Sleepy Fair' at Kennethmont, for example, was 'held between sunset and sunrise in June' until the time of the 1745 Rising.[51] Jacobitism itself was reflected in other fairs, such as 'King Charles' fair at Huntly Castle', where, in 1713, the race prize was a sword inscribed 'Pray that the Monarchie and Royall family may be Lasting/ And glorious in thes kingdomes'.[52] Lowrin (St Lawrence) Fair at Old Rayne could be a disorderly occasion (the jougs used that day are embedded in the cross at Rayne), and perhaps even a dangerous one:

> A nivver hid bit twa richt lads
> bit twa richt lads, bit twa richt
> lads, 'it ivver likit me.
> An' the t'ene wis kill't in
> Lowrin Fair, in Lowrin Fair, in
> Lowrin Fair, an' the t'ither
> wis droont in Dee.[53]

The inhabitants of Rayne parish were certainly lively at other times, being 'scandalous' in playing football on the Sabbath in the spring of 1648, for example.[54] But this was at least a common weakness of the flesh, unlike the 'charmes and sorcerie' for which Janet Forbes was arraigned at Alford in July 1663.[55] If witchcraft was no longer regarded as a major problem in Aberdeen by this time (see Chapter 3), this was not so true in the hinterland to the west and north: at Forres, witches were rolled downhill in a spiked barrel, a kind of mobile version of the Scavenger's Daughter.[56]

Other folk customs with which the authorities experienced difficulties included guysing at Alford (1663) and the continuation of fantastic dressing including cross-dressing at Christmas and New Year. Strong initiatives were also taken against 'penny weddings', budget celebrations where all the guests brought decorations and a penny for the fiddler to the bride's father's house. These could be riotous, and perhaps even themselves lead to 'handfast' marriages, which were trial unions of a year's cohabitation: naturally not popular in a Christian society.[57] Buchan appears to have remained markedly attached to its traditions, clinging on to its 'wills o-the-wisp' and water kelpies which 'haunted the fords of swollen streams'.[58] 'Rowan sticks and red thread ... over byre doors and along the eaves of farm touns' kept away the evil eye in Moray ('Raan tree and red thread mak the witches for to spread'), while charm stones were 'dipped three times ... in water from a Fairy Well or in clear running water taken from a burn near a bridge over which the living and the dead had passed'. Whether such practices were sufficient protection against opponents such as Sir Robert Gordon, the wizard Laird of Gordonstoun who allegedly 'had a Fiend imprisoned' in his service in the years before he was 'taken' in 1704, history does not relate.[59]

Beyond the level of the ballads, north-eastern culture was also rich in folk rhymes and sayings, many of them of a chauvinistic nature, such as 'Tak in yer claise-there's a Brechiner !' or 'The deil kept his thumb on Forfar/ When shewin' the rest of the world'.[60] The ambivalent sense of the north-east as a borderland, a place of inter-change between Highland and Lowland, is borne witness to in a number of songs, not least those which are set at the chief focal points of Cairn o' Mount and Bennachie, such as 'Gight's Ladye', 'The Gypsie Laddie' or 'Gin I were where Gaudie rins':

> Oh! gin I were where Gaudie rins, where Gaudie rins, where Gaudie rins,
>   Oh! gin I were where Gaudie rins, at the fit o' Bennachie,
> Oh! I should ne'er come back again (3)
> Oh! I should ne'er come back again, your Lowland lads to see.[61]

In the eighteenth century, this dual role of the north-east as expressed in the Lowland lass/Highland laddie typology of its songs would be projected onto the persons of James and Charles Edward Stuart and the Jacobite cause. Fittingly for the region's pivotal role in the Jacobite century, the troubles which eventually heralded the end of Stuart rule were ushered in by phantom drums at the Barmekin in the winter of 1637-8, which were heard playing the Scots, Irish and English marches. The war in three kingdoms followed soon after.[62]

On a different note, the role of women in north-eastern society also bespeaks the distinctiveness of its culture. Women were probably the primary transmitters of the folk tradition, and played a major role in society, even at an early period, being involved in at least some of the trades of the medieval burgh. At one point in the fifteenth century, eighty-five of the ninety brewers in the town were female (see Chapters 2 and 6).[63] Girls of fifteen were regarded as of an age to 'agree contracts, seal [a charter], alienate and sell lands and possessions',[64] while in later periods they were admitted as simple burgesses. Occasionally, their political roles could be more marked. For example, both men and women voted for the election of the parish clerk of Inverurie on 23 June 1536.[65] Such engagement with social duty suggests the importance of at least some female education (see Chapter 14). Indeed, there was some movement in this direction, for example in 1598, when John Thomson, his wife and another female teacher, were 'authorised to teach "maiden bairns"'.[66] Women themselves endowed such developments. Catherine Forbes, Lady Rothiemay's 1642 mortification 'for the Love I bear to vertue in weemen and to all weemen vertuoslie disposed and ... to the burgh of Aberdein, wherein I was educated and bred the most pairt of my youth' provided for 'ane Woman to be ane Mistress for keeping ane School ... and teaching young weemen and lassis to read ... and any other airt ... whairof they can be capable' (Plate 27). The town accepted these conditions.[67] On 30 January 1734, Lady Braco's mortification provided 'for the maintenance and education of a virtuous sober young woman of a good Character & Reputation', who must previously have attained a proficiency in reading, writing and arithmetic.[68] It appears that such provision was of some efficacy. One deed of 1609 anent the sale of property at Doocot Brae was signed by John Hay 'with my hand at the pen led by the notar under wretin at my command because I culd not wreitt', while his wife signs 'Bessie Black with my hand' (Ill. 29).[69] There is evidence that domestic mistreatment was also attended, as indeed was the case elsewhere in Scotland. In 1691, Old Aberdeen authorities commanded no brewer to sell drink to Thomas Rhind, who was guilty of 'stricking and abuseing his owne wyff and familie, and others his neighbours within the toune'.[70]

A different drum: northern counter-culture, 1560–1750

If the authority of Barbour's text survives to our own day, that of the institution he represented was overthrown in Scotland in 1560; but in this, as so often, Aberdeen's own role was somewhat more equivocal than the ubiquity of established Presbyterianism would subsequently suggest (see Chapter 13). Cultural developments by and large reflected the burgh's equivocal response to the events of the 1560s. Attempts were made to curtail games of bowls, cards and dice and in 1646 three inhabitants of Old Aberdeen were fined for playing golf instead of attending a sermon.[71] These games remained nonetheless popular. Indeed, in 1642 the town secured the services of a manufacturer of golf balls, doubtless intended for those who played on a course at the Links.[72] Meanwhile, despite the Reform-

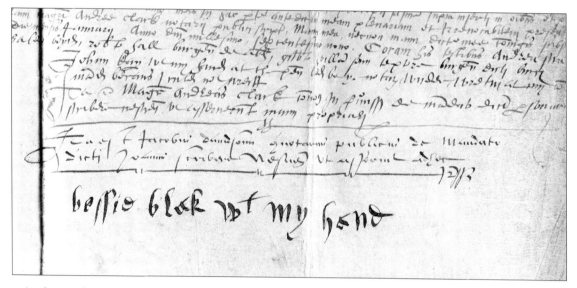

Illustration 29
Signature of Bessie
Black, 1609.

ation's attack on church music, and the decline of the song schools which maintained it, Aberdeen succeeded in maintaining its own school for a longer continuous period than any other Scottish burgh. Its composers, John Futtie and John Black, 'gained great renown throughout Scotland'. Ejected at the Reformation, Black received his place back around 1579, when James VI was making efforts to restore the condition of song schools in Scotland. Black may have composed pavanes and galliards for the court, and the tradition he exemplified was borne out by the song school's central role in early printings of Scottish music.[73]

The influence of the Reformation was felt in the establishment of a second university, Marischal College, on alienated church property in 1593 (see Chapter 15). The new kirk also enforced more stringent discipline and made repeated efforts to put an end to street festivities. Among these was included the practice of flyting, or the ritualised contest of insults, an interesting example of a popular practice which was also found in high culture, especially at court. Major flyting poems survive from both William Dunbar in the reign of James IV and Alexander Montgomerie in the reign of James VI, and a form of the custom may even have survived into the twentieth century.[74] By-laws against flyting were promulgated by the Old Aberdeen authorities in 1608 and 1644.[75] If flyting disturbed the peace of the streets, all was not quiet in the new kirk either. Charitable collections were made to relieve the poor and those held captive overseas. But toddlers were intransigent in the face of the notion of a godly community, as the kirk session minutes for 20 October 1616 make plain: 'That young bairns, quha are not at the schoole, and ar not of sic aige and dispositioun as they can take thame selffis to ane seat quhen thay cum to the kirk, bot vaig throw the same heir and their in tyme of sermoun, and mak perturbatioun and disordour, be not sufferit to cum to the kirk in tyme of sermoun, bot kepit at hame.'[76] Youngsters were also in 1576 'prohibited from going publickly through the streets' with candles at Candlemas, as savouring of 'the superstitious rites of Papestrie'.[77] If children were the same as ever, other things were changing. The Leper House, situated where the King Street bus station later stood, was falling into desuetude along with the lepers' entitlement to take 'one peat from every load exposed for sale in the market-place' in the Castlegate (see Chapter 3). Following the not uncustomary post-Reformation 'discovery' of large-scale witchcraft, which led to the mass burnings of 1596-7 in Commerce Street (see Chapter 13),[78] the town seems to have been overcome with a fit of common sense. Accused witches began to make counter-complaints of mischief-making, which were investigated.[79] In 1601, an English theatre company managed by Lawrence Fletcher played comedies at Woolmanhill, receiving 32 merks and the freedom of the burgh for their services: they were only one of the 'profane' celebrations still being used in civic amusement after the Reformation.[80]

In the aftermath of King James' removal to London in 1603, the bishop's court at Aberdeen became part of the network of cultural centres which collectively became a 'castle culture', serving in partial replacement of the loss of the Scottish court. Patrick Forbes of Corse, bishop from 1618 to 1635, was a distinguished figure who did much to cement the cause of episcopacy in what was now a flourishing city. Bishop Forbes developed the teaching of ecclesiastical history at King's and revived the old links between the staff and the church, suggesting that regents should proceed after six years 'to the charge of parochial cures'. His new chair in divinity formed the core of the movement which became known as the Aberdeen Doctors, and it was under them at King's that James Sharp, son to the sheriff clerk of Banff and future Archbishop of St Andrews, received his training.[81]

The printer Edward Raban moved from St Andrews to set up the 'first press which had ever crossed the Grampian line' in the Castlegate, becoming printer to King's and publishing much distinguished local work.[82] Raban's successor John Forbes was responsible for *Cantos, Songs and Fancies* (1662), 'the first book of secular music to be printed in Scotland ... with an introduction on the theory of music by Thomas Davidson', master of the song school. Forbes politely (and, hopefully, truthfully) described Aberdeen as 'the Sanctuary of the Sciences, the Manse of the Muses, and Nurserie of all Arts'.[83] It was certainly flourishing, providing the king with no fewer than three royal appointments.[84] Some English writers even came north: in 1618, John Taylor, the Water Poet, was the earl of Mar's guest. He appears to have been rather struck in a proto-Romantic way by the sublime scale and emptiness of west Aberdeenshire. Taylor thought it

a large country, all composed of such mountaines that Shooter's hill, Gads hill,

Highgate hill, Hampsted hill, Birdlip hill or Malvernes hill are but mole hills in Comparison, or like a liver, or a gizard under a capon's wing ... [no] habitation for any creature but deere, wilde horses, wolves, and such like creatures.[85]

If, however, Taylor was impressed by the earl of Mar's hospitality, there were still other, less civil, magnates lurking in the north-east. One Garioch laird's marginalia proclaimed: 'This day oor Jock stickit Glaister o' Glack's auldest son,/Glory be to God the Father, God the Son and God the Holy Ghost', while on a higher literary plane, the ballad *Edom o' Gordon* recalled the burning of Margaret Campbell, wife to the laird of Towie, with twenty-six others in Corgarff in 1571.[86] Indeed, the ballad tradition of the country reflects the strength and savagery of some of these 'unfortunate rencontres' between the local gentry. *The Fire of Frendraught, The Baron of Brackley* and *The Battle of Corichie* are only three of these. The eponymous Brackley's foe, Farquharson of Inverey, was supposed to be 'in league with the powers of darkness' owing to 'the miraculous expedition with which he could sweep the cattle away from a fertile district': *'Deil scaup wi' Fiddie'* became a proverb. *The Battle of Balrinnes* uses a familiar mode of reportage of the battle, famous from songs such as *The Haughs of Cromdale* and *The Sherramuir Fight*:

> On Towie Mounth I mett a man
>   Well grathed in his gear:
> Quoth I, 'Quhat newes?' then he begane
>   To tell a fitt of warre.[87]

Dr Arthur Johnston (1577-1641), *medicus regius* to James VI and sometime rector of King's, also held positions at Heidelberg, Sedan (where he was professor of logic and metaphysic in 1604) and La Rochelle. Johnston was, together with men like Thomas Reid, Latin secretary to James VI,[88] at the core of an essentially Scoto-Latin intellectual culture in north-east Scotland, which endured in some form until the death of Dr James Melvin in 1853; Thomas Ruddiman (1684-1757) was another of its leading exemplars.[89] It was associated both with the preservation of Scottish court culture in the age after the loss of the court in 1603, and with a patriotic discourse of essential or authentic Scottishness, which came into its own after 1707. In it, the Union and the overthrow of the Stuarts were seen as acts of collective disloyalty to a past of valour and simplicity, like that of Republican Rome before it was corrupted by the gold of empire. The beginnings of this critique were already evident in the seventeenth century, when poems like Johnston's lament for the earl of Stirling's absorption in English court culture, or his 1626 poem on the rupture of the Auld Alliance, foretold the shape of things to come.[90] Among such serious forebodings were works of more humorous chauvinism, such as 'De Pluvius Anglicanis et Scotia Serenitate', which celebrated Scottish weather during a two-month period of rain in England. Very much out of touch (as was not unusual in the north-east) with the tensions leading up to the National Covenant of 1638, Johnston even dedicated a version of the Psalms to Archbishop Laud.[91] Nor was he the only important exemplar of this distinctive milieu. Thomas Dempster (1579-1625), professor at Nimes and historiographer royal to James VI, was a strong Scottish patriot and Catholic, knighted by Pope Urban VIII, while James Kennedy's poem 'Aeneas Britannicus' was a forerunner of the Vergilianism which surrounded the cult of the Stuarts until well into the eighteenth century.[92] There were many others, in an efflorescence of Latin poetry which can be detected in the numerous elegies for Bishop Forbes when he died in 1635. Two hundred and fifty years later, Sir William Duguid Geddes rightly remarked of these ignored Scoto-Latinists that their 'cultural productions' were 'such as no other city in Scotland, or even in the British Isles' could match in the first half of the seventeenth century.[93]

At this time too, George Jamesone (c. 1588-1644), the son of a master mason in the town, became Scotland's first modern portrait painter. Following the securing of a commission from the king in 1633, he became well-to-do and two years later gave the burgh its first public park (see Chapter 11).[94] Jamesone proved to be the first of a dynasty of considerable Aberdeen painters, including his great-grandson John (1686-1766) and great-great-grandson Cosmo Alexander (1724-72), both of whom were Jacobites. Both studied in Italy, as did William Mosman (1700-71), who used a camera obscura to obtain his 'panoramic view' of the Dee in his *View of Aberdeen* (1756) (which decorates the cover of this volume).[95] The essentially pre-Union roots of the Scottish Enlightenment can also be seen in the activities of men such as George Dalgarno (1626-87), one of many contemporary seekers after a 'universal language', and in the career of Dr Robert Morrison (1620-83), 'King's Physician, King's Botanist and Superintendent of the Royal Gardens under Charles II'.[96] A second local man, Sir Alexander Fraser, also served as Charles II's (1649-85) physician, while Dr Patrick Abercromby (1656-1718) was physician to James VII (1685-89), and the famous Dr John Arbuthnot (1667-1735), friend of Alexander Pope, served Queen Anne (1702-14) in the same capacity. Arbuthnot is credited with inventing the quintessentially English icon of John Bull in its modern form. Both Arbuthnot and Abercromby had Jacobite connections; the latter wrote *Martial Achievements of the Scottish Nation* before joining the Stuart war effort in 1715.[97]

After 1688, Jacobitism was strong in Aberdeen and the north-east, where Jacobites proved particularly ready to join armed insurrection, thousands being involved in both risings, women as well as men (see Chapter 12). Ten women were returned as fencibles for the Jacobite forces in Peterhead in 1715, and supplied with 'ane sufficient gun, charged with powder and bullets, and ffor shots besides, and ane sufficient sword'.[98] After the failure of the '45, women carriers and such redoubtable local figures as Barbara Strachan, 'the Jacobite postmistress of Buchan', created a network which kept the fugitives informed of government movements, and thus secured them from capture. Chris Guthrie, the wife of George Cumine of Pitullie, who may have given her name and feisty nature to the heroine of Lewis Grassic Gibbon's *Scots Quair* (1932), took a more direct method of protecting her husband's life by pouring boiling water into his boots so that he could not fight.[99]

After the risings, there appears to have been a protective attitude among the continuing authorities to their Jacobite exiles, as well as support among the community for domestic fugitives. The artist Cosmo Alexander, who had fled the town in the aftermath of the '45, was sustained by Jacobite networking. In 1754, he inherited the London house of his fellow-Jacobite, Aberdeen architect and grammar school former pupil James Gibbs (1682-1754), the designer of West St Nicholas Kirk and the Radcliffe Library, whose career had been launched under the patronage of the earl of Mar. Gibbs was a close friend of Dr William King, one of the leading English Jacobites, who made explicit their common culture through a rabidly Jacobite speech at the Radcliffe's opening.[100] Despite being ensconced in London, Alexander was dependent on Scottish commissions. One of them was the 1756 portrait of the earl and countess of Findlater commissioned by the burgh authorities from their errant son, for which Alexander was paid £1,047 Scots.[101]

William Meston (*c.* 1679-1745) was the city's foremost Jacobite poet. Master at Aberdeen Grammar School and professor of philosophy at Marischal before the '15, in which he served as governor of Dunottar, Meston subsequently entered a downward spiral of scrounging, unsuccessful schoolmastering and drink, a victim of the cause's failure and his own personality. In the household of the Countess Marischal until 1729, he subsequently set up schools at Elgin, Turriff and Montrose. All failed. Tutor to Oliphant of Gask in 1736, his drinking forced a departure into poverty and final decline, though he was still composing Latin songs in praise of the provost and burgh in 1744. His poem, *Mob Contra Mob*, deals with the rabbling of Deer in 1711, when Episcopalians stoutly resisted the intrusion of a Presbyterian incumbent; as late as 1710, there were still 113 Episcopal incumbents north of Tay, twenty years after disestablishment![102] Meston apparently also tried his hand at folk styles (he allegedly wrote 'The Bonnie Laddie' while skulking in the Cabrach),[103] as did others such as Lord Duffus, who reputedly penned the Jacobite version of the song 'The Broom of Cowden Knowes' in 1716, and Murdoch McLennan, the minister of Crathie, who allegedly wrote one version at least of 'Sheriffmuir'.[104]

Among the balladeers of the period, one of the most famous was Charles Leslie, 'Mussel-mou'd Charlie', a staunch Jacobite who reputedly died at the age of 115 (possibly 95 or 105) in 1782. Leslie's stamping-ground was Aberdeenshire, Banffshire, Forfarshire and the Mearns, and may even have served as the role-model for Skirling Wattie in Violet Jacob's novel *Flemington* (1911), which charts the importance of the '45 in her own family's history. Indeed, Leslie was reputedly so popular in

Aberdeen, that 'he enjoyed a monopoly of his calling, no other person being allowed to sing in the streets of the town'.[105] When questioned in prison about his songs, 'Charlie' used to reply thus:

Q: Where had he got them?

A: Where they were cheapest.

Q: Who printed them?

A: Nobody.

Q: Why did not he sing other songs?

A: Because they would not buy them from him.[106]

Leslie might have been right: a significant number of Jacobite songs appear to have been popular in eighteenth-century Aberdeen, including 'This is not my ain hoose', 'John Roy Stewart's Rant', 'Lochyell is gane to France', 'Push about the Jorum', 'Jenny Cameron', 'White Cockade' and 'Charlie Stewart'. There is some commonplace-book evidence that these were generally permissible songs in Aberdeen long before their once-rebellious politics became more widely acceptable early in the nineteenth century.[107]

Jacobite artefacts were in local use, as well as Jacobite songs, among them silver buttons with white roses on them, pincushions with the names of those who died in the '45 and swords with inscriptions such as 'St Andreas Prosperity to Scotland No Union God Save King James The VIII'.[108] Aberdeen was also involved in the subsequent cult of romantic Jacobitism. When the Jacobite period came to be depicted in later years, models from local families were often used – for example as in S. W. Brownlow's famous 1868 picture of a baptism conducted by an imprisoned Episcopalian minister in Stonehaven tolbooth. Indeed, such was the tradition in these families that within living memory girls curtsied to the dean of Brechin and children were taught that Charles Edward had been their rightful king.[109]

Cultural innovations of very different origins were also beginning to have their impact in this period. Bowling was introduced from England after 1660, while in 1667 a twice-weekly 'foot post was established between Aberdeen and Edinburgh' at a cost of 2s Scots a sheet.[110] In 1700, George Cruickshank was granted a nineteen-year tax-free licence to 'set up a coffee-house for the sale of coffee, tea and chocolate', while the first hotel at Ship Tavern on the Shiprow was opened by Patrick Copland in 1709. Cruickshank's commercial innovation and tax exemption did not prevent him from becoming a tax collector for the Jacobites in 1715, one of the numerous examples of modern and commercially-minded Jacobites recently discovered; another more famous was Brigadier Mackintosh of Borlum, top graduate of King's in 1677, whose manifold schemes for improvement included the establishment of a college of agriculture.[111] Agricultural improvement crossed political boundaries, both on the large scale implemented by Sir Archibald Grant of Monymusk and the more elegant and domestic designs of Pitmedden Garden (1675), which were ultimately copied from Versailles, and Crathes Castle's yew hedges and formal garden, begun in 1702.[112] Sophisticated levels of silversmithing were becoming evident, both in the disc end spoons of Thomas Moncur in the seventeenth century, and later in the distinctive toddy ladles of John Leslie (1774-1837).[113] The unusually full early list (for this period) of jewellery sales in the Cochran and MacPherson papers in the City Archives indicates a flourishing community of customers for such artefacts, in a business naturally sustained by an increasingly prosperous population.[114]

Altering Enlightenment, c. 1750–c.1800

The growth in wealth and leisure manifest in such design and consumption found its cultural reflection in the participation of Aberdeen's growing *bourgeoisie* in the by-products of the Enlightenment era. It has already been clearly demonstrated that Aberdeen's role in the intellectual developments of the eighteenth century was much more profound than has historically been assumed. Aberdeen was important, if not pre-eminent, in the Enlightenment period in a number of ways. In the fields of divinity and history, Alexander Cruden (1701-70) compiled a *Complete Concordance of the Holy Scriptures*, the first work of this kind, while Fr Thomas Innes of Aboyne (1662-1744), vice-principal of the Scots College in Paris, was responsible for setting the history of the Scottish monarchy on a more critical footing than that of the old myths of Fergus and misty antiquity, which can still be seen in the 1684-6 Holyrood portraits of the Stuart dynasty. Ironically, himself a Jacobite from a Jacobite area, a Scots exile and a Catholic, Innes undermined the mystique of Scotland's status as the oldest monarchy in Europe, a belief which had sustained the special claims of the Stuarts.[115]

In the field of language, *An Essay on the Origin and Progress of Language* (1773) by James Burnett, Lord Monboddo (1714-99) was one of the first works to explore the topic in a modern manner. Monboddo became famous for thinking that orang-utangs and men were related. He was part of the Enlightenment movement towards regarding language as the reflection of culture, and 'polite language as an indispensable element in civilised culture', a view which in its turn led to assaults on the direct, mordant and bawdy elements in Scots which reflected a society unassimilable to metropolitan value. In this context, Monboddo saw 'the central position of language as a factor in the evolution of humanity', and with this in mind became the first to write in English on the position of language in 'undeveloped societies'. For many Enlightenment writers, Scotland was one of these, and the teleology of civility they espoused amounted, in fact, to submission to English speech and manners as the most 'civilised' available.[116]

In science, Sir James McGrigor helped found the British Army medical service,[117] while the Gregory family, beginning with James, whose *Optima Promota* (1663) contributed substantially to the development of the reflecting telescope, formed a remarkable academic family over a number of generations (see Chapter 8).[118] In the field of military technology, the Rev. Dr Alexander Forsyth invented the percussion lock in 1768, becoming by this 'the first to substitute fulminate for flint as a means of igniting the charge of gunpowder', while Patrick Ferguson (1744-80) patented the breech-loading rifle in 1776, 'which was capable of firing seven shots a minute and sighted for ranges 100 to 500 yards'.[119]

It was in philosophy that Aberdeen arguably achieved its greatest eminence in the Enlightenment period. Thomas Reid's (1710-96) *An Inquiry into the Human Mind. On the Principles of Common Sense* (1764) established the Scottish philosophy of 'Common Sense' and 'influenced the shapers of the American republic'. Reid and the 'Common Sense' school in their turn owed a great deal to the medieval university curriculum, and the patterns of thought it represented.[120] The application of reason to knowledge, so central a part of the whole Enlightenment enterprise, was best expressed philosophically through Reid and his school. Their conception of their discipline enabled it to relate to other modes of intellectual enquiry, without claiming essentially more privileged ways of 'knowing', accessible through philosophy alone, as writers as diverse as Hegel and Russell were to do after them. Common Sense's view that all premises in arguments are ultimately bald claims (Beattie's 'Principles which must be believed on their own Authority'), so that the most extravagant chains of metaphysical reasoning in the end rest on mere assertion, carried in it the powerful (and democratic) implication that legitimate premises must rest in consent: it was associated with the rise of the democratic intellect, and the ripening in the Scottish university system of a pattern of general educational enquiry fructified by philosophical methods. Its achievements and influence were thus prolonged in length and international in scope; yet they had their roots in the confined spaces of the Lemon Tree Inn and the Red Lion pub in the Spital, where they may now almost be forgotten.[121]

Alexander Gerard's (1728-95) *Essay on Genius* (1774) explored the idea of a 'science of human nature', George Campbell's (1719-96) *Philiosophy of Rhetoric* (1776) intersected with literary study in ranking 'among the most important rhetorical treatises in the Western tradition', while James Beattie's (1735-1803) *An Essay on the Nature and Immutability of Truth* (1770) struck a blow against the scepticism evident in Hume's view of the inherence of inductive reasoning in all models of causation.[122] Beattie's own moral premises bore out a contrary commitment to absolute value and dignity, as his misleadingly-titled *On the Lawfulness and Expediency of Slavery* (1778) bears witness:

> There is something in slavery which fills a considerate mind with horror. That a man, a rational and immortal being, should be treated on the same footing with a beast, or a piece of wood, and bought and sold, and entirely subjected to the will of another man, whose equal he is by nature, and whose superior he may be in virtue and understanding; and all this for no crime; but merely because he is born in a certain country, or of certain parents, or because he differs from us in the shape of his nose, the size of his lips, or the colour of his skin: if this be equitable, if it be excusable, if it be pardonable, it is vain to talk any longer of the eternal distinctions of right and wrong, truth and falsehood, good and evil.[123]

Beattie was not the only local figure to hold such views. James Ramsay (1733-89), a Fraserburgh man, a King's graduate and a 'life-long friend' of Reid's, was a keen abolitionist who published two works on slavery in the 1780s. His *An Address on the Proposed Bill for the Abolition of the Slave Trade* (1788) influenced Wilberforce's attacks in the Commons. A firm advocate of the view that 'the black race is equal to the white in ability', in that same year Ramsay was a witness before the privy council inquiry into slavery.[124]

Remarkably, all these works (Ramsay's excepted), as well as the books of other figures such as John Gregory's *A Comparative View of the State and Faculties of Man With Those of the Animal World* (1765) and James Dunbar's *Essays on the History of Mankind in Rude and Cultivated Ages* (1780), grew out of the 'discourses' of the Aberdeen Philosophical Society, whose members met between 1758 and 1773 in the Lemon Tree or the Red Lion. The Society, which grew out of earlier philosophical (1736) and theological (1742) clubs, lived up to the generous dimensions of contemporary intellectual endeavour in discussing 'economics, education, epistemology, government, law, literature, medicine, moral philosophy, religion, and the physical sciences'.[125]

Just as the heavily-populated, yet enclosed and isolated, professional environment of Aberdeen had made major contributions to the intellectual and cultural achievements of the two burghs in earlier times, so it did in the eighteenth century (see Chapter 8). George Campbell was educated at Aberdeen Grammar School and Marischal, where he was later principal; Thomas Reid was likewise at the Grammar and Marischal, where Gerard and Beattie were also educated: all three held university posts, while Gerard became moderator of the General Assembly in 1764. The universities which bred them were themselves developing all the time, 'a museum of natural history' was established at King's in 1754.[126] At the same time, the neglected educationalist David Fordyce, also educated at the grammar school and

Marischal, proved through his *Dialogues Concerning Education* a noteworthy influence on the English dissenting academies. Fordyce favoured a rounded and liberal educational system including 'architecture, the experimental sciences, philosophy, history, and geography' at a time when classics still dominated the curriculum. An advocate of sporting as well as intellectual education (his 'culture of the body'), Fordyce also appears to have been the first to argue for student-centred learning.[127] At the same time, by a sad and curious paradox, just as its leading educationalists were developing distinctively Scottish forms of intellectual inquiry, the curriculum at King's began to display a strong tendency to 'endorse and promote the British state and constitution'. Beattie expressed the contemporary Anglophilia in the 1770s, in statements such as: 'the English have a generosity and openness of nature, which many of us want'.[128] Nonetheless, there was (especially at King's) a strongly continuing traditional culture, which manifested its contemporary expression not only through the Elphinstone birthday celebrations, with their lashings of claret and punch,[129] but also in the teaching of such as the Blackwells, 'the younger of whom ... was a pioneer of primitivist thought'.[130] Not everyone was dedicated to the life of the intellect, however. William Forbes, reflecting on his deposition from the post of dominie in Peterculter in 1732 due to his irregular habits, admitted that:

> And to attend he was not willing
> His school, sae langs he had a shilling
> But lov'd to be where there was filling
> Good punch or ale ...[131]

The major literary achievement to emerge from the north-east in the eighteenth century (if we exclude the declining fortunes of James Beattie's once-famous *Minstrel* (1771)) was the 'Ossian' poetry of James Macpherson (1736/8–96), whose *Fingal* (1761) and *Temora* (1763) gave rise to a Europe-wide cult of Celticism. Macpherson's own cultural milieu was that of a Badenoch Highlander who had witnessed some of the conflict and destruction of the '45; intellectually speaking, his time at King's College had brought him into contact with the Scoto-Latin ethos. Inheriting the image of the classicised Highlander of Jacobite patriot rhetoric, Macpherson's inspired presentation enabled him to place oral Gaelic poetry within the lineaments of classical epic and the contemporary cult of sentiment. Just as the earl of Mar had, in 1730, proposed 'two outsize statues in Highland dress' for the 'Tuscan Doric' façade of his house in Alloa, so the classicism of the Doric heartland gave Macpherson the intellectual equipment to clothe and inflate the Ossianic songs of his own culture into the size and guise required from the epic hero by scholarly opinion. He did so by creating 'A tale of the times of old' and 'the last of the race' in an elegy on the culture of his background voiced through that of his education.[132] When Macpherson donated a copy of his translation of the *Iliad* to King's College library in 1776, it was perhaps in obeisance to the training which had given Ossian a voice in which the educated eighteenth century could recognise the familiar, though he spoke of the exotic.[133]

The more general culture of Aberdeen was also developing at a rapid rate. The *Aberdeen Journal* (Plate 36), launched in 1747, was to endure for over 200 years, while Aberdeen also began to produce innovative journalists, such as James Pirie (Perry), the future editor of the *Morning Chronicle*. The harbour, drained at the beginning of the seventeenth century by David Anderson ('Davie do a' thing') was now capable of more thorough utilisation, and overseas travel became commonplace among the more moneyed and educated inhabitants (see Chapter 7). At a 1787 graduate reunion, a quarter of former students in the city had had experience overseas.[134] Some of these became men of considerable influence. Henry Farquharson, for example, a don on the staff of Marischal in the 1690s, helped to found Russia's first naval academy, 'supervised the building of a highway' from Moscow to St Petersburg, 'published the first Tables of Logarithms in Russian', surveyed the Caspian, published textbooks and became a Russian brigadier.[135] Many other northeast Scots were involved in military service or the cause of improvement in Russia, building on Aberdeen's traditional outlook towards the Baltic (see Chapter 17).[136]

Within Aberdeen, clubs and societies, not only intellectual, but of professional, social and other kinds, began to form, including Gordon's Mill Farming Club (1758) and the Aberdeen Musical Society, which began its life ten years earlier.[137] In 1785, the Aberdeen Merchant Society, with its 'idea of a Chamber of Commerce', was inaugurated, with an entry fee of three guineas and and annual subscription of 10s (Ill. 30).[138] Circulating libraries also developed: in 1765, Angus & Son's Castlegate library had 1,150 items: by 1779, it had 2,330. Ten years later, Brown's library opened in Broad Street, the two merging in the early nineteenth century into the stock of a United Public Library.[139] The Society of Advocates founded its own library in 1787.[140] Publishing developed significantly, though it still lagged far behind Glasgow, where nine times as many titles (2,000 as against 230) were published in the eighteenth century.[141] Leisure pursuits of all kinds were clearly on the increase, with (for example) racing taking place at Banchory-Devenick.[142] Post-chaises were introduced in the early 1760s; the golf club was founded in 1780;[143] and the provision of bathing machines and the decision to erect public baths were signs of continuing urban improvement.[144]

The rise of the Musical Society, which held its first public concert at Old Trades Hall in 1748, took place at a key period in the cultural development of this new environment, perhaps assuming some of the enthusiasm which had maintained the song school, which itself survived far into the eighteenth century. Andrew Tait, organist at St Paul's Episcopal Chapel and master of the school from 1740, was one

Aberdeen 17. *Dec.* 1785.

SIR,

IT has been repeatedly recommended to the Committee of Burgesses, to frame a set of rules, upon liberal and equal principles, for the purpose of establishing a MERCHANT SOCIETY, which should combine in it, though on a small scale, the idea of a Chamber of Commerce, and whose general fund should furnish a branch for the annual support of such members as, by unforeseen misfortunes, might be reduced to circumstances which might require such aid.

To this, it was supposed, a FUND might be annexed, for the benefit of the Widows and Children of such members as might also choose to enter as contributors to this last fund.

The Committee have accordingly prepared a set of rules, on general and liberal principles, for the formation, and establishment, of THE ABERDEEN MERCHANT SOCIETY, and as the out-lines of its constitution.— In this they have been careful to secure the right of every individual, by giving him a vote, not only in the election of all its officers, and in the admission of every future member, after the society is established, but also in every material transaction of the society.——It may, perhaps, be proper to observe that the principal rules of this society, so far as circumstances would admit, are framed on the rules by which the Chamber of Commerce at Glasgow is established, altho' much more limited with respect to the entry-money, and annual payments.— Every institution for an association of this nature must be attended with beneficial consequences, not only to the members individually, but to the commerce of every town where it takes place; and, indeed, it has long been a matter both of surprize and regret, that in Aberdeen, where almost every other description of men are already associated, no such establishment has been made by the Merchants and Manufacturers.—— The present is only a foundation; but as it is upon liberal principles, no doubt, in time, considerable advantages may be derived from it.

As you have already signified your approbation of the design, it is intreated that you will meet, with other gentlemen who have also seen the out-lines of the plan, in the Concert-hall, Queen-street, on Monday evening the 19th curt. at 6 o'clock, in order to elect a Court of Directors, and to recommend to them certain other necessary measures, for the establishment, and improvement, of the Aberdeen Merchant Society. We are, Sir, with due respect,

Your humble servants,
Alexr Leslie V.P.
Jno Crum jror y

A short ABSTRACT of the RULES.

I. As soon as fifty merchants and manufacturers have signified their approbation of the design, they are to meet to choose a Court of Directors, fifteen in number, who are afterwards to elect, from among themselves, a President, Secretary, Treasurer, and Clerk. (N. B. Upwards of seventy have already expressed their approbation of the design.)

II. Four Trustees are to be chosen by the company, for the security of their property, till they shall obtain a charter, or some other public establishment.

III. The entry-money of each member to be Three Guineas, and an annual payment of Ten Shillings, for the support of the common fund.

of the leading lights of the new society in its early days.[145] The Musical Society was associated with the careers of a number of noteworthy figures. Perhaps the most prominent among these was Francis Peacock (1723-1807), 'sole dancing-master within the burgh' from 1747, who brought a mind trained in French dancing to the examination of Highland reels,[146] and thus became, on at least one view, the father of modern Scottish country dancing, carrying out the classic Enlightenment process of applying reason to knowledge. The dancing-master's role was not simply that of an instructor in the subject, but also, as was explicitly stated on the appointment of James Hunter in 1721, that of a 'Teacher of Manners and good breeding'.[147]

The enclosed world of Aberdeen was already responding to the 'civilising' penetration of English manners which followed the Union. Later in the century, Enlightenment influences similarly brought more abstracted and general formal practices to bear on such local customs as dancing: by the 1780s, the Highland Society of London (a titular juxtaposition which would have sounded most incongruous only thirty years before) began to institute competitions in Highland dancing.[148] Peacock himself was a supporter of native music, as is evidenced by his *Fifty Favourite Scotch Airs* (1762). Scots songs (as in Edinburgh and Glasgow) formed an important part of the Society's performances; yet even so 'a protest' was 'made by the members … that their national music was not being given an appropriate or timely position on the programmes'. Despite its prolonged success, interest in the Musical Society waned towards the close of the century, and it predeceased Peacock, collapsing in 1801. The site of the dancing-master's house, where the town council waited on James 'VIII' in 1715, is recalled in the name Peacock's Close in the Castlegate.[149]

Change in the physical landscape of Aberdeen, now with a population of over 10,000, was marked. Unlike heavily tenemented Edinburgh, Aberdeen had been more likely to have dwellings which retained gardens, until the 'building boom of the 1760s' created 'a network of courts, back-buildings and purpose-built tenements' (see Chapter 4). Timber and thatch finally gave way (save in Futty) to stone, infill brick, pantiles and slates; from 1730, granite was being quarried, though it was not cut for some time afterwards. Robert Gordon's College (1730) was designed by William Adam, and in 1758 a new grammar school building was sited on Schoolhill (see Chapters 14 and 18). Education was an increasing concern: in that same year, the kirk session of St Machar 'gave their official encouragement and support' to the training of midwives (see Chapter 3). Industrial development also prospered, for the Don's 'steep gradient' proved a good site for the water power needed to drive textile and paper mills. Enlightened improvement subjugated topography into civility, a condition illuminated when in 1795 the Aberdeen Police Act 'appointed thirteen commissioners to supervise services such as lighting, cleansing, and water supply'.[150]

*Illustration 30
Proposals to establish The Aberdeen Merchant Society, 6 December 1785.*

Life in Aberdeen and its hinterland still displayed the lineaments of tradition, for all the innovations of the eighteenth century, including the strong economic development of both fishing and whaling (see Chapter 7) and the rise of the Huntly linen industry. Wildlife was being pushed to the margins: forty-four wildcats were killed around Braemar and seventy eagles destroyed on Deeside in the ten years following 1776; but human experience still retained its traditional contiguities with animal life.[151] In January 1753, Alexander Martin of Westertoun, near Huntly, was charged with stealing and slaughtering an ox: 'he was wrapped in the ox hide by way of a great-coat, with the horns properly placed'. Eight years later, an advertisement placed in the *Aberdeen Journal* for 9 March 1761 evidences the continuation of 'a widespread belief in the curative properties of goats' milk for consumption and kindred ailments'.[152] A poor state of healthcare encouraged these beliefs: in one Kincardineshire parish in 1792, 20 per cent of deaths were from smallpox and consumption alone, while mortality through injury was also very common, reflecting the harshness of life (see Chapter 3).[153] More established urban communities could feel increasingly distant from the traditional condition of life on their doorstep. In 1789, a subscription was launched in Aberdeen to relieve the effects of a distemper then prevailing in Futty. Its language betrays a mix of Enlightened charity and a distaste for the medieval living conditions of the neighbouring fishing village: 'As in most other fishing towns in Scotland, there are dunghills of the most putrid materials collected in pits dug for the purpose before every fisherman's door in the town ... during the prevalence of any disorder that has the least putrid tendency, it never fails to prove a most aggravating circumstance.' In the midst of such odours, it was surely a mark of the burgh's civility that an appeal of this kind was launched: Futty was finally improved in the early nineteenth century.[154]

In the country, despite the pace of improvement driven forward by such figures as Grant of Monymusk, much of the pace of life changed slowly. The reaping scythe, for example, was not introduced into the north-east until 1810.[155] Traditional punishments were also still in evidence: as late as 1834, there was an attempt in Huntly to practise legally the punishment of 'Riding the Stang', a public humiliation inflicted on fornicators and adulterers.[156] In the folk tradition, suspicion of the new more mobile habits of an increasingly high-spending and ostentatious British aristocracy was on occasion given vent, as in the ballad 'Miss Gordon o' Gight', written against the 1785 marriage of Byron's mother:

> O, whare are ye gaun, bonnie Miss Gordon,
> O, whare are ye gaun sae bonnie and braw ?
> Ye're gaun wi' Johnny Byron
> To squander the lands o' Gight awa.

> Your Johnny's a man frae England jist come,
> The Scots dinna like his extraction ava,
> But tak' ye gude tent, for he'll spen' a' your rent,
> And fast draw the lands o' Gight awa.[157]

Religious life settled down more into the pattern of that of the rest of Scotland, although in 1792 the burgh did petition parliament in favour of the Scots Episcopal Church, still partially outlawed. Roman Catholics became slowly more active with the passage of time, acquiring the Jacobite shipmaster Alexander Scott's house in 1762; his property eventually became the residence of the Vicars Apostolic.[158] Methodists visited the town in 1761 but, in common with the rest of Scotland, did not win over many adherents.[159] There were strong geographical variations in confessional strength: for example, three fishing villages in Fetteresso parish were virtually wholly Episcopalian, as were Dunottar and Kinneff, with their strongly Jacobite history; Dounies, Portlethen and Findon, on the other hand, were almost wholly Presbyterian.[160] In Aberdeen itself, changing religious attitudes reflected the gradual impact of modernising developments in the period. In 1751, an attempt to bring a company of comedians to the town was short-lived, meeting with opposition from both magistrates and clergy. Another attempt was made with better success in 1768, and by the close of the eighteenth century a theatre had been established.[161]

By 1800, the culture of Aberdeen was strongly reflecting general trends in Scottish society. The autonomy of religious and political approach which had once characterised the old, isolated, regional capital was no longer so evident, though Old Aberdeen and areas of the north-east hinterland retained some of these traditional characteristics. At the same time, Aberdeen was making its own distinctive contributions to the new patterns of thought emerging in Scotland. If many of the changes of the eighteenth century reflected general shifts in *mentalité* concerning social habits and urban conditions, the strong intellectual climate of the city remained, as it always had been, an important part of its ability to maintain a heterogeneous distance from fashion. No large metropolis which was not a national capital, it might be claimed, possessed such a substantial body of educated people and provision at a distance so great from any rival. Nor could any other then boast two universities. Just as the north-east's wealth by land and sea served to establish a separate character in the communities of the hinterland, so Aberdeen's cultural life continued to benefit from an unusual degree of self-sufficiency derived from its status as chief market of that hinterland and the major centre of educational and professional opportunity for almost half of Scotland's land area.

Part V

PRE-MODERN ABERDEEN AND BEYOND

17

Aberdeen and the Outside World

DAVID DITCHBURN *and* MARJORY HARPER

Medieval Aberdeen was the last bastion of civilisation. According to a thirteenth-century map drawn by the English monk Matthew Paris, it was the only town on the Scottish mainland between Arbroath and Caithness. Similarly, on the famous thirteenth-century *mappa mundae*, now in Hereford Cathedral, Aberdeen is the most northerly specified location on a British Isles which lurks ominously close to the circumference of the world (Plate 37).[1] But the town lay on another frontier too. For the fourteenth-century Netherlandish writer Jean Froissart, Aberdeen was on 'the borders of wildest Scotland'.[2] Some who resided in Scotland were of a similar opinion. Describing the visit of two English clerics in 1218, the chronicler of Melrose Abbey commented that they reached Aberdeen, 'in deepest Scotland'.[3] And even in 1495 William Elphinstone, architect of the town's first university, depicted Aberdeen as an oasis, set amidst a population which was 'rude, ignorant ... and almost barbarous'.[4] For Elphinstone, Froissart and Cistercian chroniclers, all of whom had been reared in a world of French cultural domination, barbarity was to be equated with Gaeldom. Towns, meanwhile, were agents and indices of civility. And, from a southern perspective, there were few worth mentioning beyond Aberdeen.

Maritime bonds

Like any oasis, Aberdeen was attractive. In the view of one late thirteenth-century Englishman, its 'faire castell' dominated a 'good towne upon the see' and, although the castle was soon to disappear, later visitors generally concurred with the anonymous Englishman's opinion. In the early fifteenth century, John Harding, another Englishman, deemed it 'a goodly cytee [and] marchaunt towne' and his fellow countryman, Thomas Tucker, rated it as 'noe despicable burgh' in 1655.[5] Yet, beyond these bland compliments, few visitors (Defoe excepted) discerned much in the urban landscape to warrant detailed comment. Some noted the presence of the university, though an English observer of 1562 did so with implicit disdain, remarking that it was merely 'one college with fifteen or sixteen scholars'.[6] Others tended to elaborate upon the town's seaside location, rather than its size or appearance. Froissart, for instance, remarked upon an apparently timber-built jetty at the harbour.[7] The Frenchman Jean de Beaugé, following his visit in 1548, commented at even greater length on the harbour. So, in the following century, did both Thomas Tucker and Richard Franck.[8] Even the Englishman Sir William Brereton, who in 1636 considered the Brig of Balgownie to be one of the 'fairest bridges in Scotland', felt it necessary to relate this marvellous fourteenth-century construction to the sea, noting that ships of between fifty and sixty tons could still pass up-river under the stone built construction.[9] Harbours and rivers were the town's gateway to the outside world.

Aberdeen's original port was probably at the sheltered mouth of the Denburn, though by the medieval period harbour facilities were already located slightly to the east, along the north shore of the Dee. It was not an easy harbour to negotiate. Beacons (to guide ships) were installed only towards the end of the fifteenth century and a dangerous sand bed lay close to the mouth of the river.[10] Some ships failed to avoid such hazards. Wrecks necessitated the redirection of the town's trade through Futty between 1430 and 1434 and again between 1447 and 1451. During the intervening years, in 1444, a Danzig barge and a hulk had been wrecked at the harbour and a Spanish vessel came to grief in 1484.[11] Despite these examples, many of the ships which frequented the harbour were of local origin. By 1365, they included the bishop's vessel, the *Seint Marie*. In 1464, one of its successors, a 140-ton carvel, was docked in the Flemish port of Sluis, the port of Bruges; it is perhaps to be identified as the *Christopher*, which the bishop leased to an Aberdeen merchant in 1459.[12] Both ships, we may note, were named after saints, a habit which pre-Reformation secular ship owners normally copied too, sometimes with an eye to local favourites. The *Nicholas* of Aberdeen, for instance, is recorded in 1523.[13] We do not know who owned this particular vessel, but ownership of others was often shared. Quarter stakes in two ships are recorded in 1458, and in 1512 Elizabeth Sinclair sold her twenty-fourth part of *The Bark* to Thomas Riddel.[14] After the Reformation, ships were normally given secular names, but despite the change in nomenclature their size did not increase greatly: even in the mid eighteenth century those which dominated Aberdeen's North Sea and Baltic trades were of little more than forty tons.[15]

Most sailors were probably of local origin and by 1598 sums were levied to support the town's 'auld aget and decrepit masters and mariners'.[16] Nevertheless, there seems to have been a shortage of local sailors in the seventeenth century and in 1614 the town council manned the Aberdeen fishing vessel *Stella* with a Dutch crew.[17] Meanwhile, incoming foreign vessels often heralded the influx of alien mariners; they were sometimes rowdy, like the Danes who vandalised a cart in 1515.[18] Such incidents, however, were comparatively rare, not least because in European terms Aberdeen's harbour was relatively quiet. Between 1327 and 1333, an average of thirty-five vessels left Aberdeen annually with customed goods, slightly more than the equivalent number in the 1680s. In times of recession, vessel movements were considerably lower than these two snapshots would suggest. Between 1410 and 1420, for instance, an average of fewer than five vessels departed annually with customed items.[19] Likewise, the number of foreigners active in the port was modest. Although aliens purchased about 20 per cent of the wool exported between 1331 and 1333, later customs accounts reveal only limited foreign mercantile dealings in the town. Only five foreign-owned consignments are, for instance, clearly identifiable in the customs accounts of 1522-4.[20]

Once at sea, passengers and crew often faced a lengthy journey. In the medieval centuries, journeys between Scotland and the Low Countries sometimes took only a week but at other times as long as a month.[21] By the eighteenth century, transoceanic vessels spent considerably longer at sea. Jonathan Troup, who left Aberdeen on 5 December 1788, did not arrive in Dominica until 11 May 1789, having departed from England four and a half months previously (Ill. 31). A whaler that set sail from Aberdeen for Greenland on 18 February 1791 did not return until 12

Illustration 31
An eighteenth-century sailing ship.

August.[22] The time spent at sea increased the chances of both natural and man-made mishap. In 1448, a London-bound vessel was driven by gales onto the Dutch coast, and similar tales of woe were reported on the English coast.[23] Even in later centuries, by when technological innovations had led to the construction of sturdier ships and more accurate navigational tools, some vessels still fell foul of stormy weather. The Greenland-bound whaler of 1791 was blown by storms as far south as Arbroath.[24] Political enemies and pirates posed a further hazard. Aberdonians were not averse to seizing foreign vessels themselves, notably during the recession of the early fifteenth century, but on occasion they too were victims. In 1462, compensation was sought from Bremen in Germany for goods which had been captured 'in the last raiss maid til ye estland'; and in 1627 the Aberdeen merchant Andrew Burnett, together with the crew and cargo of two local ships, languished in a Dunkirk prison while negotiations went on for their ransom.[25] It was wise to take precaution against possible attack. The gathering storm over the American colonies led William Brebner & Co. to furnish their two-year old ship, *The Hercules*, with eight carriage guns for its voyage to Grenada, Dominica, Barbados and Jamaica in January 1775. And during the conflict with France nineteen years later, agent Charles Gibson intimated that the *Consolo* would sail from Aberdeen to Portsmouth, in order to join a convoy before proceeding to Grenada.[26]

Incidents and circumstances such as these (and many more could be cited) posed a threat to the livelihood, and sometimes the lives, of mariners and passengers. On a few occasions, however, the entire community was also directly affected by foreign aggressors. In 1153, a band of Norsemen, led by the Norwegian king Eystein Haraldson, reputedly plundered the town.[27] This was probably the last occasion on which hostile Vikings attacked the Scottish east coast, though it was not the last occasion on which foreign armies reached the north-east. In 1336, English forces (arriving by land and sea) are recorded as levelling the town to the ground. Another English force which arrived at the outset of the Cromwellian occupation in 1651 treated the town more kindly; perhaps this was because the council treated the army officers to a civic banquet to stave off the fate that had earlier befallen Dundee, which had been ransacked and looted.[28]

Further danger came from microbes rather than men. In 1497, it was noted that 'infirmity' – probably syphilis – had come from France (Fig. 3.1), while in 1500 'sekness' (perhaps plague) was discovered aboard an incoming Danzig ship; its passengers were quarantined until the nature of the disease had been identified (see Chapter 3).[29] Aberdeen was perhaps peripheral to the Eurocentric world, but it was clearly not isolated. Distance, however, had its advantages. The town was less likely to suffer foreign attacks than many others further south; and the limited volume of Aberdeen's maritime traffic probably meant that Aberdeen was less prone to the import of deadly diseases than busier ports.[30]

Religious bonds

Clergymen were among the earliest of the town's inhabitants who might be expected to have possessed some appreciation of the wider world. The mission of Christianity was universal and all those who entered holy orders would, to some degree, have been versed in an understanding of the world that transcended national or local boundaries. It is worth remembering that Christianity was not indigenous; its very presence in Scotland was the fruit of foreign missionaries, many of them Irish. In later centuries, the internationalism of the medieval faith was underpinned by both ecclesiastical structures and educational experiences. In Scotland, from 1189 (or perhaps 1192), when the Scottish church was declared to be a 'special daughter' of Rome, until 1472, bishops were directly answerable to the pope. Aberdeen's bishops were in frequent contact with the Holy See. Several - such as Hugh de Berham (who in 1272 journeyed to the Italian city of Orvieto) and Gilbert Greenlaw (who in 1390 probably visited Avignon) - were consecrated abroad. Subsequently, most were also liable to pay taxation to the *curia*. Different means were devised to transfer money safely. Some bishops dispatched proctors to deliver their dues to the papal treasury. Henry Lichton (bishop from 1422 to 1440) initially authorised his brother to act on his behalf in such matters, though by 1428 the dean of Aberdeen, James Scrymgeour, had been entrusted to pay 350 florins to the papal treasury on the bishop's behalf. But in the 1430s, Lichton (and others) also made use of the nascent European banking network, delivering his by now long outstanding debts through Florentine bankers with whom he presumably had made contact in the Low Countries.[31]

Consecration and taxation aside, bishops were frequently in communication with the *curia* regarding other matters. Even in the thirteenth century, the long arm of papal justice stretched into remote Scottish glens, as popes appointed judges to settle disputes in Scotland in order to save litigants the expense and ordeal of travelling to the *curia*. Aberdonian clerics often found themselves nominated to settle squabbles in a neighbouring diocese; in 1504 a marital case involving two consanguineous partners in Moray was referred to the Aberdeen bishop, William Elphinstone.[32] Sometimes, Aberdeen clerics found themselves involved as a party to litigation, as in 1250 when four monasteries questioned Bishop Peter Ramsay's attempt to limit the sums which monastic appropriators exacted from their vicars.[33] Comparatively few papal powers, however, were devolved in this manner and many approached the papacy directly to supplicate for favours or to seek justice. Henry Lichton sought papal permission to admit twelve illegitimate boys to holy orders in 1427; and towards the end of his career, in 1436, he begged permission to be excused a diocesan tour of inspection since he was 'so broken in body that he cannot travel without bodily harm'. In the intervening years, too, he supplicated the papacy and, more frequently still, witnessed others seek papal confirmation of his own grants.[34]

As the papacy's powers to appoint clerics to ecclesiastical office expanded rapidly in the fourteenth and fifteenth centuries, clergymen were increasingly drawn to the *curia* in their quest for patronage. For several Aberdeen clerics, the *curia* was far from a strange environment. Greenlaw probably spent several years at the papal court after he graduated from Paris in 1374, as did Ingram de Lindsay, bishop from 1441 to 1458, who had reportedly secured a position in the papal chancery in 1423.[35] By then the pope was as likely as the bishop of Aberdeen to appoint clerics in the diocese. It was with exasperation that in 1466 Bishop Thomas Spens supplicated Pope Paul II (1458-64) for permission to appoint priests to ecclesiastical benefices which fell vacant in the months of February, April, June, August, October and December.[36] In other months this right was reserved to the pope. Bishops, it has been claimed justifiably, had become the 'harassed agents of popes'.[37]

The clerical elite was part of a genuinely international class in others ways. While graduate status was not a prerequisite for high ecclesiastical office, from at least the thirteenth century onwards most of medieval Aberdeen's bishops received part of their education at university. Before 1412, higher education meant foreign education. A few, such as Peter Ramsay (bishop from 1247 to 1256), learnt the finer subtleties of their faith in England, in his case at Oxford.[38] Ramsay probably also spent time studying in Paris, then the most famous university north of the Alps. Following the Wars of Independence, clerics more frequently ventured in that direction than towards England. Paris was particularly renowned as a centre of theological study and it was this curriculum which was pursued by, among others, John de Rate, bishop from 1350 to 1354×5.[39] Canon law, too, was taught at Paris. It was this which William Elphinstone, already an arts graduate of Glasgow, studied at Paris from 1465-70, before proceeding to Orléans (the foremost French school of civil law) from 1470-71.[40]

Education did not cease on the acquisition of a comfortable ecclesiastical position. The senior clergy of the Aberdeen diocese had access to a well-stocked library in their local cathedral and books continued to bond Aberdeen and the outside world. John Barbour, archdeacon of Aberdeen from 1357 to 1395 (and possibly a law graduate), was fully versed in the international best sellers of his day in French and Latin, which he quoted in his own great work *The Brus*, written *c.* 1375. It is likely that Barbour was also familiar with the tomes penned by Augustine, John Duns Scotus, Thomas Aquinas and other theologians which were kept in the cathedral library. We know for certain that Barbour borrowed a copy of the Decretals, because, it was subsequently noted, he failed to return it.[41] The impressive cathedral collection included other compilations of canon law and also commentaries on them, written by some of the foremost legal minds of the twelfth, thirteenth and fourteenth centuries, including Giovanni d'Andrea, William Durand, William of Monlezun, St Ramón of Penyafort, Henry of Segusio, Tancred and Geoffrey of Trani.[42]

These laws, and the discussions of them, were no matter of mere academic

Illustration 32
Manual for the
instruction of priests
(1492), published in
Cologne and
purchased by
William Elphinstone.

interest. Canon law was international law and its remit extended into the realms of marital and sexual relations, business practices and defamation, as well as any matter involving a clergyman. The collection of legal tomes housed at St Machar's Cathedral thus provided a tangible set of guidelines for the conduct of many aspects of daily life which were as applicable to Aberdonians, as they were to Christians everywhere in Christendom. In an era when literacy was predominantly a clerical preserve, there remains an élitist whiff to the study of such texts. Nevertheless, since their application was more general, it would be a mistake to believe that the cosmopolitan experiences of the ecclesiastical élite were merely personal adventures and of little wider significance. In 1491 alone, for instance, three couples from the diocese of Aberdeen took their supplications regarding marital relations to the papal penitentiary.[43]

In other ways, too, episcopal encounters overseas rubbed off on the wider population. Very probably while abroad on diplomatic business in 1496, Elphinstone acquired a manual for the instruction of priests which had been published at Cologne in 1492: priests in his diocese were, we may presume, instructed in much the same way as their counterparts in the Rhineland (Ill. 32).[44] Other local clergymen acquired religious texts from the continent too - notably the elaborately decorated Netherlandish Books of Hours produced in the fifteenth and sixteenth centuries and the epistolary commissioned by Bishop Gavin Dunbar (1518-32) from an Antwerp workshop in 1527 (Plate 19).[45] These were valuable commodities and a gloss on the Psalter, published in Strasbourg and acquired by Aberdeen Cathedral in 1488, was chained to the choir to prevent theft.[46]

Even those unable to read cannot have escaped the internationalism of their own culture. Many of the major ecclesiastical festivals were as common to continental Europe as they were to Aberdeen. Corpus Christi Day, for instance, was marked in Aberdeen from at least 1440 by a dramatic performance: the origins of the cult of Corpus Christi lay in the Low Countries (see Chapter 13).[47] Churches in Aberdeen were adorned with statutes and artistic depictions of saints, such as Mary and Anne, who would have been as familiar to foreigners as to locals. An even stronger reminder of saintly power came in the form of their collected relics. By 1436 the cathedral's assemblage of saintly artefacts included a hair of St Edmund of Abingdon, the bones of various saints associated with the Middle East - Catherine (probably of Alexandria), Helen, Isaac the Patriarch and Margaret (possibly of Antioch) - and also Marian, Petrine and Pauline wares.[48] Edmund's relics may well be a reflection of Peter Ramsay's devotions, for the thirteenth-century bishop was perhaps a pupil of St Edmund's at Oxford and, more certainly, a visitor to the saint's shrine at Pontigny in France in 1249.[49] Acquisition of the Middle-Eastern relics is more difficult to ascribe, but they were perhaps collected by a pilgrim or crusader who had ventured to the most holy of all sites, Palestine. The familiarity of

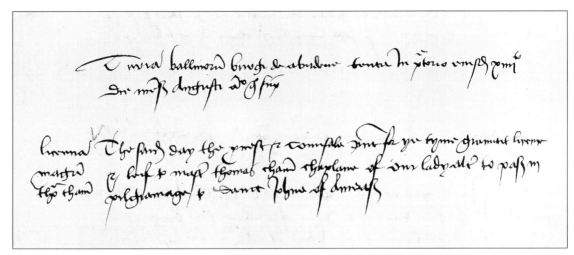

medieval Aberdeen society with the Holy Land is attested by the text *De passagio ad terram sanctam*, which was stocked in the cathedral library by 1464.[50]

Given the expense and distance of travel to the Middle East, most pilgrims made do with shrines nearer to home. Most of these would have been local. It is striking that the extensive archaeological excavations in the city have failed to uncover any of the trinkets, badges and souvenirs commonly obtained at the greatest foreign shrines. Yet some pilgrimages by Aberdeen clerics to celebrated foreign shrines are recorded. In 1363, Bishop Alexander Kininmund intended to make a pilgrimage to the shrine of St Thomas Becket at Canterbury in England. Shortly afterwards, two of his subordinates had similar notions. In 1365, John Barbour received an English safe-conduct to visit St Denis, near Paris, where the tombs of many of France's kings were to be found. In the following year, Adam de Tyningham, the dean, planned a visit to Amiens, in northern France, one of three locations which allegedly possessed St John the Baptist's head – also the location chosen by the chaplain Thomas Chalmers in 1506 (Ill. 33).[51]

Laymen, too, undertook pilgrimages. John Leith, perhaps the same Aberdeen burgess who often traded in England, received an English safe-conduct to undertake a pilgrimage to the popular destination of Amiens in 1363, while in 1445 Alexander Stephenson, who suffered from worms and sores on his feet, travelled to Canterbury.[52] There he was miraculously cured and, after dancing joyously for three days, he expressed his gratitude for divine intervention by planning another pilgrimage – to Wilsnack in Germany, which rose to fame after miracles were reported at the local church in 1383. In Stephenson's actions we can identify two motives to explain the quite voluntary, yet extraordinary lengths to which medieval men and women went in their quest for God's grace: the belief in divine cure and the quest for miracles.

*Illustration 33
The provost and
council grant
Thomas Chalmers,
chaplain, permission
to undertake a
pilgrimage to
Amiens, 14 August
1506.*

These were contacts which could not long survive the Reformation. The abolition of papal jurisdiction, the denunciation of imagery and the condemnation of conventional acts of piety were to sever many of Aberdeen's continental connections. Before 1560, Catholics had travelled abroad as pilgrims or supplicants in positive affirmation of their faith. Thereafter, recusant Catholics (such as the schoolmaster John Henderson) ventured abroad as exiles in search of shelter – in Henderson's case to France in 1573.[53] Catholicism was now a religion under threat. Yet the new religion could provide no substitute for the religious unity of earlier centuries. Calvin's Geneva lacked the eternity of St Peter's in Rome and precious few Scots, let alone Aberdonians, can be found in the Swiss town after the mid sixteenth century.[54] Although £960 6s 8d was collected in Aberdeen in 1623 for 'the distressit kirk in Franc', ultimately sympathy for their co-religionists floundered on the divided affiliations amongst Episcopalians and Presbyterians, Calvinists, Lutherans, Anglicans and many other sects.[55] Some, it is true, attempted to provide Protestantism with coherence, notably the Edinburgh minister John Durie in the 1630s. During Durie's extensive continental travels, he approached a multitude of Danes, Dutch, English, French, Germans, Irish, Poles, Prussians and Swedes, but in Scotland only Aberdeen academics and Edinburgh ministers, to achieve his irenicist ends.[56] It was to no avail. Religion had been nationalised.

Commercial bonds

Trade was the *raison d'être* of a medieval town and the second group of Aberdonians who forged contacts with the outside world were those involved in commerce. The horizons of pre-seventeenth century sailors and merchants were more limited than those of contemporary clerics. The attention of clerics was focused on faraway Rome (or, for a time, Avignon). By contrast, traders initially confined themselves to the North Sea world. Quite when these contacts began remains uncertain, but they were already well established by the later thirteenth century, when Aberdonian wool (presumably from the town's hinterland) was one of four types of Scottish wool differentiated by the authorities of St Omer.[57] Aberdeen's trade was probably boosted by the Anglo-Scottish war of 1296–1328. For much of the conflict Aberdeen was the only significant Scottish port which remained in anti-English hands, firstly during the Comyn ascendancy (to 1305) and then following Robert I's (1306-29) capture of the town in 1308 – which was apparently aided by the German merchant Herman Clipping.[58] In these years German merchants frequently delivered supplies to the resistance, though their trade was probably a carrying one which linked Aberdeen not with the Hanseatic towns of the Baltic, but rather with the Low Countries. It was the towns of Flanders and Artois that provided the biggest market for the town's principal exports of wool,

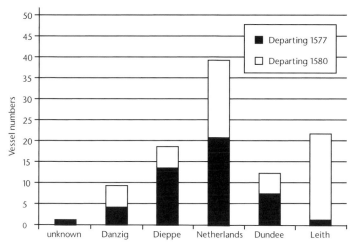

Figure 17.1
Destination of ships
departing Aberdeen
in 1577 and 1580
(bar chart).

leather and fish and the most likely source of food and weapons for the Scottish resistance. And the Low Countries continued to dominate Aberdeen's trading links until the seventeenth century.

The first detailed insight into the town's trading links survives from 1499-1500.[59] In that year, nineteen vessels left Aberdeen with customed goods, twelve bound for the Netherlandish port of Veere, five for England and two for Dieppe in France. As indicated in Figure 17.1, by the end of the sixteenth century the destination of vessels departing for the continent with customed goods was not greatly different. Even in the 1680s, over 31 per cent of departing ships still made for the Netherlands.[60] While other Scots increasingly focused their Netherlandish trade on the developing port of Rotterdam in Holland, Aberdonians clung trenchantly to the old staple port of Veere in Zeeland. Even in the second half of the eighteenth century, the vast majority of Aberdeen's increasingly lucrative stocking exports was sent to Veere.[61]

The continued dominance of the Netherlands trade is striking, and all the more so when compared with figures for other Scottish ports, such as Leith and Dundee, which diversified their commercial contacts to a much greater extent and much earlier than Aberdeen. The prime reason for this Aberdonian conservatism was economic (see Chapter 6). Wool remained a much more important element in Aberdeen's trade than it did in the trade of other towns and the main market for wool remained the cloth-producing towns of the Netherlands. And it was still in the Low Countries that Aberdonians acquired most of their imports (Fig. 17.2).

Some indication of the importance which Aberdonians placed on the import trade is afforded by a council decision of 1449 to dispatch David Menzies to Flanders 'in al haste to by a schipfull of salt and fracht a schip to this burgh'.[62] Local sources of salt were limited, but its supply was vital to a town where the economy relied

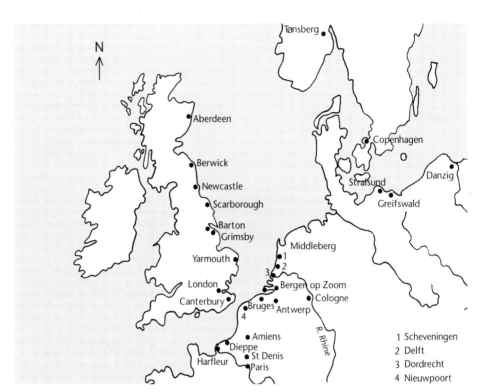

Figure 17.2
Aberdeen's foreign
contacts in the
fifteenth century
(map).

N

Tønsberg •

Copenhagen •
O
Danzig
Stralsund •
Greifswald •

Aberdeen •

Berwick •

Newcastle •

Scarborough •

Barton •
Grimsby •

Middleberg
1
2
3
Bergen op Zoom •
Cologne •

Yarmouth •

London •

Canterbury •
Bruges • Antwerp
4

Amiens •
Dieppe •
St Denis •
Harfleur •
Paris •

R. Rhine

1 Scheveningen
2 Delft
3 Dordrecht
4 Nieuwpoort

so heavily on the sale of fish, which could be most easily preserved by salting. Salt, however, was not the only commodity which lured Aberdonians to the Low Countries. Two Aberdeen-bound ships – the *Seinte Marie* of Westkapelle in Zeeland and the other sailing from Sluis in Flanders – were driven by poor weather onto the English coast in 1368 and 1369. Aside from salt, the cargo of the Sluis ship included red wine, woad, three gold rings, two silver cups and other items of silver, while that of the *Seinte Marie* included wheat, herring, gold and silver.[63] Andrew Halyburton's business ledger provides a further insight. He was the Conservator of the Scottish Staple in the Low Countries but also acted as a factor for clients, chiefly from Edinburgh and Aberdeen. These included Bishop William Elphinstone, whose transactions with Halyburton were as much financial as commercial. Between 1497 and 1499 Halyburton bought spices, cloth, canvas and chalices on Elphinstone's behalf in the markets of Bergen-op-Zoom, Bruges and Middelburg – as well as gunpowder, carts and barrows which were presumably used during the construction of King's College. He also paid for a clock to be mended in the Low Countries. All this (to the tune of £57 12s 5d) was financed by the bishop's export of wool, salmon and trout, valued at £72 19s 4d. Halyburton's financial dealings on behalf of the bishop were greater still: in the same period he arranged for the delivery of £92 16s 8d to papal bankers and Rome.[64]

Aberdeen's other trading links were partly determined by the demand for fish, for which there was an increasingly important market in France and England from the fifteenth century. Although the provost Robert Davidson visited Harfleur in 1410, attempting to sell (or reset) a cargo of pirated Hanseatic goods, regular French trade was surprisingly late to develop.[65] When it did, later in the fifteenth century, it was focused initially on the port of Dieppe in Normandy, though even in 1499-1500 only 6 per cent of Aberdeen's recorded salmon exports were sent there. Subsequently, although the proportion of salmon which Dieppe took grew, sailings remained relatively infrequent. Only three or four ships left Aberdeen for the Norman port in 1596-7.

By then the south-west of France provided another market: in 1698-9 over half of Bordeaux's salmon imports came from Scotland, mainly from Aberdeen. Although wine from this area had long since been consumed in Scotland, most was initially supplied from the French wine staple at Damme, near Bruges, or from England. Towards the end of the sixteenth century, however, direct Scottish contacts with Gascony increased. In 1596-7, one vessel arrived in Aberdeen from Bordeaux with 74 tuns of wine, which amounted to 75 per cent of the town's wine imports in that year. Other imports were minimal, though in 1698 Aberdeen merchants acquired twenty-four bales of woad. Still, Aberdeen accounted for only a miniscule proportion of late seventeenth-century Bordeaux's trade. It lagged behind Montrose, Dundee and Glasgow. In 1699-1700, its share of tonnage shipped from Bordeaux was only 8.6 per cent of that delivered to Leith and a tiny fraction (0.2 per cent) of that dispatched to Amsterdam.[66]

Trade with England was interrupted by Anglo-Scottish conflict, though it often resumed during periods of truce. William de Leith, a prominent burgess of the mid fourteenth century, obtained safe-conducts to trade in England in 1357, 1358, 1361 and 1363, as did other burgesses.[67] Although we do not know what Leith sought to sell in England, it seems likely that fish, especially salmon, would have been included in his cargoes. London fishmongers were certainly seeking salmon in Aberdeen by the later fourteenth century.[68] Leith planned to purchase wheat, barley, malt and wine: Scots routinely looked to England as the closest location to make good the shortfall in domestic grain production, while wine from the English crown's Gascon lands (until the English relinquished control of their first colony in 1453) was also readily available. Unfortunately, as the London customs accounts rarely indicate the origin of incoming vessels, it is impossible to determine the extent of this trade. While some (perhaps even most) of the fish shipped to London from Aberdeen was on English vessels, Aberdonian ships reached London at least occasionally: the *Gabrielle*, for instance, docked there on 29 May 1440.[69] It departed (as other Aberdonian ships also did) with a cargo of cloth.

There are signs from the end of the Middle Ages that the importance of the

London market was declining, at least for a time. Very little salmon reached London in either 1480-81 or 1567-8, and that which did came on continental vessels. None at all is recorded as English-bound in the levy imposed on shipping at Aberdeen in 1596-7.[70] Meanwhile, trade with other English ports was more limited still. Not one Aberdonian vessel is evident at Boston between 1528 and 1538 or between 1601 and 1640, though plenty of other Scottish ships reached the Lincolnshire port in these years.[71] Likewise, Aberdeen vessels were only very occasionally to be found in other east-coast ports frequented by Scots, such as Newcastle, Scarborough and Yarmouth, between the fourteenth and sixteenth centuries.[72]

Trade with the Baltic region (including Denmark, Sweden, northern Germany and Poland) remained occasional following its development in the early fifteenth century. Not a single Aberdonian vessel passed the Sound (the gateway to the Baltic between Elsinore and Helsingborg) in 1508 or 1528, compared with sixteen recorded passages by Dundonian ships in the same years.[73] Dundee developed its production of cloth (for which, unlike Scottish wool and fish, there was a demand in the Baltic) much earlier than Aberdeen and it is this which probably explains Aberdeen's limited direct contacts with the region until the later sixteenth century. As a consequence those Aberdonians with business interests in Danzig, the chief centre of commerce in the south-eastern Baltic littoral, were often forced to hitch a lift from others. One who bought a cargo of Prussian wheat in 1447 learned that it would be delivered 'in Rattre or Aberdene or Leith quhar it suld happen the schip to arrive'.[74] Similarly, in 1515 a cargo of tar belonging to the Aberdeen merchant Andrew Cullen was delivered via Copenhagen to Leith.[75] As Figure 17.1 indicates, Leith and to a lesser extent Dundee had become significant funnels for Aberdeen's overseas trade.

There is comparatively little evidence of trade with Scandinavia before the sixteenth century. Orkney, however, was part of the Norwegian realm until 1468, and Orcadian bishops had received grants of wine and corn from Aberdeen since at least the early fourteenth century.[76] Presumably there was sufficiently regular traffic from Aberdeen for the bishops to be able to enjoy these grants. Nevertheless, although one Norwegian merchant received a remission on his customs dues at Aberdeen in 1341-2, it was only from the later fifteenth century, once Norway began to export substantial amounts of timber, that Norwegians are again traceable in Aberdeen.[77] By the end of the sixteenth century, between seven and twelve ships arrived each year in Aberdeen with timber from Norway. The fact that Norwegian-bound vessels do not appear in the late sixteenth-century Aberdeen customs accounts suggests that there was little of value, if anything, sent in return.[78] Still, there is an important warning here. The destination of customed goods does not provide a complete picture of the town's overseas contacts. The itinerary of the *Susanna* in 1588 exemplifies the point. This Aberdonian vessel left its home port in July, laden with salmon for Dieppe. Twenty days later, it arrived in Bordeaux, returning with Gascon produce to Middelburg in Zeeland, before sailing south once more to San Lúcar de Barrameda, at the mouth of the Guadalquivir river in Spain. There, its master, John Murray, found himself involved in a row with Breton sailors and imprisoned on the spurious grounds that he and his crew were 'protestantis and luthereanis'.[79] Mariners were liable to encounter far more of the outside world than the sedentary merchants whose goods they transported.

The eighteenth century was to witness the most significant re-orientation of Aberdeen's maritime contacts in the entire period. Whereas previously trade had been focused on the North Sea and Baltic worlds, it now developed gradually in an imperial British context. Of course, Aberdonians still maintained extensive trading contacts with continental Europe; for commercial, geographical and historical reasons one would not expect otherwise. Nevertheless, by 1735 it was reported that they looked more to London than to Veere for supply of their manufactured goods.[80] This was perhaps something of an exaggeration, though there is no doubt that trade with England in general, and London in particular, had revived following the Restoration of 1660, largely on the basis of wool shipped north and stockings sent south.[81] Occasionally ships also headed for Ireland, such as the Derry-bound Aberdeen vessel that left Newburgh with a cargo of oatmeal in 1738.[82] Further afield, even in the 1630s the Aberdeen merchant John Burnett had been importing tobacco from Virginia, and, although the Navigation Act of 1660 technically prohibited Scots from trading with England's colonies, three vessels left Aberdeen for America in the 1680s.[83]

After the Union of 1707, although Glasgow benefited most from the development of transatlantic commerce, east-coast ports such as Aberdeen were also able to tap into the new markets of empire. Some of modern Aberdeen's dockside street names bear testimony to the location and nature of this trade. Commerce Street, Virginia Street and Sugarhouse Lane were all established in the mid eighteenth century, at a time when the expanding trade with the Americas was reflected in regular newspaper advertisements for outward freight and passage and in more sporadic press records of commodities imported into Aberdeen.[84] Chesapeake tobacco and, to a lesser extent, West Indian rum and sugar were the colonial imports most frequently mentioned in the local press, while goods exported included sailcloth and locally manufactured osnaburgs.[85] The vast majority of vessels were involved in the Caribbean traffic, particularly to and from Antigua and Jamaica.

Aberdeen's relationship with the West Indies remained consistently important throughout the second half of the eighteenth century. Following the Seven Years War (1756-63) the trading network expanded to include Dominica, Grenada and Tobago (three of the four Ceded Islands) as well as, more occasionally, the older British colonies of Barbados, St Kitts and St Vincent, and also Demerara, acquired after the Napoleonic Wars. Virginia had been the most regular destination among the thirteen mainland colonies until the 1770s. Thereafter it was eclipsed by traffic to more northerly ports, such as Halifax, St John's Island and Quebec, though from time to time ships also sailed for New York, Philadelphia, Boston and Baltimore. Meanwhile, the eastern Empire too was opening up. From the 1760s, a significant number of Scots were appointed to writerships by the East India Company, a position which, while ostensibly entailing administrative work on behalf of the Company, also allowed their holders to practise private trading ventures. Among the first to be appointed to such a position was John Burnett, son of an Aberdeen merchant and bailie, whose engagement with the Company dates from 1762 – but a further seven Aberdonians were to gain similar positions by 1799.[86]

Cultural bonds

Religion and commerce helped to sustain an international culture in medieval Aberdeen. This is most obvious in the use of Latin in the town's record keeping. Although official business was increasingly transacted in Scots from the fifteenth century, even in the eighteenth century the council still occasionally maintained records in Latin, usually when their content concerned foreigners. French, too, was understood by many of the élite throughout the period.[87]

This knowledge of foreign languages is also evident when examining the reading habits of two of later medieval Aberdeen's most accomplished authors – John Barbour, who wrote in the vernacular, and Hector Boece, author of the last of the full-scale medieval chronicles of Scotland, who wrote in Latin. Allusions to *Le Roman d'Alixandre*, *Le Roman de Thèbes*, Guido de Columnis's *Historia Desctructionis Troiae*, the chronicle known as *The Brut* and (perhaps) Vergil's *Aeneid* pepper Barbour's *The Brus*. Likewise, in the early sixteenth century Boece, the university's first principal, was evidently a man well read in both classical works and more modern authors, such as the Italians Marcantonio Coccio (1436–1506) and Bartolomeo Sacchi (1421–81). Nevertheless, we cannot be sure that either Barbour or Boece had access in Aberdeen to all of the authorities whom they quoted. Indeed, Boece's memory of Froissart's *Chronicles* is sketchy, suggesting that he had perhaps read (and badly remembered) the work of the great chronicler of European chivalry while a student in Paris. Hence too, perhaps, the notable lack of reference to a variety of authors with whom one might have expected Boece to have been familiar when he composed his *Scotorum Historia* in 1527.[88]

Growing secular literacy from the end of the medieval period brought others into contact with books and, thereby, with an international culture. Alain Chartier's fifteenth-century text *Le bréviaire des nobles* was translated by an Aberdeen notary in *c.* 1490.[89] The French poem *Le débat de l'omme et de la femme*, by the

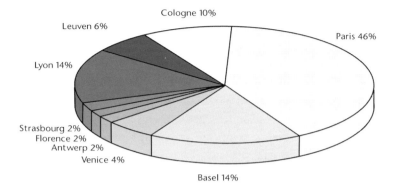

Figure 17.3
The
sixteenth-century
library of William
Gordon, bishop of
Aberdeen: places of
publication (pie
chart).

fifteenth-century monk Guillaume Alexis, from near Evreux in Normandy, was translated in early sixteenth-century Aberdeen, and its circulation suggests a familiarity with the vexed controversy concerning the nature of women which gripped literary circles across Christendom.[90] Very little evidence of Aberdeen's early modern book trade survives, but (as indicated in Figure 17.3), the extant volumes from Bishop Gordon's library were largely acquired from French and Swiss printers. These may, however, have been purchased in Netherlandish markets, rather than directly from the printers. More worrying, from the perspective of the ecclesiastical authorities, was the market which appears to have existed in Aberdeen from the early sixteenth century for imports of Protestant works.[91]

Printing was the most important technological development of the fifteenth century and, coupled with the dramatic decline in the cost of paper, it was to have a profound effect on both literacy and access to ideas (see Chapter 16). This was particularly so following the emergence of printers and bookshops in the town from the seventeenth century, Edward Raban establishing the first press on the Castlegate in 1622.[92] In the following century newspapers too began to appear, notably the *Aberdeen Journal*, established in 1747, which carried foreign reports reprinted from London newspapers, as well as advertisements for passage to the colonies (Plate 36). While this was perhaps the most important source of information regarding the outside world, eighteenth-century Aberdeen was also home to a number of booksellers. Academics bought books from London too: James Beattie's purchases including *A Journey through England, Portugal, Spain and France* (1773) and *A History of the Canary Islands* (1764).[93] It is altogether more difficult to establish how much of this global vision was shared by ordinary Aberdonians. Still, the late eighteenth-century diary of the merchant Alexander Mackie reveals a familiarity with the Greek alphabet, with news of East India Company shipping and with developments in the French Revolutionary wars.[94]

Other cultural manifestations of a cosmopolitan nature, notably in art and

music, are less easy to discern, especially for the earlier period, though Bishop William Elphinstone posed for a portrait of perhaps Netherlandish execution in the early sixteenth century (Plate 18).[95] By the eighteenth century, portraits were a more common acquisition by the élite at least and James Beattie, a Marischal College professor, commissioned Joshua Reynolds in London to paint *The Triumph of Truth* (Ill. 34).[96] By then, much art was locally produced, though Aberdeen painters, such as William Mosman (the artist whose illustration is on the cover of this book) often undertook their training abroad – in Mosman's case in London and Rome. Meanwhile, other local art, such as that which adorns the Long Gallery in Provost Skene's House and the five seventeenth-century Old Testament scenes at King's College, was probably based on engravings by foreign artists.[97] King's College itself is a fine example of fashionable early sixteenth-century European culture. The college bells were made in London and Mechelen, while the chapel's architectural design and carved choir stalls, as well as the Bishop Elphinstone's tomb, betray influences of the Low Countries.[98]

Emigrants: destinations

Religion, commerce and culture ensured a cosmopolitan streak to early Aberdonian society. There was another dimension to Aberdeen's contacts with the outside world, for people as well as commodities were exported from the town. In the fifteenth and sixteenth centuries, emigrants headed for a variety of European countries. Several Aberdonians settled in port towns with which Aberdeen was in direct contact, including London and Antwerp, Bruges and Veere in the Low Countries. It is virtually impossible to determine how many Aberdonians departed the town in this period, though at least eight of the 118 Scots who acquired denizenship in fifteenth-century England (a very small proportion of the Scots then in England) were from Aberdeen. Of those who made for the Netherlandish towns, there were six Aberdonians among the fifty-one known Scots who acquired burgess-ship in Bruges between 1418 and 1496.[99] And at least nine Aberdonians featured among almost one hundred Scots who obtained citizenship in Veere during the first half of the sixteenth century, a few others coming from Aberdeen's hinterland.[100] The numbers were not large, but at about 10 per cent of the totals, they were a good deal more than Aberdeen's likely proportion of the Scottish population as a whole.

For many, the nearest of the port towns of Europe were merely a staging post for more distant travels. The eastern Baltic lands were to prove a particularly powerful magnet for Scots, especially from about the 1470s, though it is not until the sixteenth century that Aberdonians can be traced with certainty in the Prussian/Polish hinterland. By then the town authorities were often called upon to issue testimonials, certifying the identity of those who had travelled abroad and recording their kin in Propinquity Books. In the first extant Propinquity Book, dating from 1589 to 1603, less than a fifth of the 175 emigrants noted were from New Aberdeen or Old Aberdeen, most coming from Aberdeen's vast hinterland in the north-east.[101] Whatever their origin, however, emigrants at this period headed overwhelmingly for Poland and Prussia - as indicated in Figure 17.4. Many settled in the thriving inland towns of the Baltic's hinterland. Between 1596 and 1620, at least twenty-five men from Aberdeen and its environs had become burgesses of Cracow, while between 1598 and 1650 at least eight had become burgesses of Posnan.[102] The ports of Danzig (Gdansk) and Königsberg aside, other concentrations were to be found in Warsaw and Zamosc. The eastern Baltic lands remained a popular destination of emigrants throughout the seventeenth century. Over three-quarters of those who obtained Aberdeen birth brieves between 1637 and 1699, and whose destinations are known, headed for Poland, Prussia or further east.[103] Their numbers, however, were already beginning to decline in the second half of the century.

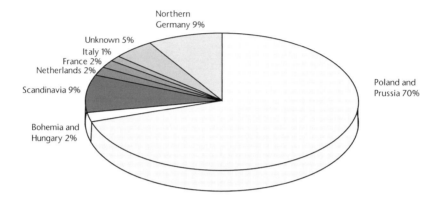

*Figure 17.4
Aberdonians
overseas, 1589-1603
(pie chart).*

The pattern of seventeenth-century emigration was to change radically follow-ing the Union of 1707. Indeed, it was changing even before then. In 1709, it was noted that John Innes, the son of an Aberdeen litster, had left in about 1670 for Surrat, in the kingdom of Guzaret in India. Innes was a comparatively early emigrant to the east, but others soon followed. Some gained employment with the Swedish East India Company and others appeared in Dutch service – and at least one mariner had ventured as far as China by 1748 (Ill. 35).[104] By the second half of the eighteenth century, several were also working for the English East India Com-pany, as administrators, cadets, sailors or soldiers.[105] Africa remained, as yet, largely uncolonised, though a few Aberdonians (most of them sailors) visited Guinea in the service of the Royal Africa Company in the first half of the eighteenth cen-tury.[106] Sailors constitute a significant number of those whose movements and deaths are recorded in the eighteenth-century Aberdeen Propinquity Books. They are included in the calculations illustrated in Figure 17.5 and arguably distort the picture of emigrant destinations. Nevertheless, even if mariners are excluded, op-portunities in the Atlantic Empire, and especially in the Caribbean, attracted early eighteenth-century Aberdonians above all others.

Aberdeen's links with North America pre-dated the Union of 1707. In 1702, for instance, the Aberdeen-educated Patrick Gordon died in New York, while the following year his doctor brother died in Barbados.[107] As demonstrated in Figure 17.5, however, it was apparently the Caribbean, rather than the North American mainland, which attracted the bulk of emigrants from Aberdeen and the north-east. As already noted, Aberdeen's commercial links with the West Indies were also significant. These contacts stand in stark contrast to the pattern of Atlantic contacts maintained by Glasgow, which were particularly focused on the mainland colonies and determined above all by the lucrative tobacco trade. Aberdonians, by contrast,

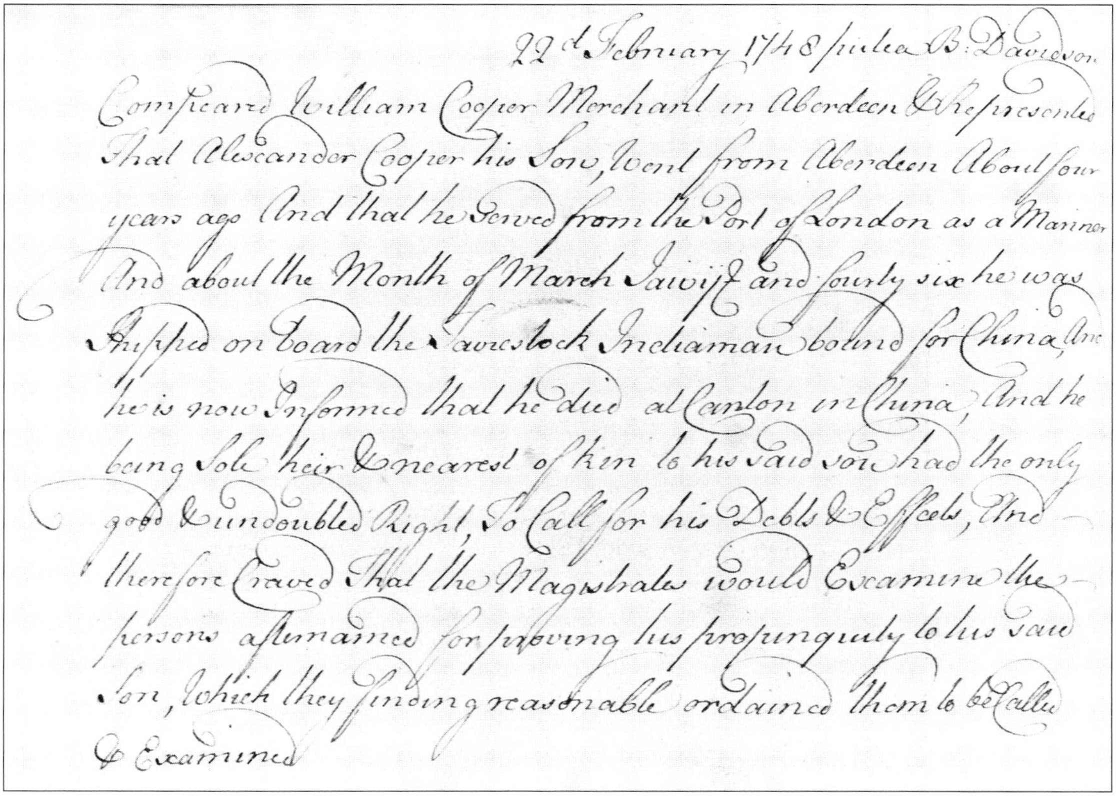

> 22ᵈ February 1748 /julia B: Davidson.
>
> Compeared William Cooper Merchant in Aberdeen & he presented
> That Alexander Cooper his Son, Went from Aberdeen About four
> years ago And that he served from the Port of London as a Mariner
> And about the Month of March Jaiviff and fourty six he was
> Shipped on board the Tavestock Indiaman bound for China, And
> he is now Informed that he died at Canton in China, And he
> being Sole heir & nearest of kin to his said son had the only
> good & undoubled Right, To Call for his Debts & Effects, And
> therefore Craved That the Magistrates would Examine the
> persons aftemamed for proving his propinquity to his said
> Son, Which they finding reasonable ordained them to be Called
> & Examined

Illustration 35
Notice of a mariner
who died in Canton,
China, 1748.

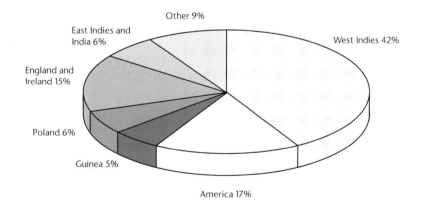

Other 9%

East Indies and
India 6%

England and
Ireland 15%

Poland 6%

Guinea 5%

America 17%

West Indies 42%

Figure 17.5
Aberdonians
overseas, 1735-1750
(pie chart).

seem to have concentrated their interests on risky and peripheral imperial areas, where competition from the west of Scotland was more limited.[108]

Emigrants: occupations

Many emigrants, according to Emerson Smith, were 'shiftless, hopeless, ruined individuals' – in other words the flotsam and jetsam of society.[109] Some Aberdonians fit this description, at least in the sense that they possessed few skills. Jan Pendrik, for instance, who acquired citizenship in Antwerp in 1537, was a labourer. Many of the Atlantic emigrants were servants. And of the fourteen Aberdonian soldiers serving in India between 1753 and 1763, most were labourers.[110] Yet, throughout the period, many of the overseas openings were for skilled tradesmen – especially blacksmiths, wheelwrights, carpenters, bricklayers, millwrights and tailors. Sailors constituted another large category, though, by contrast, the number of soldiers was modest. Most of the Scottish troops who served overseas came from the countryside rather than the towns, though the rebellion of the United Irishmen in 1797 prompted attempts to recruit soldiers and collect money for their support.[111]

Other emigrants were traders of one sort or another. Several were established merchants, and those in the continental ports often maintained commercial contact with their native country. Residence abroad was often intimately linked with family business interests at home. In 1490, David White was the Aberdeen-based 'procurator and factor' of his brother in Danzig, while in 1500 Andrew Fudes, resident in the Netherlands, was 'son and factor' of the Aberdeen burgess William Fudes.[112] Even in the eighteenth century, younger sons, such as Gavin Young (1744–1802), conducted deals on behalf of the family business – in Young's case in London.[113] Not all émigrés, however, were merchants proper. Many were small-scale hucksters or retailers. Thomas Wrichten and Arnt Davidsen, who respectively became burgesses of Antwerp in 1544 and 1598, were *kremer* (= German *Krämer*, cramer), while Hans Lesh, an Antwerp burgess from 1589, was a *tavernier*.[114] Several of those whose names appear in the late sixteenth-century Propinquity Book were described as 'travellers', probably an indication that they hawked merchandise round the rural areas of northern Europe, selling cheap produce to the poor.

There were also opportunities for professional men – clerics, teachers and doctors (see Chapter 8). Even in the fifteenth century several Scottish clergymen found positions in England; they included the Aberdonians Richard Govan (in Essex in 1467) and John Nicoll and Henry Lilburn (both in Kent in 1474).[115] The clerical exodus continued in later centuries. David Simpson, a member of the Dominican friary in 1503, had moved to the order's Newcastle house by 1539 and subsequently, as a Protestant exile, to Copenhagen and then the Netherlandish town of Emden. Patrick Copeland, a product of both the grammar school and Marischal College, entered service as a chaplain to the East India Company before heading to Bermuda in *c.* 1626.[116] Copeland was a Presbyterian, but the expanding empire provided particular opportunities for Episcopalians and Quakers whose beliefs were out of favour at home. Among a dozen Scots clergymen sent to Jamaica by the bishop of London between 1707 and 1763, two – James Spence and Alexander Mackay – came from Aberdeen. Others headed for mainland America, notably James Blair, who from 1685 until his death in 1743 was the leading Episcopalian minister in Virginia. Many of the colonists resented the bishop of London's appointment of a Scotsman as commissary and Blair was suspected, with some justification, of assembling a 'Scottish Party' in the colony. Blair acted as a facilitator for fellow Episcopalians from north-east Scotland to obtain livings in Virginia. His brother Archibald (a physician) soon appeared in the colony, as did a number of other Scottish ministers, including the Aberdeen graduates Alexander Finney and Alexander Gordon. More were to follow.[117]

Clerics, of course, were graduates, but graduates found other outlets for their talents (see Chapter 15). William Elphinstone's career is a reminder that the thirst for foreign education had not diminished with the foundation of three Scottish universities in the fifteenth century. Some gained employment abroad as teachers. On 29 October 1751, Charles Copland junior advertised for 'any young Man, who is bred to his Book and has good Education, so that he is qualified for teaching Gentlemens Children Latin, Writing and Arithmetick, and inclies to officiate in that way in Virginia.' On 14 December 1772, Provost Jopp appealed for a young man 'who understands something of Arithmetic and book-keeping' to go to the West Indies as a plantation overseer. Many others contributed to the expansion of university education, especially in northern Europe, from the fifteenth century onwards. Having studied in Paris and Cologne, the Aberdonian Peter Davidson became one of the first teachers at the new university of Copenhagen, from where he also obtained a doctorate in 1498.[118] After the Reformation, many students continued to use the Scottish universities to obtain a basic arts degree, before proceeding abroad for more specialised study and sometimes an academic career. But, in keeping with the changed religious environment from the sixteenth century, scholars were now as likely to matriculate in the Protestant Germanic-speaking world as in the French- or Italian-speaking institutions which they had attended in earlier centuries.

Catholics went elsewhere. One such was James Cheyne of Arnage, a King's College graduate, who continued his studies at Douai in Flanders in 1566.[119] Cheyne, however, was not typical in either his religion or his choice of university. Far more common, in this respect, was the career of the mathematician Duncan Liddel, who studied at Frankfurt-an-der-Oder, Breslau (Wrocław) and Rostock, before his appointment to a chair at Helmstedt in 1591.[120] Some of these wandering scholars subsequently returned home. Robert Howie, who received his initial education at the grammar school and at King's College, departed for Poitiers and Toulouse. In 1584, he made his way to Rostock (a favourite haunt of sixteenth-century Aberdonian students), before his Calvinist inclinations attracted him to the sympathetic environments of Herborn and then Basel. Howie was a well travelled and studied man when he assumed office as the first principal of Marischal College in 1593. The contacts which he had amassed during almost a decade abroad were to shape his leadership of Marischal College: he remained in contact with Swiss acquaintances throughout his term of office and encouraged his Aberdeen students to visit continental universities too.[121]

Although, in the later eighteenth century, there was considerable French and Germanic interest in the ideas of Aberdeen philosophers such as Thomas Reid and James Beattie, the vitality of academic contacts with continental Europe, developed by such contrasting figures as Elphinstone and Howie, was not to be sustained. Without the strong Calvinist bond, and the shared interest in legal and medical studies which served to maintain close ties between Edinburgh and the Netherlandish universities, Aberdeen academics increasingly gravitated towards greater interaction with the fast-expanding English-speaking world.[122] While Oxford and Cambridge continued to dominate the world of higher education in England itself, new institutions of higher education were gradually established in England's colonies. In 1693, James Blair, a graduate of Marischal College, became the first president of William and Mary College in Virginia. Further north, William Smith, like Blair an Episcopalian cleric and Aberdeenshire graduate of King's, was appointed in 1754 to teach logic, rhetoric, ethics and natural philosophy at Benjamin Franklin's new Academy of Philadelphia (now the University of Philadelphia), becoming its first provost a year later. Smith modelled the curriculum and teaching methods on his own *alma mater* and, perhaps drawing on the example of Thomas Reid at Aberdeen, he is credited with steering the curriculum - not only at Philadelphia, but throughout the American college system - away from classical learning and formal philosophy and towards natural history and philosophy as essential elements in a liberal education.[123] The process of influence was not, however, and never had been, one way. Academic émigrés (and others) also left their mark on higher education in their native town (see Chapter 15). Liddel, for instance, bequeathed a substantial number of books to Marischal College.[124]

Empire provided an outlet for medical men, as well as for clerics and academics. Similar to other migrants, Aberdeen doctors headed for the risky and less well-established imperial localities. The notoriously unhealthy climate of the Caribbean in particular provided ample opportunity for the products of Scotland's medical schools to practise their skills. Roughly half of the doctors to be found on Antigua in 1731 were Scots.[125] In 1775, the publisher of the *Aberdeen Journal* advertised for a surgeon to go Jamaica on a three-year contract, while the town's Propinquity Books identify doctors who worked in England, Barbados and Jamaica.[126] Some diversified into planting and mercantile activities – as is evident in the case of Walter Grant, who, with the patronage of the Grant family in Aberdeenshire and Jamaica, returned from the Caribbean to study at Marischal College. Following his graduation in 1753, Grant returned to Jamaica, not only to practise surgery in Kingston, but also to manage the plantation affairs of various members of his family around Kingston.[127]

Meanwhile, other doctors headed east. Since the 1780s, Alexander Balfour reported, his unnamed brother had been engaged as a surgeon with a regiment serving in India. Alexander, a native of Old Aberdeen and graduate of King's College, was also a medical man who left the north-east to teach in London, though he too hankered after a position in India.[128] Though Alexander never made the journey east, many Aberdeen medical graduates did. There were at least eleven in both Bengal and Madras between 1764 and 1800 and at least eight in Bombay during the same period.[129] Although most of the medical men in India were trained at the Corporation of Surgeons in London, Aberdeen educated 7.2 per cent of those whose training is known. This was a far greater number than any other university except Edinburgh (with 11.3 per cent). Yet Aberdeen, a much less prestigious and rigorous medical school, probably sent a higher proportion of its graduates to India.

Many emigrants spent lengthy periods abroad. David Harbert, who lived in London and took an oath of loyalty to the English crown in 1480, was still there in 1483, residing, along with many other Scots, in the Farringdon district.[130] Fourteen of those noted in the Propinquity Book of 1589–1603 were described as having been abroad for between six and thirteen years. Another seventeen were noted as burgesses of foreign towns – a status that implies not only a degree of affluence, but also an intention to settle. Nevertheless, it is difficult to establish whether these early emigrants sojourned in their new residences, or whether they intended to remain abroad permanently. Both sojourners and permanent exiles are evident in the eighteenth century, by which time staged migration was important too. James Ogilvie had gone from Aberdeen to London in 1744 and thence to Charleston, South Carolina, where he died in 1745. Meanwhile, Thomas Webster, originally from Kincardine O'Neil, had died at St Thomas in the Vale, Jamaica, by 1750, after sojourning as a chapman in Aberdeen and Galloway. Women, too, followed this pattern. By the 1750s Jean Brown had moved from Aberdeen to Philadelphia and then Barbados 'where she kept a publick house or punsch house', before marrying a carpenter and settling in St Croix.[131]

Jean Brown is of interest for another reason. While in the Caribbean she tapped into an Aberdeen network, corresponding with Alexander Harvie in Antigua, who supplied her with news of her family before he returned to settle in his native town. While those who were literate could maintain contacts with home, Patrick Copeland was unusual in his regular dispatch of missives to the Aberdeen council from various locations in the early seventeenth century.[132] Some migrants supplemented letters with visits home. Patrick Coutts, who went to Virginia in the 1740s and died in 1770, reportedly returned to Aberdeen 'once or twice' to visit friends. Coutts had another link with home, for his brother William had moved to Virginia in the 1760s.[133] It was not uncommon (even in earlier centuries) for brothers to emigrate, though some headed in completely different directions. By 1644 Alexander Burnel had made for Italy, while his brother John was a merchant in Poland.[134]

Emigrants: experiences

It is evident from the Propinquity Books that the main location of Aberdonian emigrants was Poland or Prussia in the seventeenth century and the Caribbean in the eighteenth - a shift that perhaps reveals the longer-term local impact of the Union of 1707. In their new locations, Aberdonians settled, sojourned and did business. Yet differing interpretations can be made of the testimonials entered in the Propinquity Books. It is possible that the volume and geographical origin of those who sought testimonials reflects particular problems associated with specific colonial areas (such as the repatriation of money from the Caribbean), rather than the actual volume or direction of emigration. Alternatively, the importance of establishing the kinship of those who emigrated to Poland/Prussia and the Caribbean reflects the fact that greater fortunes were to be made in these areas than others. Some emigrants to both areas certainly prospered. It was not unusual for seventeenth-century migrants in Poland and Prussia to bequeath part of their estate for charitable purposes in Aberdeen. The local hospital was one beneficiary, as was Marischal College. In 1699, the college authorities launched an appeal for renovation work on the university, soliciting a generous response from Scots resident in the Polish cities of Danzig, Elbing, Lublin, Warsaw and Zamosc, and from those resident further east in Königsberg. Most, we may presume, had Aberdonian connections, and some contributed extraordinarily large sums.[135]

Similar largesse - some private, some public - is evident among eighteenth-century migrants, such as Francis Colly, a native of Peterculter, whom the *Aberdeen Journal* described as 'a most ingenious and industrious Builder and Architecht'. Colly had emigrated in 1770 and died eleven years later in St John's, Antigua, a town which he had rebuilt, to public acclaim, after its destruction by fire. His fortune, the *Aberdeen Journal* intimated, 'will now come to his relations in this neighbourhood'.[136] How much was not specified, but other donations and legacies intimated in the press included £200 for selected poor in the town, donated by a former East India Company clerk; £600 set aside by Charles Menzies, a physician in the East Indies, for his sister in Aberdeen; £50 for the infirmary from Andrew Cassie, a Jamaican physician, in 1759; and £500 for King's College left by Alexander Moir from Banffshire, a former bursar of the college, who died at St Croix in 1766.[137]

Profit was clearly one motive that is likely to have encouraged emigration, together with the calculation that greater fortunes were to be made abroad than could be amassed at home. Presumably, until the seventeenth century such calculation was based upon hearsay, but by the eighteenth century there was another means of attracting migrants. Although specific opportunities were sometimes harnessed to shipping notices, they were more commonly intimated in free-standing advertisements. There were fifty-two such advertisements in the *Aberdeen Journal* for the Atlantic Empire alone between 1748 and 1800. Most were for the Caribbean – fourteen for Jamaica, twelve for Grenada, three for Antigua, two for Tobago, one each for St Vincent and Dominica and eight for unspecified locations – though Virginia accounted for four, West Florida for three, Maryland for two and East Florida and Canada for one each. (It is perhaps significant that the proportion of advertisements for each area roughly equates with the proportionate share of destinations in the Propinquity Books.) On one occasion, the East India Company, through its Aberdeen agent, brewer James Rigg, adopted a similar recruiting ploy, encouraging young men to indent for five years 'at the End of which they are relanded in Britain, free of any Expense'.[138] The vast majority of transatlantic advertisements either stated explicitly, or implied, that the emigrants would be recruited under indenture.

Some advertisers returned to the colonies after a spell at home and wanted to recruit servants either for their own use or for business associates. James Freeman, son of an Aberdeen baker, who in 1729 had emigrated via London to Maryland as an indentured servant, recruited Abraham and John Davidson as servants during a visit home in 1741, shipping them aboard the *Charming Nancy* to Virginia, where he owned a plantation.[139] Similarly, James Gray and William Black were both about to set out for Virginia when they advertised for tradesmen in 1748 and 1750; Black promised that all he recruited 'are sure to reside at his own House in Virginia, and they will run no manner of Risque of being disposed of to others'. They were, he assured them, going to a 'plentiful and healthy Country, inhabited by a kind and hospitable People'.[140] Assurances about the healthy nature of the climate were usually confined to advertisements for particularly suspect locations.[141] While most recruiters were looking for single men, encouragement was occasionally held out to married men with families, once in Florida and once in Maryland.[142] Indentures usually lasted for three or four years and the option of returning home was occasionally offered, at least in theory. When John Elphinston advertised for a tailor to go to Virginia in 1749, he promised 'in case they don't like the Country, when there, he shall oblige himself to bring them back to Aberdeen on his own Charge'.[143] Elphinston's tailor was offered ten pounds sterling per year, with bed, board and washing, somewhat less than the financial inducement of thirty pounds sterling per year, plus bed and board, offered to masons and joiners in Jamaica two years later.[144]

It would be misleading to assume that, whatever the enticements, all (or even most) emigrants departed willingly. In the seventeenth and eighteenth centuries, the sentence of banishment was regularly imposed on men and women alike for misdemeanours ranging from theft and housebreaking to adultery, incest and murder. David Dobson has estimated that approximately 400 Scottish criminals were banished between 1707 and 1763, their precise destinations depending on the whim of the ships' captains.[145] In the fifty-three years from 1748 to 1800 the *Aberdeen Journal* reported on at least 135 verdicts of banishment handed down by circuit courts in Inverness, Perth and Stonehaven, as well as Aberdeen itself, primarily in the years before the American War of Independence. They involved ninety-nine men and thirty-six women, who were usually sent to unspecified 'plantations', but in six cases to Virginia, for periods of five, seven, ten and fourteen years – as well as fifty-four men and thirteen women who were sent for life. Six of the life banishments were pronounced at the Aberdeen Circuit Court in May 1776 alone: Mary Lawson for child murder; Walter Annesly, John Blair and Alexander Robb for 'riotously carrying off some Meal from a ship at Banff'; Nathaniel Stewart for stealing a mare; and Alexander Ross for sheep stealing. Stewart and Ross were also forced to endure being 'whipt thro' the streets of Aberdeen' prior to transportation.[146] The final banishments recorded in the eighteenth-century *Aberdeen Journal* were of two women, Elspet Snowy and Jean Allen, who in September 1800 were exiled to an unspecified destination for life and seven years respectively, for child murder and theft.[147] By then, transportation of criminals to Australia had been underway for twelve years.

If convicted felons were unwilling exiles, so too were those individuals who fell victim to the kidnapping trade for which Aberdeen was notorious in the mid eighteenth century. This trade was possibly provoked by an influx of indigent country dwellers during the famine years of 1739–42, though initially it attracted little attention from Aberdonians, perhaps because they were unaware of the fate of the victims. This was to change as a result of the well documented action of Peter Williamson who, as a twelve-year old boy sent from Aboyne to stay with his aunt in Aberdeen in 1742, had been apprehended at the docks, detained below decks for a month and then shipped to Philadelphia. There, for the sum of £16, the captain sold Williamson into seven years of indentured service with a Scottish farmer from the Forks of Delaware. The farmer had suffered the same fate in youth and treated Williamson well, sending him to school and leaving him a substantial legacy. Sixteen years later, after acquiring and losing both a farm and a wife to native Americans and suffering ill-treatment and injury at native and French hands before and during the Seven Years War, Williamson was repatriated. He returned to Aberdeen, where in June 1758 he sold copies of an autobiographical pamphlet that described his adventures.[148]

According to Williamson, and subsequently fifteen supporting witnesses, it had been commonplace in the 1740s for Aberdeen merchants to ship gullible youths to America. He named and shamed several local worthies, including the merchants John Elphinston, George and Andrew Garioch, John Burnet, James Abernethy and Alexander Gray, as well as the saddler James Smith and the ship's captain Robert Ragg. At their behest, the Dean of Guild raised a successful libel action against Williamson, who was fined, imprisoned and then banished, while the controversial parts of his book were burned at the market cross. Williamson, however, was not silenced. He proceeded to sue the Aberdeen magistrates at the Court of Session, which in February 1762 issued a unanimous judgement in his favour, awarding him compensation of £100 and £80 costs.[149] More importantly, perhaps, even wider publicity was given to his damning indictment of an élite which connived in human traffic. This, of course, was not just in whites. In 1773, the vintner James Grant advertised the public display of 'a white negro woman from the West Indies', though in the same decade many other Aberdonians, led by James Beattie, the professor of moral philosophy at Marischal College, were in the vanguard of the nascent anti-slavery movement.[150] Still, racism died hard. In 1793, the town's inhabitants were entertained by a theatrical performance entitled *The West Indian*.[151]

The unwilling migrant was not an unusual character, and (on the basis of evidence in the Propinquity Books) we may add several who were press-ganged into naval service in the eighteenth century. There were others, too, and probably rather more of them, who can also be categorised as unwilling migrants and economic refugees. In 1515, the Aberdeen council decided to evict 'strangers, ganglers and beggars' from the town and it has been suggested that these were the rural victims of feuing.[152] Later migrants (especially those of the seventeenth century) may well have been forced to depart by periodic famines.[153] Emigration was not always a panacea for insecurity or poverty at home. In *c.* 1470 Walter of Dyce was apprehended, along with several other Scots, by the authorities of Wrocław in Poland on the grounds of vagrancy. Many of his companions were ill and sick.[154] Countless other, unknown Aberdonians may well have suffered a similar fate.

Conclusion

There is a great danger when writing a chapter such as this in exaggerating Aberdeen's role in the wider world between 1100 and 1800. For much of the period most Europeans, including many who were educated, would never have heard of the place. It is telling that when southern Europeans started to compile portolan charts from the later thirteenth century they did not include Aberdeen.[155] Although by the sixteenth century Aberdeen appeared on maps devised by Italians and Portuguese, such as Vesconte de Maiollo, Baptista Agnese and Diogo Homen, other Iberian cartographers still sometimes placed Aberdeen south of Dundee.[156] It is significant, too, that several north Europeans visiting Scotland relied on others for their information about Aberdeen, preferring to concentrate their tours in the Lowlands or to head for the Highlands.[157]

While the world could survive without knowledge of Aberdeen, Aberdonians themselves encountered more regular reminders of the outside world – even if they themselves were not always aware of the fact. Their diet was largely fashioned by continental influences and some of the food and drink that they consumed came from abroad. While many delicacies, such as spices and figs, were too dear to be anything other than the preserve of the élite, even the humbler members of society at least occasionally supped wine. Perhaps they also made use of Polish grain to make bread, especially in times of famine. A list of debtors compiled between 1396 and 1417 by the Teutonic Order (whose domain then included Prussia) includes not just the aristocratic élite of Scottish society, but also a litster's wife from Aberdeen, who had purchased a boll of grain from the Order's merchants.[158] Meanwhile, the community's culture was fashioned by foreign fads. Although the wealthy might dabble in the distant art market, the poor, too, participated in a cosmopolitan culture when they witnessed pre-Reformation religious iconography and when they viewed (or participated in) the various ecclesiastical and secular pageants staged in the town. Iconography and festivities followed patterns established elsewhere in Europe. And those who wandered into St Machar's Cathedral, and gazed up, were treated from the early sixteenth century to a splendid heraldic representation of the place of their university, their town and their king in the wider world. And this, we may note, was probably based on an Antwerp prototype.[159]

To some extent the Reformation marked a diminution of cosmopolitan culture, though not of economic integration with Europe. The seventeenth century witnessed the beginnings of another shift in the horizons of Aberdonians with the development of transoceanic empires, both in the east and across the Atlantic. Nicholas Canny has warned against assuming that Scots (or for that matter English) viewed 'transoceanic enterprise as a single enterprise'.[160] Yet it is perhaps significant that the first exception to this attitude which he cites was not only a Scot, but an Aberdonian, Patrick Copeland, who served as a chaplain to the East India Company before settling in Bermuda. By the eighteenth century, there were others who shared, if not Copeland's vision, then at least his horizons. They included William

Jack, an Aberdeenshire blacksmith, who left the north-east for London and then the East Indies, before returning to London and then passing on to Jamaica, where he was still plying his trade as a blacksmith in about 1773.[161] 'Little men' (and women) like Jack, as much as statesmen and soldiers, made a reality of Empire; and in his own probably inadvertent way Jack helped to sketch what contemporary European society considered new frontiers of barbarity, far distant from those which Froissart had identified in the fourteenth century.

18

The Growth of a New Town

JAMES MACAULAY

'As I entered New Aberdeen, I beheld amongst the first objects, the active and liberal hand of improvement before me, and on every side ... I was much gratified by observing that the streets were spacious, and the houses in general very handsome'.[1] This was the view of a visitor in 1807. Yet, less than a generation before, the scene had been very different.[2]

This becomes obvious from the description of the town made by a surveyor in 1794: 'the situation of the whole is so much confined by the Don on one (side), the harbour; and hilly or uneven ground on the other sides',[3] with the result that 'the city is chiefly built upon three ... hills and the greatest part upon the highest. It have [*sic*] an access by an ascent every way'.[4] The Heading Hill and Castle Hill were to the east; St Katherine's Hill to the west of Castlegate, the market thoroughfare; and Woolmanhill stood to the north. Within the burgh the only open ground was St Nicholas churchyard and Castlegate, with its impressive market cross, although this merit did not hinder the town council's desire to remove it in 1806. From the western end of Castlegate, Broad Street marked the start of the route out of town northwards. All of this snapshot of 1794 still closely corresponded to the map of New Aberdeen made by James Gordon of Rothiemay in 1661 (Plate 38). As yet, little had changed.

Today, alas, Broad Street is unrecognisable compared to what was seen within living memory. Indeed, of the town's early architecture the very few visible monuments include the partially obscured tolbooth, within the present Town House, Provost Ross's House and Provost Skene's House, the latter shorn of its pitched roof and 'conserved' in a bleak and unworthy setting (see Chapter 4). These are couthy dwellings, not to be confused in point of style with the erudite, if slightly old fashioned (for its date), Robert Gordon's Hospital, designed by William Adam,[5] described by a son-in-law as 'a man of distinguished genius, inventive enterprise and engaging address'.[6] By commissioning Adam, the hospital trustees indicated that what was wanted was a 'good show'. Yet Adam's first important public commission is plain externally, unlike the published elevation which in its decorative parts was lifted from *A Book of Designs* by James Gibbs, an Aberdonian who gave a design *gratis*, out of filial piety, in 1741 for the church of West St Nicholas.[7] Built in 1751, it introduced metropolitan standards to Aberdeen.[8]

In 1708, the population was only around 7,000. By the 1740s it had risen to nearly 11,000 and by 1801 to between 17,000 and 18,000. This does not count the growing suburbs which included Gilcomston, Windmill Brae, the Hardgate and Printfield. The population of the parish of Old Machar had risen from about 5,000 in 1755 to nearly 10,000 in 1801 (see Chapter 5).[9] With the town bursting at the seams there was no alternative but to break through the enclosing natural barriers in much the same way that Edinburgh had done. 'Placed upon a ridge of a hill, it admits but of one good street, running from east to west, and even this is tolerably accessible only from one quarter.'[10] So Edinburgh (although it could equally have been Aberdeen) was described in the 'Proposals' of 1752 which aimed to make Scotland's capital 'the centre of trade and commerce, of learning and the arts, of politeness, and refinement of every kind'.[11] By leap-frogging across the Nor' Loch by means of the North Bridge, begun in 1765, and the artificial Mound, the New Town of Edinburgh could be ventured upon. Perhaps the most spectacular and certainly the most celebrated example of economics driving physical expansion occurred in Bath, where the taking of the waters and the consequent rise in tourism had increased the town's population from 2,000 at the beginning of the eighteenth century to 28,000 a hundred years later.[12] The demolition of the city walls and subsequent outward spread provided opportunities for John Wood, father and son, to create Queen's Square, the Circus and Royal Crescent, the first such in the world.

By comparison with such elegancies in Bath, the surveyor reporting to the councillors of Aberdeen in 1794 touched on 'the great irregularity and inconvenience of your streets, especially towards the south, some places measuring little more than from fifteen to twelve feet wide, besides being so exceedingly crooked, that it is with difficulty a stranger can find his way in or out.'[13] That stranger approaching Aberdeen from the south crossed the River Dee by the sixteenth-century bridge, proceeded with difficulty to the Hardgate, down Windmill Brae, crossing the Denburn at its foot, and then through the Green, before toiling up the curving slope of the Shiprow or Marischal Street, which was laid out in 1767, as a direct route from Castlegate to the harbour (see Chapter 4). Its regular incline was achieved by underbuilding with arches and incorporating the single arch of Bannerman's Bridge (replaced in the 1970s) as a flyover across Virginia Street, an undertaking which left Alexander Bannerman, the mason, out of pocket.[14] The road north to the River Don by way of Broad Street and through Old Aberdeen was described as the worst in the county. What was required were 'wide and direct streets as much laid at right angles as the nature of the ground will admit, by that means the area of the town can be greatly enlarged, and in place of being one of the most irregular, may become one of the most regular towns in the kingdom.'[15]

This was the prediction of Charles Abercrombie, the surveyor, who despatched his report from Glasgow in December 1794. The previous year, the magistrates had been recommended to meet with him 'and to employ him to make a survey of the city and neighbouring country and to point out the most convenient line of roads and avenues from the south and north.'[16] Little is known of Abercrombie. In 1805, he built Cranston Bridge, Midlothian; both before and after this he was setting out the lines of roads in Ayrshire; and he was paid £420 in 1811 for superintending the harbour works at Dunure.[17]

For Aberdeen, Abercrombie set out three choices (Ill. 36): 'The first is by the riverside, the second by a bridge at the Marischal Street, and the third by the Justice Mills, and then by a direct straight street on to Castle Street [Castlegate]'. The riverside route was level and direct, although with the disadvantage that at 'the wharf at the Old Peir [sic]' it would be necessary 'to raise its surface some feet above

Illustration 36
Charles
Abercrombie,
Proposals for
Aberdeen, 1794.

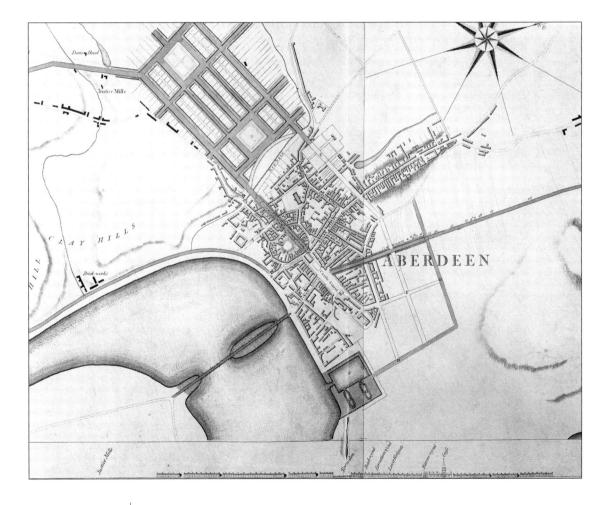

ABERDEEN BEFORE 1800

the tide ... it would then in my opinion be going round the place in order to seek the longest way in to it.' The second option was to bridge the Dee across the Inches, low lying banks, as a continuation of Marischal Street, although, as Abercrombie pointed out, 'it has no manner of command in improving the town of Aberdeen ... no advantage would be given for building or inlarging the town except Aberdeen were to pass to the south side the river'. And that was not a foreseeable eventuality. The third proposal was to proceed via the high ground to the north of the Dee bridge 'and then by some cutting and banking I continue the direction by Justice Mills on to the regular ground between that and the Den when I then form one direct straight street continued on to the cross; I propose crossing the Den by a bridge of three arches, and then by cutting about fifteen feet off St Katherine's Hill and arching the winds between [it] and the Den.' The cost of the arches was to be recouped by letting or selling the vaults as cellars for the neighbouring proprietors. Next, Abercrombie 'laid down a large addition to the town by a regular plan devided [sic] into building lotts on that space of ground between the Den and Justice Mills.' A second parallel street to the north 'continued through Gordon's Hospital garden ... would in a manner form the town with a grand square'. Abercrombie costed the riverside route as outlined in his first proposal at £3,741 10s 0d and the third route at almost £1,000 more. A road northwards from the Castlegate to the River Don would cost only £1,100, as the ground was level.[18] Two years later, Abercrombie would still hold to his view 'that the line passing Justice Mills and so in a straight line to Castle Street is the best, and most commodious approach into Aberdeen.'[19]

In 1796, the newly formed Police Commissioners presented a 'memorial', or memorandum, urging the adoption of a route 'deriving the greatest advantages from natural situation, and terminating so favourably as to combine excellency of free, short and easy access to the harbour and market-place'. The gain that such a road would bring was that 'a communication is opened southward to all intermediate places, and to the farthest extremities of Great Britain'.[20] Even so, the council held back, being afraid of the expense, particularly the cost of purchasing the requisite private property. Some was bought, however, before the council accepted in 1799 that the burgh's physical bondage had to be broken, albeit with the caveat that 'in a work of this kind, where no tax whatever was proposed to be raised, a temporary advance of a large sum of money would be necessary'.[21] Therein lay the seed of future trouble.

'An Act for opening and making two new streets in the city of Aberdeen' was given the royal assent on 4 April 1800, ten years after the first intimation that leave to introduce a bill would be sought; this was despite the opposition of the convener and deacons of the seven Incorporated Trades of the city. The act provided for trustees, although none 'should be any wise concerned as a contractor for carrying on any part of the proposed improvements'.[22] The trustees, who were to meet quarterly in the Town House, were to be nominated from among the magistrates, members of parliament, the principal of Marischal College, the president of the Society of Advocates, the convener of the Incorporated Trades and the president of the Society of Shipmasters. The new streets were to be 160 feet wide, allowing sixty feet for the roadway and fifty feet on each side for building. For the south road, much property had to be acquired from many folk who included salmon fishers, weavers, a barber, a reed-maker, a soapmaker, a cooper and 'James Elmslie mason in Midmar … Patrick Milne Esq. of Crimongate … James Massie wright', in whose office Archibald Simpson (see below) was engaged for a time. Those who had to be compensated on the northern line included the Incorporations of Tailors, Wrights and Coopers. By the close of 1800, offers of sale had been received from seventy-three owners to the south and twenty-one to the north. It was stipulated that no construction was to commence until the trustees had 'raised and secured, by subscription, loan or otherwise' £15,000 for the south road and £5,000 for the north one. A copy of the act was laid before the trustees at their first meeting together with 'the principal copies of the plans of the said two streets … subscribed by Charles Abercrombie and Colin Innes surveyors'. At their second meeting, the trustees decided to seek 'the best information from skillful engineers or architects' and from the magistrates or town clerks of Edinburgh and Glasgow regarding 'any of the new streets which may have been lately opened in any of these cities'; and to advertise accordingly in the *Aberdeen Journal* and other newspapers in Edinburgh, Glasgow, London and Liverpool, offering premiums for forming the two new streets, as well as bridges, 'agreeably to which buildings might be executed in the most regular and commodious manner'. The premiums were 150 guineas and one hundred guineas, plus two shillings for every mile travelling to Aberdeen.[23]

Although the 'Proposals' for Edinburgh had been published in 1752, it was not until 1767 that an act of parliament sanctioned an extension of the capital.[24] This became reality once James Craig, the winner of the planning competition, laid the foundation stone of the first house in the New Town of Edinburgh. Some twenty years later, one inhabitant noted: 'The New Town was then … limited to St. Andrew's Square, Princes Street, George Street and Queen Street, the former only extending to a few houses west of Castle Street, and the two others nearly to a parallel extent. Charlotte Square was only commenced … there were but a few houses built and inhabited on the north side of it.'[25] In St Andrew Square, the house fronts were not identical; for Charlotte Square Robert Adam designed a palace front, as in Wood's Queen's Square in Bath. In 1819, the poet Southey (who also visited Aberdeen) when in the capital criticised 'the enormous length of the streets in the New Town where there is neither protection nor escape from the severe winds to which Edinburgh is exposed'.[26] Craig's plan of the New Town was a self-contained, finite entity, with no room for expansion and matched its European antecedents. Glasgow, on the other hand, looked to America, from where it took the grid plan which can be laid down, then gradually infilled and is limitless. A visitor to Glasgow in 1776 recorded: 'Find Glasgow the best of any modern second-rate city we have ever seen, the houses being of stone and in good taste. The principal street is upwards of a mile in length, running east and west, but unfortunately is not straight.'[27] Half a century later, the Trongate was still attracting encomiums, 'Not solely from its being spacious, and bordered by rows of lofty houses, but because, with those houses, are intermingled stately public edifices; while the domestic buildings themselves are of varied aspect, and the lines of them interrupted by frequent breaks, arising chiefly from varied height, or from the openings of divergent streets'.[28] Perhaps, then, it was the Trongate and Argyle Street, moving west from the Cross, on the flat and unoccupied high ground parallel to the River Clyde, that was Abercrombie's model for Aberdeen.

The inquiries made by the Aberdeen town council brought differing responses. Since beginning the New Town, Edinburgh had not advertised for engineers or architects. Neither had Glasgow, although its town clerk sent a copy of the feuing conditions for stances in 'the New Town' and St Andrew's Square. The newspaper advertisements produced, in early 1800, seven sets of drawings of streets and elevations of houses and bridges – sent in by James Savage and John Young, London; David Hamilton, Glasgow; Robert Reid and Richard Crichton, Edinburgh; and James Littlejohn and John Chisholme, Aberdeen.[29] These were all young men hoping to make a name for themselves by gaining an opening in Aberdeen. Littlejohn remains obscure. Chisholme, an Aberdeen graduate, soon left his native city to become a bridge-builder with John Rennie and Thomas Telford. Savage was also a bridge-builder,[30] but is remembered today as the architect of St Luke's Church, Chelsea (1825), the first Gothic revival church since the Middle Ages to use constructional rib and panel roof vaults. That the Glasgow and Edinburgh men had not thrown off the inheritance of Robert Adam can be seen in Hamilton's copy drawing[31] of Adam's garden bridge at Syon House and later in Crichton's Rossie Castle, Angus (1801) and Reid's St George's Church, Edinburgh (1811). Nothing is known of four of the submitted schemes. Of the remainder, Chisholme proposed a bridge with a single arch, while Hamilton and Young opted for three arches, as Abercrombie had proposed. The drawing by Young, the sole competition entry to survive, also shows an unbroken terrace of houses, occasionally above arcades, filling both sides of the eastern section of the proposed street between the Denburn and the Castlegate.[32]

The first prize was awarded to Hamilton, with Savage being placed second. Hamilton was then invited to the town to prepare specifications to allow advertisements to be placed for contractors. Hamilton accepted 'the design for laying the street on vaults'. Indeed, one cannot help but speculate that he and Abercrombie, both with Glasgow connections, might have been working together. At any rate, the result for 'the traveller of taste in making his entry to the city, would look exceedingly picturesque, when viewed in the distance, especially from the south, on account of the shelves formed with the new buildings lowering over that of the present old part of the city, and would likewise give elegant situations, views etc., especially on the south side of the street, for the arrangement of the principal rooms in the lodgings that may be built'.

The candidate selected to oversee the trustees' works was 'Thomas Fletcher, engineer at present in Lancashire, and who lately had the superintendence of the Aberdeenshire Canal'.[33] In July 1801, the foundation stone of the new bridge over the Denburn was laid and it was announced that the new streets were to be named in honour of the king and the new union of the parliaments of Great Britain and Ireland. Among the throng of spectators were Charles Abercrombie and David Hamilton. 'It is remarkable,' ran one account, 'that tho' it rained heavily all the morning, it cleared up entirely during the time of the procession and ceremony; but immediately after they had returned, the rain began with greater violence, and lasted all the evening ... is this not an auspicious omen?'[34] Well, not quite, for when, two years later, the keystone of the arch was lowered into position, Hamilton had been ousted because of rising costs and faulty levels.

Design revisions were sought from John Rennie, already noted for his Kelso Bridge and at that time working on the Aberdeenshire Canal. His three suggestions included the daring novelty of a bridge with a cast iron arch and another with three forty-two feet arches. Thomas Telford, when passing through Aberdeen in the autumn of 1801, was 'desired by the magistrates to examine their intended bridge. On considering the excellent granite stone which was used, he prevailed with them to abandon the scheme of having three arches. At their desire, he gave a plan of one arch of 150 feet span, being larger than any stone arch in Britain.' This was considered to be too expensive. It was deemed more prudent, therefore, to accept Fletcher's more economical proposal of a single span of 130 feet (Plate 40). The alternative would have been 'to take down and remove the materials of the piers already built', despite the contractor's wish to increase the span to 142 feet so that 'it would be largest stone arch in Great Britain' by two feet.[35]

Eventually, paved with 'causeway stones' and with a foot pavement on either side,[36] the Union Bridge opened on 5 June 1805 when 'the mail coach ... left town by the new bridge over the Denburn'.[37] Much time and thought had been devoted to its construction and appearance as the architectural centrepiece of Union Street, providing 'a noble opening at once into the centre of the town; while at the same time it will afford an opportunity of extending the limits of the city'.[38] Pride in the beauty and magnificence of the Union Bridge was not merely Aberdonian self-satisfaction. The bridge has more than a local significance in the history of arched bridge building. Bannerman's Bridge, which was a continuation in its incline and width of Marischal Street and was abutted by houses, was designed solely for utility, whereas the Union Bridge combined usefulness and ornamentation. Thus it was to be viewed from all points as a bridge with a constricted roadway carried on gigantic piers; their bulk was lessened by arched niches. Undoubtedly, the substitution of the triple arches by a single span, the largest in Scotland, gave an air of lightness so that the level roadway, unusual for its time, has a fine tension between the opposing but retired houses. The bridge can be ranked with Edinburgh's North Bridge and the Regent Bridge, with a span of fifty feet, and with Rennie's celebrated Kelso Bridge of 1803.

It was now time to attend to the buildings that were to line the new roads. James Burn of Haddington (who had erected the Aberdeen Bank on the south side of Castlegate in 1801) was invited to prepare 'an elevation and design' for the stretch of King Street between Castlegate and North Street. The result disappointed the trustees, who wanted 'as much variety as might suit the ideas of the different purchasers and at the same time preserve uniformity and regularity in the street', so that once again Fletcher was called in; he gave an outline scheme of front walls, floor levels and roofs, leaving the disposition of apertures to the needs and tastes of others.[39] In time, the western stretch of King Street received a handsome set of public buildings, opposite which the Episcopal cathedral occupied what would have been the pedimented centre of the intended composition. Lord Cockburn was moved to write in 1841: 'Aberdeen is improving rapidly in public taste, and King Street, a creation within these five or six years, is really beautiful.'[40]

Because of the need for revenue, it was essential to develop the ground to the west of the Denburn, so 'the committee had under consideration what plan would be the most proper to be laid down for the buildings along both sides of Union Street', although it was not until 1806 that Fletcher was directed 'to make out a sketch or draught'.[41] As inducements, there would be a remission of the first year's feu duty and minimum building controls. These controls were similar to those adopted earlier in Edinburgh, to ensure that 'the houses between each opening or cross street … should form one compartment, and be of the same height of fore wall, number of floors and pitch of roof'. The front walls were to be 'retired eight feet … to form a sunk floor or area … having an iron railing' which would 'tend much to beautify the street itself'.[42] Later, in 1825, at least one house had iron balconies, causing one owner to complain that 'they would obstruct Mr. Massie's view of processions etc., and, being made of iron, drops of water from them would damage ladies' dresses'.[43] Between the bridge and Castlegate, the permitted building height was four storeys 'of granite stone dressed at least as well as the Athenaeum'. Although houses were intended, it was not long before shops appeared, a development that had soon occurred also in Edinburgh's Princes Street. In 1809, temporary shops are mentioned at the end of Broad Street, which led to the consideration of 'the ground at same time turned to some account, if two or three small temporary shops were erected along the north side of Union Street'.

Building work, of course, is always disruptive, with the result that in pushing on with Union Street 'it had occurred to the committee', in 1806, 'as proper to open up the communication of Union Street by pulling down the houses situated within its line upon the south side of the narrow wynds'. The tenants had to remove themselves by Whitsunday and the house materials sold, which brought in £560 5s 0d.[44] The opportunity was also taken to straighten old routes, such as Broad Street, so that they met Union Street at right angles and, later, spurs such as Dee Street and Bon Accord Street were laid out in 1809 and 1814 respectively.

The western stretch of Union Street became linked in people's minds with ideas of a new town which had been outlined by Abercrombie as a parallelogram, subdivided by thoroughfares connected to twin squares, as in Edinburgh. By 1806, this plan was ready for development and Fletcher was directed by the trustees 'to make out a sketch or draught thereof agreeably to the ideas they had formed on the subject'. Fletcher resigned, however, in 1807 'on account of some private business he had undertaken' and was replaced as overseer by 'Mr. John Smith junior, wright and architect', but his scheme did not deviate from earlier ones.[45] In 1819, Southey praised the new Aberdeen: 'Here all is life, bustle, business and improvement, for in outward and visible improvement this place may almost be said to keep pace with Edinburgh. Union Street, where our hotel stands, is new and many houses are still building'.[46] The one piece of open ground was alongside the Denburn. When the bridge was being talked of, there was an objection that it would obstruct a walk alongside the burn.[47] Now, in imitation perhaps of Princes Street Gardens in Edinburgh, the slopes of the Den were to be planted so that 'a sketch' was called for 'of a terrace along the top of the bank, having building areas upon the west side'. This was the origin of Union Terrace, which early on was attracting potential buyers although the ground had to be cut and levelled at '3d per yard'.

By the autumn of 1808, 'now that the road towards the Bridge of Dee is so far completed', there was a quick and modern entrance to and exit from the city. Yet, although Union Street was described in 1808 as 'one of the most crowded and frequented public streets in the town',[48] there was considerable reluctance on the part of individuals to move so far west, just as there had been in removing to the New Town of Edinburgh from the hugger mugger of the Old Town. The inability to dispose of sites meant that the trustees were not raising income quickly enough. Moreover, the prices demanded from existing proprietors by way of compensation were 'considerably too high, and as such should not be acceeded to'.[49] In addition, there was 'the expense of certain permanent improvements, highly beneficial to the community at large, as well as to the town', which did not yield a return such

as the Union Bridge, which was estimated to have cost with interest 'little short of £24,000' by 1817.[50] It was impossible to meet the interest payments on the borrowed capital. By 1817, the debt stood at just over £250,000, on which the accumulated interest was over £57,000, whereas the annual revenue was £10,000.[51] Within seven years solvency would be restored and it was reported that 'in every direction round the city, buildings have been rapidly increasing since the opening of the new streets'.[52]

West of the Denburn, building progress had been erratic and slow with little of the early visionary formal layout, save for Golden Square, the city's first square (Ill. 37).[53] This was developed on the Longlands which belonged to the Incorporation of Hammermen; the streets were named, therefore, after the trade's precious metals. Thus, Diamond Street is mentioned in 1809, a year after Golden Square, 'lately formed and lined out',[54] where the proprietors would 'pay ... a proportion of the expense of forming and enclosing the circle in the middle of the square' and have the 'privilege of walking in the circle ... and the use of the pump well'.[55] Golden Square arose piecemeal. As late as 1823, an offer was made to feu forty feet

*Illustration 38
Bon Accord Square,
Aberdeen, and the
Archibald Simpson
Memorial.*

of frontage at 1s 9d per foot and three years later complaints were made against one William Pirie for not building on his feu.[56] But Golden Square was never wholly residential, since a Gothic Episcopal chapel filled the south-west corner.[57]

The Incorporation of Tailors was also a developer, authorising in 1805 payment 'in part of the expense ... for forming and making out Chapel Street', to the west of Golden Square; and in the next year John Innes, a land surveyor, was 'to get a new plan of the feus in Chapel Street, similar to the one already made out, which is nearly worn out'. By 1820, the instruction for a plan 'made out by a professional man' indicated a desire by the tailors to develop comprehensively the lands to the south of Union Street. Alexander Gildowie and John Smith were each asked to provide two plans, 'one of a square and another of streets without a square'. Then Archibald Simpson supplanted first Gildowie and then Smith. His scheme 'varies from former measurements of said ground' and was to be submitted 'to a scientific man'. In 1822, Simpson's proposal of a square and a terrace was approved and soon the first feu was being built upon according to the overall specification 'to build a dwelling house ... of stone and lime and covered with slates or lead, the stone to be of granite and dressed equal to ashlar work', whereas new buildings in the nearby Hardgate could be 'of cottage height and slated'.[58] Although Simpson resigned in 1825 as 'architect for and taking charge of the execution of the plans', the tailors agreed 'to increase Mr Simpson's salary five pounds', which was augmented by ten pounds in the next year 'on account of his great trouble and moderate charges in relation to the planning and laying out of the terrace and other grounds.' By the end of the year, it was resolved 'to discontinue retaining Mr Archibald Simpson as the architect with a stated salary'. The demand for feus in Bon Accord Square (Ill. 38) and Crescent, despite advertisements in the *Edinburgh Advertiser* and the *Aberdeen Journal*, was slow. Simpson offered on more than one occasion to take up a feu for 'my employer' and in 1837 he gave 'to my brother Mr A. Simpson half of the building area in Bon Accord Square feued by me'; and there are references, too, to 'Mr John Simpson, junior, builder' offering to feu ground in the terrace.[59]

The Bon Accord development was unique in Aberdeen, for not only was it executed as the architect had intended, but it combined in miniature some of the contemporary planning developments in Edinburgh, although the concept of a crescent overlooking open ground goes back to the Royal Crescent in Bath. A more contemporary source would have been found in Archibald Elliot's published proposals 'for feuing the Dam Lands of Rubislaw' in 1820 (Ill. 39), in response to 'the uncommon spirit of improvement, in the extension and embellishment of the town of Aberdeen, which has lately manifested itself'. As a spur, it was noted that in Edinburgh, where 800 new houses were in hand, 'a third new town has just been laid out ... calculated for an increase of at least 20,000 inhabitants', while in

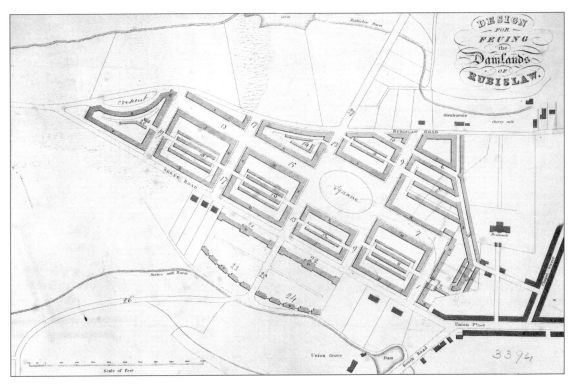

*Illustration 39
Archibald Elliot,
Design for Feuing
the Dam Lands of
Rubislaw, Aberdeen.*

Glasgow 'no less than 500 houses are in progress .... At Paisley and Greenock the enlargement has been still more remarkable and rapid.'[60]

As with the Blythswood estate in Glasgow and the Moray estate in Edinburgh, the lands of Rubislaw were a family estate with 'every advantage requisite for health, convenience and beauty of prospect ... all the amenity, free air, and attractions of the country, with every facility for drainage ... and its vicinity of the finest building materials at the Rubislaw quarries.' There would be a square greater in extent than that of St Andrew in Edinburgh, to the north of the Skene Road, from which the houses would be set back 'to admit of shrubbery in front'. To the south, there would be villas and on the western edge 'a crescent ... which will command a fine view of the country'. Perhaps Aberdonians were reluctant to move so far west for, with only a few villas built, the scheme was revised in 1849 (Ill. 40). That Simpson's understated neo-classicism still had a hold is evident when the major part of the Rubislaw estate was being developed. The Rubislaw Terrace houses were 'to be of a similar character and height to those of Bonaccord Terrace or of such other style as may be agreed'.[61] Given the date of 1849 and Queen Victoria's recent purchase of Balmoral Castle, Scottish-baronialism was chosen instead of Simpson's understated neo-classicism.

By then, Union Street had been graced with major public works, including

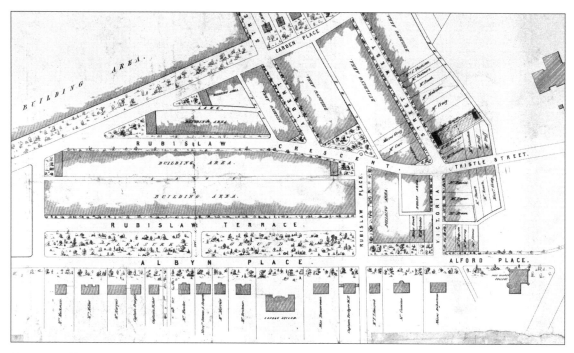

Trinity Hall, the screen in front of St Nicholas Church and the Music Hall where the portico, encompassing the street, benignly watched over the lesser one fronting the neighbouring Crimongate House, the one grand private mansion in the street.[62] Indeed, with its mixture of commercial, ecclesiastical, public and private building, Union Street can be compared with George Street in Edinburgh. It should also be bracketed with the development of Regent Street in London after 1812 and of Grey Street in Newcastle-upon-Tyne, laid out in the early 1830s – the most beautiful and handsomest of them all.

So, how does one rate Union Street? With its fine cut granite, elegant public edifices displaying local pride and sophisticated manners, Union Street has an austere nobility which comes not just from the use of granite but from the nobility of thought that marked the age of neo-classicism. Today, alas, these qualities are scarcely visible. Much has been lost, but not irretrievably so, and one day perhaps the dignity which once graced Union Street will be restored. Union Street is not only the centrepiece of Aberdeen's new town; it fulfilled the vision that 'a communication is opened southward to all intermediate places … and to the farthest extremities of Great Britain'. It was also a symbol that, for the first time, Aberdonians had broken free from the geographical and geological constrictions of the hilly setting that had determined their townscape from earliest times (see Introduction and Chapter 1).

Illustration 40 Feuing Plan for Rubislaw Estate, Aberdeen, 1849.

APPENDIX 1

Aberdeen Council Register, viii, 752-5.

Extract from the session of the Aberdeen guild court held on 8 October 1507.

[*Marginated*] Statuta[1]

The said day it was statut and ordanit for the comone proffit weill and gud reull of this burgh be the provest bailzes and consaile that nay burges withtin this burgh sale have nay forstallar under him to pas in quintray to forstale the burgh in bing of woll hidis nor skynnis under the pane of fiwe markis; and that nay merchand sale tak ane uthir mannis merchand out of his hand unto the tyme that he have coimptit and raknit finaly witht his merchand and be fred of him under the pain of fiwe markis.

Item that nay merchand man oppin his butht dur to sell or by or do ony merchandice one ane Sonday under the payn of ane pund of walx or the waile of it to be applyit to the Haly Blud licht.[2]

Item it is statut and ordanit that na taulche[3] be barrellit nor schippit under the pane of eschet to the toune quhar it may be comprehendit and viij s' of the sellar for any amerciament and thar personis and gudis to be dangerit be the kingis hienes.[4]

Item it [is][5] statut and ordanit that nay swyne be haldin withtin this toune utenthe[6] band or ane ring in thar wort under the pane of eschet of thame and viij s' uneforgevin; and gif thai befundin utenthe band and wort ring in thar wort fifteen dais beand run' thai salbe eschet and lesum to be sclane quarevere thai ma be fundin.

[*p. 753*]

Item that ale forstallaris salbe accusit and punist for thar forstalling be the lowabill statutis and consuetud of the burghe.

Item that ale futchepman berand paxis one thar bakis salbe free to cum and pas saiffly to the said burghe withtout ony accusacioune or perall of forstalling of the burghe.

Item it [is][7] statut etc. that nay litstaris bercaris blekstaris[8] skynnaris nor craftismen'[9] sale wesche thar claithtis hidis skynis nor uthir stuf in the commone rinolis[10] loche nor watteris and that nay red fische quhit fische claithtis nor uthir stuf that may infect' the watter be cassin[11] nor weschin in it.

Item that nay drauchtis[12] be haldin apoun the said loche nor rinolis nor watteris in preve nor appert bot uterly distroyt.

Item that ane preve inquest be takin of ale unelauchfull personis housis draucht haldaris walcaris[13] and of ale utheris poyntis pertenying tharto oppin and punist be the law.

Item that ale candilmakaris has candile reddy to sell to ale mane and thai salbe sellit be richt wecht the pund for iij d' smale weikit and dry.

Item that nay aill be sellit derar this zeir than viij d' the gallone be fre folkis and vj d' the gallone be unefrehaldaris.

Item that ale baxtaris sale have breid of quhet reddy sufficient gud and clene stuf penny breid and tua penny breid to serve the toune.[14]

Item that dilegent inquesitioune be takin of ale infectit personis witht this strange seiknes of Nappillis for the sawite of the toune; and the personis beand infectit thar witht be chargit to keip thame seicerly in thar housis and uther placis fra the haill folkis, etc.

[p. 754][15]

Item that the four sergeandis witht thar cunnaris pas' ilkane oulk throu thar quarteris of the toune ande tast ande cun the aile ande set it eftir thar aithtis, that is to say, gude provable aile for viii d' the gallone ande uthiris for vj d' the gallon.

Item that the flescharis sale sel na flesch quhile it be prisit ande evere Settirday the bailzeis about cirtualy sale pas witht the flesch prisaris ande set it[16] eftir thar aithtis.

Item that quhit fischaris sale present the fisch to the mercat and sele na fisch to land men nor zhit in gret quhile the toun be servit, and that nay[17] regratouris of quhit fisch quhile the toun be servit.

Item that thar salbe certane personis ordanit to cleng the toun ande dicht the causais[18] ilkane fyr house payand thane[19] ane penny.

Item that nayne infeckit folkis witht the seiknes of Napillis be haldin at the commone fleschouse or witht the flescharis baxstaris broustaris or ladinaris[20] for savite of the toun; ande the personis infeckit sale keip thame quyat in thar houssis zhardis or uthr quiat placis quhill thai be haill for the infectioun of thar nychtbouris.

Item that na wittoll be housit quhile it be present to the mercat and at the mercat be kepit and ale caik baxstaris and huxstaris be expellit thar fray.

Item that na craftis men by hidis bot as the law requiris that is to say the loug ande the horne elik lang.

Item that na craftis men bark ande schaip batht eftir the forme of oure souerane lordis lawis.

Item that craftis mennis wiffis litstaris cordonaris using browing have a leid to brew in ande ane uthir for thar craft.

Item that na persone hald swyne fyr ande elding[21] in a house and that the bailzeis cersch thar quarteris four tymes in the zeir and expell unlauchfull folkis and unlauchfull houssis.

[p. 755][22]

Item that nay one[23] freman keipe oppin butht withtin this burghe nor have licence to saile in merchandice undir the pane of xl s'; ande gif the denys of the gilde sufferis tham to saile or keip oppin butht thai sale ansuer for the said xl s'.[24]

Item that the mettis and mesoris be assait throw the haile toune and quhar thai be fundin unrichtius' be distroit and the aunaris of tham punist be the lawe.[25]

Item that ale couparis mak sufficient barrellis of mesour after the law of the realme and consuetud of this burghe and ilkan mane set his aune merk to his aune wirk; and quhay falzeis herintile to be punist after the tenour and rigour of the law.[26]

Item that nay man intromett nor merchandice mak witht uthir mennys gudis undir colour allegeand thame to be thar propir gudis undir the pane of x merkis.[27]

Item that nay muk laid withtin this burghe at ony mannis zet or dur ly langer thar thane xxiiij houris undir the pane of viij s' unforgavin and the said muk to be fre tile evere persone that sale plese to tak or leid it avay.

Editorial notes

Capital letters and punctuation marks have been standardised according to modern usage.

The medieval Scottish letters 'y' and 'ʒ' have been rendered as 'th' and 'z' respectively; 'c's and 't's, and 'u's and 'v's have been standardised according to modern derivations and modern pronunciations of the words concerned; 'w's and 'v's have been left as found in the text. '&' has been extended to 'and'.

An apostrophe has been inserted on words where there is a contraction mark but where it is unclear what the missing letter or letters ought to be. Units of currency have been left as in the text.

Notes to the Text

Notes to Introduction:
Aberdeen Before Aberdeen

1. A. S. Cameron and J. A. Stones (eds), *Aberdeen: An In-depth View of the City's Past* (Edinburgh, 2001); personal comment from J. A. Stones.
2. I am indebted to Judith Stones for all her assistance with archaeological information.
3. J. S. Smith (ed.), *New Light on Medieval Aberdeen* (Aberdeen, 1985), 1-4; E. Patricia Dennison and J. Stones, *Historic Aberdeen: The Archaeological Implications of Development* (Scottish Burgh Survey, 1997), 5-6.
4. J. Robertson, *The Book of Bon-Accord* (Aberdeen, 1839) 22-4.
5. See the report by A. S. Cameron in *Discovery and Excavation Scotland* (Council for Scottish Archaeology, 2002, forthcoming).
6. The stones were removed to Edinburgh for conservation work, but returned to Dyce in 2002.
7. *The Charters of David I: The Written Acts of David I, King of Scots, 1124-53, and of His Son, Henry, Earl of Northumberland, 1139-52*, ed. G. W. S. Barrow (Woodbridge, 1999), *no. 136.*
8. *Early Sources of Scottish History, 500-1286*, ed. A. O. Anderson (Edinburgh, 1922), 68; A. Stevenson, 'Trade with the south', in M. Lynch, M. Spearman and G. Stell (eds), *The Scottish Medieval Town* (Edinburgh, 1988), 180; *Libellus de Vita et Miraculis Sancti Godrici* (Surtees Soc., 1847), 28-30.
9. *APS*, i, 11.
10. *RRS*, i, no. 243.
11. *RRS*, ii, no. 153.
12. *Abdn Reg.*, i, 4.
13. *St Nich. Cart.*, pp. vii-ix.
14. J. Cripps, 'Establishing the topography of medieval

Aberdeen: an assessment of the documentary sources', in Smith, *New Light*, 22-3.
15. E. P. D. Torrie, *Medieval Dundee: A Town and its People* (Dundee, 1990), 60-2.
16. *Liber S. Thome de Aberbrothoc* (Bannatyne Club, 1848), i, no. 140; *Abdn Recs.*, 13, 15, 17.
17. E. P. D. Torrie, 'The early site of New Aberdeen: a reappraisal of the evidence', *Northern Scotland*, 12 (1992), 14.
18. J. Milne, *Aberdeen: Topographical, Antiquarian and Historical Papers in the City of Aberdeen* (Aberdeen, 1911), 33.
19. *ER*, i, 12.
20. J. Gordon, *Abredoniae Utriusque Descriptio* (1660), ed. C. Innes (Spalding Club, 1842), 9.
21. *Ibid.*, 9.
22. Cameron and Stones, *Aberdeen.*
23. For fuller discussion see Torrie, 'The early urban site of New Aberdeen', 1-18; and Dennison and Stones, *Historic Aberdeen*, 14-15.
24. L. J. Macfarlane, 'St Machar's through the ages', in J. S. Smith (ed.), *Old Aberdeen; Bishops, Burghers and Buildings* (Aberdeen, 1991), 14, where he cites the legend's origin as stemming from the life of St Columba written by Adomnan (627-704), abbot of Iona, for which see Adomnan, *Life of Columba*, eds A. O. and M. O. Anderson (Edinburgh, 1961).
25. Macfarlane, 'St Machar's', 16.
26. I. B. Cowan, *St Machar's Cathedral in the Early Middle Ages* (Aberdeen, 1980), 2.
27. G. G. Simpson, 'The medieval topography of Old Aberdeen', in Smith, *Old Aberdeen*, 2.

Notes to Chapter 1:
The Growth of Two Towns

1. For discussion of this name, and proof that it was not a 'burgh green', but a roadway to a public green on the east bank of the Denburn, see G. M. Fraser, *Historical Aberdeen: The Green and its*

Story (Aberdeen, 1904).
2. See G. M. Fraser, *The Old Deeside Road* (Aberdeen, 1921).
3. *Ibid.*, 231.

4. W. Kennedy, *Annals of Aberdeen*, (London, 1818), i, 415-18.

5. R. K. Marshall, *Mary of Guise* (London, 1977), 94.

6. St Fiacre (died *c.* 670) was apparently Irish and, as Ireland was known as Scotia in the Dark Ages, this may have led to a later erroneous belief that he was identical with a similarly named Scottish saint. See J. M. Mackinlay, *Ancient Church Dedications in Scotland: Non-scriptural Dedications* (Edinburgh, 1914), 332-5; D. H. Farmer, *The Oxford Dictionary of Saints* (Oxford, 1982), 148-9; *Aberdeen Breviarium*, fos xciv-xcv.

7. *RRS*, ii, 337.

8. F. Wyness, *City by the Grey North Sea: Aberdeen* (2nd edn, Aberdeen, 1972), 227. (Primary sources on the settlement at Potters' Creek have not currently been traced.)

9. *RMS*, ii, no 2292; *Liber S. Thome de Aberbrothoc* (Bannatyne Club, 1848-56), ii, 212-527 *passim*.

10. G. M. Fraser, *Aberdeen Street Names* (2nd edn, Aberdeen, 1986), 36-8; Kennedy, *Annals*, ii, 59-60.

11. H. Scott, *Fasti Ecclesiae Scoticanae* (2nd edn; Edinburgh, 1915-61), vi, 27.

12. Could the present council committee responsible for street naming be persuaded to return to the form 'Futty' or 'Fittie'? That is certainly what its present inhabitants call it.

13. *RRS*, v, 430-1.

14. 'Aberdoniae Utriusque Descriptio Topographica Autore J.G.', in *Macfarlane's Geographical Collections* (SHS, 1907), ii, 507.

15. Kennedy, *Annals*, i, 420-2.

16. *Aberdeen Description*, 498.

17. *ER*, i, 12.

18. *Rot. Scot.*, i, 55.

19. *Ibid.*, i, 9.

20. *Abdn Recs.*, 13, 15, 17.

21. *Abdn Chrs.*, xv.

22. *Abdn Recs.*, 238.

23. *Abdn Counc.*, i, 37, 123.

24. ACA, MS Inventory of Charters, Papers, etc (2.26.3), Box II, no. 43.

25. J. C. Murray (ed.), *Excavations in the Medieval Burgh of Aberdeen, 1973-81* (Edinburgh, 1982), 247.

26. *CDS*, iv, 459.

27. E. Patricia Dennison and J. Stones, *Historic Aberdeen: The Archaeological Implications of Development* (Scottish Burgh Survey, 1997), 11.

28. *Aberdeen Description*, 496.

29. ACA, CR, iv, 33.

30. *Abdn Counc.*, i, 395.

31. See, for example, ACA, CR, viii, 1164.

32. *Abdn Recs.*, 106.

33. Murray, *Excavations*, 37-45; A. H. Diverres, 'Britain in Froissart's *Meliador*', in F. Whitehead, A. H. Diverres and F. G. Sutcliffe (eds), *Medieval Miscellany Presented to Eugene Vinaver* (Manchester, 1965), 100.

34. *RMS*, i, 415.

35. J. Robertson, *The Book of Bon Accord* (Aberdeen, 1839), 275.

36. ACA, MSS Guildry Accounts, 1453-1812, no folio numbers.

37. Murray, *Excavations*, 42.

38. Robertson, *Book*, 275.

39. *Ibid.*, 276.

40. ACA, MSS Guildry Accounts, 1453-1812, no folio numbers.

41. *Ibid.*

42. *Abdn Reg.*, i, 54.

43. *St Nich. Cart.*, pp. vii-ix.

44. *Abdn Counc.*, 56, 102.

45. *St Nich. Cart.*, ii, 335.

46. *Aberdeen Description*, 499; G. M. Fraser, *Historical Aberdeen: The Castle and the Castle-hill ..., the Snow Church* (Aberdeen, 1905), 31.

47. *Abdn Counc.*, i, 181.

48. *St Nich. Cart.*, ii, no. lxxxiv.

49. Robertson, *Book*, 26; *Aberdeen Friars*, 11; Cowan & Easson, *Religious Houses*, 116; *ER*, i, 60ff; *Aberdeen Friars*, 108.

50. Cowan & Easson, *Religious Houses*, 108.

51. *RMS*, i, no. 259.

52. *Aberdeen Friars*, 12-17.

53. Cowan & Easson, *Religious Houses*, 130; W. M. Bryce, *The Scottish Greyfriars* (Edinburgh, 1909), 307, 314-16.

54. ACA, MS Inventory of Charters, Papers etc (2.26.3), Box II, no. 33.

55. ACA, MS Old Aberdeen Town Council Minutes, ii, 3-11.

56. G. G. Simpson, *Old Aberdeen in the Early Seventeenth Century: A Community Study* (Aberdeen, 1975), 5.

57. I. Campbell, 'Crown steeples and crowns imperial', in L. Golden (ed.), *Raising the Eyebrow: John Onians and World Art Studies* (Oxford, 2001), 25-34.

58. L. J. Macfarlane, *King's College* (Aberdeen, 1982), 3. See also J. Geddes (ed.), *King's College Chapel, Aberdeen, 1500-2000* (Leeds, 2000).

59. *Abdn Fasti*, 77, 80-108.

60. R. G. Cant, *The Building of St Machar's Cathedral, Aberdeen* (Aberdeen, 1976), 3-6.

61. W. Orem, *A Description of Old Aberdeen, the Chanonry, Cathedral and King's College of Old Aberdeen in the Years 1724-25* (Aberdeen, 1832), 79, 127.

62. *Ibid.*, 3.

63. *Abdn Reg.*, i, 401-6.

64. *Ibid.*, i, 11; ii, 39.

65. *St Nich. Cart.*, ii, 384-5.

66. J. Cripps, 'Establishing the topography of medieval Aberdeen: an asssessment of the documentary

sources', in J.S.Smith (ed.), *New Light on Medieval Aberdeen* (Aberdeen, 1985), 20-31.

67. *Aberdeen Description*, 500-01.
68. *St Nich. Cart.*, ii, p.xli.
69. *Aberdeen Friars*, 98, 100.
70. Source quoted in A.White, 'The Regent Morton's visitation: the Reformation of Aberdeen, 1574', in A.A.MacDonald, M.Lynch and I.B.Cowan (eds), *The Renaissance in Scotland: Studies in Literature, Religion, History and Culture* (Leiden, 1994), 255.
71. Fraser, *Historical Aberdeen* (1905), 79-100.
72. D.Stevenson, *King's College, Aberdeen, 1560-1641: From Protestant Reformation to Covenanting Revolution* (Aberdeen, 1990), 63-4.
73. *Aberdeen Description*, 506.
74. Orem, *Description of Old Aberdeen*, 118-19.
75. *Ibid.*, 141-4.
76. *Ibid.*, 185.
77. G.D.Henderson, *The Founding of Marischal College, Aberdeen* (Aberdeen, 1947).
78. C.A McLaren, 'New work and old: building at the colleges in the seventeenth century', *AUR*, 53 (1989-90), 208-17.
79. *St Nich. Cart.*, ii, 380; Scott, *Fasti*, vi, 36, 461, 466. See too ACA, CR, xxxvi, 117-18.
80. Kennedy, *Annals*, ii, 239-41.
81. *Ibid.*, i, 141.
82. *Aberdeen Description*, 501-2.
83. Kennedy, *Annals*, i, 411.
84. *Ibid.*, i, 420-3.
85. *Ibid.*, i, 403.
86. *Shore Work Accounts*.
87. H.Carter, *An Introduction to Urban Historical Geography* (London, 1983), 114.
88. R.J.Morris, 'Urbanisation', in J.Langton and R.J.Morris (eds), *Atlas of Industrializing Britain, 1780-1914* (London, 1986), 164.
89. M.Lynch, 'Urbanisation and urban networks in seventeenth-century Scotland: some further thoughts, *SESH*, 12 (1992), 26; *OSA*, xiv, 285-6; *Minutes of the Aberdeen Philosophical Society, 1758-73*, ed. H.L.Ulman, (Aberdeen, 1990), 14; *Census of 1801*.
90. *OSA*, xiv, 286.
91. An Urban Ethic of Europa. Internet www page, at url: http://web.inter.nl.net/users/Paul.Treanor/urban.ethic.html (version current at 12 July 2001).
92. P.Hume Brown (ed.), *Early Travellers in Scotland* (Edinburgh, 1891), 203.
93. *Aberdeen Description*, 491.
94. *Ibid.*, 496.
95. M.Girouard, *The English Town: A History of Urban Life* (New Haven, 1990), 68.
96. RCHAMS, *Aberdeen on Record: Images of the Past* (Edinburgh, 1997), 16.
97. Hume Brown, *Early Travellers*, 203.
98. M.Reed, 'The urban landscape, 1540-1700', in P.Clark (ed.), *Cambridge Urban History of Britain* (Cambridge, 2000), ii, 289.
99. *Aberdeen Description*, 496.
100. *Ibid.*, 502.
101. Hume Brown, *Early Travellers*, 173.
102. *Aberdeen Description.*, 502.
103. *Abdn Counc.*, iii, 291.
104. C.Graham, *Historical Walkabout of Aberdeen* (Aberdeen, 1973), 10.
105. Fraser, *Aberdeen Street Names*, 6.
106. Reed, 'Urban Landscape', 292.
107. Girouard, *The English Town*, 68.
108. Reed, ' Urban Landscape', 292.
109. Kennedy, *Annals*, i, 402.
110. A.J.Mill, *Medieval Plays in Scotland* (Edinburgh, 1927), 349.
111. G.M.Trevelyan, *English Social History* (London, 1948), 347.
112. P.Slack, 'The English urban landscape', in P.Clark (ed.), *The Urban Setting* (Milton Keynes, 1977), 107.
113. *OSA*, xiv, 286.
114. Simpson, *Old Aberdeen*, 2.
115. *Old Aberdeen Recs.*, i, 25.
116. RCHAMS, *Aberdeen on Record*, 19.
117. *Aberdeen Description*, 503.
118. P.Marren, *A Natural History of Aberdeen* (Aberdeen, 1982), 57.
119. Kennedy, *Annals*, i, 395.
120. Ulman, *Minutes*, 14.
121. I.Maver, 'Urbanisation', in A.Cooke *et al.* (eds), *Modern Scottish History, 1707 to the Present* (East Linton, 1998), i, 164.
122. W.Robbie, *Aberdeen: Its Traditions and History with Notices of Some Eminent Aberdonians* (Aberdeen, 1893), 298.
123. A.Vickery, 'In Pursuit of Pleasure. Part Two: The Pleasures of Town', www page, at url: http://www.open.ac.uk/Arts/18c-society/introduction.htm (version current at 12 July 2001).
124. K.Thomas, *Man and the Natural World: Changing Attitudes in England, 1500-1800* (London, 1983), 243.
125. Ulman, *Minutes*, 15.
126. Kennedy, *Annals*, i, 155.
127. Maver, 'Urbanisation', i, 161.
128. J.Robertson, 'The Scottish Contribution to the Enlightenment': Electronic Seminars in History Presentation Internet www page, at url: http://www.treeofliberty.com/scotcontrib.html (version current at 12 July 2001); Ulman, *Minutes*; A.Keith, *A Thousand Years of Aberdeen* (Aberdeen, 1972), 380.
129. E.Meldrum, *Aberdeen of Old* (Aberdeen, 1987), 14.
130. Fraser, *Aberdeen Street Names*, 83.

131. I. Adams, *The Making of Urban Scotland* (London, 1978), 81.
132. H. Hamilton, *An Economic History of Scotland in the*

Eighteenth Century (Oxford, 1963), 27.
133. Robbie, *Aberdeen: Its Traditions and History*, 298.
134. Hamilton, *Economic History of Scotland*, 27.

Notes to Chapter 2:
Life in the Two Towns

1. P. Hume Brown (ed.), *Early Travellers in Scotland* (Edinburgh, 1891), 205.
2. *Ibid.*, 205. In 1648, the music school in New Aberdeen was described as 'altogidder decayed throw the iniquitie of [the] tyme' (ACA, CR, liii (1), 23 Feb. 1648). Older members of the congregation, however, had grown up under the influence of the music school and its choirmasters. See W. Walker (ed.), *Extracts from the Commonplace Book of Andrew Melville, Doctor and Master in the Song School of Aberdeen, 1621-40* (Aberdeen, 1899).
3. E. Bain (ed.), *Merchant and Craft Guilds: A History of the Aberdeen Incorporated Trades* (Aberdeen, 1887), 47-72.
4. *Abdn Counc.* i, 136-7; E. Patricia Dennison and J. Stones, *Historic Aberdeen: The Archaeological Implications of Development* (Scottish Burgh Survey, 1997), 62.
5. See, for example, *St Nich. Cart.*, i, nos 11-13, 15; *Abdn Reg.*, i, 35-6, 234, 239-40.
6. W. Kennedy, *Annals of Aberdeen* (Aberdeen, 1818), ii, 46.
7. For example, on licensing and aisles, see ACA, CR, lii (1), 21 March 1638 & 16 Sept. 1640; on pew rent, ACA, CR, lv, 22 July 1674; and on burials, ACA, CR, lii (1), 15 July 1635.
8. ACA, CR, liv, 8 July 1663.
9. By law, everyone was obliged to attend church services on Sunday, morning and afternoon. There were also services on Tuesday and Thursday evenings. In practice, a certain proportion of the population was always absent on Sunday, and the weekday turnout (judging by the offerings) tended to be sparse. Children under six were barred from services because of the disruption they caused, and mothers and servants who stayed home to mind them were excused, as were the sick and the infirm. Catholics, Quakers and other dissenters tended to stay away as a matter of principle.
10. *ACA, CR*, lvii, 20 Sept. 1682.
11. On standing, see ACA, CR, liv, 23 Dec. 1661; on students, CR, liii (1), 10 Dec. 1656; CR, lv, 30 Oct. 1667; on under sixes, NAS, CH 2/448/4 (St Nicholas Kirk Session Minutes), 11 May 1651; *Abdn Counc.*, iv, 213.
12. *Abdn Ecc. Recs.*, 62-3, 136.
13. A. Skene, *Memorialls For the Government of the Roy-*

all-Burghs in Scotland (Aberdeen, 1685), 50.
14. H. Morland Simpson (ed.), *Bon Record: Records and Reminiscences of Aberdeen Grammar School* (Aberdeen, 1906), 5. On misconduct, see *Abdn Counc.*, ii, 39-40, 251. On educating girls, see *ibid.*, ii, 171, and G. DesBrisay, 'City limits: female philanthropists and wet nurses in seventeenth-century Scottish towns', *Journal of the Canadian Historical Association*, new series, 8 (1997), 42-7.
15. C. A. McLaren, 'Affrichtment and riot: student violence in Aberdeen, 1659-69', *Northern Scotland*, 10 (1990).
16. ACA, CR, lii (1), 22 Feb. 1632.
17. ACA, CR, liv, 23 Oct. 1661. In 1667, mischievous servants stole into empty seats in the town council's own pew, and apprentices were warned to stop menacing students in the grammar school loft (ACA, CR, lv, 9 Oct. 1667).
18. ACA, CR, lii (1), 22 Feb. 1632.
19. Such conduct was also said to endanger the lives of 'Meake and tender weemen' generally: ACA, CR, lv, 22 March 1671.
20. ACA, CR, lii (1), 22 Jan. 1640.
21. *Abdn Counc.*, iv, 193. These small stools were portable, as 'Jenny Geddes' demonstrated in St Giles', Edinburgh in 1637.
22. ACA, CR, liv, 4 Dec. 1661.
23. ACA, CR, lvi, 24 Jan. 1677.
24. ACA, CR, lvi, 24 Jan., 7 & 14 Feb. and 4 April 1677.
25. Skene, *Memorialls*, 62.
26. See for example *Abdn Recs*, 21, 100.
27. Anon., *The Freedom Lands and Marches of Aberdeen, 1319-1929* (Aberdeen, 1929), 4-7.
28. ACA, CR, lv, 7 Dec. 1670; lvi, 21 June 1676.
29. P. Yeoman, *Medieval Scotland: An Archaeological Perspective* (Edinburgh, 1995), 68-9, 57; E. Ewan, *Townlife in Fourteenth-Century Scotland* (Edinburgh, 1990), 22; J. A. Stones (ed.), *A Tale of Two Burghs: The Archaeology of Old and New Aberdeen* (Aberdeen, 1987) 40-7; J. C. Murray (ed.), *Excavations in the Medieval Burgh of Aberdeen 1973-81* (Edinburgh, 1982), 224.
30. ACA, CR, lii (1), 4 May 1642.
31. For example, on the building wall, see ACA, CR, lvii, 8 July & 1 Aug. 1688; on gutters, see ACA, CR, lii (1), 28 Nov. 1632; on smoke, see ACA, CR, liii (1), 6 Sept. 1648; on forestairs, see ACA, CR, lvii, 27 July 1687.

32. ACA, CR, lv, 1 May 1667. See also ACA, CR, lvii, 25 Oct. 1693.
33. ACA, CR, lv, 8 Oct. 1673; *Abdn Counc.*, iv, 207.
34. ACA, CR, liv, 13 July 1659; ACA, Register of Delinquents for Forestalling and Regrating, 23 Oct. 1668.
35. ACA, CR, liii (1), 15 July 1657.
36. ACA, CR, lv, 23 Dec. 1668; lvii, 22 March 1683 & 15 Aug. 1688; *Old Aberdeen Recs*, i, 143.
37. *Abdn Counc.*, iv, 143, 319-20.
38. *Abdn Counc.*, i, 70 (10 May 1511, misdated 1501), 81-2.
39. *Abdn Counc.*, iv, 289; *Abdn Counc.*, iii, 55-8; ACA, CR, lvi, 16 Feb. 1678 & 26 March 1679; lvii, 11 April 1683. See also ACA, CR, iv, 19 (29 June 1434).
40. For early examples, see ACA, CR, i, 6, 13 (28 Oct. & 9 Dec. 1398). See also E. Gemmill and N. Mayhew, *Changing Values in Medieval Scotland* (Cambridge, 1995), 30-41, 48-53.
41. See, for example, ACA, CR, liv, 21 July 1659; lv, 29 April 1674; lvii, 27 March & 10 April 1695.
42. ACA, CR, lvi, 4 Dec. 1678. Wooden stoups were notoriously easy to modify, and the council tried to insist that everyone use pewter: ACA, CR, liv, 14 Feb. 1666; lv, 10 Dec. 1672 & 11 Nov. 1674.
43. ACA, CR, lvii, 18 Nov. 1696.
44. See ACA, CR, liv, 19 Aug. 1663; *RPC*, 3rd. Ser., i, 406-7.
45. ACA, CR, liii (1), 1 Sept. 1658 (see also *ibid*, 7 April & 6 Oct. 1658); liv, 15 Jan. 1662 & 8 Feb 1666; lv, 21 June 1671; lvi, 30 May 1682; lvii, 14 June, 1693.
46. ACA, CR, lvi, 12 Dec. 1677.
47. L. Ewen, 'Debtors, imprisonment and the privilege of girth', in L. Leneman (ed.), *Perspectives in Scottish Social History: Essays in Honour of Rosalind Mitchison* (Aberdeen, 1988).
48. ACA, CR, iv, 349 (18 May 1444).
49. ACA, Bailie Court Books, xii, 8 Nov. 1673.
50. *Ibid.*, xiv, 19 Nov. & 6 Dec. 1687.
51. ACA, CR, iv, 409 (26 July 1445).
52. ACA, Bailie Court Books, xii, 18 Oct. 1673.
53. *Abdn Recs*, 23-9 (26 Oct. 1398).
54. *Abdn Recs*, 8.
55. *Abdn Recs*, 68; *Abdn Counc.*, i, 24, 417.
56. ACA, Register of Delinquents, 2 July 1684.
57. *Abdn Recs*, 217.
58. ACA, Justice Court Records, i, Feb. 1666.
59. *RPC*, 3rd ser., iii, 92-3. An apology was probably the best the town could hope for, given Irvine's friends in high places. See G. DesBrisay, 'Catholics, Quakers, and religious persecution in Restoration Aberdeen', *IR*, 47 (1996), 154-6.
60. *Abdn Counc.*, i, 330-1; ACA, Register of Delinquents, 8 Oct. 1684.
61. Figure based on a sample from ACA, Register of Delinquents, of 81 cases of verbal or physical assault between 1683 and 1687. Women were sole aggressors in 31 cases (16 directed at women, 15 against men).
62. NAS, CH 2/448/5 (Aberdeen St Nicholas Kirk Session), 4 June 1637.
63. ACA, Register of Delinquents, 23 June and 5 May 1685, 19 July 1664. Court officials must have heard every oath imaginable, but one poor scribe could not bring himself to record a particularly gruesome patch of 'veray ewill and injurious langaige, undvordy [i.e. unworthy] of heiring': *Abdn Counc.*, i, 285.
64. *Abdn Counc.*, i, 159-60.
65. ACA, Justice Court Records, i, 6 June 1664.
66. ACA, CR, xvi, 325 (6 July 1543).
67. NAS, CH 2/448/5, 15 Aug. 1630.
68. *Abdn Counc.*, i, 345.
69. Persecution was at its height from March 1676 to Nov. 1679: DesBrisay, 'Catholics, Quakers, and religious persecution'.
70. NAS, CH 10/3/36 ('A Brieff Historicall Account and Record of the First Rise and Progress of the Blessed Truth, Called in Derision Quakerism, in and about Aberdeen').
71. C. B. Boog Watson (ed.), *Register of Edinburgh Apprentices, 1666-1700* (Edinburgh, 1929), 65.
72. W. F. Miller, 'The Record Book of Friends of the Monethly Meeting att Urie', *Journal of the Friends Historical Society*, 7 (1910), 93.
73. *Diary of Alexander Jaffray ... To Which Are Added Particulars of His Subsequent Life, Given in Connexion With Memoirs of the Rise, Progress, and Persecutions of the People Called Quakers in the North of Scotland*, ed. J. Barclay (3rd edn, Aberdeen, 1856).
74. Jaffray's editor sometimes moderated his language. This quotation is taken from the original manuscript, ACA, MS Diary of Alexander Jaffray, fo. 5, top. The authors wish to thank Judith Cripps, City Archivist, for making this document available.
75. *Diary*, 43.
76. A. M. Munro (ed.), *Memorials of the Alderman, Provosts, and Lord Provosts of Aberdeen* (Aberdeen, 1897), 157-65.
77. *Diary*, 43.
78. ACA, MS Diary, fo. 145, bottom. The relevant passage was expunged from the printed diary.
79. *Diary*, 54.
80. *Diary*, 81.
81. *Diary*, 48.
82. *Diary*, 53. See also Jaffray's entry in the *Dictionary of National Biography*.
83. *Diary*, 75.
84. *Diary*, 80.
85. DesBrisay, 'City limits', 49.
86. J. Stuart (ed.), *List of Pollable Persons Within the*

Shire of Aberdeen, 1696 (Aberdeen, 1844), ii, 595-632.

87. I.D.Whyte and K.A.Whyte, 'The geographical mobility of women in early modern Scotland', in Leneman, *Perspectives in Social History*, 97.

88. ACA, Justice Court Records, i (1), 9 July 1660.

89. Servants from out of town, however, were more likely to encounter social and economic disparity, and were more vulnerable to abuse, sexual and otherwise: R. Mitchison and L. Leneman, *Sin in the City: Sexuality and Social Control in Urban Scotland 1660-1780* (Edinburgh, 1998), 60.

90. Bain, *Aberdeen Incorporated Trades*, 219, 226, 301.

91. The following discussion of illegitimacy and wet-nursing is based on G. DesBrisay, 'Wet nurses and unwed mothers in seventeenth-century Aberdeen', in E. Ewan and M. Meikle (eds), *Women in Scotland, c. 1100-1750* (East Linton, 1999).

92. Skene, *Memorialls*, 121. He was specifically referring to Deuteronomy 15:7-11.

93. Calculation based on figures for 1669, when a tax roll (ACA, Stent Roll Bundles) and a list of guild burgesses from 1668 (ACA, Press 18/Bundle 12, Election Leet Bundles) together suggest a community of 350 burgesses of guild and 250 burgesses of trade, with a further 100 households headed by guild or trade widows. Together, these 700 or so 'corporate' households accounted for about 40 per cent of a total of about 1,750 households in 1695, when the poll book affords the first reliable population estimate. G. DesBrisay, 'Authority and Discipline in Aberdeen: 1650-1700' (University of St Andrews, unpublished Ph.D. thesis, 1989), 178-81, 129; R.E.Tyson, 'The population of Aberdeenshire, 1695-1755: a new approach', *Northern Scotland*, 6 (1985), 125.

94. Trinity Hall, Aberdeen Incorporated Trades, Convener Court Book, i, 29 Oct. 1698. The authors thank the Deacon Convener and other Trades officers past and present, especially Ron Taylor, Master of the Trades Hospital, for granting access to the Trinity Hall archives.

95. See, for example, *Abdn Counc.*, ii, 124; *Abdn Counc.*, iv, 112; ACA, Letter Books (Incoming), vii, no. 243 (*c.* April 1699).

96. *Old Aberdeen Recs*, i, 142.

97. *Abdn Counc.*, i, 117.

98. DesBrisay, 'City limits', 39-40.

99. A. Clark, *A Short History of the Shipmaster Society, or the Seamen's Box of Aberdeen* (Aberdeen, 1911), 45-6. Mariners may well have identified more by vocation than location. The masons, another group whose peripatetic vocation made them exceptional, seem to have extended charity to needy masons from elsewhere, but only on an occasional basis. See D. Stevenson, *The First Free-masons: Scotland's Early Lodges and Their Members* (Aberdeen, 1988), 133-4.

100. *Abdn Counc.*, iv, 112; ACA, CR, lii (1), 9 April 1634; lv, 4 March 1674; lvii, 30 Sept. 1696 & 7 July 1697; ACA, Letter Books (Incoming), vii, no. 243 (*c.* April 1699).

101. See, for example, *Abdn Counc.*, iv, 112; ACA, CR, lv, 4 March 1674.

102. C.R.Friedrichs, *The Early Modern City, 1450-1750* (New York, 1995), 220.

103. DesBrisay, 'Wet nurses', 214.

104. *Abdn Counc.*, ii, 124, 359-61; ACA, CR, lvii, 23 Dec. 1696.

105. The remainder of Aberdeen's seventeenth-century funding came from fees paid by marrying couples, occasional gifts from grateful survivors of illness or hazardous voyages (though these gifts became less common over time) and the generally unreliable investment returns on legacies or 'mortifications' directed to the common poor (most were directed elsewhere). Glasgow and Edinburgh also directed burial fees to the poor, but in Aberdeen that money went to kirk upkeep.

106. The following discussion of public poor relief in New Aberdeen is based on a study of relevant entries and lists scattered throughout the St Nicholas Kirk Session Records for 1620-1700 (NAS, CH 2/448/4-24), and ACA, Kirk Session Accounts (1680, 1683, 1688, 1690, and 1692); ACA, Justice Court Records, ii (1660-90, 1693-1700).

107. NAS, CH 2/448/20, 9 Dec. 1689.

108. Murray, *Excavations*, 197-200.

109. *Abdn Counc.*, ii, 27, 161.

110. F.J.Stones, 'Sumptuary legislation in Scotland', *Juridical Review* (1979), 81-90, 104-7.

111. *Abdn Counc.*, ii, 191-7; Yeoman, *Medieval Scotland*, 81; Stones, *Tale of Two Burghs*, 32.

112. ACA, CR, vii, 73 (4 Sept. 1488); Murray, *Excavations*, 186.

113. ACA, CR, iv, 467 (22 Jan. 1447). For rings, see ACA, CR, iv, 373 (1 Dec. 1444), 406 (12 July 1445); Murray, *Excavations*, 186.

114. For example, ACA, CR, i, 404 (18 Oct; 1405), ii, 39 (June 1409); iv, 94 (22 April 1437).

115. See, for example, on doctors, ACA, CR, liv (21 Nov. 1660 & 14 Sept. 1664); schoolmasters, DesBrisay, 'City limits', 42-7; girls in service, ACA, CR, lvii, 23 Dec. 1696; apprentices, NAS, CH 2/448/5, 18 April 1630 & 20 June 1630; public payroll, ACA, CR, lv, 18 Sept. 1667 & 29 Jan. 1668.

116. DesBrisay, 'Authority and Discipline', 316-17; R. Jütte, *Poverty and Deviance in Early Modern Europe* (Cambridge, 1994), 40-1.

117. The only seemingly complete lists of pensioners date from the famine year of 1697 (NAS, CH 2/448/24, 1 Feb. 1697). For other years, partial lists

of pensioners added or deleted from the poor rolls can suggest the average amounts received, and where these lists coincide with session accounts indicating the total yearly expenditure on pensions, the number of pensioners can be calculated.

118. Friedrichs, *Early Modern City*, 227; Jütte, *Poverty and Deviance*, 50-4; R. A. Houston, *Social Change in the Age of Enlightenment: Edinburgh, 1660-1760* (Oxford, 1994), 253-4.

119. The low figure is for 1680, a year of low mortality and low prices, while the high figure is for 1691, a year of high prices and high mortality. Records for the famine of 1695-9 are incomplete, but the proportion of households on relief must have soared.

120. Jütte, *Poverty and Deviance*, 141.

121. H. M. Dingwall, *Late Seventeenth-Century Edinburgh: A Demographic Study* (Aldershot, 1994), 255.

122. Weekly collections, communion services, and fines garnered the kirk session about £2,000 per year in the 1630s, and about £1,850 in the 1680s.

123. The common poor of Old Aberdeen probably received even less on average: R. E. Tyson, 'Famine in Aberdeenshire, 1695-99: anatomy of a crisis', in D. Stevenson (ed.), *From Lairds to Louns: Country and Burgh in Aberdeen, 1600-1800* (Aberdeen, 1986), 36.

124. For example, a weaver named James Hay and his wife Catherine Chapman paid £8 6s 8d for a half year's rent on a house in New Aberdeen: ACA, Bailie Court Books, xii, 14 Oct. 1673.

125. ACA, Kirk Session Accounts, 1680 (references to Thomas Stevin and Christian Brown, respectively).

126. Male day-labourers earned 6s 8d per day in Aberdeen from *c.* 1630 to 1700, and could expect to work an average of four days per week, which would yield £67 6s (A. Gibson and T. C. Smout, *Prices, Food and Wages in Scotland, 1550-1780* (Cambridge, 1995), 284).

127. In 1697, during a relative respite from the famine, 6d would buy 10.5 ounces of bread. But oats were trading at £7 a boll at that point (up from £4 earlier in the decade), and the price eventually rose to a fatal £13 6s 8d a boll, by which point the council had stopped pricing a notional oat loaf. See Tyson, 'Famine in Aberdeenshire', 33-4; Gibson and Smout, *Prices, Food and Wages in Scotland*, 56.

128. G. Parker, *The Military Revolution: Military Innovation and the Rise of the West, 1500-1800* (Cambridge, 1988), 75, 80.

129. NAS, CH 2/448/5, Nov. 1634; see also Oct. 1629 for injunction against pensioners begging.

130. ACA, Letter Books (Incoming), vii, no. 243 (*c.* April 1699).

131. *Ibid.* On sixteen as the cut-off age, see, for example, NAS, CH 2/448/5, 25 Jan. 1635.

132. NAS, CH 2/448/5, 19 May 1633.

133. NAS, CH 2/448/14, 29 Dec. 1675.

134. *Abdn Counc.*, iii, 106-12.

135. For a son sent to the Correction House by his father, see NAS, CH 2/448/4, 17 Jan. 1640. The thirty prisoners sent to the Correction House by the kirk session between 1637 and 1639 were all women. The records are less complete thereafter.

136. NAS, CH 2/448/4, 12 Jan. 1640.

137. *Abdn Counc.*, iii, 109. On Edinburgh's workhouse, see M. Wood, 'St Paul's Work', *The Book of the Old Edinburgh Club*, 17 (1930).

138. *Abdn Counc.*, iv, 38-9, 69.

139. ACA, CR, liii (1), 12 Aug. 1657; liv, 20 Jan., 3 & 27 Feb., 20 April, 10 Sept., 15 Oct. 1664; lvi, 31 March 1675); lvii, 30 Jan. 1683. See also *Abdn Counc.*, iv, 215.

140. *Abdn Counc.*, iv, 320-2. In 1695-6, well over 400 Aberdeen households (the list is incomplete) drew small payments totalling £1,530 out of Mr Robert Johnston's mortification for the Correction House: ACA, Mortification Accounts, ii.

141. Kennedy, *Annals*, i, 258.

142. *Mortifications Under the Charge of the Provost, Magistrates, and Town Council of Aberdeen*, (Aberdeen, 1849).

143. *Ibid.*, 156, 150, 149.

144. *Ibid.*, Appendix no. ii, 21.

145. *Ibid.*, 3-8.

146. Bain, *Merchant and Craft Guilds*, 166; ACA, CR, li (2), 16 Nov. 1631. On Gordon of Rothiemay's 1661 map, St Thomas was referred to simply as the 'Toun's Hospital'.

147. Bain, *Merchant and Craft Guilds*, 166-73; *Mortifications*, 94.

148. *Mortifications*, 101-2.

149. ACA, CR, liv, 17 Feb. 1664; lii (1), 29 May 1633.

150. A. Skene, 'A Succinct Survey of the Famous City of Aberdeen' in *idem*, *Memorialls for the Government of the Royall-Burghs in Scotland* (Aberdeen, 1685), 221. The accounts of the litsters' craft were discovered by the late Mr Peter Vasey (NAS, E 870/4/29).

151. Kennedy, *Annals*, ii, 315.

152. ACA, CR, vi, 459 (20 Nov. 1476).

153. ACA, CR, lii (2), 16 Jan. 1639. Gordon of Rothiemay depicted the sick house as a ruin on his map published in 1661.

154. Ewan, *Townlife*, 12.

155. ACA, CR, liv, 21 Dec. 1659.

156. *Ibid.*

157. Much the same strictures applied to burgesses of craft entering the Trades' Hospital: Bain, *Merchant and Craft Guilds*, 167-8.

158. Entitlements are spelled out in a complaint the bedesmen lodged against the Master of the Hospital in July 1675. ACA, Press 17/ Parcel H, Guild Brethren Hospital Papers (1 of 2).
159. Trinity House, Aberdeen Incorporated Trades, Convener Court Book, i, fo.79 (5 Oct. 1685); ACA, Mortification Accounts, ii (Lady Drum's Mortification, 1673-4).
160. ACA, CR, liv, 21 Dec. 1659.
161. H. L. Diack, 'Women, Health and Charity: Women in the Poor Relief Systems in Eighteenth-century Scotland and France' (University of Aberdeen, unpublished Ph.D., 1999).
162. NHSA, GRHB 1/1/3.
163. A. Walker, *The History of the Workhouse or Poor's Hospital of Aberdeen* (Aberdeen, 1885), 8.
164. *Ibid.,* 8.
165. *OSA*, xiv, 305.
166. ACA, Ledger Book of the Poor's Hospital, ii.
167. *Ibid.*
168. Walker, *Workhouse*, 9.
169. *OSA*, Aberdeen, 305.
170. ACA, Ledger of the Poor's Hospital.
171. RGC, MS Daily Tasks Work Book, 1741-3.
172. C. Whatley, 'Women and the economic transformation of Scotland, *c.* 1740-1830', *SESH*, 14 (1994), 25-46.
173. RGC, Daily Tasks Work Book, 1741-3.
174. *Old Aberdeen Recs*, i, 49; ACA, CR, liii (2), 3 June & 2 Dec. 1640.

Notes to Chapter 3:
Health in the Two Towns

1. ACA, MSS Guildry Accounts, 1453-1812 (10-1/1), Compt of David Mar, 1548-52, fo. 4v.
2. *Abdn Counc.*, i, 81.
3. ACA, CR, viii, 615.
4. This word is peculiar to Aberdeen. The porters were the forerunners of the Shore Porters; their numbers included both men and women - an indication of the strength and stamina of Aberdeen women! See too J. Bulloch, *The Pynours: Historical Notes on an Ancient Aberdeen Craft* (Aberdeen, 1887).
5. *Abdn Counc.*, i, 82.
6. *Ibid.*, i, 80, 82-3.
7. J. Stones (ed.), *A Tale of Two Burghs* (Aberdeen, 1987), 30.
8. A. Gibson and T. C. Smout, 'Scottish food and Scottish history', in R. A. Houston and I. D. Whyte (eds), *Scottish Society, 1500-1800* (Cambridge, 1989), 60-6.
9. Stones, *Two Burghs*, 30.
10. *Abdn Reg.*, i, 54.
11. *Ibid.*, i, 54.
12. ACA, CR, ix, 156; xii, 132, 145; xiv, 197; xv, 705; xvi, 602, 704, 873.
13. P. Richards, *The Medieval Leper and his Northern Heirs* (Cambridge, 2000), *passim*.
14. *Liber Sancte Marie de Calchou* (Bannatyne Club, 1846), ii, 448, no. 559.
15. M. Flinn (ed.), *Scottish Population History from the Seventeenth Century to the 1930s* (Cambridge, 1977), 112.
16. P. Slack, *The Impact of Plague in Tudor and Stuart England* (Oxford, 1985), 7.
17. J. F. D. Shrewsbury, *A History of Bubonic Plague in the British Isles* (Cambridge, 1970), 1-6.
18. D. Hamilton, *The Healers: A History of Medicine in Scotland* (Edinburgh, 1982), 9.
19. Flinn, *Scottish Population*, 133-6. See also G. Twigg, 'Plague in London: spatial and temporal aspects of mortality,' in J. A. I. Champion (ed.), *Epidemic Disease in London* (London, 1993), 1-6. The even deadlier pneumonic form of plague was very rare in Britain after about 1500: Slack, *Impact of Plague*, 8-9.
20. Flinn, *Scottish Population*, 135.
21. Preparing and administering remedies was one of the main skills expected of a wife, and recipes for all sorts of medicines were widely published and exchanged. Apothecaries carried the more exotic ingredients, and had their own special blends for sale. Physicians tended to bleed plague victims. One of the most common internal medicines for plague was theriac, known as treacle (Slack, *Impact of Plague*, 30-9). Treacle is referred to in a 1665 poem by the Aberdeen poet Lilias Skene (AUL, MS 2774 (Poems of Lilias Skene, 1665-96, transcribed by William Walker)).
22. Slack, *Impact of Plague*, 7-8; A. B. Appleby, 'The disappearance of plague: a continuing puzzle,' *Economic History Review*, 2nd ser., 33 (1980), 163-4; Flinn (ed.), *Scottish Population*, 133-4.
23. A. Fitch, 'Assumptions about plague in late medieval Scotland', *Scotia*, 11 (1987), 31-2.
24. ACA, CR, vii, 934-6.
25. *Ibid.*, vii, 963.
26. *Ibid.*, vii, 969.
27. *Ibid.*, vii, 993, 994.
28. *Ibid.*, vii, 963.
29. *Ibid.*, vii, 1067.
30. *Ibid.*, vii, 1105.
31. *Ibid.*, viii, 576, 594.
32. *Ibid.*, vii, 8, 582.
33. *Ibid.*, xii (2), 454, 706-7.

34. *Abdn Counc.*, i, 177.
35. ACA, CR, vii, 797.
36. *Edin. Recs.*, i, 71-2.
37. ACA, CR, viii, 753, 754.
38. Stones, *Two Burghs*, 35.
39. J. A. Stones (ed.), *Three Scottish Carmelite Friaries: Excavations at Aberdeen, Linlithgow and Perth, 1980-86* (Edinburgh, 1989), 132-3.
40. *Ibid.*, 35-6.
41. *Ibid.*, 139.
42. *Ibid.*, 36-7; A. K. J. Jones, 'Parasite remains from Oslogatgate 7', in *De Arkologiske Letgravinger* (Norway, 1979).
43. Stones, *Carmelite Friaries*, 134.
44. *Abdn Reg.*, i, 11; ii, 39.
45. J. C. Murray (ed.), *Excavations in the Medieval Burgh of Aberdeen, 1973-81* (Edinburgh, 1982), 242.
46. P. Holdsworth (ed.), *Excavations in the Medieval Burgh of Perth* (Edinburgh, 1987), 206-7.
47. O. Hufton, *The Prospect before Her: A History of Women in Western Europe, 1500-1800* (London, 1995), 282.
48. D. Andrew, 'Two medical charities in eighteenth-century London: the Lock Hospital and the lying-in charity for married women,' in J. Barry and C. Jones (eds), *Medicine and Charity before the Welfare State* (London, 1991), 89.
49. G. M. Cullen, 'Concerning sibbens [sic] and the Scottish yaws', *Caledonian Medical Journal* (April, 1911). A doctor in Fort William has conducted some preliminary studies into the matter, but most doctors and venereologists consulted had not heard of a disease by that name.
50. A Warrack, *A Scots Dialect Dictionary* (Edinburgh, 1930) describes sibbens as 'the itch; venereal disease, cf. Sivven.' For sivven, the *Dictionary* gives the following explanation, 'the raspberry; in plural, a venereal disease resembling a raspberry.' R. Quain (ed.), *A Dictionary of Medicine* (London, 1882) defines sibbens as a term 'derived from a Scots word signifying kindred; and is suggestive of a disease prevalent in families and presumed to be a form of chronic syphilis'. In personal correspondence, the consultant venereologist J. D. Milne characterises it as a type of endemic non-venereal syphilis and also suggests that it could be 'derived from the Gaelic word for raspberry - *subhag*'.
51. J. D. Comrie, *A History of Medicine* (London, 1932), i, 431.
52. NHSA, GRHB 1/1/4.
53. The Black Death killed about one-third of the population of England in 1348-9 before making its way north to Scotland. Subsequent outbreaks of the plague never matched that first catastrophic mortality.
54. Flinn, *Scottish Population*, 6-7, 133-49. It has often been stated that the plague returned to Aberdeen in 1649 (e.g. Flinn, *Scottish Population*, 146), but this derives from an error in the published extracts of the town council minutes, where an entry dating from 11 Oct. 1648 was misdated 1649 (*Abdn Counc.*, iv, 99-100).
55. The last plague tended to be especially deadly elsewhere as well. See Appleby, 'The disappearance of plague', 165 and *passim*. It has been suggested that Scottish burghs as a whole lost about 20 per cent of their population to the final plague epidemic of the 1640s: Flinn, *Scottish Population*, 147.
56. Flinn, *Scottish Population*, 136-40.
57. *Abdn Counc.*, iv, 51. Old Aberdeen seems not to have mounted a public response to the 1645 plague alarm.
58. The figure of 600 burgesses is based on an estimate for 1669. See G. DesBrisay, 'Authority and Discipline in Aberdeen, 1650-1700' (University of St Andrews, unpublished Ph.D. thesis, 1989), 12. Gatherings of craft and guild burgesses were routinely said, apparently without irony, to have constituted 'the haill toun'.
59. *Abdn Counc.*, iv, 54-5.
60. *Ibid.*, iv, 51, 58-9. Labourer's wages were fixed at 6s 8d per day.
61. *Ibid.*, iv, 55.
62. *ACL*, iii, 14.
63. *Abdn Counc.*, iv, 58-9.
64. It seems clear that quarantine measures could at least slow the spread of plague, but historians disagree as to what role, if any, quarantine and other human interventions played in the plague's eventual disappearance from western Europe. For an introduction to the debate, see Appleby, 'Disappearance of plague' and P. Slack, 'The disappearance of the plague: an alternative view', *Economic History Review*, 2nd ser., 34 (1981).
65. Flinn, *Scottish Population*, 142-3.
66. *Abdn Counc.*, iv, 77-9. For an earlier effort to encourage burials in the churchyard see *Abdn Counc.*, ii, 55.
67. *Ibid.*, iv, 81.
68. The General of Artillery's Foot of the Scottish New Model Army left on 10 April (ACA, CR, liii (1), 21 April 1647. See also E. M. Furgol, *A Regimental History of the Covenanting Armies, 1639-51* (Edinburgh, 1990), 252-3.
69. *Abdn Counc.*, iv, 81-3.
70. The kirk session records for New Aberdeen do not survive for the 1640s. As the plague grew near in 1608, the ministers of the day called for a fast to appease the Almighty before it was too late, 'seein God is drawen nerer to the citie be the vistitatioun

of the plague', while the bishop reminded the town that it was 'the innumberable sinnis of this citie that procuris Goddis wraith' (*Abdn Ecc. Recs.* 63-5). It is likely that similar responses and sentiments issued from the pulpits in 1647 and 1648.

71. *Abdn Counc.*, iv, 82. From about the middle of the seventeenth century, it became normal for girls as well as boys to attend junior schools: G. DesBrisay, 'City limits: female philanthropists and wet nurses in seventeenth-century Scottish towns,' *Journal of the Canadian Historical Association*, 8 (1997), 45-8. The grammar school and colleges were only for boys.

72. *Abdn Counc.*, iv, 82.

73. Slack, *Impact of Plague*, 26-7.

74. *Abdn Counc.*, iv, 81-3.

75. It is hard to know what effect this last measure, if implemented, might have had. Poisoning infected rats (who would likely to crawl back into the walls or roof or under the floors to die) might have encouraged the infected fleas they carried to seek a new (probably human) host sooner rather than later, whereas killing healthy rats in time should have helped limit the chain of transmission.

76. *Abdn Counc.*, iv, 83-4.

77. Kempt had been banished several times before, but the order had not been put in effect: *Abdn Counc.*, iv, 84 .

78. Slack, *Impact of Plague*, 43.

79. By 1639, people with infectious diseases were sometimes given money from the funds intended to support the sickhouse, suggesting the house itself was no longer in use: ACA, CR, lii (1), 16 Jan. 1639.

80. It was depicted as a ruin in Rothiemay's map of 1661.

81. W. Kennedy, *Annals of Aberdeen* (Aberdeen, 1818), ii, 315.

82. Kennedy, *Annals*, i, 271-2.

83. On the shunning of plague victims, survivors and workers, see Slack, *Impact of Plague*, 273-9.

84. ACA, CR, liii (1), 22 March 1648; A. M. Munro, 'Aberdeen Burgess Register, 1631-1700', *Miscellany of the New Spalding Club*, ii (1908), 39.

85. As a cleanger she was referred to in the records as the 'relict of Alexander Brebner': ACA, CR, liii (1), 16 Feb. 1648; NAS, CH 2/448/14 (Aberdeen St Nicholas Kirk Session), 10 Nov. 1674. Women elsewhere were sometimes compelled to become plague workers in order to continue to collect poor relief, but there is no evidence of this in Aberdeen. See R. Munkhoff, 'Searchers of the dead: authority, marginality, and the interpretation of plague in England, 1574-1665', *Gender and History* 11 (1999).

86. Kennedy, *Annals*, i, 272; *ACL*, iii, p. xiv.

87. *Abdn Counc.*, iv, 83.

88. *Abdn Counc.*, iv, 85. See also *ibid.*, ii, 56 .

89. Patrick Watson, the offending constable, was also fined 100 merks (£66 13s 4d). He could 'redeime himselff' from the shaming ritual by paying double the fine - an option most people in his position took: ACA, CR, liii (1), 8 Mar. 1648. In 1585, two women were sentenced to death for sheltering strangers during a plague emergency, but at the instigation of two noblemen their sentences were commuted to banishment: *Abdn Counc.*, ii, 57.

90. This seasonal pattern was probably due to fleas hibernating or slowing down in cold weather. When an epidemic remained virulent over the winter months other diseases besides bubonic plague were probably involved: Flinn, *Scottish Population*, 134-5.

91. *Abdn Counc.*, iv, 85; ACA, CR, liii (1), 27 Sept. 1647.

92. Kennedy, *Annals*, i, 271.

93. *Old Aberdeen Recs.*, ii, 27.

94. *Ibid.*, i, 78.

95. *Ibid.*, i, 78-9.

96. *Ibid.*, ii, 28.

97. Alexander Jaffray, *Diary … to which are added particulars of his subsequent life, given in connection with memoirs of the rise, progress, and persecutions of the people called Quakers in the North of Scotland*, ed. J. Barclay (3rd edn, Aberdeen, 1856), 54.

98. *Abdn Chrs.*, 345-51. See also A. Skene, *Memorialls For the Government of the Royall Burghs in Scotland* (Aberdeen, 1685), esp. *A Succinct Survey of the Famous City of Aberdeen*, printed with it.

99. ACA, CR, liii (1), 27 Sept. 1647.

100. *Abdn Counc.*, iv, 99-100 (actually 11 Oct. 1648, but misdated 1649).

101. *Old Aberdeen Recs*, ii, 28. It is not clear whether New and Old Aberdeen shared the huts.

102. *Abdn Counc.*, iv, 118.

103. *Ibid.*, iv, 118. Leslie continued to attend to the poor free of charge, but his tax exemption attracted controversy as he became very wealthy. He was a fiery character, and challenged at least two men to duels over the matter. See *ACL*, iv, 83.

104. Leslie's concern was to provide some oversight of medical providers - ensuring that apothecaries' old drugs were thrown out annually, for example - and to see that apothecaries, surgeons, and physicians did not intrude on each other's work. Surgeons were not to treat 'internal diseases' without consulting a physician first. Midwives, probably the most numerous and among the most necessary and effective medical practitioners in town, were not considered part of the emerging medical profession, which consisted solely of men.

105. *ACL*, iii, 228.

106. The weekly collections normally provided well over half of the money spent on the poor. There were other mechanisms for collecting donations, but these may not have filled the gap. The ministers of Old Aberdeen, for example, took up collections whenever they could, and a woman named Issobel Hunter left just over £100 in her will 'for the use of the poore people in the hutts ye tyme of the lait visitation' (*Old Aberdeen Recs*, ii, 28; ACA, CR, liii (1), 13 Sept. 1648).

107. Flinn, *Scottish Population*, 145. After the town council resumed meeting in December 1647 there were references to the importation of grain 'for the common use of the toun'. See, for example, ACA, CR, liii (1), 15 Dec. 1647.

108. *ACL*, iii, 228. The surviving records do not break down expenditure. The materials and labour involved in constructing the huts was one plague cost, and another involved the relatively high salaries paid to searchers and cleangers. The (suspiciously round) figure of £30,000 probably included interest charges, lawyers' fees and the cost of sending officials to Edinburgh to lobby (and bribe) for the remission of taxes as soon as the infection lifted, but bulk food purchases were most likely to have been the chief expense.

109. The classic expression of and response to this fear is Thomas Hobbes, *Leviathan* (1651).

110. *Abdn Counc.*, iv, 84-5.

111. In 1639, the council declared its preference for borrowing from the mortifications in its trust rather than outside creditors, as was the norm. ACA, CR, lii (1), 27 Nov. 1639.

112. In 1654, the town council owed £99,000 to its mortifications, and in 1695 the town still owed £92,392. *ACL*, iii, 228; ACA, Press 18/Bundle 12 ('State of the toun', 24 Sept. 1695).

113. *Abdn Counc.*, iv, 85.

114. For example, the provost was advised to come to terms with James Campbell, cleanger, 'for his residence and service heir for a certaine tyme to come' (ACA, CR, liii (1), 23 Dec. 1647.

115. *Old Aberdeen Recs*, ii, 29; i, 80.

116. Reports that the plague returned in 1649 are incorrect. See n. 55, above.

117. For plague alarms see, for example, *Abdn Counc.*, iv, 208, 211-12, 221-2; *ACL*, iv, 381-3.

118. Kennedy, *Annals*, i, 272, based on records no longer extant. Old Aberdeen was less populous and less congested than New Aberdeen, so a lower rate of mortality is to be expected. But the burial registers for Old Machar are clearly incomplete for 1647: with a population about one-eighth the size of New Aberdeen, it seems unlikely that Old Aberdeen, just one mile away, would suffer one-eightieth the mortality. See the comments in Flinn, *Scottish Population*, 135-6.

119. In other towns the plague usually, but not always, killed more men than women. Since women outnumbered men in Aberdeen by a ratio of about 100:71, it is to be expected that more of them died. In the absence of the original burial registers, however, there is no way to be sure. See Slack, *Impact of Plague*, 179-81.

120. On plague and infant mortality, see Slack, *Impact of Plague*, 182. For the hospital, see *Abdn Counc.*, iv, 90.

121. *ACL*, iii, pp. xiv-xv, n. 4.

122. See Slack, *Impact of Plague*, 164-72; J. A. I. Champion, 'Epidemics and the built environment', in Champion, *Epidemic Disease in London* (London, 1993), i, 6-7.

123. N. J. Alldridge, 'House and household in Restoration Chester,' *Urban History Yearbook* (1983), 45; Slack, *Impact of Plague*, 183-4.

124. ACA, CR, liii (1), 15 & 22 Dec. 1647.

125. Lorimers, blacksmiths, and other members of the hammermen's trade were especially hard hit; perhaps their work in stables put them closer to rats and fleas, perhaps they continued to congregate when other trades stopped meeting, or perhaps they were just unlucky. See Munro, 'Aberdeen Burgess Register', 39; ACA, CR, liii (1), 22 Dec. 1647.

126. *ACL*, iii, 102.

127. *Abdn Counc.*, iv, 90. Bonnetmakers, who also knitted stockings, were particularly associated with Dundee: the Aberdeen magistrates presumably wished to encourage economic diversity, but the business did not catch on. For plague in Dundee, see Flinn, *Scottish Population*, 146.

128. ACA, CR, liii (1), 22 Dec. 1647; *Abdn Counc.*, iv, 86.

129. See DesBrisay, 'Authority and Discipline', Appendix I.

130. Slack, *Impact of Plague*, 3.

131. DesBrisay, 'Authority and Discipline', 77; Flinn, *Scottish Population*, 115. Smallpox outbreaks in 1610 and 1635 were severe and noted in the public records. See *Abdn Ecc. Recs*, 74; Flinn, *Scottish Population*, 131-2.

132. This was common in burghs confronting smallpox. See Flinn, *Scottish Population*, 112.

133. *APS*, ix, 195.

134. R. E. Tyson, 'Famine in Aberdeenshire, 1695-9', in D. Stevenson (ed.), *From Lairds to Louns* (Aberdeen, 1986), 50.

135. An account of the Poor's Hospital can be found in Chapter 2.

136. F. Watson, *In Sickness and in Health* (Aberdeen, 1988), 3.

137. NHSA, GRHB 1/10/22 (Account of the Rise and Progress of the Infirmary at Aberdeen, 1754).

138. ACA, CR, lxi, 17 Nov. 1741.
139. NHSA, GRHB 1/1/2.
140. *Ibid.*
141. *Ibid.* Until the opening of Royal Cornhill Hospital in 1801, all patients for Bedlam were housed in the Infirmary.
142. H. Marland, 'Lay and medical conceptions of medical charity during the nineteenth century: the case of Huddersfield General Dispensary and Infirmary', in Barry and Jones, *Medicine and Charity*, 157-8.
143. NHSA, GRHB 1/1/4 (Minute Book of the Infirmary, 1758-67).
144. L. Diack, 'A woman's greatest adventure: the development of maternity care in Aberdeen since the eighteenth century', in T. Brotherstone and D. J. Withrington (eds), *The City and its Worlds: Aspects of Aberdeen's History since 1794* (Glasgow, 1996), 115-29.
145. NHSA, GRHB 1/1/5 (Minute Book of the Infirmary, 1767-7, labelled Clinical Register).
146. NHSA, GRHB 1/10/22 (Minute Book, 1754), 1/10/23 (Minute Book, 1758), 1/10/24 (Minute Book, 1768).
147. R. Wilson, *An Historical Account and Delineation of Aberdeen* (Aberdeen, 1822), 179.
148. NHSA, GRHB 1/3/9 (Admission and Discharge Registers).
149. NAS, GD 136/1194 (Sinclair of Freswick Papers) include a list of diseases treated in 1792-3. *OSA*, xiv, 310-15, also includes tables of diseases for the early 1790s. The nineteenth-century annual reports of the Dispensary (or Aberdeen Dispensary, Vaccine and Lying-in Institution, as it came to be called), are held in AUL and Aberdeen Public Library, although neither has a complete set.
150. AUL, MS 632; (A. Gordon, *A Treatise of the Epidemic Puerperal Fever of Aberdeen* (London, 1795).
151. *OSA*, xiv, 310-15.
152. L. Diack, 'Dr David Skene and his contribution to women's health', in A. Adam, D. Smith and F. Watson (eds), '*To the Greit Support and Advancement of Helth*' (Aberdeen, 1996), 12-19.
153. W. R. Humphries, 'The letters of David Skene, part iii', *Postgraduate Medical Bulletin* (June, 1972), 5.
154. AUL, MS 476 (Papers of David Skene), pp. 63, 103.
155. AUL, MS 38 (Letter from Dr David Skene, Edinburgh, 13 Mar. 1752). The four diseases mentioned are iron deficiency anaemia, leucorrhoea, haemoptysis and uterine disorders. Further details on David Skene and his attitudes to women's health can be found in L. Diack, 'Dr David Skene', 12-19.
156. AUL, MS 37 (Papers of David Skene), fos 11-12 (undated): *Whether by the encouragement of proper Laws the number of Births in Great Britain might not be greatly increased.*
157. AUL, MS 475 (Papers of David Skene).
158. L. Diack, 'Motherhood and poverty in eighteenth-century Aberdeen', in T. Brotherstone, D. Simonton and O. Walsh (eds), *Gendering Scottish History: An International Approach* (Glasgow 2000), 172-85.

Notes to Chapter 4:
Housing in the Two Towns

1. The author wishes to acknowledge the help given by Nicholas Bogdan, Pat Dennison, Ian Fisher, Iain Fraser and Judith Stones in the preparation of this essay.
2. *Aberdeen Description.*
3. For descriptive summaries, see W. A. Brogden, *Aberdeen: An Illustrated Architectural Guide* (Aberdeen, 1986; 2nd edn, 1998); E. Meldrum, *Aberdeen of Old* (Inverness, 1986); N. Q. Bogdan and I. B. D. Bryce, 'A compendium of the castles, manors and town houses (*c.* 1052-*c.* 1707) of Scotland, Grampian Region, Aberdeen City District' (Aberdeen, Scottish Castle Survey, typescript 1988), 1-13 (items A1/1-78 *passim*); J. A. Stones (ed.), *A Tale of Two Burghs: The Archaeology of Old and New Aberdeen* (Aberdeen, 1987); E. Patricia Dennison and J. Stones, *Historic Aberdeen: The Archaeological Implications of Development* (Scottish Burgh Survey, 1997).
4. Collections of old photographs are conveniently published in, for example, F. Wyness, *Aberdeen, Century of Change* (Aberdeen, 1971); A. Cluer, *Walkin' the Mat* (Aberdeen, 1976); and H. F. C. Lyall, *Vanishing Aberdeen. In the Steps of George Washington Wilson* (Aberdeen, 1988).
5. RCAHMS, *Aberdeen on Record, Images of the Past* (Edinburgh, 1997).
6. Brogden, *Aberdeen*; Meldrum, *Aberdeen of Old*; Stones, *Two Burghs, passim*. See also J. S. Smith, 'Old Aberdeen - the Buildings' in J. S. Smith (ed.), *Old Aberdeen: Bishops, Burghers and Buildings* (Aberdeen, 1991), 79-98; and for the historical background L. J. Macfarlane and A. G. Short, *The Burgh and Cathedral of Old Aberdeen* (Aberdeen, 1989); G. G. Simpson, *Old Aberdeen in the Early Seventeenth Century* (Aberdeen, 1975).
7. D. Walker, 'Aberdeen: the planning of the central area, 1750-1850', *St Andrews Studies in the History of Scottish Architecture and Design*, 4 (2000), 51-68. See also ch. 18.

8. RCAHMS, National Monuments Record of Scotland (NMRS), Record Sheet ABR/13/1 and Drawings ABD/371/1-2 (published in RCAHMS, NMRS Report, 1972-4).

9. E. Meldrum, 'Sir George Skene's house in the Guestrow, Aberdeen - its history and architecture', *PSAS*, 92 (1958-9), 85-103.

10. C. Carter, 'The *Arma Christi* in Scotland', *PSAS*, 90 (1956-7), 116-29.

11. E. Meldrum, 'Benholm's Tower, Nether Kirkgate, Aberdeen', *PSAS*, 95 (1961-2), 249-61.

12. R. W. Billings, *The Baronial and Ecclesiastical Antiquities of Scotland* (Edinburgh, 1845-52), i, Plate 5 and commentary; D. MacGibbon and T. Ross, *The Castellated and Domestic Architecture of Scotland* (Edinburgh, 1887-92), v, 76; G. M. Fraser, *Historical Aberdeen* (Aberdeen, 1905), 136; Wyness, *Century of Change*, no. 67; Meldrum, *Aberdeen of Old*, 95; Brogden, *Aberdeen* (1998 edn), 36-7; Dennison & Stones, *Historic Aberdeen*, 40-1.

13. Billings, *Baronial and Ecclesiastical Antiquities*.

14. For example, Meldrum, *Aberdeen of Old*, 31.

15. Wyness, *Century of Change*, nos 45, 48; Stones, *Two Burghs*, 43.

16. RCAHMS, NMRS, plans by Fenton Wyness, ABD/40/2-11. See also Meldrum, *Aberdeen of Old*, 154.

17. Stones, *Two Burghs*, 44; Dennison & Stones, *Historic Aberdeen*, 80-1; Meldrum, *Aberdeen of Old*, 174.

18. *Aberdeen Description*, 9.

19. Daniel Defoe, *A Tour through the Whole Island of Great Britain* (London, 1724-26; 1968 reprint), ii, 693, cited in M. Lynch, M. Spearman and G. Stell (eds), *The Scottish Medieval Town* (Edinburgh, 1988), 73.

20. Cluer, *Walkin' the Mat*, not paginated (s. n. Upper Denburn, Mutton Brae, Jack's Brae, Guestrow, Old Torry); Meldrum, *Aberdeen of Old*, 87; Stones, *Two Burghs*, 46-7. See also G. G. Burr and A. M. Munro,

Old Landmarks of Aberdeen (Aberdeen, 1886), Plate 11 (Old House in Guestrow).

21. Cited in Stones, *Two Burghs*, 47.

22. This summary closely follows Stones, *Two Burghs*, 41-2. For the working and use of granite, see W. Kelly, 'On work in granite', in W. Douglas Simpson (ed.), *A Tribute Offered by the University of Aberdeen to the memory of William Kelly, LLD, ARSA* (Aberdeen, 1949), 76-90; W. Diack, *The Rise and Progress of the Granite Industry of Aberdeen* (Aberdeen, 1949); and T. Donnelly, *The Aberdeen Granite Industry* (Aberdeen, 1994).

23. For popular accounts of urban excavations in Aberdeen see G. G. Simpson (ed.), *Aberdeen's Hidden History* (Aberdeen, 1974); J. C. Murray (ed.), *Aberdeen: The Town beneath the City* (Aberdeen, 1978); Stones, *Two Burghs*.

24. H. Murray, 'The excavated secular buildings', in J. C. Murray (ed.), *Excavations in the Medieval Burgh of Aberdeen, 1973-81* (Edinburgh, 1982), 224-8; J. C. Murray, 'The archaeological evidence', in J. S. Smith (ed.), *New Light on Medieval Aberdeen* (Aberdeen, 1985), 10-19.

25. *Abdn Recs.*, pp. lix-lx, 14. The use of documentary sources for building histories and property boundaries in medieval Aberdeen is discussed by J. Cripps, 'Establishing the topography of medieval Aberdeen: an assessment of the documentary sources', in Smith, *New Light*, 20-31.

26. J. S. Dent, 'Building materials and methods of construction, the evidence from the archaeological excavations at Broad Street, Aberdeen', in *Building Construction in Scotland, Some Historical and Regional Aspects* (Scottish Vernacular Buildings Working Group, 1974), 65-71.

27. The summary that follows is closely based on the excellent account in Stones, *Two Burghs*, 12-14, 40-7.

Notes to Chapter 5:
People in the Two Towns

1. 'Introduction', in M. Lynch, M. Spearman and G. Stell (eds), *The Scottish Medieval Town* (Edinburgh, 1988), 6.

2. P. G. B. McNeill and H. I. MacQueen (eds), *Atlas of Scottish History to 1707* (Edinburgh, 1996), 35.

3. E. Ewan, 'The age of Bon-Accord: Aberdeen in the fourteenth century', in J. S. Smith (ed.), *New Light on Medieval Aberdeen* (Aberdeen, 1985), 35.

4. W. Kennedy, *Annals of Aberdeen* (Aberdeen, 1818), i, 36-7.

5. *Old Parish Registers [OPRs]*, Parish of St Nicholas, Baptisms, vol. i.

6. *Abdn Counc.*, iv, 179.

7. *Old Aberdeen Recs*, ii, 92.

8. *Ibid.*, ii, 7; NRA(S), CH 2/1/4 (Presbytery of Aberdeen Register), 120-8; CH 2/1020/8 (Old Machar Kirk Session Records), 124-5.

9. *OSA*, xiv, 285-7, 294-5.

10. *OPRs*, Parish of St Nicholas, vols i-iii.

11. M Lynch, 'Urbanisation and urban networks in seventeenth-century Scotland: some further thoughts', *SESH*, 12 (1992), 26.

12. *Old Aberdeen Recs*, i, 346-55; R. E. Tyson, 'The population of Aberdeenshire, 1695-1755: a new

approach', *Northern Scotland*, 6 (1985), 125.

13. *OSA*, xiv, 285-6; *Census of 1801*.

14. Kennedy, *Annals*, i, 27.

15. C. Brown, *The Battle for Aberdeen, 1644* (Stroud, 2002), 59-82 for an account of the battle of Justice Mill.

16. John Spalding, *Memorialls of the Trubles in Scotland and England, 1624-1645*, ed. J. Stuart (Spalding Club, 1851), ii 406-12; Kennedy, *Annals*, i, 221-3.

17. P. Slack, *The Impact of Plague in Tudor and Stuart England* (Oxford, 1990), 7-13.

18. J. A. Stones, *A Tale of Two Burghs: the Archaeology of Old and New Aberdeen* (Aberdeen, 1987), 12-14, 40-4.

19. M. Flinn (ed.), *Scottish Population History from the 17th Century to the 1930s* (Cambridge, 1977), 33-5.

20. H. Booton, 'Burgesses and Landed Men in North-east Scotland in the Late Middle Ages: A Study in Social Interaction' (University of Aberdeen, unpublished Ph.D. thesis, 1987), 6; *Abdn Counc.*, ii, 245; Kennedy, *Annals*, i, 78, 237; C. Creighton, *A History of Epidemics in Britain* (London, 1965), i, 361-2, 370, 564.

21. *Abdn Recs*, 211; *Abdn Counc.*, i, 66, 88-91, 123-8, 130, 222, 240, 273; ii, 52-6; iv, 81.

22. *Abdn Counc.*, i, 246; ii, 245; Kennedy, *Annals*, i, 271.

23. *Abdn Counc.*, iv, 81-2.

24. Kennedy, *Annals*, i, 100; *Abdn Counc.*, i, 89-91, 123-5; iv, 81-5; *Old Aberdeen Recs*, i, 78; ii, 28; D. Morgan, *The Villages of Aberdeen: Old Aberdeen* (Aberdeen, 2000), 186.

25. Kennedy, *Annals*, i, 271-2; *ACL*, iii, pp. xiv, 228; Flinn, *Scottish Population History*, 145-6.

26. *Abdn Ecc. Recs*, i, 427.

27. Flinn, *Scottish Population History*, 116-17, 155-6; Spalding, *Memorialls of the Trubles*, i, 338.

28. *OSA*, xiv, 311-15; Flinn, *Scottish Population History*, 290-3.

29. Flinn, *Scottish Population History*, 289-90.

30. Creighton, *History of Epidemics*, i, 99; J. D. Comrie, *A History of Scottish Medicine* (London, 1932), 189.

31. *Abdn Counc.*, i, pp. xxvii, 425, 437; Creighton *History of Epidemics*, i, 361, 417, 419.

32. Kennedy, *Annals*, i, 28-9.

33. Flinn, *Scottish Population History*, 20, 150-2.

34. R. E. Tyson, 'Famine in Aberdeenshire, 1695-9: anatomy of a crisis', in D. Stevenson (ed.), *From Lairds to Louns: Country and Burgh Life in Aberdeen, 1600-1800* (Aberdeen, 1986), 32-6.

35. *Ibid.*, 36-50.

36. Flinn, *Scottish Population History*, 216-23, 233-7.

37. Stone, *Tale of Two Burghs*, 32-6; A. Cardy, 'Excavating in the Carmelite friary, the Green' (manuscript), *passim*.

38. G. DesBrisay, '"Menacing their persons and exacting their purses": the Aberdeen Justice

Court, 1657-1700', in Stevenson, *From Lairds to Louns*, 72-3.

39. E. A. Wrigley *et al.*, *English Population History from Family Reconstitution, 1580-1837* (Cambridge, 1997), 121-6; *Census of 1861*.

40. R. E. Tyson, 'Household size and structure in a Scottish burgh: Old Aberdeen in 1636', *Local Population Studies*, 40 (1988), 48.

41. Tyson, 'Population of Aberdeenshire', 122; G. DesBrisay, 'Wet nurses and unwed mothers in seventeenth-century Aberdeen', in E. Ewan and M. Meikle (eds), *Women in Scotland, c. 1100-1750* (East Linton, 1999), 210-32.

42. *OPRs*, Parish of St Nicholas, Baptisms, vol. i.

43. L. Leneman and R. Mitchison, *Sin in the City* (Edinburgh, 1998), 69-80.

44. *Abdn Counc.*, iv, 86.

45. A. M. Munro, 'Aberdeen burgess register', *New Spalding Misc.*, ii (1908), 386-98.

46. *ACL*, iii, 44.

47. *Abdn Recs, passim*.

48. A. E. Smith (ed.), 'Register of St Paul's episcopal chapel, Aberdeen', *New Spalding Misc.*, ii (1908), 337.

49. I. D. Whyte and K. A. Whyte, 'Patterns of migration of apprentices to Aberdeen and Inverness during the seventeenth and eighteenth centuries', *The Scottish Geographical Magazine*, 102 (1986), 81-91.

50. *OPRs*, Parish of St Nicholas, Marriages, vol. ii; Parish of Old Machar, vol. i.

51. *Abdn Counc.*, i, 367; Taylor, *ACL*, i, 16; *Old Aberdeen Recs*, i, 60-2.

52. E. P. D. Torrie, 'The guild in fifteenth-century Dunfermline', in Lynch, *Medieval Town*, 245.

53. T. Pagan, *The Convention of the Royal Burghs of Scotland* (Glasgow, 1926), 134.

54. Booton, 'Burgesses and Landed Men', 149; G. DesBrisay, 'Authority and Discipline in Aberdeen, 1650-1700' (University of St Andrews, unpublished Ph.D. thesis, 1989), 182, 438.

55. D. Macniven, 'Merchants and traders in early seventeenth century Aberdeen', in Stevenson, *From Lairds to Louns*, 57; M. Lynch, 'The social and economic structure of the larger towns, 1450-1600', in Lynch, *Medieval Town*, 273.

56. 'Register of the burgesses of the burgh of Aberdeen, 1399-1691', ed. J. Moir, *New Spalding Misc.*, i (1890), 1-161; Munro, 'Aberdeen burgess register', 13-126; DesBrisay, 'Authority and Discipline', 180-1, 218.

57. DesBrisay, 'Authority and Discipline', 180-1, 218.

58. *List of pollable persons within the shire of Aberdeen, 1696*, ed. J. Stuart (Aberdeen, 1844), ii, 595-632.

59. AUL, MS 57 (Taxation Book of Aberdeen from Martinmas 1748 to Martinmas 1749); R. E. Tyson, 'The rise and fall of manufacturing in Aberdeenshire', in J. S. Smith and D. Stevenson (eds), *Fermfolk*

and Fisherfolk: Rural Life in the North of Scotland in the Eighteenth and Nineteenth Centuries (Aberdeen, 1989), 66; DesBrisay, 'Authority and Discipline', 184; T. Devine, 'The merchant class of the larger Scottish towns in the late seventeenth and eighteenth centuries', in G. Gordon and B. Dicks (eds), Scottish Urban History (Aberdeen 1983), 95.

60. Kennedy, Annals, ii, 234-54; E. Bain, Merchant and Craft Guilds: A History of the Aberdeen Incorporated Trades (Aberdeen, 1887), 115.

61. Booton, 'Burgesses and Landed Men', 168.

62. DesBrisay, 'Authority and Discipline', 171-2, 202, 204.

63. Ibid., 138-40.

64. Old Aberdeen Recs, i, 347-55; R. E. Tyson, 'The economic and social structure of Old Aberdeen in the seventeenth century', in J. S. Smith (ed.), Old Aber-

deen: Bishops, Burghers and Buildings (Aberdeen, 1991), 39-56.

65. Tyson, 'The rise and fall of manufacturing', 67.

66. ACA, Burial Registers of St Peter's Cemetery, the Spital, vols i and ii; Bain, Merchant and Craft Guilds, 262-3, 294.

67. H. Booton, 'Economic and social change in late medieval Aberdeen', in Smith, New Light, 47; Booton, 'Burgesses and Landed Men', 116-17, 169-72.

68. Abdn Chrs., 312-17; ACA, Stent Rolls, 1637, 1669; ACL, i, 372-406; DesBrisay, 'Authority and Discipline', 129.

69. AUL, Aberdeen Taxation Book, 1748-9.

70. DesBrisay, 'Authority and Discipline', 132-4.

71. Stuart, List of Pollable Persons, ii, 583-632.

72. Kennedy, Annals, ii, 275.

*Notes to Chapter 6:
The Economy: Town and Country*

1. I. Blanchard, 'Lothian and beyond: the economy of the "English empire of David I"', in R. Britnall and J. Hatcher (eds), Progress and Problems in Medieval England. Essays in Honour of Edward Miller (Cambridge, 1996), 46-67.

2. Ailred of Rievaulx, Eulogium Davidis, in Lives of Scottish Saints: Vitae Antiquae Sanctorum, ed. J. Pinkerton (London, 1889), 439-56.

3. G. W. S. Barrow, 'The Scots charter', in H. Mayr-Harting and R. I. Moore (eds), Studies in Medieval History Presented to R. H. C. Davis (London, 1985), 154.

4. Liber S Thome de Aberbrothoc, ed. C. Innes and P. Chalmers (Bannatyne Club, 1848-56), i, no. 1; RRS, ii, nos 166, 475; Ancient Laws and Customs of the Burghs of Scotland, 1124-1707, ed. C. Innes (SBRS, 1868-1910), i, 'Leges Burgorum', cc. 8, 9, 16, 25.

5. G. W. S. Barrow, Kingship and Unity: Scotland, 1000-1306 (Edinburgh, 1989), 99-100.

6. Ibid., 99-100.

7. I should like to express my thanks to Geoffrey Barrow for drawing to my attention the similarity between the suburb of the Gaelic-speaking traders (vicus hybernicorum) at Carlisle and those western suburbs of Scottish burghs inhabited by Gaelic-speakers usually called 'Argyll', for example, in Glasgow (whence Argyle Street), St Andrews (Argyle, just west of the West Port), Dundee and elsewhere.

8. J. D. A. Thompson, Inventory of British Coin Hoards, AD 600-1500 (London, 1956).

9. Blanchard, 'Lothian and beyond', 37-9; idem, Mining, Metallurgy and Minting. Volume 2:

Afro-European Supremacy, 1125-1225 (Stuttgart, 2001), 583-666.

10. Even fixed rents, established during the years 1125-55, were worth less as the silver content of coinage diminished. Because of the large role of imports in aristocratic consumption, the long-term fall (by c. 25%) in the exchange value of the currency resulting from this decline in the silver content of the coinage, particularly when coupled from the 1170s with inflation abroad (E. Waschinski, Währung, Preisentwicklung und Kaufkraft des Geldes in Schleswig-Holstein von 1226-1864 (Neumünster, 1952); C. T. Inama-Sternegg, Deutsche Wirtschaftsgeschichte in dem letzten Jahrhunderten des Mittelalter (Leipzig, 1879-1901), seriously compromised the ability of the Scottish aristocracy to maintain their desired levels of purchases of such wares.

11. G. W. S. Barrow, The Anglo-Norman Era in Scottish History (Oxford, 1980), 90.

12. Ibid., 31-2.

13. APS, i, 382, 387-8. The former document, quoted above, is an assize transcribed in the early seventeenth century which may be a forgery, but see A. Stevenson, 'Trade with the south, 1070-1513', in M. Lynch, M. Spearman and G. Stell (eds), The Scottish Medieval Town (Edinburgh, 1988), 183.

14. Based on the listing of G. S. Pryde, The Burghs of Scotland. A Critical List (Oxford, 1965).

15. David's charter to Holyrood in Liber Cartarum Sancte Crucis. Munimenta Ecclesie Sancte Crucis Edwinesburg (Bannatyne Club, 1840), no. 1, reveals Rutherglen in the crown's hands in c. 1143-7, but

before the end of that king's reign it had passed to Walter, son of Alan, the Stewart: *RRS*, i, no. 184; *Registrum Episcopatus Glasguensis*, ed. C. Innes (Bannatyne Club, 1843), i, no. 40; *RRS*, ii, no. 190; *Charters of the City of Glasgow*, i, pt ii, no. 1; N. F. Shead, 'Glasgow: an ecclesiastical burgh', in Lynch, *Medieval Town*, 116–32; *Chronica de Mailros*, ed. J. Stevenson (Bannatyne Club, 1835), 103; *Charters of the Royal Burgh of Ayr* (Ayr, 1883), 1-2.

16. In a papal confirmation to Newbattle Abbey in 1174, a property is referred to as existing within the *villa* of Inveresk (*Registrum S Marie de Neubotle*, ed. C. Innes (Bannatyne Club, 1849), 316), but a decade later there is reference to an existing *burgus et portus* (*Registrum de Dunfermlyne* (Bannatyne Club, 1842), no. 239); Barrow, *Kingship and Unity*, 89. Following Pryde, *Burghs of Scotland*, no. 17 (p. 9), its foundation is dated at the height of the mining boom in 1159x65.

17. *Early Scottish Charters prior to 1153*, ed. A. C. Lawrie (Glasgow, 1905), nos 169, 268, quoted in W. M. MacKenzie, *The Scottish Burghs* (Edinburgh, 1949), 18–19; Barrow, *Kingship and Unity*, 92; A. A. M. Duncan, 'Perth: the first century of the burgh', *Transactions of the Perth Society of Natural Sciences*, Special Issue (1974), 32. The topographical development of the town can best be followed from the archaeological reports: N. Q. Bogdan and J. W. Wordsworth, *The Medieval Excavations at the High Street, Perth* (Perth, 1978); L. M. Thoms, 'Trial excavations at St Ann's Lane, Perth', *PSAS*, 112 (1982), 437-56; L. M. Blanchard, 'An excavation at 45 Canal Street, Perth, 1978-79', *PSAS*, 113 (1983), 489-519; P. Holdsworth (ed.), *Excavations in the Medieval Burgh of Perth, 1979-81* (Edinburgh, 1988), the last work providing a valuable retrospective survey of earlier work. The analysis of these materials differs somewhat from that of R. M. Spearman, 'The medieval townscape of Perth', in Lynch, *Medieval Town*, 42-59. *RRS*, ii, no. 278 (dated 1178x95) following Pryde, *Burghs of Scotland*, no. 94 (pp. 39-40). On the subsequent rivalry between these two centres during the thirteenth century, see Barrow, *Kingship and Unity*, 100.

18. *APS*, i, 308.

19. The following topographical description is based on materials in J. C. Murray (ed.), *Excavations in the Medieval Burgh of Aberdeen, 1973-81* (Edinburgh, 1982) and may, in the event of future excavations in Castle Street, require to be significantly modified.

20. 'Leges Burgorum', cc. 8, 9, 16, 25, and 'Assise Regis Willelmi', c. 41, in Innes, *Ancient Burgh Laws*, i. For the application of these laws in relation to particular localities, see *APS*, i, 88; *RRS*, ii, no. 475.

21. Blanchard, *Mining, Metallurgy and Minting*, ii, Appendix B.

22. From 1275 these changes in Scotland's and Aberdeen's overseas trade may be traced from the records of the Scottish customs administration. Access to the relevant data from these collections has been graciously afforded me by Martin Rorke, whose research has since appeared as 'Scottish Overseas Trade, 1275/86-1597' (University of Edinburgh, unpublished Ph.D. thesis, 2001).

23. I. Blanchard, *The Middle Ages: A Concept Too Many? Inaugural Lecture* (Edinburgh, 1996), 17-23.

24. I should like to express my gratitude to Dr Grant Simpson for extremely stimulating discussions concerning his research on the forms of land ownership in Scotland after the death of David I.

25. *Taxatio Ecclesiastica Angliae et Wallia. Auctoritate Papae Nicholae IV* (London, 1802).

26. Stevenson, 'Trade with the south', 182, 185; D. Ditchburn, 'Trade with northern Europe, 1297-1540', in Lynch, *Medieval Town*, 162; A. Tuck, 'A medieval tax haven: Berwick on Tweed and the English crown, 1333-1461', in Britnall and Hatcher, *Progress and Problems*, 148-67.

27. Rorke, 'Scottish Overseas Trade'.

28. E. M. Carus-Wilson and O. Coleman, *England's Export Trade, 1275-1547* (Oxford, 1963).

29. The pattern of Scottish commercial activity in 1338-40 is revealed in Francesco B Pegalotti, *La Practica della Mercatura*, ed. A. Evans (Cambridge, Mass., 1936). It can be set in the context of earlier documents dating from *c*. 1275, illustrating Flemish knowledge of British wool markets at that time, which are printed in E. Varenbergh, *Histoire des relations diplomatiques entre le comté de Flandre et l'Angleterre au moyen age* (Brussels, 1874), 214; G. Espinas, *Vie urbaine de Douai au moyen age* (Paris, 1913), iii, 230. It can also be compared with the very similar pattern of activity in the Scottish wool trade through Edinburgh, which can be constructed from *Halyburton's Ledger*.

30. Pegalotti, *La Practica della Mercatura*, suggests that Scots monastic wool could be obtained not only at the ports of the realm - Perth, the Fife havens, Edinburgh, and North Berwick as well as on the west coast in Kirkcudbright and Wigtownshire - but also from a dense network of burghs spanning Lothian, Roxbugh, Kelso, Jedburgh and Coldingham.

31. On Scottish trading activity at the Netherlands marts in *c*. 1500 see *Halyburton's Ledger*; I. Blanchard, 'Northern wools and Netherlands markets at the close of the Middle Ages', in G. G. Simpson (ed.), *Scotland and the Low Countries, 1124-1994* (East Linton, 1996), 76-88; D. Ditchburn, *Scotland and Europe: The Later Medieval Kingdom and its*

Contacts with Christendom. Volume I: Religion, Culture and Commerce (East Linton, 2001), ch. 4, *passim*; and, for Dieppe, *Comptabilité du port de Dieppe au XVe siècle*, ed. M. Mollat (Paris, 1951); *idem, Le commerce maritime normand à la fin du Moyen Age: étude d'histoire économique et sociale* (Paris, 1952).

32. I should like to express my gratitude to Dawn Griesbach, for affording me access to the fruits of her researches, prior to the completion of her study on 'The Neighbourhood to the South-west of St Giles' in 1500-13' (University of Edinburgh, unpublished M. Sc. thesis, 2000).

33. A similar pattern of exports was observable during the 'boom' years of 1240-1310. See *CDS*, ii, no. 9.

34. A vivid picture of Aberdeen's trade with the Netherlands in 1499 can be constructed from *Halyburton's Ledger, De Tol van Iersekerood, 1321-1572*, ed. W. S. Unger (s' Gravenhage, 1939); and NAS, E 71/1/1.

35. Murray, *Excavations in Aberdeen* suggests the relatively low level of material culture enjoyed by the inhabitants of Aberdeen through the periods from the late 12th to 14th and late 15th to early 16th centuries.

36. This section is based substantially on research carried out by Elizabeth Gemmill, developing work done in connection with a study of prices in medieval Scotland, published as E. Gemmill and N. Mayhew, *Changing Values in Medieval Scotland* (Cambridge, 1995). Just as the chapter on Aberdeen in that work was substantially the work of Dr Gemmill, so this part-chapter was written by her with minor additions by Mr Mayhew. Nevertheless, both authors subscribe to, and endorse, the whole.

37. E. Ewan, *Townlife in Fourteenth Century Scotland* (Edinburgh, 1990), 66-7, speaks of two possible market sites at Aberdeen and of the importance of the fair from the late thirteenth century. See also E. Ewan, 'The age of Bon Accord: Aberdeen in the fourteenth century', in J. S. Smith (ed.), *New Light on Medieval Aberdeen* (Aberdeen, 1985), 37-8.

38. Innes, *Ancient Burgh Laws*, i, esp. 4-58 ('Leges Burgorum'), 60-2 ('Assise Willelmi Regis'), 64-88 ('Statuta Gilde'), 114-26 ('Articuli Inquirendi in Itinere Camerarii'), 132-54 ('Modus Procedendi in Itinere Camerarii'), and 160-86 ('Fragmenta Collecta').

39. ACA, CR, vi, 742; and see Gemmill and Mayhew, *Changing Values*, 45-6, 125-8.

40. See Gemmill and Mayhew, *Changing Values*, esp. 3-57, for a discussion of these regulations.

41. There were fixed maximum prices for shoes by the 16th century: see ACA, CR, viii, 25; x, 17.

42. E.g. in Nov. 1511 a statute for skinners, to which

four of them gave their explicit consent, required them to have good, sufficiently made gloves, well-sewed and 'querelit' for all those who wanted to buy for a great or small price and especially to supply the university. All gloves were to be marked with the skinner's own mark so that the workmanship and the material would be guaranteed: ACA, CR, ix, 55.

43. A statute made in Oct. 1503 forbade smiths to sell horseshoes for more than 2d, 3d, or 4d each; they were to make a horseshoe for a penny and put it on the horse's foot. The fee for removing a horseshoe was to be a penny: ACA, CR, viii, 266.

44. See Gemmill and Mayhew, *Changing Values*, esp. 103-07.

45. It is interesting that maximum prices were frequently set for lamb and mutton but that beef never seems to have been subject to such an assize: Gemmill and Mayhew, *Changing Values*, 44.

46. *Ibid.*, 47-8.

47. ACA, CR, vi, 227.

48. ACA, CR, vi, 733.

49. See N. J. Mayhew, 'The status of women and the brewing of ale in medieval Aberdeen', *ROSC*, 10 (1996-7), 17, for the equipment needed for brewing. People sometimes handed over their possessions instead of paying a monetary fine, and these were often cooking pots of various kinds: e.g. *Abdn Recs.*, 220-1.

50. Gemmill and Mayhew, *Changing Values*, 54, 63-4.

51. ACA, CR, vii, 846.

52. See R. Nicholson, *Scotland: The Later Middle Ages* (Edinburgh, 1975), 115, 367; J. R. Maddicott, *The English Peasantry and the Demands of the Crown, 1294-1341* (P & P, Supplement, 1975).

53. ACA, CR, vii, 851. On the issue of whether there was endemic rivalry between merchants and craftsmen, see M. Lynch, 'Social and economic structure of the larger towns, 1450-1600', in Lynch, *Medieval Town*, 261-86.

54. On Aberdeen's reliance on regional produce, see also H. W. Booton, 'Inland trade: a study of Aberdeen in the later Middle Ages', in Lynch, *Medieval Town*, esp. 154-5.

55. Examples are in ACA, CR, vi, 758; viii, 615, 752 (printed above); ix, 35. For England, see also R. H. Hilton, 'The small town as part of peasant society', in *idem, The English Peasantry in the Later Middle Ages* (Oxford, 1975).

56. E.g. in a statute of March 1505, it was confirmed that all corn growing in the freedom of the burgh must be brought to the burgh's common mill: ACA, CR, viii, 427.

57. ACA, CR, vii, 183; see also ix, 38.

58. On medieval Scotland's imports of food and raw materials, see Ditchburn, 'Trade with northern Eu-

rope', esp. 168-9; Stevenson, 'Trade with the south', esp. 183-4, 189, 193, and 201-2; and P. G. B. McNeill and H. L. MacQueen (eds), *Atlas of Scottish History to 1707* (Edinburgh, 1996), esp. 264-5.

59. ACA, CR, v (1), 642-4. The ships, or in some cases their masters, were said to be from Dordrecht, Delft, Veere, 'Armove' in Zeeland, Antwerp, and 'Hundfleit'. Their cargoes included wheat, rye, muslin, malt, bere, meal, butter, cheese, salt, onions, apples, wine, and rice, as well as linen cloth, iron, timber products, soap, lint, and other goods.

60. Gemmill and Mayhew, *Changing Values*, 72-6.

61. ACA, CR, vii, 99-100.

62. ACA, CR, ix, 659.

63. *Abdn Chrs.*, 5-8. By the late 15th century, however, there is evidence that there was a twice-weekly market. In Nov. 1489, the bailies were ordered to supervise the market on Wednesdays and Saturdays, in a rota: see ACA, CR, vii, 150.

64. ACA, CR, vii, 8-9.

65. Gemmill and Mayhew, *Changing Values*, 66-8.

66. For a detailed discussion of the operation of the corn market in medieval Aberdeen, see Gemmill and Mayhew, *Changing Values*, 57-65.

67. The town made an arrangement in Jan. 1493 that John and Robert, their common minstrels, should have their board from the neighbours of the town. If anyone refused to receive them they were to pay them instead 12d per day for meat, drink and wage: ACA, CR, vii, 386.

68. The account of William Rolland of the costs of repairing the tolbooth in 1522, including full details of the costs of materials and of wages, was received by the provost and council on 17 April 1523 and was copied into the register: ACA, CR, xi, 280. For other examples of payments for the upkeep of the tolbooth, see ACA, CR, vii, 478; viii, 750-1; ix, 210.

69. E.g. ACA, CR, vii, 12; viii, 519.

70. ACA, CR, xiii, 439.

71. ACA, CR, xiii, 330.

72. ACA, CR, ix, 197-8.

73. E.g. ACA, CR, vi, 502, 527-8. In 1477 and 1478, bakers were fined for buying wheat at home before it was presented to the market, and in the countryside: ACA, CR, vi, 727. In 1482, fleshers were amerced for buying fish before they were allowed to do so, that is, before the burgesses and the community had been served: ACA, CR, xi, 458. In 1524, fleshers and their servants were forbidden to buy lambs coming to market until they had been presented to the cross and had remained there for sufficient time to enable the neighbours to be served.

74. E.g. ACA, CR, i, 326; vii, 653; xii, 355, 396; xiii, 139.

75. Gemmill and Mayhew, *Changing Values*, 60-4.

76. ACA, CR, xi, 187. See N. J. Mayhew, 'Women in Aberdeen at the end of the Middle Ages', in T. Brotherstone, D. Simonton and O. Walsh (eds), *Gendering Scottish History: An International Approach*, (Glasgow, 1999), 142-55, and references cited there.

77. ACA, MSS Guildry Accounts, i 1453; Acc. 1000/7 (photocopy from Gordon of Gordonstoun MSS in Yale University Library) (1470-1). See also ACA, CR, vii, 839: an entry recording the king's propine in Oct. 1497 included sums for gifts of wine to the earl of Huntly, Lord Oliphant, and Lord Gordon.

78. ACA, CR, ii, 52.

79. *Abdn Counc.*, i, 380; see Gemmill and Mayhew, *Changing Values*, 69.

80. ACA, CR, vi, 35. The manuscript is torn and some letters of the word 'wool' are missing, but this is the word that seems to be intended. For further examples of Aberdeen's economic links with local nobles, see Booton, 'Inland trade', 148-60.

81. ACA, CR, ii, 113.

82. ACA, CR, vii, 392.

83. See ACA, CR, vii, 670; viii, 753 (extracted in Appendix); ix, 35; but cf. CR, xii, 47-8: it was made clear in Oct. 1526 that chapmen's ability to sell in town was limited, as was that of the unfree, to one day per week.

84. Gemmill and Mayhew, *Changing Values*, 64-5.

85. See Appendix 1.

86. ACA, CR, ix, 268.

87. ACA, CR, ix, 305.

88. ACA, CR, ix, 468. For other examples of the effects of plague on Aberdeen's commerce, see Booton, 'Inland trade', 156.

89. ACA, CR, viii, 1027.

90. *Abdn Recs.*, 156.

91. E.g. *Abdn Recs.*, 222-31; ACA, CR, ii, 11-14.

92. *Abdn Recs.*, 224.

93. A series of fines were levied on fishermen, boatmen and women from Futty, Cove Bay and Findon between 1499 and 1511 for various offences regarding the selling of fish: ACA, CR, vii, 933; viii, 805-06, 1035; ix, 37.

94. Gemmill and Mayhew, *Changing Values*, 42-3.

95. See Appendix.

96. ACA, CR, viii, 614.

97. As in Stirling, where they made up 18.7% of householders in 1550: *Scottish Antiquary*, 6 (1892), 175-8.

98. ACA, CR, vi, 27; x, 207. See E. Ewan, '"For whatever ales ye": women as consumers and producers in late medieval Scottish towns', in E. Ewan and M. Meikle (eds), *Women in Scotland, c. 1100-c. 1750* (East Linton, 1999), 129.

99. ACA, CR, viii, 1205-9. The list is printed with a discussion by N. J. Mayhew in 'The brewsters of

Aberdeen in 1509', *Northern Studies*, 32 (1997), 71-81. See also Mayhew 'The status of women and the brewing of ale', 16-21.

100. A. J. S. Gibson, and T. C. Smout (eds), *Prices, Food and Wages in Scotland, 1550-1780* (Cambridge, 1995), 19.

101. G. DesBrisay, 'Authority and Discipline in Aberdeen, 1650-1700' (University of St Andrews, unpublished Ph.D. thesis, 1989).

102. DesBrisay, 'Authority and Discipline', 77; R. E. Tyson, 'Famine in Aberdeenshire, 1695-1699: anatomy of a crisis', in D. Stevenson (ed.), *From Lairds to Louns: Country and Burgh Life in Aberdeen, 1600-1800* (Aberdeen, 1986), 50.

103. Tyson, 'Famine', 50; J. G. Kyd (ed.), *Scottish Population Statistics* (SHS, 1952), 51.

104. *ACL*, i, p. xix.

105. Tyson, 'The rise and fall of manufacturing in rural Aberdeenshire', 66-7.

106. *ACL*, i, 241.

107. R. Leitch, '"Here chapmen billies tak their stand": a pilot study of Scottish chapmen, packmen and pedlars', *PSAS*, 120 (1990), 177.

108. *Ibid.*, 177.

109. Alexander, *Notes and Sketches*, 157.

110. *ACL*, i, pp. xi, 101,.

111. *Abdn Counc.*, ii, 20, 81.

112. *Abdn Counc.*, ii, 336.

113. *Abdn Counc.*, ii, 142.

114. R. E. Tyson, 'The economic and social structure of Old Aberdeen in the seventeenth century', in J. S. Smith (ed.), *Old Aberdeen: Bishops, Burghers and Buildings* (Aberdeen, 1991), 43-50.

115. *Old Aberdeen Recs*, i, 24.

116. *Abdn Counc.*, iv, 99.

117. *Abdn Counc.*, iv, 106.

118. DesBrisay, 'Authority and Discipline', 230.

119. Lynch, 'Introduction', in *idem, The Early Modern Town in Scotland* (London, 1987), 26.

120. H. W. Booton, 'The craftsmen of Aberdeen between 1400 and 1550', *Northern Scotland*, 13 (1993), 9.

121. *Abdn Counc.*, ii, 30.

122. *Abdn Counc.*, ii, 28, 31.

123. *Abdn Counc.*, ii, 38, 55.

124. *Old Aberdeen Recs*, i, 33, 70.

125. Gibson and Smout, *Prices, Food and Wages*, 23.

126. *Abdn Counc.*, ii, 54.

127. *Abdn Counc.*, ii, 167-8.

128. *Old Aberdeen Recs*, i, 55.

129. *Old Aberdeen Recs*, i, 33-4.

130. *Abdn Counc.*, iii, 112, 189, 260.

131. *Abdn Counc.*, iv, 133.

132. Booton, 'Inland trade', 153.

133. I. D. Whyte, 'The occupational structure of Scottish burghs in the late seventeenth century', in Lynch (ed.), *Early Modern Town*, 236-40.

134. *RCRB (1677-1711)*, 98, 162.

135. *RCRB (1677-1711)*, 665.

136. J. E. Thomas, 'Elgin notaries in burgh society and government, 1549-1660', *Northern Scotland*, 13 (1993), 21-30; M. Lynch, 'Urbanisation and urban networks in seventeenth-century Scotland', *SESH*, 12 (1991), 24-41.

137. Lynch, 'Urbanisation and urban networks'; *RCRB (1615-77)*, 60, 84, 87, 106, 196, 244, 251.

138. R. E. Tyson, 'The rise and fall of manufacturing in rural Aberdeenshire', in J. S. Smith and D. Stevenson (eds), *Fermfolk and Fisherfolk: Rural Life in Northern Scotland in the Eighteenth and Nineteenth Centuries* (Aberdeen, 1989), 72.

139. M. Lynch, 'Introduction', in *idem, Early Modern Town*, 11.

140. *Abdn Counc.*, ii, 331.

141. DesBrisay, 'Authority and Discipline', 139, 145; Lynch, 'Social and economic structure', 273.

142. Whyte, 'Occupational structure', 234.

143. Lynch, 'Social and economic structure', 273.

144. D. Macniven, 'Merchants and traders in early seventeenth-century Aberdeen', in Stevenson, *From Lairds to Louns*, 57.

145. H. W. Booton, 'Economic and social change in later medieval Aberdeen', in Smith, *New Light*, 46-7.

146. Booton, 'Economic and social change', 49.

147. A. Mitchell (ed.), *Macfarlane's Geographical Collections* (SHS, 1906), i, *passim*.

148. W. Alexander, *Notes and Sketches Illustrative of Northern Rural Life in the Eighteenth Century* (Edinburgh, 1877), 79.

149. Lynch, 'Social and economic structure', 273.

150. *Ibid.*, 283.

151. *OSA*, iv, 322 (Methlick); 426 (Logie Buchan); vi, 65 (Foveran).

152. *Abdn Counc.*, iii, 53.

153. *OSA.*, v, 375 (Strachan).

154. Mitchell, *Macfarlane's Geographical Collections, passim*.

155. *OSA*, vi, 214 (Leochel); vi, 233 (Tarland).

156. *Old Aberdeen Recs*, i, 145.

157. *Old Aberdeen Recs*, i, Appendix I, 347-55.

158. See www.nls.uk/pont. The map is no. 11 in the collection. It is also printed in I. C. Cunningham (ed.), *The Nation Survey'd; Timothy Pont's Maps of Scotland* (East Linton, 2001), 132, Ill. 135.

159. *Abdn Counc.*, ii, 322.

160. Alexander, *Notes and Sketches*, 119.

161. Booton, 'Inland trade', 149.

162. Tyson, 'Famine in Aberdeenshire', 38; Gibson and Smout, *Prices, Food and Wages*, 51, 231-2.

163. A. Fenton, 'Skene of Hallyards' *Manuscript of Husbandrie*, *Agricultural History Review*, 11 (1963), 68; I. D. Whyte, *Agriculture and Society in Seventeenth-*

Century Scotland (Edinburgh, 1979), 74-9.

164. Gibson and Smout, Prices, Food and Wages, 248.
165. DesBrisay, 'Authority and Discipline', 236.
166. Shore Work Accounts.
167. Lynch, 'Social and economic structure', 277.
168. DesBrisay, 'Authority and Discipline', 268; Macniven, 'Merchants and traders', 66.
169. Shore Work Accounts, 610-17.
170. Abdn Counc., ii, 167.
171. Whyte, Agriculture and Society, 224.
172. Shore Work Accounts, 19.
173. Alexander, Notes and Sketches, 79.
174. J. A. Stones, A Tale of Two Burghs: The Archaeology of Old and New Aberdeen (Aberdeen, 1987), 40-2.

175. Alexander, Notes and Sketches, 155.
176. Old Aberdeen Recs, i, 77, 124.
177. Mitchell, Macfarlane's Geographical Collections, i, 85, 99-100, 108, 248.
178. Tyson, 'The rise and fall of manufacturing in rural Aberdeenshire', 63-82.
179. Ibid., 66.
180. I. C. M. Barnes, 'The Aberdeen stocking Trade', Textile History, 8 (1977), 77.
181. Macniven, 'Merchants and traders', 58; see too Barnes, 'Aberdeen stocking trade', 81-3, 87-8.
182. R. Perren, 'The nineteenth-century economy', in W. H. Fraser and C. H. Lee (eds), Aberdeen, 1800-2000: A New History (East Linton, 2000), 75, 80.

Notes to Chapter 7:
The Economy: Aberdeen and the Sea

1. The later part of this chapter is based on a research project 'Aspects of Scottish trade and shipping, 1789-1829', supported by the Economic and Social Research Council.
2. I. F. Grant, The Social and Economic Development of Scotland before 1603 (Edinburgh, 1930), 122.
3. A. Stevenson, 'Medieval commerce', in G. Jackson and S. G. E. Lythe (eds), The Port of Montrose (Tayport, 1993), 19-20.
4. D. Ditchburn, 'Cargoes and commodities: Aberdeen's trade with Scandinavia and the Baltic, c. 1302-c. 1542', Northern Studies, 27 (1990), 12-22; A. Stevenson, 'Trade with the south, 1070-1513', in M. Lynch, M. Spearman and G. Stell (eds), The Scottish Medieval Town (Edinburgh, 1988), 180-206; idem, 'Medieval Scottish associations with Bruges', in T. Brotherstone and D. Ditchburn (eds), Freedom and Authority: Scotland c. 1050-c. 1650 (East Linton, 2000), 93-107.
5. D. Ditchburn, 'Piracy and war at sea in late medieval Scotland', in T. C. Smout (ed.), Scotland and the Sea (Edinburgh, 1992), 48-9.
6. D. Ditchburn, 'The pirate, the policeman and the pantomime star: Aberdeen's alternative economy in the early fifteenth century', Northern Scotland, 12 (1992), 19-34; idem, 'Piracy and war', 40. It is worth noting that both the Scottish and English kings recognised the detrimental effects of piracy and declared 'piracy truces' from time to time: ibid., 44.
7. D. Ditchburn, Scotland and Europe: The Medieval Kingdom and its Contacts with Christendom, 1215-1545. Volume 1: Religion, Culture and Commerce (East Linton, 2000), 149-52; I. D. Whyte, Scotland before the Industrial Revolution (London, 1995), ch. 3.
8. Grant, Social and Economic Development, 113.

9. Ibid., 354; M. Lynch, 'The social and economic structure of the larger towns, 1450-1600', in Lynch, Medieval Town, 269-70.
10. J. A. van Houtte, An Economic History of the Low Countries, 800-1800 (London, 1977), 83, 99, 179.
11. T. Riis, 'The Baltic trade', in Jackson and Lythe, Montrose, 104; Grant, Social and Economic Development, 340.
12. E. Gillett, A History of Grimsby (London, 1970), 26-7. Like Aberdeen, Grimsby was already an important centre for fish, caught along the Yorkshire and Lincolnshire coasts. Yarmouth acted for East Anglia.
13. Based on customs statistics compiled by Isobel Guy, and contained in 'The Scottish Export Trade, 1469-1599' (University of St Andrews, unpublished M. Litt. thesis, 1982), passim. See also idem, 'The Scottish export trade, 1460-1599', in T. C. Smout (ed.), Scotland and Europe, 1200-1850 (Edinburgh, 1986), 62-80.
14. Quoted in Grant, Social and Economic Development, 315. The council was objecting to infringements of its rights over the salmon fishery.
15. Shore Work Accounts, Appendices IV and V (converted from original tuns and lasts).
16. 4 Sept. 1669, Shore Accounts, 596 (spelling modernised).
17. Stevenson, 'Trade with the south', 186.
18. J. R. Coull, The Sea Fisheries of Scotland (Edinburgh, 1996), ch. 4, and map 40.
19. APS, ii, 235.
20. S. G. E. Lythe, The Economy of Scotland in its European Setting, 1550-1625 (Edinburgh, 1960), 57-9.
21. Quoted in K. H. D. Haley, The British and the Dutch: Political and Cultural Relations Through the Ages (London, 1988), 60. This volume contains a useful summary of disputes regarding herring and whales.

22. *Shore Work Accounts*, 592.
23. *Ibid.*, 358.
24. For this side of port history, see I. Frial, *Ships, Shipbuilding and Technology in England, 1200-1520* (London, 1995), *passim*. The lack of progress before the early modern period is clear from a comparison with very large, seaworthy vessels, discussed in L. Casson, *Ships and Seafaring in Ancient Times* (Austin, Texas, 1994), *passim*.
25. These names are not unique to Aberdeen: fitty, link, sand and ness are commonly found on the east coast of Britain.
26. It is an interesting thought that if the new town had been more port than regional centre it might have finished up as Gawpool - the pool in the navigable channel.
27. *A Succinct Survey of the Famous City of Aberdeen* (Aberdeen, 1685), 214, quoted in *Shore Work Accounts*, 1, n. 3.
28. In local histories the quay is often called a pier, which it was not, at least in the common usage of the word in maritime history.
29. T. Tucker, 'The settlement of the revenues of excise and customs in Scotland', printed in *Miscellany of the Scottish Burgh Records Society*, ed. J. D. Marwick (SBRS, 1908), 23.
30. Quoted in *Shore Work Accounts*, 12.
31. Tucker gave the Montrose sizes in lasts, which are converted to tons in D. G. Adams, 'Montrose ships and shipowners', in Jackson & Lythe, *Montrose*, 151. Tucker has no detailed figures for Leith.
32. Aberdeen's losses are listed in *ACL*, iii, 68-169, though it should be noted that burghs sometimes exaggerated distress to gain funding! Aberdeen's situations during the Wars of the Covenant and their aftermath are explored in T. M. Devine, 'The Cromwellian Union and the Scottish burghs', in J. Butt and J. T. Ward (eds), *Scottish Themes: Essays in Honour of Professor S. G. E. Lythe* (Edinburgh, 1976), 1-16.
33. *ACL*, iii, 228.
34. *Shore Work Accounts*, 120.
35. *Ibid.*, 125.
36. *Ibid.*, 120.
37. Montrose's contrasting grain trade is detailed in I. D. Whyte, '"All Kynds of Graine": the trade in victual, 1680-1825', in Jackson and Lythe, *Montrose*, 115-24, and the general background is best followed in his *Agriculture and Society in Seventeenth Century Scotland* (Edinburgh, 1979).
38. Quoted in T. C. Smout, *Scottish Trade on the Eve of the Union, 1660-1707* (Edinburgh, 1963), 11. See, however, ch. 6, for a more up-beat assessment of land routes.
39. The main drove roads ignored Aberdeen, though they crossed the Don at Inverurie and the Dee at Durris and Banchory; see the roads map in A. R. B. Haldane, *The Drove Roads of Scotland* (Edinburgh, 1952).
40. Analysis based on *Shore Work Accounts*, *passim*.
41. *Ibid.*, 100.
42. *Ibid.*, 288, 100.
43. Lythe, *Economy of Scotland*, 244.
44. *Ibid.*, 108, 123. (See also ch. 6).
45. *Ibid.*, 240.
46. *ibid.*, 235.
47. Quoted in *Shore Work Accounts*, 15.
48. Smout, *Scottish Trade*, 27.
49. Grant, *Social and Economic Development*, Appendix I.
50. Smout, *Scottish Trade*, Appendix I, Table II.
51. This may explain Aberdeen's omission from the agent for royal burghs' proposed convention regarding 'a union of trade betwixt Scotland and England', discussed by the Glasgow council on 2 Feb. 1689.
52. For geographical reasons, Aberdeen played little part in cross-border Anglo-Scottish trade.
53. Sample years 1668-70 and 1690-91: Smout, *Scottish Trade*, 234-5.
54. *Shore Work Accounts*, 526; Smout, *Scottish Trade*, 287.
55. NAS, RH 18/1/93.
56. The originals for Scotland appear to be lost, but Scottish data analysed for Robert Harley, Chancellor of the Exchequer, are in BL, Harleian MS 6269. I owe these figures to Eric Graham.
57. Figures for 1707 are depressed: some vessels lack specified port or were absent during 1707. The error in Glasgow numbers, 1712, is unidentifiable ['Glasgow' = Glasgow, Port Glasgow and Greenock]. Aberdeen details were omitted from a royal burgh survey in 1692, which would have given a better comparison of trend.
58. Discussed, most recently, in P. van Royen, J. Bruijn and J. Lucassen (eds), *'Those Emblems of Hell'? European Sailors and the Maritime Labour Market, 1570-1870* (Research in Maritime History No. 13, St John's, Newfoundland, 1997), *passim*. For Scotland, see G. Jackson, 'Scottish sailors', in *ibid*, 119-57.
59. Copenhagen, Rigsarkivet, Øresundstolregnskaber, *passim*. I owe these figures to Dr Graham.
60. Daniel Defoe, *A Tour Through the Whole Island of Great Britain* (Harmondsworth, 1971), 655.
61. Quoted in A. R. B. Haldane, *The Great Fishmonger of the Tay* (Dundee, 1981), 11. 1766 was actually a very poor year for catches: *ibid*, 35. (This is a detailed excellent account of the organisation of salmon trading.)
62. V. Clark, *The History of the Port of Aberdeen* (Aberdeen, 1921), 79.
63. For the background, see G. Jackson, *The British*

Whaling Trade (London, 1978), ch. 3, and for the impact of bounties, G. Jackson, 'Government bounties and the establishment of the Scottish whaling industry', in Butt and Ward, Scottish Themes, 46-66.

64. Two articles in Northern Scotland, 3 (1977-8) offer an excellent coverage of Aberdeen whaling: R. C. Michie, 'North-east Scotland and the northern whale fishing' for financial analysis; and W. R. H. Duncan, 'Aberdeen and the early development of the whaling industry, 1750-1800' for local detail based on the Aberdeen Journal.

65. G. Jackson, The Trade and Shipping of Dundee, 1780-1850 (Dundee, 1991), 30-1.

66. Quoted by M. Fry, The Dundas Despotism (Edinburgh, 1992), 167.

67. A. Smith, The Wealth of Nations (Everyman edn, London, 1910), ii, 19.

68. Based on an analysis of NAS, E 504/1/19-20 (Aberdeen Customs Quarterly Accounts). Errors result from confused spelling of names. Partnerships count as one importer, but partners may also act independently.

69. The details of the count undertaken a year earlier, in September 1787, have recently come to light, and show only minor variations. Aberdeen had 141 registered ships, totalling 10,338 tons. Four ships were over 200 tons, and 47 were under 47 tons, with another 67 under 100 tons: Pasadena, Henry Huntingdon Library, Stowe Collection, ST34 (Abstract of ships registered in Great Britain, September 1787). I am grateful to Andrew Mackillop for this information.

70. PRO, Customs, 17/17, 17/22, 17/27.

71. PRO, Customs, 17/22.

72. Parliamentary Papers, 1826/7 (327), XVIII, 290-1, Ships Built and Registered, from 1814 to 1826 inclusive.

Notes to Chapter 8:
Elite Society in Town and Country

1. A. Skene, A Succinct Survey of the Famous City of Aberdeen (Aberdeen, 1685; repr. 1835). The references are from the 1835 edition. Skene was also the author of Memorialls for the Government of Royal Burghs in Scotland (Aberdeen, 1685). See F. Wyness, Spots from the Leopard (Aberdeen, 1971), 110-12.

2. G. Desbrisay, '"Menacing their persons and exacting on their purses": the Aberdeen Justice Court, 1657-1700', in D. Stevenson (ed.), From Lairds to Louns: Country and Burgh Life in Aberdeen, 1600-1800 (Aberdeen, 1986), 70-90; Skene, Succinct Survey, 160-2.

3. E. Patricia Dennison, 'Power to the people? The myth of the medieval burgh community', in S. Foster et al., Scottish Power Centres from the Early Middle Ages to the Twentieth Century (Glasgow, 1998), 100-31.

4. Skene, Memorialls, 162, 173.

5. ACA, CR, xxvi, 12.

6. ACA, MSS Kirk and Bridge Work Accounts, 1571-1660, fos 28r-31v.

7. Ibid., 31v.

8. J. G. Dunbar, 'The emergence of the reformed church in Scotland, c. 1560-c. 1700', in J. Blair and C. Pyrah (eds), Church Archaeology: New Directions for the Future (York, 1996), 131.

9. Abdn Counc., i, 395.

10. E. Bain, Merchant and Craft Guilds: A History of the Aberdeen Incorporated Trades (Aberdeen, 1887), 49-61. For the cult of the Holy Blood in Edinburgh, see D. McRoberts, 'The Fetternear banner', IR, 7 (1956).

11. R. Hutton, The Stations of the Sun: A History of the Ritual Year in Britain (Oxford, 1996), 304-10.

12. Dennison, 'Power to the people', 113.

13. Hutton, Stations of the Sun, 233, 249.

14. Dennison, 'Power to the people', 114-15.

15. Abdn Counc., i, 438; A. J. Mill (ed.), Medieval Plays in Scotland (Oxford, 1927), 22-32, 137-286; Hutton, Stations of the Sun, 273.

16. Abdn Counc., i, 9; I. Fraser, 'The Later Medieval Burgh Kirk of St Nicholas, Aberdeen' (University of Edinburgh, unpublished Ph.D. thesis, 1989), 119; Hutton, Stations of the Sun, 141.

17. Abdn Counc., i, 432, 438, 542.

18. Wyness, Spots from the Leopard, 10-12; ACA, CR, xxxvi (1), 426.

19. J. Goodare and M. Lynch (eds), The Reign of James VI (East Linton, 2000), 17-18.

20. ACA, CR, xxxvi (1), 426.

21. Wyness, Spots from the Leopard, 12.

22. ACA, CR, xxxviii, 483-8; xliii, 193-4; xlix, 333.

23. W. A. Brogden, Aberdeen: An Illustrated Architectural Guide (Aberdeen, 1986), 7-8; E. Patricia Dennison and J. Stones, Historic Aberdeen: The Archaeological Implications of Development (Edinburgh, 1997), 67-8, 71; Wyness, Spots from the Leopard, 135.

24. ACA, CR, iv, 512-18; V (i), 37-42, 112-16, 141-5, 158-9, 203-6, 257-62, 314-18, 333-6, 353-7, 386-8, 404-8, 551-5. The lowest figure is 290 and the highest 445.

25. ACA, MSS Stent Roll Bundles, 1608 and 1637. The 1608 roll is printed in ACL, i, 392-406.

26. M. Lynch, 'Whatever happened to the medieval

burgh? Some guidelines for sixteenth and seven-teenth century historians', *SESH*, 4 (1984), 5-20, at 9-11.

27. P. G. B. McNeill and H. L. MacQueen (eds), *Atlas of Scottish History to 1707* (Edinburgh, 1996), 316-17.

28. Dennison, 'Power to the people', 114.

29. ACA, CR, v (2), 651; iv, 463; M. Lynch, 'Towns and townspeople in fifteenth-century Scotland', in J. A. F. Thomson (ed.), *Towns and Townspeople in the Fifteenth Century* (Aldershot, 1988), 184.

30. M. Lynch, 'The social and economic structure of the larger towns, 1450-1600', in M. Lynch, M. Spearman and G. Stell (eds), *The Scottish Medieval Town* (Edinburgh, 1988), 274.

31. *Ibid.*, 272-5.

32. As in 1517: ACA, CR, ix, 708.

33. D. Macniven, 'Merchants and traders in early seventeenth century Aberdeen', in Stevenson, *From Lairds to Louns*, 57; *idem*, 'Merchant and Trader in Early Seventeenth Century Aberdeen' (University of Aberdeen, unpublished M. Litt., 1977), 134.

34. See ACA, CR, ix, 708.

35. ACA, CR, xviii, 351; A. White, 'Religion, Politics and Society in Aberdeen, 1543-93' (University of Edinburgh, unpublished Ph.D. thesis, 1985), 73; M. Lynch, 'The crown and the burghs, 1500-1625', in M. Lynch (ed.), *The Early Modern Town in Scotland* (London, 1987), 72; Skene, *Succinct Survey*, 48-9.

36. *Abdn Counc.*, i, 309; *APS*, iv, 141-2.

37. Macniven, 'Merchant and Trader', 65.

38. ACA, CR, xxxii, 640.

39. McNeill and MacQueen, *Atlas*, 316-17. This is based on a comparison of an Edinburgh tax roll of 1583 and an Aberdeen one of 1608.

40. ACA, CR, xxxii, 632, 637.

41. Lynch, 'Larger towns', 272: E. Ewan, *Townlife in Fourteenth-Century Scotland* (Edinburgh, 1990), 107-8; H. W. Booton, 'Burgesses and Landed Men in North-East Scotland in the Later Middle Ages: A Study in Social Interaction' (University of Aberdeen, unpublished Ph.D. thesis, 1987), 112, 311-50; White, 'Religion, Politics and Society'; 14-15; Macniven, 'Merchant and Trader', 104-6, 134, 145, 231, 236.

42. *Abdn Recs*, 15-16; Ewan, *Townlife*, 116.

43. Macniven, 'Merchant and Trader', 280.

44. Booton, 'Burgesses and Landed Men', 115; James Gordon of Rothiemay, *Abredoniae Utriusque Descriptio: A Description of Both Towns of Aberdeen* (Spalding Club, 1842), 8.

45. See www.nls.uk/pont. The map is no. 11 in the collection. It is also printed in I. C. Cunningham (ed.), *The Nation Survey'd; Timothy Pont's Maps of Scotland* (East Linton, 2001), 132, Ill. 135.

46. J. C. Stone, *The Pont Manuscript Maps of Scotland: Sixteenth Century Origins of a Blaeu Atlas* (Tring, 1989); Cunningham, *Nation Survey'd*, 32.

47. Booton, 'Burgesses and Landed Men', 80.

48. J. Goodare, *State and Society in Early Modern Scotland* (Oxford, 1999), 251; Cunningham, *Nation Survey'd*, 113-20.

49. The massive tower was built soon after Robert I's grant in 1323 to William Irvine. Pont's drawing is of the tower before it was extended in 1619. The drawing of Drum is printed in Cunningham, *Nation Survey'd*, Ill. 110. There may, however, have been inaccuracies in it: see *ibid.*, 116.

50. Dennison and Stones, *Historic Aberdeen*, 53-4.

51. D. Ditchburn, 'The pirate, the policeman and the pantomine star: Aberdeen's alternative economy in the early fifteenth century', *Northern Scotland*, 12 (1992), 19-34.

52. Booton, 'Burgesses and Landed Men', 271.

53. Booton, 'Burgesses and Landed Men', 338-9; Lynch, 'Towns and townspeople', 180.

54. 'Chronicle of Aberdeen', *Spalding Misc.*, ii (1842), 31.

55. Booton, 'Burgesses and Landed Men', 283.

56. *Ibid.*, 283-4; ACA, Treasury Accounts, I (i), show that Crawford was still being paid £40 per annum in 1559-60.

57. *Abdn Counc.*, i, 6; ACA, CR, v (2), 652; Booton, 'Burgesses and Landed Men', 286-7.

58. *Abdn Counc.*, i, 22-3.

59. Booton, 'Burgesses and Landed Men', 290-4; *Abdn Counc.*, i, pp. xxiv, xxxvi; ACA, CR, vi, 39; xi, 767; xii, 817.

60. Wyness, *Spots from the Leopard*, 57-8, opposite p. 64.

61. Gordon, *Description*, 13; Dennison and Stones, *Historic Aberdeen*, 65.

62. H. W. Booton, 'Sir John Rutherford: a fifteenth century Aberdeen burgess', *SESH*, 10 (1990), 28-30.

63. *RCRB*, i, 313-14; White, 'Religion, Politics and Society', 304-7.

64. ACA, CR, vii, 27, 34; xii, 626, 800; Booton, 'Burgesses and Landed Men', 118-19, 297-8.

65. ACA, CR, xii, 626, 800.

66. *APS*, ii, 226-7, 245. The act of 1503 was repeated in 1505: *ibid*, ii, 252. See also Balfour, *Practicks*, 58.

67. *Abdn Counc.* i, p. xxxiv; ACA, CR, xii, 626, 800; Booton, 'Burgesses and Landed Men', 266; ACA, MS Guildry Accounts (1581-2).

68. Lynch, 'Crown and the burghs', 57, 64-5.

69. J. Spalding, *Memorialls of the Trubles in Scotland and in England, A. D. 1624-A. D. 1645* (Spalding Club, 1850), i, 68-9; *The Book of Bon Accord* (Aberdeen, 1839), 181-8.

70. For clergymen and teachers, see Chs. 14 and 15; for notaries, see H. W. Booton, 'John and Andrew Cadiou: Aberdeen notaries of the fifteenth and early

sixteenth centuries', *Northern Scotland*, 9 (1989), 17-20.

71. J.J. Carter and J.H. Pittock (eds), *Aberdeen and the Enlightenment* (Aberdeen, 1987); A.A. MacLaren, 'Privilege, patronage and the professions: Aberdeen and its universities, 1760-1860', in J.J. Carter and D.J. Withrington (eds), *Scottish Universities: Distinctiveness and Diversity* (Edinburgh, 1992), 96-104.

72. J.A. Henderson (ed.), *History of the Society of Advocates in Aberdeen* (New Spalding Club, 1912).

73. Most of these individuals paid poll tax at the lowest level and may not have been eligible to pay other sorts of taxation.

74. By the end of the 17th century Edinburgh professionals outnumbered the merchants. H.M. Dingwall, *Late Seventeenth-Century Edinburgh: A Demographic Study* (Aldershot, 1994), 274-5.

75. J. Durkan, 'The early Scottish notaries', in I.B. Cowan and D. Shaw (eds), *The Renaissance and Reformation in Scotland* (Edinburgh, 1983), 36.

76. *History of the Society of Advocates*, 121.

77. *Ibid.*, 318-19. Scougal was also MP for Kintore from 1693 to 1702, and voted consistently for the Court Party: R.L. Emerson, *Professors, Patronage and Politics: The Aberdeen Universities in the Eighteenth Century* (Aberdeen, 1992), 18-19.

78. *History of the Society of Advocates*, 149.

79. His term of office was ended in 1717 because of his overtly Jacobite sympathies (Emerson, *Professors*, 20; *History of the Society of Advocates*, 207). In-fighting among the academic Gordons is described in Emerson, *Professors*, 24-6. See too Ch. 15.

80. See C. Pennington, *The Modernisation of Medical Teaching at Aberdeen in the Nineteenth Century* (Aberdeen, 1994) for a full account of the subsequent development of medical education.

81. The first formal medical school in Scotland was established in Edinburgh in 1726. Progress in Glasgow was hindered by the friction between the university and the faculty of physicians and surgeons: H.M. Dingwall, *Physicians, Surgeons and Apothecaries: Medical Practice in Seventeenth-Century Edinburgh* (East Linton, 1995), 229-35; D. Hamilton, *The Healers: A History of Medicine in Scotland* (Edinburgh, 1981), 124-5.

82. The difficulties with occupational designation are well demonstrated by Dr McKaill, who was professor of medicine in King's College in 1717 and wrote many treatises on medical matters, but styled himself either 'apothecarie and chirurgeone' or 'chirurgico-medicus'.

83. Chalmers was professor of medicine in King's College in the early 1780s, but a surviving apprentice indenture concluded between Chalmers and the son of a weaver describes him as 'physician and surgeon': E.H.B. Rodger, *Aberdeen Doctors* (Edinburgh, 1893), 51. (Rodger's book contains a wealth of anecdotal details of members of the medical profession in Aberdeen.

84. The high number of physicians admitted to the Burgess Register in the seventeenth century may well be inflated by the admission of a number of physicians not normally resident in the burgh. It was customary to award burgess status to royal and military retinues, and these individuals are not always clearly identifiable on the register.

85. J.D. Comrie, *History of Scottish Medicine* (London, 1932), i, 371.

86. For a description of Skene's book in Comrie, *History of Scottish Medicine*, i, 372.

87. D. Stevenson, *King's College Aberdeen 1560-1641: From Protestant Reformation to Covenanting Revolution* (Aberdeen, 1990), 134.

88. Dun's name appeared on the list of contributors to the expenses of the tables in the Band of Relief of 1639. In addition to the medicinership, he held posts as regent, professor of logic, rector and principal of Marischal College. His *Ars Conservandi Sanitatem* was published posthumously in 1651.

89. Stevenson, *King's College*, 82.

90. The pull of Edinburgh was such that William Cullen, Joseph Black and others were drawn to the capital to pursue their academic medical careers.

91. For a full account of early years of the infirmary, see I. Levack and H. Dudley, *Aberdeen Royal Infirmary: The People's Hospital of the North-East* (London, 1992), 9-31.

92. J.L.M. Jenkinson, *Scottish Medical Societies* (Edinburgh, 1993), 120-1. The Society was renamed the Aberdeen Medico-Chirurgical Society in 1911, and seems to have been regarded highly, as it was consulted by the managers of the Aberdeen Infirmary during a fever outbreak in 1818.

93. Pennington, *Modernisation of Medical Training*.

94. Details of Gordon's medical education are sparse, though he may have studied at Edinburgh and Leiden briefly in the 1770s. After naval service and a spell in London, he was instrumental in the foundation of the Aberdeen Dispensary in 1781 and was appointed physician to the institution in 1786 (Levack and Dudley, *Aberdeen Royal Infirmary*, 27). He published on other areas of medicine, including extra-uterine conception and the effects of cold baths in the prevention of disease. For a full account of his life, see I.A. Porter, *Alexander Gordon, M.D. of Aberdeen* (Edinburgh, 1958).

95. ACA, CR, iv, 373.

96. Bain, *Merchant and Craft Guilds*. The Police Commissioner's Rent Roll of 1695, however, does list a 'hall for the Barber Society'.

97. Unlike their Edinburgh counterparts, the Aberdeen barbers had never held high civic status, coming last in the Corpus Christi procession in 1531 (Comrie, *History of Scottish Medicine*, i, 366).

Notes to Chapter 9:
The Burgh and the Realm: Medieval Politics, c. 1100-1500

1. John of Fordun's *Chronica Gentis Scotorum* (1371x87), Andrew of Wyntoun's *Original Chronicle* (1408-24) and Walter Bower's *Scotichronicon* (1441-7) were all heavily reliant on a chronicle maintained at St Andrews. Wyntoun was prior of St Serf's in Loch Leven and Bower abbot of Inchcolm.

2. Hector Boece, *The Chronicles of Scotland*, translated into Scots by John Bellenden, 1531 (STS, 1938-41); Hector Boece, *Murthlacensium et Aberdonensium Episcoporum Vitae*, ed. J. Moir (New Spalding Club, 1894).

3. Here of course, Donaldson was drawing a deliberate contrast with the (later) 'radical' south-west. G. Donaldson, 'Scotland's conservative north', *TRHS*, 16 (1966), 191-203.

4. I. H. Stewart, *The Scottish Coinage* (London, 1955), 14, 18-19, 38-9, 44, 49, 65; *ER, passim*.

5. In the 15th century a 'king's house' was maintained at an unknown location within the burgh, although when James IV visited in 1505 he and his household stayed at an inn in the town. E.g. *ER*, vi, 364, 407, 508, 600; vii, 160: 'pro reparacione hospicii domini regis in Aberdene'; vii, 304: 'pro certis reparacionibus factis in hospicio Regis in Aberdene in lez penteis, et aliis reparacionibus tempore adventus regis ibidem'. There were no parliaments held in Aberdeen, although there were some exchequer sessions held in the burgh.

6. The place-date maps in P. G. B. McNeill and H. L. MacQueen (eds), *Atlas of Scottish History to 1707* (Edinburgh, 1996), 158-82, reflect the primacy of southern Scotland in all reigns from David I onwards.

7. The financial implications of a visit by the royal household were clear from the council's arrangements for 'propynes' or gifts to welcome and support various 15th century monarchs on their visits to the burgh: e.g. *Abdn Counc.*, i, 17. See too ch. 6, for James IV's visit of 1497.

8. Prolonged stays in the north-east, such as the forty days James II was resident in the area in 1457, usually reflected the king dealing with particular emergencies or issues affecting his own rights and status in the locality. In 1479 the least itinerant of Stewart monarchs, James III, faced parliamentary demands to intervene directly in various regional feuds, including a number in the north-east.

9. E.g. *ER*, i, 13; iii, 412; vii, 559: 'equitancium in partibus boreales pro terries assedandis in Aberdene, Marr, et Gariauch.' See also, *ER*, vii, 569. The sense of the burgh as part of a 'provincial' society, one step removed from the political and bureaucratic core of the kingdom, is perhaps reflected in the terminology employed of royal records in the 14th and 15th centuries. The use of 'northern parts' or 'lords of the Northland' is far commoner than use of the term 'southern part', although the latter did also occur. See, for example, *ER*, vii, 555: 'et revertendo versus partes australes'.

10. For translation, see P. Contamine, 'Froissart and Scotland', in G. G. Simpson (ed.), *Scotland and the Low Countries, 1124-1994*, 54; Jean Froissart, *Oeuvres*, ed. K. de Lettenhove (Brussels, 1867-75), ii, 281. See also Ch. 17.

11. *ER*, i, 12.

12. *Nat. MSS. Scot.*, iii, no. 8; L. J. Macfarlane, *William Elphinstone and the Kingdom of Scotland, 1431-1514* (Aberdeen, 1985), 293.

13. A. Young, *Robert the Bruce's Rivals: The Comyns, 1212-1314* (East Linton, 1997); G. W. S. Barrow, 'The Highlands in the lifetime of Robert the Bruce', in *idem, The Kingdom of the Scots* (London, 1973), 377-9.

14. Young, *The Comyns*, ch. 8.

15. *Ibid.*, 203-6.

16. The fortress was evidently still holding out in July 1308 when the English administration issued instructions to a Hartlepool skipper as the captain of a fleet from that port sailing to the relief of the English king's besieged castle of Aberdeen: *Rot. Scot.*, i, 55.

17. Boece, *Vitae*, 16-18. The impossible chronology of Boece's story has long been recognised: see *The Book of Bon-Accord* (1839), i, 32-4.

18. J. H. Stevenson and M. Wood, *Scottish Heraldic Seals* (Glasgow, 1940), i, 52; *Descriptive Catalogue of Impressions from Ancient Scottish Seals*, ed. H. Laing (Bannatyne Club, 1850), i, nos 1146-7; ii, nos 1197-8. Between 1357 and 1408 no surviving impressions of the burgh seal carry the double tressure. The new seal matrices of 1430 (now in ACA) include a shield bearing arms showing a castle within a royal tressure, supported by two lions bearing a scroll inscribed 'Bon Accord'. These various elements thus all link with the tale relating to Robert I, but whether the narrative existed and dictated the choice of visual symbols in 1430, or developed

after that date, in order to explain the imagery, is uncertain. The former, however, is more likely.

19. *ER*, iv, 511.

20. S. Boardman, *The Early Stewart Kings: Robert II and Robert III, 1371-1406* (East Linton 1996), 91n.

21. Boece, *Chronicles* (Bellenden), ii, 277-8.

22. *ER*, i, 60, and *passim*; *ER*, iii, 307; iv, 259. The annuity was still being paid in 1559-60, on the eve of the Reformation: ACA, Treasury Accounts I (i), 1559-60.

23. *RRS*, v, nos 37, 158; *RSS*, ii, no. 2185; *Abdn Counc.*, i, 53-4. Robert I's charter of 24 October 1313 granted the burgh custody of Stocket, while that of 10 December 1319 granted the burgh feu-ferme of Stocket. A delegation from the burgh lobbying the young James VI in 1580 similarly recalled the 'blessed memory' of Robert I: *RPC*, iii, 294-5.

24. Boece, *Vitae*, 16-18.

25. *SP*, v, 581-5. Both Earl Donald and his son Thomas retained strong ties to the English crown.

26. *Chron. Bower* (Watt), vii, 3.

27. E.g. *ER*, i, 451, 453-4, for payment to Yon, sire de Garencières (who would return to Scotland in 1355), and for his accidental burning of the house of William Chapman, provost of Aberdeen, as he returned to France. See also C. McNamee, *The Wars of the Bruces: Scotland, England and Ireland, 1306-28* (East Linton, 1997), 209; and Ch. 17, below.

28. See *ER*, i, 6 (1 Jan. 1327-8): a remission of 20 merks for ten years to the burgh because of the 'combustionum dicti burgi … de quibus unus annus cum dimidio est elapses'; *ER*, i, 90, 155, 308.

29. *Chron. Fordun*, i, 360; *Chron. Wyntoun*, ii, 422-3; *ER*, i, 449; *Chron. Bower* (Watt), vii, 119.

30. S. Boardman, 'Lordship in the north-east: the Badenoch Stewarts (I). Alexander Stewart, earl of Buchan, lord of Badenoch', *Northern Scotland* 16 (1996), 1-29.

31. It was a curious, and presumably accidental, feature of Robert I's settlement of the north-east that the two principal honorary military offices of the realm, those of Constable and Marischal, were given to families which he had inserted into Buchan.

32. Boardman, *Early Stewart Kings*, 81-2.

33. *ER*, iii, 441, 475.

34. Boardman, *Early Stewart Kings*, 236-7.

35. A. Grant, 'Scotland's "Celtic fringe" in the later Middle Ages: the Macdonald lords of the Isles and the kingdom of Scotland', in R. R. Davies (ed.), *The British Isles, 1100-1500: Comparisons, Contrasts and Connections* (Edinburgh, 1988), 127-31.

36. See *Chron. Bower* (Watt), viii, 10-11, for Lindsay's involvement in central Highland politics and policing. Although the title was not derived from any óf their holdings in Angus, the collection of territories, offices and social ties that the Lindsays possessed made them the effective overlords of the ancient earldom. The titular earl of Angus had little real territorial or political power within the boundaries of the earldom.

37. Boardman, *Early Stewart Kings*, ch. 1.

38. *RMS*, i, no. 556.

39. Boardman, *Early Stewart Kings*, 168-70, 175-9.

40. *Ibid.*, 260-6.

41. D. Ditchburn, 'The pirate, the policeman and the pantomine star: Aberdeen's alternative economy in the early fifteenth century', *Northern Scotland*, 12 (1992), 19-34.

42. W. Junghans and K. Koppmann (eds), *Die Recesse und andere Akten der Hansetage von 1256-1430* (Leipzig, 1870-97), vi, no. 333. For other evidence of contact between Mar and Chalmers, see *RMS*, ii, nos 56, 1239; *A. B. Ill.*, iv, 168, 178, 382, 453; and for Chalmers' rural interests, see E. Ewan, *Townlife in Fourteenth-Century Scotland* (Edinburgh, 1990), 110-11, 114-15, 134.

43. Ditchburn, 'Pirate', 29; M. H. Brown, 'The Badenoch Stewarts (II), Alexander, earl of Mar', *Northern Scotland*, 16 (1996), 33.

44. See W. Mackay, 'The battle of Harlaw: its true place in history', *TGSI*, 30 (1919-22), 267-85, for an early critique of this view exemplified in *The Book of Bon-Accord* (1839), i, 37, where the battle was described as 'one of the conflicts in that great war between the Celtic and the Saxon races – between barbarism and civilisation, which beginning with the Pretender Donalbane, in the 11th century, was only finally ended on the Moor of Culloden.'(!)

45. Mackay, 'Battle of Harlaw', 269-70; Ditchburn, 'Pirate', 30.

46. For a discussion of the evidence suggesting that the aim of the Harlaw campaign extended beyond securing Donald's hold on Ross, see J. Bannerman, 'The lordship of the Isles', in J. M. Brown (ed.), *Scottish Society in the Fifteenth Century* (London, 1977), 214.

47. *Moray Reg.*, 382-3.

48. Nor, indeed, the Douglas retainers who burned and looted the burgh of Stirling on 17 March 1452 in retaliation for the killing of William, eighth earl of Douglas, by James II and his courtiers in Stirling Castle in the previous month: 'Auchinleck Chronicle', as produced in C. McGladdery, *James II* (Edinburgh, 1990), 165-6.

49. *Chron. Bower* (Watt), viii, 74-7.

50. S. Mapstone, 'Bower on kingship', in *Chron. Bower* (Watt), ix, 321-38; M. H. Brown, '"Vile times": Walter Bower's last book and the minority of James II', *SHR*, 79 (2000), 165-88.

51. William Worcestre, *Itineraries*, ed. J. H. Harvey (Oxford, 1969), 6-7.

52. *Abdn. Counc.*, i, 10-11.
53. *Chron. Bower* (Watt), viii, 74-7.
54. *Abdn Counc.*, i, 389.
55. ACA, CR, ii, 126.
56. M. H. Brown, 'Badenoch Stewarts', 45-6.
57. *RMS*, ii, no. 53.
58. One later source suggested that the host of Donald of the Isles, presumably starting from a mustering point in Easter Ross or the Inverness area, passed through Strathbogie on its march to Harlaw in 1411.
59. The change of surname might, indeed, have been one of the conditions of inheritance. Alternatively, it may have reflected a desire clearly to differentiate George and his descendants from the family of his elder half-brother Alexander Seton, who had been excluded not only from inheriting his father's estates, but also those lands and lordships that were the property of Alexander's own mother. The latter properties were at the centre of a long-running dispute between the two brothers and their descendants.
60. For Mar's burial, see J. A. Twemlow (ed.), *Calendar of Entries in the Papal Registers relating to Great Britain and Ireland* (London, 1895-), viii, 601; 'The chronicle of Fortingall', in *The Black Book of Taymouth*, ed. C. Innes (Bannatyne Club, 1855), 112.
61. *A. B. Ill.*, iii, 582-3.
62. For a summary of Erskine's relationship with Forbes and Crawford, see McGladdery, *James II*, 19-22. Erskine had essentially bought Forbes' support by an agreement of 17 Nov. 1435. By the terms of the indenture Forbes agreed to uphold Robert and his son Thomas' claims to Mar in return for certain estates (*A. B. Ill.*, 188-9; NAS, GD 124/7/7). Alexander Lindsay, second earl of Crawford (d. 1439) may have been Robert Erskine's brother-in-law. Certainly, an agreement of Dec. 1400 between David, first earl of Crawford, and Thomas Erskine had made arrangements for Robert Erskine's marriage to one of Earl David's daughters: NAS, GD 124/7/3; *SP*, iii, 17.
63. McGladdery, *James II*, 20-1.
64. *Abdn Counc.*, i, 394. This rather unusual move may have been designed to allow the burgesses to offer Erskine full political support without infringing royal legislation forbidding burgesses from serving in the retinues of lords from outwith the burgh. In another clear indication of Erskine involvement in Aberdeen, in January 1441 the new earl of Mar, granted lands to the burgess, Andrew Cullane, in a grant issued in Aberdeen and witnesssed by David Hay of Yester, Alexander Forbes, Henry Douglas of Logton, and James Rutherford (*A. B. Ill.*, iv, 48).
65. *ER*, v, 57.
66. *ER*, v, 58.
67. NAS, GD 124/1/148. Alexander Seton was instructed before 22 August 1438 to deliver Kildrummy to the new earl of Mar, but never obeyed the instruction.
68. The exact date of Seton's marriage to Crichton's daughter is unclear (perhaps 1438-9), but the match was so desirable for the Lord of Gordon that he seems to have divorced his first wife and disinherited their son, Alexander, in order to secure his Crichton bride. For Seton's marital adventures, see NAS, GD 44/4/1/2, 44/4/1/3; 44/1/1/26 (Gordon Castle Muniments); *RMS*, ii, no. 73; Sir Richard Maitland of Lethington, *The History of the House of Seytoun to the year 1559* (Maitland Club, 1829), 30-1. For a detailed examination of the ongoing dispute between the descendants of the half-brothers, see S. Boardman, 'Politics and the Feud in Late Medieval Scotland' (University of St Andrews, unpublished Ph.D. thesis, 1989), 133-41.
69. See NAS, GD 52/402 (Lord Forbes Collection), for the establishment of Forbes claims to land in Aboyne in October 1431.
70. *Spalding Misc.*, v, 262-3.
71. NAS, GD 52/63 (Lord Forbes Collection).
72. NAS, GD 44/13/8/1, 44/40/10 (Gordon Castle Muniments); GD 52/406 (Lord Forbes Collection).
73. *RMS*, ii, no. 278; NLS, Ch. No. 17088 (Titles of Keith Earl Marischal Papers); NAS, GD 203/12/3 (Lindsay Papers).
74. ACA, CR, v (2), 651-2, 724. For the interest of local lords in the burgh's fishings, see too Chs. 8 and 10.
75. *Abdn Counc.*, i, 6.
76. ACA, CR, iv, 253, 281; v (2), 660.
77. ACA, CR, v (2), 706. This pronouncement was connected to a general reassertion of royal rights, probably connected with the coming of age of James II (b. Oct. 1430).
78. McGladdery, *James II*, 37. The notion, found in *Extracta e Variis Cronicis Scocie* (Abbotsford Club, 1842), that Huntly had simply been staying with the Ogilvies and was obliged to take their part because of the rules of hospitality is rather unlikely.
79. *A. B. Ill.*, iii, 404. In 1445, Menzies had acted as procurator for William Forbes of Kinnaldie in Aberdeen: ACA, CR, iv, 405, 418.
80. McGladdery, *James II*, 40-1; *A. B. Ill.*, iv, 196; *Abdn. Counc.*, i, 17; W. Fraser, *History of the Carnegies, Earls of Southesk* (Edinburgh, 1867), 69; *ER*, v, 306; *APS*, ii, 60.
81. *RMS*, ii, no. 442; McGladdery, *James II*, 62; 'Auchinlek Chronicle', 169.
82. For a summary of these developments see McGladdery, *James II*, 61-4.
83. *Abdn Counc.*, i, 19-20.

84. McGladdery, *James II*, 117-18.
85. *A. B. Ill.*, iv, 205-13; *APS*, ii, 61.
86. *A. B. Coll.*, 606. In 1456 Huntly and his son George received a general remission for their undated attacks on Thomas Lord Erskine and his property in the earldom of Mar: *A. B. Ill*, iv, 203. The remission was presumably applied for once it became apparent the king was about to review the rights of the respective parties in Mar: *ER*, vi, 364.
87. *ER*, vi, 70, 269, 361, 436, 514, 650.
88. *ER*, vii, 86, 163, 462, 555.
89. *Abdn Counc.*, i, 22-3.
90. *APS*, ii, 50, repeated in the parliament of April 1491: *APS*, ii, 226-7.
91. *Abdn Counc.*, i, 24-5.
92. *Ibid.*, i, 24.
93. *Ibid.*, i, 25.
94. In 1595, when the population was in the region of 6,250, a muster roll of 400 was drawn up and in 1619, when both free and unfree were involved, 550 inhabitants took part in a wappinschaw: ACA, CR, xxx (1), 426; xlix, 333. See also Ch. 8. In the 15th century, when the population was rising from a figure of *c.* 3,000 in 1408, it seems likely that a levy would have numbered between 200 and 300 men.
95. *ER*, vii, 560, 649; viii, 78.
96. *Abdn Counc.*, i, 34-5. For contact between Mar and Aberdeen burgesses, see too ACA, CR, vi, 417, 457.
97. N. Macdougall, *James III* (Edinburgh, 1982), 130-3.
98. N. Macdougall, '"It is I, the earle of Mar": in search of Thomas Cochrane', in R. Mason and N. Macdougall (eds), *People and Power in Scotland* (Edinburgh 1992), 41.
99. Macdougall, 'Thomas Cochrane', 44-5.
100. *Moray Reg.*, 234-6; *APS*, ii, 210.
101. *APS*, ii, 210.
102. *APS*, ii, 214-15; N. Macdougall, *James IV* (Edinburgh, 1989), 68.
103. W. Fraser, *The Lennox* (Edinburgh, 1874), ii, 128-31; Macdougall, *James IV*, 69-70.
104. *Abdn Counc.*, i, 45-6.
105. *Ibid.*, i, 42-4, 415.
106. NAS, GD 33/52/1 (Haddo House Muniments); *RMS*, ii, nos 1616, 1812; *ER*, ix, 386, 525; x, 15.
107. See Boardman, 'Feud', 204.
108. *Abdn Counc.*, i, 421.
109. *RMS*, ii, nos 1910-11.

Notes to Chapter 10:
The Menzies Era: Sixteenth-century Politics

1. H. W. Booton, 'Burgesses and Landed Men in North-East Scotland in the Later Middle Ages: A Study in Social Interaction' (University of Aberdeen, unpublished Ph.D. thesis, 1987), ch. 6.
2. *Abdn Counc.*, i, p. xxiv. See also Booton, 'Burgesses and Landed Men', 341-8.
3. *Abdn Counc.*, i, p. xxxvi; ACA, CR, xi, 767.
4. A. M. Munro, *Memorialls of the Aldermen, Provosts and Lord Provosts of Aberdeen, 1357-1895* (Aberdeen, 1897), 85. Gilbert and Thomas Menzies served in a number of other important offices too, including as custumars of the burgh, and as the burgh's commissioners to parliament. See M. D. Young (ed.), *The Parliaments of Scotland: Burgh and Shire Commissioners* (Edinburgh, 1992), ii, 488, 490-1.
5. H. W. Booton, 'Economic and social change in later medieval Aberdeen,' in J. Smith (ed.), *New Light on Medieval Aberdeen* (Aberdeen 1985), 47-8.
6. H. W. Booton, 'Sir John Rutherford: A fifteenth-century Aberdeen burgess', *SESH*, 10 (1990), 21-37.
7. *Spalding Misc.*, ii, 186.
8. ACA, CR, vii, 26, 34, 79.
9. *Maitland Misc.*, iv, 79.
10. M. Lynch, 'The crown and the burghs, 1500-1625', in M. Lynch (ed.), *The Early Modern Town in Scotland* (London, 1987), 58.
11. *ER*, xviii, 33.
12. *APS*, ii, 414; *Letters and Papers, Foreign and Domestic, of the Reign of Henry VIII* (London, 1862-1932), xviii (2), nos 76, 79.
13. *Abdn Counc.*, i, 189.
14. *RSS*, iii, 820.
15. *Abdn. Counc.*, i, 214.
16. *TA*, viii, 409.
17. 'The Chronicle of Aberdeen', *Spalding Misc.*, ii, 34.
18. *Abdn Counc.*, i, 98, 107.
19. *Abdn. Counc.*, i, 110-11.
20. *The Acts of the Lords of Council in Civil Causes*, eds T. Thomson *et al.* (Edinburgh, 1839), i, 423.
21. *Abdn Counc.*, i, 211.
22. *StAKSR*, i, 9.
23. ACA, CR, xxiv, 22.
24. *Abdn Counc.*, i, 186, 249.
25. NAS, GD 45/26/53 (Dalhousie MSS, Commissary Maule), fo. 65.
26. W. M. Bryce, *The Scottish Grey Friars* (Edinburgh, 1909), i, 319.
27. *Abdn Counc.*, i, 323.
28. R. Keith, *An Historical Catalogue of the Scottish Bishops, down to the year 1688* (Edinburgh, 1824), 125-9; *Abdn Reg.*, i, 427-8.
29. R. S. Rait, *The Universities of Aberdeen* (Aberdeen, 1895), 98.
30. *Abdn Counc.*, i, 325.

31. *Abdn Counc.*, i, 325-6.
32. *Abdn Counc.*, i, 315.
33. ACA, CR, xxiii, 257.
34. *Abdn Counc.*, i, 319.
35. ACA, CR, xxiv, 10.
36. *Abdn Ecc. Recs*, 3, 10.
37. ACA, CR, xxiv, 159, 273.
38. *CSP Scot.*, iv, 168; ACA, CR, xxvii, 172.
39. *Abdn Counc.*, i, 362.
40. ACA, CR, xxviii, 544.
41. D. Stevenson, *King's College, Aberdeen, 1560-1641: From Protestant Reformation to Covenanting Revolution* (Aberdeen, 1990) 14-19.
42. *Abdn Counc.*, i, 366. See ch. 8 for discussion of the community of the burgh.
43. For a more detailed assessment of what follows in this paragraph, see A. White, 'The Regent Morton's visitation: the Reformation of Aberdeen, 1574', in A. A. MacDonald, M. Lynch and I. B. Cowan (eds), *The Renaissance in Scotland: Studies in Literature, Religion, History and Culture* (Leiden, 1994), 246-63.
44. *RPC*, ii, 390.
45. *Abdn Counc.*, i, 366.
46. J. Durkan, 'Early humanism and King's College', *AUR*, 48 (1980), 272.
47. *Abdn Ecc. Recs*, 19.
48. ACA, CR, xxxvi, 556; *St Nich. Cart.*, ii, 386.
49. *RPC*, ii, 343.
50. NAS, RH 3/20, 34.
51. White, 'Regent Morton's visitation', 258.
52. *RPC*, iv, 533; *RCRB*, i, 313; *RSS*, i, no. 1738.
53. *RCRB*, i, 313-15.
54. ACA, CR, xxxii, 54-5; *Abdn Counc.*, ii, 60.
55. ACA, CR, xxxii, 443, 452-7.
56. *RCRB*, i, 312; ACA, CR, xxxiv (1), 395.
57. *Spalding Misc.*, ii, 59; *RCRB*, i, 314.
58. *Spalding Misc.*, iv, 240.
59. *ACL*, i, 49.
60. G. D. Henderson, *The Founding of Marischal College, Aberdeen* (Aberdeen, 1946), 15.
61. *RPC*, iv, 525, 533-4.
62. ACA, CR, xxxii, 78.
63. *RCRB*, i, 312. See too *RPC*, iv, 533-4.
64. ACA, CR, xxxiv (1), 510.
65. ACA, CR, xxxiv (1), 1.
66. *Abdn Counc.*, ii, 119.

Notes to Chapter 11:
'The civill warrs did overrun all': Aberdeen, 1630-1690

1. ACA, CR, lii (2) (frontispiece, in the hand of the 1640s clerk, and probably copied when the volume was started in June 1644); see also ACA, CR, lvii (10 March 1696).
2. I would like to thank Miss Judith Cripps, Aberdeen City Archivist, for her help and kindness over many years. Her colleagues, Iain Gray and Siobhan Convery, have gone out of their way to help, as have the staff in Special Collections at the Aberdeen University Library. I am most grateful to the Deacon Convener and Master of Hospital of the Aberdeen Incorporated Trades for their help and hospitality.
3. B. Donagan, 'Codes and conduct in the English Civil War', *P & P*, 118 (1988), 65-7.
4. *Aberdeen Description*, 5.
5. R. E. Tyson, 'The rise and fall of rural manufacturing in Aberdeenshire', in J. S. Smith and D. Stevenson (eds), *Fermfolk & Fisherfolk: Rural Life in Northern Scotland in the Eighteenth and Nineteenth Centuries* (Aberdeen, 1989), 64-5; D. MacNiven, 'Merchants and traders in early seventeenth century Aberdeen', in D. Stevenson (ed.), *From Lairds to Louns: Country and Burgh Life in Aberdeen, 1600-1800* (Aberdeen, 1986), 64.
6. ACA, CR, lii (1) (26 Sept. 1632).
7. David Aedye was permitted to rebuild his old family home in the Green, the council hoping it would 'decore that pairt of the towne in a more decent maner nor abefoir.' ACA, CR, lii (1) (6 March 1633).
8. ACA, CR, lii (1) (22 Aug. 1632).
9. G. DesBrisay, 'Authority and Discipline in Aberdeen: 1650-1700' (unpublished Ph.D. thesis, University of St Andrews, 1989), 35-6, 91. See also *Aberdeen Shore Work Accounts*, introduction; and V. E. Clark, *The Port of Aberdeen* (Aberdeen, 1921), ch. 3.
10. ACA, CR, lii (1) (17 Sept. 1634; 4 March 1635). *Abdn Counc.*, iii, 38, 74-6; RCAHMS, *Tolbooths and Town-Houses: Civic Architecture in Scotland to 1833* (Edinburgh, 1996), 24-32.
11. *Abdn Counc.*, iii, 61-2.
12. *Abdn Counc.*, ii, 348-9; iii, 61-2; J. Gordon, 'A Topographical Description of Both Towns of Aberdeen', in A. Mitchell (ed.), *Geographical Collections relating to Scotland made By Walter Macfarlane* (SHS, 1907), 496.
13. ACA, CR, lii (1) (22 July 1635). One week later, the council paid £335 for a plot of land next to the guild hospital in the Green, to make a yard for the residents. ACA, CR, lii[1] (29 July 1635).
14. G. Donaldson, 'Scotland's conservative north in the 16th and 17th centuries', *TRHS*, xvi (1966).
15. See D. MacMillan, *The Aberdeen Doctors* (London, 1909); G. D. Henderson, *The Burning Bush: Studies*

in *Scottish Church History* (Edinburgh, 1957), ch. 5;
D. Stewart, 'The Aberdeen Doctors and the Covenanters', *RSCHS*, 29 (1984); D. Stevenson, *King's
College, Aberdeen, 1560-1641: From Protestant Reformation to Covenanting Revolution* (Aberdeen,
1990), 105-23; and D. G. Mullan, *Scottish Puritanism,
1590-1638* (Oxford, 2000).

16. Stevenson, *King's College*, 4, ch. 5. On the political
structure of Old Aberdeen, see A. Short, *Old Aberdeen in the Eighteenth Century* (Aberdeen, 1985), 2;
Old Abdn. Recs, i, 24-6. The Merchant Society
of Old Aberdeen was founded in 1680. *Ibid.*, i,
294 6.

17. New Aberdeen's council of 19 was elected annually. Only four members at a time could serve
consecutive terms. 17 seats were reserved for the
350-odd members of the merchant guild, and two
for the 250 odd members of the incorporated
trades. Outgoing merchants on council produced
a shortlist of about 60 merchants each year, from
which they then chose new councillors. The
trades chose their councillors from among the
outgoing deacons of six of the seven trades (the
fleshers were not included). The system managed
to be both ingrown and inclusive: one-third of all
merchants served at least one term on council. See
A. Skene, *A Succinct Survey of the Famous City of
Aberdeen* (Aberdeen, 1833), 30-4; DesBrisay, 'Authority and Discipline', 257-78.

18. New Aberdeen also sent the town clerk, Walter
Robertson. Two of the Aberdeen Doctors, John
Forbes and Robert Baron, preached before the
king, and George Jamesone painted him. J. Spalding, *Memorialls of the Trubles in Scotland and in
England. A. D. 1624 - A. D. 1645* (Aberdeen, 1850), i,
32-41 {hereafter Spalding}. Other Aberdonians
were there as spectators, including the young
Alexander Jaffray: J. Barclay (ed.), *Diary of Alexander Jaffray*, 3rd edn (Aberdeen, 1856), 44;

19. A. I. Macinnes, *Charles I and the Making of the Covenanting Movement, 1625-1641* (Edinburgh, 1991),
86-9.

20. Aberdeen, for example, was keen to have its salmon fishers exempted from laws against working
on the Sabbath. *ACL*, ii, 385-6.

21. D. Stevenson, 'The burghs and the Scottish Revolution', in M. Lynch (ed.), *The Early Modern Town
in Scotland* (London, 1987), 175; *ACL*, ii, 24-5. Menzies told the town council everything had gone
well. ACA, CR, lii (1) (14 Aug. 1633).

22. *Abdn Counc.*, iii, 70-4.

23. Stevenson, 'Burghs and the Scottish Revolution',
175.

24. *ACL*, ii, 28-31; *Abdn Counc.*, iii, 80-8.

25. *Abdn Counc.*, ii, 89-95.

26. *Abdn Counc.*, ii, 95. M. Lee, *The Road to Revolution:*

Scotland Under Charles I, 1625-1637 (Urbana, 1985),
175.

27. He lived in New Aberdeen in a house on Upperkirkgate. A. A. Bonar (ed.), *Letters of Samuel
Rutherford* (Edinburgh, 1891), 14, n 3.

28. J. Coffey, *Politics, Religion and the British Revolutions: The Mind of Samuel Rutherford* (Cambridge,
1997), 45-8.

29. *Letters of Samuel Rutherford*, 163, 275; see also 239,
300, 346; Stevenson, *King's College*, 107; Coffey,
Rutherford, 47.

30. On Catholics, see G. DesBrisay, 'Catholics, Quakers,
and religious persecution in Restoration Aberdeen', *IR*, 47 (1996), 143, 152-6; see also P. F. Anson,
Underground Catholicism in Scotland, 1622-1878
(Montrose, 1970), 25. On Arminianism, see the per-
ceptive comments of Mullan, *Scottish Puritanism*,
224-6. On Aberdeen and godly discipline, see
G. DesBrisay, '"Menacing their persons and exacting on their purses": the Aberdeen Justice Court,
1657-1700', in Stevenson (ed). *From Lairds to Louns*;
M. F. Graham, *The Uses of Reform: 'Godly Discipline'
and Popular Behavior in Scotland and Beyond, 1560-
1610* (Leiden, 1996), 114-25; and L. Leneman and
R. Mitchison, *Sin in the City: Sexuality and Social
Control in Urban Scotland 1660-1780* (Edinburgh,
1998), ch. 2.

31. Mullan, *Scottish Puritanism*, 1. Even Rutherford
had to admit that there were a few receptive souls
in Aberdeen: 'I find folks here kind to me; but in
the night, and under their breath.' The ministers,
he claimed, sought his removal to Orkney or
Caithness, 'far from them, because some people
here (willing to be edified) resort to me.' *Letters of
Samuel Rutherford*, 149, 301, 189.

32. D. Stevenson, *The Covenanters: The National Covenant and Scotland* (Edinburgh, 1988), 21.

33. Stevenson, 'Burghs in the Scottish Revolution',
167.

34. Stevenson, *Covenanters*, 27-8.

35. *Ibid.*, 35-44; R. Mason, 'The aristocracy, episcopacy
and the revolution of 1638', in T. Brotherstone
(ed.), *Covenant, Charter, and Party: Traditions of Revolt and Protest in Modern Scottish History*
(Aberdeen, 1989), 13-14.

36. *ACL*, ii, 73, 76-7; ACA, CR, lii (1) (10 May 1637; 8
Nov. 1637).

37. In a sign of just how sensitive this matter was,
minutes of the council meeting of 16 March were
not copied into the council register until 4 July,
'in respect of that quhilk hes followit' (i.e. the
imminent arrival of a delegation of powerful
Covenanter nobles). The minutes are printed in
ACL, ii, 88-9.

38. Spalding, i, 100. Spalding, son of an Old Aberdeen
lawyer, entered King's College in 1640 and grad-

uated in 1644. He signed the King's Covenant in 1638, as a youth. See D. Stevenson, *King or Covenant? Voices from Civil War* (East Linton, 1996), 95-103.

39. J. Gordon, *History of Scots Affairs, from MDCXXXVII to MDCXLI* (Aberdeen, 1841), i, 34.

40. NAS, GD406/1/639 (John Forbes of Corse to Huntly, 20 July 1638).

41. Macinnes, *Covenanting Movement*, 185; Stevenson, *King's College*, 107-12. For a summary of the debate and a different interpretation, see Stewart, 'Aberdeen Doctors', 35-44.

42. *Abdn Counc.*, iii, 128-30.

43. Description of Cant is from R. Baillie, *The Letters and Journals of Robert Baillie, M.DC.XXXVII. -M. DC. LXII* (Edinburgh, 1841), i, 86. The other barons were Lord Couper, the Master of Forbes, the Laird of Leyis, and the Laird of Morphie; the other ministers were David Dickson and Alexander Henderson (co-author of the National Covenant). These details and the following account of the visit are taken from Spalding, i, 91. See also Baillie, *Letters and Journals*, i, 97.

44. Spalding, i, 94. D. Stevenson, *The Scottish Revolution, 1637-1644: The Triumph of the Covenanters* (Newton Abbot, 1973), 101, accepts this figure. J. Row, *The History of the Kirk of Scotland, From the Year 1558 to August 1637* (Edinburgh, 1842), 495, put the figure at 65, whereas Baillie, writing from Glasgow and probably mistaken, suggested between 400 and 500: *Letters and Journals*, i, 97.

45. Gordon, *Scots Affairs*, i, 83.

46. Stevenson, *King's College*, 110.

47. Spalding, i, 92-3.

48. NAS, GD406/1/669 (Johnston, Bailies Thomas Gray and George Morison, to Huntly, 16 Aug. 1638).

49. NAS, GD406/1/531 (Montrose to Lauderdale, 28 Aug. 1638).

50. John Stuart was normally the most scrupulous of editors, but he made the unusual decision to cut the printed extracts of the council minutes of 26 Sept. before the Covenanters began to respond to the objections lodged by Johnston and his supporters. This has helped to obscure the fact that Covenanters won the election. *Abdn Counc.*, iii, 134-5; ACA, CR, lii (1) (26 Sept. 1638). See also Row, *History*, 501.

51. Spalding, i, 93.

52. ACA, CR, lii (1) (26 Sept. 1638).

53. NAS, GD406/1/447 (Johnston, Gray, Morrison to Huntly, 27 Sept. 1638). Huntly then reported to the king's commissioner, the Marquis of Hamilton, putting the best gloss on events that he could by claiming that a plot to elect that 'most factious Covenanter' Patrick Leslie provost had been thwarted. NAS, GD406/1/757 (Huntly to Hamilton, 29 Sept. 1638). Lesley was elected as an ordinary councillor, however.

54. He is said to have collected 12,000 of the 28,000 signatures nation-wide. Macinnes, *Covenanting Movement*, 185.

55. Spalding, i, 113; NAS, GD 406/1/450 (Huntly to Hamilton. Incomplete, undated, Oct. 1638).

56. Spalding, i, 113; Row, *History*, 501. Referring to the Covenanters, Huntly wrote he was 'behoved to enterpose my self for preventing that the paper might not be torne out of theyr handes'. NAS, GD 406/1/450 (see n. 55, above).

57. *Abdn Counc.*, iii, 137-9.

58. The Doctors saw that part of the King's Covenant could be construed, probably inadvertently, as endorsing the abolition of episcopacy. See Stevenson, *Scottish Revolution*, 111.

59. NAS, GD 406/1/450 (see n. 55, above). Unlike most of his predecessors, Huntly was Protestant.

60. The National Covenant and the King's Covenant were not entirely incompatible in terms of content. Stevenson, *Scottish Revolution*, 108-13.

61. NAS, GD406/1/446 (Aberdeen Doctors to Huntly, 5 Oct. 1638).

62. Stevenson, *King's College*, 112.

63. *Abdn Counc.*, iii, 142.

64. On the difficulty of fortifying Aberdeen, see R. Gordon of Straloch, 'Notes for a Description of the Two Shires of Aberdeen and Banff in Scotland beyond the Mountains', in Mitchell (ed.) *Geographical Collections*, 287; and Gordon, 'A Topographical Description', 496.

65. *Abdn Counc.*, iii, 144-5, 147-9.

66. Spalding, i, 131, 134.

67. In February 1638, Huntly lead his forces to confront a Covenanter gathering at Turriff. (Not to be confused with the subsequent 'Trot of Turriff'.) He had many more men on his side, but withdrew rather than fight. He may have been under instructions from the king not to fight just yet but, if so, none of his followers knew it. For whatever reason, he succeeded only in encouraging the Covenanters and disheartening his own side. Stevenson, *Scottish Revolution*, 139-40.

68. *Abdn Counc.*, iii, 151; Spalding, i, 146.

69. See for example C. Russell, 'The Scottish party in English parliaments, 1640-42, OR The myth of the English Revolution', *Historical Research*, 66 (1993).

70. Spalding, i, 147; J. Gordon, *Scots Affairs*, ii, 225. The bishop fled to New Aberdeen and left for good on 27 March 1640.

71. Spalding, i, 147, 149-50.

72. *Abdn Counc.*, iii, 154; Spalding, i, 150.

73. Spalding, i, 153, 155.

74. Montrose was one of the worst offenders. For an

example of local merchants forcing up prices, see *ACL*, iii, 9-10.

75. *Abdn Counc.*, i, 154-6; E.M. Furgol, *A Regimental History of the Covenanting Armies, 1639-1651* (Edinburgh, 1990), 27.
76. *Abdn Counc.*, iii, 156-7.
77. *Abdn Counc.*, iii, 156-7; Spalding, i, 160-1, 167.
78. *Abdn Counc.*, iii, 158.
79. S. Reid, *The Campaigns of Montrose: A Military History of the Civil War in Scotland, 1639 to 1646* (Edinburgh, 1990), 16-20.
80. *Abdn Counc.*, iii, 164-5.
81. *Abdn Counc.*, iii, 161-5.
82. Marischal arrived on 24th, Montrose on or before 27th. *Abdn Counc.*, iii, 166-9.
83. W. Kennedy, *Annals of Aberdeen*, 2 vols (Aberdeen, 1818), i, 210-11n; Spalding, i, 197.
84. Stevenson, *Scottish Revolution*, 147-8.
85. Spalding, i, 199-203.
86. A meeting on 7 June of all male residents attracted just 20 men, about one per cent of those eligible. *Abdn Counc.*, iii, 169-70. It is not suggested that these were literally the only men in town, but clearly the numbers were down.
87. *Abdn Counc.*, iii, 171-2; Spalding, i, 206; Row, *History*, 518.
88. NAS, GD406/1/859 (William Johnston to Hamilton, 10 June 1639). Lt Col. William Johnston was Huntly's commissioner in Aberdeen, and a professional soldier in charge of the town's defences. He distinguished himself at the Trot of Turriff and the Bridge of Dee.
89. Aboyne may still have expected help from England but, in May, Hamilton had written to the king advising that troops were not to be sent to Aberdeen. S.R. Gardiner (ed.), *The Hamilton Papers, 1638-1650* (Westminster, 1880), 80-1.
90. *Abdn Counc.*, iii, 173; Spalding, i, 209. Five times as many townsmen faced Montrose when he returned, as a royalist, in 1644.
91. See Spalding, 209-12; Gordon, *Scots Affairs*, ii, 276-82; Row, *History*, 519-20. For a modern description of the battle, see Reid, *Campaigns of Montrose*, 24-7.
92. Gordon, *Scots Affairs*, ii, 277-9.
93. Spalding, i, 212.
94. Baillie insisted that it had been 'resolvit to have sacked it orderlie, that hereafter that Town should have done our nation no more cumber'. *Letters and Journals*, i, 222.
95. The Aberdeen Doctor John Forbes fled on the evening of the 19th, returning on the 22nd after Montrose left. He noted in his diary that: 'Peace cometh to Aberdne by letters from the king and from the covenanters declairing the same wch letters were deliverd in Abd upon Thursday the 20 day of June in the morning earlie, wherby the

town was wonderfully delivered from present ro-wine'. AUL, MS 635A, 'Diary or Spiritual Exercises of John Forbes of Corse, 1624-47'. (Hereafter 'Forbes, Diary')
96. NAS, GD 406/1/1085. (Bp of Aberdeen to Hamilton, 7 Oct. 1639).
97. *Abdn Counc.*, iii, 176, 180.
98. ACA, CR, lii (1) (13 Sept. 1637).
99. *Abdn Counc.*, iii, 187-9.
100. ACA, CR, lii (1) (27 Nov. 1639).
101. At a meeting on 19 Dec., the townsfolk unanimously agreed to comply with a demand from Covenanting nobles that they help pay the salaries of a dozen Scottish officers returning from the continental wars to train and lead Covenanting forces in the north-east, and unanimously refused to comply with the Marquis of Huntly's demand that they pay for weapons which he had provided the year before. *Abdn Counc.*, iii, 193-5. They also consented to the Tenth Penny tax, and promptly paid it. *ACL*, ii, 172.
102. Comments on discipline and recusancy based on an analysis of the Aberdeen St Nicholas kirk session registers for 1629/30, 1634/5 1637/8, 1638/9, and 1639/40. NAS, CH2/448/4-5. Unfortunately, there is a break in the registers from Sept. 1640 to May 1651.
103. *Abdn Counc.*, iii, 252.
104. Spalding, i, 236.
105. 'Forbes, Diary', 224, 231, 248, 253.
106. *ACL*, ii, 202-3, 177-9, 280-1. See ACA, CR, lii (1) (25 Dec 1639), not printed in Abdn Counc., iii. The council could hire ministers, but only a provincial or general assembly of the kirk could remove them.
107. *Abdn Counc.*, iii, 221-2; *ACL*, ii, 204, 211; Spalding, i, 273-4.
108. *ACL*, ii, 205-7. The nine anti-Covenanters were among 26 men from the region arrested and sent to Edinburgh, where they languished for six months before being fined and released. *ACL*, ii, 212; Spalding i, 283-6.
109. For a breakdown of the costs involved, see J. Stuart, 'Extracts from the Accounts of the Burgh of Aberdeen' in *Spalding Misc.*, v, 154.
110. *Abdn Counc.*, iii, 234.
111. Scott, *Fasti*, vi, 19, 37-8, 14, 2. On Cant's election, see *Abdn Counc.*, iii, 235-6; and *ACL*, ii, p. xx. On Strachan's popularity, see *ACL*, ii, 358-9.
112. William Robertson at Futtie was also a Covenanter. Oswald was translated to Edinburgh in 1643, and replaced in 1647 (not 1649, as the *Fasti* has it) by John Menzies.
113. *Abdn Counc.*, iii, 233-4, 236-7, 238; iv, 44-5; Furgol, *Regimental History*, 61; *ACL*, ii, 216.
114. *Abdn Counc.*, iii, 238, 241-2; Furgol, *Regimental His-*

tory, 61; Stevenson, *Scottish Revolution*, 205.

115. *ACL*, ii, 244-5.
116. Spalding, i, 338; Furgol, *Regimental History*, 52; *ACL*, ii, 241-3.
117. Spalding, ii, 102. Before the war, cases of illegitimacy among Aberdeen civilians averaged under 30 a year. Spalding's testimony here is particularly valuable, as the St Nicholas kirk session registers are missing for the period.
118. Spalding, ii, 102
119. E. Ewan, '"For whatever ales ye": women as consumers and producers', in E. Ewan and M. Meikle (eds), *Women in Scotland, c. 1100-c. 1750* (East Linton, 1999), 125-36.
120. Spalding, ii, 102. See also G. DesBrisay, 'Twisted by definition: women under godly discipline in seventeenth century Scottish towns', in Y. F. Brown and R. Ferguson (eds), *Twisted Sisters: Women, Crime and Deviance in Scotland since 1400* (East Linton, 2002) 137-55. As for the men, the authorities could do no more than inform their officers.
121. *Abdn Counc.*, iii, 286.
122. *Abdn Counc.*, iii, 284-5.
123. *Abdn Counc.*, iv, 5-6; iii, 279; M. Lynch, *Scotland: A New History* (London, 1992), 277.
124. *Abdn Counc.*, iii, 279-81.
125. *Abdn Counc.*, iv, 11-15; Spalding, ii, 309.
126. *Abdn Counc.*, iv, 17-18; Spalding, ii, 324-5. Jaffray's sickly wife died soon after the attack, and he blamed Haddo. Jaffray, *Diary*, 48-50.
127. ACA, CR, lii (1) (3 July 1643).
128. D. Stevenson, *Revolution and Counter-Revolution in Scotland, 1644-1651* (London, 1977), 6-9.
129. *Abdn Counc.*, iv, 19-20, 21.
130. Spalding, ii, 351-3; Jaffray was on hand when Haddo was captured, and confronted him face-to-face about his wife's death. He also took back some of her jewellery. *Diary*, 48. See also P. Gordon of Ruthven, *A Short Abridgement of Britane's Distemper From the Yeare of God MDCXXXIX to MDCXLIX* (Aberdeen, 1844), 57-8.
131. *Abdn Counc.*, iv, 22-3.
132. Spalding reports predictably mixed emotions at the army's arrival: 'covenanteris wes no less blythe [than] the non covenanteris wes wo'. Spalding, ii, 354.
133. G. D. Henderson, 'John Forbes of Corse in exile', *AUR*, 17 (1929), 25.
134. *Abdn Counc.*, iv, 24-5; Spalding, ii, 371.
135. *Abdn Counc.*, iv, 24-5. Robert Baillie and David Dickson were also nominated, but they did not come either. The place was eventually filled by John Menzies, a much younger and more junior man.
136. Stevenson, *Revolution and Counter-Revolution*, 20,

21. In April 1639 Huntly rode into Aberdeen to meet with Covenanter leaders, having been assured of safe passage by Montrose. Other Covenanter leaders were less inclined to compromise, and Huntly was kidnapped and taken to Edinburgh. He never forgave Montrose. Stevenson, *Scottish Revolution*, 146.
137. *Abdn Counc.*, iv, 28. According to Spalding, Burleigh warned the inhabitants as early as 26 Aug. to prepare to defend 'the covenant and wark of reformatioun' and their own lives, against 'Irish rebellis and vagabound people'. Spalding, ii, 398-9.
138. Spalding, ii, 399; D. Stevenson, *Highland Warrior: Alasdair MacColla and the Civil Wars* (Edinburgh, 1994), 132.
139. Stevenson, *Highland Warrior*, 131. See also the unflattering remarks about Burleigh in Gordon of Ruthven, *Britane's Distemper*, 83.
140. Stevenson, *Highland Warrior*, 131.
141. *Ibid.*, 131-2.
142. All accounts, including this, rely mainly on Spalding's classic description (Spalding, ii, 405-15), and for military details on Gordon of Ruthven, *Britane's Distemper*, 80-5, but there are many fine modern renderings. Besides Stevenson, *Highland Warrior*, 131-7, see for example Reid, *The Campaigns of Montrose*, 64-73; P. Marren, *Grampian Battlefields: The Historic Battles of North East Scotland from AD 84 to 1745* (Aberdeen, 1990); E. J. Cowan, *Montrose: For Covenant and King* (London, 1977), 164-8; J. Buchan, *Montrose: A History* (Edinburgh, 1928), 198-205; and C. Brown, *The Battle for Aberdeen, 1644* (Stroud, 2002), 67-82.
143. *ACL*, ii, 380; Spalding, ii, 406; *Abdn Counc.*, iv, 29. The drummer is sometimes assumed to have been a boy, but most such positions were usually filled by men in the seventeenth century. Reid, *Campaigns of Montrose*, 182, n. 7.
144. Gordon of Ruthven, *Britane's Distemper*, 82; E. Furgol, 'The civil war in Scotland', in J. Kenyon and J. Ohlmeyer (eds), *The Civil Wars: A Military History of England, Scotland, and Ireland 1638-1660* (Oxford, 1998), 55.
145. Spalding, ii, 406.
146. Bailie Mathew Lumsden, Master of Kirkwork Thomas Buck, and Master of Hospital Robert Leslie were killed. *Abdn Counc.*, iv, 29. Alexander Jaffray the younger was 'evilly horsed' but got away. *Diary*, 50.
147. The dead included about 15 merchants and burgesses, as against 38 tradesmen (including 11 weavers and ten tailors) and 25 'unfree'. The merchant guild outnumbered the incorporated trades by about 3:2. Spalding, ii, 410-12.
148. Spalding, ii, 407.
149. The figure of 160 ('eight score') townsmen appears

in virtually all sources, beginning immediately after the battle. *Abdn Counc.*, iv, 29. *ACL*, iii, 115, specifies 'men'. Jaffray refers to eight score men 'besides women and children.' *Diary*, 50. 'Many' of the Fife regiment are said to have died, but the number has never been established.

150. Spalding, ii, 407.
151. Stevenson, *Revolution and Counter-Revolution*, 22; Spalding, ii, 409.
152. B. Donagan, 'Atrocity, war crime and treason in the English Civil War', *American Historical Review*, 99 (1994), 1144; Stevenson, *Highland Warrior*, 135-6. The quotation is from the Roman Emperor Justinian, and was frequently cited in the 17th century. Donagan, 'Atrocity', 1144, n. 25.
153. Stevenson, *Highland Warrior*, 136.
154. *Abdn Counc.*, iv, 31-2; Spalding, ii, 421.
155. *Abdn Counc.*, iv, 43-4, 45-6, 48-9, 52.
156. *ACL*, iii, 12. See also 9-11, 21-2.
157. *Abdn Counc.*, iv, 52.
158. Spalding referred in particular to Lord Lothian's regiment of foot, who garrisoned Aberdeen from Nov. 1644 to March 1645, at vast cost to the locals, and then ran away at Montrose's approach. Spalding, ii, 101; Furgol, *Regimental History*, 101.
159. Gordon of Ruthven, *Britane's Distemper*, 188-9; *Abdn Counc.*, iv, 68; Gordon, 'A Topographical Description', 493.
160. ACL, iii, 51-2; 243.
161. Stevenson, *Revolution and Counter-Revolution*, 50.
162. Spalding, ii, 418.
163. *Abdn Counc.*, iv, 102-5 (misdated 8 Nov. 1649; the correct date is 8 Nov. 1648); ACA, CR, liii (1) (11 Oct. 1648); *ACL*, iv, 103-5. Ministers overwhelmingly rejected the Engagement. 'We were fashed with Patrick Lesley of Aberdeen', reported Baillie, 'Mr. Andrew Cant gave in against him a foule libell: he gave in another against the ministers ... Mr Andrew Cant could hardly live in Aberdeen, if that man were enraged.' *Letters and Journals*, iii, 61-2. Jaffray, *Diary*, 54, notes the death of Jaffray the elder.
164. ACA, CR, liii (1) (11 Oct. 1648).
165. Jaffray, *Diary*, 54-6.
166. *ACL*, iv, p. xviii. See DesBrisay, 'Catholics, Quakers and religious persecution', 148-9, 151.
167. A. M. Munro, *Memorials of the Alderman, Provosts, and Lord Provosts of Aberdeen* (Aberdeen, 1897), 138. This is not quite as odd as it sounds. Most Covenanters were probably sincere in their willingness to support Charles I if he would only secure their kirk. Robert Farquhar, moderate Covenanter and financier, was also knighted on this occasion.
168. *Abdn Counc.*, iv, 87-8. This is an early example of social and spacial differentiation of the sort found in Restoration and Enlightenment Edinburgh.

R. A. Houston, *Social Change in the Age of Enlightenment: Edinburgh, 1660-1760* (Oxford, 1994), ch. 2.
169. According to the magistrates, 'the disciplin of the kirk is weakint be reason that the ministers hes not [allowed] ane session to be electit since Sept 1644 and did not suffer the pnt counsell and magistrats to be sessioners as hes beine the laudable custome of this burt'. ACA, CR, liii (1) (11 Nov. 1646).
170. *ACL*, iv, 112.
171. *Abdn Ecc. Recs*, 122.
172. See DesBrisay, 'Aberdeen Justice Court, 1657-1700', *passim*.
173. Jaffray, *Diary*, 57-66.
174. DesBrisay, 'Authority and Discipline', 42-80.
175. *Abdn Counc.*, iv, 186-8.
176. *Abdn Counc.*, iv, 189-90, 196.
177. DesBrisay, 'Catholics, Quakers and religious persecution', 137-41.
178. *ACL*, iii, 124. Even the lower figure was more than double the annual rental of the shire. R. E. Tyson, 'The economy and social structure of Old Aberdeen in the seventeenth century', in J. S. Smith (ed.), *Old Aberdeen: Bishops, Burghers, and Buildings* (Aberdeen, 1991), 43.
179. ACA, CR, lii (1) (13 Sept. 1637); *ACL*, iii, 42-7, 106.
180. *ACL*, iii, 243.
181. T. M. Devine, 'The Cromwellian union and the Scottish burghs: the case of Aberdeen and Glasgow, 1652-1660', in J. Butt and J. T. Ward (eds), *Scottish Themes: Essays in Honour of Prof. S. G. E. Lythe* (Edinburgh, 1976).
182. ACA, CR, liii (1) (25 June 1645, 20 May 1646, 20 Sept. 1648); lvi (13 Nov. 1678).
183. *Abdn Counc.*, iv, 40.
184. *Mortifications under the Charge of the Provost, Magistrates, and Town Council of Aberdeen* (Aberdeen, 1849).
185. Tyson, 'Rise and fall of manufacturing', 64.
186. A. Skene, *A Succinct Survey of the Famous City of Aberdeen* (Aberdeen, 1833), 50. *Idem, Memorialls For the Government of the Royall-Burghs in Scotland* (Aberdeen, 1685), 105.
187. ACA, Stent Roll Bundles, 1669.
188. *Abdn Chrs*, 207-11.
189. ACA, Press 18/Bundle 12 ('State of the town', 24 Sept. 1695).
190. G. Donaldson (ed.), *Scottish Historical Documents* (Edinburgh, 1974), 237-8.
191. Tyson, 'Economy and social structure of Old Aberdeen', 44.
192. Skene, *Memorialls*, 108.
193. Tyson, 'Economy and social structure of Old Aberdeen', 45.
194. *Ibid, passim*.
195. Gordon, 'A Topographical Description', 493.

Notes to Chapter 12:
Revolution to Reform: Eighteenth-century Politics, c. 1690-1800

1. ACA, CR, lvii, 324 (2 Nov. 1688).
2. Scott, *Fasti*, vi, 2.
3. ACA, CR, lvii, 302.
4. *Spalding Misc.*, ii, 296 (William Hay to the Countess of Errol, 20 Nov. 1688).
5. *RPC*, xv, 668.
6. *RPC*, xvi, 347-55.
7. ACA, CR, lvii; A. M. Munro, *Memorials of the Aldermen, Provosts and Lord Provosts of Aberdeen* (Aberdeen, 1897), 187-8.
8. ACA, CR, lvii, esp. 592, 604.
9. M. D Young (ed.), *The Parliaments of Scotland: Burgh and Shire Commissioners* (Edinburgh, 1992), i, 14; *APS*, xi, 323, 327, 330.
10. *Old Aberdeen Recs*, ii, 120.
11. A. & H. Tayler, *The Jacobites of Aberdeenshire and Banffshire in the Rising of 1715* (Edinburgh, 1934), p. xix.
12. *Old Aberdeen Recs*, 171.
13. M. Lynch, *Scotland: A New History* (London, 1991), 327; *Historical Papers relating to the Jacobite Period, 1699-1750*, ed. J. Allardyce (New Spalding Club, 1896), ii, 585-6.
14. ACA, CR, lviii (3 Aug. 1715).
15. ACA, Letters Books (Incoming), viii, no. 198 (30 Aug. 1714).
16. *Ibid.*
17. Munro, *Memorials of the Aldermen*, 207; Tayler, *Jacobites*, p. xx.
18. R. L. Emerson, *Professors, Patronage and Politics: The Aberdeen Universities in the Eighteenth Century* (Aberdeen, 1992), 11-12; Allardyce, *Historical Papers*, 588.
19. A. & H. Tayler, *The Jacobites of Aberdeenshire*, p. xxvi.
20. Scott, *Fasti*, vi, 27.
21. ACA, CR, lviii, 419 (Michaelmas 1715).
22. ACA, CR, lviii, 413-504.
23. ACA, Letter Books (Incoming, Supplementary), 1615-1729, no. 38, fos 1, 4 (2 Dec. 1726).
24. NLS, MS 16555, fo. 1 (William Cruikshank and Hugh Hay to Lord Milton, 15 May 1734).
25. J. Carter, 'The office of chancellor at Aberdeen university', *AUR*, 52 (1987), 110.
26. NLS, MS 16545, fos 1-4 (Provost of Aberdeen and others to Lord Milton, 1 Feb. 1731).
27. ACA, CR, lx, 386 (23 June 1735).
28. NLS, MS 16559, fo. 1 (William Cruikshank to Lord Milton, 21 Feb. 1735). See too J. S. Shaw, *The Management of Scottish Society, 1707-47* (Edinburgh, 1983), 110-12.
29. J. Simpson, 'Who steered the gravy train?', in N. T. Phillipson and R. Mitchison (eds), *Scotland in the Age of Improvement* (Edinburgh, 1970), 66.
30. R. Sedgwick, *The House of Commons, 1715-54* (London, 1970), ii, 14.
31. *Ibid.*, i, 395. Middleton had been made an honorary burgess of Old Aberdeen in 1712: *Old Aberdeen Recs*, i, 280.
32. Shaw, *Scottish Society*, 107-8.
33. *Old Aberdeen Recs*, i, 229, 286.
34. R. L. Emerson, 'Lord Bute and the Scottish universities', in K. W. Schweizer (ed.), *Lord Bute: Essays in Re-interpretation* (Leicester, 1988), 160-9.
35. ACA, CR, lx, 644 (19 July 1740).
36. *Ibid.*, 646.
37. C. A. Whatley, 'How tame were the Scottish Lowlanders during the eighteenth century?', in T. M. Devine (ed.), *Conflict and Stability in Scottish Society, 1700-1850* (Edinburgh, 1990), 19.
38. ACA, CR, lxi, 211 (31 Aug. 1745).
39. *Spalding Misc.*, i, 360; *Old Aberdeen Recs*, ii, 132.
40. *Old Aberdeen Recs*, i, 284.
41. ACA, Press 17/Parcel L/J/2, i-ii (1745-6).
42. NLS, MS 17522 (Saltoun Papers). See too *A List of the Persons Concerned in the Rebellion*, ed. W. Macleod (SHS, 1890), 2-23, 298-301.
43. NLS, MS 17257 (Saltoun Papers).
44. *Old Aberdeen Recs*, i, 229; ii, 132.
45. NLS, Adv. MS 31.6.22, fo. 38 (James Morison and others to Lord Albemarle, 3 Aug. 1746). See also NLS, MS 16613 (Saltoun Papers), fo. 5.
46. ACA, Press 17/Parcel L/L/2 ('Memorial for the Magistrates of Aberdeen', 4 Aug. 1746).
47. *Ibid.*, fo. 295 (James Morison and others to Lord Albemarle, 29 Aug., 1746).
48. *Ibid.*, fo. 76.
49. *Ibid.*, fo. 103.
50. NLS, Adv. MS 31.6.22, fo. 103 (8 Aug. 1746).
51. *Ibid.*, fo. 104 (Lord Albemarle to Lord Ancram, 29 Aug. 1746).
52. ACA, Press 17/Parcel L/Q/1 (14 Nov. 1746).
53. *Ibid.*, fo. 48.
54. See the entries on the Aberdeen district of burghs in Sedgwick, *House of Commons*, i, 395-6; L. Namier and J. Brooke (eds), *The House of Commons, 1754-90* (London, 1964), i, 498-9; and R. Thorne, *The House of Commons, 1790-1820* (London, 1986), ii, 590-2.
55. Sedgwick, *House of Commons, 1715-54*, ii, 230-40.
56. *Old Aberdeen Recs*, i, 285.
57. *Ibid.*, ii, 411-12.
58. Namier and Brooke, *House of Commons*, i, 498-9.
59. Thorne, *House of Commons*, ii, 590-1.
60. *Ibid.*, iii, 61-2.
61. *Ibid.*, iii, 727-8.
62. AUL, MS King 81/10 (Alexander Gerard, *Liberty the*

Cloke of Maliciousness, both in The American Rebellion and in the manners of the time (Aberdeen, 1778), 6).

63. *Further Proceedings of the Burgesses of Aberdeen, in the Years 1785, 1786, and 1787, ...* (Aberdeen, 1787).

64. *To the Burgesses of Aberdeen*, n. d. [1783]. There is a copy in NLS. See H. W. Meikle, *Scotland and the French Revolution* (Glasgow, 1912), 16.

65. *Proceedings of the Burgesses of Aberdeen; in Examining the Public Accounts; in the Annual Head Court, September 21, 1784; and in an Examination of the Public Records ...* Appendix 2, *A Letter to the Burgesses of Scotland, who have declared for the necessity of a reform in the elections of the magistrates and council, and representatives in parliament for the different towns, particularly those of Aberdeen, in answer to the letter of CASSIUS, which appeared in the Aberdeen Journal of June 2, June 4 1783, A BURGESS of Aberdeen*, p. 49. There are two copies of this pamphlet in NLS: X. 225. a. 1 (23); and A. 115. e. 1(1).

66. See n. 64, above.

67. Meikle, *Scotland and the French Revolution*, 57.

68. See n. 65, above.

69. W. L. Mathieson, *The Awakening of Scotland: A History from 1747 to 1797* (Glasgow, 1910); Meikle, *Scotland and the French Revolution*, ch. 1.

70. *To the Burgesses of Aberdeen*, n. d. [1783].

71. *Proceedings of the Burgesses of Aberdeen ... 1784*, pp. i-v, 5-7.

72. *Proceedings of the Burgesses of Aberdeen ... 1784*, and *Further Proceedings of the Burgesses of Aberdeen, in the Years 1785, 1786 and 1787*.

73. NLS, X. 225. a. 1 (untitled leaflet, dated 'Aberdeen, July 22, 1786', giving James Chalmers printer and publisher of the *Aberdeen Journal* as author, included in a volume of printed broadsheets and pamphlets, compiled by James Gordon of Craig, the clerk of the Aberdeen Sheriff Court at this period).

74. NLS, X. 225. a. 1, nos 11, 33, 35-6 ('Vindex', *To the Burgesses of Guild, and Incorporated Trades of Aberdeen* (Aberdeen, 1784), NLS copy, annotated in a contemporary hand 'by George Forbes Advocate in Aberdeen'; 'Anti-Covenanter', *To the Burgesses, Citizens, and Inhabitants of Aberdeen* (Aberdeen, '4

July 1784'); 'Geo. Forbes', untitled (Aberdeen, 'July 29th, 1786'); 'Oliver', *Serious Letters to the Committees of Burgesses in Scotland by a Gentleman of Aberdeen* (Edinburgh, 1786), NLS copy inscribed 'To John Gordon Esq. Of Craig humbly presented By The Author').

75. NLS, X. 225. a. 1, nos 33, 35.

76. ACA, CR, lxv, 140 (28 July 1786). See also the report of tradesmen rioting in K. Logue, *Popular Disturbances in Scotland, 1780-1815* (Edinburgh, 1979), 161-2.

77. Meikle, *Scotland and the French Revolution*, 44.

78. W. H. Fraser, *Conflict and Class: Scottish Workers, 1700-1838* (1988), 51; ACA, Press 18/Bundle 9 (Memorial for the Woollen Manufacturers in Aberdeen, 10 July 1762).

79. Logue, *Popular Disturbances*, 160; Meikle, *Scotland and the French Revolution*, 97.

80. Logue, *Popular Disturbances*, 40. Also see C. A. Whatley, *Scottish Society 1707-1830* (Manchester, 2000), 164, for details of a justiciary case relating to fear of the mob by a meal merchant in Aberdeen in 1753.

81. R. Tyzack, 'No mean city? The growth of civic consciousness in Aberdeen, with particular reference to the work of the police commissioners', in T. Brotherstone and D. J. Withrington (eds), *The City and its Worlds: Aspects of Aberdeen's History since 1794* (Glasgow, 1996), 150-2.

82. *In a General Meeting of the Citizens, Burgesses and Inhabitants of Aberdeen, called by public Advertisement in Handbills, and in the Aberdeen Journal of the 11th instant, to consider the Heads of a Police Bill published by the Magistrates, and circulated among the Citizens for their Consideration and Opinion*, 'Trinity Hall, 12 March 1793'. I have consulted the copy in the NLS, X. 225. a. 1 (57). There is a copy of the Police Bill as circulated at NLS, X225. a. 1 (56).

83. W. Thom, *The History of Aberdeen* (Aberdeen, 1811), ii, 32.

84. C. H. Lee, 'Local government', in W. H. Fraser and C. H. Lee (eds), *Aberdeen 1800-2000: A New History* (East Linton, 2000), 237. Also see *Ibid.*, 22-4.

Notes to Chapter 13:
The Faith of the People

1. G. Donaldson, 'Scotland's conservative north in the 16th and 17th centuries', *TRHS*, 5th series, 16 (1966), 65-79; reprinted in idem, *Scottish Church History* (Edinburgh, 1985), 191-203.

2. I. Fraser, 'The Later Medieval Burgh Kirk of St Nicholas, Aberdeen' (University of Edinburgh,

unpublished Ph.D. thesis, 1989), 68-83; W. Kennedy, *Annals of Aberdeen* (London, 1818), ii, 57-60, 65-82.

3. G. Donaldson, 'Aberdeen University and the Reformation', *Northern Scotland*, 1 (1973), 130; J. Robertson, *Reformation in Aberdeen* (Aberdeen,

1887), 5-8. Donaldson's estimate of 6,000 for the combined population of the two burghs, however, is almost certainly too high, whereas that for Old Aberdeen, of 500, is probably too low. The smaller burgh had some 900 inhabitants in 1636: G. G. Simpson, *Old Aberdeen in the Early Seventeenth Century: A Community Study* (Aberdeen, 1975), 5. His conclusion as to the 'extraordinarily' high proportion of clerics in Old Aberdeen, however, is sound.

4. *Old Aberdeen Recs.*, ii, 266-75; *Abdn Reg.*, i, 226-7; L. J. Macfarlane, *William Elphinstone and the Kingdom of Scotland, 1431-1514* (Aberdeen, 1985), 314-16.

5. E. Cinthio, 'The churches of St Clemens in Scandinavia', *Archaeologia Lundensia*, 3 (1968), 103-16.

6. Cowan & Easson, *Religious Houses*, 108, 116, 130, 135; Macfarlane, *Elphinstone*, 251-8. Strictly, the Trinitarians were not a mendicant order, though widely known as the Red Friars.

7. Special Lenten preachers were appointed at St Machar's in the 1540s but, as with other cathedrals, it is likely that their audience was the clergy rather than the laity (G. Hill, 'The sermons of John Watson, canon of Aberdeen', *IR*, 15 (1964), 3-34).

8. A. Whyte, 'The Reformation in Aberdeen', in J. Smith (ed.), *New Light on Medieval Aberdeen* (Aberdeen, 1985), 60; Calderwood, *History*, i, 171-2; also Pitcairn, *Trials*, i, 286, for another example. In Perth, this had followed the interruption of a friar's sermon.

9. Macfarlane, *Elphinstone*, 270; R. Fawcett, *Scottish Architecture from the Accession of the Stewarts to the Reformation, 1371-1560* (Edinburgh, 1994), 161-3, 210-11; I. G. Lindsay, *The Scottish Parish Kirk*, (Edinburgh, 1960), 22; D. Hay, *The Architecture of Scottish Post-Reformation Churches, 1560-1843* (Oxford, 1957), 24-5; A. L. Drummond, *The Church Architecture of Protestantism* (Edinburgh, 1934), 23; Fraser, 'St Nicholas', 38-67.

10. They are listed in *St Nich. Cart.*, ii, pp. lv-lvi; Fraser, 'St Nicholas', 278-302, and Kennedy, *Annals*, ii, 13-38.

11. Fraser, 'St Nicholas', 16, n. 4-5: *St Nich. Cart.*, i, 50; *Abdn Reg.*, ii, 280.

12. Fraser, 'St Nicholas', 279, 280-81; ACA, CR, iv, 411; *St Nich. Cart.*, i, 144

13. Fraser, 'St Nicholas', 26-7, 98-9.

14. *St Nich. Cart.*, i, 17; ii, 426; *Abdn Reg.*, i, 282; Fraser, 'St Nicholas', 286.

15. Cf N. Yates, 'Unity in diversity: attitudes to the liturgical arrangement of church buildings between the late seventeenth and early nineteenth centuries', in W. M. Jacob and N. Yates (eds), *Crown and Mitre: Religion and Society in Northern Europe since the Reformation* (Woodbridge, 1993), 46-54.

16. A. Grant, *Independence and Nationhood: Scotland, 1306-1469* (London, 1984), 110-11. Cf G. Donaldson, *The Faith of the Scots* (London, 1990), 49, where it is maintained that 'the Mass had come to be, above all else, a Mass for the dead'.

17. *St Nich. Cart.*, i, 255-7.

18. ACA, CR, viii, 777.

19. *St Nich. Cart.*, i, 260-2.

20. D. Howard, *Scottish Architecture: Reformation to Restoration, 1560-1660* (Edinburgh, 1995), 178-82, 191-3.

21. *St Nich. Cart.*, ii, pp. xli, 380.

22. J. Dawson, '"The face of ane perfyt reformed kyrk": St Andrews and the early Scottish Reformation', in J. Kirk (ed.), *Humanism and Reform: The Church in Europe, England, and Scotland, 1400-1643* (Oxford, 1991), 413-35. There is evidence, in the case of St Machar's, that even the pillars in the nave were painted in brightly coloured bands of blue, red and yellow: D. McRoberts, *The Heraldic Ceiling of St Machar's Cathedral, Aberdeen* (Aberdeen, 1981), 11.

23. *St Nich. Cart.*, ii, 384-5; A. White, 'The Regent Morton's visitation: the Reformation of Aberdeen, 1574', in A. A. Macdonald, M. Lynch and I. B. Cowan (eds), *The Renaissance in Scotland: Studies in Literature, Religion, History and Culture* (Leiden, 1994), 248-57.

24. Fraser, 'St Nicholas', 51-6; Macfarlane, *Elphinstone*, 270.

25. ACA, CR, ix, 336-7.

26. Fraser, 'St Nicholas', 35, 296-7.

27. ACA, CR, viii, 878; J. P. Foggie, 'The Dominicans in Scotland, 1450-1560' (University of Edinburgh, unpublished Ph.D. thesis, 1998).

28. *Abdn Ecc. Recs.*, 4-12. J. Bossy, *Christianity in the West, 1400-1700* (Oxford, 1985), 38, 126-31, 135.

29. *Statutes of the Scottish Church* (SHS, 1907), 144-5.

30. Bossy, *Christianity in the West*, 118-20.

31. M. Graham, *The Uses of Reform: 'Godly Discipline' and Popular Behavior in Scotland and Beyond, 1560-1610* (Leiden, 1996), 119, 122-3; *Statutes of the Scottish Church*, 142; Bossy, *Christianity in the West*, 122-4.

32. Graham, *Uses of Reform*, 119-20.

33. *APS*, iii, 272; *BUK*, i, 212.

34. *Abdn Ecc. Recs.*, 6.

35. Graham, *Uses of Reform*, 199.

36. *Abdn Counc.*, i, 323-4; Whyte, 'Reformation in Aberdeen', 66; D. Hay Fleming, *The Reformation in Scotland: Causes, Characteristics, Consequences* (London, 1910), 319-21; *Edin Recs*, iii, 70, 74-5, 77, 78-9.

37. See Kennedy, *Annals*, i, 113; Hay Fleming, *Reformation*, 319.

38. *Abdn Counc.*, i, 325-6; W. J. Couper, *Our Lady of Aberdeen* (Aberdeen, 1930), 3-8; F. Wyness, *Spots from the Leopard* (Aberdeen, 1971), 22-6.

39. *Abdn Counc.*, i, 329; ACA, CR, xxiii, 30.
40. *Abdn Ecc. Recs*, 16, 19-20; Whyte, 'Regent Morton's visitation', 256, citing NAS, GD 149/265, pt. 3, fo. 33; *St Nich. Cart.*, ii, 384.
41. *St Nich. Cart.*, ii, 390, 392-3.
42. R. A. Houston, *Scottish Literacy and the Scottish Identity* (Cambridge, 1985), 84-109.
43. W. Kelly, 'Four needlework panels attributed to Mary Jamesone, in the West Church of St Nicholas, Aberdeen', *Miscellany of the Third Spalding Club*, ii (1940), 161-81.
44. The first volume of session records ends in 1578. The next surviving volume dates only from 1602: NAS, CH 2/448/1-2. See Graham, *Uses of Reform*, 14-17, 124-5.
45. D. Campbell, 'Notes on church music in Aberdeen', *Trans. Aberdeen Ecclesiological Soc.* (1887), 16-17, 19.
46. 'The Chronicle of Aberdeen', in *Spalding Misc.*, ii (1842), 37-8, 42-7, 50, 55-6, 58; Graham, *Uses of Reform*, 115-16.
47. 'Chronicle of Aberdeen', 51.
48. E. P. Dennison, 'Power to the people? The myth of the medieval burgh community', in S. Foster, A. Macinnes and R. Macinnes (eds), *Scottish Power Centres from the Early Middle Ages to the Twentieth Century* (Glasgow, 1998), 100-31, esp. 112-14
49. *Abdn Ecc. Recs*, 40.
50. *Ibid.*, 40.
51. There are documented examples for Dundee in 1521 and 1523 and Edinburgh in 1565: Dennison, 'Power to the people?', 116. Similarly, an Edinburgh council ordinance of 1585 urged attendance only on burgesses and their wives (*Edin. Recs*, iv, 400).
52. Cf. P. H. Maxwell-Stuart, 'Witchcraft and the kirk in Aberdeenshire, 1596-7', *Northern Scotland*, 18 (1998), 1-14; J. Goodare, 'The Aberdeenshire witchcraft panic of 1597', *Northern Scotland*, 21 (2001), 17-37.
53. 'Trials for witchcraft, 1596-1597', in *Spalding Misc.*, i, 167.
54. Cf. Maxwell-Stuart, 'Witchcraft', 12-13, and Goodare, 'Witchcraft panic', 29-31.
55. *Abdn Ecc. Recs*, 38; W. D. Maxwell, *A History of Worship in the Church of Scotland* (Oxford, 1955), 110-11; M. Lynch, 'Preaching to the converted? Perspectives on the Scottish Reformation', in MacDonald., *The Renaissance in Scotland*, 331-2.
56. 'Trials for Witchcraft', 36-8.
57. *Ibid.*, 25.
58. P. Hume Brown (ed.), *Early Travellers in Scotland* (Edinburgh, 1891), 205. See Ch. 2 for an extended analysis of Franck's impressions of burgh life and the scene in St Nicholas.
59. The same point can be made about St Machar's,

which by the 1680s had a series of elaborate lofts for lairds, scholars, merchants and craftsmen, leaving others to occupy the floor of the church: D. Stevenson, *St Machar's Cathedral and the Reformation, 1560-1690* (Aberdeen, 1981), 15.
60. Cf. D. Szechi (ed.), *Letters of George Lockhart of Carnwath* (SHS, 1989).
61. W. Watt, *A History of Aberdeen and Banff* (Edinburgh and London, 1900), 218; D. Macmillan, *The Aberdeen Doctors* (London, 1909), 173-4.
62. Kennedy, *Annals*, ii, 311; A. M. Mackenzie, *Scottish Pageant* (1946-50), iii, 103; Stevenson, *St Machar's*, 10-11.
63. ACA, Letter Books (Incoming), vii (1682-99).
64. J. Davidson, *Inverurie and the Earldom of the Garioch* (Edinburgh and Aberdeen, 1878), 423; G. D. Henderson, *Mystics of the North-East* (Third Spalding Club, 1934), 5.
65. Cf. M. G. H. Pittock, *Jacobitism* (Basingstoke, 1998), ch. 3; *idem*, 'The political thought of Alexander, Lord Forbes of Pitsligo', *Northern Scotland*, 16 (1996), 73-86.
66. B. McLennan, 'The Reformation in the burgh of Aberdeen', *Northern Scotland*, 1 (1975), 133.
67. Davidson, *Inverurie and Garioch*, 249, 307.
68. *Old Aberdeen Recs*, ii, 31, 44-5; Kennedy, *Annals*, ii, 355; *Passages from the Diary of General Patrick Gordon of Auchleuchries AD 1635-AD 1699* (Spalding Club, 1859), 148n.
69. D. McRoberts, 'Provost Skene's house in Aberdeen and its Catholic chapel', *IR*, 5 (1954), 119-24.
70. Davidson, *Inverurie and Garioch*, 319.
71. *Abdn Counc.*, iii, 9, 279-80.
72. D. Stewart, 'The Aberdeen Doctors and the Covenanters', *RSCHS*, 22 (1984), 35-44; D. Stevenson, *King's College, Aberdeen 1560-1641; From Protestant Reformation to Covenanting Revolution* (Aberdeen, 1990), 105-15.
73. A. B. Birchler, 'The Influence of the Scottish Clergy on Politics, 1616-38' (University of Nebraska, unpublished Ph.D. thesis, 1966), 66, 68, 75.
74. R. Hutton, *The Rise and Fall of Merry England: the Ritual Year 1400-1700* (Oxford, 1994), 223-6, 229.
75. Mackenzie, *Scottish Pageant, 1707-1802*, iv, 10; *Aberdeen Journal Notes and Queries*, 7 (1914), 120.
76. G. DesBrisay, 'Catholics, Quakers, and religious persecution in Restoration Aberdeen', *IR*, 47 (1996).
77. *Abdn Counc.*, iv, 252, 292.
78. Davidson, *Inverurie and Garioch*, 423; P. Anson, *Underground Catholicism in Scotland 1622-1878* (Montrose, 1970), 113; J. Watts, *Scalan: The Forbidden College, 1716-99* (East Linton, 1999), 1-30.
79. J. R. N. Macphail (ed.), *Highland Papers* (SHS, 1920), iii, 56-7, 60.
80. *Topographies and Antiquities of the Shires of Aberdeen and Banff* (Spalding Club, 1869), ii, 182.

81. *Aberdeen Journal Notes and Queries*, 4 (1911), 145-6.

82. Wyness, *Spots from the Leopard*, 153-4.

83. Mackenzie, *Scottish Pageant, 1707-1802* (1950), 329.

84. The army was already cracking down on Quakers: *A Collection of the State Papers of John Thurloe, ed.* J. Thurloe, (London, 1742), vi, 145-6, 136. See also W. C. Braithwaite, *The Beginnings of Quakerism* (Cambridge, 1961), 228-9.

85. NAS, CH 10/3/36 (Alexander Skene *et al.,* 'A Brieff Historicall Account and Record of the First Rise and Progress of the Blessed Truth, Called in Derision Quakerism in and about Aberdeen' (*c.* 1681) ['Historicall Account']), 1. This chronicle dates the first conversions to 'the end of the year 1662', but Scottish Quakers followed the English old-style calendar until 1752, so it was probably 1663, new-style. See also W. Braithwaite, *The Second Period of Quakerism* (Cambridge, 1955), 328-47; G. B. Burnet, *The Story of Quakerism in Scotland, 1650-1850* (London, 1952), 51-5.

86. G. DesBrisay, 'Catholics, Quakers, and religious persecution'. See also A. I. Macinnes, 'Repression and conciliation: the Highland dimension, 1660-88', *SHR*, 65 (1986); and *idem,* 'Catholic recusancy and the penal laws, 1603-1707', *RSCHS*, 23 (1987).

87. Composed and first published in Latin in 1676, the first English edition of *An Apology for the True Christian Divinity as the Same is Held Forth, Preached By The People, Called in Scorn, the Quakers* appeared in 1678 and has seldom been out of print since. On Barclay, see D. E. Trueblood, *Robert Barclay* (New York, 1968); *DNB;* and the *New DNB* (forthcoming, 2004).

88. J. P. Wragge, *The Faith of Robert Barclay* (London, 1948), 25.

89. NAS, GD 244/1/84 (Sir George Mackenzie to Provost George Skene of Aberdeen, Edinburgh, 25 Sept. 1679).

90. NAS, CH 10/3/35: Alexander Skene *et al.,* 'A Breiffe Account of the Most Materiall Passages and Occurrances ... During That Great and Long Tryall of Sufferings and Persecution in Aberdene' (*c.* 1687) ['Materiall Passages'], 26-7.

91. By 1675, there were some 60,000 Quakers in England, English colonies, Ireland, and pockets on the continent. (R. T. Vann, *The Social Development of English Quakerism, 1655-1755* (Cambridge, Mass., 1969), 159).

92. W. F. Miller, 'Gleanings from the records of the yearly meeting of Aberdeen, 1672 to 1786', *Journal of the Friends Historical Society*, 8 (1911), 40.

93. W. F. Miller, 'Notes on early Friends' schools in Scotland', *Journal of the Friends Historical Society*, 7 (1910), 105, 110-12.

94. The Aberdeen Quakers drew up an especially strict dress code in 1698: J. Kendall, 'The development of a distinctive form of Quaker dress', *Costume*, 19 (1985), 61-2; Braithwaite, *Second Period of Quakerism*, 512-14.

95. The 'mountebank' was probably a quack doctor or other con artist who attracted crowds with jokes and tricks. (Hume Brown, *Early Travellers*, 20). The tolbooth window was 'four or five Story high and double grated,' and Friends could be 'distinctly heard all over the street by the people': 'Materiall Passages', 54.

96. G. DesBrisay, 'Quakers and the university: the Aberdeen debate of 1675', *History of Universities*, 13 (1994), 87-98.

97. Born Lilias Gillespie, she married Alexander Skene in 1646 and took his name, English-style, upon turning Quaker in 1666 (five years before he did). She was known by both names locally, but is best known to posterity as Lilias Skene. On her reputation among Presbyterians prior to her conversion, see 'Historicall Account', 29. Selections of her poetry were published in W. Walker, *The Bards of Bon-Accord, 1375-1860* (Aberdeen, 1887), 85-102.

98. H. Scougal, 'Of the importance and difficulty of the ministerial function', in his *The Life of God in the Soul of Man: Or the Excellency of the Christian Religion. With Nine Other Discourses on Important Subjects. To Which is Added, A Sermon Preached at His Funeral by G. G.* [George Garden] (London, 1726), 370.

99. DesBrisay, 'Catholics, Quakers, and religious persecution', esp. 143, 145, 151-7, 165-8.

100. 'Historicall Account', 46-7; ACA, CR, li, 8 April 1674. Aberdeen Friends were still renting space for their meetings at this point. Through much of the 1670s they met in the hall and upper chamber of the home of Alexander and Lilias Skene, where visiting Friends also stayed. The house on the Guestrow stood into the 19th century (NAS, CH 10/3/57; Miller, 'Gleanings', 45; R. Wilson, *An Historical Account and Delineation of Aberdeen ...* (Aberdeen, 1822), 138). Long since demolished, this house should not be confused with that on the same street known today as Provost Skene's House after Provost George Skene, a contemporary but no close relation of Bailie Skene.

101. *Abdn Counc.,* iv, 277-8.

102. Such a bye-law seems to have been passed in the wake of the next Quaker burial, however (*Abdn Counc.,* iv, 281-3). See also W. McMillan, *The Worship of the Scottish Reformed Church 1550-1638* (Edinburgh, 1931), 290.

103. 'Historicall Account', 46-9; ACA, CR, li, 8 April, 1674; 'Materiall Passages', 53.

104. ACA, CR, li, 8 April, 1674; *Abdn Counc.,* iv, 281-3. Edinburgh town council raised similar objections against a Quaker burial ground established there

in 1675, but there were no reprisals: Burnet, *The Story of Quakerism in Scotland*, 105-6.

105. *Abdn Counc.*, iv, 292. A further amendment in 1678 required all prospective burgesses to swear an oath against 'Poperie and Quakerisme', though this was quietly dropped in 1686 in deference to James VII & II, a Catholic (*Abdn Counc.*, iv, 299, 307). The magistrates were careful all along not to impinge upon Catholic and Quaker property-holders (Des-Brisay, 'Catholics, Quakers, and religious persecution', 162-3).

106. On Jaffray see Alexander Jaffray, *Diary*, ed. J. Barclay (Aberdeen, 1856); and on Skene see J. Robertson, 'Alexander Skene of Newtyle', *Scottish Notes and Queries* (March 1896) and the *New DNB* (forthcoming, 2004).

107. 'Historicall Account', 32. See also DesBrisay, 'Catholics, Quakers, and religious persecution', 146-52; G. D. Henderson, *Religious Life in Seventeenth Century Scotland* (Cambridge, 1937), 100-16.

108. Miller, 'Gleanings', 40; Friends' House Library, London, W. F. Miller MSS., Box P.

109. Margaret Smith was one of the first Quakers in Aberdeen, converting in 1662 ('Historicall Account', 1). It was not until 1671, five years after Lilaias Skene's own conversion, that her magistrate husband followed suit; in the intervening years, he exercised a 'blind forward zeal' against Quakers ('Historicall Account', 29-30).

110. W. F. Miller, 'The Record Book of Friends of the Monethly Meeting att Urie', *Journal of the Friends Historical Society*, 3 (1910), 93; *Register of Edinburgh Apprentices, 1666-1700*, ed. C. B. B. Watson (SRS, 1929), 65.

111. *RPC*, 3rd ser., iv, 547-51, 578.

112. The authorities would not arrest Quaker women, but increased by half the fines of three Quaker men 'for their wives transgressions' ('Materiall Passages', 23).

113. *Ibid.*, 54; Quakers filled the building; the room where many of them slept had to be cleared of bedding and bags twice a week and the prisoners marched upstairs so that the burgh court and sheriff's court could meet ('Materiall Passages', 34).

114. *Ibid.*, 36.

115. Several élite Quakers, including Barclay and Keith, were removed from the tolbooth to a cramped room in the abandoned chapel atop the Castle Hill, where they vied for the light of a single small window ('Materiall Passages', 34-5). Barclay's *Universal Love* (1677) was composed there. His correspondents at the time included Elisabeth, Princess Palatine of the Rhine (first cousin of the king), with whom Lilias Skene also corresponded (R. Barclay, *Reliquiae Barclaianae: Correspondence of Colonel David Barclay and Robert Barclay of Urie and*

His Son Robert, (London, 1870), 1-35). Keith spent thirty years as a leading Quaker writer and agitator, but ended his days leading the Church of England's anti-Quaker campaign. See E. W. Kirby, *George Keith* (New York, 1942); and R. Clark, '"The gangreen of Quakerism": an anti-Quaker Anglican offensive in England after the Glorious Revolution', *Journal of Religious History*, 11 (1981). For Keith's influence on Barclay, see Wragge, *Faith of Robert Barclay*, 21-34.

116. L. Skene, 'A Word of Warning to the Magistrats and Inhabitants of Aberdene, Writt the 31 of [March] 1677', in 'Materiall Passages', 38. Friends repeated this theme when they complained that 'though we wer many of us their towns Children (and our predecessoars befor us) and had been usefull in our and their places and payed a very considerable part at the present tyme of all publick taxations and Burthens in the place, Yet did they seek to cull us off' (*ibid.*, 51).

117. DesBrisay, 'Catholics, Quakers, and religious persecution', 160-62.

118. Col. David Barclay (Robert's father) and George Keith were released with him. Robert Barclay spoke plainly to the Duke of York, urging him to 'write effectually to the Duke of Lauderdale in that stile wherein Lauderdale might understand that he was serious,' but it was two more years before James intervened decisively (*Reliquiae Barclaianae*, 28-9).

119. Miller, 'Gleanings', 63; *Reliquiae Barclaianae*, 66-7.

120. W. F. Miller, 'Gleanings', 55-9.

121. In 1697, Thomas Mercer, minister of Kinnellar and nephew of a Quaker by the same name, reported that his uncle's funeral attracted 'the wholl convention of quakers in or neir Abd ... rekooned to be above the number of an hundreth.' They were there partly to protest the family's insistence on a churchyard burial: A. M. Munro (ed.), 'Diary of John Row, principal of King's College', in *Scottish Notes and Queries* (April 1894), 164-5.

122. *Memorials of the Family of Skene of Skene*, ed. W. F. Skene (Aberdeen, 1887), 78. John Skene became deputy governor of West New Jersey, and possibly America's first freemason: *The Papers of William Penn: Vol. II, 1680-84*, ed. M. Maples Dunn and R. S. Dunn (Philadelphia, 1982), 96n, 105n; D. Stevenson, *The First Freemasons: Scotland's Early Lodges and Their Members* (Aberdeen, 1988), 143-5.

123. Barclay helped send about 700 Scots to East New Jersey in the 1680s: Trueblood, *Robert Barclay*, 95-110; G. P. Insch, *Scottish Colonial Schemes, 1620-86* (Glasgow, 1922), 157, 233-7, 266; N. C. Landsman, *Scotland and Its First American Colony, 1683-1765* (Princeton, 1985), 114, 121.

124. *Abdn Counc.*, iv, 342-3.

Notes to Chapter 14:
Schooling the People

1. *Abdn. Reg.* i, p.lxxiv.
2. J.Durkan, 'Education in the century of the Reformation', in D.McRoberts (ed.), *Essays on the Scottish Reformation, 1513-1625,* (Glasgow, 1962), 146.
3. *St Nich. Cart.,* i, pp.ix, 50; H.F.Morland Simpson (ed.), *Bon Record: Records and Reminiscences of Aberdeen Grammar School from the earliest times by many writers* (Aberdeen, 1906), 6.
4. *St Nich. Cart.,* ii, pp.xxvi, xx; I.B.Cowan and D.E.Easson (eds.), *Medieval Religious Houses: Scotland* (2nd edn, London, 1976), 214-15; I.Fraser, 'The Later Mediaeval Burgh Kirk of St Nicholas, Aberdeen' (University of Edinburgh unpublished Ph.D. thesis, 1989), 16-18, 38-67, 279-302.
5. *Bon Record,* 7.
6. W.Walker (ed.), *Extracts from the Commonplace Book of Andrew Melville, Doctor and Master in the Song School of Aberdeen, 1621-1640* (Aberdeen, 1899), pp.xviii, xix.
7. *Commonplace Book of Andrew Melville,* p.xxi.
8. *Bon Record,* 12.
9. J.MacQueen (ed.), *Humanism in Renaissance Scotland* (Edinburgh, 1990), 10-11.
10. Printed in *Spalding Misc.,* v, 309-402, and, in an English translation, in *Bon Record,* 105-8.
11. J.Grant, *History of the Burgh and Parish Schools of Scotland. Volume I: Burgh Schools* (Glasgow, 1876), 47.
12. See e.g. J.M.Beale, *A History of the Burgh and Parochial Schools of Fife,* ed. D.J.Withrington (Edinburgh, 1983), 89; R.O'Day, *Education and Society, 1500-1800: The Social Foundation of Education in Early Modern Britain* (London, 1982), 230.
13. *Abdn Counc.,* i, 4.
14. *Commonplace Book of Andrew Melville,* p.xxi.
15. Grant, *Burgh Schools,* i, 94; *Bon Record,* 7.
16. *Bon Record,* 9. My italics.
17. See e.g. G.DesBrisay, 'Authority and Discipline in Aberdeen, 1650-1700', (University of St. Andrews unpublished Ph.D. thesis, 1989), *passim,* on attempts at imposing civic control on urban life.
18. L.J.Macfarlane, *William Elphinstone and the Kingdom of Scotland, 1431-1514: The struggle for order* (Aberdeen, 1985), 308. See also Ch. 15.
19. The Dominicans had probably settled in Aberdeen by 1257, the Trinitarians and Carmelites by 1273, and the Franciscans by 1461. See Ch. 13.
20. Durkan, 'Education in the century of the Reformation', 156.
21. *Bon Record,* 8.
22. J.K.Cameron (ed.), *The First Book of Discipline* (Edinburgh, 1972), 130.
23. *Ibid.,* 133.
24. *Abdn Counc.,* ii, 22-3.
25. J.Durkan, 'Education: the laying of fresh foundations', in MacQueen (ed.), *Humanism in Renaissance Scotland,* 127; *RPC,* i, 202.
26. For Aberdeen, see *RSS,* v, 2638; vi, 1322, 2345. For other burghs, *RSS,* v, 3342, 3417, 3419, 3425, 3452; vi, 1997.
27. This issue is treated in greater depth in S.M.Vance, 'Godly citizens and civic unrest: tensions in schooling in Aberdeen in the era of the Reformation', *European Review of History,* 7 (2000).
28. *Commonplace Book of Andrew Melville,* pp.xxvii-viii.
29. *Ibid.,* p.xxviii.
30. *Abdn Ecc. Recs,* 16.
31. *Commonplace Book of Andrew Melville,* p.xxx.
32. *Ibid.,* pp.xxxi, xxxvi.
33. *Abdn Ecc. Recs,* 25.
34. *Old Abdn Recs,* ii, 39.
35. *Ibid.,* ii, 46.
36. *Bon Record,* 168.
37. *Ibid.,* 18.
38. *Abdn Counc.,* ii, 39.
39. *Bon Record,* 41.
40. *Ibid.,* 43.
41. Extracts from both are printed in Grant, *Burgh Schools,* i, 336-42.
42. *Commonplace Book of Andrew Melville,* p.xxviii.
43. *Abdn Counc.,* iii, 96.
44. *Ibid.,* iii, pp.i, 5, 21, 34-47, 49-51.
45. *Old Abdn Recs,* ii, 15.
46. *Old Abdn Recs,* ii, 23.
47. Durkan, 'Education in the century of the Reformation', 145.
48. ACA, CR, lvi, 292.
49. See e.g. *Old Abdn Recs,* ii, 61.
50. *Abdn Counc.,* ii, 29; ACA, Treasury Accounts, i (3), 35.
51. *Commonplace Book of Andrew Melville,* p.xxx.
52. *Abdn Counc.,* ii, 267; E.P.Dennison and J.Stones, *Historic Aberdeen:The archaeological implications of development* (Edinburgh, 1997), 38.
53. *Abdn Counc.,* ii, 312.
54. *Abdn Counc.,* ii, 293.
55. ACA, CR, liii (1), 7.
56. ACA, CR, liv, 261.
57. ACA, CR, liv, 335.
58. ACA, CR, lvi, 9.
59. *Old Abdn Recs,* ii, 61, 66-7, 81-2.
60. The last complaint by a master of the grammar school about competition from other teachers was by David Wedderburn, who complained

about the 'multitude of schooles everiequhar' (*Bon Record*, 53).

61. *Abdn Counc.*, iii, 19.
62. *Bon Record*, 107; *Abdn Counc.*, iii, 19.
63. ACA, CR, liii (1), 448.
64. ACA, CR, liii (1), 533.
65. ACA, CR, l, 332. I have found no evidence for the assertion by W. Kennedy, *Annals of Aberdeen*, (London, 1818), ii, 136, that Italian was also taught in the burgh on an *ad hoc* basis from the beginning of the 17th century.
66. ACA, CR, lii (1), 214.
67. ACA, CR, lvii, 246.
68. See ch. 6, above, and especially Table 6.4.
69. *BUK*, iii, 1120.
70. *Abdn Counc.*, ii, 171; G. DesBrisay, 'City limits: female philanthropists and wet nurses in seventeenth-century Scottish towns', *Journal of the Canadian Historical Association*, new series, 8 (1997), 42-3.
71. *Abdn Counc.*, iii, 98.
72. *Commonplace Book of Andrew Melville*, 51. I am grateful to Dr. Gordon DesBrisay for pointing out this reference to me.
73. ACA, CR, lii (1), 733.
74. ACA, CR, lii (1), 733.
75. ACA, CR, liii (1), 208-14.
76. ACA, CR, liii (1), 214.
77. DesBrisay, 'Authority and Discipline', 165.
78. *Mortifications under the Charge of the Provost, Magistrates, and Town Council of Aberdeen* (Aberdeen, 1849), 140.
79. As in Feb. 1662, when certain women were exempted from the council's prohibition on independent teachers on condition they restricted themselves to teaching 'the grounds of reading' (ACA, CR, lix, 355).
80. Mortifications were charitable endowments made in perpetual trust, usually for education, the old or the poor, to the burgh council of Aberdeen.
81. Excerpts from all the mortifications for education entrusted to the burgh of Aberdeen in the period are printed in *Mortifications under the Charge of the Provost*.
82. ACA, CR, liv, 686.
83. *Abdn Counc.*, ii, 293.
84. ACA, CR, liii (1), 533.

85. *Abdn Ecc. Recs*, 144.
86. ACA, CR, liii (1), 577.
87. G. G. Simpson, *Scottish Handwriting, 1150-1650* (Edinburgh, 1973), 11; R. A. Houston *Literacy in Early Modern Europe: Culture and Education, 1500-1800* (London, 1988), ch. 6.
88. ACA, CR, li (1), 20.
89. ACA, CR, liii (1), 550.
90. *Abdn Counc.*, iv, 316.
91. ACA, CR, lviii, 713.
92. ACA, CR, lxi, 59.
93. ACA, CR, lxi, 68.
94. *The Sang Schule of Sanct Nicholace Paroche* (Aberdeen City Council, n.d.); *Minutes of the Aberdeen Philosophical Society*, ed. H. L. Ulman (Aberdeen, 1990), 15.
95. *Old Abdn Recs*, ii, 164.
96. ACA, CR, lxvi, fo. 46v.
97. *Mortifications under the Charge of the Provost*, 188.
98. *Ibid.*, 208.
99. Kennedy, *Annals*, ii, 137.
100. R. Anderson, *The History of Robert Gordon's Hospital, Aberdeen, 1729-1881*, (Aberdeen, 1896), 122.
101. *Ibid.*, 122-37.
102. *Ibid.*, 37.
103. *Ibid.*, 40-3.
104. *Ibid.*, 43.
105. *Ibid.*, 48
106. ACA, CR, lviii, 10.
107. *MUCPMTCA*, 181.
108. *Old Abdn Recs*, ii, 160.
109. *Old Abdn Recs*, ii, 165, 183, 185.
110. ACA, CR, lxi, 210.
111. ACA, CR, lviii, 28.
112. ACA, CR, lxi, 154.
113. *Bon Record*, 169.
114. ACA, CR, lxi, 438.
115. *Bon Record*, 173.
116. *Bon Record*, 92.
117. *Bon Record*, 95-6.
118. Kennedy, *Annals*, ii, 132.
119. *Bon Record*, Appendix 1, 288.
120. Ulman, *Minutes*, 232.
121. ACA, CR, lviii, 59.
122. Kennedy, *Annals*, ii, 128n.
123. ACA, CR, lxvi, fos 150r-153v.
124. ACA, CR, lxvi, fo. 154r.

Notes to Chapter 15:
Educating the Elite: Aberdeen and its Universities

1. For a full consideration of the plans to develop the university, see L. J. Macfarlane, *William Elphinstone and the Kingdom of Scotland, 1431-1514* (Aberdeen, 1985), 290-402.
2. *Halyburton's Ledger*, 183-4.

3. W. Frijhoff, 'Patterns', in H. de Ridder-Symoens (ed.), *A History of the University on Europe. Volume II: Universities in Early Modern Europe* (Cambridge, 1996), 78.
4. M. Napier, *Memoir of John Napier of Merchistoun*

(Edinburgh, 1834), 67.

5. *Nat. MSS. Scot.*, iii, no. 8.

6. *Aberdeen Reg.*, ii, 129-34; W. M. Bryce, *The Scottish Greyfriars* (Edinburgh, 1909), ii, 334; J. Durkan and A. Ross, 'Early Scottish libraries', *IR*, 9 (1958), 164.

7. ACA, Sasine Register, 2, p. 460; P. Bawcutt, 'An early Scottish debate-poem on women', *Scottish Literary Journal*, 23 (1996), 35-42.

8. D. E. R. Watt, *A Biographical Dictionary of Scottish Graduates to AD 1410* (Oxford, 1977), 28-9.

9. *Nat. MSS. Scot.*, iii, no. 8.

10. R. Swanson, 'The university of St Andrews and the Great Schism, 1410-1419', *Journal of Ecclesiastical History*, 26 (1975), 230-1; Macfarlane, *Elphinstone*, 319.

11. For the foundation of Marischal, see D. Stevenson, *King's College, Aberdeen, 1560-1641: From Protestant Reformation to Covenanting Revolution* (Aberdeen, 1990), 35-7; G. D. Henderson, *The Founding of Marischal College, Aberdeen* (Aberdeen, 1947).

12. Stevenson, *King's College*, 14-18.

13. For the text of the New Foundation, see G. P. Edwards (ed.), 'The New Foundation', in Stevenson, *King's College*, 149-66, and for the controversy surrounding it, Stevenson, *King's College*, 29-40.

14. Stevenson, *King's College*, 36.

15. J. Fletcher, 'The foundation of the university of Aberdeen in its European context', in P. Dukes (ed.), *The Universities of Aberdeen and Europe: The First Three Centuries* (Aberdeen, 1995), 9-56; J. Fletcher, 'The college-university: its development in Aberdeen and beyond', in J. J. Carter and D. J. Withrington (eds), *Scottish Universities: Distinctiveness and Diversity* (Edinburgh, 1992), 16-25. Trinity College Dublin, Zamość, Saumur and Montauban were founded in the 1590s, while Frankfurt-an-der Oder and Alcalá de Henares were founded in the 1490s.

16. W. R. Humphries, *William Ogilvie and the Projected Union of the Colleges, 1786-7* (Aberdeen, 1940); R. L. Emerson, 'Lord Bute and the Scottish universities', in K. W. Schweizer (ed.), *Lord Bute: Essays in Re-interpretation* (Leicester, 1988), 163-9.

17. On the origins and development of the Caroline university, see *Fasti Academiae Mariscallanae Aberdonensis*, ed. P. J. Anderson (New Spalding Club, 1889-98) [hereafter *FAM*], i, 255-63; Stevenson, *King's College*, 120-2.

18. Thomas Gordon, 'Reasons and proposals for an union', in *A Complete Collection of the Papers relating to the Union of the King's and Marischal Colleges of Aberdeen* (Aberdeen, 1787), 6-7.

19. See, for example, *Abdn Counc.*, iv, 385-7.

20. C. A. McLaren, 'Affrichtment and riot: student violence in Aberdeen, 1659-1669', *Northern Scotland*, 10 (1990), 1-17.

21. Stuart, *Extracts*, 247.

22. D. B. Johnston, 'James Beattie and his students at Marischal College, Aberdeen', *Northern Scotland*, 11 (1991), 18.

23. Fletcher, 'The foundation of the university of Aberdeen', 24.

24. ACA, CR, viii, 278; Macfarlane, *Elphinstone*, 301, 322-3, 384-5.

25. W. F. Skene (ed.), *Tracts by Dr Gilbert Skeyne, Mediciner to His Majesty* (Bannatyne Club, 1860). See too R. French, 'Medical teaching in Aberdeen from the foundation of the university to the middle of the seventeenth century', *History of the Universities*, 3 (1983), 134-9.

26. *Abdn Grads.*, 121-44.

27. P. B. Wood, *The Aberdeen Enlightenment: The Arts Curriculum in the Eighteenth Century* (Aberdeen, 1993), 71, 80-1, 84; G. P. Milne (ed.), *Aberdeen Medico-Chirurgical Society: A Bicentennial History, 1789-1989* (Aberdeen, 1989); E. H. B. Rodger, *Aberdeen Doctors at Home and Abroad: The Narrative of a Medical School* (Edinburgh, 1893), 61-99. For overseas recruitment of doctors, see ch. 17.

28. Macfarlane, *Elphinstone*, 358, 377.

29. John Spalding, *Memorialls of the Trubles in Scotland and England, 1624-45* (Spalding Club, 1850-51), i, 166; G. Donaldson, 'Aberdeen University and the Reformation', *Northern Scotland*, 1 (1973), 141; Stevenson, *King's College*, 116-17.

30. Stevenson, *King's College*, 49.

31. J. J. Carter and C. A. McLaren, *Crown and Gown, 1495-1995: An Illustrated History of the University of Aberdeen* (Aberdeen, 1994), 76.

32. AUL, MS K/144 (Papers relating to The Catanach Case, 1744); MS K/214 (Papers of James Catanach); N. Clyne, 'The Advocates in Aberdeen' and P. J. Anderson, 'The advocates in Aberdeen: the Catanach case', *Scottish Notes and Queries*, 1 (1888), 114-15, 129-31.

33. Macfarlane, *Elphinstone*, 373-4. See too G. P. Edwards, 'The place of theology in the foundation of the university', in A. Main (ed.), *But Where Shall Wisdom Be Found?* (Aberdeen, 1995), 11-16, and, for a recent summary of Lombard's work and its significance, M. L. Colish, 'Peter Lombard', in G. R. Evans (ed.), *The Medieval Theologians* (Oxford, 2001), 168-83.

34. William Hay, *Lectures on Marriage*, ed. J. C. Barry (Stair Soc., 1967), 209-11.

35. G. D. Henderson, "The Aberdeen doctors" in *idem*, *The Burning Bush: Studies in Scottish Church History* (Edinburgh, 1957), 75-93; D. Stewart, 'The 'Aberdeen Doctors' and the Covenanters', *RSCHS*, 22 (1984), 35-44; H. R. Sefton, 'Scotland's greatest theologian', *AUR*, 45 (1973-4), 348-52; Stevenson, *King's College*, 105-19. See also Ch. 17.

36. Macfarlane, *Elphinstone*, 363-70. For the reception of Aristotle's work in the medieval west, see the classic account by C. H. Haskins, *The Renaissance of the Twelfth Century* (Cambridge, Mass., 1927), 278-302, 341-8.

37. J. Le Goff, *Intellectuals in the Middle Ages* (Oxford, 1993) 137.

38. Stevenson, *King's College*, 155-6.

39. Stuart, *Extracts*, 9.

40. On Lawson, see J. Durkan, 'George Hay's oration at the purging of King's College, Aberdeen, in 1569: commentary', *Northern Scotland*, 6 (1985), 103-8.

41. Wood, *Aberdeen Enlightenment*, 55-9; Carter and McLaren, *Crown and Gown*, 41, 43.

42. Le Goff, *Intellectuals*, 154; J. Pelikan, '1491-1500: *decennium mirabile* or *zwischen den Zeiten?*', in Main, *Wisdom*, 3-4.

43. W. S. Watt, 'George Hay's oration at the purging of King's College, Aberdeen, in 1569: a translation', *Northern Scotland*, 6 (1985), 91.

44. C. Shepherd, 'The arts curriculum at Aberdeen at the beginning of the eighteenth century', in J. J. Carter and J. H. Pittock (eds), *Aberdeen and the Enlightenment* (Aberdeen, 1987), 146-54; Wood, *Aberdeen Enlightenment*, 3-8.

45. Stevenson, *King's College*, 42-4.

46. H. Kearney, *Scholars and Gentlemen: Universities and Society in Pre-industrial Britain, 1500-1700* (London, 1970), 89; Wood, *Aberdeen Enlightenment*, 5-8, 36, 49.

47. I owe this observation to my colleague, Howard Hotson, who is currently examining the mediation of central European ideas, such as those of Bartholomew Keckermann, from Danzig to Aberdeen.

48. Shepherd, 'The arts curriculum at Aberdeen', 146-9.

49. C. Shepherd, 'A national system of university education in seventeenth-century Scotland?', in Carter and Withrington, *Scottish Universities*, 26-33.

50. There is a wealth of literature on Reid, Beattie, others and 'Common Sense' philosophy. For its reception abroad, see M. Kühn, *Scottish Common Sense Philosophy in Germany, 1768-1800* (Kingston, 1987); J. W. Manns, *Reid and His French Disciples* (Leiden, 1994).

51. M. A. Stewart, 'George Turnbull and educational reform', and K. A. B. Mackinnon, 'George Turnbull's common sense jurisprudence', in Carter and Pittock, *Aberdeen and the Enlightenment*, 95-110; Wood, *Aberdeen Enlightenment*, 29-30, 40-9, 63-73, 82-3, 89-90; R. L. Emerson, *Professors, Patronage and Politics: The Aberdeen Universities in the Eighteenth Century* (Aberdeen, 1992), 21-2; J. S. Reid, 'The

Castle Hill observatory, Aberdeen', *Journal for the History of Astronomy*, 13 (1982), 84-95; idem, 'Patrick Copland, 1748-1822: aspects of his life and times at Marischal College', *AUR*, 172 (1984), 359-79; B. Ponting, 'Mathematics at Aberdeen: developments, characteristics and events, 1717-1860', *AUR*, 162 (1979), 162-75.

52. *FAM*, i, 433-4; Brodie Castle, Brodie of Brodie Papers, Box 4/2. I am very grateful to Andrew Mackillop for the latter reference. The Macpherson bursary still exists. For others, donated from abroad, see *Abdn Fasti*, nos 147-8, 151-2, 156; *FAM*, i, 337-40, 403-5, 412-15, 419-22, 431-2.

53. *Abdn Grads.*, 177-91.

54. For attendance numbers, see Donaldson, 'Reformation', 135, 137; Stevenson, *King's College*, 55-6; Emerson, *Professors*, 133 (Appendix 1); *Abdn Grads.*, 97-309; R. C. Schwinges, 'Admissions', in H. de Ridder-Symoens (ed.), *A History of the University in Europe. Volume 1: The University in the Middle Ages* (Cambridge, 1992), 189; H. Hotson, 'A dark Golden Age: the Thirty Years War and the universities of northern Europe', in A. I. Macinnes, T. Riis and F. Pedersen (eds), *Guns, Ships and Bibles in the North Sea and Baltic States, c. 1350-c. 1700* (East Linton, 2000), 235-70.

55. Edwards, 'New Foundation', 164. See too *FAM*, i, 69-74.

56. See, for example, *Abdn Grads.*, 179, 187, 195, 249, 254, 265; *FAM*, ii, 341, 346, 353-4, 358, 364, 369, 371-9.

57. *Abdn Grads.*, passim; *FAM*, ii, 340-86.

58. The following paragraphs draw on C. A. McLaren, 'Discipline and decorum: the law-codes of the universities of Aberdeen, 1605-86', in Carter and Withrington, *Scottish Universities*, 128-37; Macfarlane, *Elphinstone*, 385-7; Edwards, 'The New Foundation', 158-9, 162-3; *Abdn Fasti*, 225-55; *FAM*, i, 69-74.

59. L. J. Macfarlane, 'The Divine Office and the Mass', and C. A. McLaren, 'The chapel, the college and the university, 1560-1945', in J. Geddes (ed.), *King's College Chapel, Aberdeen, 1500-2000* (Leeds, 2000), 6-27, 157-60.

60. Macfarlane, *Elphinstone*, 347, 363.

61. *Abdn Fasti*, 575-77; *Abstracts from Some Statutes and Orders of King's College in Old Aberdeen, 1753* (Aberdeen, 1754), 6; Letter from Thomas Reid to Archibald Dunbar (4 Sept. 1755), published in *Alma Mater*, 20 (1902), 62-3.

62. AUL, MS K/232 (Account for the supply of candles, 1712-13).

63. C. A. McLaren, 'Visiting the charter chest: the early records of the university and King's College, Aberdeen', in T. Brotherstone and D. Ditchburn (eds), *Freedom and Authority: Scotland, c. 1050-c. 1650*

(East Linton, 2000), 195-7; Carter and McLaren, *Crown and Gown*, 62.

64. D. M. Walker, 'The rebuilding of King's and Marischal Colleges, 1723-1889', *AUR*, 190 (1993), 123-6.
65. *Abstracts from Some Statutes*, 5.
66. *Ibid.*, 17; 'Letter from Thomas Reid', 62-3.
67. C. A. McLaren, 'The college and the community, 1600-1860', in J. S. Smith (ed.), *Old Aberdeen: Bishops, Burghers and Buildings* (Aberdeen, 1991), 66.
68. Johnston, 'James Beattie', 21.
69. McLaren, 'The college and the community', 60-1; Johnston, 'James Beattie', 19.
70. McLaren, 'The college and the community', 67; Carter and McLaren, *Crown and Gown*, 63-6.
71. AUL, MS K/231/8 (Papers 'concerning the falling out between the Colledges of New and Old Aberdeen'), p. 3.
72. McLaren, 'The college and the community', 61-5.

73. Wood, *Aberdeen Enlightenment*, 1, 11-14; Emerson, *Professors*, 11-12, 32-4.
74. Emerson, *Professors*, 19.
75. Emerson, *Professors*, 151-6 (Appendix VI).
76. C. A. McLaren, 'Enlightened men at law: litigation at King's College in the eighteenth century', in Carter and Pittock, *Aberdeen and the Enlightenment*, 129-35; McLaren, 'The college and the community', 70-2.
77. *Abdn. Counc.*, iv, 368-9; Wood, *Aberdeen Enlightenment*, 16-19, 31, 77-8; H. W. Turnbull, *Bi-centenary of the Death of Colin Maclauren, 1698-1746* (Aberdeen, 1951).
78. Wood, *The Aberdeen Enlightenment*, 14-16.
79. Emerson, *Professors*, 173 (Appendix VI).
80. Emerson, *Professors*, 14.
81. AUL, MS K/4 (Album Amicorum), fos 101-87. For appeals to overseas communities, see ch. 17.

Notes to Chapter 16:
Contrasting Cultures: Town and Country

1. G. Donaldson, 'Scotland's conservative north in the 16th and 17th centuries', *TRHS*, 16 (1966), 65-79.
2. M. Glendinning, G. Ritchie and J. Thomas, *Aberdeen on Record: Images of the Past* (Edinburgh, 1997), ch. 2.
3. W. Kennedy, *Annals of Aberdeen* (London, 1818), i, 99.
4. J. S. Smith 'The physical site of historical Aberdeen', in *idem* (ed.), *New Light on Medieval Aberdeen* (Aberdeen, 1985), 4-5; J. C. Murray, 'The archaeological evidence' in *ibid*, 13, 16, 18.
5. *Spalding Misc.*, ii, p. x. In fairness, it should be noted that other journeys at the time could be quicker, but the state of the 'roads' invited such disasters as Lovat suffered.
6. E. Ewan, 'The age of Bon-Accord: Aberdeen in the fourteenth century', in Smith, *New Light*, 32, 34; Glendinning, *Aberdeen on Record*, ch. 2 (cf. H. Booton, 'Economic and social change in later medieval Aberdeen', in Smith, *New Light*, 46 for a more cautious estimate).
7. *Abdn Counc.*, i, p. xv.
8. *Abdn Counc.*, i, 81; W. Kennedy, 'An alphabetical index of the first 67 volumes of the Council Register', i, 361 (ACA, CR, vol. xviii).
9. *Abdn Counc.*, i, 81; Kennedy, 'Index', i, 361 (ACA, CR, vol. xviii); L. J. Macfarlane, *William Elphinstone and the Kingdom of Scotland, 1431-1514* (Aberdeen, 1985), 273.
10. Kennedy, *Annals*, i, 61-3; ACA, Register of Sasines, ii, 460.
11. Kennedy, *Annals*, i, 63; J. Bulloch, *Aberdeen Three Hundred Years Ago* (Aberdeen, 1884), 20.

12. Watt, *Aberdeen and Banff*, 115.
13. William Dunbar, *Selected Poems*, ed. P. Bawcutt (London, 1996), 68n, 69.
14. *Abdn Counc.*, i, 339; Kennedy, 'Index', i, 365 (ACA, CR, vol. xii).
15. J. C. Murray (ed.), *Excavations in the Medieval Burgh of Aberdeen, 1973-81* (Edinburgh, 1982), 182; A. Cameron and J. Stones (eds), *Aberdeen: An Indepth View of the City's Past* (Edinburgh, 2001), 219.
16. W. A. Cragie *et al.*, *Dictionary of the Older Scottish Tongue* (Chicago etc., 1931-2002), ii, 677; *APS*, ii, 48, 100, 226.
17. F. Wyness, *Spots from the Leopard* (Aberdeen, 1971), 45; *Abdn Counc.*, i, p. xxi.
18. Watt, *Aberdeen and Banff*, 93-4; *Abdn Counc.*, i, pp. xxiii, 413.
19. E. P. Dennison, 'Power to the people? The myth of the medieval burgh community', in S. Foster, A. Macinnes and R. MacInnes (eds), *Scottish Power Centres from the Early Middle Ages to the Twentieth Century* (Glasgow, 1998), 114-15, 129, n. 114.
20. E. Bain, *Merchant and Craft Guilds. A History of the Aberdeen Incorporated Trades* (Aberdeen, 1887), 51.
21. *Abdn Counc.*, i, pp. xxi-xxiv, 459.
22. Kennedy, *Annals*, i, 181; Watt, *Aberdeen and Banff*, 197.
23. Kennedy, *Annals*, i, 97.
24. *Ibid.*, i, 182; examples of grave slabs bearing trade signs are to be found in Marischal Museum.
25. *A. B. Coll.*, 152-3, 157-8.
26. L. J. Macfarlane, *St. Machar's Cathedral in the Later Middle Ages* (Aberdeen, 1979), 8-9; D. Bruce, 'The

Society of Advocates in Aberdeen', *AUR*, 56 (1995-96), 301.

27. L.J.Macfarlane, 'St Machar's Cathedral through the Ages', in J.S.Smith (ed.), *Old Aberdeen: Bishops, Burghers and Buildings* (Aberdeen, 1991), 16.

28. K.E.Trail, *The Story of Old Aberdeen* (Aberdeen, 1929), 12.

29. M.Glendinning, R.MacInnes and A.MacKechnie, *A History of Scottish Architecture* (Edinburgh, 1996), 6.

30. *Ibid.*, 3; I.Campbell, 'Bishop Elphinstone's tomb', in J.Geddes (ed.), *King's College Chapel, Aberdeen, 1500-2000* (Leeds, 2000), 115-29.

31. R.Smith, *Discovering Aberdeenshire* (Edinburgh, 1988), 36.

32. S.Simpson, 'The choir stalls and rood screen', in Geddes (ed.), *King's College*, 74-97.

33. Macfarlane, *William Elphinstone*, 299.

34. John Barbour, *Bruce*, ed. M.P.MacDiarmid and J.A.C. Stevenson (Scottish Text Soc., 1985), i, 3 (Book I, ll. 225-8).

35. *Ibid.*, i, 8.

36. *Ibid.*, i, 45, 50.

37. D.Webster, 'Agriculture in Aberdeenshire in the olden days', in *A Scientific Survey of Aberdeen*, by Various Hands (London, 1934), 82.

38. D.Buchan, *The Ballad and the Folk* (London, 1972), 4, 5, 41.

39. *Ord's Bothy Songs and Ballads of Aberdeen, Banff & Moray Angus and the Mearns, with an introduction by Alexander Fenton* (Edinburgh, 1930), 19.

40. *A.B.Coll.*, 73; D.Murison, 'The speech of Moray', in D.Omand (ed.), *The Moray Book* (Edinburgh, 1976), 280.

41. Wyness, *Spots from the Leopard*, 169-71.

42. Watt, *Aberdeen and Banff*, 9.

43. *Abdn Reg.*, i, p.xxix; A.Smith, *A New History of Aberdeenshire* (Aberdeen, 1875), ii, 1182-4.

44. J.Ritchie, *Some Antiquities of Aberdeenshire and its Borders* (Edinburgh, 1927), 270-2.

45. *Ibid.*, 272; P.Crowl, *The Intelligent Traveller's Guide to Historic Scotland*, (London, 1986), 535.

46. J.Pratt, *Buchan* (Aberdeen, 1858), 20.

47. *Abdn Ecc. Recs.*, pp.xxvi, xxvii; *A.B.Ill.*, ii, 48; N.Pennick, *Celtic Sacred Landscapes* (London, 1996), 202.

48. R.Smith, *The Granite City: A History of Aberdeen*, (Edinburgh, 1989), 64; Glendinning, *Aberdeen on Record*, ch. 2.

49. *A.B.Ill.*, ii, pp.xvi, 94.

50. Smith, *Granite City*, 171.

51. *Scottish Notes and Queries* (Series iii, 1929), 100.

52. A.V.B.Norman, *Culloden* (National Trust for Scotland, 1996), 17-18.

53. M.J.S.Harris, 'Memories of the Garioch', *AUR*, 44 (1971-2), 372.

54. J.Davidson, *Inverurie and the Earldom of the Garioch* (Edinburgh, 1878), 302.

55. *Records of the Meeting of the Exercise of Alford*, ed. T.Bell (Aberdeen, 1897), 21-2.

56. A memorial to this still (1992) stands on the hill at the entrance to Forres on the A96.

57. *Records of Alford*, 31, 407n, 408n, 410n, 416.

58. Pratt, *Buchan*, 49, 334-5

59. C.Huie, 'Folklore', in Omand, *Moray Book*, 288, 290. The water was often from chalybeate springs.

60. AUL, MS 2124 (Collection or Rhymes from Counties of Aberdeen, Forfar and Angus), nos 7, 86.

61. *Ord's Bothy Songs and Ballads*, 347, 408, 411.

62. *A.B.Ill.*, ii, 46-7.

63. ACA, CR, vi, 27.

64. ACA, Burgh Court Roll, 1317.

65. ACA, Register of Burgesses, 1632-94, p.27.

66. Watt, *Aberdeen and Banff*, 196.

67. ACA, Charter M/1, no. 21.

68. ACA, CR, lx, 352-3.

69. ACA, Charter C/2, no. 1 (Ducat Brae Deed).

70. *Old Aberdeen Recs*, i, 155.

71. *Abdn Ecc. Recs.*, 38; *Old Aberdeen Recs.*, ii, 153.

72. *Abdn Counc.*, iii, 2, 286. The first reference, from 1625, includes mention of the 'first hole' and the 'queen's hole' on the Links.

73. C. Foster, *Homage to Schirr Johnne Blak*, (Aberdeen, n.d.).

74. Cf. the description of 'the Sherricking' in A.McArthur and H.K.Long, *No Mean City* (London, 1978), 43ff.

75. *Old Aberdeen Recs*, i, 43, 74.

76. *Abdn Ecc. Recs*, 84.

77. Kennedy, 'Index', i, 102 (ACA, CR, vol. xli).

78. Wyness, *Spots from the Leopard*, 28, 32.

79. *Spalding Misc.*, ii, 54-5.

80. Kennedy, *Annals*, i, 173; Wyness, *Spots from the Leopard*, 46.

81. Watt, *Aberdeen and Banff*, 227; J.Buckroyd, *The Life of James Sharp* (Edinburgh, 1987), 4, 9, 11.

82. W.D.Simpson, *The Earldom of Mar* (Aberdeen, 1959), 94-5; Watt, *Aberdeen and Banff*, 226; *Fasti Aberdonenses* (Spalding Club,1854), pp.xxxvi, xliv, xlv; D.Stevenson, *King's College, Aberdeen, 1560-1641* (Aberdeen, 1990), 83, 85ff.

83. Foster, *Homage to Schirr Johnne Blak*.

84. Cf. *Musae Latinae Aberdonensis* (Aberdeen, 1892-1910); see n. 89, below.

85. Simpson, *Earldom of Mar*, 96.

86. *Ibid*, 106, 145.

87. F.J.Child (ed.), *English and Scottish Popular Ballads* (Boston, 1857), vi, 173, 188; vii, 210, 214.

88. *Musae Latinae Aberdonensis*, ii, p.xv; J.Cameron, 'Some Scottish students and teachers at the university of Leiden in the late sixteenth and early seventeenth centuries', in G.G. Simpson (ed.),

Scotland and the Low Countries, 1124-1994 (East Linton, 1996), 122, 127-8. Cf. A. Keith, *Eminent Aberdonians* (Aberdeen, 1984), 32 ff.

89. Cf. D. Duncan, *Thomas Ruddiman* (Edinburgh, 1965); M. G. H. Pittock, *The Invention of Scotland* (London and New York, 1991); and *idem, Poetry and Jacobite Politics in Eighteenth-Century Britain and Ireland* (Cambridge, 1994).

90. *Musae Latinae Aberdonensis*, i, 180, 219.

91. *Ibid.*, i, p. xxiii; ii, 241.

92. *Ibid.*, iii, 38, 167 ff, 173.

93. *Ibid.*, i, p. vii.

94. Wyness, *Spots from the Leopard*, 38-41. Cf. D. Thomson, *The Life and Art of George Jamesone* (Oxford, 1974).

95. Mosman's painting is held in the City Art Gallery.

96. J. Laird, 'George Dalgarno', *AUR*, 23 (1935-6), 19; G. M. Fraser, 'Scientists of the north-east of Scotland', *A Scientific Survey* (1934), 110; Keith, *Eminent Aberdonians*, 118 ff.

97. Fraser, 'Scientists', 113; A. and H. Tayler, *Jacobites of Aberdeenshire and Banffshire in the Rising of 1715* (Edinburgh, 1934); A. M. Mackenzie, *Scottish Pageant 1707-1832*, (Edinburgh, 1950), 185; cf. D. Dobson, *Jacobites of the '15* (Aberdeen, 1993) and J. Geddes, *Ye Ken Noo!* (Durham, 1993).

98. Smith, *New History of Aberdeenshire*, ii, 1144.

99. *Spalding Misc.*, iv, 324, 325.

100. Glendinning, *Scottish Architecture*, 102 ff; J. Holloway, 'An Aberdeen bi-centenary: James Gibbs, architect, 1682-1754', *AUR*, 35 (1953-4), 341; cf. D. Greenwood, *William King* (Oxford, 1969).

101. ACA, MSS Guildry Accounts, 1756-7.

102. A. Keith, 'The laureate of the Jacobites: William Meston', *AUR*, 22 (1934-35), 9, 12, 13; Keith, *Eminent Aberdonians*, 139; ACA Letter Books (Incoming), x, 77-81; Watt, *Aberdeen and Banff*, 276.

103. Tayler, *Jacobites*, 156-8.

104. A. Smith, *A New History of Aberdeenshire* (Aberdeen, 1875), i, 403; W. Donaldson, 'The Jacobite Song in 18th and Early 19th Century Scotland' (University of Aberdeen, unpublished Ph.D. thesis, 1974).

105. Tayler, *Jacobites*, 146.

106. J. Davidson, *Inverurie and the Earldom of the Garioch* (Edinburgh, 1878), 408.

107. AUL, MS 795/2 (Collection of Scottish Folk Songs with Music, 1777).

108. Examples of these are on show in Marischal Museum.

109. Wyness, *Spots from the Leopard*, 122; the paternal grandmother of Miss Adeline Masson, a lady well-known to the author, held the baby in Brownlow's 1868 picture.

110. Kennedy, *Annals*, i, 256; *Abdn Counc.*, iv, p. xxxv.

111. Wyness, *Spots from the Leopard*, 128; Mackenzie, *Scottish Pageant*, 275, 283-4; Kennedy, *Annals*, ii, 284.

112. Cf. Crowl, *Intelligent Traveller's Guide*, 543, 546.

113. These are on show in the City Art Gallery.

114. ACA, ACC5, Cochran Family Papers, A/1 (1765-78).

115. J. J. Carter and J. Pittock (eds), *Aberdeen and the Enlightenment* (Aberdeen, 1987); Geddes, *Ye Ken Noo!*.

116. C. McIntosh, 'Style as a key to the Scottish Enlightenment', *Eighteenth-Century Scotland* (1997), 9-10.

117. Fraser, 'Scientists', 113.

118. Keith, *Eminent Aberdonians*, 54 ff.

119. Fraser, 'Scientists', 107.

120. *The Minutes of the Aberdeen Philosophical Society, 1758-73*, ed. H. L. Ulman (Aberdeen, 1990), 12. Cf. A. Broadie's plenary address to the 1998 Thomas Reid Conference at King's College, Aberdeen, for 'Common Sense's' medieval links.

121. P. Wood, *The Aberdeen Enlightenment: The Arts Curriculum in the Eighteenth Century* (Aberdeen, 1993), 120; G. D. Henderson, 'A member of the Wise Club', *AUR*, 24 (1936-7), 4.

122. Ulman, *Minutes*, 12.

123. S. Manning, review of Robinson (ed.), *James Beattie: Collected Works*, in *Eighteenth-Century Scotland* (1997), 17.

124. E. Duncan, 'James Ramsay, 1733-89 - abolitionist', *AUR*, 53 (1989-90), 129, 132, 134.

125. Ulman, *Minutes*, 12.

126. *Ibid.*, 20, 25, 28, 35, 37.

127. W. H. G. Armytage, 'David Fordyce: a neglected thinker', *AUR*, 36 (1995-6), 289-90.

128. Wood, *Aberdeen Enlightenment*, 129, 162.

129. G. D. Henderson, 'Ephinstone[sic] birthday celebrations in the eighteenth century', *AUR*, 18 (1930-31), 255-7.

130. J. Pittock, 'James Beattie: a friend to all', in D. Hewitt and M. Spiller (eds), *Literature of the North* (Aberdeen, 1983), 55.

131. J. A. Henderson, *Annals of Lower Deeside* (Aberdeen, 1892), 133-4.

132. Glendinning, *Scottish Architecture*, 106-7.

133. AUL, MS K114 (1776).

134. Keith, *Eminent Aberdonians*, 30, 74; information displayed at entrance to AUL, Special Collections and through the themed collection at Marischal Museum.

135. N. Hans, 'Henry Farquharson, pioneer of Russian education, 1698-1739', *AUR*, 38 (1959-60), 27.

136. P. Dukes, 'The Aberdeen Enlightenment and Russia', in Carter and Pittock, *Aberdeen and the Enlightenment*, 20-1, 23.

137. Ulman, *Minutes* 15.

138. ACA, Squibs Cartoons, ii, no. 1.

139. J. and M. Lough, 'Aberdeen circulating libraries in the eighteenth century', *AUR*, 31 (1944-6), 18-19, 23.

140. Bruce, 'Society of Advocates', 307.
141. I. Beavan, 'Bibliography of the Enlightenment', in Carter and Pittock, *Aberdeen and the Enlightenment*, 319.
142. AUL, MS 2037 (Papers of John Henderson), fo. 9.
143. Kennedy, *Annals*, ii, 170, 277.
144. AUL, MS 2037 fo. 1 ff ('Essay on *Aberdeen Journal*'); Keith, *Eminent Aberdonians*, 94; Kennedy, Index, i, 44 (ACA, CR, vol. lxiv).
145. A. Short, *Old Aberdeen in the Eighteenth Century* (Aberdeen, 1985), 11; H. G. Farmer, *Music Making in the Olden Days:The Story of the Aberdeen Concerts, 1748-1801* (London, 1950), 9-10, 19-20.
146. I. Cramb, 'Francis Peacock, 1723-1807: dancing master in Aberdeen', *AUR*, 43 (1969-70), 251, 256.
147. ACA, Kennedy, 'Index', i, 235 (ACA, CR, vol. lviii).
148. J. F. and T. M. Flett, 'Some early Highland dancing competitions', *AUR*, 36 (1955-6), 346.
149. Farmer, *Music Making*, 21, 57, 78.
150. Short, *Old Aberdeen*, 7; Glendinning, *Guide to Aberdeen*, ch. 3.
151. M. Gray, 'Fishing villages, 1750-1880' in O'Dell and Mackintosh, *North-east of Scotland*, 100; cf. also Walton, 'Regional settlement', in *ibid*, 98; J. Ritchie, 'Animal life of north-east Scotland', *A Scientific Survey* (1934), 22-3, 25.
152. AUL, MS 2037, fos 6, 8.
153. M. Steven, *Parish Life in Eighteenth-Century Scotland: A Review of the Old Statistical Account* (Aberdeen, 1995), 75.
154. ACA, Squibs Cartoons, ii; Glendinning, *Aberdeen on Record*, ch. 3.
155. *Ord's Bothy Songs and Ballads*, 15.
156. *Maitland Misc.*, i, 488.
157. *Ord's Bothy Songs and Ballads*, 390.
158. Wyness, *Spots from the Leopard*, 55-6.
159. ACA, Kennedy, 'Index', i, 253; ii, 415.
160. W. Paul, *Past and Present of Aberdeenshire* (Aberdeen, 1881), 38-9.
161. Kennedy, *Annals*, ii, 279-80.

Notes to Chapter 17:
Aberdeen and the Outside World

1. P. D. A. Harvey, *Medieval Maps* (London, 1991), Plates 30 and 57.
2. Jean Froissart, *Oeuvres*, ed. K. de Lettenhove (Brussels, 1867-75), xiii, 201.
3. *The Chronicle of Melrose* (London, 1936), eds. A. O. Anderson and M. O. Anderson, 70.
4. *Nat. MSS. Scot.*, iii, no. 8.
5. P. Hume Brown (ed.), *Early Travellers in Scotland* (Edinburgh, repr., 1978), 5, 20, 173.
6. Daniel Defoe, *A Tour Through the Whole Island of Great Britain*, ed. P. Rogers (Folio Soc., 1983), 281-5; *CSP Scot*, i, no. 1136.
7. Jean Froissart, *Méliador*, ed. A. Longnon (Paris, 1895-99), ii, 73, 145.
8. Hume Brown, *Early Travellers*, 66, 173, 204.
9. William Brereton, *Travels in Holland, The United Provinces, England, Scotland and Ireland, 1634-5*, ed. E. Hawkins (Chetham Soc., 1844), 116.
10. ACA, CR, vi, 598; Alexander Lindsay, *A Rutter of the Scottish Seas*, eds. A. B. Taylor, I. H. Adams and G. Fortune (National Maritime Museum, 1980), 48.
11. *ER*, iv, 535, 566; v, 306, 341, 389, 431; ACA, CR, v (1), 394; v (2), 684; vi, 598.
12. *Rot. Scot.*, i, 893-4; R. Degryse, 'De schepen, in de haven van Sluis, in het voorjaar 1464', *Mededelingen van de Marineakademie van Belgie*, 20 (1968), 101.
13. NAS, E71/1/2, fo. 2v. See too *CDS*, v, nos 1040, 1050.
14. ACA, CR, v (1), 342, 358; 9, 86.
15. I. C. M. Barnes, 'The Aberdeen stocking trade', *Textile History*, 8 (1977), 89. See ch. 7.
16. ACA, CR, xxxviii, 323-4; AUL, MS 3070 (Records of Aberdeen Shipmasters Society, 1590-1946), especially MS 3070/6/24; 3070/8/1.
17. *ACL*, i, no. 120. See ch. 7.
18. ACA, CR, ix, 490.
19. *ER*, i, 75, 99, 275, 321, 366, 426; iv, 144, 170, 199, 225, 248, 273, 314; T. C. Smout, *Scottish Trade on the Eve of the Union, 1660-1707* (Edinburgh, 1963), 286-7.
20. P. G. B. McNeill and H. L. Macqueen (eds.), *Atlas of Scottish History to 1707* (Edinburgh, 1996), 250-1; NAS, E71/1/2.
21. D. Ditchburn, *Scotland and Europe: The Medieval Kingdom and its Contacts with Christendom* (East Linton, 2000), 19-21.
22. AUL, MS 2070 (Journal of Jonathan Troup), fos 1-11; MS 2238 (Journal of George Kerr). See too *James Beattie's Day-Book, 1773-98*, ed. R. S. Walker (Spalding Club, 1948), 107, 136-7, 157, for journey times by land, or by land and sea, to London.
23. ACA, CR, v (1), 29; *CDS*, iv, no. 158; v, nos 328, 1050, for example.
24. AUL, MS 2238, fo. 3.
25. ACA, CR, v (1), 446. On the background to this incident, see D. Ditchburn, 'Bremen piracy and Scottish periphery: the North Sea world, in the 1440s', in A. I. Macinnes, T. Riis and F. Pedersen (eds.), *Guns, Ships and Bibles in the North Sea and the Baltic States, c. 1350-c. 1700* (East Linton, 2000), 1-23. See too D. Ditchburn, 'The pirate, the policeman and the pantomime star: Aberdeen's alternative economy, in the early fifteenth centu-

ry', *Northern Scotland*, 12 (1992), 19-34.

26. *AJ*, 7 Nov. 1774; 7 Oct. 1794. We are grateful to David Worthington for assistance in abstracting material from the *Aberdeen Journal*.

27. *Early Sources of Scottish History, 500 to 1286*, ed. A. O. Anderson, 2 vols (Edinburgh, 1922), ii, 216.

28. *Chron. Fordun*, i, 360-1; *Chron. Wyntoun*, vi, 60; *ER*, i, 472.

29. ACA, CR, vii, 797, 1067-68.

30. See Ch. 5.

31. *CSSR*, ii, 219; *The Apostolic Camera and Scottish Benefices, 1418-88*, ed. A. I. Cameron (Oxford, 1934), 9, 11, 17.

32. J. P. Foggie, 'Archivium Sacræ Pænitentiariæ Apostilicæ, in the Vatican archives as a source for Scottish historians', *IR*, 47 (1996), 118.

33. P. C. Ferguson, *Medieval Papal Representatives in Scotland: Legates, Nuncios and Judges-delegate, 1125-1286* (Stair Soc., 1997), Appendix 1, nos 69, 71-3, 92, 107, 113, 125, 135, 144, 154.

34. *CSSR*, ii, 174, 219, 233-4; iii, 2, 219-20, 265; iv, nos 19, 245, 248, 500, 561, 700, 1333; v, no. 12.

35. D. E. R. Watt (ed.), *A Biographical Dictionary of Scottish University Graduates to AD 1410* (Oxford, 1977), 237, 348; *CSSR*, ii, 37.

36. *CSSR*, v, no. 1089.

37. A. A. M. Duncan, *Scotland: The Making of the Kingdom* (Edinburgh, 1975), 285.

38. Watt, *Dictionary*, 460-3.

39. Watt, *Dictionary*, 465-6.

40. L. J. Macfarlane, *William Elphinstone and the Kingdom of Scotland, 1431-1514* (Aberdeen, 1985), 20-47.

41. John Barbour, *The Bruce*, ed. A. A. M. Duncan (Edinburgh, 1997), 64, 72, 106, 114, 138, 146, 186, 232, 236; *Abdn Reg.*, ii, 128. The cathedral possessed a copy of *The Brus*, donated by Bishop Alexander Kinnimund (*Ibid.*, ii, 131). For the book which Barbour lost, see *Ibid.*, ii, 133; and for Barbour's career, see Watt, *Dictionary*, 28-9.

42. *Abdn Reg.*, ii, 129-34. For a brief synopsis of the life and works of these and other prominent canon lawyers, see J. A. Brundage, *Medieval Canon Law* (Harlow, 1995), 202-30.

43. Rome, Vatican Archives, Archivium Sacræ Pænitentiariæ Apostilicæ, 40, fos 90r, 101r, 126r, 169r. We are grateful to Irene Furneaux for this information.

44. AUL, Inc. 34.

45. *Angels, Nobles and Unicorns: Art and Patronage in Medieval Scotland* (Edinburgh, 1982), nos E51-2, E54, E56.

46. J. Durkan and A. Ross, 'Early Scottish libraries', *IR*, 9 (1958), 11.

47. M. Rubin, *Corpus Christi: The Eucharist In Late Medieval Culture* (Cambridge, 1991), 164-85; *Chron. Bower* (Watt), v, 325-9. For its celebration, in Aber-

deen, see A. J. Mill, *Mediaeval Plays in Scotland* (Edinburgh, 1927), 61-3.

48. *Abdn Reg.*, ii, 143-4.

49. C. H. Lawrence, *St Edmund of Abingdon* (Oxford, 1960), 323; Watt, *Dictionary*, 462.

50. *Abdn Reg.*, ii, 156.

51. *Rot. Scot.*, i, 872, 897, 901; ACA, viii, 600.

52. *Rot. Scot.*, i, 877; J. Stuart, 'Notice of an original, instrument recently discovered among the records of the dean and chapter of Canterbury ...', *PSAS*, 10 (1875), 528-35; S. C. Wilson, 'Scottish Canterbury pilgrims', *SHR*, 24 (1926-7), 263.

53. A. White, 'The Regent Morton's visitation: the Reformation of Aberdeen, 1574', in A. A. MacDonald, M. Lynch and I. B. Cowan (eds), *The Reformation in Scotland: Studies in Literature, Religion, History and Culture* (Leiden, 1994), 254.

54. We are grateful to William G. Naphy for this information, based on his studies in the Genevan archives.

55. *ACL*, i, no. 209. See too *ACL*, iv, no. 193, for a similar collection for Polish Protestants, in 1658.

56. *The Hartlib Papers* (Ann Arbor, 1995), 6/4, fo. 85a; 14/2/1, fo. 2b; 19/11/106; 19/11, fos 102a-105b.

57. *Recueil de documents relatifs à l'histoire de l'industrie drapière en Flandre. Première partie: des origines à l'époque bourguignonne*, eds. G. Espinas and H. Pirenne (Brussels, 1906-24), iii, no. 651(6). See too *CDS*, ii, nos 9-10, 20; v, nos 35, 37.

58. *Calendar of Close Rolls* (London, 1900) [hereafter *CCR*], *1313-18*, 271, 288-9; *Urkundenbuch der Stadt Lübeck* (Lübeck, 1843-1905), ii, no. 1043-5.

59. NAS, E71/1/1.

60. Smout, *Scottish Trade*, 286-7.

61. Barnes, 'Aberdeen stocking trade', 95 (Appendix 4), based on analysis of quarterly customs accounts (E 504), in NAS.

62. ACA, CR, v (2), 741.

63. *CCR, 1364-68*, 440-1; *CCR, 1369-74*, 27; *CDS*, iv, no. 146.

64. *Halyburton's Ledger*, 182-5.

65. Paris, Archives Nationales, Parlement, Lettres-Arrets-Juges X57, fos 109-10.

66. C. Huetz de Lemps, *Géographie du commerce de Bordeaux à la fin du règne de Louis XIV* (Paris, 1975), 110-11, 297, 399; *Shore Work Accounts*, 26.

67. *Rot. Scot.*, i, 802, 822-3, 838, 855, 869-70, 874.

68. *Abdn Recs*, 33, 52; ACA, CR, v (1), 29; 6, 230, 376, 422; *CDS*, iv, nos 992, 1061, 1078, 1107, 1114, 1117, 1130, 1134, 1145, 1194, 1234, 1253; v, nos 994, 1018, 1040, 1050.

69. PRO, E 122/76/38, m. 2r, 4v, 5v.

70. *The Overseas Trade of London: Exchequer Customs Accounts, 1480-81*, ed. H. S. Cobb (London Record Soc., 1990), nos 57, 64, 120, 123, 134, 166; *The Port and Trade of Early Elizabethan Documents*, ed.

B. Dietz (London Record Soc., 1972), nos 217, 406; *Shore Work Accounts*, 24-30.

71. PRO, E 122/12/8-12; *The Port Books of Boston, 1601-40*, ed. R. W. K. Hinton (Lincoln Record Soc., 1956).

72. PRO, E 122/106/15; E 122/106/16; E 122/202/5, fo. 28v; Norwich, Norfolk Record Office, Y/C4/170, m. 12r.

73. Copenhagen, Rigsarkivet, Øresundstolregnskaber, 1503; 1528. Four Aberdonian entries, however, are recorded, in the 1497 toll: *Ibid.*, 1497, pp. 4, 12, 20, 22.

74. ACA, CR, iv, 498.

75. ACA, CR, ix, 441-2.

76. *ER*, i-iii, passim.

77. *ER*, i, 474; ACA, CR, ix, 40, 61, 130, 721-2; ACA, Sasine Register 1, pp. 650, 750.

78. *Shore Work Accounts*, 28-9, 33-4, 39-40, 44.

79. 'Testimonialis grantit be ye ballies', ed. L. B. Taylor, *Miscellany of the Third Spalding Club*, 2 (1940), no. 36.

80. J. Davidson and A. Gray, *The Scottish Staple at Veere* (London, 1909), 254-5.

81. Barnes, 'Aberdeen stocking trade', 77-80.

82. ACA, Propinquity Book, 3, fo. 66v.

83. *Calendar of State Papers, Colonial Series, 1574-1600* (London, 1860), 277; Smout, *Scottish Trade*, 286-7.

84. G. M. Fraser and M. Henderson, *Aberdeen Street Names: Their History, Meaning and Personal Associations* (repr., Aberdeen, 1986), 41.

85. *AJ*, 23 May 1749; 4 Sept. 1750; 26 July 1757; 1 May 1760; 20 Nov. 1760; 1 Dec. 1769, for example.

86. BL, India Office Records, J/1/4, pp. 386-7; J/1/7, pp. 125-8; J/1/8, pp. 254-8; J/1/12, pp. 4-6a; J/1/15, pp. 104-7; J/1/15, pp. 417-21; J/1/16, pp. 173-7; J/1/17, pp. 287-90. We are grateful to Andrew Mackillop for these references.

87. *ACL*, i, nos 119, 183, 187, for example.

88. John Barbour, *The Bruce*, ed. A. A. M. Duncan (Edinburgh, 1997), passim; N. R. Royan, 'The *Scotorum Historia* of Hector Boece: A Study' (University of Oxford, unpublished D. Phil. thesis, 1996), 195-6.

89. I. Cunningham, 'The Asloan manuscript', in MacDonald, Lynch and Cowan (eds.), *The Renaissance, in Scotland*, 109-10; C. van Buuren, 'John Asloan and his manuscript: an Edinburgh notary and scribe, in the days of James III, James IV and James V, *c.* 1470-*c.* 1530', in J. H. Williams (ed.), *Stewart Style, 1513-1542: Essays on the Court of James V* (East Linton, 1996), 23-4.

90. P. Bawcutt, 'Images of women, in the poems of Dunbar', *Études Écossaises*, 1 (1991), 49-58.

91. *Abdn Counc.*, i, 110-11.

92. D. Stevenson, *King's College, Aberdeen, 1560-1641: From Protestant Reformation to Covenanting Revolution* (1990), 66, 83-5.

93. *James Beattie's Day-Book*, 54, 124.

94. AUL, MS 2113 (Diary of Alexander Mackie), fos 9-10, 62.

95. L. Campbell and J. Dick, 'The portrait of William Elphinstone', in J. Geddes (ed.), *King's College Chapel, Aberdeen, 1500-2000* (Leeds, 2000), 98-108.

96. *James Beattie's Day-Book*, 69.

97. E. Bricegirdle, 'Kings for King's: the Old Testament paintings', in Geddes, *King's College Chapel*, 206-7.

98. Geddes, *King's College Chapel*, 35-65, 74-97, 109-29.

99. W. H. Finlayson, 'The Scottish Nation of Merchants, in Bruges' (University of Glasgow, unpublished Ph.D. thesis, 1951), 254-9.

100. Middelburg, Zeeuwsarchief, Archief Veere, inv. no. 920 (Poorterboeken), *passim*.

101. AUL, MS 1050 (Propinquity Book, 1589-1603), available in published format as 'Testimonialis grantit be ye ballies sen ye last day of Merche 1589', ed. L. B. Taylor, *The Miscellany of the Third Spalding Club* (Spalding Club, 1940), ii, 3-88.

102. *Papers relating to the Scots in Poland, 1576-1793*, ed. A. F. Steuart (SHS, 1915), 39-58; T. A. Fischer, *The Scots in Eastern and Western Prussia* (Edinburgh, 1903), 205-11.

103. ACA, Propinquity Book, 1, partially printed as 'Birth brieves from the registers of the burgh of Aberdeen, 1637-1705', *Miscellany of the Spalding Club*, v (1852), 323-68. For a rare example of contact with Ireland (Co. Waterford), see Propinquity Book, 1, fo. 137r.

104. ACA, Propinquity Book, 2, fo. 40r; A. A. Cormack, 'Scots in the Swedish East India Company', *AUR*, 42 (1967-8), 40-1. We are grateful to Steve Murdoch for allowing us to read his draft article 'Scots in the Dutch East Indies, 1612-1707', which includes a consideration of George Forbes (*fl.* 1582-1631), an Aberdonian steward at the castle of Ambon, in the Dutch East Indies.

105. BL, India Office Records, L/MIL/9/85, p. 92; L/MIL/9/107-109; A. Farrington, *A Biographical Index of East India Company Maritime Officers, 1600-1834* (London, 1999), 1, 34, 401, 471, 549. See too the references and acknowledgement in n. 86, above.

106. ACA, Propinquity Book, 2, fos 177r, 187v; 3, fos 41r, 91v, 99r, 133r.

107. *James Gordon's Diary, 1692-1710*, ed. G. D. Henderson and H. H. Porter (Spalding Club, 1949), 114, 118.

108. See H. V. Bowen, *Elites, Enterprise and the Making of the British Overseas Empire, 1688-1775* (London, 1996), for a fuller discussion how Scots generally concentrated on the underdeveloped spheres of imperial commerce.

109. A. E. Smith, *Colonists, in Bondage: White Servitude and Convict Labour in America, 1606-1776* (Chapel Hill, NC, 1947), 300. The precise reference was to English emigrants.

110. BL, India Office Records, L/MIL/9/85, 1-255, *passim*. We are indebted to Andrew Mackillop for these references.

111. *James Beattie's Day-Book*, 204. For soldiers in India, see BL, India Office Records, L/MIL/9/85, though this source confirms that more soldiers came from Aberdeenshire than from Aberdeen.

112. ACA, CR, vii, 167; *Halyburton's Ledger*, 233.

113. A. W. S. Johnston, *A Short Memoir of James Young, Merchant Burgess of Aberdeen …* (Aberdeen, 1860), 7-8.

114. Antwerp, Stadarchief, Poortersboeken, Vierschaar 142, 42; 144, 36; 152, 50; 153, 13.

115. *Calendar of Patent Rolls 1467-77* (London, 1906), 14, 447.

116. J. Durkan, 'Heresy in Scotland: the second phase, 1546-58', *RSCHS*, 24 (1992), 331-2; R. Anderson, 'The Aberdonian abroad', *AUR*, 9 (1921-2), 130.

117. D. Dobson, *Scottish Emigration to Colonial America, 1607-1785* (Athens, GA, 1994), 59, 99; W. R. Brock, *Scotus Americanus: A Survey of the Sources for the Links between Scotland and America in the Eighteenth Century* (Edinburgh, 1982), 7-8, 31-3, 87-92; James Gammack, 'An Aberdeen graduate in Virginia', *AUR*, 9 (1921-2), 146-7; *Idem*, 'Aberdeen University men in Virginia', *AUR*, 10 (1921-2), 147-8.

118. T. Riis, *Should Auld Acquaintaince Be Forgot … Scottish-Danish relations, c. 1450-1707* (Odense, 1988), i, 113; ii, 187.

119. W. P. D. Wightman, 'James Cheyne of Arnage', *AUR*, 35 (1954), 369-83.

120. A. G. Molland, 'Scottish-continental, intellectual relations as mirrored in the career of Duncan Liddel, 1561-1613', in P. Dukes (ed.), *The Universities of Aberdeen and Europe: The First Three Centuries* (Aberdeen, 1995), 79-101.

121. J. Durkan, 'The French connection in the sixteenth and seventeenth centuries', in T. C. Smout (ed.), *Scotland and Europe, 1200-1850* (Edinburgh, 1986), 26; *Letters of John Johnston, c. 1565-1611, and Robert Howie, c. 1565-c. 1645*, ed. J. K. Cameron (Edinburgh, 1963).

122. P. B. Wood, 'Aberdeen and Europe in the Enlightenment', in Dukes, *The Universities of Aberdeen and Europe*, 119-42.

123. P. Rouse, *James Blair of Virginia* (Chapel Hill, NC, 1971); P. J. Anderson, 'Aberdeen, influence on American universities', *AUR*, 5 (1917-18), 27-30; R. Lawson-Peebles, 'The problem of William Smith: an Aberdonian in revolutionary America', in J. J. Carter and J. H. Pittock (eds.), *Aberdeen and the Enlightenment* (Aberdeen, 1987), 52-60.

124. A. G. Molland, 'Duncan Liddel, 1561-1613: an early benefactor of Marischal College Library', *AUR*, 51 (1986), 485-99.

125. R. B. Sheridan, 'Mortality and the medical treatment of slaves in the British West Indies', in H. Beckles and V. Shepherd (eds), *Caribbean Slave Society and Economy* (1991), 204-6.

126. ACA, Propinquity Book, 2, fo. 177r; 3, fos 53r, 78v, 147r.

127. *Fasti Academiae Marischallanae Aberdonensis: Selections from the Records of the Marischal College and University, 1593-1860*, ed. P. J. Anderson (Spalding Club, 1889-98), ii, 117. See also NAS, GD345/1180/1761 (110), Letter from Dr Walter Grant, Kingston, to Captain Archibald Grant, Monymusk, 14 April 1761. For other examples of this correspondence, see NAS, GD 345/1180/1762-1763.

128. NLS, MS 49 (Melville Papers), fo. 60; MS 1055 (Melville Papers), fo. 12. We are grateful to Andrew Mackillop for these references.

129. D. G. Crawford, *Roll of the Indian Medical Service, 1615-1930* (London, 1930), 639-41.

130. *CCR, 1476-85*, 204; *The Alien Communities of London in the Fifteenth Century*, ed. J. L. Bolton (Stamford, 1998), 101.

131. ACA, Propinquity Book, 3, fos 135v, 162, 202. For other instances of sojourners, see *Ibid.*, fo. 169r; 4, pp. 7, 53.

132. E. g. AUL, MS 991 (Letter from Bermuda, 1631); *ACL*, i, nos 134, 156, 212, 215, 220, 319, 354; ii, no. 1; iii, nos 38, 116; *Fasti Academiae*, 159-78.

133. ACA, Propinquity Book, 4, pp. 106-8.

134. ACA, Propinquity Book, 1, fo. 17v.

135. *ACL*, i, nos 168, 269; *Fasti Academiae*, i, 356-60; A. Bieganska, 'Subscribers from Poland to the restoration of Marischal College in the late seventeenth century', in Dukes, *The Universities of Aberdeen and Europe*, 143-65; T. A. Fischer, *The Scots in Germany* (Edinburgh, 1902), 268-9.

136. *AJ*, 21 Jan. 1782.

137. *AJ*, 21 Feb. 1758; 8 Dec. 1760; 2 Oct. 1759; 8 Dec. 1766.

138. *AJ*, 29 Nov. 1773.

139. Dobson, *Scottish Emigration*, 98; Dobson, 'James Freeman of Maryland, 1730', *National Genealogical Society Quarterly*, 73 (1985), 291. See also Brock, *Scotus Americanus*, 34-5.

140. *AJ*, 30 Jan. 1750.

141. *AJ*, 19 Sept. 1763; 10 June 1765; 19 Sept. 1797; in each case the island in question was Grenada.

142. *AJ*, 27 June 1774; 9 Oct. 1785.

143. *AJ*, 2 May 1749.

144. *AJ*, 15 Oct. 1751. These were the only two advertisements for emigrants which specified wages and conditions.

145. Dobson, *Scottish Emigration*, 93.

146. *AJ*, 26 May 1766.

147. *AJ*, 29 Sept. 1800.

148. Peter Williamson, *The Life and Curious Adventures*

of Peter Williamson, who was carried off from Aberdeen and sold for a slave (Aberdeen, 1801).

149. W. Kennedy, *Annals of Aberdeen*, (Aberdeen, 1818), i, 294-6; ACA, CR, lxii, 320.

150. *AJ*, 7 June 1773; J. D. Hargreaves, *Aberdeenshire to Africa: North-east Scots and British Overseas Expansion* (Aberdeen, 1981), 11-15.

151. *AJ*, 9 Dec. 1793.

152. ACA, CR, ix, 444; Ditchburn, *Scotland and Europe*, 257-65.

153. See Ch. 2. For the general context of seventeenth- and eighteenth-century emigration, see T. C. Smout, N. C. Landsman and T. M. Devine, 'Scottish emigration in the seventeenth and eighteenth centuries', in N. Canny (ed.), *European on the Move: Studies on European Migration, 1500-1800* (Oxford, 1994), 76-112.

154. Fischer, *Germany*, 241.

155. E. g. Harvey, *Medieval Maps*, Plate 46.

156. M. C. Andrews, 'Scotland, in the portolan charts', *Scottish Geographic Magazine*, 42 (1926), 195, 198, 203. For Homen's map of 1559, see M. Mollat du Jourdin and M. de la Roncière *et al.* (eds) *Sea Charts of the Early Explorers, 13th to 17th Century* (Fribourg, 1984), Plate 52.

157. E. g. Brereton, *Travels in Holland*, 116; AUL, MS 2464 (Voyages en Angleterre).

158. *Handelsrechnungen des Deutshen Ordens*, ed. C. Sattler (Leipzig, 1887), 77.

159. D. McRoberts, *The Heraldic Ceiling of St Machar's Cathedral, Aberdeen* (Aberdeen, 1976).

160. N. Canny, 'The origins of empire: an, introduction', in *idem.* (ed.), *The Origins of Empire: British Overseas Enterprise to the Close of the Seventeenth Century* (Oxford, 1988), 18-19.

161. ACA, Propinquity Book, 4, pp. 75-6.

Notes to Chapter 18:
The Growth of a New Town

1. Sir John Carr, *Caledonian Sketches or a Tour through Scotland in 1807* (London, 1809), 279. Generally, quotations have been given modern spellings and capitalisations.

2. The author gratefully acknowledges the help received in the preparation of this chapter from Miss J. Cripps, the City Archivist, Aberdeen, and her staff; Mr W. Bruce, Boxmaster of the Incorporation of Tailors, and Mr G. Hunter, Clerk and Assessor of the Incorporation of Hammermen, generously made available the many records in their keeping.

3. ACA, Press 17/ Parcel N/1, Abercrombie Report.

4. J. Slezer, *Theatrum Scotiae* (London, 1693), 29.

5. ACA, Index to the Minute Books of Commissioners of Police, 1795-1844.

6. H. M. Colvin, *A Biographical Dictionary of British Architects, 1660-1840* (3rd edn, New Haven and London, 1995), 62, quoting John Clerk of Eldin who was married to Susan Adam.

7. *Vitruvius Scoticus* (re-issued Edinburgh, 1980), Plates 107-8.

8. Colvin, *Dictionary*, 402.

9. M. Lynch, 'Urbanisation and urban networks in seventeenth-century Scotland: some further thoughts', *SESH*, 12 (1992), 26; *OSA*, xiv, 285-6; *Census of 1801*. See ch. 5.

10. A. J. Youngson, *The Making of Classical Edinburgh, 1750-1840* (Edinburgh, 1966), 5.

11. *Ibid.*, 4.

12. B. Cunliffe, *The City of Bath* (reprinted Stroud, 1990), 112.

13. ACA, Abercrombie Report.

14. ACA, Council Register, Alphabetical Index to the first 67 Volumes, vol. ii.

15. ACA, Abercrombie Report.

16. ACA, Alphabetical Index, vol. i; ACA, CR, lxvii, 1.

17. Inf. ex National Monuments Record of Scotland.

18. ACA, Abercrombie Report.

19. ACA, CR, lxvii, 119.

20. *Aberdeen Journal*, 29 March 1796.

21. W. Kennedy, *Annals of Aberdeen* (London, 1818), i, 347-8.

22. ACA, CR, lxvi, 161, 233.

23. ACA, NStT/1/1 ('New Street Act of Parliament and Minutes of the Trustees Appointed for It's [sic] Execution 3d June 1800').

24. Youngson, *Classical Edinburgh*, 301, n. 1.

25. Philo Scotus, *Reminiscences of a Scottish Gentleman* (London, 1861), 146.

26. R. Southey, *Journal of a Tour in Scotland in 1819* (Edinburgh, 1972), 15.

27. NLS, MS 1021 ('A Tour in Scotland, 21 May 1776').

28. W. M. Wade, *The History of Glasgow*, (Glasgow, 1821), 166.

29. ACA, NStT/1/1.

30. Colvin, *Dictionary*, 246-7, 850-1.

31. In the David Hamilton collection of drawings held in the Hunterian Art Gallery, University of Glasgow, there are several studies of bridges including one for an iron bridge at Eglinton Castle, Ayrshire.

32. Young's drawing is in Aberdeen City Library.

33. ACA, NStT/1/1. The outline scheme, dated 21 Jan. 1804, is in Aberdeen City Library.

34. *Aberdeen Journal*, 8 July 1801.

35. T. Ruddock, *Arch Bridges and their Builders* (Cambridge, 1979), 175. See also J. Rickman (ed.), *Life of Thomas Telford* (London, 1838), i, 125-8, and N. Murray, 'Union Bridge widening, Aberdeen', *Minutes of Proceedings of the Aberdeen Association of Civil Engineers*, 8 (1907-08), 69-70.

36. ACA, NStT/1/1. An ink and colour wash drawing is signed 'Ja. Hadden Provost/ Will. Ross/ Thos. Fletcher/ Aberdeen Oct. 28th 1802'.

37. *Aberdeen Journal*, 5 June 1805.

38. *Ibid.*, 31 Aug. 1803. The original appearance of the Union Bridge is recorded in old prints and photographs. Its width was increased on both sides with steel arches in 1906-07.

39. ACA, NStT/1/1.

40. Lord Cockburn, *Circuit Journeys* (Hawick, 1983), 86.

41. ACA, Minute Book, New Street Trustees, no. 2; NStT/1/2.

42. ACA, NStT/1/1.

43. Index, Commisioners of Police.

44. ACA, NStT/1/1.

45. ACA NStT/1/1.

46. Southey, *Journal of a Tour in Scotland in 1819*, 69.

47. Index, Commisioners of Police (1803).

48. ACA, Minute Book, New Street Trustees.

49. ACA, NStT/1/1.

50. W. Kennedy, *Sketch of the Affairs of the Treasury of Aberdeen* (Aberdeen, 1820), 1.

51. Kennedy, *Annals*, i, 353; *New Statistical Account of Scotland* (Edinburgh and London, 1845), xii, 25.

52. Trinity Hall, Aberdeen Hammermen Incorporation, Charter Book, no. 1.

53. See W. H. Fraser and C. H. Lee (eds), *Aberdeen, 1800-2000. A New History* (East Linton, 2000), ch. 1, for a discussion of the extension of the town.

54. Aberdeen Hammermen Incorporation., Charter Book, no. 2.

55. Notes from the ACA, Minute Book, NStT/1/2, 22-3.

56. Aberdeen Hammermen Incorporation, Charter Book, no. 1.

57. A. Gammie, *The Churches of Aberdeen, Historical and Descriptive* (Aberdeen, 1909), 295. A report in 1847 by John and William Smith recommended that, because of the poor state of the roof, St John's chapel should be rebuilt. Although plans and tenders were submitted by John Henderson of Edinburgh and James Matthews of Aberdeen, St John's was rebuilt in Crown Terrace to the design of Thomas Mackenzie in 1849 (NRA(S), 2698).

58. Trinity Hall, The Tailor Trade of Aberdeen, Minute Book, 1795-1813.

59. Trinity Hall, The Tailor Trade of Aberdeen, Sederunt Book, vol. 3.

60. 'Report and Observations on a Plan for Feuing the Dam Lands of Aberdeen as laid out by Mr. Elliot, Architect' (Edinburgh, 1820).

61. NAS, RHP 1763.

62. For the later development of Union Street, see W. A. Brogden, *Aberdeen* (Edinburgh, 1986), 38-51; and W. A, Brogden, 'From classic to Caledonian', in J. S. Smith and D. Stevenson (eds), *Aberdeen in the Nineteenth Century* (Aberdeen, 1988), 45-90.

Notes to Appendix 1

1. Corrected from *Satuta* in MS.

2. A contribution to the Holy Blood light was a penalty frequently imposed on offending burgesses. It is thought that the cult of the Holy Blood was due to the influence of Bruges: see Lynch *et al.* (eds), *The Scottish Medieval Town*, 8.

3. Tallow.

4. That is, they would come under the jurisdiction of the king.

5. Omitted in MS.

6. Outwith.

7. Omitted in MS.

8. Preceded by *blex*, struck through.

9. Preceded by *vthir*, omitted?

10. Streams.

11. Sic; cast in.

12. Fishing nets?

13. Preceded by *nycht*, omitted?

14. There is a space in between this clause and the next, perhaps because it was intended at the time of writing to insert the assize of bread (i.e. to prescribe the weight of the penny and two penny loaves.)

15. A new scribe is at work on this page.

16. Followed by 'y', i.e. Th, struck through.

17. Preceded by *to*, omitted?

18. That is, to clear the roads?

19. Sic; recte *thame*.

20. Sic.

21. Fuel.

22. A new scribe is at work on this page.

23. Suprascript.

24. This ruling confirmed that it was unlawful for the unfree (non-burgesses) to trade in town from a booth or to trade overseas as merchants. There were, however, some opportunities for the unfree to trade in town, for example, by selling ale. While it is true that retail trade by the unfree was limited in times of scarcity, there is also evidence of occasional encouragement being given to unfree

traders. In June 1529, for example, all unfree traders - fleshers, bakers, cordwainers, skinners and all others - were given licence to sell their wares on two days in the week: ACA, CR, xii, 601. See Gemmill and Mayhew, *Changing Values in Medieval Scotland*, 49, 59-60, and E. Ewan 'The Community of the Burgh in the Fourteenth Century', in Lynch *et al.* (eds) *The Scottish Medieval Town*, esp. 236.

25. For discussion of the difficulty of enforcing standard weights and measures see Gemmill and Mayhew, *Changing Values in Medieval Scotland*.

26. and ... law interlined at the end of the previous line.

27. Of ... merkis interlined at the end of the previous line.

Bibliography

Manuscript Sources

ABERDEEN

Aberdeen City Archives (ACA)
ACA, Baillie Court Books, vols. i-xiv, 1572-1691.
ACA, Burgh Court Roll, 1317.
ACA, Burial Register, St Peter's Cemetery, The Spital, vols. i-ii, 1769-1831.
ACA, Charter C/2, Church & Bridge Works, no. 1 (Ducat Brae Deed).
ACA, Charter M/1, no. 21.
ACA, Council Register, vols i-lxvii, 1398-1800.
ACA, Council Register, Alphabetical Index to the First 67 Volumes, by W. Kennedy.
ACA, Guildry Accounts, vols i-ix, 1453-1800.
ACA, Index to Minutes Books of Commissioners of Police, 1795-1844.
ACA, Justice Court Records, vols i-iv, 1657-1783.
ACA, Kirk and Bridge Works Accounts, vols i-viii, 1571-1660.
ACA, Kirk Session Accounts, 1679-1705.
ACA, Letter Books (Incoming), vols vii-xiv, 1682-1799.
ACA, Letter Books (Incoming, Supplementary), vols i-vi, 1615-1827.
ACA, Mortification Accounts, vols i-xii, 1615-1800.
ACA, NStT/1/1-2, New Street Trustees, Minute Books, vols i-ii, 1800-11.
ACA, Old Aberdeen, Town Council Minutes, vols i-vii, 1603-1823.
ACA, Police Commissioners' Rent Roll, 1795.
ACA, Press 17/Parcel H, Guild Brethren Hospital Papers [17th & 18th centuries].
ACA, Press 17/Parcel L, Jacobite Papers, 1745-7.
ACA, Press 17, Parcel N/1, Abercrombie Report, 1794.
ACA, Press 18, Miscellaneous bundles.
ACA, Propinquity Books, vols i-iv, 1637-1797.
ACA, Register of Burgesses, vols i-v, 1632-1800.
ACA, Register of Delinquents for Forestalling and Regrating, etc., 1648-85.
ACA, Register of Sasines, vols i-lxxii, 1494-1800.
ACA, Stent Roll Bundles, 1594-1707.
ACA, Treasury Accounts, vols i-x, 1559-1800

Deposits
ACA, ACC5, Cochran Family Papers, A/1, 1775-8.
ACA, DD78, MS Diary of Alexander Jaffray, 1659-1752.
ACA, Ledger Book of the Poor's Hospital, vol. ii, 1741-58.
ACA, Squibs Cartoons, vols i-ii, c. 1607-1890.

Aberdeen University Library (AUL)
AUL, Inc 34 Manuale parrochialium sacerdotum.
AUL, MSS 37-8, 475-6 (Papers of David Skene).
AUL, MS 57 (Taxation Book of Aberdeen, Martinmas 1748 to Martinmas 1749).
AUL, MS 632 (A. Gordon, *A Treatise of the Epidemic Puerperal Fever of Aberdeen* (London, 1795).
AUL, MS 635A (Diary or Spiritual Exercises of John Forbes of Corse, 1624-47).
AUL, MS 795/2 (Collection of Scottish Folk Songs with Music, 1777).
AUL, MS 991 (Letter from Bermuda, 1631).
AUL, MS 1050 (Propinquity Book, 1589-1603).
AUL, MS 2037 (Papers of John Henderson).
AUL, MS 2070 (Journal of Jonathan Troup).
AUL, MS 2113 (Diary of Alexander Mackie).
AUL, MS 2124 (Collection or Rhymes from Counties of Aberdeen, Forfar and Angus).
AUL, MS 2238 (Journal of George Kerr).
AUL, MS 2464 (Voyages en Angleterre).
AUL, MS 2774 (Poems of Lilias Skene, 1665-96).
AUL, MS 3070 (Records of Aberdeen Shipmasters Society, 1590-1946).
AUL, MS K/4 (Album Amicorum).
AUL, MS K114 Catalogue of Books presented to the Library, 1740-1860.
AUL, MS K/144 (Papers relating to The Catanach Case, 1744).
AUL, MS K/214 (Papers of James Catanach).
AUL, MS K/231/8 (Papers 'concerning the falling out between the Colledges of New and Old Aberdeen').
AUL, MS K/232 (Account for the supply of candles, 1712-13).
AUL, MS King 81/10 (Alexander Gerard, *Liberty the Cloke of Maliciousness, both in The American*

Rebellion and in the manners of the time (Aberdeen, 1778)).

Northern Health Services Archives (NHSA)
NHSA, GRHB 1/1/2-5 (Minute Books of the Infirmary, 1742-67).
NHSA, GRHB 1/10/22-24 (Miscellaneous Pamphlets, 1754, 1758, 1768).
NHSA, GRHB 1/3/9 (Admission and Discharge Registers 1790-97).

Robert Gordon's College, Aberdeen (RGC)
RGC, MS Daily Tasks Work Book, 1741-43.

Trinity Hall, Aberdeen
Aberdeen Incorporated Trades, Convener Court Book, vol. i.
Aberdeen Hammerman Incorporation, Charter Books, 1-2.
Tailor Trade of Aberdeen, Minute Book, 1795-1813.
Tailor Trade of Aberdeen, Sederunt Books.

EDINBURGH

General Register Office for Scotland
Old Parochial Registers, 168A: Aberdeen.
Old Parochial Registers, 168B: Old Machar.

National Archives of Scotland (NAS)
NAS, CH 2/448 (Aberdeen St Nicholas Kirk Session).
NAS, CH 10/3/35: Alexander Skene *et al.*, 'A Breiffe Account of the Most Materiall Passages and Occurrances ... During That Great and Long Tryall of Sufferings and Persecution in Aberdene' (*c.* 1687).
NAS, CH 10/3/35: L. Skene, 'A Word of Warning to the Magistrats and Inhabitants of Aberdene, Writt the 31 of [March] 1677', in 'Materiall Passages'.
NAS, CH 10/3/36: 'A Brieff Historicall Account and Record of the First Rise and Progress of the Blessed Truth, called in Derision Quakerism, in and about Aberdeen'.
NAS CH 10/3/57 (papers relating to Guestrow Property, Aberdeen).
NAS, E 71/1/1-2 (Custom Accounts).
NAS, E 540 (Aberdeen Customs Quarterly Accounts, 1789).
NAS, E 504 (Quarterly Custom Accounts).
NAS, E 870/4/29 (Accounts of the Aberdeen Litsters' Craft).
NAS, GD 33/52/1 (Haddo House Muniments).
NAS, GD 44/1/1/26 (Gordon Castle Muniments).
NAS, GD 44/4/1/2-3 (Gordon Castle Muniments).
NAS, GD 44/13/8/1 (Gordon Castle Muniments).
NAS, GD 44/40/10 (Gordon Castle Muniments).
NAS, GD 45/26/53 (Dalhousie MSS, Commissary Maule).
NAS, GD 52/63, 402, 406 (Lord Forbes Collection).
NAS, GD 124/7/3, 7 (Mar and Kellie Muniments).
NAS, GD 136/1194 (Sinclair of Freswick Papers).
NAS, GD 203/12/3 (Lindsay Papers).
NAS, GD 244/1/84 (Skene, Edwards and Garson WS).
NAS, GD 345/1180 (Grant of Monymusk Muniments).
NAS, GD 406 (Hamilton Muniments).
NAS, RH 4/1921/1-24 (St Nicholas and St Nicholas South Kirk Session Records, Aberdeen, 1562-1889).
NAS, RH 18/1/93: Advertisement, Emigration to New Jersey.
NAS, RHP 1762: Aberdeen, Feuing Plan of Lands of Rubislaw, 1849.

National Library of Scotland, Edinburgh (NLS)
NLS, A. 115. e. 1: Pamphlets, 1784-1793.
NLS, Adv. 31.6.22, fo. 38 (James Morison and others to Lord Albemarle, 3 August 1746).
NLS, Ch. No. 17088 (Keith Earl Marischal Papers).
NLS, MS 49 (Melville Papers).
NLS, MS 1021: 'A Tour in Scotland, 21 May 1776.'
NLS, MS 1055 (Melville Papers).
NLS, MSS 16545, 16555, 16559, 16613, 17257, 17522 (Saltoun Papers).
NLS, X 225. a. 1: Pamphlets, 1784-1793.

National Register of Archives (NRA(S))
NRA(S), 2698: Report of 1847 on roof of St John's Chapel.
NRA(S), CH 2/1/4 (Presbytery of Aberdeen Register).
NRA(S), CH 2/1020/8 (Old Machar Kirk Session Records).

Royal Commission on the Ancient and Historical Monuments of Scotland, National Monuments Record (NMRS)
NMRS, ABD/40/2-11: Plans by Fenton Wyness.
NMRS, Record Sheet ABR/13/1 and Drawings ABD/371/1-2.

LONDON

British Library, London
BL, Harleian MS 6269.
BL, India Office Records, J/1/4.
BL, India Office Records, L/MIL/9/85.

Public Record Office, London (PRO)
PRO, Customs 17/17.
PRO, E 122/12 (K. R. Customs Accounts).

ROME
Vatican Archives
Archivium Sacræ Pænitentiariæ Apostilicæ.

Reg. Suppl. 1000.

OTHER ARCHIVES

Antwerp, Stadarchief, Poortersboeken.
Brodie Castle, Brodie of Brodie Papers, Box 4/2.
Copenhagen, Rigsarkivet, Øresundstolregnskaber.
Friends' House Library, London, W.F.Miller MSS.,
Box P.
Middelburg, Zeeuwsarchief, Archief Veere, inv. no.

920 (Poorterboeken).
Norwich, Norfolk Record Office, Y/C4/170,
Yarmouth Customs Accounts.
Paris, Archives Nationales, Parlement,
Lettres-Arrets-Juges X57.
Pasadena, Henry Huntingdon Library, Stowe
Collection, ST34: Abstract of ships registered in
Great Britain, Sept. 1787.

Printed Primary Sources

Aberdeen Charters and Other Writs Illustrating the History of the Royal Burgh of Aberdeen, ed. P.J. Anderson (Aberdeen, 1890).

Aberdeen Council Letters, ed. L.Taylor (Oxford, 1942-61).

Aberdeen Friars: Red, Black, White, Grey, ed. P.J. Anderson (Aberdeen, 1909).

Aberdeen Journal (1747-1805).

Aberdeen Shore Work Accounts, 1596-1670, ed. L.B.Taylor (Aberdeen, 1972).

Abstracts from Some Statutes and Orders of King's College in Old Aberdeen, 1753 (Aberdeen, 1754).

Accounts of the (Lord High) Treasurer of Scotland, eds T.Dickson *et al.* 13 vols (Edinburgh, 1877-).

The Acts of the Lords of Council in Civil Causes, eds T.Thomson *et al.* (Edinburgh, 1839-).

The Acts of the Parliaments of Scotland, eds T.Thomson and C.Innes, 12 vols (Edinburgh, 1814-75).

Adomnan, *Life of Columba*, eds A.O. and M.O. Anderson (Edinburgh, 1961).

The Alien Communities of London in the Fifteenth Century, ed. J.L. Bolton (Stamford, 1998).

Ancient Laws and Customs of the Burghs of Scotland, 1124-1424 and 1424-1707, ed. C.Innes, 2 vols (SBRS, 1868-1910).

The Apostolic Camera and Scottish Benefices, 1418-88, ed. A.I. Cameron (Oxford, 1934).

Baillie, R., *The Letters and Journals of Robert Baillie, M.DC.XXXVII.-M.DC.LXII*, 3 vols (Bannatyne Club, 1841).

Balfour of Pittendreich, Sir James, *Practicks*, ed. P.G.B. McNeill, 2 vols (Stair Soc., 1962).

Barbour, John, *The Bruce*, ed. A.A.M. Duncan (Edinburgh, 1997).

Barbour, John, *The Bruce*, eds M.P. MacDiarmid and J.A.C.Stevenson (STS, 1985).

Barclay, Robert, *An Apology for the True Christian Divinity as the Same is Held Forth, Preached By The People, Called in Scorn, the Quakers* (London, 1678).

Barclay, R., *Reliquiae Barclaianae: Correspondence of Colonel David Barclay and Robert Barclay of Urie and His Son Robert* (London, 1870).

Barclay, Robert, *Universal Love Contained* (Holland, 1677).

The Black Book of Taymouth, ed. C. Innes (Bannatyne Club, 1855).

Boece, Hector, *The Chronicles of Scotland, translated into Scots by John Bellenden, 1531*, 2 vols (STS, 1938-41).

Boece, Hector, *Murthlacensium et Aberdonensium Episcoporum Vitae*, ed. J. Moir (New Spalding Club, 1894).

Bon Record: Records and Reminiscences of Aberdeen Grammar School, ed. H.F. Morland Simpson (Aberdeen, 1906).

Booke of the Universall Kirk: Acts and Proceedings of the General Assembly of the Kirk of Scotland, ed. T. Thomson, 3 vols (Bannatyne Club, 1839-45).

Bower, Walter, *Scotichronicon*, ed. D.E.R. Watt, 8 vols (Aberdeen, 1987-98).

Brereton, William, *Travels in Holland, The United Provinces, England, Scotland and Ireland, 1634-35*, ed. E. Hawkins (Chetham Soc., 1844).

Breviarum Aberdonense (Bannatyne Club, 1854).

Calderwood, David, *History of the Kirk of Scotland*, eds T. Thomson and D. Laing, 8 vols (Wodrow Soc., 1842-9).

Calendar of the Close Rolls preserved in the Public Record Office (London, 1892-1963).

Calendar of Documents Relating to Scotland, eds J. Bain *et al.*, 5 vols (Edinburgh, 1881-1986).

Calendar of Entries in the Papal Registers Relating to Great Britain and Ireland, ed. J.A. Twemlow (London, 1895-).

Calendar of the Patent Rolls preserved in the Public Record Office (London, 1901-).

Calendar of Scottish Supplications to Rome, 3 vols (SHS, 1934-).

Calendar of State Papers, Colonial Series, 1574-1600 (London, 1860).

Calendar of the State Papers relating to Scotland and Mary, Queen of Scots 1547-1603, eds J. Bain *et al.*, 14 vols (Edinburgh, 1898-1969).

Carr, Sir John, *Caledonian Sketches or a Tour Through Scotland in 1807* (London, 1809).

Cartularium Ecclesiae Sancti Nicholai Aberdonensis, ed. J. Cooper, 2 vols (New Spalding Club, 1888-92).

Carus-Wilson, E. M. and Coleman, O., *England's Export Trade, 1275-1547* (Oxford, 1963).

Charters and other Documents Relating to the City of Glasgow, 2 vols (SBRS, 1894-1906).

Charters of the Royal Burgh of Ayr (Ayr, 1883).

Chronica de Mailros, ed. J. Stevenson (Bannatyne Club, 1835).

The Chronicle of Melrose, eds A.O. Anderson and M.O. Anderson (London, 1936).

Collections for a History of the Shires of Aberdeen and Banff (Spalding Club, 1843).

A Collection of the State Papers of John Thurloe, ed. J. Thurloe, 7 vols (London, 1742).

Comptabilité du port de Dieppe au XVe siècle, ed. M. Mollat (Paris, 1951).

Cowan, I. B. and Easson, D. E. (eds), *Medieval Religious Houses: Scotland* (2nd edn, London, 1976).

Criminal Trials in Scotland, 1488-1624, ed. R. Pitcairn, 3 vols (Edinburgh, 1833).

[David I] *The Charters of David I: The Written Acts of David I, King of Scots, 1124-53, and of His Son, Henry, Earl of Northumberland, 1139-52*, ed. G.W.S. Barrow (Woodbridge, 1999).

Defoe, Daniel, *A Tour Through the Whole Island of Great Britain* (Harmondsworth, 1971).

Descriptive Catalogue of Impressions from Ancient Scottish Seals, ed. H. Laing (Bannatyne Club, 1850).

De Tol van Iersekerood, 1321-1572, ed. W.S. Unger (s' Gravenhage, 1939).

Dictionary of National Biography (1885-).

Die Recesse und andere Akten der Hansetage von 1256-1430, eds W. Junghans and K. Koppmann (Leipzig, 1870-97).

Dunbar, William, *Selected Poems*, ed. P. Bawcutt (London and New York, 1996).

Early Records of the Burgh of Aberdeen, 1317, 1398-1407, ed. W. C. Dickinson (SHS, 1957).

Early Scottish Charters prior to 1153, ed. A.C. Lawrie (Glasgow, 1905).

Early Sources of Scottish History, 500-1286, ed. A.O. Anderson, 2 vols (Edinburgh, 1922).

Early Travellers in Scotland, ed. P. Hume Brown (Edinburgh, repr., 1978).

English and Scottish Popular Ballads, ed. F.J. Child (Boston, 1857).

The Exchequer Rolls of Scotland, eds J. Stuart *et al.*, 23 vols (Edinburgh, 1878-1908).

Extracta e Variis Cronicis Scocie (Abbotsford Club, 1842).

Extracts from the Commonplace Book of Andrew Melville, Doctor and Master in the Song School of Aberdeen 1621-1640, ed. W. Walker (Aberdeen, 1899).

Extracts from the Council Register of the Burgh of Aberdeen, ed. J. Stuart, 4 vols (Spalding Club &

SBRS, 1844-72).

Extracts from the Records of the Burgh of Edinburgh, eds J.D. Marwick *et al.*, 13 vols (SBRS & Edinburgh, 1869-1967).

Facsimiles of the National Manuscripts of Scotland, 3 vols (London, 1867-71).

Fasti Aberdonenses: Selections from the Records of the University and King's College of Aberdeen, ed. C. Innes (Spalding Club, 1854).

Fasti Academiae Mariscallanae Aberdonensis: Selections from the Records of the Marischal College and University, 1593-1860, ed. P.J. Anderson, 3 vols (New Spalding Club, 1889-98).

Fasti Ecclesiae Scoticanae, ed. H. Scott, 7 vols (2nd edn, Edinburgh, 1915-61).

The First Book of Discipline, ed. J.K. Cameron (Edinburgh, 1972).

[Fordun] *Johannis de Fordun, Chronica Gentis Scotorum*, ed. W.F. Skene, 2 vols (Edinburgh, 1871-2).

Froissart, Jean, *Méliador*, ed. A. Longnon (Paris, 1895-99).

[Froissart, Jean] *Oeuvres de Froissart*, ed. K. de Lettenhove, 25 vols (Brussels, 1867-77).

Further Proceedings of the Burgesses of Aberdeen, in the Years 1785, 1786, and 1787 … (Aberdeen, 1787).

Gordon, J., *History of Scots Affairs, from MDCXXXVII to MDCXLI* (Aberdeen, 1841).

Gordon, T., 'Reasons and proposals for an union', in *A Complete Collection of the Papers Relating to the Union of the King's and Marischal Colleges of Aberdeen* (Aberdeen, 1787).

Gordon of Rothiemay, James, *Abredoniae Utriusque Descriptio 1660*, ed. C. Innes (Spalding Club, 1842).

Gordon of Ruthven, P., *A Short Abridgement of Britane's Distemper From the Yeare of God MDCXXXIX to MDCXLIX* (Aberdeen, 1844).

The Hamilton Papers: being selections from original letters in the possession of His Grace the Duke of Hamilton and Brandon, relating to the years 1638-1650, ed. S.R. Gardiner (Camden Society, 1880).

Handelsrechnungen des Deutshen Ordens, ed. C. Sattler (Leipzig, 1887).

The Hartlib Papers (Ann Arbor, 1995).

Hay, William, *Lectures on Marriage*, ed. J.C. Barry (Stair Soc., 1967).

Hectoris Boetii Murthlacensium et Aberdonensium Episcoporum Vitae, ed. J. Moir (New Spalding Club, 1894).

Highland Papers, ed. J.R.N. Macphail, 4 vols (SHS, 1914-34).

Historical Papers Relating to the Jacobite Period, 1699-1750, ed. J. Allardyce, 2 vols (New Spalding Club, 1895-6).

Illustrations of the Topography and Antiquities of the

Shires of Aberdeen and Banff, 4 vols (Spalding Club, 1847-69).

Jaffray, Alexander, *Diary*, ed. J. Barclay (Aberdeen, 1856).

James Beattie's Day-Book, 1773-98, ed. R.S. Walker (Spalding Club, 1948).

James Gordon's Diary, 1692-1710, eds G.D. Henderson and H.H. Porter (Spalding Club, 1949).

Keith, Robert, *An Historical Catalogue of the Scottish Bishops, down to the Year 1688*, ed. M. Russel (Edinburgh, 1824).

Kyd, J.G. (ed.), *Scottish Population Statistics* (SHS, 1952).

Ledger of Andrew Halyburton, 1492-1503, ed. C. Innes (Edinburgh, 1892).

Letters and Papers, Foreign and Domestic, of the Reign of Henry VIII, 21 vols (London, 1862-1932).

Letters of George Lockhart of Carnwath, ed. D. Szechi (SHS, 1989).

Letters of John Johnston, c. 1565-1611, and Robert Howie, c. 1565-c. 1645, ed. J.K. Cameron (Edinburgh, 1963).

Letters of Samuel Rutherford, ed. A.A. Bonar (Edinburgh, 1891).

Letter from Thomas Reid to Archibald Dunbar (4 Sept. 1755), *Alma Mater*, 20 (1902).

Libellus de Vita et Miraculis Sancti Godrici (Surtees Soc., 1847).

Liber Cartarum Sancte Crucis. Munimenta Ecclesie Sancte Crucis Edwinesburg (Bannatyne Club, 1840).

Liber Sancte Marie de Calchou, 2 vols (Bannatyne Club, 1846).

Liber S Thome de Aberbrothoc, eds C. Innes and P Chalmers, 2 vols (Bannatyne Club, 1848-56).

Life of Thomas Telford, ed. J. Rickman, (London, 1838).

Lindsay, Alexander, *A Rutter of the Scottish Seas*, eds A.B. Taylor, I.H. Adams and G. Fortune (National Maritime Museum, 1980).

List of the Persons Concerned in the Rebellion, ed. W. Macleod (SHS, 1890).

List of Pollable Persons within the Shire of Aberdeen, 1696, ed. J. Stuart, 2 vols (Aberdeen, 1844).

Macfarlane's Geographical Collections, ed. A. Mitchell, 2 vols (SHS, 1907).

Maitland of Lethington, Sir Richard, *The History of the House of Seytoun to the Year 1559* (Maitland Club 1829).

Memorials of the Alderman, Provosts, and Lord Provosts of Aberdeen, 1357-1895, ed. A.M. Munro (Aberdeen, 1897).

Memorials of the Family of Skene of Skene, ed. W.F. Skene (Aberdeen, 1887).

The Minutes of the Aberdeen Philosophical Society, 1758-1773, ed. H.L. Ulman (Aberdeen, 1990).

Miscellany of the Maitland Club, 4 vols (Maitland Club, 1833-47).

Miscellany of the New Spalding Club, 2 vols (New Spalding Club, 1890-1908).

Miscellany of the Scottish Burgh Records Society, ed. J.D. Marwick (SBRS, 1908).

Miscellany of the Spalding Club, 5 vols (Spalding Club, 1844-52).

Mortifications Under the Charge of the Provost, Magistrates, and Town Council of Aberdeen (Aberdeen, 1849).

Musae Latinae Aberdonensis, 3 vols (New Spalding Club, 1892-1910).

Napier, M., *Memoir of John Napier of Merchistoun* (Edinburgh, 1834).

New Dictionary of National Biography (forthcoming, 2004).

New Statistical Account of Scotland, 15 vols (Edinburgh and London, 1845).

Officers and Graduates of University and King's College, Aberdeen (New Spalding Club, 1893).

Ord's Bothy Songs and Ballads of Aberdeen, Banff & Moray Angus and the Mearns, with an Introduction by Alexander Fenton (Edinburgh, 1990).

Orem, W., *A Description of Old Aberdeen, the Chanonry, Cathedral, and King's College of Old Aberdeen in the Years 1724-25* (Aberdeen, 1832).

The Original Chronicle of Andrew Wyntoun, 6 vols (STS, 1903-14).

The Overseas Trade of London: Exchequer Customs Accounts, 1480-1, ed. H.S. Cobb (London Record Soc., 1990).

Papers of William Penn: Vol. II, 1680-84, eds M. Maples Dunn and R.S. Dunn (Philadelphia, 1982).

Papers relating to the Scots in Poland, 1576-1793, ed. A.F. Steuart (SHS, 1915).

Parliamentary Papers, 1826/7 (327) XVIII, 290-1, Ships Built and Registered, from 1814 to 1826.

Passages from the Diary of General Patrick Gordon of Auchleuchries AD 1635-AD 1699 (Spalding Club, 1859).

Pegalotti, Francesco B, *La Practica della Mercatura*, ed. A. Evans (Cambridge, Mass., 1936).

The Port and Trade of Early Elizabethan Documents, ed. B. Dietz (London Record Soc., 1972).

The Port Books of Boston, 1601-1640, ed. R.W.K. Hinton (Lincoln Record Soc., 1956).

Pryde, G.S. (ed.), *The Burghs of Scotland: A Critical List* (Oxford, 1965).

RCAHMS, *Report of National Monuments Record of Scotland* (1972-4).

Records of the Convention of the Royal Burghs of Scotland, eds J.D. Marwick and T. Hunter, 8 vols (Edinburgh, 1866-1918).

Records of the Meeting of the Exercise of Alford, ed. T. Bell (Aberdeen, 1897).

Records of Old Aberdeen, ed. A.M. Munro, 2 vols (New Spalding Club, 1899-1909).

Recueil de documents relatifs à l'histoire de l'industrie drapière en Flandre. Première partie: des origines à l'époque bourguignonne, eds G. Espinas and H. Pirenne, 4 vols (Brussels, 1906-24).

Regesta Regum Scottorum, eds G. Barrow et al. (Edinburgh, 1960-).

Register of Edinburgh Apprentices, 1666-1700, ed. C. B. B. Watson (SRS, 1929).

Register of the Ministers, Elders and Deacons of St Andrews, ed. D. Hay Fleming, 2 vols (1889-90).

Register of the Privy Council of Scotland, eds J. H. Burton et al., 38 vols (Edinburgh, 1877-).

Registrar General, Census 1801, England, Wales and Scotland (London, 1801-2).

Registrar General, Census 1861, England and Scotland (London, 1862).

Registrum de Dunfermelyn (Bannatyne Club, 1842).

Registrum Episcopatus Aberdonensis, ed. C. Innes, 2 vols (Spalding & Maitland Clubs, 1845).

Registrum Episcopatus Glasguensis, ed. C. Innes, 2 vols (Bannatyne Club, 1843).

Registrum Episcopatus Moraviensis (Bannatyne Club, 1837).

Registrum Magni Sigilii Regum Scotorum, eds J. M. Thomson et al., 11 vols (Edinburgh, 1882-).

Registrum S. Marie de Neubotle, ed. C. Innes (Bannatyne Club, 1849).

Registrum Secreti Sigilli Regum Scotorum, eds M. Livingstone et al., 8 vols (Edinburgh, 1908-).

Report and Observations on a Plan for Feuing the Dam Lands of Aberdeen as laid out by Mr. Elliot, Architect (Edinburgh, 1820).

Rievaulx, Ailred of, Eulogium Davidis, in Lives of Scottish Saints: Vitae Antiquae Sanctorum, ed. J. Pinkerton (London, 1889).

Rotuli Scotiae in Turri Londinensi et in Domo Capitalari Westmonasteriensi Asservati, ed. D. MacPherson, 2 vols (London, 1814-19).

Row, J., The History of the Kirk of Scotland, From the Year 1558 to August 1637 (Wodrow Soc., 1842).

The Scots Peerage, ed. Sir J. Balfour Paul, 9 vols (Edinburgh, 1906-14).

Scotus, Philo, Reminiscences of a Scottish Gentleman (London, 1861).

Scougal, H., 'Of the importance and difficulty of the ministerial function', in idem, The Life of God in the Soul of Man: Or the Excellency of the Christian Religion. With Nine Other Discourses on Important Subjects. To Which is Added, A Sermon Preached at His Funeral by G. G. [George Garden] (London, 1726).

Selections from the Records of the Kirk Session, Presbytery and Synod of Aberdeen (Spalding Club, 1846).

Skene, A., Memorialls For the Government of the Royall Burghs in Scotland (Aberdeen, 1685).

Skene A., A Succinct Survey of the Famous City of Aberdeen (Aberdeen, 1685; repr. 1835).

[Skeyne] Tracts by Dr Gilbert Skeyne, Mediciner to His Majesty, ed. W. F. Skene (Bannatyne Club, 1860).

Slezer, J., Theatrum Scotiae (London, 1693).

Smith, Adam, The Wealth of Nations (London, 1910).

Southey, R., Journal of a Tour in Scotland in 1819 (Edinburgh, 1972).

Spalding, John, Memorialls of the Trubles in Scotland and in England, 1624-1645, ed. J. Stuart, 2 vols (Spalding Club, 1850-1).

The Statistical Account of Scotland, 1792-99, ed. Sir John Sinclair, 21 vols (repr. Wakefield, 1982).

Statutes of the Scottish Church (SHS, 1907).

Stevenson, H. and Wood, M., Scottish Heraldic Seals, 3 vols (Glasgow, 1940).

Taxatio Ecclesiastica Angliae et Wallia. Auctoritate Papae Nicholae IV (London, 1802).

Urkundenbuch der Stadt Lübeck (Lübeck, 1843-1905).

Williamson, Peter, The Life and Curious Adventures of Peter Williamson, who was Carried off from Aberdeen and Sold for a Slave (Aberdeen, 1801).

Worcestre, William, Itineraries, ed. J. H. Harvey (Oxford, 1969).

Young, M. D. (ed.), The Parliaments of Scotland: Burgh and Shire Commissioners, 2 vols (Edinburgh, 1992).

Secondary Works

Published Books and Articles

Aberdeen Journal Notes and Queries.

Adam, William, *Vitruvius Scoticus William Adam* (1812, reprinted Edinburgh, 1980).

Adams, D.G., 'Montrose ships and shipowners', in G.Jackson and S.G.E.Lythe (eds), *Port of Montrose.*

Adams, I., *The Making of Urban Scotland* (London, 1978).

Alexander, W., *Notes and Sketches Illustrative of Northern Rural Life in the Eighteenth Century* (Edinburgh, 1877).

Alldridge, N.J., 'House and household in restoration Chester', *Urban History Yearbook*, 10 (1983).

Anderson, P.J., 'Aberdeen influence on American universities', *AUR*, 5 (1917-18).

Anderson, P.J., 'The advocates in Aberdeen: the Catanach Case', *Scottish Notes and Queries*, 1 (1888).

Anderson, R., 'The Aberdonian abroad', *AUR*, 9 (1921-22).

Anderson, R., *The History of Robert Gordon's Hospital, Aberdeen, 1729-1881* (Aberdeen, 1896).

Andrew, D., 'Two medical charities in eighteenth-century London: the Lock Hospital and the lying-in charity for married women', in J.Barry and C.Jones (eds), *Medicine and Charity before the Welfare State.*

Andrews, M.C., 'Scotland in the portolan charts', *Scottish Geographical Magazine*, 42 (1926).

Angels, Nobles and Unicorns: Art and Patronage in Medieval Scotland (Edinburgh, 1982).

Anon, *The Freedom Lands and Marches of Aberdeen, 1319-1929* (Aberdeen, 1929).

Anson, P., *Underground Catholicism in Scotland, 1622-1878* (Montrose, 1970).

Appleby, A.B., 'The disappearance of plague: a continuing puzzle', *Economic History Review*, 2nd series, 33 (1980).

Armytage, W.H.G., 'David Fordyce: a neglected thinker', *AUR*, 36 (1995-6).

Bain, E., *Merchant and Craft Guilds: A History of the Aberdeen Incorporated Trades* (Aberdeen, 1887).

Bannerman, J., 'The Lordship of the Isles', in J.M.Brown (ed.), *Scottish Society in the Fifteenth Century.*

Barnes, I.C.M., 'The Aberdeen stocking trade', *Textile History*, 8 (1977).

Barrow, G.W.S., *The Anglo-Norman Era in Scottish History* (Oxford, 1980).

Barrow, G.W.S., 'The Highlands in the lifetime of Robert the Bruce', in G.W.S.Barrow, *The Kingdom of the Scots* (London, 1973).

Barrow, G.W.S., *Kingship and Unity: Scotland, 1000-1306* (Edinburgh, 1989).

Barrow, G.W.S., 'The Scots charter', in H.Mayr-Harting and R.I.Moore (eds), *Studies in Medieval History Presented to R H C Davis* (London, 1985).

Barry, J.and Jones, C. (eds), *Medicine and Charity before the Welfare State* (London, 1991).

Bateson, J.D., *Coinage in Scotland* (London, 1997).

Bawcutt, P., 'An early Scottish debate-poem on women', *Scottish Literary Journal*, 23 (1996).

Bawcutt, P., 'Images of women in the poems of Dunbar', *Études Écossaises*, 1 (1991).

Beale, J.M., *A History of the Burgh and Parochial Schools of Fife*, ed. D.J.Withrington (Edinburgh, 1983).

Beavan, I., 'Bibliography of the Enlightenment', in J.J. Carter and J. Pittock (eds), *Aberdeen and the Enlightenment.*

Bieganska, A., 'Subscribers from Poland to the restoration of Marischal College in the late seventeenth century', in P.Dukes (ed.), *Universities of Aberdeen and Europe.*

Billings, R.W., *The Baronial and Ecclesiastical Antiquities of Scotland*, 4 vols (Edinburgh, 1845-52).

Blanchard, I., 'Lothian and beyond: the economy of the "English empire of David I"', in R. Britnall and J. Hatcher (eds), *Progress and Problems in Medieval England* (Cambridge, 1996).

Blanchard, I., *The Middle Ages: A Concept Too Many? Inaugural Lecture* (Edinburgh, 1996).

Blanchard, I., *Mining, Metallurgy and Minting in the Middle Ages. Volume 2: Europe and Africa Supreme, 1125-1225* (Stuttgart, 2001).

Blanchard, I., 'Northern wools and Netherlands markets at the close of the middle ages', in G.G. Simpson (ed.), *Scotland and the Low Countries, 1124-1994.*

Blanchard, L.M., 'An excavation at 45 Canal Street, Perth, 1978-9', *PSAS*, 113 (1983).

Boardman, S., *The Early Stewart Kings: Robert II and Robert III, 1371-1406* (East Linton, 1996).

Boardman, S., 'Lordship in the north-east: The Badenoch Stewarts (I). Alexander Stewart, earl of Buchan, lord of Badenoch', *Northern Scotland*, 16 (1996).

Bogdan, N.Q. and Bryce, I.B.D., *Directory of the Castles, Manors, and 'Town Houses' of Scotland (c. 1052-c. 1707), Scottish Castle Survey and Architectural Heritage Society of Scotland* (NE Group, 1988).

Bogdan, N.Q. and Wordsworth, J.W., *The Medieval Excavations at the High Street, Perth* (Perth, 1978).

Booton, H.W., 'The craftsmen of Aberdeen between 1400 and 1550', *Northern Scotland*, 13 (1993).

Booton, H., 'Economic and social change in later medieval Aberdeen', in J.S. Smith (ed.), *New Light on Medieval Aberdeen.*

Booton, H.W., 'Inland trade: a study of Aberdeen in the later middle ages', in M. Lynch *et al.* (eds), *Scottish Medieval Town.*

Booton, H., 'Sir John Rutherford: A fifteenth-century Aberdeen burgess', *SESH*, 10 (1990).

Bossy, J., *Christianity in the West, 1400-1700* (Oxford, 1985).

Bowen, H.V., *Elites, Enterprise and the Making of the British Overseas Empire, 1688-1775* (London, 1996).

Braithwaite, W.C., *The Beginnings of Quakerism* (Cambridge, 1961).

Braithwaite, W.C., *The Second Period of Quakerism* (Cambridge, 1955).

Bricegirdle, E., 'Kings for King's: the Old Testament paintings', in J. Geddes (ed.), *King's College Chapel, Aberdeen, 1500-2000.*

Britnall, R. and Hatcher J. (eds), *Progress and Problems in Medieval England: Essays in Honour of Edward Miller* (Cambridge, 1996).

Brock, W.R., *Scotus Americanus: A Survey of the Sources for the Links between Scotland and America in the Eighteenth Century* (Edinburgh, 1982).

Brogden, W.A., *Aberdeen, an Illustrated Architectural Guide* (Aberdeen, 1986; 2nd edn, 1998).

Brogden, W.A., 'From classic to Caledonian', in J.S. Smith and D. Stevenson (eds), *Aberdeen in the Nineteenth Century* (Aberdeen, 1988).

Brotherstone, T. and Ditchburn, D. (eds), *Freedom and Authority: Scotland, c. 1050-c. 1650* (East Linton, 2000).

Brotherstone, T., Simonton, D. and Walsh, O. (eds), *Gendering Scottish History: An International Approach* (Glasgow, 2000).

Brotherstone, T. and Withrington, D.J. (eds), *The City and its Worlds: Aspects of Aberdeen's History Since 1794* (Glasgow, 1996).

Brown, C., *The Battle for Aberdeen, 1644* (Stroud, 2002).

Brown, M.H., 'The Badenoch Stewarts (II), Alexander, earl of Mar', *Northern Scotland*, 16 (1996).

Brown, M.H., '"Vile times": Walter Bower's last book and the minority of James II', *SHR*, 79 (2000).

Bruce, D., 'The Society of Advocates in Aberdeen', *AUR*, 56 (1996).

Brundage, J.A., *Medieval Canon Law* (Harlow, 1995).

Bryce, W.M., *The Scottish Greyfriars*, 2 vols (Edinburgh, 1909).

Buchan, D., *The Ballad and the Folk* (London, 1972).

Buchan, J., *Montrose: A History* (Edinburgh, 1928).

Buckroyd, J., *The Life of James Sharp* (Edinburgh, 1987).

Bulloch, J., *Aberdeen Three Hundred Years Ago* (Aberdeen, 1884).

Bulloch, J., *The Pynours: Historical Notes on an Ancient Aberdeen Craft* (Aberdeen, 1887).

Burnet, G.B., *The Story of Quakerism in Scotland, 1650-1850* (London, 1952).

Burr, G.G. and Munro, A.M., *Old Landmarks of Aberdeen* (Aberdeen, 1886).

Butt, J. and Ward, J.T. (eds), *Scottish Themes: Essays in Honour of Professor S.G.E. Lythe* (Edinburgh, 1976).

Buuren, C. van, 'John Asloan and his manuscript: an Edinburgh notary and scribe in the days of James III, James IV and James V, c. 1470-c. 1530', in J.H. Williams (ed.), *Stewart Style, 1513-1542: Essays on the Court of James V* (East Linton, 1996).

Cameron, A.S. and Stones, J.A. (eds), *Aberdeen: An In-depth View of the City's Past* (Edinburgh, 2001).

Cameron, J.K., 'Some Scottish students and teachers at the University of Leiden in the late sixteenth and early seventeenth centuries', in G.G. Simpson (ed.), *Scotland and the Low Countries, 1124-1994.*

Campbell, D., 'Notes on church music in Aberdeen', *Trans Aberdeen Ecclesiological Soc.* (1887).

Campbell, I., 'Bishop Elphinstone's tomb', in J. Geddes (ed.), *King's College Chapel, Aberdeen, 1500-2000.*

Campbell, I., 'Crown steeples and crowns imperial', in L. Golden (ed.), *Raising the Eyebrow: John Onians and World Art Studies* (Oxford, 2001).

Campbell, L. and Dick, J., 'The portrait of William Elphinstone', in J. Geddes (ed.), *King's College Chapel, Aberdeen, 1500-2000.*

Canny, N., 'The origins of empire: an introduction', in N. Canny (ed.), *The Origins of Empire: British Overseas Enterprise to the Close of the Seventeenth Century* (Oxford, 1988).

Cant, R.G., *The Building of St Machar's Cathedral, Aberdeen* (Aberdeen, 1976).

Carter, C., 'The Arma Christi in Scotland', *PSAS*, 90 (1956-7).

Carter, H., *An Introduction to Urban Historical Geography* (London, 1983).

Carter, J.J, 'The office of chancellor at Aberdeen University', *AUR*, 52 (1987).

Carter, J.J. and McLaren, C.A., *Crown and Gown, 1495-1995: An Illustrated History of the University of Aberdeen* (Aberdeen, 1994).

Carter, J.J. and Pittock, J. (eds), *Aberdeen and the Enlightenment* (Aberdeen, 1987).

Carter, J.J. and Withrington, D.J. (eds), *Scottish Universities: Distinctiveness and Diversity* (Edinburgh, 1992).

Casson, L., *Ships and Seafaring in Ancient Times* (Austin, Texas, 1994).

Champion, J.A.I. (ed.), *Epidemic Disease in London* (London, 1993).

Champion, J.A.I., 'Epidemics and the built environment', in J.A.I. Champion (ed.), *Epidemic Disease in London.*

Cinthio, E., 'The churches of St Clemens in Scandinavia', *Archaeologia Lundensia*, 3 (1968).

Clark, A., *A Short History of the Shipmaster Society, or the Seamen's Box of Aberdeen* (Aberdeen, 1911).

Clark, R., '"The gangreen of Quakerism": an anti-Quaker Anglican offensive in England after the Glorious Revolution', *Journal of Religious History*, 11 (1981).

Clark, V. E., *The History of the Port of Aberdeen* (Aberdeen, 1921).

Cluer, A., *Walkin' the Mat* (Aberdeen, 1976).

Clyne, N., 'The Advocates in Aberdeen', *Scottish Notes and Queries*, 1 (1888).

Cockburn, Henry, Lord, *Circuit Journeys* (repr., Hawick, 1983).

Coffey, J., *Politics, Religion and the British Revolutions: The Mind of Samuel Rutherford* (Cambridge, 1997).

Colish, M. L., 'Peter Lombard', in G. R. Evans (ed.), *The Medieval Theologians* (Oxford, 2001).

Colvin, H. M., *A Biographical Dictionary of British Architects, 1660-1840* (3rd edn, New Haven and London, 1995).

Comrie, J. D., *A History of Scottish Medicine*, 2 vols (London, 1932).

Contamine, P., 'Froissart and Scotland', in G. G. Simpson (ed.), *Scotland and the Low Countries, 1124-1994*.

Cormack, A. A., 'Scots, in the Swedish East India Company', *AUR*, 42 (1967-8).

Coull, J. R., *The Sea Fisheries of Scotland* (Edinburgh, 1996).

Couper, W. J., *Our Lady of Aberdeen* (Aberdeen, 1930).

Cowan, E. J., *Montrose: For Covenant and King* (London, 1977).

Cowan, I. B., *St Machar's Cathedral in the Early Middle Ages* (Aberdeen, 1980).

Cramb, I., 'Francis Peacock, 1723-1807: dancing master in Aberdeen', *AUR*, 43 (1969-70).

Crawford, D. G., *Roll of the Indian Medical Service, 1615-1930* (London, 1930).

Creighton, C., *A History of Epidemics in Britain* (London, 2nd edn, 1965).

Cripps, J., 'Establishing the topography of medieval Aberdeen: an assessment of the documentary sources', in J. S. Smith (ed.), *New Light on Medieval Aberdeen*.

Crowl, P., *The Intelligent Traveller's Guide to Historic Scotland* (London, 1986).

Cullen, G. M., 'Concerning sibbens [sic] and the Scottish yaws', *Caledonian Medical Journal* (April 1911).

Cunliffe, B., *The City of Bath* (repr., Stroud, 1990).

Cunnigham, I., 'The Asloan manuscript', in A. A. MacDonald *et al.* (eds), *The Renaissance in Scotland*.

Cunningham, I. C., *The Nation Survey'd: Timothy Pont's Maps of Scotland* (East Linton, 2001).

Davidson, J., *Inverurie and the Earldom of the Garioch* (Edinburgh, 1878).

Davidson, J. and Gray, A., *The Scottish Staple at Veere* (London, 1909).

Dawson, J., '"The Face of ane perfyt Reformed Kyrk": St Andrews and the early Scottish Reformation', in J. Kirk (ed.), *Humanism and Reform: the Church in Europe, England, and Scotland, 1400-1643* (Oxford, 1991).

Degryse, R., 'De schepen in de haven van Sluis in het voorjaar, 1464', *Mededelingen van de Marineakademie van Belgie*, 20 (1968).

Dennison, E. P., 'Power to the people? The myth of the medieval burgh community', in S. Foster, A. Macinnes, and R. MacInnes (eds), *Scottish Power Centres from the Early Middle Ages to the Twentieth Century* (Glasgow, 1998).

Dennison, E. P. and Stones, J., *Historic Aberdeen: The Archaeological Implications of Development* (Scottish Burgh Survey, 1997).

Dent, J. S., 'Building materials and methods of construction, the evidence from the archaeological excavations at Broad Street, Aberdeen', in *Building Construction in Scotland, Some Historical and Regional Aspects* (Scottish Vernacular Buildings Working Group, 1974).

DesBrisay, G., 'Catholics, Quakers, and religious persecution in Restoration Aberdeen', *IR*, 47 (1996).

DesBrisay, G., 'City limits: female philanthropists and wet nurses in seventeenth-century Scottish towns,' *Journal of the Canadian Historical Association*, new series, 8 (1997).

DesBrisay, G., '"Menacing their persons and exacting their purses": the Aberdeen Justice Court, 1657-1700', in D. Stevenson (ed.), *From Lairds to Louns*.

DesBrisay, G., 'Quakers and the University: the Aberdeen debate of 1675', *History of Universities*, 13 (1994).

DesBrisay, G., 'Twisted by definition: women under godly discipline in seventeenth century Scottish towns', in Y. F. Brown and R. Ferguson (eds), *Twisted Sisters: Women, Crime and Deviance in Scotland Since 1400* (East Linton, 2002).

DesBrisay, G., 'Wet nurses and unwed mothers in seventeenth century Aberdeen', in E. Ewan and M. Meikle (eds), *Women in Scotland*.

Devine, T. M., 'The Cromwellian Union and the Scottish burghs: the case of Aberdeen and Glasgow, 1652-1660', in J. Butt and J. T. Ward (eds), *Scottish Themes*.

Devine, T. M., 'The merchant class of the larger Scottish towns in the seventeenth and early eighteenth centuries', in G. Gordon and B. Dicks (eds), *Scottish Urban History* (Aberdeen, 1983).

Diack, L., 'Dr David Skene and his contribution to women's health', in A. Adam, D. Smith and F. Watson (eds), *'To the Greit Support and*

Advancement of Helth' (Aberdeen, 1996).

Diack, L., 'Motherhood and poverty in eighteenth-century Aberdeen', in T. Brotherstone *et al.* (eds), *Gendering Scottish History.*

Diack, L., 'A woman's greatest adventure: the development of maternity care in Aberdeen since the eighteenth century', in T. Brotherstone and D. J. Withrington (eds), *The City and its Worlds.*

Diack, W., *The Rise and Progress of the Granite Industry of Aberdeen* (Aberdeen, 1949).

Dingwall, H. M., *Late Seventeenth-Century Edinburgh: A Demographic Study* (Aldershot, 1994).

Dingwall, H. M., *Physicians, Surgeons and Apothecaries: Medical Practice in Seventeenth-Century Edinburgh* (East Linton, 1995).

Ditchburn, D., 'Bremen piracy and Scottish periphery: the North Sea world in the 1440s', in A. I. Macinnes *et al.* (eds), *Guns, Ships and Bibles.*

Ditchburn, D., 'Cargoes and commodities: Aberdeen's trade with Scandinavia and the Baltic, c.1302-c.1542', *Northern Studies*, 27 (1990).

Ditchburn, D., 'Piracy and war at sea in late medieval Scotland', in T. C. Smout (ed.), *Scotland and the Sea* (Edinburgh, 1992).

Ditchburn, D., 'The pirate, the policeman and the pantomime star: Aberdeen's alternative economy in the early fifteenth century', *Northern Scotland*, 12 (1992).

Ditchburn, D., *Scotland and Europe: The Medieval Kingdom and its Contacts with Christendom. Volume I: Religion, Culture and Commerce* (East Linton, 2000).

Ditchburn, D., 'Trade with northern Europe, 1297-1540', in M. Lynch *et al.* (eds), *The Scottish Medieval Town.*

Diverres, A. H., 'Britain in Froissart's "Meliador"', in F. Whitehead, A. H. Diverres, and F. G. Sutcliffe (eds), *Medieval Miscellany Presented to Eugene Vinaver* (Manchester, 1965).

Dobson, D., *Jacobites of the '15* (Aberdeen, 1993).

Dobson, D., 'James Freeman of Maryland, 1730', *National Genealogical Society Quarterly*, 73 (1985).

Dobson, D., *Scottish Emigration to Colonial America, 1607-1785* (Athens, GA, 1994).

Donagan, B., 'Atrocity, war crime, and treason in the English Civil War', *American Historical Review*, 99 (1994).

Donagan, B., 'Codes and conduct in the English Civil War', *P & P*, 118 (1988).

Donaldson, G., 'Aberdeen University and the Reformation', *Northern Scotland*, 1 (1973).

Donaldson, G., *The Faith of the Scots* (London, 1990).

Donaldson, G., 'Scotland's conservative north', *Transactions of the Royal Historical Society*, 5th series, 16 (1966).

Donaldson, G., *Scottish Church History* (Edinburgh, 1985).

Donaldson, G. (ed.), *Scottish Historical Documents* (Edinburgh, 1974).

Donnelly, T., *The Aberdeen Granite Industry* (Aberdeen, 1994).

Drummond, A. L., *The Church Architecture of Protestantism* (Edinburgh, 1934).

Dukes, P., 'The Aberdeen Enlightenment and Russia', in J. J. Carter and J. Pittock (eds), *Aberdeen and the Enlightenment.*

Dukes, P. (ed.), *The Universities of Aberdeen and Europe: The First Three Centuries* (Aberdeen, 1995).

Dunbar, J. G., 'The emergence of the reformed church in Scotland, c. 1560-c. 1700', in J. Blair and C. Pyrah (eds), *Church Archaeology: New Directions for the Future* (York, 1996).

Duncan, A. A. M., 'Perth: the first century of the burgh', *Transactions of the Perth Society of Natural Sciences*, Special Issue (1974).

Duncan, A. A. M, *Scotland: The Making of the Kingdom* (Edinburgh, 1973).

Duncan, D., *Thomas Ruddiman* (Edinburgh, 1965).

Duncan, E., 'James Ramsay 1733-1789 - abolitionist', *AUR*, 53 (1989).

Duncan, W. R. H., 'Aberdeen and the early development of the whaling industry, 1750-1800', *Northern Scotland*, 3 (1977-8).

Durkan, J., 'Early humanism and King's College', *AUR*, 48 (1980).

Durkan, J. and Ross, A., 'Early Scottish libraries', *IR*, 9 (1958).

Durkan, J., 'Education in the century of the Reformation', in D. McRoberts (ed.), *Essays on the Scottish Reformation, 1513-1625* (Glasgow, 1962).

Durkan, J, 'Education: the laying of fresh foundations', in J. MacQueen (ed.), *Humanism in Renaissance Scotland.*

Durkan, J., 'The French connection in the sixteenth and seventeenth centuries', in T. C. Smout (ed.), *Scotland and Europe.*

Durkan, J., 'George Hay's oration at the purging of King's College, Aberdeen, in 1569: commentary', *Northern Scotland*, 6 (1985).

Durkan, J., 'Heresy in Scotland: the second phase, 1546-58', *RSCHS*, 24 (1992).

Edwards, G. P., 'The New Foundation', in D. Stevenson, *King's College, Aberdeen.*

Edwards, G. P., 'The place of theology in the foundation of the university', in A. Main (ed.), *But Where Shall Wisdom Be Found?*

Emerson, R. L., 'Lord Bute and the Scottish universities', in K. W. Schweizer (ed.), *Lord Bute: Essays in Re-interpretation* (Leicester, 1988).

Emerson, R. L., *Professors, Patronage and Politics: The Aberdeen Universities in the Eighteenth Century* (Aberdeen, 1992).

Espinas, G., *Vie urbaine de Douai au moyen age* (Paris, 1913).

Ewan, E., 'The age of Bon-Accord: Aberdeen in the fourteenth century', in J.S.Smith (ed.), *New Light on Medieval Aberdeen*.

Ewan, E., '"For whatever ales ye": women as consumers and producers in late medieval Scottish towns', in E.Ewan and M.Meikle (eds), *Women in Scotland*.

Ewan, E., *Townlife in Fourteenth-Century Scotland* (Edinburgh, 1990).

Ewan, E.and Meikle M., (eds), *Women in Scotland, c. 1100-c. 1750* (East Linton, 1999).

Ewen, L., 'Debtors, imprisonment and the privilege of girth', in L.Leneman (ed.), *Perspectives in Scottish Social History*.

Farmer, D.H., *The Oxford Dictionary of Saints* (Oxford, 1982).

Farmer, H.G., *Music Making in the Olden Days: The Story of the Aberdeen Concerts, 1748-1801* (London, 1950).

Farrington, A., *A Biographical Index of East India Company Maritime Officers, 1600-1834* (London, 1999).

Fawcett, R., *Scottish Architecture from the Accession of the Stewarts to the Reformation, 1371-1560* (Edinburgh, 1994).

Fenton, A., 'Skene of Hallyards' *Manuscript of Husbandrie*, *Agricultural History Review*, 11 (1963).

Ferguson, P.C., *Medieval Papal Representatives, in Scotland: Legates, Nuncios and Judges-delegate, 1125-1286* (Stair Soc., 1997).

Fischer, T.A., *The Scots in Eastern and Western Prussia* (Edinburgh, 1903).

Fischer, T.A., *The Scots in Germany* (Edinburgh, 1902).

Fitch, A., 'Assumptions about plague in late medieval Scotland', *Scotia*, 11 (1987).

Fleming, D.Hay, *The Reformation in Scotland: Causes, Characteristics, Consequences* (London, 1910).

Fletcher, J., 'The college-university: its development in Aberdeen and beyond', in J.J. Carter and D.J.Withrington (eds), *Scottish Universities*.

Fletcher, J., 'The foundation of the university of Aberdeen in its European context', in P.Dukes (ed.), *Universities of Aberdeen and Europe*.

Flett, J.F.and Flett, T.M., 'Some early Highland dancing competitions', *AUR*, 36 (1955-6).

Flinn M. (ed.), *Scottish Population History from the Seventeenth Century to the 1930s* (Cambridge, 1977).

Foggie, J.P., '*Archivium Sacræ Pænitentiariæ Apostilicæ* in the Vatican archives as a source for Scottish historians', *IR*, 47 (1996).

Foster, C. *Homage to Schirr Johnne Black* (Aberdeen, n.d.).

Fraser, G.M., *Historical Aberdeen: The Castle and the Castle-hill … the Snow Church* (Aberdeen, 1905).

Fraser, G.M., *Historical Aberdeen: The Green and its Story* (Aberdeen, 1904).

Fraser, G.M., *The Old Deeside Road* (Aberdeen, 1921).

Fraser, G.M., 'Scientists of the north-east of Scotland', in *A Scientific Survey of Aberdeen and District*, by Various Authors (London, 1934).

Fraser, G.M.and Henderson, M., *Aberdeen Street Names: Their History, Meaning and Personal Associations* (repr., Aberdeen, 1986).

Fraser, W., *History of the Carnegies, Earls of Southesk* (Edinburgh, 1867).

Fraser, W., *The Lennox* (Edinburgh, 1874).

Fraser, W.H., *Conflict and Class: Scottish Workers, 1700-1838* (Edinburgh, 1988).

Fraser, W.H.and Lee, C.H. (eds), *Aberdeen 1800-2000: A New History* (East Linton, 2000).

French, R., 'Medical teaching in Aberdeen from the foundation of the university to the middle of the seventeenth century', *History of the Universities*, 3 (1983).

Frial, I., *Ships, Shipbuilding and Technology in England, 1200-1520* (London, 1995).

Friedrichs, C.R., *The Early Modern City, 1450-1750* (New York, 1995).

Frijhoff, W., 'Patterns', in H.de Ridder-Symoens (ed.), *A History of the University in Europe. Volume II: Universities in Early Modern Europe* (Cambridge, 1996).

Fry, M., *The Dundas Despotism* (Edinburgh, 1992).

Furgol, E., 'The civil war in Scotland', in J.Kenyon and J.Ohlmeyer (eds), *The Civil Wars: A Military History of England, Scotland, and Ireland 1638- 1660* (Oxford, 1998).

Furgol, E.M., *A Regimental History of the Covenanting Armies, 1639-1651* (Edinburgh, 1990).

Gammack, J., 'An Aberdeen graduate in Virginia', *AUR*, 9 (1921-2).

Gammack, J., 'Aberdeen University men in Virginia', *AUR*, 10 (1922-3).

Gammie, A., *The Churches of Aberdeen, Historical and Descriptive* (Aberdeen, 1909).

Geddes, J. (ed.), *King's College Chapel, Aberdeen, 1500-2000* (Leeds, 2000).

Geddes, J., *Ye Ken Noo!* (Durham, 1993).

Gemmill, E.and Mayhew, N., *Changing Values in Medieval Scotland* (Cambridge, 1995).

Gibson, A.and Smout, T.C., *Prices, Food and Wages in Scotland, 1550-1780* (Cambridge, 1995).

Gibson, A.and Smout, T.C., 'Scottish food and Scottish history', in R.A. Houston and I.D. Whyte (eds), *Scottish Society, 1500-1800* (Cambridge, 1989).

Gillett, E., *A History of Grimsby* (London, 1970).

Girouard, M., *The English Town: A History of Urban Life* (New Haven, 1990).

Glendinning, M., MacInnes, R.and MacKechnie, A., *A History of Scottish Architecture* (Edinburgh, 1996).

Glendinning, M., Ritchie, G.and Thomas, J., *Aberdeen*

on Record: Images of the Past: Photographs and Drawings of the National Monuments Record of Scotland (Edinburgh, 1997).

Goodare, J., 'The Aberdeenshire witchcraft panic of 1597', Northern Scotland, 21 (2001).

Goodare, J., State and Society in Early Modern Scotland (Oxford, 1999).

Goodare, J. and Lynch, M. (eds), The Reign of James VI (East Linton, 2000).

Graham, C., Historical Walkabout of Aberdeen (Aberdeen, 1973).

Graham, M., The Uses of Reform: 'Godly Discipline' and Popular Behavior in Scotland and Beyond, 1560-1610 (Leiden, 1996).

Grant, A., Independence and Nationhood: Scotland, 1306-1469 (London, 1984).

Grant, A., 'Scotland's "Celtic fringe" in the later Middle Ages: the Macdonald lords of the Isles and the kingdom of Scotland', in R. R. Davies (ed.), The British Isles, 1100-1500: Comparisons, Contrasts and Connections (Edinburgh, 1988).

Grant, I. F., The Social and Economic Development of Scotland before 1603 (Edinburgh, 1930).

Grant, J., History of the Burgh and Parish Schools of Scotland. Volume I: Burgh Schools (Glasgow, 1876).

Gray, M., 'Fishing villages, 1750-1880', in A. C. O'Dell and J. Mackintosh (eds), The North-East of Scotland.

Greenwood, D., William King (Oxford, 1969).

Guy, I., 'The Scottish export trade, 1460-1599', in T. C. Smout (ed.), Scotland and Europe.

Haldane, A. R. B., The Drove Roads of Scotland (Edinburgh, 1952).

Haldane, A. R. B., The Great Fishmonger of the Tay (Dundee, 1981).

Haley, K. H. D., The British and the Dutch: Political and Cultural Relations through the Ages (London, 1988).

Hamilton, D., The Healers: A History of Medicine in Scotland (Edinburgh, 1982).

Hamilton, H., An Economic History of Scotland in the Eighteenth Century (Oxford, 1963).

Hans, N., 'Henry Farquharson, pioneer of Russian education, 1698-1739', AUR, 38 (1959-60).

Hargreaves, J. D., Aberdeenshire to Africa: North-east Scots and British Overseas Expansion (Aberdeen, 1981).

Harris, M. J. S., 'Memories of the Garioch', AUR, 44 (1971-2).

Harvey, P. D. A., Medieval Maps (London, 1991).

Haskins, C. H., The Renaissance of the Twelfth Century (Cambridge, Mass., 1927).

Hay, D., The Architecture of Scottish Post-Reformation Churches, 1560-1843 (Oxford, 1957).

Henderson, G. D., 'The Aberdeen doctors', in G. D. Henderson (ed.), The Burning Bush.

Henderson, G. D. (ed.), The Burning Bush: Studies in Scottish Church History (Edinburgh, 1957).

Henderson, G. D., 'Ephinstone [sic] birthday celebrations in the eighteenth century', AUR, 18 (1930-1).

Henderson, G. D., The Founding of Marischal College, Aberdeen (Aberdeen, 1946).

Henderson, G. D., 'John Forbes of Corse in exile', AUR, 17 (1929).

Henderson, G. D., 'A member of the Wise Club', AUR, 24 (1936-7).

Henderson, G. D., Mystics of the North-East (Third Spalding Club, 1934).

Henderson, G. D., Religious Life in Seventeenth Century Scotland (Cambridge, 1937).

Henderson, J. A., Annals of Lower Deeside (Aberdeen, 1892).

Henderson, J. A. (ed.), History of the Society of Advocates in Aberdeen (New Spalding Club, 1912).

Hill, G., 'The sermons of John Watson, canon of Aberdeen', IR, 15 (1964).

Hilton, R. H., 'The small town as part of peasant society', in R. H. Hilton (ed.), The English Peasantry in the Later Middle Ages (Oxford, 1975).

Holdsworth, P. (ed.), Excavations in the Medieval Burgh of Perth 1979-81 (Edinburgh, 1988).

Holloway, J., 'An Aberdeen bi-centenary: James Gibbs, architect, 1682-1754', AUR, 35 (1953-4).

Hotson, H., 'A dark golden age: The Thirty Years War and the universities of northern Europe', in A. I. Macinnes et al. (eds), Guns, Ships and Bibles.

Houston, R. A., Literacy in Early Modern Europe: Culture and Education, 1500-1800 (London, 1988).

Houston, R. A., Scottish Literacy and the Scottish Identity (Cambridge, 1985).

Houston, R. A., Social Change in the Age of Enlightenment: Edinburgh, 1660-1760 (Oxford, 1994).

Houtte, J. A. van, An Economic History of the Low Countries, 800-1800 (London, 1977).

Howard, D., Scottish Architecture: Reformation to Restoration, 1560-1660 (Edinburgh, 1995).

Huetz de Lemps, C., Géographie du commerce de Bordeaux à la fin du règne de Louis XIV (Paris, 1975).

Hufton, O., The Prospect Before Her: A History of Women in Western Europe 1500-1800 (London, 1995).

Huie, C., 'Folklore', in D. Omand (ed.), The Moray Book.

Humphries, W. R., 'The letters of David Skene, part iii', Postgraduate Medical Bulletin (1972).

Humphries, W. R., William Ogilvie and the Projected Union of the Colleges, 1786-87 (Aberdeen, 1940).

Hutton, R., The Rise and Fall of Merry England: The Ritual Year 1400-1700 (Oxford, 1994).

Hutton, R., The Stations of the Sun: A History of the Ritual Year in Britain (Oxford, 1996).

Inama-Sternegg, C. T., Deutsche Wirtschaftsgeschichte in dem letzten Jahrhunderten des Mittelalter (Leipzig, 1879-1901).

Insch, G. P., Scottish Colonial Schemes, 1620-1686 (Glasgow, 1922).

Jackson, G., *The British Whaling Trade* (London, 1978).

Jackson, G., 'Government bounties and the establishment of the Scottish whaling industry', in J. Butt and J. T. Ward (eds), *Scottish Themes*.

Jackson, G., 'Scottish Sailors', in P. van Royen *et al.* (eds), *'Those Emblems of Hell'?*

Jackson, G., *The Trade and Shipping of Dundee, 1780-1850* (Dundee, 1991).

Jackson, G. and Lythe, S. G. E. (eds), *The Port of Montrose* (Tayport, 1993).

Jenkinson, J. L. M., *Scottish Medical Societies* (Edinburgh, 1993).

Johnston, A. W. S., *A Short Memoir of James Young, Merchant Burgess of Aberdeen* (Aberdeen, 1860).

Johnston, D. B., 'James Beattie and his students at Marischal College, Aberdeen', *Northern Scotland*, 11 (1991).

Jones, A. K. J., 'Parasite remains from Oslogatgate 7', in *De Arkologiske Letgravinger* (Norway, 1979).

Jütte, R., *Poverty and Deviance in Early Modern Europe* (Cambridge, 1994).

Kearney, H., *Scholars and Gentlemen: Universities and Society in Pre-industrial Britain, 1500-1700* (London, 1970).

Keith, A., *Eminent Aberdonians* (Aberdeen, 1984).

Keith, A., 'The laureate of the Jacobites: William Meston', *AUR*, 22 (1934-5).

Keith, A., *A Thousand Years of Aberdeen* (Aberdeen, 1972).

Kelly, W., 'Architecture in Aberdeen: a survey', in *A Scientific Survey of Aberdeen and District*, by Various Authors (London, 1934).

Kelly, W., 'On Work in Granite', in W. Douglas Simpson (ed.), *A Tribute offered by the University of Aberdeen to the Memory of William Kelly, LLD, ARSA* (Aberdeen, 1949).

Kendall, J., 'The development of a distinctive form of Quaker dress', *Costume*, 19 (1985).

Kennedy, W., *Annals of Aberdeen*, 2 vols (London, 1818).

Kennedy, W., *Sketch of the Affairs of the Treasury of Aberdeen* (Aberdeen, 1820).

Kirby, E. W., *George Keith* (New York, 1942).

Kühn, M., *Scottish Common Sense Philosophy in Germany, 1768-1800* (Kingston, 1987).

Laird, J., 'George Dalgarno', *AUR*, 23 (1935-6).

Landsman, N. C., *Scotland and its First American Colony, 1683-1765* (Princeton, 1985).

Lawrence, C. H., *St Edmund of Abingdon* (Oxford, 1960).

Lawson-Peebles, R., 'The problem of William Smith: an Aberdonian in revolutionary America', in J. J. Carter and J. H. Pittock (eds), *Aberdeen and the Enlightenment*.

Le Goff, J., *Intellectuals in the Middle Ages* (Oxford, 1993).

Lee, C. H., 'Local government', in W. H. Fraser and C. H. Lee (eds), *Aberdeen 1800-2000*.

Lee, M., *The Road to Revolution: Scotland Under Charles I, 1625-1637* (Urbana, 1985).

Leitch, R., '"Here chapmen billies tak their stand": a pilot study of Scottish chapmen, packmen and pedlars', *PSAS*, 120 (1990).

Leneman, L. (ed.), *Perspectives in Scottish Social History: Essays in Honour of Rosalind Mitchison* (Aberdeen, 1988).

Leneman, L. and Mitchison, R., *Sin in the City: Sexuality and Social Control in Urban Scotland 1660-1780* (Edinburgh, 1998).

Levack, I. and Dudley, H., *Aberdeen Royal Infirmary: The People's Hospital of the North-East* (London, 1992).

Lindsay, I. G., *The Scottish Parish Kirk* (Edinburgh, 1960).

Logue, K., *Popular Disturbances in Scotland, 1780-1815* (Edinburgh, 1979).

Lough, J. and Lough, M., 'Aberdeen circulating libraries in the eighteenth century', *AUR*, 31 (1944-6).

Lyall, H. F. C., *Vanishing Aberdeen: In the steps of George Washington Wilson* (Aberdeen, 1988).

Lynch, M., 'The crown and the burghs, 1500-1625', in M. Lynch (ed.), *The Early Modern Town*.

Lynch, M. (ed.), *The Early Modern Town in Scotland* (London, 1987).

Lynch, M., 'Introduction', in M. Lynch *et al.* (eds), *The Scottish Medieval Town*.

Lynch, M., 'Preaching to the converted? Perspectives on the Scottish Reformation', in A. A. MacDonald *et al.* (eds), *The Renaissance in Scotland*.

Lynch, M., *Scotland: A New History* (London, 1991).

Lynch, M., 'The social and economic structure of the larger towns, 1450-1600', in M. Lynch *et al.* (eds), *The Scottish Medieval Town*.

Lynch, M., 'Towns and townspeople in fifteenth-century Scotland', in J. A. F. Thomson (ed.), *Towns and Townspeople in the Fifteenth Century* (Aldershot, 1988).

Lynch, M., 'Urbanisation and urban networks in seventeenth-century Scotland: some further thoughts', *SESH*, 12 (1992).

Lynch, M., 'Whatever happened to the medieval burgh? Some guidelines for sixteenth- and seventeenth-century historians', *SESH*, 4 (1984).

Lynch, M., Spearman, M. and Stell, G. (eds), *The Scottish Medieval Town* (Edinburgh, 1988).

Lythe, S. G. E., *The Economy of Scotland in its European Setting, 1550-1625* (Edinburgh, 1960).

McArthur, A. and Long, H. K., *No Mean City* (London, 1978).

MacDonald, A. A., Lynch, M. and Cowan, I. B. (eds), *The Renaissance in Scotland: Studies in Literature, Religion, History and Culture* (Leiden, 1994).

Macdougall, N., "'It is I, the earle of Mar'': in search of Thomas Cochrane', in R. Mason and N. Macdougall (eds), *People and Power in Scotland* (Edinburgh 1992).

Macdougall, N., *James III* (Edinburgh, 1982).

Macdougall, N., *James IV* (Edinburgh, 1989).

Macfarlane, L. J., 'The Divine Office and the Mass', in J. Geddes (ed.), *King's College Chapel, Aberdeen, 1500-2000*.

Macfarlane, L. J., *King's College* (Aberdeen, 1982).

Macfarlane, L. J., *St Machar's Cathedral in the Later Middle Ages* (Aberdeen, 1979).

Macfarlane, L. J., 'St Machar's through the ages', in J. S. Smith (ed.), *Old Aberdeen*.

Macfarlane, L. J., *William Elphinstone and the Kingdom of Scotland, 1431-1514: The Struggle for Order* (Aberdeen, 1985).

Macfarlane, L. J. and Short, A. G., *The Burgh and Cathedral of Old Aberdeen* (Aberdeen, 1989).

MacGibbon, D. and Ross, T., *The Castellated and Domestic Architecture of Scotland*, 5 vols (Edinburgh, 1887-92).

McGladdery, C., *James II* (Edinburgh, 1990).

Macinnes, A. I., 'Catholic recusancy and the penal laws, 1603-1707', *RSCHS*, 23 (1987).

Macinnes, A. I., *Charles I and the Making of the Covenanting Movement, 1625-1641* (Edinburgh, 1991).

Macinnes, A. I., 'Repression and conciliation: the Highland dimension, 1660-1688', *SHR*, 65 (1986).

Macinnes, A. I., Riis, T. and Pedersen, F. (eds), *Guns, Ships and Bibles in the North Sea and Baltic States, c. 1350-c. 1700* (East Linton, 2000).

McIntosh, C., 'Style as a key to the Scottish Enlightenment', *Eighteenth-Century Scotland* (1997).

Mackay, W., 'The battle of Harlaw: its true place in history', *TGSI*, 30 (1919-22).

Mackenzie, A. M., *Scottish Pageant*, 4 vols (1946-50).

MacKenzie, W. M., *The Scottish Burghs* (Edinburgh, 1949).

Mackinlay, J. M., *Ancient Church Dedications in Scotland: Non-scriptural Dedications* (Edinburgh, 1914).

Mackinnon, K. A. B., 'George Turnbull's common sense jurisprudence', in J. J. Carter and J. H. Pittock (eds), *Aberdeen and the Enlightenment*.

MacLaren, A. A., 'Patronage and professionalism: the "forgotten middle class", 1760-1860', in D. McCrone, S. Kendrick and P. Straw (eds), *The Making of Scotland: Nation, Culture and Social Change* (Edinburgh, 1989).

MacLaren, A. A., 'Privilege, patronage and the professions: Aberdeen and its universities, 1760-1860', in J. J. Carter and D. J. Withrington (eds), *Scottish Universities*.

McLaren, C. A., 'Affrichtment and riot: student violence in Aberdeen, 1659-1669', *Northern Scotland*, 10 (1990).

McLaren, C. A., 'The Chapel, the College and the University, 1560-1945', in J. Geddes (ed.), *King's College Chapel, Aberdeen, 1500-2000*.

McLaren, C. A., 'The college and the community, 1600-1860', in J. S. Smith (ed.), *Old Aberdeen*.

McLaren, C. A., 'Discipline and decorum: the law-codes of the universities of Aberdeen, 1605-86', in J. J. Carter and D. J. Withrington (eds), *Scottish Universities*.

McLaren, C. A., 'Enlightened men at law: litigation at King's College in the eighteenth century', in J. J. Carter and J. H. Pittock (eds), *Aberdeen and the Enlightenment*.

McLaren, C. A, 'New work and old: building at the Colleges in the seventeenth century', *AUR*, 53 (1989-90).

McLaren, C. A., 'Visiting the charter chest: the early records of the university and King's College, Aberdeen', in T. Brotherstone and D. Ditchburn (eds), *Freedom and Authority*.

McLennan, B., 'The Reformation in the burgh of Aberdeen', *Northern Scotland*, 1 (1975).

Macmillan, D., *The Aberdeen Doctors* (London, 1909).

McMillan, W., *The Worship of the Scottish Reformed Church 1550-1638* (Edinburgh, 1931).

McNamee, C., *The Wars of the Bruces: Scotland, England and Ireland, 1306-28* (East Linton, 1997).

McNeill, P. G. B. and MacQueen, H. L. (eds), *Atlas of Scottish History to 1707* (Edinburgh, 1996).

MacNiven, D., 'Merchants and traders in early seventeenth-century Aberdeen', in D. Stevenson (ed.), *From Lairds to Louns*.

MacQueen, J. (ed.), *Humanism in Renaissance Scotland* (Edinburgh, 1990).

McRoberts, D., 'The Fetternear Banner', *IR*, 7 (1956).

McRoberts, D., *The Heraldic Ceiling of St Machar's Cathedral, Aberdeen* (Aberdeen, 1976).

McRoberts, D., 'Provost Skene's House in Aberdeen and its Catholic chapel', *IR*, 5 (1954).

Maddicott, J. R., *The English Peasantry and the Demands of the Crown, 1294-1341* (P & P, Supplement, 1975).

Main, A. (ed.), *But Where Shall Wisdom Be Found?* (Aberdeen, 1995).

Manning, S., review of R. J. Robinson (ed.), *The Works of James Beattie* (London, 1996), in *Eighteenth-Century Scotland* (1997).

Manns, J. W., *Reid and His French Disciples* (Leiden, 1994).

Marland, H., 'Lay and medical conceptions of medical charity during the nineteenth century: the case of Huddersfield General Dispensary and Infirmary', in J. Barry and C. Jones (eds), *Medicine and Charity before the Welfare State*.

Marren, P., *Grampian Battlefields: The Historic Battles*

of North-East Scotland from AD 84 to 1745 (Aberdeen, 1990).

Marren, P., A Natural History of Aberdeen (Aberdeen, 1982).

Marshall, R.K., Mary of Guise (London, 1977).

Mason, R., 'The Aristocracy, episcopacy and the revolution of 1638', in T.Brotherstone (ed.), Covenant, Charter, and Party: Traditions of Revolt and Protest in Modern Scottish History (Aberdeen, 1989).

Mathieson, W.L., The Awakening of Scotland: A History from 1747 to 1797 (Glasgow, 1910).

Maver, I., 'Urbanisation', in A.Cooke et al. (eds), Modern Scottish History, 1707 to the Present (East Linton, 1998).

Maxwell, W.D., A History of Worship in the Church of Scotland (Oxford, 1955).

Maxwell-Stuart, P.H., 'Witchcraft and the kirk in Aberdeenshire, 1596-7', Northern Scotland, 18 (1998).

Mayhew, N.J., 'The brewsters of Aberdeen in 1509', Northern Studies, 32 (1997).

Mayhew, N.J., 'The status of women and the brewing of ale in medieval Aberdeen', ROSC, 10 (1996-7).

Mayhew N.J., 'Women in Aberdeen at the end of the middle ages', in T.Brotherstone et al. (eds), Gendering Scottish History.

Meikle, H.W., Scotland and the French Revolution (Glasgow, 1912).

Meldrum, E., Aberdeen of Old (Aberdeen, 1987).

Meldrum, E., 'Benholm's Tower, Nether Kirkgate, Aberdeen', PSAS, 95 (1961-2).

Meldrum, E., 'Sir George Skene's house in the Guestrow, Aberdeen - its history and architecture', PSAS, 92 (1958-9).

Michie, R.C., 'North-east Scotland and the northern whale fishing', Northern Scotland, 3 (1977-8).

Mill, A.J., Mediaeval Plays in Scotland (Oxford, 1927).

Miller, W.F., 'Gleanings from the records of the yearly meeting of Aberdeen, 1672 to 1786', Journal of the Friends Historical Society, 8 (1911).

Miller, W.F., 'Notes on early Friends' schools in Scotland', Journal of the Friends Historical Society, 7 (1910).

Miller, W.F., 'The record book of Friends of the monethly meeting att Urie', Journal of the Friends Historical Society, 7 (1910).

Milne, G.P. (ed.), Aberdeen Medico-Chirurgical Society: A Bicentennial History, 1789-1989 (Aberdeen, 1989).

Milne, J., Aberdeen: Topographical, Antiquarian and Historical Papers on the City of Aberdeen (Aberdeen, 1911).

Molland, A.G., 'Duncan Liddel, 1561-1613: an early benefactor of Marischal College Library', AUR, 51 (1986).

Molland, A.G., 'Scottish-continental intellectual relations as mirrored in the career of Duncan

Liddel, 1561-1613', in P.Dukes (ed.), Universities of Aberdeen and Europe.

Mollat, M., Le commerce maritime normand à la fin du Moyen Age: étude d'histoire économique et sociale (Paris, 1952).

Mollat du Jourdin, M., Roncière, M.de la et al. (eds), Sea Charts of the Early Explorers, 13th to 17th Century (Fribourg, 1984).

Morgan, D., The Villages of Aberdeen: Old Aberdeen (Aberdeen, 2000).

Morris, R.J., 'Urbanisation', in J.Langton and R.J.Morris (eds), Atlas of Industrializing Britain, 1780-1914 (London, 1986).

Mullan, D.G., Scottish Puritanism, 1590-1638 (Oxford, 2000).

Munkhoff, R., 'Searchers of the dead: authority, marginality, and the interpretation of plague in England, 1574-1665', Gender and History, 11 (1999).

Munro, A.M. (ed.), 'Diary of John Row, principal of King's College', Scottish Notes and Queries (April 1894).

Murison, D., 'The speech of Moray', in D.Omand (ed.), The Moray Book.

Murray, H., 'The excavated secular buildings', in J.C.Murray (ed.), Excavations in the Medieval Burgh of Aberdeen.

Murray, J.C. (ed.), Aberdeen: The Town beneath the City (Aberdeen, 1978).

Murray, J.C., 'The archaeological evidence', in J.S.Smith (ed.), New Light on Medieval Aberdeen.

Murray, J.C. (ed.), Excavations in the Medieval Burgh of Aberdeen, 1973-81 (Edinburgh, 1982).

Murray, N., 'Union Bridge widening, Aberdeen', Minutes of Proceedings of the Aberdeen Association of Civil Engineers, 8 (1907-8).

Namier, L. and Brooke, J. (eds), The House of Commons, 1754-90 (London, 1964).

Nicholson, R., Edward III and the Scots, 1327-1335 (Oxford, 1965).

Nicholson, R., Scotland: The Later Middle Ages (Edinburgh, 1975).

Norman, A.V.B., Culloden (National Trust for Scotland, 1996).

O'Day, R., Education and Society, 1500-1800: The Social Foundation of Education in Early Modern Britain (London, 1982).

O'Dell, A.C. and Mackintosh, J. (eds), The North-East of Scotland (Aberdeen, 1963).

Omand, D. (ed.), The Moray Book (Edinburgh, 1976).

Pagan, T., The Convention of the Royal Burghs of Scotland (Glasgow, 1926).

Parker, G., The Military Revolution: Military Innovation and the Rise of the West, 1500-1800 (Cambridge, 1988).

Paul, W., Past and Present of Aberdeenshire (Aberdeen, 1881).

Pelikan, J., '1491-1500: *decennium mirabile* or *zwischen den Zeiten?*', in A. Main (ed.), *But Where Shall Wisdom Be Found?*

Pennick, N., *Celtic Sacred Landscapes* (London, 1996).

Pennington, C., *The Modernisation of Medical Teaching at Aberdeen in the Nineteenth Century* (Aberdeen, 1994).

Perkin, H., *The Rise of Professional Society* (London, 1989).

Perren, R., 'The nineteenth-century economy', in W. H. Fraser and C. H. Lee (eds), *Aberdeen, 1800-2000*.

Pittock, J., 'James Beattie: a friend to all', in D. Hewitt and M. Spiller (eds), *Literature of the North* (Aberdeen, 1983).

Pittock, M. G. H., *The Invention of Scotland* (London, 1991).

Pittock, M. G. H., *Jacobitism* (Basingstoke, 1998).

Pittock, M. G. H., *Poetry and Jacobite Politics in Eighteenth-Century Britain and Ireland* (Cambridge, 1994).

Pittock, M. G. H., 'The political thought of Alexander, Lord Forbes of Pitsligo', *Northern Scotland*, 16 (1996).

Ponting, B., 'Mathematics at Aberdeen: developments, characteristics and events, 1717-1860', *AUR*, 162 (1979).

Porter, I. A., *Alexander Gordon, M. D. of Aberdeen* (Edinburgh, 1958).

Pratt, J., *Buchan* (Aberdeen, 1858).

Quain, R. (ed.), *A Dictionary of Medicine* (London, 1882).

Rait, R. S., *The Universities of Aberdeen* (Aberdeen, 1895).

RCHAMS, *Aberdeen on Record: Images of the Past* (Edinburgh, 1997).

RCAHMS, *Tolbooths and Town-Houses: Civic Architecture in Scotland to 1833* (Edinburgh, 1996).

Reed, M., 'The urban landscape 1540-1700', in P. Clark (ed.), *Cambridge Urban History of Britain*. Vol. II, *1540-1840* (Cambridge, 2000).

Reid, J. S., 'The Castle Hill observatory, Aberdeen', *Journal for the History of Astronomy*, 13 (1982).

Reid, J. S, 'Patrick Copland, 1748-1822: aspects of his life and times at Marischal College', *AUR*, 172 (1984).

Reid, S., *The Campaigns of Montrose: A Military History of the Civil War in Scotland, 1639 to 1646* (Edinburgh, 1990).

Richards, P., *The Medieval Leper and his Northern Heirs* (Cambridge, 2000).

Ridder-Symoens, H. de (ed.), *A History of the University in Europe. Volume 1: The University in the Middle Ages* (Cambridge, 1992).

Riis, T., 'The Baltic trade', in G. Jackson and S. G. E. Lythe (eds), *The Port of Montrose*.

Riis, T., *Should Auld Acquaintaince Be Forgot ... Scottish-Danish Relations, c. 1450-1707* (Odense, 1988).

Ritchie, J., 'Animal life of north-east Scotland', in *A Scientific Survey of Aberdeen and District*, by Various Authors (1934).

Ritchie, J., *Some Antiquities of Aberdeenshire and its Borders* (Edinburgh, 1927).

Robbie, W., *Aberdeen: Its Traditions and History with Notices of Some Eminent Aberdonians* (Aberdeen, 1893).

Robertson, J., 'Alexander Skene of Newtyle', *Scottish Notes and Queries* (March 1896).

Robertson, J., *The Book of Bon Accord* (Aberdeen, 1839).

Robertson, J., *Reformation in Aberdeen* (Aberdeen, 1887).

Rodger, E. H. B., *Aberdeen Doctors at Home and Abroad: The Narrative of a Medical School* (Edinburgh, 1893).

Rouse, P., *James Blair of Virginia* (Chapel Hill, NC, 1971).

Royen, P. van, Bruijn, J. and Lucassen, J. (eds), *'Those Emblems of Hell'? European Sailors and the Maritime Labour Market, 1570-1870* (Research in Maritime History No. 13, St John's, Newfoundland, 1997).

Rubin, M., *Corpus Christi: The Eucharist in Late Medieval Culture* (Cambridge, 1991).

Ruddock, T., *Arch Bridges and their Builders* (Cambridge, 1979).

Russell, C., 'The Scottish party in English parliaments, 1640-2 OR The myth of the English revolution', *Historical Research*, 66 (1993).

Schwinges, R. C., 'Admissions', in H. de Ridder-Symoens (ed.), *A History of the University in Europe. Volume 1*.

Seaby's Coins of Scotland, Ireland and the Islands, Standard Catalogue of British Coins (London, 1984).

Sedgwick, R., *The House of Commons, 1715-54* (London, 1970).

Sefton, H. R., 'Scotland's greatest theologian', *AUR*, 45 (1973-4).

Shaw, F. J., 'Sumptuary laws in Scotland', *Juridical Review* (1979).

Shaw, J. S., *The Management of Scottish Society, 1707-1747* (Edinburgh, 1983).

Shead, N. F., 'Glasgow: an ecclesiatical burgh', in M. Lynch *et al.* (eds) *The Scottish Medieval Town*.

Shepherd, C., 'The arts curriculum at Aberdeen at the beginning of the eighteenth century', in J. J. Carter and J. H. Pittock (eds), *Aberdeen and the Enlightenment*.

Shepherd, C., 'A national system of university education in seventeenth-century Scotland?', in J. J. Carter and D. J. Withrington (eds), *Scottish Universities*.

Sheridan, R. B., 'Mortality and the medical treatment of slaves, in the British West Indies', in H. Beckles and V. Shepherd (eds), *Caribbean Slave Society and Economy* (Oxford, 1991).

Short, A., *Old Aberdeen in the Eighteenth Century* (Aberdeen, 1985).

Shrewsbury, J.F.D., *A History of Bubonic Plague in the British Isles* (Cambridge, 1970).

Simpson, G.G. (ed.), *Aberdeen's Hidden History* (Aberdeen, 1974).

Simpson, G.G., 'The medieval topography of Old Aberdeen', in J.S.Smith (ed.), *Old Aberdeen*.

Simpson, G.G., *Old Aberdeen in the Early Seventeenth Century: A Community Study* (Aberdeen, 1975).

Simpson, G.G. (ed.), *Scotland and the Low Countries, 1124-1994* (East Linton, 1996).

Simpson, G.G., *Scottish Handwriting, 1150-1650* (Edinburgh, 1973).

Simpson, J., 'Who steered the gravy train?', in N.T.Phillipson and R.Mitchison (eds), *Scotland in the Age of Improvement* (Edinburgh, 1970).

Simpson, S., 'The choir stalls and rood screen', in J.Geddes (ed.), *King's College Chapel, Aberdeen, 1500-2000*.

Simpson, W.Douglas, 'The region before 1700', in A.C.O'Dell and J.Mackintosh (eds), *The North-East of Scotland*.

Simpson, W.Douglas, *The Earldom of Mar* (Aberdeen, 1959).

Slack, P., 'The disappearance of the plague: an alternate view,' *Economic History Review*, 2nd series, 34 (1981).

Slack, P., 'The English urban landscape', in P.Clark (ed.), *The Urban Setting* (Milton Keynes, 1977).

Slack, P., *The Impact of Plague in Tudor and Stuart England* (Oxford, 1985).

Smith, A., *A New History of Aberdeenshire* (Aberdeen, 1875).

Smith, A.E., *Colonists in Bondage: White Servitude and Convict Labour in America, 1606-1776* (Chapel Hill, NC, 1947).

Smith, J.S. (ed.), *New Light on Medieval Aberdeen* (Aberdeen, 1985).

Smith, J.S. (ed.), *Old Aberdeen: Bishops, Burghers and Buildings* (Aberdeen, 1991).

Smith, J.S., 'Old Aberdeen - the buildings', in J.S.Smith (ed.), *Old Aberdeen*.

Smith, J.S., 'The physical site of historical Aberdeen', in J.S.Smith (ed.), *New Light on Medieval Aberdeen*.

Smith, R., *Discovering Aberdeenshire* (Edinburgh, 1988).

Smith, R., *The Granite City: A History of Aberdeen* (Edinburgh, 1989).

Smout, T.C. (ed.), *Scotland and Europe, 1200-1850* (Edinburgh, 1986).

Smout, T.C., *Scottish Trade on the Eve of the Union, 1660-1707* (Edinburgh, 1963).

Smout, T.C., Landsman, N.C. and Devine, T.M., 'Scottish emigration in the seventeenth and eighteenth centuries', in N.Canny (ed.), *European on the Move: Studies on European Migration, 1500-1800* (Oxford, 1994).

Spearman, R.M., 'The medieval townscape of Perth', in M.Lynch *et al.* (eds), *The Scottish Medieval Town*.

Steven, M., *Parish Life in Eighteenth-Century Scotland: A Review of the Old Statistical Account* (Aberdeen, 1995).

Stevenson, A., 'Medieval commerce', in G.Jackson and S.G.E.Lythe (eds), *The Port of Montrose*.

Stevenson, A., 'Medieval Scottish associations with Bruges', in T.Brotherstone and D.Ditchburn (eds), *Freedom and Authority*.

Stevenson, A.W.K., 'Trade with the south, 1070-1513', in M.Lynch *et al.* (eds), *The Scottish Medieval Town*.

Stevenson, D., 'The burghs and the Scottish revolution', in M.Lynch (ed.), *Early Modern Town*.

Stevenson, D., *The Covenanters: The National Covenant and Scotland* (Edinburgh, 1988).

Stevenson, D., *The First Freemasons: Scotland's Early Lodges and Their Members* (Aberdeen, 1988).

Stevenson, D. (ed.), *From Lairds to Louns* (Aberdeen, 1986).

Stevenson, D., *Highland Warrior: Alasdair MacColla and the Civil Wars* (Edinburgh, 1994).

Stevenson, D., *King or Covenant? Voices from Civil War* (East Linton, 1996).

Stevenson, D., *King's College, Aberdeen 1560-1641: From Protestant Reformation to Covenanting Revolution* (Aberdeen, 1990).

Stevenson, D., *Revolution and Counter-Revolution in Scotland, 1644-1651* (London, 1977).

Stevenson, D., *St Machar's Cathedral and the Reformation, 1560-1690* (Aberdeen, 1981).

Stevenson, D., *The Scottish Revolution, 1637-1644: The Triumph of the Covenanters*, (Newton Abbot, 1973).

Stewart, D., 'The Aberdeen doctors and the Covenanters', *RSCHS*, 22 (1984).

Stewart, I.H., *The Scottish Coinage* (London, 1955).

Stewart, M.A., 'George Turnbull and educational reform', in J.J.Carter and J.H.Pittock (eds), *Aberdeen and the Enlightenment*.

Stone, J.C., *The Pont Manuscript Maps of Scotland: Sixteenth Century Origins of a Blaeu Atlas* (Tring, 1989).

Stones, J.A., *A Tale of Two Burghs: The Archaeology of Old and New Aberdeen* (Aberdeen, 1987).

Stones, J.A. (ed.), *Three Scottish Carmelite Friaries: Excavations at Aberdeen, Linlithgow and Perth, 1980-86* (Edinburgh, 1989).

Stuart, J., 'Notice of an original instrument recently discovered among the records of the dean and chapter of Canterbury', *PSAS*, 10 (1875).

Swanson, R., 'The University of St Andrews and the Great Schism, 1410-1419', *Journal of Ecclesiastical History*, 26 (1975).

Tayler, A. and Tayler, H., *The Jacobites of Aberdeenshire and Banffshire in the Rising of 1715* (Edinburgh, 1934).

The Sang Schule of Sanct Nicholace Paroche (Aberdeen

City Council, n.d.).

Thom, W., *The History of Aberdeen* (Aberdeen, 1811).

Thomas, J. E., 'Elgin notaries in burgh society and government, 1549-1660', *Northern Scotland*, 13 (1993).

Thomas, K., *Man and the Natural World: Changing Attitudes in England, 1500-1800* (London, 1983).

Thompson, J. D. A., *Inventory of British Coin Hoards, AD 600-1500* (London, 1956).

Thoms, L. M., 'Trial excavations at St Ann's Lane, Perth', *PSAS*, 112 (1982).

Thomson, D., *The Life and Art of George Jamesone* (Oxford, 1974).

Thorne, R., *The House of Commons, 1790-1820* (London, 1986).

Torrie, E. P. D., 'The early urban site of New Aberdeen: a reappraisal of the evidence', *Northern Scotland*, 12 (1992).

Torrie, E. P. D., 'The guild in fifteenth-century Dunfermline', in M. Lynch *et al.* (eds), *The Scottish Medieval Town*.

Torrie, E. P. D., *Medieval Dundee: A Town and its People* (Dundee, 1990).

Trail, K. E., *The Story of Old Aberdeen* (Aberdeen, 1929).

Trevelyan, G. M., *English Social History* (London, 1948).

Trueblood, D. E., *Robert Barclay* (New York, 1968).

Tuck, A., 'A medieval tax haven: Berwick on Tweed and the English crown, 1333-1461', in R. Britnall and J. Hatcher (eds), *Progress and Problems in Medieval England*.

Turnbull, H. W., *Bi-centenary of the Death of Colin Maclauren, 1698-1746* (Aberdeen, 1951).

Twigg, G., 'Plague in London: spatial and temporal aspects of mortality', in J. A. I. Champion (ed.), *Epidemic Disease in London*.

Tyson, R. E., 'The economic and social structure of Old Aberdeen in the seventeenth century', in J. S. Smith (ed.), *Old Aberdeen*.

Tyson, R. E., 'Famine in Aberdeenshire, 1695-1699: anatomy of a crisis', in D. Stevenson (ed.), *From Lairds to Louns*.

Tyson, R. E., 'Household size and structure in a Scottish burgh: Old Aberdeen in 1636', *Local Population Studies*, 40 (1988).

Tyson, R. E., 'The population of Aberdeenshire, 1695-1755: a new approach', *Northern Scotland*, 6 (1985).

Tyson, R. E., 'The rise and fall of manufacturing in rural Aberdeenshire', in J. S. Smith and D. Stevenson (eds), *Fermfolk and Fisherfolk* (Aberdeen, 1989).

Tyzack. R., 'No mean city? the growth of civic consciousness in Aberdeen, with particular reference to the work of the police commissioners', in T. Brotherstone and D. J. Withrington (eds), *The City and its Worlds*.

Vance, S. M., 'Godly citizens and civic unrest: tensions in schooling in Aberdeen in the era of the Reformation', *European Review of History*, 7 (2000).

Vann, R. T., *The Social Development of English Quakerism, 1655-1755* (Cambridge, Mass., 1969).

Varenbergh, E., *Histoire des relations diplomatiques entre le comté de Flandre et l'Angleterre au moyen age* (Brussels, 1874).

Wade, W. M., *The History of Glasgow* (Glasgow, 1821).

Walker, A., *The History of the Workhouse or Poor's Hospital of Aberdeen* (Aberdeen, 1885).

Walker, D., 'Aberdeen: the planning of the central area, 1750-1850', *St Andrews Studies in the History of Scottish Architecture and Design*, 4 (2000).

Walker, W., *The Bards of Bon-Accord, 1375-1860* (Aberdeen, 1887).

Warrack, A, *A Scots Dialect Dictionary* (Edinburgh, 1930).

Waschinski, E., *Währung, Preisentwicklung und Kaufkraft des Geldes in Schleswig-Holstein von 1226-1864* (Neumünster, 1952).

Watson, F., *In Sickness and in Health* (Aberdeen, 1988).

Watt, D. E. R. (ed.), *A Biographical Dictionary of Scottish University Graduates to A. D. 1410* (Oxford, 1977).

Watt, W., *A History of Aberdeen and Banff* (Edinburgh, 1900).

Watt, W. S., 'George Hay's oration at the purging of King's College, Aberdeen, in 1569: a translation', *Northern Scotland*, 6 (1985).

Watts, J., *Scalan: the Forbidden College, 1716-1799* (East Linton, 1999).

Webster, D., 'Agriculture in Aberdeenshire in the olden days', in *A Scientific Survey of Aberdeen and District*, by Various Authors (London, 1934).

Whatley, C. A., 'How tame were the Scottish Lowlanders during the eighteenth century?', in T. M. Devine (ed.), *Conflict and Stability in Scottish Society, 1700-1850* (Edinburgh, 1990).

Whatley, C. A., *Scottish Society 1707-1830* (Manchester, 2000).

Whatley, C. A., 'Women and the economic transformation of Scotland, c. 1740-1830', *SESH*, 14 (1994).

White, A., 'The Reformation in Aberdeen', in J. Smith (ed.), *New Light on Medieval Aberdeen*.

White, A., 'The Regent Morton's visitation: the reformation of Aberdeen, 1574', in A. A. MacDonald *et al.* (eds), *The Renaissance in Scotland*.

Whyte, I. D., *Agriculture and Society in Seventeenth Century Scotland* (Edinburgh, 1979).

Whyte, I. D., '"All kynds of graine": the trade in victual, 1680-1825', in G. Jackson and S. G. E. Lythe (eds), *Port of Montrose*.

Whyte, I. D., 'The occupational structure of Scottish burghs in the late seventeenth century', in M. Lynch (ed.), *The Early Modern Town*.

Whyte, I. D., *Scotland before the Industrial Revolution*

(London, 1995).

Whyte, I. D. and Whyte, K. A., 'The geographical mobility of women in early modern Scotland', in L. Leneman (ed.), *Perspectives in Social History*.

Whyte, I. D. and Whyte, K. A., 'Patterns of migration of apprentices to Aberdeen and Inverness during the seventeenth and eighteenth centuries', *Scottish Geographical Magazine*, 102 (1986).

Wightman, W. P. D., 'James Cheyne of Arnage', *AUR*, 35 (1954).

Wilson, R., *An Historical Account and Delineation of Aberdeen* (Aberdeen, 1822).

Wilson, S. C., 'Scottish Canterbury pilgrims', *SHR*, 24 (1926-27).

Wood, M., 'St Paul's Work', *The Book of the Old Edinburgh Club*, 17 (1930).

Wood, P. B., 'Aberdeen and Europe in the Enlightenment', in P. Dukes (ed.), *Universities of Aberdeen and Europe*.

Wood, P. B., *The Aberdeen Enlightenment: The Arts Curriculum in the Eighteenth Century* (Aberdeen, 1993).

Wragge, J. P., *The Faith of Robert Barclay* (London, 1948).

Wrigley, E. A. *et al., English Population History from Reconstitution, 1580-1837* (Cambridge, 1997).

Wyness, F., *Aberdeen, Century of Change* (Aberdeen, 1971).

Wyness, F., *A. Cluer, Walkin' the Mat* (Aberdeen, 1976).

Wyness, F., *City by the Grey North Sea: Aberdeen* (2nd edn, Aberdeen, 1972).

Wyness, F., *Spots from the Leopard* (Aberdeen, 1971).

Yates, N., 'Unity in diversity: attitudes to the liturgical arrangement of church buildings between the late seventeenth and early nineteenth centuries', in W. M. Jacob and N. Yates (eds), *Crown and Mitre: Religion and Society in Northern Europe since the Reformation* (Woodbridge, 1993).

Yeoman, P., *Medieval Scotland: An Archaeological Perspective* (Edinburgh, 1995).

Young, A., *Robert the Bruce's Rivals: The Comyns, 1212-1314* (East Linton, 1997).

Youngson, A. J., *The Making of Classical Edinburgh, 1750-1840* (Edinburgh, 1966).

Unpublished Theses and Papers

Birchler, A. B., 'The Influence of the Scottish Clergy on Politics, 1616-1638' (University of Nebraska, unpublished Ph.D. thesis, 1966).

Boardman, S., 'Politics and the Feud in Late Medieval Scotland' (University of St Andrews, unpublished Ph.D. thesis, 1989).

Bogdan, N. Q. and Bryce, I. B. D., 'A compendium of the castles, manors and town houses (*c.* 1052-*c.* 1707) of Scotland, Grampian Region, Aberdeen City District' (Aberdeen, Scottish Castle Survey, typescript 1988).

Booton, H., 'Burgesses and Landed Men in North-East Scotland in the Later Middle Ages: A Study in Social Interaction' (University of Aberdeen, unpublished Ph.D. thesis, 1987).

Broadie, A., 'Plenary address to the 1998 Thomas Reid Conference at King's College, Aberdeen, on Common Sense's medieval links'.

Cardy, A., 'Excavating in the Carmelite Friary, The Green' (manuscript).

DesBrisay, G., 'Authority and Discipline in Aberdeen: 1650-1700' (University of St Andrews, unpublished Ph.D. thesis, 1989).

Diack, H. L., 'Women, Health and Charity: Women in the Poor Relief Systems in Eighteenth-Century Scotland and France' (University of Aberdeen, unpublished Ph.D. thesis, 1999).

Donaldson, W., 'The Jacobite Song in 18th and early 19th Century Scotland' (University of Aberdeen, unpublished Ph.D. thesis, 1974).

Finlayson, W. H., 'The Scottish Nation of Merchants, in Bruges' (University of Glasgow, unpublished Ph.D. thesis, 1951).

Foggie, J. P., 'The Dominicans in Scotland, 1450-1560' (University of Edinburgh, unpublished Ph.D. thesis, 1998).

Fraser, I., 'The Later Medieval Burgh Kirk of St Nicholas, Aberdeen' (University of Edinburgh, unpublished Ph.D. thesis, 1989).

Griesbach, D., 'The Neighbourhood to the South-west of St Giles' in 1500-13'. (University of Edinburgh, unpublished M. Sc. thesis, 2000).

Guy, I., 'The Scottish Export Trade, 1469-1599' (University of St Andrews, unpublished M. Litt. thesis, 1982).

MacNiven, D., 'Merchants and Traders in Early Seventeenth-Century Aberdeen' (University of Aberdeen, unpublished M. Litt. thesis, 1977).

Murdoch, S., 'Scots in the Dutch East Indies, 1612-1707' (draft article).

Royan, N. R., 'The *Scotorum Historia* of Hector Boece: a Study' (University of Oxford, unpublished D. Phil. thesis, 1996).

Rorke, M., 'Scottish Overseas Trade, 1275/86-1597' (University of Edinburgh, unpublished Ph.D. thesis, 2001).

White, A., 'Religion, Politics and Society in Aberdeen, 1543-1593' (University of Edinburgh, unpublished Ph.D. thesis, 1985).

Web Sites

www.nls.uk/pont.

An Urban Ethic of Europa. Internet www page, at url: http://web.inter.nl.net/users/Paul.Treanor/urban.ethic.html (version current at 12 July 2001).

Vickery, A., 'In Pursuit of Pleasure Part Two: The Pleasures of Town', www page, at url:http://www.open.ac.uk/Arts/18c-society/introduction. htm (version current at 12 July 2001).

Robertson, J., 'The Scottish Contribution to the Enlightenment': Electronic Seminars in History Presentation Internet www page, at url: http://www.treeofliberty.com/scotcontrib.html (version current at 12 July 2001).

Index

Dam of ẏ Barkmills

Inclosures

Broadfoord
Meadow
Ground

Mou

Galloway Port

Porthi

Old

ins abound
of Small
ogether
for what
ain.

Mid. Gilcumstoun

Dam

Gallowgate

An Aquaduct suplying ẏ City ẉ Water

2 Stones of 12 & 6 Feet high

The Steps

The Loch
of
New Aberdeen

Chapel

Marischal Colle

Nether Gilcumstoun

Rottenholes

Silverton
Hospital

Brandgate

Guetk Row

Hard Ward

ẏ to Robslaw

Cardanshaugh

Blinkbly

Corbhaugh

School Hill

Uper Kirkgate

Mill

Shuple

Nether Kirkgate

Corn Fields

Den Barn

New old Kirk

Green

law

aw

The Damhead

Old Dovecau

Wind Mill

Justice Mills

Longstone

Crabstone

An Inch
overflow'd
at Spring
Tydes

ther Couperstoun

ardgate

New-bridge

Den
barn

30

12

A good Soil for
Turnips, Parsnips,
Carrots & all
sort of Potherbs,
which ẏ Inhabitants
daily use.

Fairy-hill

Inch

The Boggs Fenns

Marsh

Inch

& Marshes of